ICHI-F

CONTENTS

The Simple Testimony of a Fighting Man

An Introduction to *Ichi-F*

What happened in the days following March 11, 2011 at the Fukushima Daiichi Nuclear Plant, 200 kilometers northeast of Tokyo? While thousands of reports exist, there will probably never be a single, fully comprehensive account of the enormous, 9.0-magnitude earthquake, or the catastrophic tsunami it caused. At Fukushima, the towering wave destroyed the reactor's backup cooling systems, which caused the reactor's fuel rods to heat up and eventually melt down. Hydrogen that then built up inside some of the reactor buildings led to a dramatic explosion, and radioactive substances were released in massive amounts. Tens of thousands of residents evacuated, and the whole world looked on with deep concern. It took six months to regain control over the power plant, and its dismantling and renaturation will take 40 years.

Today, thousands of workers have struggled with the innards of the nuclear cadaver. They battle scorching heat and freezing cold in their work to clean up the site. Some have no background at all in nuclear power, but all are determined to find a way to cope with this, the world's worst nuclear accident since the Chernobyl incident in Ukraine in 1986.

One of these men is manga artist Kazuto Tatsuta, whose talent has given us a rare and unusual look behind the scenes of Fukushima Daiichi, or "Ichi-F" (which means "1-F" in Japanese). Do not expect titillating details about how many will contract radiation sickness, the ecological or agricultural impact, or the astronomical sums and cutting-edge technology it would take to salvage the melted fuel rods.[1] Tatsuta, like many others, has no definitive answers to these questions, but in this book he does share something that no journalist, doctor, radiation expert, politician, anti-nuclear activist, or anyone else could. He shows us how the workers of Fukushima live every day and night, the condition of their work, what they think, what they see, and what they talk about. Because he is one of them.

Luckily, this unique testimony also comes to us from a new manga artist. Tatsuta is gifted with an extraordinary talent, one that has already won him many accolades. Of

1 According to the latest information on Ichi-F, there have been no deaths or recorded instances of radiation sickness or major ecological or agricultural impacts.

course, because it is necessarily subjective, his testimony is incomplete and sometimes controversial, but it is an essential contribution to the literature. Tatsuta is one of the few who can furnish us with a realistic impression of what it's like to live at Fukushima – a name that will be forever entwined with the tragedy that happened there after March 11, 2011. It should also be noted that, while this is perhaps the most unique, dozens of manga about the catastrophe have been published in Japan in the years since, because, for Japanese people, manga is a shared way of seeing that goes beyond entertainment.

Few of the workers at Fukushima have the ability, the will, the right, or the courage to share their knowledge. They are possibly not aware of the significance of their experiences to the public. But Tatsuta's brave work creating this book shows us a new side of the work at Fukushima. However onerous it may be, it's not all bleak pain and fear. For these men, part of the story is also friendship, laughter, and a shared purpose. In other words, this is a human story, one that will deeply move its readers. One comes to imagine the workers of Fukushima as a team of Sisyphuses, working at an absurd task, one that involves neither creating anything nor enriching anyone, and one that they will not see the end of, because their time on the crew is limited by their total radiation exposure.

One could read *Ichi-F* and object: The protagonist is a little too compliant, a little too naïve, a little too unaware of the extent of the danger. Some have even accused him of taking the "side" of TEPCO, the power company. Some of that may be true, but Tatsuta is a man who has made a choice to offer his insight. He never claims to be delivering the one and only truth; he merely drew what he lived through, like a soldier who comes home from war and puts his small part of the sweeping battle down on paper. He may not grasp the whole picture, but that does not lessen the value of his experience.

Karyn Nishimura Poupée

A journalist and Japan correspondent for Agence France-Presse (AFP), Poupée was in Tokyo on March 11, 2011, experiencing the catastrophe and its impact firsthand. Since then, she has covered the disaster extensively. She is also the author of several books on Asia, Japan, and manga.

This introduction was arranged by Dargaud-Lombard s.a. (Kana), the publisher of French edition of *Au coeur de Fukushima* published in March 2016. It was also published in German edition of *Reaktor 1F - Ein Bericht aus Fukushima* by Carlsen Verlag in March 2016.

CHAPTER 0

ふれあい交差点
VRRM...
KTUNK
KTUNK
Sign: Fureai Intersection
BWOM
SCREE
CHK
YUP.
HERE WE GO.

CHAPTER 0: STAY SAFE!

たつたかず
TDF
竜田

月 日
この付近の空間線量
0.8 mSv/h
です
月 日 時の
WBGT値は
30℃です
TDF 大野
TDF 竜田
TDF 木戸
TNK
KANK
KANK
MY NAME IS KAZUTO TATSUTA. PLEASE FORGIVE THE PSEUDONYM.
I WORK AT TEPCO FUKUSHIMA DAIICHI NUCLEAR POWER PLANT.
TDF 竜田
I'M GOING TO GIVE YOU A GUIDED TOUR OF OUR WORKPLACE, "1-F."
HERE WE SAY "ICHI-F."
THE WORKERS AND LOCALS ALL CALL IT THAT. APPARENTLY SOME PEOPLE SAY "FUKU-ICHI," BUT NOT AROUND HERE.
JUST AT DAWN.
RIGHT ABOUT THE TIME THAT HIRONO POWER STATION'S SMOKESTACK CATCHES THE LIGHT...
6
J J-ヴィレッジ
J-Village
...THE WORKERS' CARS CONVERGE ON NEARBY J-VILLAGE.

Sign: Local Radiation level - 0.8 mSv/h / WBGT level - 30°C
Sign (right): Road Blocked

WHEN THE PLANT WAS EXPANDED, TEPCO ADDED A SOCCER FACILITY FOR THE LOCAL CITIZENS.

NOW THE FORMERLY GREEN PITCH IS A TRAMPLED, TORN-UP LOT FOR THE 1-F CLEAN-UP WORKERS.

GOOD MORNING, MR. ONO.

MORNING, TATSUTA.

NEARLY ALL OF THE ICHI-F WORKERS ARE LOCALS. MANY WERE EVACUATED OUTSIDE OF THE RESTRICTED ZONE AND CAME TO WORK HERE.

HEYA.

HEADING HOME FROM THE NIGHT SHIFT, EH?

Sign: Do your best with courage and hope, for the sake of a brighter future for Japan! Please understand how grateful we all are! Saitama City Tsuchiai Middle School 1-8

Sign (right): Workers at Fukushima Daiichi, thank you! Keep doing your best!

日本の未来の為に勇気
い望を持ち頑張って下さ
る！最高の感謝の気持ち
明た 埼玉市立土合中学校1-8
い希けい
と届さ

Sign: Watch for loose cattle!

FIRST, WE GO TO THE TENT IN THE CENTER OF THE GROUNDS TO GEAR UP FOR THE TRIP TO ICHI-F.

Door Sign: JV Store
8AM-5PM

Sign: Do not take excess protective clothing

GOOD MORNING.

HI!

DuPont Tyvek Softwear

Sign: Monitor your valuables

Sign (top): Masks

THE EQUIPMENT IS LAID OUT ON THE RIGHT AS YOU ENTER.

Signs (L-R): Cover/One Set Per Person/Cotton Gloves/Rubber Gloves

マスク →

カバー

人一足で お願いします

綿手

ゴム手

GROCERY BAGS

COTTON GLOVES

RUBBER GLOVES

COTTON CAPS (BLUE OR WHITE)

SURGICAL MASKS

SOCKS

SHOE COVERS

THERE ARE BLUE AND WHITE PROTECTIVE SUITS. WE USE BLUE WHEN GOING TO ICHI-F.

YOU PUT ON DOUBLE PAIRS OF SOCKS.

YOUR LAST NAME AND COMPANY MUST BE WRITTEN ON THE CHEST AND BACK OF THE SUIT.

Caps are stuck in the desk so the markers stand on their own

MOST COMPANIES INVOLVED HAVE THEIR OWN INITIALS. I'LL USE MADE-UP NAMES AGAIN FOR THE PURPOSE OF ANONYMITY.

SQUIK

F SQUIK

NEXT COME THE COTTON GLOVES, CAP, AND A SURGICAL MASK THAT HOOKS OVER THE EARS.
NOW WE'RE READY FOR THE TRIP TO ICHI-F.
We call this a "blue Tyvek" (makes you look fat)
Bring your own lunch
Grocery bag with full-face mask (only holding rubber gloves)
Don't forget the shoe covers
WE'LL GET OUR FULL-FACE MASKS AT THE NEXT BUILDING.
Signs (L-R): Dust Koken Unisize/Dust 3M M size/Dust Shigematsu L size
THERE ARE THREE MASK MANUFACTURERS, AND THEY COME WITH EITHER DUST OR CHARCOAL FILTERS.
KOKEN
SUMITOMO 3M
→ Comes in half masks, too
SUMITOMO 3M
SHIGEMATSU
MY FAVORITE IS THE SHIGEMATSU. YOU USE A CHARCOAL FILTER FOR INDOOR WORK, WHERE RADIATION AND CONTAMINATION IS HIGHER.
TSSST
THEY STERILIZE THE MASKS TO REUSE THEM, SO SOME WILL SMELL AWFUL.
TSST
APD
MAKE SURE TO USE THE SPRAY AND WET WIPES BEFORE YOU PUT IT ON.

AT THE EXIT, SOME PEOPLE BORROW ALARM POCKET DOSIMETERS (APD) FOR MEASURING RADIATION, BUT WE CAN DO THAT LATER.
線量計貸出所
Sign: APD Desk
THE RULES FOR USING AND TRANSPORTING THIS SORT OF EQUIPMENT CHANGE ALL THE TIME, AND WE DON'T WANT THEM BEING MISUSED, SO KEEP IN MIND THAT THIS IS ALL SPECIFIC TO 2012.
No re-entry after leaving
THIS IS THE ROTARY WHERE WE LEAVE FOR ICHI-F.
FROM HERE WE TAKE OUR SPECIFIC COMPANY VEHICLES TO THE SITE, OR A TEPCO AFFILIATE'S BUS.
Last smoking area before leaving J-Village
HI.
GOOD MORNING.
ANYONE CAN TAKE THE TEPCO BUS, BUT YOU MUST HAVE A PROTECTIVE SUIT AND FULL-FACE MASK ON.
THE WHOLE INTERIOR IS COVERED IN PINK SHEETS TO PROTECT AGAINST CONTAMINATION.
IT'S SO PACKED DURING RUSH HOUR, YOU OFTEN NEED TO WAIT FOR A SECOND BUS.

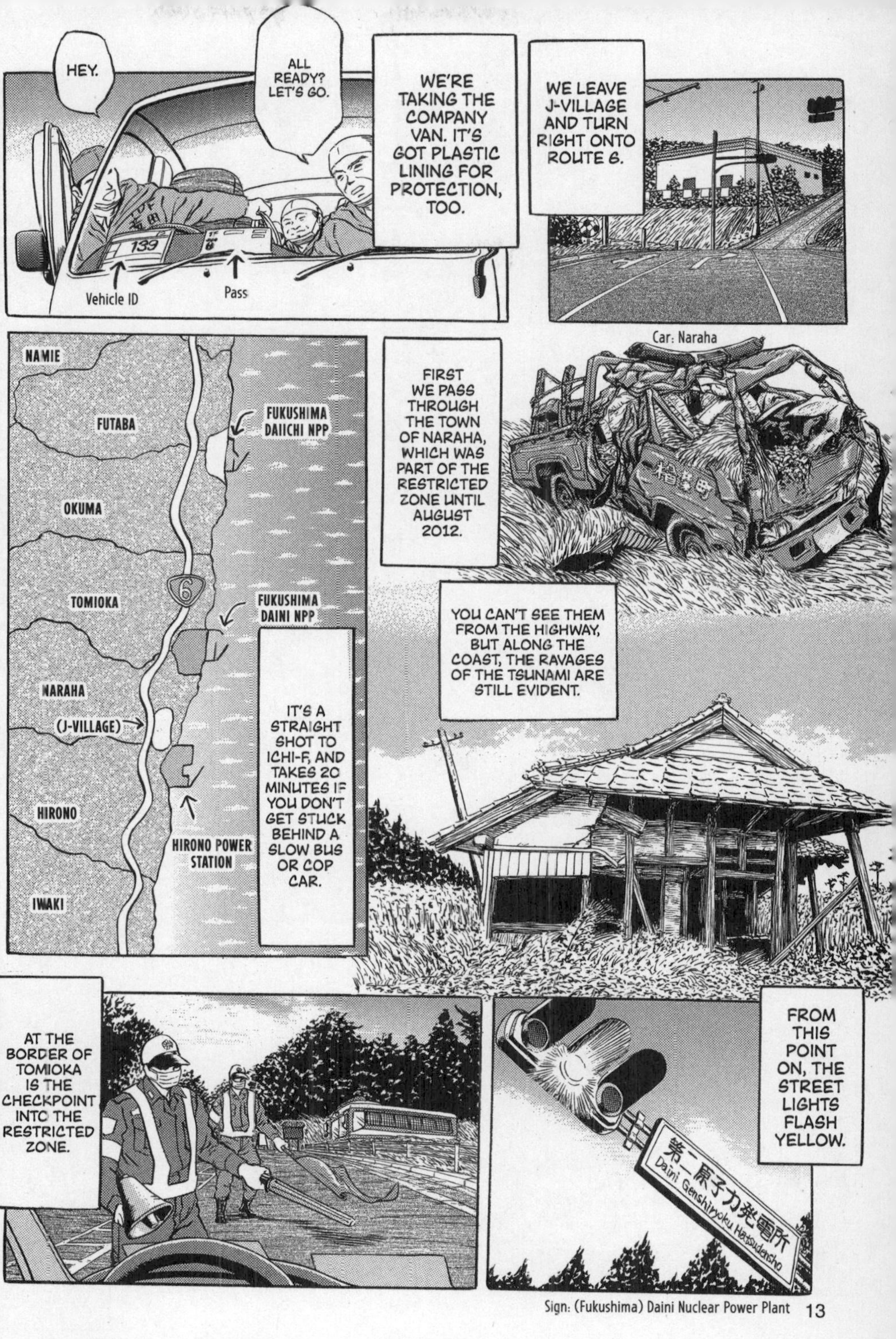
HEY.
ALL READY? LET'S GO.
WE'RE TAKING THE COMPANY VAN. IT'S GOT PLASTIC LINING FOR PROTECTION, TOO.
139
Vehicle ID
Pass
WE LEAVE J-VILLAGE AND TURN RIGHT ONTO ROUTE 6.
NAMIE
FUTABA
OKUMA
TOMIOKA
NARAHA
(J-VILLAGE)
HIRONO
IWAKI
FUKUSHIMA DAIICHI NPP
6
FUKUSHIMA DAINI NPP
HIRONO POWER STATION
IT'S A STRAIGHT SHOT TO ICHI-F, AND TAKES 20 MINUTES IF YOU DON'T GET STUCK BEHIND A SLOW BUS OR COP CAR.
Car: Naraha
FIRST WE PASS THROUGH THE TOWN OF NARAHA, WHICH WAS PART OF THE RESTRICTED ZONE UNTIL AUGUST 2012.
YOU CAN'T SEE THEM FROM THE HIGHWAY, BUT ALONG THE COAST, THE RAVAGES OF THE TSUNAMI ARE STILL EVIDENT.
AT THE BORDER OF TOMIOKA IS THE CHECKPOINT INTO THE RESTRICTED ZONE.
FROM THIS POINT ON, THE STREET LIGHTS FLASH YELLOW.
第二原子力発電所
Daini Genshiryoku Hatsudensho
Sign: (Fukushima) Daini Nuclear Power Plant

VWAAA
ALONG THE HIGHWAY, THE EMPTY BUILDINGS OF TOMIOKA SPEAK TO THE DESTRUCTIVE MIGHT OF THE EARTHQUAKE.
THE FIELDS OF OKUMA.
IN THE FALL, THE ABANDONED FIELDS BLAZE YELLOW AS THE FLOWERS OF THE INVASIVE GOLDENROD WEED BLOOM.
MR. ONO IS FROM OKUMA.
IT'S PRETTY, BUT THESE ARE SUPPOSED TO BE RICE PADDIES.

Stacks: Rice of Fukushima

Side of building: Okuma

WELL, HERE WE GO.
SHHP
TUG
TUG
TIME FOR THE RUBBER GLOVES AND HOODS.
AT THIS POINT, THE LIGHTS AREN'T EVEN ON. AFTER A RIGHT TURN AT THIS INTERSECTION, ICHI-F IS JUST AHEAD.
中央台
Chuo-dai
ようこそ
福島第一原子力発電所へ
直進
この先1.5Km
東京電力
TEPCO
Sign: Welcome to Fukushima Daiichi Nuclear Power Plant, continue straight, 1.5 km ahead. Inset: Tokyo Electric Power (TEPCO)
HERE COMES THE FRONT ENTRANCE TO ICHI-F.

GOOD MORNING. HOW MANY?
THEY ALLOW US ACCESS ONCE THEY'VE CHECKED OUR VEHICLE PASS AND ID CARDS.
EIGHT.
OKAY, YOU'RE GOOD TO GO.
INSIDE ICHI-F, THE FIRST THING YOU NOTICE IS THE STUNNING NUMBER OF ENORMOUS TANKS ON THE RIGHT-HAND SIDE.
FWOHHHH
OCEAN
UNITS 5 & 6
ANTI-EARTHQUAKE BUILDING
UNIT 1
UNIT 2
UNIT 3
UNIT 4
CONTAMINATED WATER TANKS
CHUO (CENTRAL) RD.
WE ARE HERE
FRONT GATE
COMPANY RECREATION BLDG
VEHICLE SURVEY
IT USED TO BE YACHO-NO-MORI (WILD BIRD FOREST), BUT NOW IT'S A CLEARING SPACE FOR TANKS OF CONTAMINATED WATER. MANY STILL CALL IT YACHO-NO-MORI.
OUR FIRST DESTINATION IS THE ANTI-QUAKE BUILDING.

ICHI-F IS PACKED WITH SERVICE VEHICLES, AND FINDING PARKING IS A CONSTANT STRUGGLE.
COOLING TOWER FOR UNITS 1 & 2
OOF, ANOTHER FULL HOUSE TODAY.
KSHUNK
GET ON THAT ALREADY, TEPCO.
THE ENTRANCE TO THE ANTI-EARTHQUAKE BUILDING IS A PREFAB STRUCTURE.
IT HAS MANNED DOUBLE DOORS TO PREVENT THE OUTSIDE AIR FROM GETTING IN.
KSHUNK
GOOD MORNING.
THERE WE GO ...
WE REMOVE OUR SHOE COVERS AS WE CROSS THE THRESHOLD.
AND THE RUBBER GLOVES.
GOOD MORNING.
NOW WE'RE INSIDE THE BUILDING AT LAST.

Sign: Gloves

Floor and walls are fireproof plastic

NOW WE NEED OUR EQUIPMENT FOR WORKING ON-SITE.
THERE ARE TWO LAYERS OF PRO-TECTIVE SUITS. WHITE FOR ON-SITE.
THE NAME TYVEK IS A REGIS-TERED TRADE-MARK OF DUPONT.
LONG-SLEEVED SHIRTS AND LONG-JOHNS GO UNDER THE SUIT (NAVY, GRAY, OR WHITE).
上 LL
上 XL
THERE ARE OTHER BRANDS PRESENT, BUT WE JUST CALL ALL OF THEM "TYVEKS."
DON'T FORGET, TWO PAIRS OF GLOVES.
Signs: Tops
NOW WE'RE FINALLY READY TO ENTER THE MAIN PART OF THE ANTI-QUAKE BUILDING.
ON THE SECOND FLOOR IS THE FAMOUS EMERGENCY PLANNING ROOM, AS SEEN IN THE PRESS CON-FERENCES ON TV, BUT THAT'S NOT FOR US.
0.8 mSv (millisieverts)
WE WANT THE ROOM ON THE RIGHT TO GET OUR APDs.
WHAT'S YOUR SETTING?
POINT-EIGHT.
I CAN HELP YOU RIGHT HERE!
大野
APD
YOU LET THEM SCAN YOUR COMPANY ID AND ASSIGNMENT BARCODE.
WHAT'S YOUR SET-TING?
BEEP
1.8 FOR ME.

HERE YOU GO, 1.8. STAY SAFE.
THANKS.
WE GET HANDED APDs SET TO OUR PLANNED EXPOSURE AMOUNT FOR THE DAY.
CHAK
YOU ATTACH THE APD TO THE ID LANYARD AROUND YOUR NECK WITH THE "GLASS BADGE" DOSIMETER. DON'T LOSE IT!
REMOVE YOUR SHOES AND HEAD DOWN THE LONG HALLWAY...
Lights alternate to save power
...AND YOU ARRIVE AT THE ANTI-QUAKE BUILDING'S BREAK ROOM.
IT'S SPLIT UP FOR THE DIFFERENT COMPANIES, WITH SILVER ALUMINUM MATS ATOP THE STERILIZED PLASTIC SHEETS.
THIS IS WHERE WE CHANGE INTO OUR ON-SITE GEAR, BUT FIRST LET'S HIT THE JOHN.
LAST CHANCE.
SAME FOR THIS.
THERE'S A SMOKING ROOM HERE, TOO. IT'S ALL YELLOWED FROM THE TOBACCO.
AIR'S WORSE IN HERE THAN IN THE REACTORS.

OKAY, HERE'S TODAY'S RUN-DOWN.
WE'LL HAVE TWO SHIFTS DUE TO HIGH DOSAGE...
EVERY ASSIGNMENT AT ICHI-F IS DANGEROUS. GOTTA LISTEN CLOSE TO THE BRIEFING AND SUIT UP CAREFULLY.
FIRST COMES UNDERWEAR. STASH YOUR APD AND ID IN YOUR SHIRT POCKET.
NEXT IS YOUR FIRST TYVEK. ALWAYS WRITE YOUR NAME ON EVERY-THING.
ZIIIIP
NEXT, THE FIRST PAIR OF GLOVES. SEAL THE WRISTS WITH TAPE.
KRIIP
NOW COMES THE FULL MASK.
TUG
TUG
CAREFUL NOT TO FASTEN THE STRAPS TOO TIGHT, OR YOUR HEAD WILL HURT AFTER A WHILE.
PWOF
Cover the filters
If the mask seals to your face when you breathe in, you're fine
CHECK-ING FOR LEAKS IS CRUCIAL!
ZZZP
I'M ALL READY.
OKAY.
SEALING AROUND THE MASK IS EASIER WHEN SOMEONE ELSE DOES IT FOR YOU.

THEN THE OTHER TYVEK GOES ON OVER.
THEN THE RUBBER GLOVES, AND...
WHOOPS! HANG ON, THERE!
WHAP
WHEN GOING TO A HIGH-EXPOSURE SITE, YOU PLACE THIS STICKER ON YOUR BACK.
防護区域内作業者
1F防護管理G
NOW WE'RE SAFELY OUT-FITTED FOR WORK.
OKAY, OFF I GO!
STAY SAFE!
THERE'S ALSO MORE ADVANCED STUFF LIKE ANORAKS AND FIREPROOF SUITS, BUT THIS IS THE BASIC OUTFIT.
WHEN LEAVING FOR THE SHIFT, WE EXIT THROUGH A DIFFERENT PREFAB STRUCTURE.
I'M DOING APD CHECKS.
APD装着ヨシ!
THEY CRACKED DOWN ON THE APD CHECKS AFTER INCIDENTS OF LEAD COVERS PREVENTING PROPER READINGS.
YOU TAKE IT OUT TO SHOW THEM DIRECTLY.
IF YOU'VE SEALED YOUR SUIT WITH TAPE, THEY NEED TO FEEL IT UNDER THE TYVEK TO MAKE SURE YOU HAVE IT.
OKAY, GOOD TO GO.
IT'S ODD TO SEE MEN FEELING EACH OTHER LIKE THIS.

Sticker: Protected Zone Work Crew

Sign: One last check. Have APD equipped!

IN THE NEXT ZONE, WE GET OUR BOOTS.
THE BOOTS GET CONTAMINATED, SO THEY'RE ONLY REUSED FOR WORKING ON-SITE.
ANKLE-LENGTH, BLUE
HALF-BOOTS, YELLOW
ALL ARE SAFETY SHOES
LONG BOOTS, WHITE OR BLACK
OF COURSE, WE ALL WEAR MULTIPLE PAIRS OF DISPOSABLE SOCKS, SO THERE'S NO WORRY ABOUT ATHLETE'S FOOT...I THINK.
LASTLY, BORROW A HELMET AND HEAD OUT THE DOUBLE DOORS.
KSHUNK KSHUNK
APD
STAY SAFE!
THIS PHRASE MIGHT SOUND OMINOUS TO PEOPLE WHO DON'T HEAR IT THIS OFTEN, BUT I FIND IT REASSURING.
STAY SAFE!
Sign: APD Check
WHEN BOARDING A CAR WITH CONTAMINATED SHOES, YOU MUST USE COVERS.
THIS IS SUCH A PAIN TO DO EVERY TIME.
DON'T COMPLAIN.
ALL RIGHT, LET'S GO.
OKAY!
VOOOM

DRUNNN

TO GET TO UNITS 1 TO 4, WE RETURN TO CHUO ROAD, THE WAY WE CAME, THEN GO DOWN THIS HILL STRAIGHT TOWARD THE WATER.
OCEAN
①
②
OKUMA AVE.
QUAKE BLDG.
CHUO RD.
CHUO (CENTER) INTERSECTION
FUREAI INTERSECTION

Sign: Okuma Avenue, Okuma Town Flower: The Pear Blossom

WE TURN RIGHT BEFORE THE SEASIDE STREET.
VWUM
ネバーギブアップ!福島

Trailer: Never Give Up! Fukushima Hitachi

...IS THE ADMIN OFFICE ANNEX. ITS WINDOWS AND WALLS WERE BLOWN OFF IN THE HYDROGEN EXPLOSION. AND...
RATTL
RATTL
HITACHI
VISIBLE BEHIND US...

UNIT 1
...ON THE LEFT ARE THE UNIT 1 AND UNIT 2 REACTORS.
UNIT 2
UNIT 1 IS UNDER A COVER, WHILE UNIT 2 STILL LOOKS LIKE IT ALWAYS HAS ON THE OUTSIDE.
BWUM
SKREE
BUT THERE'S NO DENYING ...
KCHAK
...THAT THE SIGHT OF THE UNIT 3 BUILDING IS SIMPLY BREATH-TAKING.
JUST BLOWS MY MIND EVERY TIME I SEE IT.
...
TDF
竜田
TDF

HERE I AM AT LAST...
I AM NOT FROM FUKU-SHIMA.

Sign: Job Guidance

WHEN THE EXPLOSION HAPPENED, I WAS LIVING IN THE TOKYO AREA AND LOOKING FOR WORK.
I'D LIKE TO WORK AT FU-KUSHIMA DAIICHI.
ARE YOU... SERIOUS?
YES. VERY MUCH SO.
I WAS SWAYED BY HIGH PAY, CURIOSITY, AND JUST A BIT OF ALTRUISM FOR THOSE AFFECTED.

Window: Hello Work

I'D BE LYING IF I SAID I WASN'T CONCERNED ABOUT THE RADIATION EXPOSURE, BUT MY OWN RESEARCH ON THIS CASE SHOWED ME THAT IT WASN'T AS BAD AS THE MEDIA AND CERTAIN CITIZEN GROUPS CLAIMED.

IN FACT, I TOLD MYSELF, IF THERE REALLY WAS A "HIDDEN TRUTH OF FUKUSHIMA" LIKE THEY SAID, I'D GO THERE AND SEE WHAT IT WAS FOR MYSELF.

RADIATION SAFETY TRAINING

HOWEVER, THE PROCESS FOR A NON-LOCAL CITIZEN TO WORK THERE WAS RATHER BYZANTINE, AND AFTER MANY DETOURS, I FINALLY GOT CLEARANCE TO WORK AT ICHI-F IN EARLY SUMMER 2012, MORE THAN A YEAR LATER.

IF I GET THE CHANCE, I'D LIKE TO TELL YOU ALL ABOUT THAT SOMEDAY.

J-VILLAGE'S WBC (WHOLE-BODY COUNTER)

Booklet: Radiation Control Handbook

THE FIRST COMPANY I WORKED WITH WAS A SENARY (SIXTH-HAND) SUBCONTRACTOR UNDER LAYERS AND LAYERS OF LARGER COMPANIES. TECHNICALLY, IT WASN'T A CONSTRUCTION JOB, BUT MANAGEMENT WORK.

EVEN AT 1-F, I ONLY MAKE 8,000 YEN A DAY.

AND SUBTRACT A THOUSAND OF THAT FOR RENT.

IT'S BARELY ENOUGH TO SURVIVE...

AND THERE'S NO EXTRA HAZARD PAY.

NO FOOD IN-CLUD-ED...

I HAVE TO GET CHEAP FAST FOOD FOR EVERY MEAL.

THE OTHERS HIRED AT THE SAME TIME AS ME CAME FROM ALL OVER THE COUNTRY, AND HAD THEIR OWN PROBLEMS TO MANAGE.

*1 USD = approximately 100 yen.

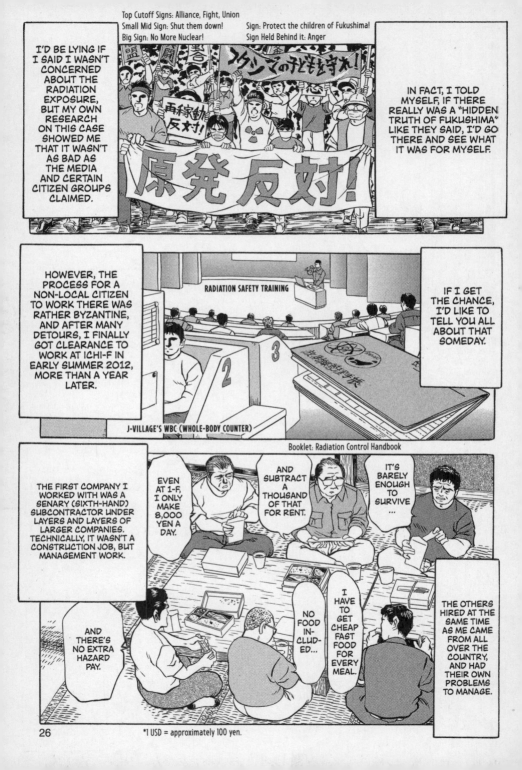

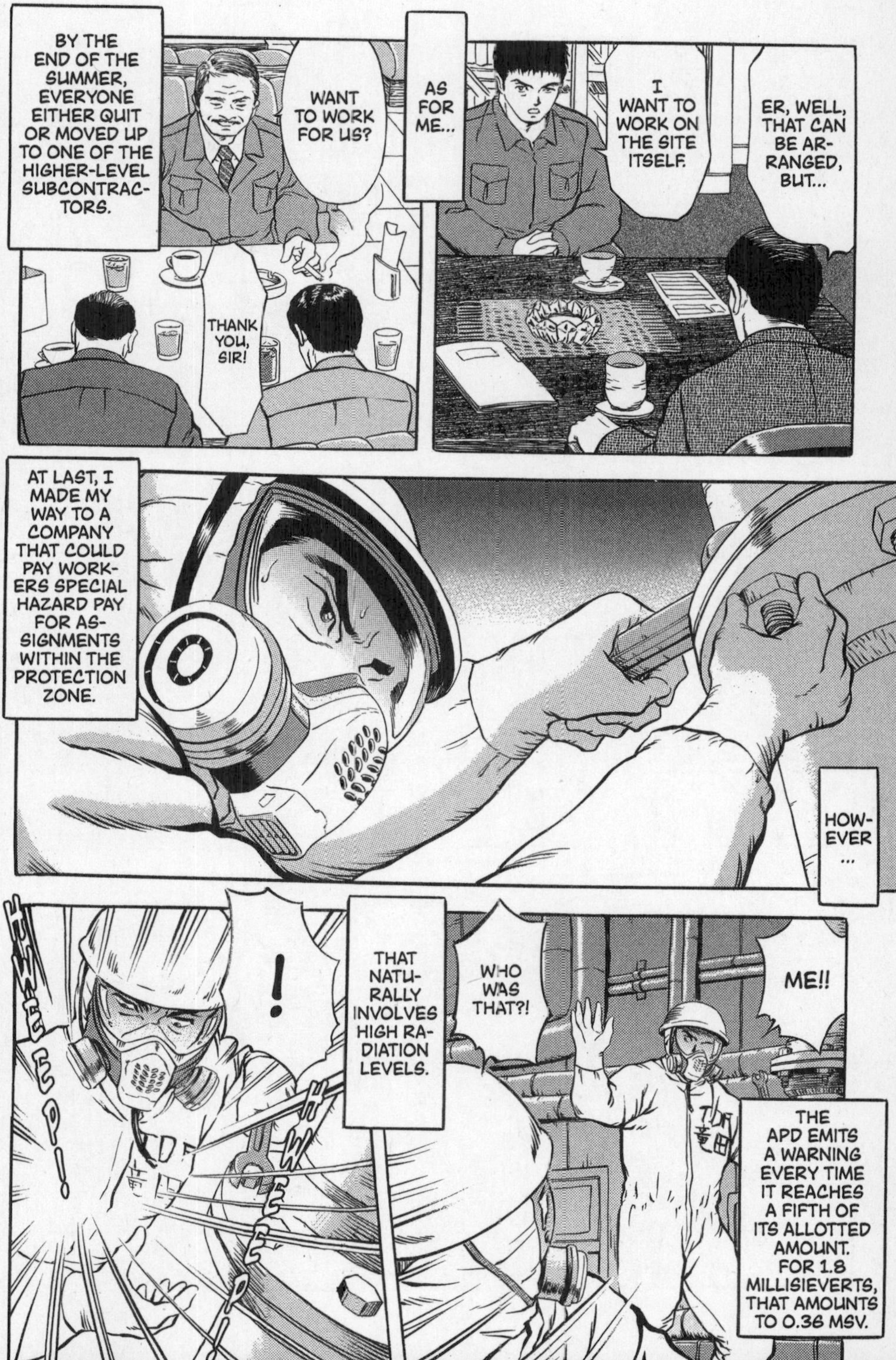
BY THE END OF THE SUMMER, EVERYONE EITHER QUIT OR MOVED UP TO ONE OF THE HIGHER-LEVEL SUBCONTRACTORS.
WANT TO WORK FOR US?
THANK YOU, SIR!
AS FOR ME...
I WANT TO WORK ON THE SITE ITSELF.
ER, WELL, THAT CAN BE ARRANGED, BUT...
AT LAST, I MADE MY WAY TO A COMPANY THAT COULD PAY WORKERS SPECIAL HAZARD PAY FOR ASSIGNMENTS WITHIN THE PROTECTION ZONE.
HOWEVER...
HWEEEP!
!
HWEEEP!
THAT NATURALLY INVOLVES HIGH RADIATION LEVELS.
WHO WAS THAT?!
ME!!
THE APD EMITS A WARNING EVERY TIME IT REACHES A FIFTH OF ITS ALLOTTED AMOUNT. FOR 1.8 MILLISIEVERTS, THAT AMOUNTS TO 0.36 MSV.

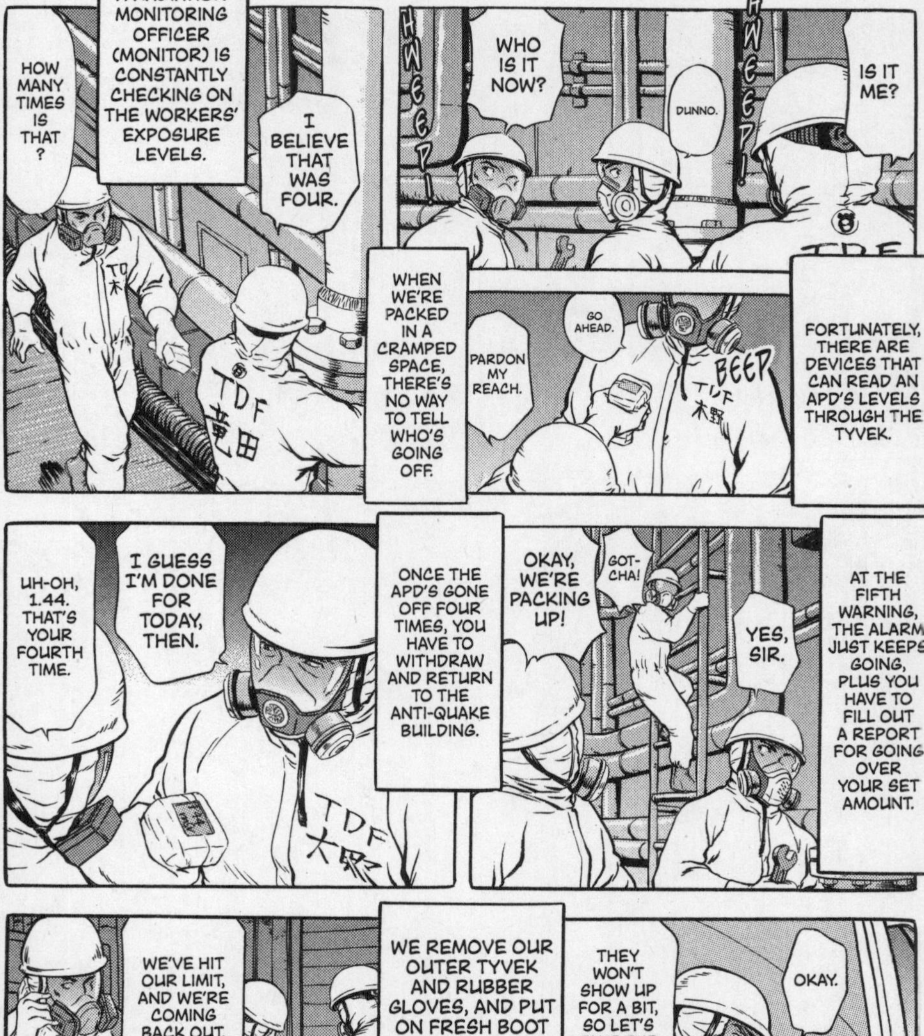

A RADIATION MONITORING OFFICER (MONITOR) IS CONSTANTLY CHECKING ON THE WORKERS' EXPOSURE LEVELS.
HOW MANY TIMES IS THAT?
I BELIEVE THAT WAS FOUR.
HWEEP!
WHO IS IT NOW?
DUNNO.
HWEEP!
IS IT ME?
WHEN WE'RE PACKED IN A CRAMPED SPACE, THERE'S NO WAY TO TELL WHO'S GOING OFF.
PARDON MY REACH.
GO AHEAD.
BEEP
FORTUNATELY, THERE ARE DEVICES THAT CAN READ AN APD'S LEVELS THROUGH THE TYVEK.
UH-OH, 1.44. THAT'S YOUR FOURTH TIME.
I GUESS I'M DONE FOR TODAY, THEN.
ONCE THE APD'S GONE OFF FOUR TIMES, YOU HAVE TO WITHDRAW AND RETURN TO THE ANTI-QUAKE BUILDING.
OKAY, WE'RE PACKING UP!
GOT-CHA!
YES, SIR.
AT THE FIFTH WARNING, THE ALARM JUST KEEPS GOING, PLUS YOU HAVE TO FILL OUT A REPORT FOR GOING OVER YOUR SET AMOUNT.
WE'VE HIT OUR LIMIT, AND WE'RE COMING BACK OUT. GET READY TO TAKE OVER.
WE REMOVE OUR OUTER TYVEK AND RUBBER GLOVES, AND PUT ON FRESH BOOT COVERS TO GET IN THE CAR.
THEY WON'T SHOW UP FOR A BIT, SO LET'S TAKE THE LONG WAY BACK.
OKAY.

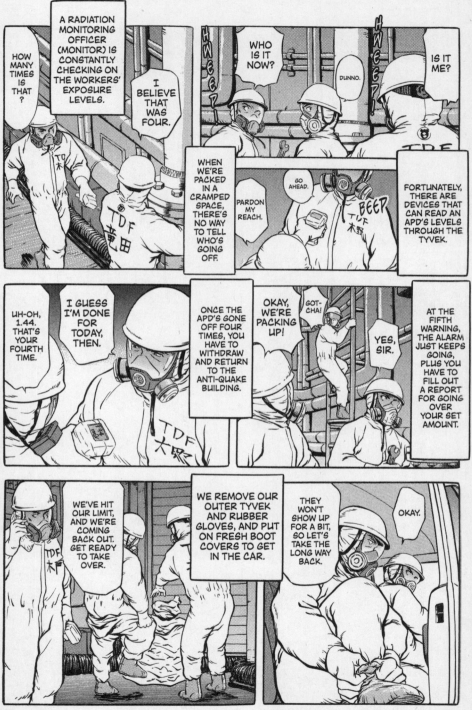

SINCE WE'RE HERE, WE MIGHT AS WELL LOOK AT THE REAR SIDE OF ICHI-F.
VWOM
AFTER THE TSUNAMI, A HUGE CRUDE OIL TANK WASHED UP RIGHT DOWN THIS PATH.
PASS UNIT 1 GOING BACK TO OKUMA AVE. AND TURN RIGHT, AND THE OCEAN IS STRAIGHT AHEAD.
TURN RIGHT AGAIN, AND YOU'LL PASS THE URBINE BUILD-INGS.
← OCEAN IS ON THIS SIDE
ALL THE SEASIDE BUILDINGS ARE IN TATTERS—THE BASES FROM THE TSUNAMI, AND THE UPPER LEVELS FROM THE EXPLOSIONS.
Tank: Condensate Tank
復水タンク
3
ALONG THE TURBINE BUILDINGS ARE CARS THAT WASHED UP IN THE TSUNAMI.
4
Y'KNOW, THE GRAVEL AND STEEL PLATES THEY PUT DOWN LOWERED THE RADIATION LEVEL A WHOLE LOT.
YEAH, I'M IMPRESSED WITH HOW MUCH EASIER IT IS TO GET AROUND.

WE'LL MAKE A TURN AROUND THE WASTE DISPOSAL BUILDINGS, NOW SURROUNDED BY TEMPORARY BREAKWATERS ...

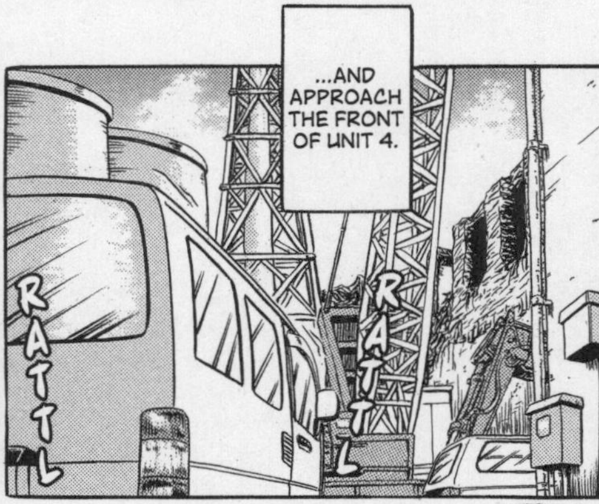
...AND APPROACH THE FRONT OF UNIT 4.
RATTL
RATTL

Sign: Let all our hearts be one! Fukushima

OOOOH, THEY'VE BEEN HARD AT WORK HERE.
RIPPED OFF ALL THE STUFF ON TOP ALREADY.
ALL THOSE FOLKS SAYIN' THAT JAPAN IS DOOMED IF THIS THING COLLAPSES REALLY OUGHTA SEE THIS FOR THEMSELVES.

REMOVED SECTION

IF YOU CLIMB TO THE SIDE OF UNIT 4...

UNIT 4 IS VISIBLY SMALLER NOW THAT THEY''VE REMOVED THE UPPER LEVEL OF THE BUILDING EXTERIOR.

...YOU PASS THE TANKS AT YACHO-NO-MORI.

WHEN WE GET BACK TO THE ANTI-EARTHQUAKE BUILDING, THE REPLACEMENT SHIFT IS JUST ABOUT GEARED UP TO LEAVE.

WEL-COME BACK!

WE COVERED OUR SCHEDULED WORK. THE REST IS UP TO YOU.

GOT-CHA!

WE LEFT THE TOOLS IN THE BACK WHERE THE RAD COUNT IS LOW.

THANKS.

THE ENTRANCE SEEMS TO HAVE A HIGH ATMOSPHERE (AIRBORNE RADIATION LEVEL), SO GET IN THERE QUICK.

I WON'T LIE, IT'S ALWAYS A RELIEF TO GET BACK TO THE ANTI-QUAKE BUILDING SAFELY...

HERE WE GO!

VWUM

STAY SAFE!

PASSING ALONG INFO ON THE WORK STATUS AND CONDI-TIONS IS CRUCIAL.

KSHUNK KSHUNK
WELCOME BACK!
BUT THE TRIP BACK TO THE BREAK AREA IS LONG AND TIRESOME.
WE ENTER THROUGH A SPECIAL RETURN-TRIP DOOR, WHICH IS DIFFERENT FROM OUR MORNING ENTRANCE AND OUR ORIGINAL EXIT.
RIP
WE RETURN OUR HELMETS AND UNDO THE TAPE ON THE MASKS AND WRISTS.
RIP
RIP
テープ
Sign: Tape
HI THERE.
IN THE NEXT ZONE, WE RETURN OUR SHOES.
THEN WE REMOVE OUR TYVEKS AND TAKE OFF OUR RUBBER GLOVES AND SOCKS.
Signs: Tyveks/Socks
AT LAST, WE CAN TAKE OFF OUR MASKS.
WHEW ...
Still wearing cotton gloves
THE MASKS GET SWEATY EVEN IN THE WINTER. SO IN THE SUMMER, WELL, YOU CAN IMAGINE WHAT IT'S LIKE.
You must announce this
LAST COMES THE PERSONAL SURVEY, WHERE THEY MEASURE YOU TO MAKE SURE YOU'RE NOT STILL WEARING ANYTHING WITH HIGH RADIATION.
UNIT 4 EXTERIOR.
WORK STATION ?
THERE ARE ABOUT TEN LANES FOR SURVEYS, BUT IT CAN GET REALLY BACKED UP WHEN A BUNCH OF TEAMS RETURN FROM THEIR SHIFTS AT ONCE.
Mask in the grocery bag
Cotton gloves discarded here

WE GET SCANNED THOROUGHLY FROM THE TOPS OF OUR HEADS TO THE BOTTOMS OF OUR FEET.
UNDER FEET, PLEASE.
THE MOST LIKELY SOURCE OF CONTAMINATION IS THE FILTERS ON THE FULL MASKS.
THE FILTERS ARE HOT, SO YOU'LL NEED TO SWITCH THEM OUT.
THANKS.
REPLACEMENT, PLEASE.
GOING BACK OUT THERE?
K-R-K KRK
NO, I'M DONE FOR THE DAY.
DUST IT IS, THEN.
THEY WON'T GIVE ME THE EXPENSIVE CHARCOAL KIND ANYMORE.
BRR! THE SWEAT'S CHILLY ON MY SKIN.
AT THE PLACE WHERE I PICKED UP MY STUFF COMING IN, I SWITCH OUT MY UNDERWEAR AND CAP.
NICE WORK OUT THERE.
THEN YOU RETURN YOUR APD TO THE SAME DESK.
ZEET
GACHUNK

Sign: Bottoms

THEY'LL PRINT OUT A SHEET OF THE DAY'S RADIATION EXPOSURE.
HOW MUCH?
1.48 MILLISIEVERTS.
HOW MUCH DO YOU HAVE LEFT, MR. ONO?
ONLY 5 FOR THE REST OF THE YEAR.
THERE ARE LIMITS ON HOW MUCH RADIATION EXPOSURE YOU CAN SUFFER IN A YEAR BY LAW. IT'S 50 MSV FOR A SINGLE YEAR, AND 100 MSV OVER FIVE YEARS.
THEREFORE, MOST COMPANIES LIMIT THEIR WORKERS TO 20 OR LESS IN A YEAR.
I'LL BE DONE RIGHT ABOUT WHEN WE FINISH THIS JOB.
WON'T BE BACK IN ICHI-F UNTIL THE SPRING.
THE YEARLY DOSAGE TALLY IS RESET IN APRIL.
THE DOSAGE LIMIT ISSUE HAS AN EFFECT ON THE NUMBER OF WORKERS TEPCO AND THE SUBCONTRACTORS CAN HIRE.
WE'RE BACK!
NICE WORK OUT THERE.
IT'S TROUBLE FOR US, TOO, SINCE IT AFFECTS OUR INCOME.
OKAY, LET'S EAT.
I'M TAKING SOME HOT WATER.
EACH COMPANY BRINGS ITS OWN HOT WATER POTS INTO THE BREAK ROOM, SO YOU CAN AT LEAST HAVE INSTANT NOODLES, BUT THERE'S NO PLACE TO DUMP OUT THE REST OF THE LIQUID. GOTTA DRINK THAT BROTH!
SHUK SHUK
WE GET PLASTIC BOTTLES OF WATER, AND THERE ARE BOTH HOT AND COLD WATER COOLERS.
THE COMPANY RECREATION FACILITY AND SOME OF THE REST AREAS OF THE VARIOUS CONTRACTORS HAVE REFRIGERATORS WITH SPORTS DRINKS.
IN THE SUMMER OF 2012, ONE WEEKLY TABLOID SAID, "ONLY TEPCO EMPLOYEES GET COLD WATER TO DRINK," BUT THIS WAS A MALICIOUS FABRICATION.

THERE WAS ANOTHER CASE OF TABLOID LIES.
HEY! WHAT'S WRONG?!
AGAIN, IN SUMMER 2012, THERE WAS A WORKER WHO WENT INTO CARDIAC ARREST IN THE REC CENTER.
BRING THE AED!
CALL THE AMBU-LANCE FROM UNITS 5 AND 6!
HMP
HMP
THEY TRIED LIFESAVING MEASURES LIKE HEART MASSAGE AND AN AED, TO NO AVAIL.
BY THE TIME THE DOCTOR GOT THERE FROM THE MEDICAL OFFICE AT UNITS 5 AND 6...
HE'S DEAD.
ACCORDING TO THE "UNDER-COVER JOURNALIST"...
HIS PULSE IS BACK!
...THE AED SUCCEEDED IN REVIVING HIM BRIEFLY. THE REPORT CLAIMED THAT HE DIED DUE TO "LACK OF PROPER MEDICAL FACILITIES."
THANK GOOD-NESS.
WHEW
ACCORD-ING TO SOMEONE WHO WAS ACTUALLY PRESENT...
HE NEVER CAME BACK. ALL THAT NONSENSE WAS A TOTAL LIE.
HOWEVER, IN TEPCO'S INCIDENT REPORT, HE WAS ONLY PRONOUNCED DEAD ONCE TAKEN TO A HOSPITAL IN IWAKI. PERHAPS THEY DID NOT WANT THE DEATH TO BE OFFICIALLY LISTED AS OCCURRING AT ICHI-F.
EITHER WAY, THE CAUSE WAS A HEART ATTACK WITH NO RELATION TO RADIATION EXPOSURE. IF THEY *WERE* RELATED, WE'D ALL BE DEAD BY NOW. HE WAS THE FIFTH VICTIM IN THE DECOMMISSION EFFORT. MAY HE REST IN PEACE.

THE MEDIA'S SHADY EXPOSÉS ON "THE TRUTH OF FUKUSHIMA" ARE FULL OF NONSENSE LIKE THAT, AND WE GET SICK OF IT HERE.
AHH, I FEEL BETTER AFTER EATING.
YEP.
THEY SAY THAT ICHI-F IS LIKE HELL ON EARTH, AND HERE WE ARE EATING LUNCH AND TAKING NAPS IN THE BREAK ROOM.
THIS IS "THE REALITY OF FUKUSHIMA" THAT THE MEDIA RARELY EVER BOTHERS TO SHOW.
頼むぞ福一!!
GZZZZ
SNORR
WEL-COME BACK.
Z Z
MM ...?
HERE WE ARE.
OH! WELCOME BACK...
MADE IT THROUGH ANOTHER DAY.
TDF
ALL RIGHT, LET'S GO.
SO LONG, EVERY-ONE.
WE PUT ON BLUE TYVEKS AND FULL MASKS TO LEAVE, TOO.
SO LONG.
GOOD WORK OUT THERE!
WE LEAVE THE ANTI-QUAKE BUILDING FROM THE SAME ENTRANCE AS IN THE MORNING.
MAT

Sign: Do it for us, Fuku-Ichi!!

A poster from an association of ex-TEPCO employees. (They call it Fuku-Ichi for some reason.)

You can wear just cotton gloves on the way back

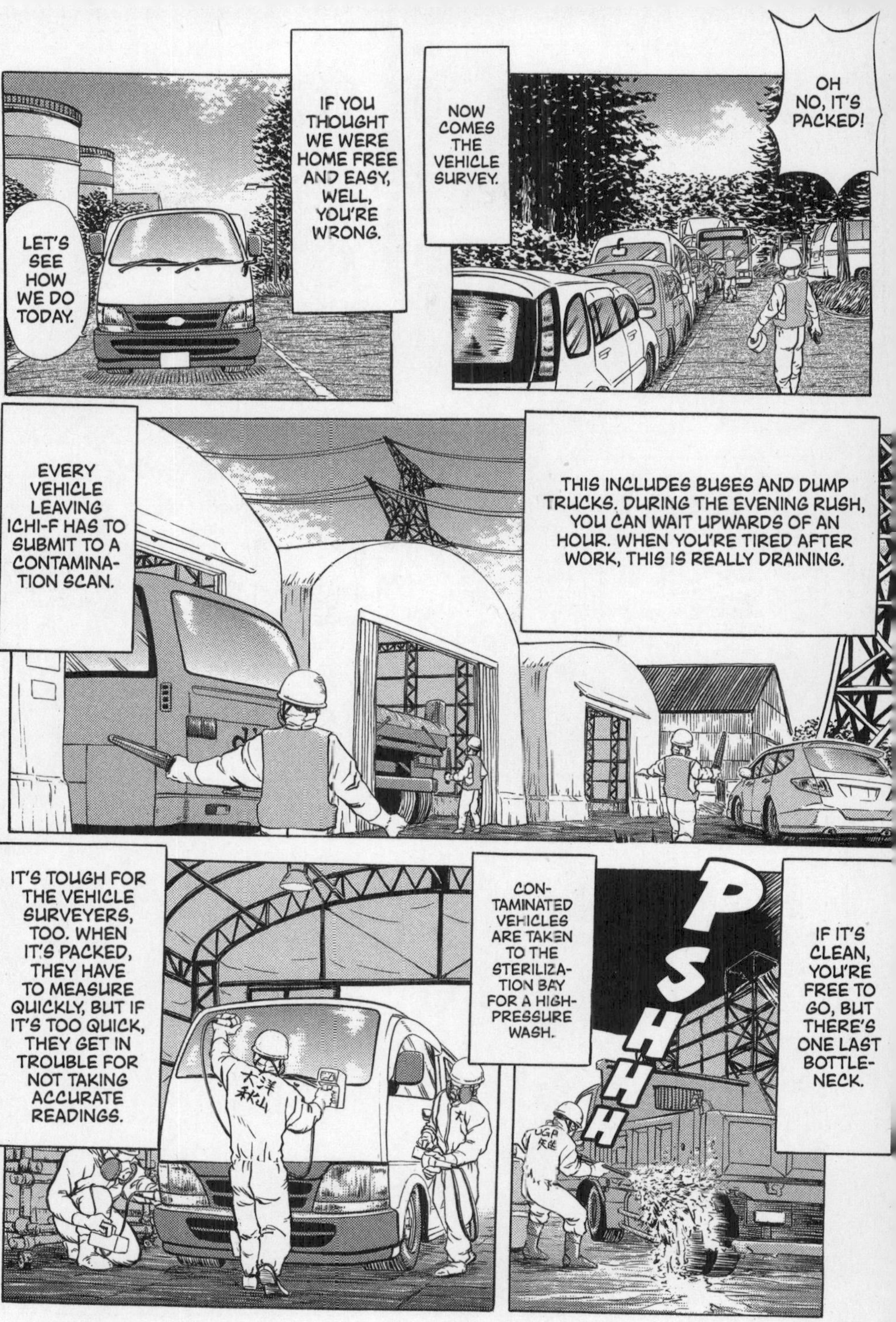
IF YOU THOUGHT WE WERE HOME FREE AND EASY, WELL, YOU'RE WRONG.
LET'S SEE HOW WE DO TODAY.
NOW COMES THE VEHICLE SURVEY.
OH NO, IT'S PACKED!
EVERY VEHICLE LEAVING ICHI-F HAS TO SUBMIT TO A CONTAMINATION SCAN.
THIS INCLUDES BUSES AND DUMP TRUCKS. DURING THE EVENING RUSH, YOU CAN WAIT UPWARDS OF AN HOUR. WHEN YOU'RE TIRED AFTER WORK, THIS IS REALLY DRAINING.
IT'S TOUGH FOR THE VEHICLE SURVEYERS, TOO. WHEN IT'S PACKED, THEY HAVE TO MEASURE QUICKLY, BUT IF IT'S TOO QUICK, THEY GET IN TROUBLE FOR NOT TAKING ACCURATE READINGS.
CONTAMINATED VEHICLES ARE TAKEN TO THE STERILIZATION BAY FOR A HIGH-PRESSURE WASH.
PSHHHH
IF IT'S CLEAN, YOU'RE FREE TO GO, BUT THERE'S ONE LAST BOTTLENECK.

Sign: Thank you very much! We are grateful for your visit.
Fukushima Daiichi Nuclear Power Plant

Sign: Fir Tree Parking

AFTER THE DISASTER, THERE WERE GRISLY PHOTOS OF COWS THAT DIED OF STARVATION...

Sign: Nuclear power is gentle on the earth
Okuma Town is gentle to people

LOOK, A CALF!

SWEET LITTLE THING.

LOOK CLOSELY.

...BUT THE ONES LIVING THERE NOW LOOK STURDY—STRONG AND HEALTHY EVEN.

SEE? NO EAR TAG.

THIS ONE HAS NO INDIVIDUAL ID TAG.

IT WAS BORN AFTER THE DISASTER.

I'VE NEVER SEEN ANY MUTANTS, OF COURSE.

TAKE CARE!

BOING

SAME GOES FOR THE OTHER FLORA AND FAUNA. LIFE IS HARDY AND FREE, EVEN IN THIS RESTRICTED ZONE.

LET'S GO HOME.

YEAH.

THE REST OF THE WORLD THINKS OF OUR WORKPLACE AS A GHASTLY HELL ON EARTH.

BUT DESPITE OUR MANY COMPLAINTS, EVEN WE ARE PROUD OF OUR WORLD, AND OUR PLACE IN IT.

WE'LL CONTINUE DRIVING THIS ROAD UP TO ICHI-F TOMORROW, AND HOWEVER LONG IT TAKES AFTER THAT.
Sign: Tomioka will never give up!
Sign: Don't use normal tires during icy or snowy conditions!
富岡は負けん！
50
凍結・積雪道路のノーマルタイヤ

Sign: Let all our hearts be one! Fukushima
MAYBE WE WON'T STILL BE ALIVE TO SEE IT FOR OURSELVES...
心をひとつにがんばろう！福島
...BUT OUR MISSION WILL CONTINUE UNTIL THE DAY WE'VE ERASED THIS WORKPLACE FROM FUKUSHIMA.
CHAPTER 0 - END

Chapter 0: "Stay Safe!" was originally the winner of the 34th Manga Open Grand Prize, and ran in *Morning* issue 44, 2013, under the title, "Ichi-F: An Interior Guide to the Fukushima Daiichi Nuclear Power Plant."

WHICH IS WHY ICHI-F'S SITE IS STILL BEING WORKED ON TODAY.

WHAT ARE THEY BUILDING HERE?

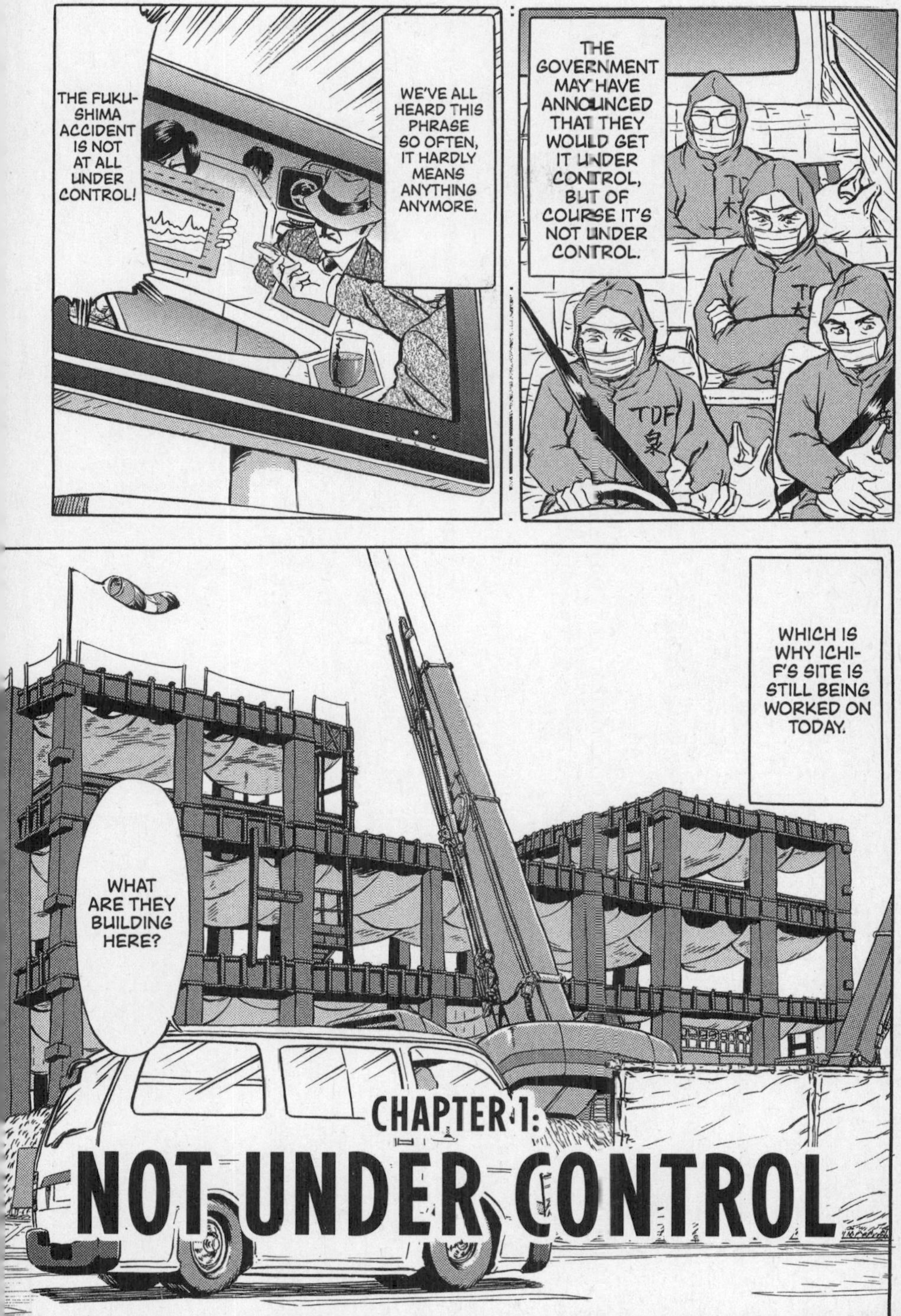

CHAPTER 1: NOT UNDER CONTROL

OH, THIS IS THE NEW RESTRICTED-ZONE ACCESS FACILITY. THEY'RE GOING TO TRANSFER ALL THE J-VILLAGE FUNCTIONS HERE WHEN IT'S DONE.
AHH.
TDF 竜田
THAT MEANS THAT WE'LL BE ABLE TO CHANGE CLOTHES AND GET OUR APDs AND STUFF THERE INSTEAD.
FINISHED VERSION OF THE ACCESS MANAGEMENT FACILITY
DURING THE PERIOD I'M DEPICTING HERE IN 2012, THIS BUILDING WAS UNDER CONSTRUCTION. AS OF JULY 2013, IT'S NOW FULLY FUNCTIONAL. PEOPLE SAY THAT ICHI-F'S SITUATION IS GOING NOWHERE, BUT THINGS ARE CHANGING BIT BY BIT.
THESE ARE THE WATER TANKS, WHICH LATER ENDED UP HAVING ISSUES WITH LEAKS.
SO ALL THESE TANKS ARE HOLDING CONTAMINATED WATER.
YEP. AND MORE AND MORE BY THE WEEK.

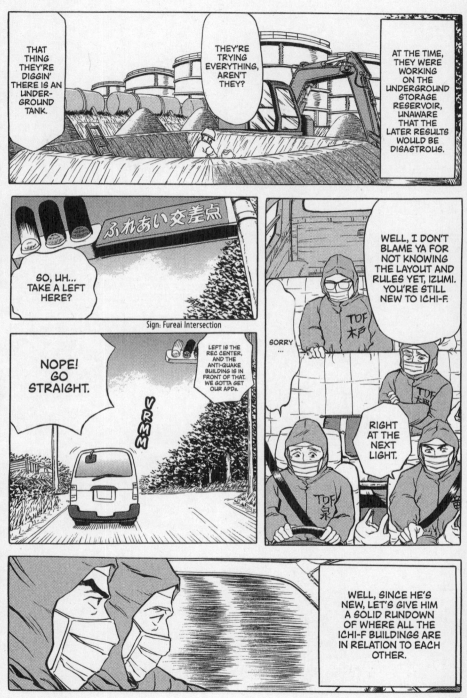

THAT THING THEY'RE DIGGIN' THERE IS AN UNDER-GROUND TANK.
THEY'RE TRYING EVERYTHING, AREN'T THEY?
AT THE TIME, THEY WERE WORKING ON THE UNDERGROUND STORAGE RESERVOIR, UNAWARE THAT THE LATER RESULTS WOULD BE DISASTROUS.
WELL, I DON'T BLAME YA FOR NOT KNOWING THE LAYOUT AND RULES YET, IZUMI. YOU'RE STILL NEW TO ICHI-F.
SORRY ...
RIGHT AT THE NEXT LIGHT.
ふれあい交差点
SO, UH... TAKE A LEFT HERE?
Sign: Fureai Intersection
LEFT IS THE REC CENTER, AND THE ANTI-QUAKE BUILDING IS IN FRONT OF THAT. WE GOTTA GET OUR APDs.
NOPE! GO STRAIGHT.
VRMM
WELL, SINCE HE'S NEW, LET'S GIVE HIM A SOLID RUNDOWN OF WHERE ALL THE ICHI-F BUILDINGS ARE IN RELATION TO EACH OTHER.

SUPPRESSION POOL SURGE TANK (BROKEN)
UNIT 6
UNIT 5
THERE'S A MEDICAL STATION, TOO.
HERE'S YOUR APD.
ADMIN. OFFICE
ANTI-QUAKE BLDG.
FUTABA RD.
FALLEN UTILITY TOWER
The collapse of this tower was a partial cause of the external power supply loss
HERE'S THE ADVANCED LIQUID PROCESSING SYSTEM (ALPS), OUR SECRET WEAPON AGAINST CONTAMINATED WATER.
TSUNAMI/RADIATION JUNKED VEHICLE STORAGE
CHUO INTERSECTION
CHUO (CENTER) RD.
THIS IS ICHI-F, OUR WORKPLACE.
(AS OF 2012)
AFFILIATE SHELTERS

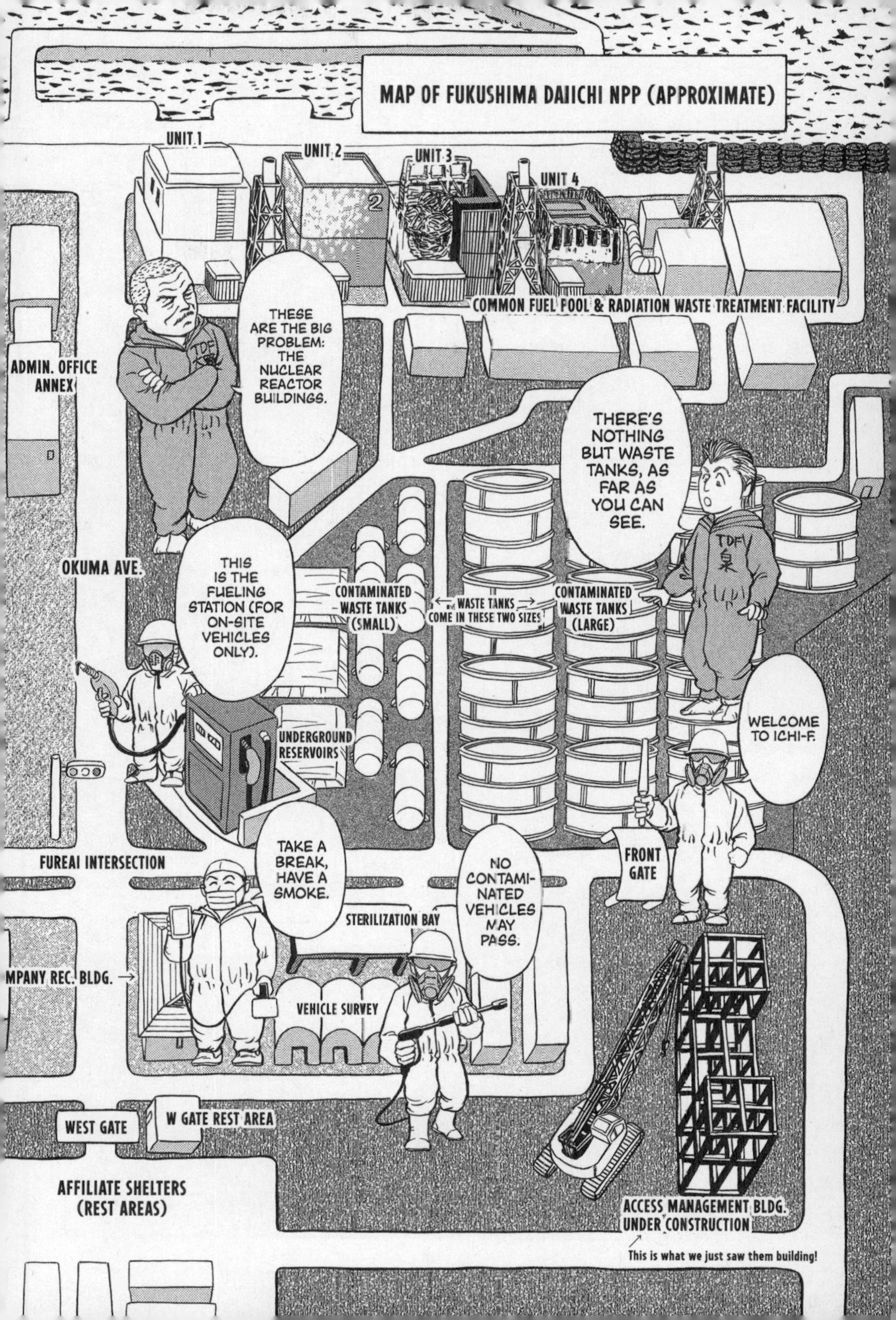

MAP OF FUKUSHIMA DAIICHI NPP (APPROXIMATE)
UNIT 1
UNIT 2
UNIT 3
UNIT 4
COMMON FUEL POOL & RADIATION WASTE TREATMENT FACILITY
THESE ARE THE BIG PROBLEM: THE NUCLEAR REACTOR BUILDINGS.
ADMIN. OFFICE ANNEX
THERE'S NOTHING BUT WASTE TANKS, AS FAR AS YOU CAN SEE.
OKUMA AVE.
THIS IS THE FUELING STATION (FOR ON-SITE VEHICLES ONLY).
CONTAMINATED WASTE TANKS (SMALL)
WASTE TANKS COME IN THESE TWO SIZES
CONTAMINATED WASTE TANKS (LARGE)
WELCOME TO ICHI-F.
UNDERGROUND RESERVOIRS
FUREAI INTERSECTION
TAKE A BREAK, HAVE A SMOKE.
NO CONTAMINATED VEHICLES MAY PASS.
FRONT GATE
STERILIZATION BAY
MPANY REC. BLDG.
VEHICLE SURVEY
WEST GATE
W GATE REST AREA
AFFILIATE SHELTERS (REST AREAS)
ACCESS MANAGEMENT BLDG. UNDER CONSTRUCTION
This is what we just saw them building!

Depending on the time and company, our break areas switch between the anti-quake building and the rec center. Plant construction companies like Hitachi and Toshiba have their own break areas.

AT THE ANTI-EARTHQUAKE BUILDING, WE PICK UP OUR APDs.
HERE WE ARE, 1.8 MSV. STAY SAFE!
AT THIS POINT IN TIME, WE WERE USING THE RECREATION CENTER AS OUR BREAK AREA, SO WE CHANGE INTO OUR GEAR THERE.
TDF
NOW TO OUR ASSIGNMENT.
HEY, LET'S GO DOWN THE RIGHT PATH UP THERE.
HUH?
TDF
泉
UNIT 2
UNIT 3
UNIT 4
THIS WAY?
YEAH. WE CAN GET TO UNIT 4 THAT WAY.

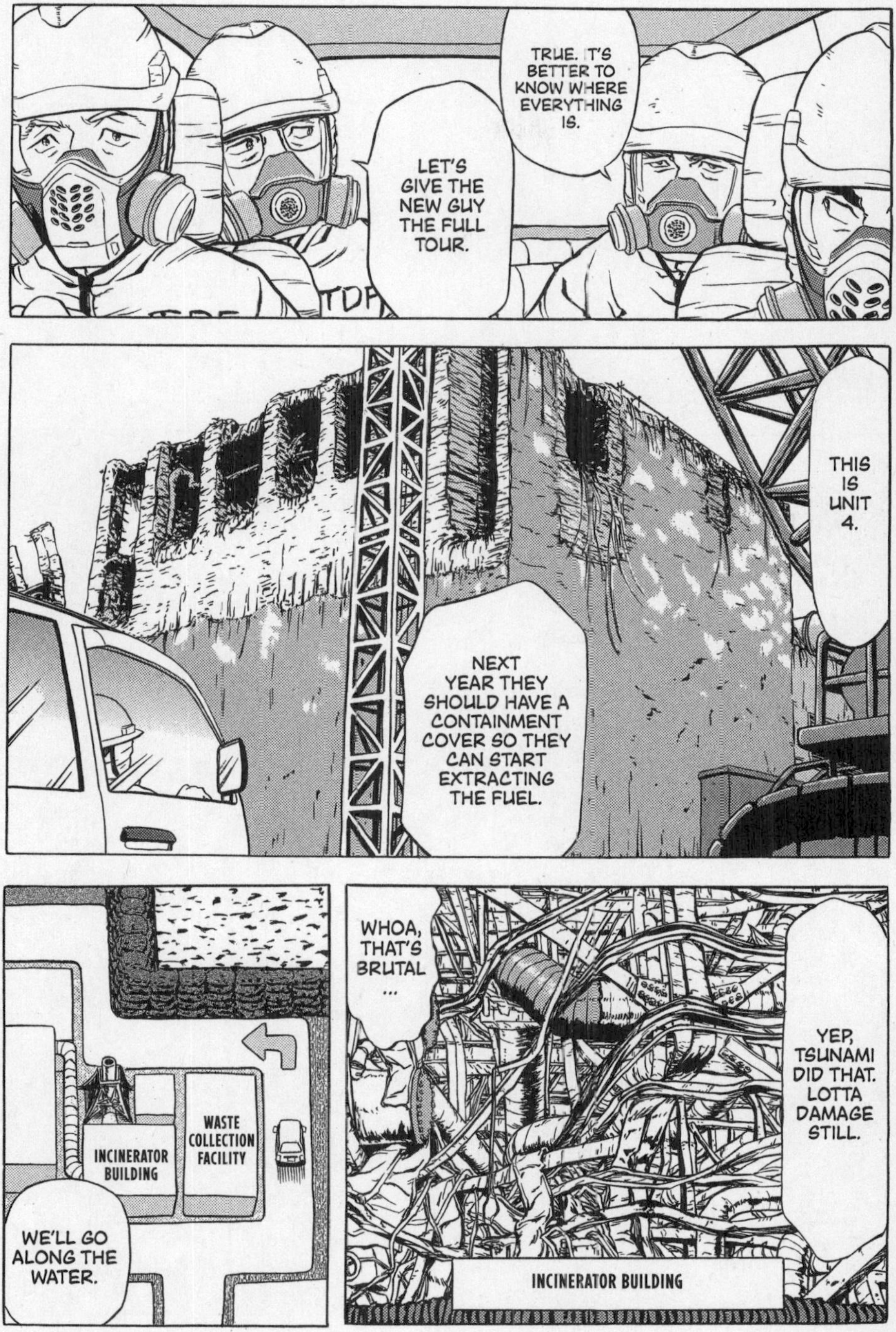
LET'S GIVE THE NEW GUY THE FULL TOUR.
TRUE. IT'S BETTER TO KNOW WHERE EVERYTHING IS.
THIS IS UNIT 4.
NEXT YEAR THEY SHOULD HAVE A CONTAINMENT COVER SO THEY CAN START EXTRACTING THE FUEL.
WASTE COLLECTION FACILITY
INCINERATOR BUILDING
WE'LL GO ALONG THE WATER.
WHOA, THAT'S BRUTAL ...
YEP, TSUNAMI DID THAT. LOTTA DAMAGE STILL.
INCINERATOR BUILDING

ンプール水サージタンク
3500KL
SUPPRESSION POOL SURGE TANK

YONOMORI LINE NO. 27 UTILITY TOWER
(ALONG FUTABA RD.)
This is the "fallen utility tower" mentioned in the previous map
that helped cause the loss of external power.

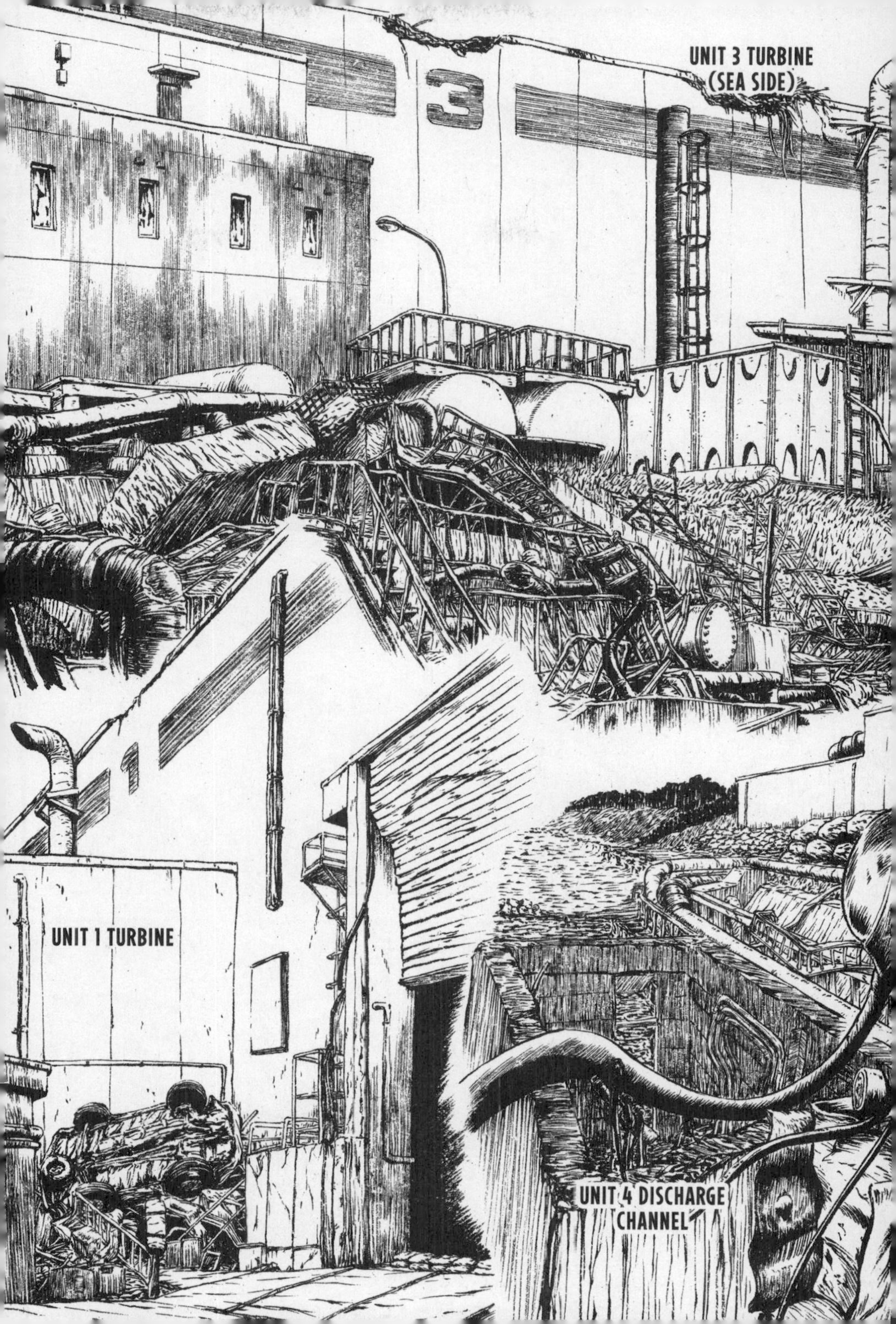
UNIT 3 TURBINE
(SEA SIDE)
UNIT 1 TURBINE
UNIT 4 DISCHARGE
CHANNEL

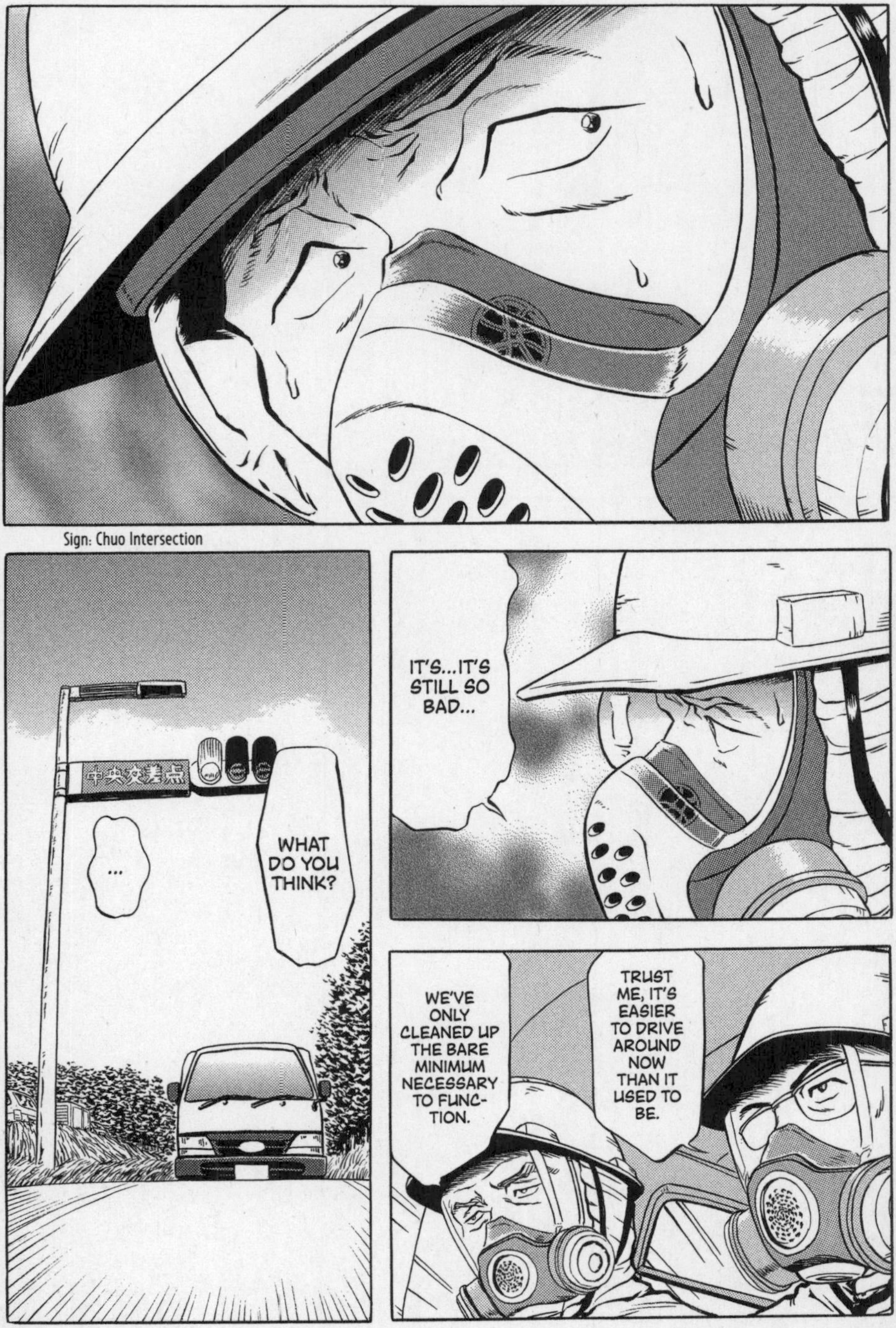

Sign: Chuo Intersection

...

WHAT DO YOU THINK?

IT'S...IT'S STILL SO BAD...

WE'VE ONLY CLEANED UP THE BARE MINIMUM NECESSARY TO FUNCTION.

TRUST ME, IT'S EASIER TO DRIVE AROUND NOW THAN IT USED TO BE.

Sign: Okuma Avenue, Okuma Town Flower: The Pear Blossom

THE EXPLOSION AT UNIT 1 DID THIS ONE IN.

GOTTA RESPECT THE POWER OF A HYDROGEN BLAST.

ADMINISTRATIVE OFFICE ANNEX

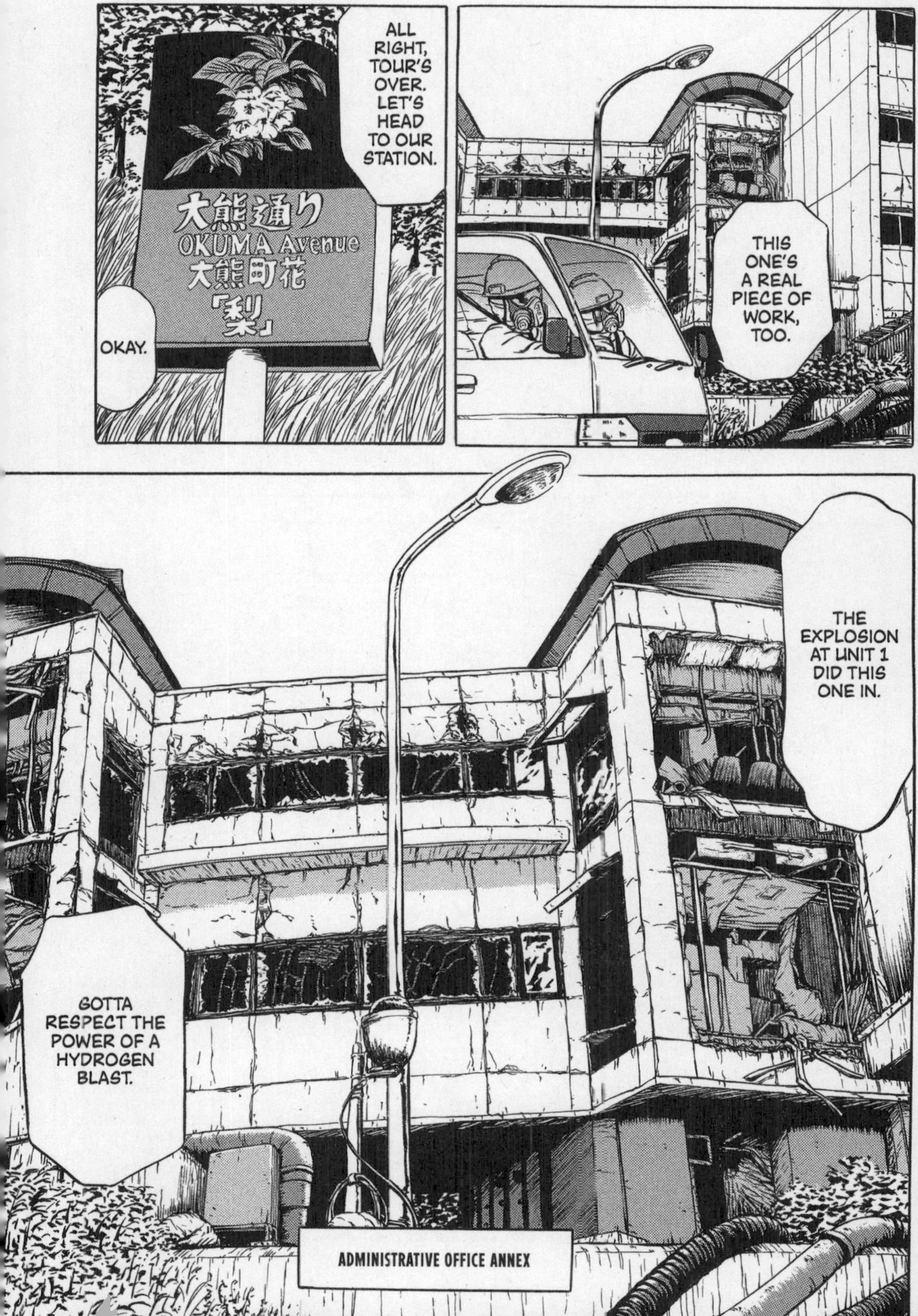

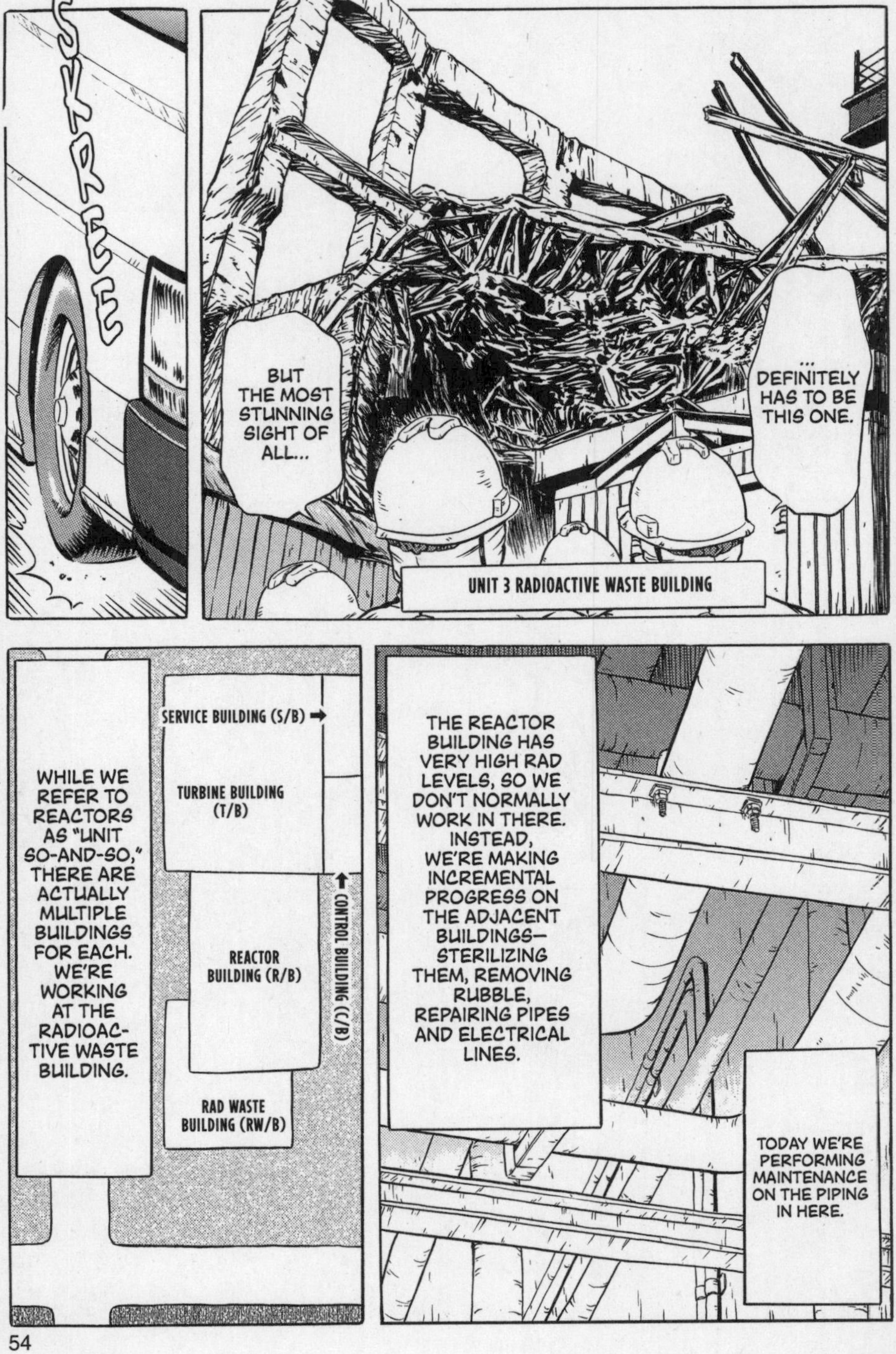
SKREEE
BUT THE MOST STUNNING SIGHT OF ALL...
...DEFINITELY HAS TO BE THIS ONE.
UNIT 3 RADIOACTIVE WASTE BUILDING
WHILE WE REFER TO REACTORS AS "UNIT SO-AND-SO," THERE ARE ACTUALLY MULTIPLE BUILDINGS FOR EACH. WE'RE WORKING AT THE RADIOACTIVE WASTE BUILDING.
SERVICE BUILDING (S/B)
TURBINE BUILDING (T/B)
CONTROL BUILDING (C/B)
REACTOR BUILDING (R/B)
RAD WASTE BUILDING (RW/B)
THE REACTOR BUILDING HAS VERY HIGH RAD LEVELS, SO WE DON'T NORMALLY WORK IN THERE. INSTEAD, WE'RE MAKING INCREMENTAL PROGRESS ON THE ADJACENT BUILDINGS—STERILIZING THEM, REMOVING RUBBLE, REPAIRING PIPES AND ELECTRICAL LINES.
TODAY WE'RE PERFORMING MAINTENANCE ON THE PIPING IN HERE.

OKAY, WE'VE GOT TO TAKE THIS LINE OFF.
RIGHT.
WE TAKE THE BOLTS OFF THE PIPES TO MAKE IT EASIER TO WORK ON THEM.
Atmospheric radiation monitor
KCHAK
KCHAK
HRG
DAMN, THIS ONE'S STUCK ...
GONK
GONK
GOTTA USE THIS TRICK.
HEY, PASS THAT HAMMER OVER HERE, TOO.
OKAY.

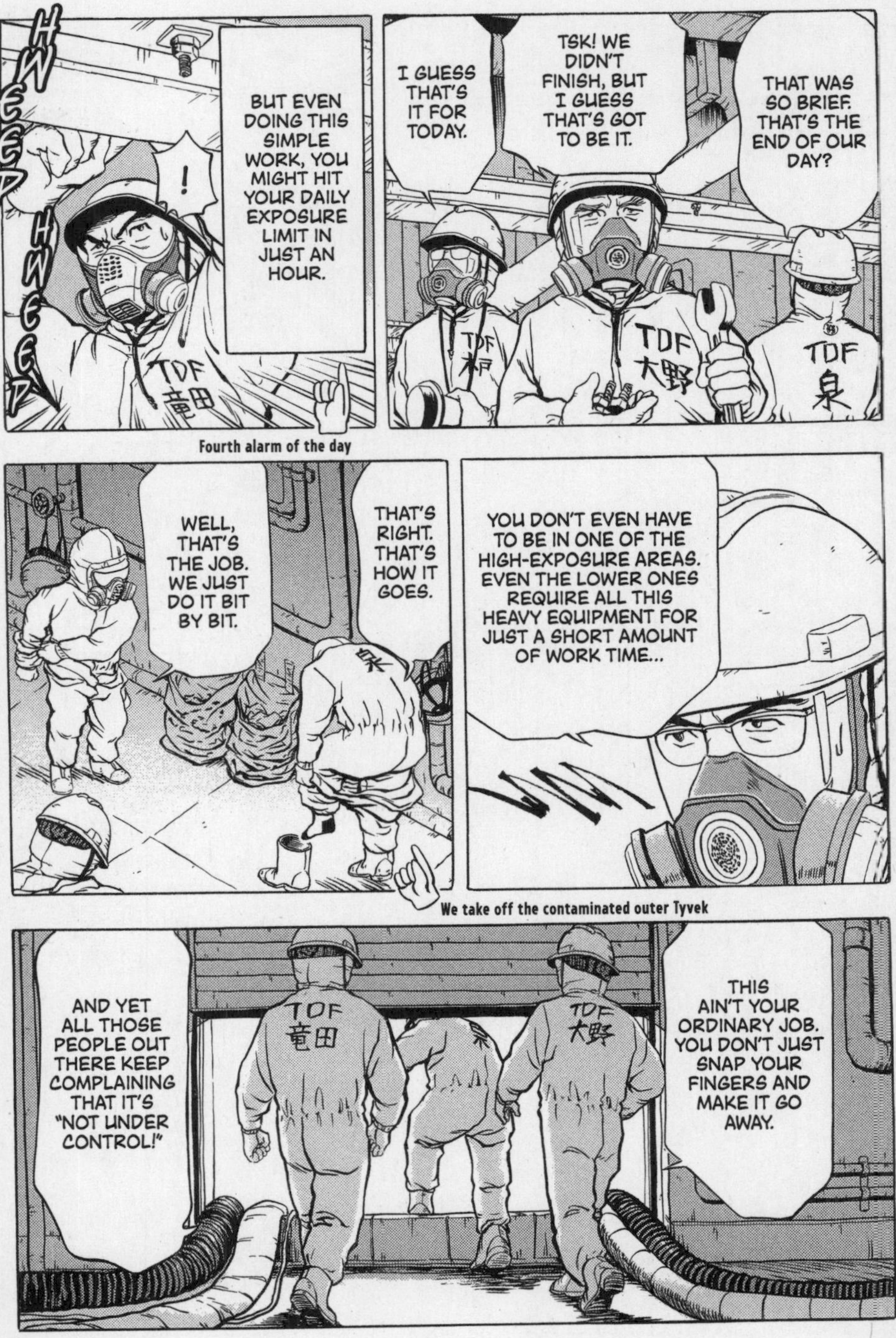
HWEEP
HWEEP
!
BUT EVEN DOING THIS SIMPLE WORK, YOU MIGHT HIT YOUR DAILY EXPOSURE LIMIT IN JUST AN HOUR.
TDF 竜田
I GUESS THAT'S IT FOR TODAY.
TSK! WE DIDN'T FINISH, BUT I GUESS THAT'S GOT TO BE IT.
THAT WAS SO BRIEF. THAT'S THE END OF OUR DAY?
TDF 大野
TDF 泉
Fourth alarm of the day
WELL, THAT'S THE JOB. WE JUST DO IT BIT BY BIT.
THAT'S RIGHT. THAT'S HOW IT GOES.
YOU DON'T EVEN HAVE TO BE IN ONE OF THE HIGH-EXPOSURE AREAS. EVEN THE LOWER ONES REQUIRE ALL THIS HEAVY EQUIPMENT FOR JUST A SHORT AMOUNT OF WORK TIME...
We take off the contaminated outer Tyvek
AND YET ALL THOSE PEOPLE OUT THERE KEEP COMPLAINING THAT IT'S "NOT UNDER CONTROL!"
TDF 竜田
TDF 大野
THIS AIN'T YOUR ORDINARY JOB. YOU DON'T JUST SNAP YOUR FINGERS AND MAKE IT GO AWAY.

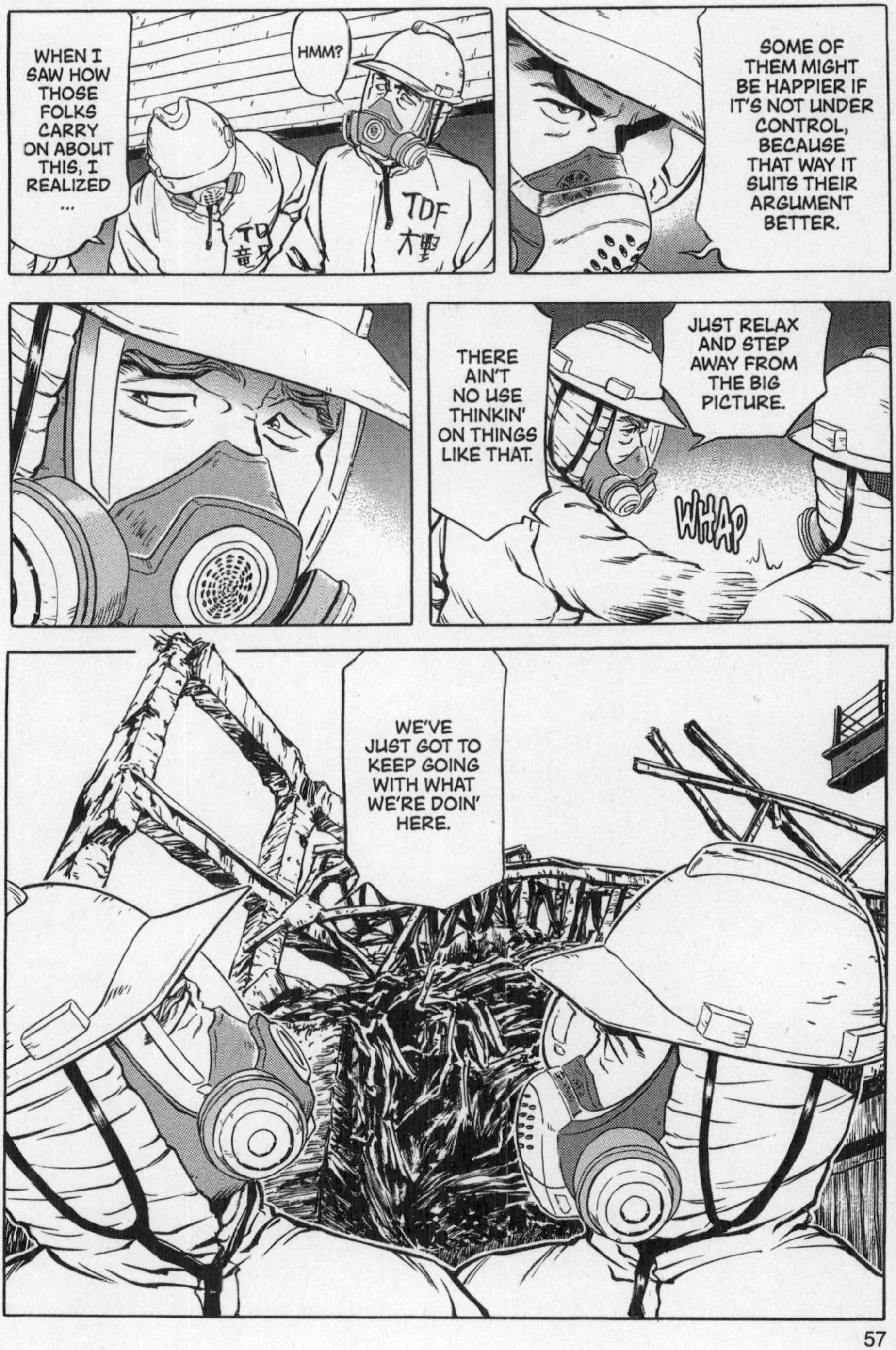
WHEN I SAW HOW THOSE FOLKS CARRY ON ABOUT THIS, I REALIZED ...
HMM?
SOME OF THEM MIGHT BE HAPPIER IF IT'S NOT UNDER CONTROL, BECAUSE THAT WAY IT SUITS THEIR ARGUMENT BETTER.
JUST RELAX AND STEP AWAY FROM THE BIG PICTURE.
THERE AIN'T NO USE THINKIN' ON THINGS LIKE THAT.
WHAP
WE'VE JUST GOT TO KEEP GOING WITH WHAT WE'RE DOIN' HERE.

WELL, FOLKS GET ORNERY WHEN THEY'RE HUNGRY.
C'MON, LET'S EAT LUNCH AND GET BACK HOME.
...YOU'RE RIGHT. I'M SORRY FOR GETTING ALL WORKED UP...
YEAH!
THANKS.
WEL-COME BACK!
ALL RIGHT, LUNCH TIME!
REC CENTER REST AREA
THEY'RE NOT REALLY FULL "LUNCHES" MOST OF THE TIME, JUST PASTRIES OR RICE BALLS FROM THE CONVENIENCE STORE.
HOT WATER, PLEASE.
SURE.
OR IN-STANT RAMEN.
SHLUB
SHLUB

SOME GUYS BRING A BENTO BOX FROM HOME.
SO YOU'RE THE ONLY ONE WHOSE WIFE MADE HIM A LUNCH?
AWW, SHUT UP.
IT'S A FUNNY THING, BUT...
PEEL
COMING HERE REALLY MAKES ME HUNGRY...
I KNOW WHAT YOU MEAN. ESPECIALLY FOR HOW LITTLE TIME WE ACTUALLY WORK.
EVEN FOR ICHI-F, THE FOOD YOU EAT AFTER WORKING TASTES GREAT.
MAYBE IT'S THE HORMESIS* EFFECT?
DON'T BE CRAZY. IT'S JUST 'CUZ WE GOT UP BEFORE DAWN!
"THE FUKUSHIMA DISASTER IS STILL NOT UNDER CONTROL!" THAT'S RIGHT, IT'S NOT.
OH, GOOD POINT.
THAT'S WHY WE'RE HERE TODAY.
BWA HA HA HA HA!

Carton: Cafe Au Lait

*Radiation hormesis: the hypothesis that low doses of radiation induce healthy body processes.

CHAPTER 1 - END

JOBAN LINE, TATSUTA STATION

THIS STATION WENT OUT OF SERVICE DUE TO THE GREAT EAST JAPAN EARTHQUAKE. AS OF MARCH 2014, IT IS STILL OFFLINE, BUT JR EAST IS WORKING HARD TO RESUME SERVICE FROM HIRONO TO TATSUTA THIS YEAR. THIS STATION IS THE SOURCE OF THE PEN NAME, "KAZUTO TATSUTA." BY THE WAY, THE STATIONS STILL CLOSED IN THE FORMER RESTRICTED ZONE ARE, FROM THE SOUTH GOING UPWARD, KIDO STATION, TATSUTA STATION, TOMIOKA STATION, YONOMORI STATION, ONO STATION, FUTABA STATION, NAMIE STATION, MOMOUCHI STATION, ODAKA STATION, AND IWAKI-OTA STATION. OUT OF THOSE, THE RECONFIGURING OF THE RESTRICTED ZONE MEANS THAT SEVEN OF THOSE (ASIDE FROM YONOMORI, ONO, AND FUTABA) ARE NOW ACCESSIBLE AGAIN.

AFTER THE ZONE RECONFIGURATION, WHEN KAZUTO TATSUTA FIRST VISITED THE STATION, THERE WERE STILL WANTED POSTERS UP FOR AUM SHINRIKYO'S MAKOTO HIRATA. THIS WAS MANY MONTHS AFTER HE HAD ALREADY BEEN APPREHENDED, SO IT FELT LIKE TIME HAD STOPPED AT THE STATION.

CHAPTER 2

PFAA...
KURRRRR...
KURR
WORKING AT ICHI-F, PEOPLE OFTEN ASK YOU...
"ISN'T IT HARD TO BREATHE IN THOSE MASKS?"
CLANK
OF COURSE IT MAKES BREATHING DIFFICULT. BUT IT'S NOT AS BAD AS YOU'RE PROBABLY IMAGINING.
WHAM
TDF
竜田
WHAM
WHAT'S WORSE IS THE HEAT.
SWEAT BUILDS UP INSIDE THE MASK, EVEN IN WINTER.
IN THE SUMMER, IT'S A SWAMP THAT THREATENS TO DRIVE YOU CRAZY.
BUT THE WORST THING OF ALL IS...

CHAPTER 2:
ITCHY NOSE

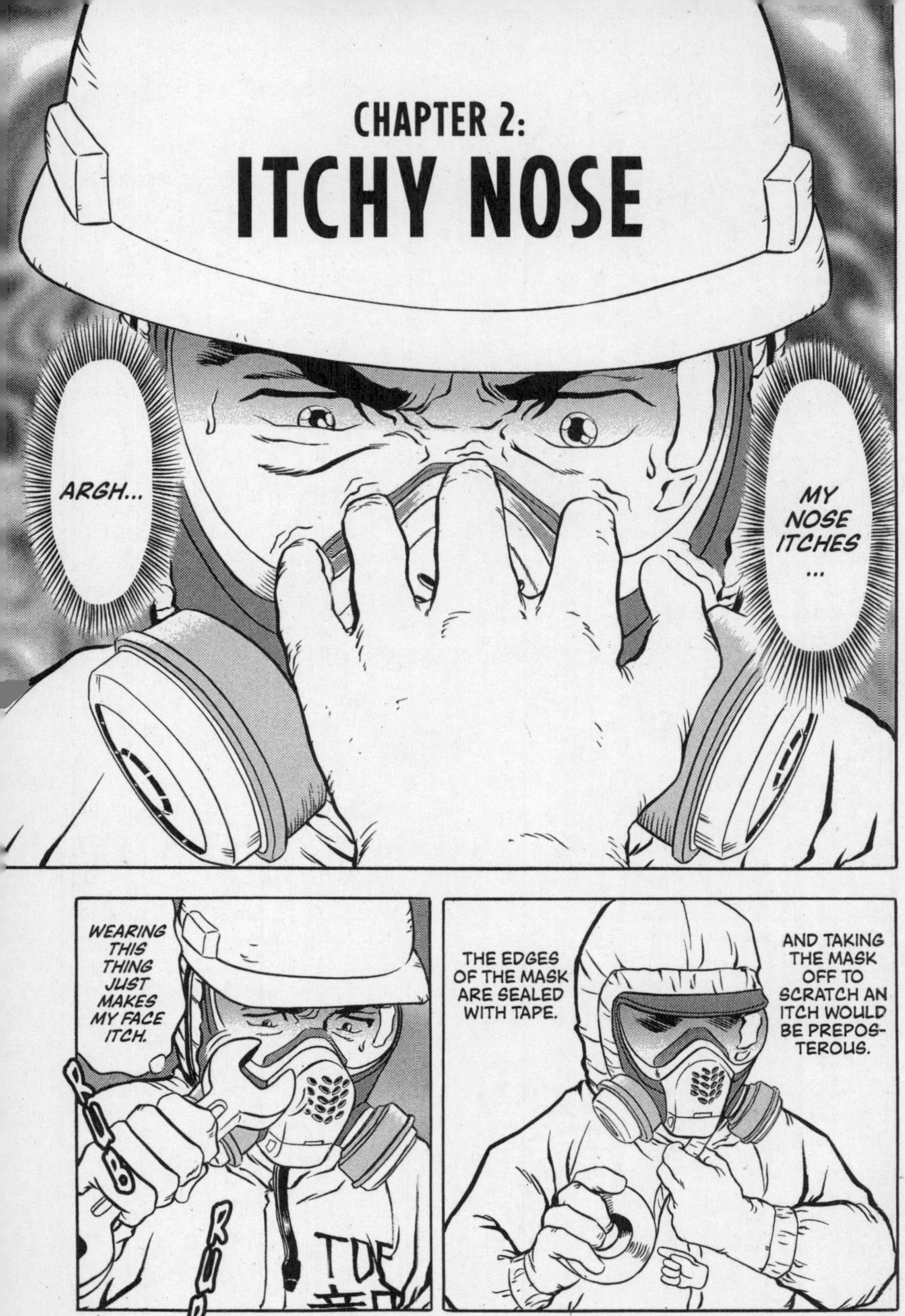

ARGH...
MY NOSE ITCHES ...
WEARING THIS THING JUST MAKES MY FACE ITCH.
RUB
RUB
THE EDGES OF THE MASK ARE SEALED WITH TAPE.
AND TAKING THE MASK OFF TO SCRATCH AN ITCH WOULD BE PREPOS-TEROUS.

AFTER ALL, THIS IS THE UNIT 3 REACTOR OF FUKUSHIMA DAIICHI, SYMBOL OF TERROR TO ALL THE WORLD!
TEPCO FUKUSHIMA DAIICHI NUCLEAR POWER PLANT, ABBREVIATED 1-F (ICHI-F).
1 FOR DAIICHI (FIRST), F FOR FUKUSHIMA. THE NEARBY FUKUSHIMA DAINI IS 2-F (NI-F).
SO Y'ALL WORK OVER AT ICHI-F?
WELL, TAKE A LOAD OFF.
IT WAS JUST A TEPCO INTERNAL ABBREVIATION, BUT NOW EVEN NORMAL FOLKS AROUND HERE USE IT CASUALLY.
I GUESS IT'S WIDE-SPREAD NOW.
MY FRIENDS WHO KNOW THAT I WORK AT ICHI-F SEEM...
IS IT SAFE TO BE AT FUKU-ICHI?
DON'T DO IT! WHAT IF SOMETHING HAPPENS TO YOU?!
...TO BE VERY WORRIED ABOUT ME.
YES, THE WORK AT ICHI-F IS DIFFICULT...
GANK
BUT THE WORST TROUBLE PLAGUING ME IS AN ITCHY NOSE...
GANK
作業員死亡!
TDF
竜田

Headline: 10,000 millisieverts

Headline: Worker Dies! Radiation

Headline: 100 quadrillion becquerels

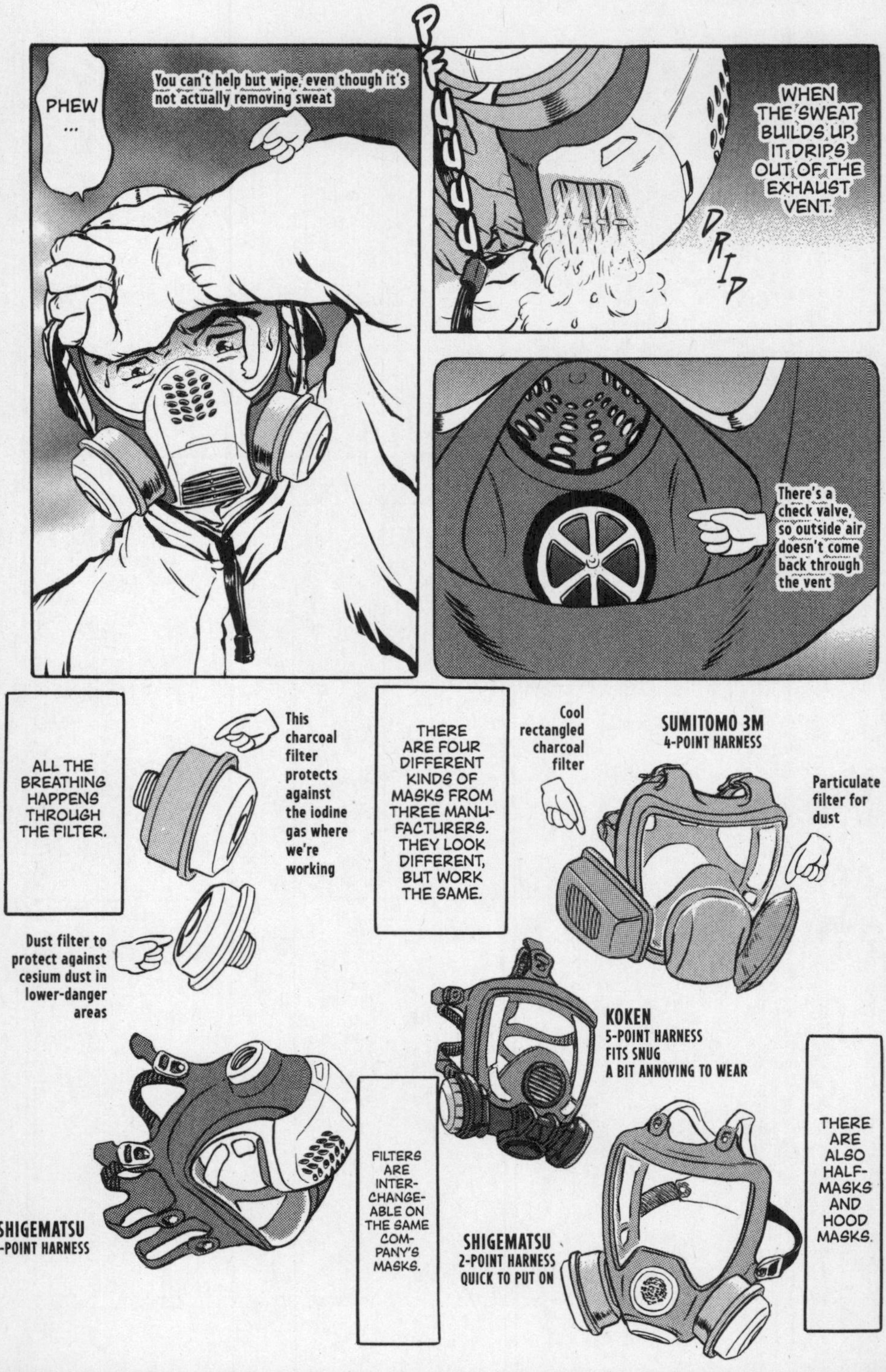
PHEW ...
You can't help but wipe, even though it's not actually removing sweat
PFUUUUU
WHEN THE SWEAT BUILDS UP, IT DRIPS OUT OF THE EXHAUST VENT.
DRIP
There's a check valve, so outside air doesn't come back through the vent
ALL THE BREATHING HAPPENS THROUGH THE FILTER.
This charcoal filter protects against the iodine gas where we're working
Dust filter to protect against cesium dust in lower-danger areas
THERE ARE FOUR DIFFERENT KINDS OF MASKS FROM THREE MANU-FACTURERS. THEY LOOK DIFFERENT, BUT WORK THE SAME.
Cool rectangled charcoal filter
SUMITOMO 3M
4-POINT HARNESS
Particulate filter for dust
KOKEN
5-POINT HARNESS
FITS SNUG
A BIT ANNOYING TO WEAR
SHIGEMATSU
4-POINT HARNESS
FILTERS ARE INTER-CHANGE-ABLE ON THE SAME COM-PANY'S MASKS.
SHIGEMATSU
2-POINT HARNESS
QUICK TO PUT ON
THERE ARE ALSO HALF-MASKS AND HOOD MASKS.

IT MIGHT BE HOT, ITCHY, AND SMELLY, BUT THIS IS OUR MOST CRUCIAL LIFE-SAVING ITEM.

KOHHH!

MR. TATSUTA!

HMM? WHAT IS IT, IZUMI?

TODAY IS IZUMI'S FIRST SHIFT INDOORS.

SORRY... MY HEAD'S REALLY HURTING...

TDF 泉

WHAT'S WRONG?

IZUMI'S HEAD IS HURTING, MR. ONO.

IS IT HEATSTROKE?

I SEE. LET'S CALL OFF WORK FOR NOW, THEN.

MR. ONO IS A LOCAL VETERAN WHO'S BEEN WORKING AT ICHI-F SINCE BEFORE THE DISASTER.

WE DON'T ALL HAVE TO LEAVE. I'LL TAKE HIM BACK TO THE REST AREA IN THE CAR.
YOU CAN'T DO THAT.
HMM.
TDF
竜田
TDF
木戸
THAT WOULD LEAVE US UNDERMANNED IN AN EMERGENCY.
MR. KIDO, OUR MONITOR (FOR MANAGING EXPOSURE) IS ALSO A LOCAL FROM NARAHA.
BUT I'LL BE RIGHT BACK.
NO, SAFETY FIRST. WE'RE LEAVING.
LET'S DO THAT.
I'M SO SORRY FOR CAUSING THIS...
DON'T WORRY. ONO JUST WANTS TO GET BACK SO HE CAN SMOKE.
HEY, DON'T BLOW MY COVER!
2
VRRRM...
HA HA HA!
AT THIS POINT (FALL 2012) OUR REST AREA IS IN A BUILDING CALLED THE COMPANY RECREATION FACILITY.

THERE ARE MORE AND MORE AREAS WITHIN THE GROUNDS OF ICHI-F WHERE WE DON'T NEED FULL MASKS OUTSIDE, JUST A FEW HUNDRED METERS FROM THE NUCLEAR REACTORS.
GOOD WORK OUT THERE.
TDF 竜田
RIP RIP
HERE, I'LL TAKE IT OFF.
THANKS AGAIN.
TDF 竜田
AAAAAH!
SWEET LIBERATION!
WE GET A MASK-AND-BODY SURVEY (FOR RAD LEVELS) BEFORE WE CAN GO INTO THE REST AREA.
Mask goes into a plastic bag
THE REC BUILDING'S REST AREA HAS ROLLED ALUMINUM MATS THAT EACH COMPANY SETS DOWN FOR ITS OWN EMPLOYEES.

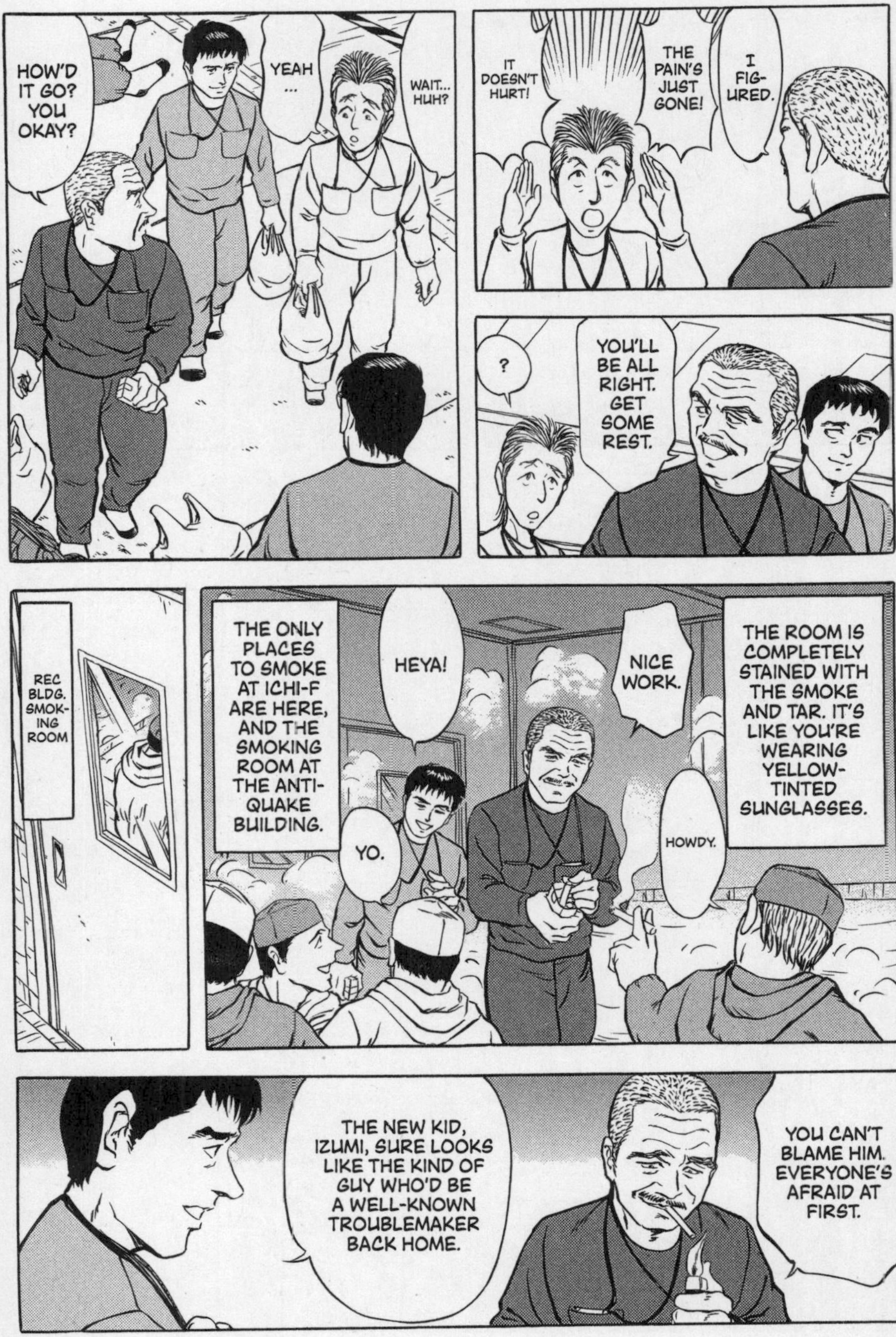

68

WHICH TOWN IS HE FROM? KAWA-UCHI?
YEAH. THEY LIFTED THE EVACUATION ORDER, BUT THE JOBS HAVEN'T RETURNED. THAT'S WHY HE'S HERE.
THEY FORCED ALL OF KAWAUCHI TO EVACUATE AT FIRST, BUT NOW THEY'RE ALLOWING THE RESIDENTS TO RETURN.
FEWER THAN HALF HAVE DONE SO.
負けないぞ!!かわうち
Sign: Don't give up, Kawauchi!!
IT'S HARD WITHOUT A LOCAL INDUSTRY, HUH?
THAT WAS TRUE BEFORE THE DISASTER, THOUGH.
THE CLEANUP IS PROCEEDING AND INFRASTRUCTURE IS COMING BACK, BUT THAT DOES NOT SOLVE THE UNDERLYING ISSUES FACING THE AREA.
A YOUNG MAN IN THE PRIME OF HIS LIFE, AND HE'S GOT NO BETTER JOB PROSPECTS THAN *THIS.*
THE PRESENCE OR ABSENCE OF AN EVACUATION ZONE DON'T CHANGE HIS CHANCES IN LIFE AROUND HERE.
AND WHERE YOU LIVE IS STILL THE RED ZONE.
THERE'S NOTHIN' TO BE DONE FOR MY HOME NOW.

The plastic sheets over the roofs damaged by the quake are still left there
MR. ONO'S HOME IS IN THE TOWN OF OKUMA, WHICH IS IN THE FULLY RESTRICTED ZONE, SO HE CAN'T LIVE THERE NOW.
BUT AT LEAST THE FOLKS FROM THE RESTRICTED ZONE GET A LITTLE PAYOUT.
THERE'S NOTHIN' I CAN DO ABOUT THAT.
BUT IT WAS A NEW HOME, WASN'T IT?
I'VE GOT IT BETTER THAN THOSE FOLKS WHOSE HOMES AND FAMILIES GOT WASHED AWAY IN THE TSUNAMI.
WELL... THAT'S A GOOD POINT...
IT'S IRONIC, THOUGH—I GOT KICKED OUTTA THE RESTRICTED ZONE, BUT CAME BACK IN HERE TO WORK.
LOTTA PEOPLE AT ICHI-F IN THAT SITUATION.
HMMM ...
DON'T YOU FEEL ANGER OR HATRED AT TEPCO FOR THIS MESS?

BUT IT WAS OUR WORKPLACE THAT CAUSED THE ACCIDENT.
I LOST MY HOME. OF COURSE I'M ANGRY.
AND IF WE DON'T, THE PEOPLE WHO WANNA COME BACK WILL BE SHUT OUT FOREVER.
WE'RE THE ONLY ONES WHO CAN DO ANYTHING ABOUT IT.
I'M JUST AN OUTSIDER COMING IN FROM TOKYO TO WORK.
MR. ONO WAS BOTH A VICTIM AND A PERPETRATOR IN THIS DELICATE SITUATION, AND I HAD NO RIGHT TO QUIBBLE WITH HIS VIEWS.
ANGER AS A RESIDENT, AND DUTY AS A WORKER...
MR. ONO...

BUT GIVEN THAT I'VE BEEN USING THE ELECTRICITY SENT TO TOKYO FROM FUKUSHIMA ALL ALONG, I FEEL THAT I HAVE A RESPONSIBILITY IN THE MATTER, TOO.
TEPC サトウ
IT'S WHY I FELT LIKE I NEEDED TO DO SOMETHING TO HELP THIS PLACE.
RAGING ABOUT SOMETHING THAT'S ALREADY HAPPENED WON'T SET THINGS RIGHT AGAIN. JUST GOTTA GET ON WITH THE JOB.
AIN'T THAT RIGHT?
... RIGHT!
LET'S GET BACK THERE. KID'S PROBABLY FEELIN' BETTER BY NOW.
GOOD IDEA.
PSHHHH
カフェオレ
酪王
カフェオレ

Carton: Rakuou Cafe Au Lait

HOW YA DOIN'?
OH!
I THINK HE'S GOOD TO GO.
I'M SORRY ABOUT THE TROUBLE.
I GUESS IT WASN'T HEATSTROKE AFTER ALL.
WHAT HAPPENED TO ME, THEN? AS SOON AS I LEFT THE SITE, I FELT BETTER...
THAT WAS YOUR FIRST TIME WORKING ON-SITE WITH THE FULL MASK, WASN'T IT?
YES.
BE HONEST: WERE YOU SCARED TO GO INTO THE BUILDING?
Y-YEAH, A LITTLE ...
THAT'S IT!
YOU FREAK OUT ABOUT IRRADIATED MATTER WORKING ITS WAY UNDERNEATH YOUR MASK AND IRRADIATING YOUR INSIDES ...
...AND YOU END UP FASTENING YOUR MASK TOO TIGHT.

OH.
IT HAPPENS A LOT AT FIRST, WHEN YOU DON'T KNOW HOW TIGHT TO DO IT.
OH, GEEZ.
I WAS SO SURE...
THAT IT WAS RADIATION SICKNESS?
YES.
THEN WHY WOULD THE REST OF US BE FINE?
B-BECAUSE ...YOU'RE ALL USED TO IT...?
DON'T BE A FOOL! YOU CAN'T JUST GET "USED" TO RADIATION!!
IF WE WERE TAKING EXPOSURE STRONG ENOUGH TO CAUSE PHYSICAL AILMENTS EVERY DAY, WE'D ALL BE DEAD BY NOW!
!
I...I'M SORRY, SIR!

LISTEN TO ME: DON'T MESS AROUND WITH RADIATION.
IF YOU'RE SERIOUSLY SCARED OF IT, THEN SHOW THAT YOU'RE SERIOUS—STUDY IT!
... YES, SIR.
...I'M MORE SCARED OF YOU...
B-BUT DON'T WORRY, I'M MEASURING THE RADIATION WHILE WE WORK.
STILL, THIS IS JUST A VETERAN WORKER'S KINDNESS TOWARD THE NEW KID. FEAR OF THE UNKNOWN BECOMES MANAGEABLE WHEN YOU LEARN ITS TRUE NATURE AND HOW TO COUNTERACT IT.

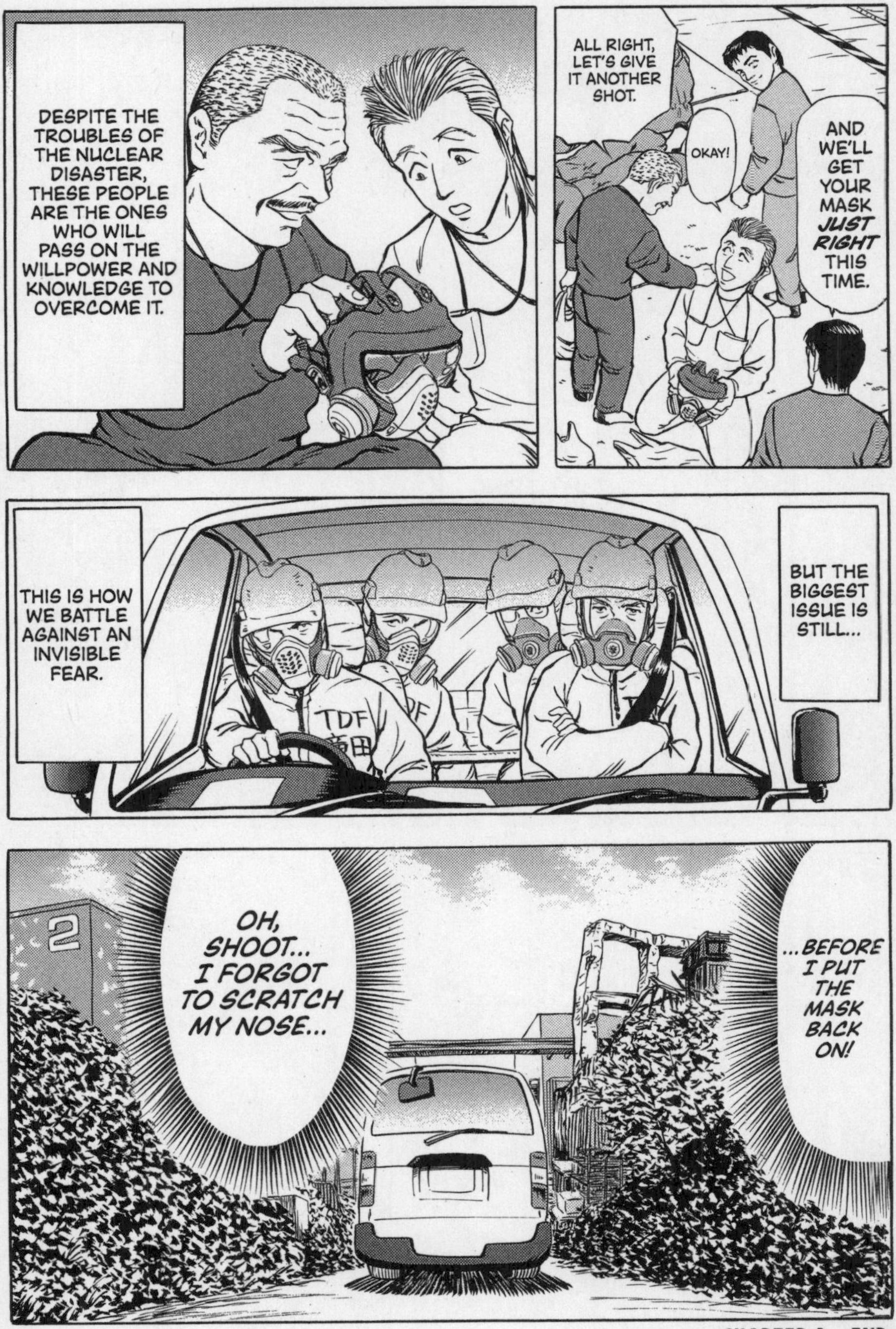
DESPITE THE TROUBLES OF THE NUCLEAR DISASTER, THESE PEOPLE ARE THE ONES WHO WILL PASS ON THE WILLPOWER AND KNOWLEDGE TO OVERCOME IT.
ALL RIGHT, LET'S GIVE IT ANOTHER SHOT.
OKAY!
AND WE'LL GET YOUR MASK *JUST RIGHT* THIS TIME.
THIS IS HOW WE BATTLE AGAINST AN INVISIBLE FEAR.
TDF
BUT THE BIGGEST ISSUE IS STILL...
2
OH, SHOOT... I FORGOT TO SCRATCH MY NOSE...
...BEFORE I PUT THE MASK BACK ON!

CHAPTER 2 - END

LIFE AT ICHI-F CROSS-SECTION (PART 1)

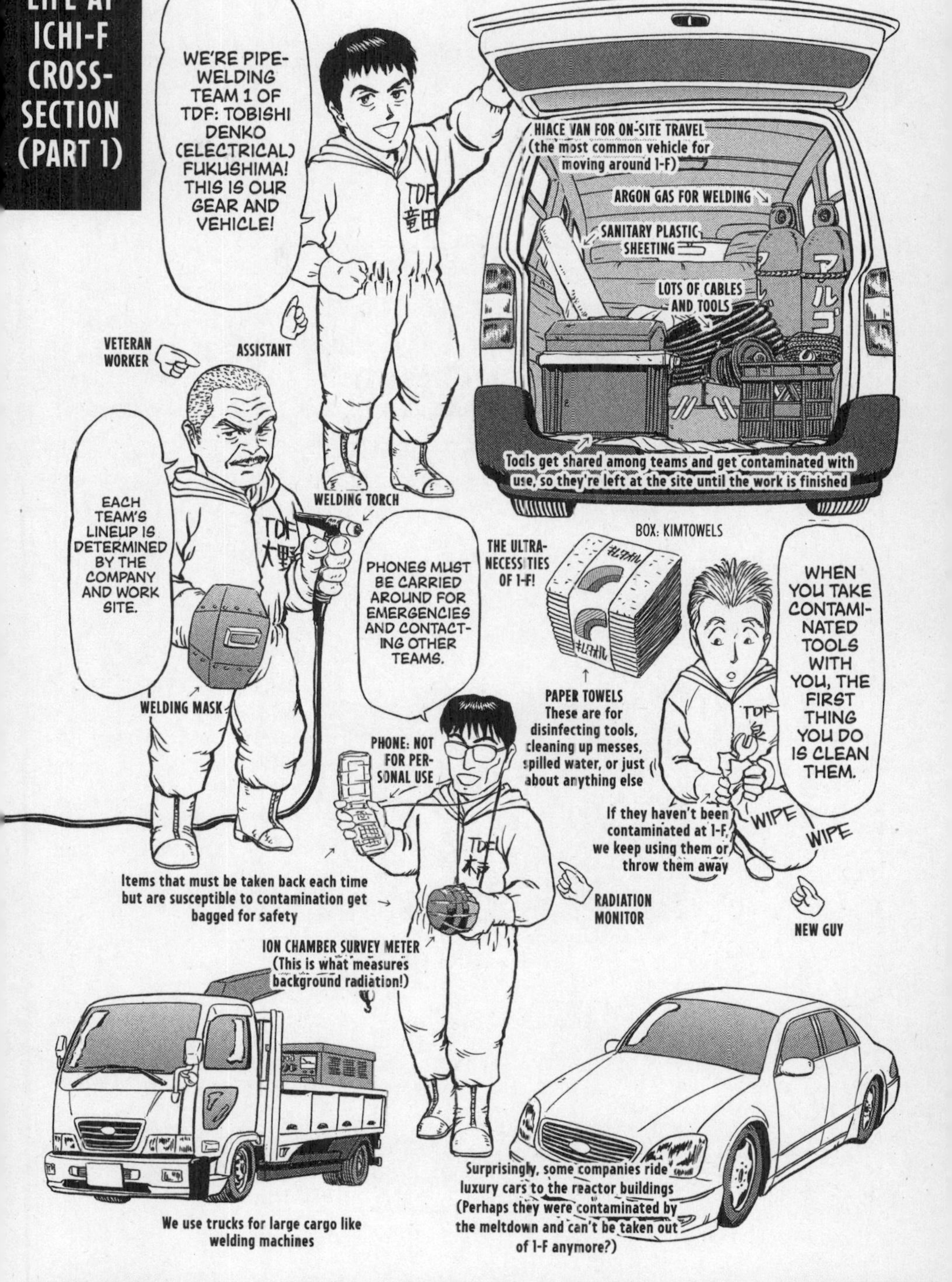

WE'RE PIPE-WELDING TEAM 1 OF TDF: TOBISHI DENKO (ELECTRICAL) FUKUSHIMA! THIS IS OUR GEAR AND VEHICLE!
HIACE VAN FOR ON-SITE TRAVEL (the most common vehicle for moving around 1-F)
ARGON GAS FOR WELDING
SANITARY PLASTIC SHEETING
LOTS OF CABLES AND TOOLS
Tools get shared among teams and get contaminated with use, so they're left at the site until the work is finished
VETERAN WORKER
ASSISTANT
EACH TEAM'S LINEUP IS DETERMINED BY THE COMPANY AND WORK SITE.
WELDING TORCH
WELDING MASK
PHONES MUST BE CARRIED AROUND FOR EMERGENCIES AND CONTACTING OTHER TEAMS.
BOX: KIMTOWELS
THE ULTRA-NECESSITIES OF 1-F!
PAPER TOWELS These are for disinfecting tools, cleaning up messes, spilled water, or just about anything else
WHEN YOU TAKE CONTAMINATED TOOLS WITH YOU, THE FIRST THING YOU DO IS CLEAN THEM.
If they haven't been contaminated at 1-F, we keep using them or throw them away
WIPE
WIPE
PHONE: NOT FOR PERSONAL USE
Items that must be taken back each time but are susceptible to contamination get bagged for safety
RADIATION MONITOR
NEW GUY
ION CHAMBER SURVEY METER (This is what measures background radiation!)
Surprisingly, some companies ride luxury cars to the reactor buildings (Perhaps they were contaminated by the meltdown and can't be taken out of 1-F anymore?)
We use trucks for large cargo like welding machines

RESTRICTED ZONE

IN CHAPTER 2, MR. ONO SAYS "THERE'S NOTHING [HE] CAN DO ABOUT" HIS HOME IN OKUMA. HE REFERS TO THE RADIATION, OF COURSE, BUT NOT JUST THAT. MANY WORKERS WHO WERE ALLOWED TO TEMPORARILY VISIT THEIR HOMES IN THE RESTRICTED ZONES FOUND THEY HAD BEEN SOILED BY WILD ANIMALS.

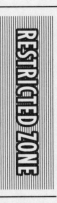

AND NOT JUST ANIMALS—MANY WERE OVERRUN WITH PLANTS, TOO. NATURE CAN BE FIERCE TO HUMAN HABITATS WITH NO RESIDENTS ANYMORE.

CHAPTER 3:
HELLO WORK, 2011

I'M HOME!
OCTOBER 2012: I'M LIVING IN A CHEAP APARTMENT WITH TWO OTHER MEN IN THE CITY OF IWAKI, FUKUSHIMA PREFECTURE.
WELCOME BACK.
I MET MY FLATMATES WHEN I FIRST CAME TO FUKUSHIMA.
COME IN, SIT DOWN.
YOU'RE HOME LATE TODAY.
MR. TSURUMI IS 59, WITH A FAMILY AND GRANDKIDS IN KANAGAWA.
OUR CAR GOT HELD UP AT THE VEHICLE SURVEY.
FIGURES. YOU GUYS GET SENT TO THE REAL HOT (IRRADIATED) AREAS.
YOU EAT DINNER ALREADY?
MR. TAMANA IS 52, FROM KUMAMOTO. HE WAS A PUBLIC EMPLOYEE BEFORE THIS.
BOUGHT A CHEAP DINNER FROM BENI-MARU.*
GREAT MINDS THINK ALIKE.
WE WERE HIRED BY THE SAME COMPANY AND ORIGINALLY WORKED TOGETHER...

*Local chain supermarket

...BUT NOW WE WORK FOR DIFFERENT COMPANIES ON DIFFERENT SPOTS AROUND ICHI-F.
SEEMS LIKE WE ALWAYS END UP BUYING A MEAL FROM THE STORE.
THE WATER'S STILL HOT.
THANKS.
HEY, AT LEAST WE'RE ABLE TO AFFORD WHICHEVER MEAL WE LIKE NOW.

WELL, I SUPPOSE YOU'RE RIGHT.
IT WAS REAL BAD BACK IN KORIYAMA AND THE OLD DORM.
RIGHT?
IT'S AN ODD LIVING ARRANGEMENT WITH THREE TOTAL STRANGERS TOGETHER.
THERE WERE MANY THINGS THAT LED UP TO US LIVING LIKE THIS, BUT THAT'S A STORY FOR ANOTHER TIME.

Sign: Hello Work

THIS TAKES US BACK A YEAR AND ALL THE WAY TO TOKYO.
THIS TIME, I'LL BE TELLING YOU THE STORY OF HOW I GOT TO ICHI-F!
公共職業安定所

Sign: Employment Service Center

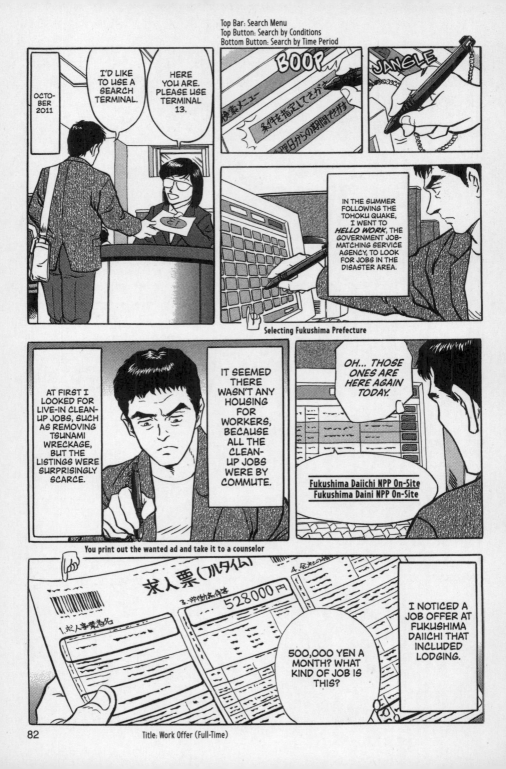

Top Bar: Search Menu
Top Button: Search by Conditions
Bottom Button: Search by Time Period

OCTOBER 2011
I'D LIKE TO USE A SEARCH TERMINAL.
HERE YOU ARE. PLEASE USE TERMINAL 13.
BOOP
JANGLE
IN THE SUMMER FOLLOWING THE TOHOKU QUAKE, I WENT TO ***HELLO WORK***, THE GOVERNMENT JOB-MATCHING SERVICE AGENCY, TO LOOK FOR JOBS IN THE DISASTER AREA.
Selecting Fukushima Prefecture
AT FIRST I LOOKED FOR LIVE-IN CLEAN-UP JOBS, SUCH AS REMOVING TSUNAMI WRECKAGE, BUT THE LISTINGS WERE SURPRISINGLY SCARCE.
IT SEEMED THERE WASN'T ANY HOUSING FOR WORKERS, BECAUSE ALL THE CLEAN-UP JOBS WERE BY COMMUTE.
OH... THOSE ONES ARE HERE AGAIN TODAY.
Fukushima Daiichi NPP On-Site
Fukushima Daini NPP On-Site
You print out the wanted ad and take it to a counselor
求人票(フルタイム)
528000円
500,000 YEN A MONTH? WHAT KIND OF JOB IS THIS?
I NOTICED A JOB OFFER AT FUKUSHIMA DAIICHI THAT INCLUDED LODGING.

Title: Work Offer (Full-Time)

PLEASE CALL UP THIS ONE AND THIS ONE.
ALL RIGHT.
FUKU-SHIMA, I SEE.
HMM?!
DAI-ICHI ...
He really did a double-take!
YOU'RE SERIOUS ?
YES, SIR.
JUST ABOUT ALL OF THE JOB COUNSELORS HAD THIS REACTION.
BUT... WHY?
WELL, I FIGURED THAT I COULD TAKE ON A JOB THAT WILL HELP THOSE AFFECTED BY THE DISASTER...
PLUS THE PAY IS GOOD.
ARE YOU SURE YOU WANT TO DO THIS?
I'VE DONE MY OWN RESEARCH ON THE MATTER AND DECIDED THAT IT WAS SAFE ENOUGH.
WHAT ARE YOU TRYING TO SAY? THAT YOUR EMPLOYMENT SERVICE IS OFFERING UNSAFE JOBS?
AND IF THE GUYS WHO THINK IT'S SAFE DON'T GO, I FIGURE THEY'LL HAVE TROUBLE GETTING ENOUGH HELP.
IF IT TURNS OUT THAT THE CONDITIONS ARE WORSE THAN I THINK, I CAN ALWAYS COME BACK WITH MY TAIL BETWEEN MY LEGS.

Some company numbers go right to the owner's cell phone (sole proprietor/contractor)

Fukui has many companies in the nuclear industry

Form: Introduction

Form: Applicant Name: Kazuto Tatsuta

Okay, you're hired.

THANKS!

WOW, THAT WAS EASY.

I GOT BACK POSITIVE ANSWERS FROM FIVE OR SIX JOB LEADS...

But we don't know when work might start. I'll call you back when things get settled, so can ya hang on until then?

THEY ALL HAD THE SAME ANSWER, AND NEVER LED ANYWHERE.

ALL OF YOU FOLKS IN CHARGE OF HIRING FOR THOSE COMPANIES: I STILL HAVEN'T HEARD BACK FROM YOU YET!

It's already the next year

THERE WAS JUST ONE JOB...

COME OVER ON JANUARY XXST. I'LL LET YOU KNOW WHEN AND WHERE TO MEET ME.

...THAT HAD MORE DE-TAILS.

SO I WENT AHEAD...

THANKS FOR ALL OF YOUR HELP.

YOU SURE? TAKE CARE OVER THERE.

...AND QUIT MY PART-TIME JOB IN PREPARATION.

THERE WAS NO WORD FROM THEM, EVEN THE DAY BEFORE THE MEETING.

CLICK CLICK

WHAT'S GOING ON?

HUH?

The number you have dialed is not currently in service...
ARE YOU KIDDING ME?!
THIS WAS A MAJOR SETBACK ...
IF ALL THESE SOURCES OF WORK ARE SO FLAKY, IS IT REALLY WORTH IT?
MY FRIEND WAS ALREADY WORRIED, AND I HAD ONLY SAID I WAS GOING TO THE FUKUSHIMA DISASTER AREA, NOT THE DAIICHI PLANT SPECIFICALLY.
WHAT? YOU'RE STILL HERE?
HA HA, IT'S BEEN TOUGH...
OTHERS WHO KNEW WHEN I WAS "LEAVING" MADE IT EVEN MORE AWKWARD.
LATER ON I LEARNED THAT THESE INCIDENCES WERE NOT UNCOMMON EVERYWHERE. MY COTENANT MR. TSURUMI SAID...
YEAH, I WENT THROUGH THE SAME THING. THE CONTRACTORS JUST UP AND LEAVE.
THEY COLLECT AS MANY NAMES AS THEY CAN JUST TO DRAW UP A SUBCONTRACTOR LIST DURING THE PLANNING STAGES OF A JOB.
IT'S THE UNSCRUPULOUS ONES WHO TAKE THE HIRING FUNDS FOR ALL THOSE WORKERS AND VANISH INTO THE NIGHT.
OH, MAN. MAYBE THAT'S WHAT HAPPENED WITH ME...

I PICKED UP ANOTHER SHORT-TERM JOB AND KEPT LOOKING FOR WORK.
AT THIS POINT, IT'S SHEER CUSSEDNESS!
BUT THAT WASN'T ENOUGH TO STOP ME.
IN ORDER TO MAKE MYSELF MORE DESIRABLE AND USEFUL IN COMPETING FOR A POSITION...
...I WENT TO GET LICENSES AT THE EQUIPMENT MAKERS' INSTRUCTION FACILITIES.
CRANE OPERATION
QUALIFICATIONS FOR HOISTING LOADS WITH CRANES
ARC WELDING
SMALL CONSTRUCTION VEHICLES
BACKHOES AND OTHER EQUIPMENT UNDER 3 TONS
It's almost Golden Week, a weeklong holiday in the spring
AND FINALLY, MORE THAN A YEAR AFTER THE DISASTER, AND TEN MONTHS SINCE I STARTED LOOKING FOR ONE OF THESE JOBS...
Can you come to Koriyama over the holiday ahead?
I've got a job clearing wreckage at the plant, 20,000 yen a day.
Ship your stuff to this address.
THIS ACTUALLY SOUNDS PRETTY SOLID!
ALL RIGHT, LET'S GO AND CHECK IT OUT!
VWAA
MAY 2012
郡山駅

Sign: Koriyama Station

WELCOME TO KUROMORI CONSTRUCTION (FICTIONAL NAME). SHALL WE GO?
HELLO, I'M TATSUTA! IT'S GOOD TO BE HERE.
WHAT?
WE'RE OFF TO THE HOSPITAL.
FOR YOUR RADIATION EXAM. WE'VE GOT TO TAKE THEM BEFORE WE'RE ALLOWED TO WORK AT THE PLANT.
WE'RE ABOUT TO TAKE IT, TOO.
OH, I SEE! THANKS.
MR. TSURUMI
MR. TAMANA
First meeting with my future roommates
WE'LL GO TO THE OFFICE ONCE THE EXAM IS DONE.
THIS WAS OUR CARE-TAKER AT THE DORM IN KORIYAMA.
IONIZING RADIATION HEALTH EXAMINA-TION
THIS IS AN EXAM THAT ANY WORKER INVOLVED IN HIGH-EXPOSURE JOBS OR OTHERWISE GOING INTO THE RADIATION MANAGEMENT ZONE MUST TAKE REGULARLY.
LET ME SEE YOUR HANDS.
ON TOP OF TAKING HEIGHT, WEIGHT, BLOOD PRESSURE, BLOOD TYPE, URINALYSIS, AND CHEST X-RAYS, THEY ALSO EXAMINE THE EYES AND SKIN TO FIND CATARACTS OR RADIATION DERMATITIS.

YOU DO IT AT A LOCAL HOSPITAL AMONG NORMAL PATIENTS, AND IT'S OVER QUICKLY.
HOW WAS YOUR BLOOD PRES-SURE?
142, BUT IT'S USUALLY A BIT HIGHER.
IF YOU HAVE HIGH SYSTOLIC PRESSURE, LIKE 150 OR 160, YOU CAN'T WORK AT THE PLANT, SO THERE ARE RUMORS THAT THEY TWEAK IT TO LOOK LOWER.
IT'S AN URBAN LEGEND AMONG THE WORK-ERS.
I HEARD A NUMBER OF THESE URBAN LEGENDS, OR "NUCLEAR LEGENDS," BUT WAS NEVER ABLE TO FIND EVIDENCE OF ANY OF THEM.
THE WORST ONE I HEARD WAS THAT A DEAD FOREIGN-BORN WORKER WAS SECRETLY BURNED IN A BARREL OUT BEHIND ICHI-F. (AND WHERE IS "BEHIND ICHI-F"? WHY FOREIGN? THE RUMOR-MONGERS REALLY LOVE THEIR BARRELS.)
↑ Do the people making these things up imagine it looks like this?
THAT NON-SENSE ASIDE...
THIS IS OUR OFFICE AND DORM HOUSE.
SKREE
LOOKS JUST LIKE AN ORDI-NARY HOUSE.
KUROMORI CONSTRUCTION IS A GENERAL CONTRACTOR IN KORIYAMA, AND THEY LATCHED ONTO CLEAN-UP WORK AT ICHI-F AFTER THE NUCLEAR ACCIDENT.

GOOD TO SEE YOU BACK HERE.
I'M LOOKING FORWARD TO THE FRUITS OF YOUR HARD WORK, TATSUTA!
MANAGING DIRECTOR OF KUROMORI CONSTRUCTION
YOU FINISH THE TESTS?
YES.
THEN WE'RE GOING TO IWAKI TO APPLY FOR HANDBOOKS.*
CAN WE TAKE THE HIGHWAY?
JANGLE

*Radiation Control Handbook: necessary to work at a nuclear plant!

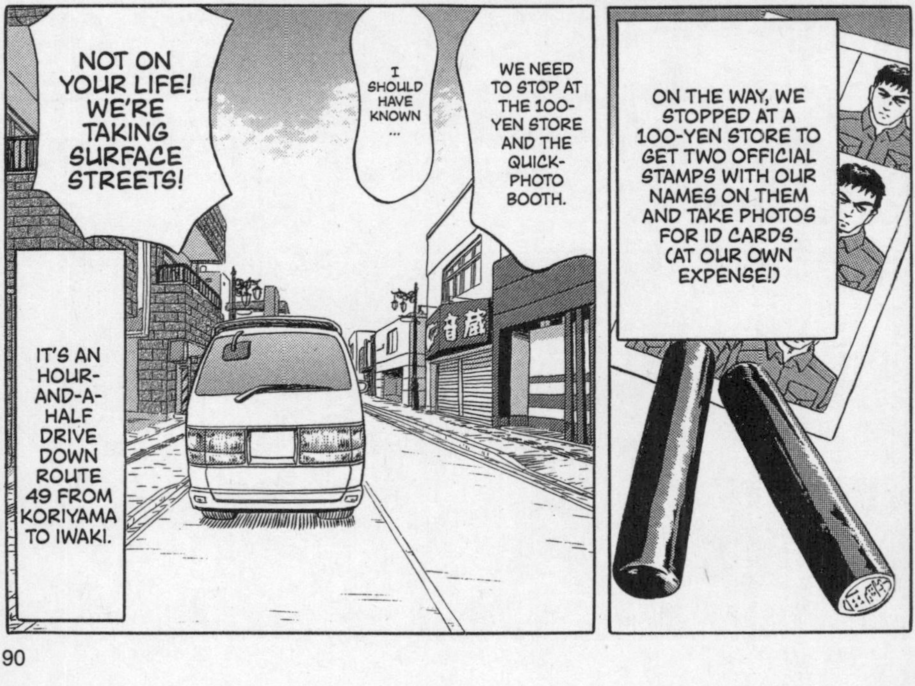
NOT ON YOUR LIFE! WE'RE TAKING SURFACE STREETS!
I SHOULD HAVE KNOWN ...
WE NEED TO STOP AT THE 100-YEN STORE AND THE QUICK-PHOTO BOOTH.
IT'S AN HOUR-AND-A-HALF DRIVE DOWN ROUTE 49 FROM KORIYAMA TO IWAKI.
ON THE WAY, WE STOPPED AT A 100-YEN STORE TO GET TWO OFFICIAL STAMPS WITH OUR NAMES ON THEM AND TAKE PHOTOS FOR ID CARDS. (AT OUR OWN EXPENSE!)

株式会社
八千代テクノス
福島営業所
WE TOOK OUR RADIATION EXAM RESULTS TO THE APPLICATION OFFICE FOR OUR HANDBOOKS.
NOW JUST USE YOUR STAMP ON THIS FORM.
FORTUNATELY, THE COMPANY AT LEAST PICKED UP THE COST OF THE RADIATION EXAM AND THIS APPLICATION FEE.
THEY'LL SEND THE HANDBOOKS TO THE COMPANY LATER.
OH, AND I'LL HOLD ONTO THESE STAMPS FOR YOU.
?
福島県庁を
郡山市へ
WE TOOK SURFACE STREETS BACK TO KORIYAMA.
HERE WE ARE, BACK AT LAST...
SKREE
YOU CAN SLEEP IN THAT ROOM THERE. YOUR LUGGAGE IS SET ON TOP OF YOUR BED.
THANK YOU, SIR.
THIS IS WHEN I FIRST SAW WHERE I'D SLEEP.
NO WAY ...

Sign: Yachiyo Technos Fukushima Office

Sign: Move the Fukushima Prefectural Office to Koriyama City

I hear some companies even make you pay this

You see these signs here and there

THREE BUNKBEDS IN A SMALL ROOM...
THIS IS BARELY MORE THAN A SQUARE METER PER PERSON...
OTHER ROOMS WERE EVEN SMALLER, WITH TWO BUNKBEDS.
WELL, IT'S STILL BETTER THAN DENMA-CHO (AN EDO-PERIOD PRISON).
THUMP
I CAN JUST THINK OF THIS LIKE ONE OF THOSE PRISON REHABILITATION CAMPS...
History buff
HEY, FOOD'S UP!
COMING!
THERE WERE EVEN BEDS IN THE LARGE LIVING ROOM THAT DOUBLED AS OUR DINING AREA. OVER TEN MEN WERE CRAMMED INTO THIS HOUSE TOGETHER.

Sign: Lights out at 10!
Manage your own valuables!

Sign: No smoking in bed!
Make sure the gas is off!

LOTS OF NUCLEAR PLANT JOBS GET PUT TOGETHER REAL QUICK.
I DON'T KNOW ABOUT OTHER PLANTS, BUT IT'S TRUE THAT JOBS AT ICHI-F TEND TO BE DECIDED VERY PROMPTLY. (I WOULD LATER HAVE FIRSTHAND EXPERIENCE WITH THIS.)
YOU JUST HANG OUT HERE AND SIT TIGHT.
OKAY ...
THE OTHER MEN HIRED AT THIS TIME WERE OF DIFFERENT AGES AND LOCATIONS. OVER TIME, THE GROUP WOULD GROW AND SHRINK AS PEOPLE CAME AND WENT.
FROM SAITAMA, 28
HOW LONG WILL THEY KEEP US WAITIN'?
DUNNO ...
FROM IWATE, 39
WELL, THIS ISN'T GREAT...
FROM KANAGAWA, 59
BUT SINCE WE'VE ALL COME THIS FAR, I'M SURE IT WON'T BE VERY LONG AT ALL!
FROM KUMAMOTO, 52
FUTURE ROOMMATES
FROM THE TOKYO AREA, 47
BUT A WEEK PASSED, AND THERE WAS NO INDICATION OF WORK COMING.

MAN, THIS IS BORING.
WE'RE DOING ABSOLUTELY NO GOOD HERE.
SO CLOSE, AND WE HAVEN'T EVEN SEEN ANY TSUNAMI DAMAGE YET.
WE'RE GOING TO BORROW A VAN. WE'LL FILL UP THE TANK ON THE WAY BACK.
ALL RIGHT, DRIVE SAFE.
MINAMI-SOMA

WHEN I FIRST SAW THE AFTERMATH OF THE TSUNAMI AND THE MOUNTAIN OF WRECKAGE IT LEFT, I COULDN'T FIND WORDS TO DESCRIBE IT.
WE HAD SO MUCH TIME, WE WENT SIGHTSEEING.
HOW LONG ARE WE JUST GOING TO WANDER AROUND?
LAKE INAWASHIRO
WE AIN'T HERE AS TOURISTS (THOUGH IT IS NICE).
THE ENTIRE TIME WE'RE JUST WAITING AROUND, WE'RE LOSING MONEY ON THE LODGING AND FOOD.
TSURUGA CASTLE
WE CAN'T JUST SIT AROUND LIKE THIS!
OH DEAR, THIS WON'T DO.
HOW ABOUT YOU HELP OUT AT THIS OTHER WORK SITE?
SO WE WOUND UP ON A NORMAL CONSTRUCTION SITE (7,000 YEN/DAY) WITH NO RELATION TO THE DISASTER AREA OR NUCLEAR PLANT.

*Backhoes come in one of two general lever control systems: JIS pattern or Komatsu pattern
ASSEMBLING REBAR
I DON'T KNOW HOW TO USE THESE KOMATSU* LEVERS!
Practicing on the job
WHAT ARE YOU DOING?!
WUB WUB
I'M SORRY, SIR!
Wheelbarrows are unstable if you're not used to them
I CAME TO THIS PART OF THE COUNTRY TO HELP THE DISASTER AREA. WHAT AM I DOING HERE...?
THAT'S WHAT WE ALL WANT TO KNOW.
Cans: Tea
WE WERE LURED HERE ON THE PROMISE OF 20,000 YEN A DAY, SO SOME PEOPLE WEREN'T INCLINED TO STICK AROUND.
THANK YOU FOR THE OPPOR-TUNITY.
NO, THANKS FOR YOUR WORK. GOOD LUCK.
JUST AS WE ALL WERE READY TO GIVE UP...
WE GOT A JOB AT ICHI-F! GO ON DOWN TO IWAKI, NOW!
HUH?!
WE'VE GOTTA MEET THE CONTRACTING COMPANY TOMORROW! MOVE, MOVE, MOVE!
RIGHT NOW?!
YOU'RE KIDDING ME. WE'RE MOVING AT NINE IN THE EVE-NING?
AFTER ALL THE TIME WE WASTED, NOW WE DON'T HAVE ENOUGH.
A LITERAL FLY-BY-NIGHT.

THIS IS YOUR HOUSING HERE.
IT'S JUST ANOTHER NORMAL HOUSE.
NOTHING WILL SURPRISE ME ANYMORE.
A ONE-STORY PLACE WITH THREE ROOMS AND A KITCHEN. WE HAD OVER TEN CRAMMED IN HERE WHEN IT WAS BUSIEST, TOO.
Man from the local office in Iwaki

THE NEXT DAY, WE WENT UP THE CHAIN OF CONTRACTING COMPANIES IN ORDER.
WE WENT THROUGH THE EMPLOYMENT CONTRACTS.
YES, SIR?
GO AHEAD AND PUT YOUR STAMP THERE.
OH.
Sign: Yonomori Engineering

THIS IS WHAT WE BOUGHT IN KORIYAMA ...
THESE ARE YOUR RADIATION HANDBOOKS. WE'LL SEND 'EM TO THE MASTER CONTRACTOR.
THIS WAS THE FIRST TIME I SAW MY OWN HANDBOOK. (THEY DON'T COME BACK TO YOU UNTIL YOU QUIT).
Handbook: Tatsuta, Kazuto Radiation Control Handbook

Sign: Ottozawa Electric

夫沢電工
WE WENT TO ABOUT THREE DIFFERENT COMPANIES AND SIGNED OR STAMPED A BUNCH OF FORMS, BUT NONE OF THEM GAVE US ANYTHING LIKE A FINISHED CONTRACT.
PEOPLE OFTEN ASK, "DO YOU HAVE TO SIGN NON-DISCLOSURE FORMS?" BUT I CAN SAY FOR SURE THAT I WAS NEVER GIVEN ONE TO SIGN.
WHEN I QUIT THIS COMPANY, I ONLY GOT MY HANDBOOK AND A SINGLE STAMP BACK.
HOWEVER, I ALSO DON'T KNOW HOW MY STAMP MIGHT HAVE BEEN USED WHILE IT WAS CIRCULATING AMONG THE HIGHER COMPANIES.
HOW MANY COMPANIES ARE ABOVE US IN THE CHAIN?
LET'S SEE. TEPCO IS THE WORK SOURCE. THE MASTER CONTRACTOR IS...
WE'RE THE SENARY, SIXTH FROM THE MASTER...
THEN THERE'S THE PRIMARY AND SECONDARY SUBCONTRACTORS UNDER THE MASTER, AND WE HAVEN'T VISITED ANY OF THEM TODAY...
Work Source ☞ TEPCO
Master Contractor ☞ Toyo Enex
Primary Subcontractor ☞ Shibahama Technol Fukushima
Banetsu Industrial
Nucreal
Ottozawa Electric
Yonomori Engineering
We only visited these three today ☞
Note: All names made up aside from TEPCO!

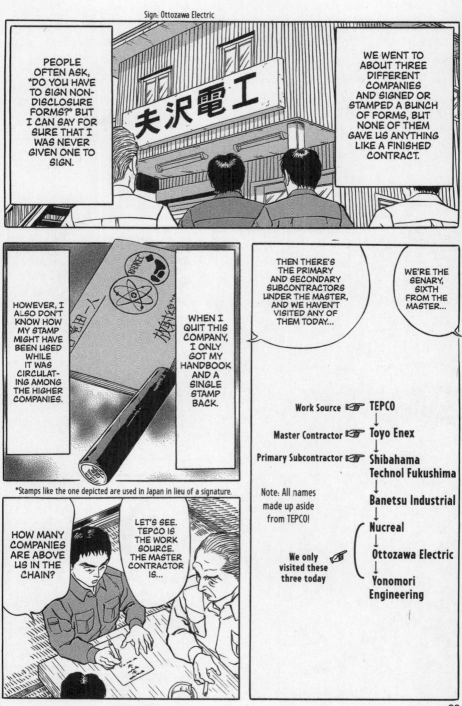

*Stamps like the one depicted are used in Japan in lieu of a signature.

HERE'S KURO-MORI AGAIN.
YOU DID THE ROUNDS? NICE WORK.
YOU'LL BE WORKING SURVEY AT THE BREAK AREA, 8,000 YEN A DAY.

Shows up in Iwaki sometimes

WE'RE ACTUALLY GOING TO ICHI-F, AND THE PAY'S STILL THAT LOW?
IT'S JUST TOO CHEAP FOR THE RISKS.
I CAN'T HELP IT. THE STUFF THAT COMES DOWN THIS FAR IS LOW-PAY BY NATURE. WE'RE NOT MAKING ANY PROFIT FROM IT.
WELL, WITH THIS MANY GO-BETWEENS ...
LOOK, WE'RE THE SEVENTH COMPANY DOWN, STARTING FROM THE MASTER CONTRACTOR.
THERE ARE *THAT* MANY?!
YOU MEAN EVEN *YOU* DIDN'T KNOW?!
ACTUALLY, I WAS ONLY AWARE OF ONE OR TWO COMPANIES ABOVE US...
GOOD GRIEF ...
IT SOUNDS LIKE I MADE THIS UP, BUT IT'S ALL TRUE. IT'S SO SILLY I COULDN'T EVEN BE MAD ABOUT IT.

Sign: Hang in there, Iwaki!!

Iwaki's bicycle racetrack was a base for disaster supplies, but as of June 2011, it was open again.

WHOOOO...
I'VE COME ALL THIS WAY...
YET I HAVEN'T DONE ANYTHING YET...
FSHHH...

Slide: Radiation, Safety
BUT FINALLY, THE FRUSTRATION CAME TO AN END.
IT'S FINALIZED! WE START TRAINING TOMORROW!
AT LAST!
放射線
安全
AT J-VILLAGE'S LECTURE HALL, WE HAD A DAY-LONG COURSE ABOUT RADIATION PROTECTION, SEPARATED INTO "a EDUCATION" AND "b EDUCATION."
THE a COURSE IN THE MORNING, THE b COURSE IN THE AFTERNOON, WITH A TEST AT THE END OF EACH SESSION.
THESE ARE REALLY EASY.
I'M SURE THEY JUST DON'T WANT TO FAIL ANYONE.
THE NEXT DAY, WE FINALLY WENT TO THE MASTER CONTRACTOR AND PRIMARY SUBCONTRACTOR FOR ANOTHER EASY TRAINING SESSION.
THE HIGHER WE GO, THE FANCIER THE OFFICES.
NOW THAT I THINK ABOUT IT, WE NEVER EVEN VISITED SOME OF THE SUBCONTRACTORS IN THE CHAIN. (DO THEY EVEN EXIST?!)
THIS IS THE J-VILLAGE WBC (WHOLE-BODY COUNTER).
5

IDs: Tokyo Electric WID (1-F); Tatsuta, Kazuto
BY THE TIME I FINALLY GOT INTO ICHI-F...
...A MONTH HAD PASSED SINCE I CAME TO KORIYAMA, AND OVER A YEAR SINCE I STARTED LOOKING FOR THIS JOB.
THEY TOOK TWO PHOTOS TO MAKE OUR WORKER ID AND ENTRY ID.
CLICK
THE MASTER CONTRACTOR SUPPLIES THE GLASS BADGE AND WORK ASSIGNMENT BARCODE.
東京電力WID(1F)
竜田一人
Needed to borrow your APD
Glass badge (personal one-month dosimeter)
IT'S GOTTEN SO MUCH BETTER SINCE THEN.
WELL, WE'VE ALL FOUND OUR WAY TO DIFFERENT COMPANIES NOW.
BOY, YOU WANT TO TALK ABOUT SOME UNSCRUPULOUS BUSINESS PRACTICES!
THAT WAS MY LONG JOURNEY TO ICHI-F.
I FERVENTLY HOPE THAT THE CONDITIONS FOR WORKERS AT ICHI-F CONTINUE TO IMPROVE, NO MATTER WHAT ROUTE THEY TOOK!
公共 所
竜田
FINDING MY JOB THROUGH THE HELLO WORK SERVICE WAS A VERY ROUNDABOUT WAY TO GET HERE, BUT THE EXPERIENCES WERE INTERESTING. I'M GRATEFUL THAT THEY HELPED ME REACH ICHI-F.
Sign: Hello Work Employment Service Center

CHAPTER 3 - END

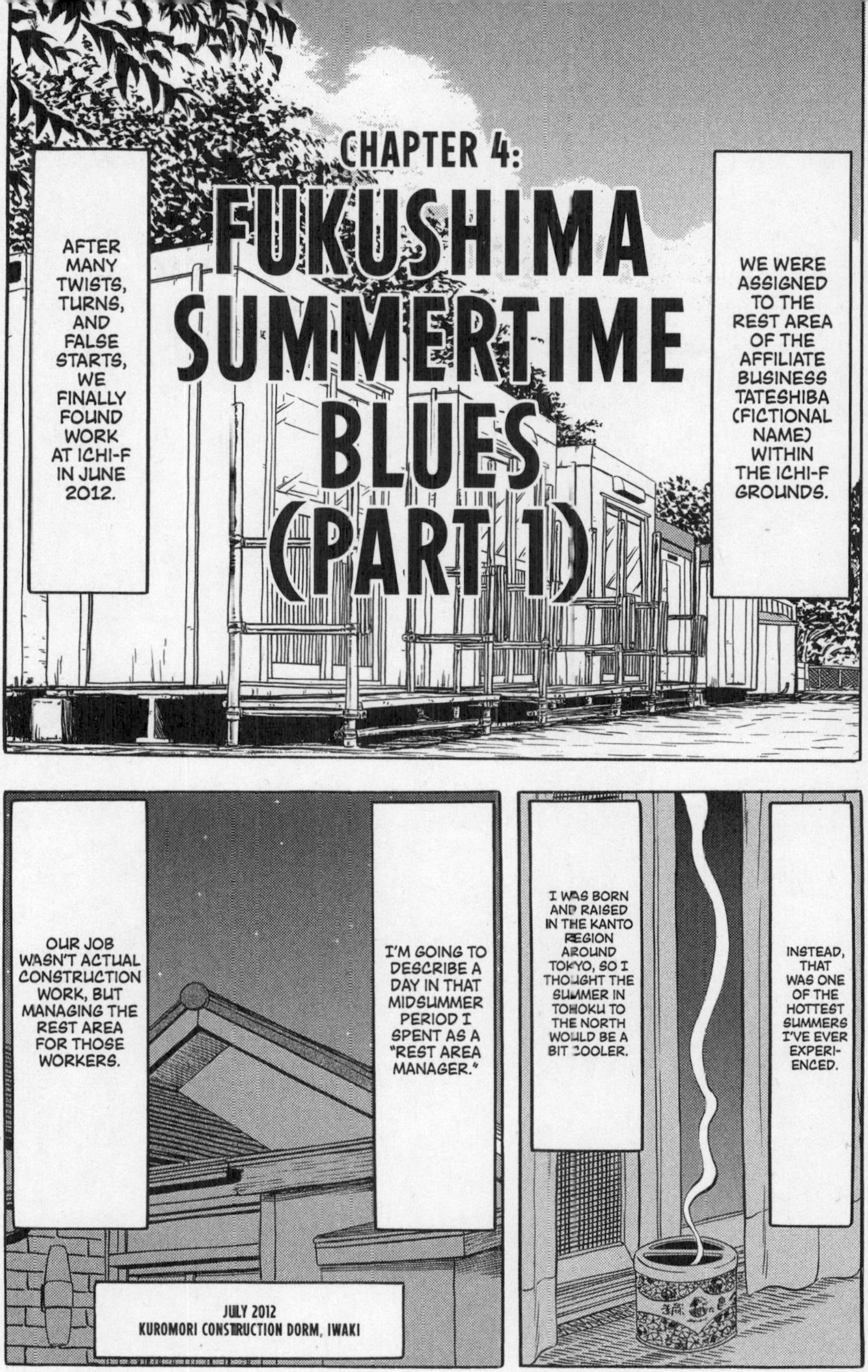

CHAPTER 4:
FUKUSHIMA SUMMERTIME BLUES (PART 1)
AFTER MANY TWISTS, TURNS, AND FALSE STARTS, WE FINALLY FOUND WORK AT ICHI-F IN JUNE 2012.
WE WERE ASSIGNED TO THE REST AREA OF THE AFFILIATE BUSINESS TATESHIBA (FICTIONAL NAME) WITHIN THE ICHI-F GROUNDS.
JULY 2012
KUROMORI CONSTRUCTION DORM, IWAKI
OUR JOB WASN'T ACTUAL CONSTRUCTION WORK, BUT MANAGING THE REST AREA FOR THOSE WORKERS.
I'M GOING TO DESCRIBE A DAY IN THAT MIDSUMMER PERIOD I SPENT AS A "REST AREA MANAGER."
I WAS BORN AND RAISED IN THE KANTO REGION AROUND TOKYO, SO I THOUGHT THE SUMMER IN TOHOKU TO THE NORTH WOULD BE A BIT COOLER.
INSTEAD, THAT WAS ONE OF THE HOTTEST SUMMERS I'VE EVER EXPERIENCED.

BEEP BEEP
BEEP BEEP
3:45
...GOOD MORNING...
MORN-ING.
URGH ...
UGH ...
BEEP...
AS A COUNTERMEASURE AGAINST HEATSTROKE, ICHI-F HAS A SUMMER-TIME SYSTEM WHERE WORK STARTS ONE OR TWO HOURS EARLIER IN THE DAY.
AS REST AREA MANAGERS, WE HAVE TO GET IT READY TO "OPEN" BEFORE THE WORKERS LEAVE, SO WE WAKE UP BEFORE FOUR.
It's treated like a business
LURCH...

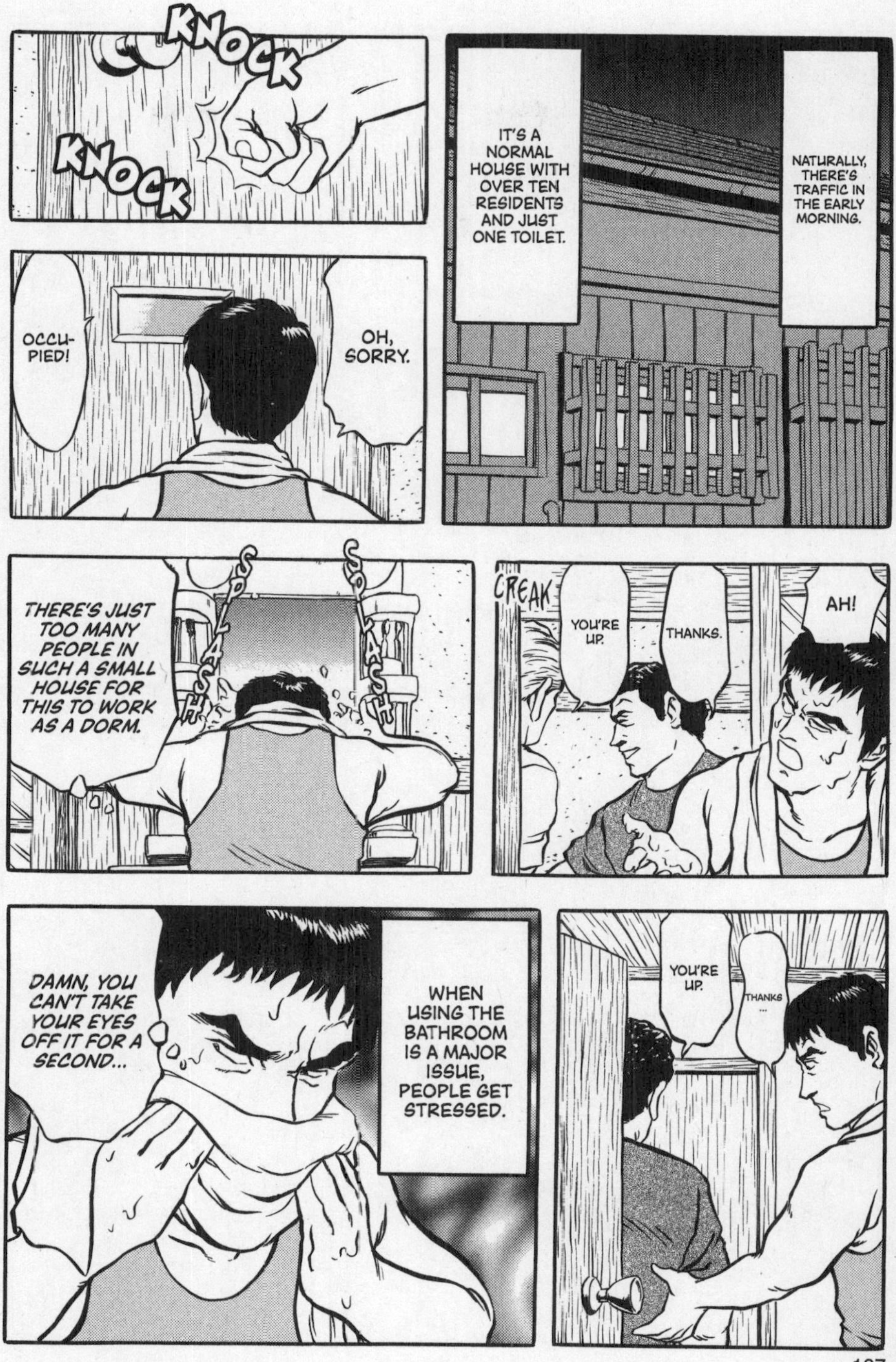
KNOCK
KNOCK
IT'S A NORMAL HOUSE WITH OVER TEN RESIDENTS AND JUST ONE TOILET.
NATURALLY, THERE'S TRAFFIC IN THE EARLY MORNING.
OCCU-PIED!
OH, SORRY.
SPLASH
SPLASH
THERE'S JUST TOO MANY PEOPLE IN SUCH A SMALL HOUSE FOR THIS TO WORK AS A DORM.
CREAK
YOU'RE UP.
THANKS.
AH!
DAMN, YOU CAN'T TAKE YOUR EYES OFF IT FOR A SECOND...
WHEN USING THE BATHROOM IS A MAJOR ISSUE, PEOPLE GET STRESSED.
YOU'RE UP.
THANKS...

BETWEEN THE SMELL AND THE STAINS, THIS IS DEFINITELY NOT SOMETHING I CAN DEPICT IN A MANGA.
Self-censoring
I CLEAN THE PLACE, TOO, BUT WITH THIS MANY PEOPLE, YOU JUST CAN'T KEEP UP.
I HAVE TO GET OUT OF HERE.
THIS EXPERIENCE CAUSES A TEMPORARY LOSS OF APPETITE.
KLCHAK
BUT I'VE GOT TO EAT, OR SUFFER THE RISK OF HEAT-STROKE.
At this point, it was so early that you couldn't even get a storebought meal
IT'S PRACTICALLY A NECESSITY TO GET PLENTY OF WATER AND SODIUM IN PREPARATION FOR THE JOB. THESE SOUR DRIED PLUMS WILL DO THE TRICK.
MMMM ...

Label: Dried Plums

IN MY GROUP ARE THESE TWO FELLOWS AGAIN FROM OUR TIME IN KORIYAMA...
ALL RIGHT, HERE WE GO.
TAMANA FROM KUMAMOTO (52)
TSURUMI FROM KANAGAWA (59)
DURING SUMMER-TIME HOURS, WE LEAVE AFTER FOUR.
4:15 AM
A line you hear later at work
DO YOU HAVE YOUR ID CARD AND GLASS BADGE?
YOU CAN'T GET INTO THE WORKPLACE WITHOUT YOUR CARD AND BADGE, SO I MAKE SURE I HAVE THEM EVERY MORNING.
Just worried about myself
...AND THESE TWO GUYS, WHICH MAKES US FIVE.
TAKAGI FROM MOTOMIYA, FUKUSHIMA (39)
SEKIMOTO FROM IBARAKI (47)
EVERYBODY GOT ALL THEIR STUFF?
YES, SIR!
WELL, IT'S NOT EXACTLY ROMANTIC HAVING FIVE OLDER MEN CRAMMED INTO A TINY VAN IN THE MIDDLE OF THE NIGHT...

Oddly, you really do feel this way

4:30 AM
OOOH!
GOOD ONE TODAY.
...BUT SOMETIMES YOU GET TO SEE A BRILLIANT SUNRISE ON THE DRIVE.
IT'S A BLESSING TO SEE IT!
I PRAY FOR OUR SAFETY TODAY.
WE STOP AT A CONVENIENCE STORE TO GET LUNCHES.
ALL RIGHT, LET'S GET SOME FOOD.
SKREE
ALL THE STORES ALONG THE WAY TO ICHI-F ARE PACKED FOR SUCH AN EARLY HOUR.
焼肉
慶州
AS WE GET TO THE TOWN OF HIRONO, TRAFFIC THICKENS.
WE STOP AT J-VILLAGE ON THE BORDER TO NARAHA.

Sign: Yakiniku, Keishu

HERE'S THE J-VILLAGE PARKING LOT (WHICH IS JUST A FIELD).
AROUND FIVE O'CLOCK IT STARTS TO FILL UP.
KTHUD
KTHUD
HEY!
GOOD MORNING.
Local pachinko chains
THERE'S A SMOKING AREA NEAR THE REAR DOOR OF THE MAIN BUILDING. SOME COMPANIES MAKE THAT THEIR MORNING MEETING SPACE.
HOW'D IT GO YESTERDAY?
NO GOOD. NEITHER TSUBAME NOR N-1 WERE PAYING OUT.
MOST MORNING GREETINGS CONSIST OF TALKING ABOUT PACHINKO.
I THINK TODAY'S MAIN EVENT IS THE NORTH KANTO LINE.
STILL, TAKEDA-KAMIYAMA IS A LOCK FOR THE FINISH, SO WHERE'S THE FUN IN BETTING?
WHEN THE BICYCLE TRACK IS IN SEASON, WE TALK ABOUT THAT, TOO.
ALL TOGETHER? LET'S GO.
OKAY!
GIVEN WHAT WE WERE BEING PAID AT THIS POINT, THERE WASN'T ENOUGH MONEY TO BOTHER GAMBLING, BUT GUYS CAN DREAM...

LATER, WEARING BLUE TYVEKS WOULD BE THE ONLY WAY TO GAIN ACCESS TO ICHI-F, BUT AT THIS TIME, WHITE TYVEKS WERE ALSO ACCEPTABLE.
ALL THE MORE EX-PERIENCED WORKERS ARE FROM THE LOCAL AREA.
STF 塩田
STF 江田
STF 北目
STF 川前
STF ナカジマ
STF 赤井
THE FIVE OF US WERE ADDITIONAL MEMBERS AFTER THE REST AREA WAS EXPANDED.
WE HAVE A DOZEN MEMBERS THAT SPLIT INTO TWO VANS AND HEAD FOR ICHI-F.
5:20 AM
AT THE J-VILLAGE EXIT, WE GET AN ID CHECK.
AT THIS TIME, THERE WAS A RESTRICTED ZONE CHECKPOINT RIGHT AT THE ENTRANCE TO NARAHA ON ROUTE 6 AFTER LEAVING J-VILLAGE.

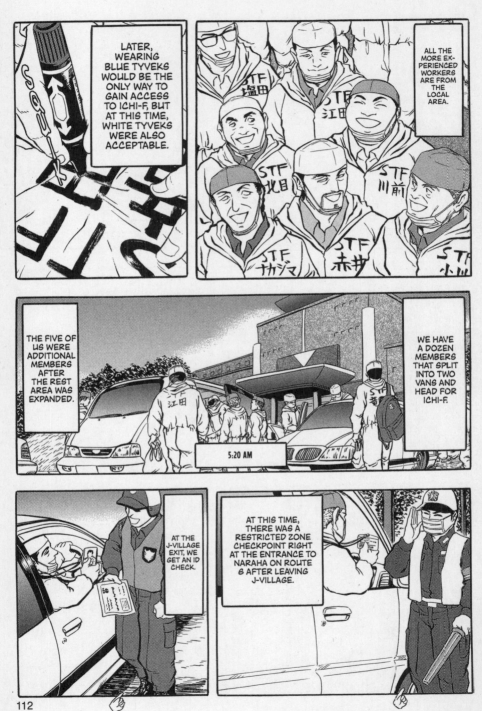

This is a guard from the security company

These are nationwide riot police units who came to help

AFTER NARAHA, WE PASS THROUGH EMPTY TOMIOKA AND OKUMA.
50
WHAT'S WORSE THAN NOT SEEING ANY PEOPLE AT ALL...
アトム

Sign: Revolving Sushi Atom Banner: Revolving Sushi

...IS THE SIGHT OF THE PLANTLIFE GROWING OUT OF CONTROL WITHOUT ANY HUMAN SUPERVISION. IT'S REALLY STUNNING TO BEHOLD.
BUT IN CONTRAST TO THE SCENERY...
I'M TELLING YOU! THERE'S LOT OF YOUNG WOMEN AT THAT PLACE!
BWA HA
YEAH, BUT TO YOU, "YOUNG" IS ANYONE UNDER 70!
HA
HA
...THE INTERIOR OF THE VAN IS OFTEN FULL OF RAUCOUS LAUGHTER ON THE WAY TO WORK.
WHEN YOU SEE IT ENOUGH, ANY SIGHT BECOMES ORDINARY.

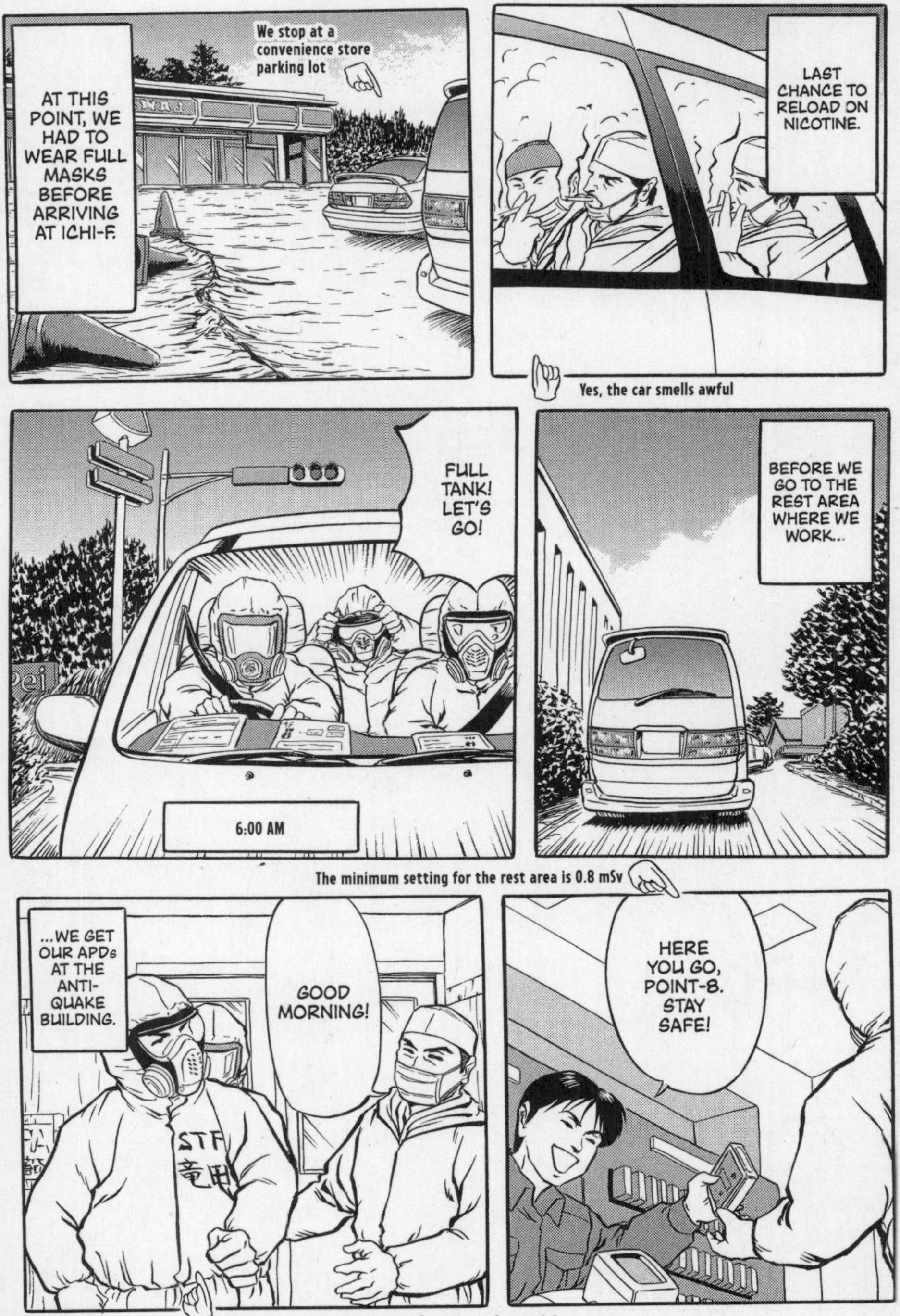
AT THIS POINT, WE HAD TO WEAR FULL MASKS BEFORE ARRIVING AT ICHI-F.
We stop at a convenience store parking lot
LAST CHANCE TO RELOAD ON NICOTINE.
Yes, the car smells awful
FULL TANK! LET'S GO!
6:00 AM
BEFORE WE GO TO THE REST AREA WHERE WE WORK...
The minimum setting for the rest area is 0.8 mSv
...WE GET OUR APDs AT THE ANTI-QUAKE BUILDING.
GOOD MORNING!
HERE YOU GO, POINT-8. STAY SAFE!
I leave the mask on because we leave just after arriving

WE GOTTA HAUL WATER TODAY.
THERE'S A BIG STORE OF BOTTLES OF WATER IN A STORAGE AREA OF THE QUAKE BUILDING.
UGH ...
24-packs of 500 ml bottles
WE JUST GOTTA DO IT. THE STOCK'S RUNNING LOW.
THERE WE GO!
THERE'S NO RUNNING WATER AT THE REST AREA, SO WE HAVE TO CARRY THEM OURSELVES.
CAN'T PACK ANY MORE.
SET THE REST ON YOUR LAP.
THERE ARE NO SINKS IN THE REST AREA. NO TOILETS, NO WASHING.
WE'RE JUST FERRYING DRINKING WATER. IT'S THE LIFELINE OF THE REST AREA.
A NUMBER OF LARGE AFFILIATE COMPANIES LIKE TATESHIBA HAVE SO MANY WORKERS THAT THEY'VE SET UP THEIR OWN REST AREAS OUTSIDE OF THE ANTI-QUAKE BUILDING AND RECREATION CENTER.
TO REACTOR BUILDINGS
ANTI-QUAKE BLDG.
OKUMA AVE.
FUELING STATION
ALPS
THESE REST AREAS ARE BUILT INTO CONTAINERS SHIPPED HERE AFTER THE ACCIDENT. WE ALSO CALL THEM "SHELTERS."
TATESHIBA REST AREA
RECREATION BLDG.
STERILIZATION BAY
VEHICLE SURVEY
AFFILIATE COMPANY CAMPUS (master contractor storehouse is here)
There are more company shelters down here

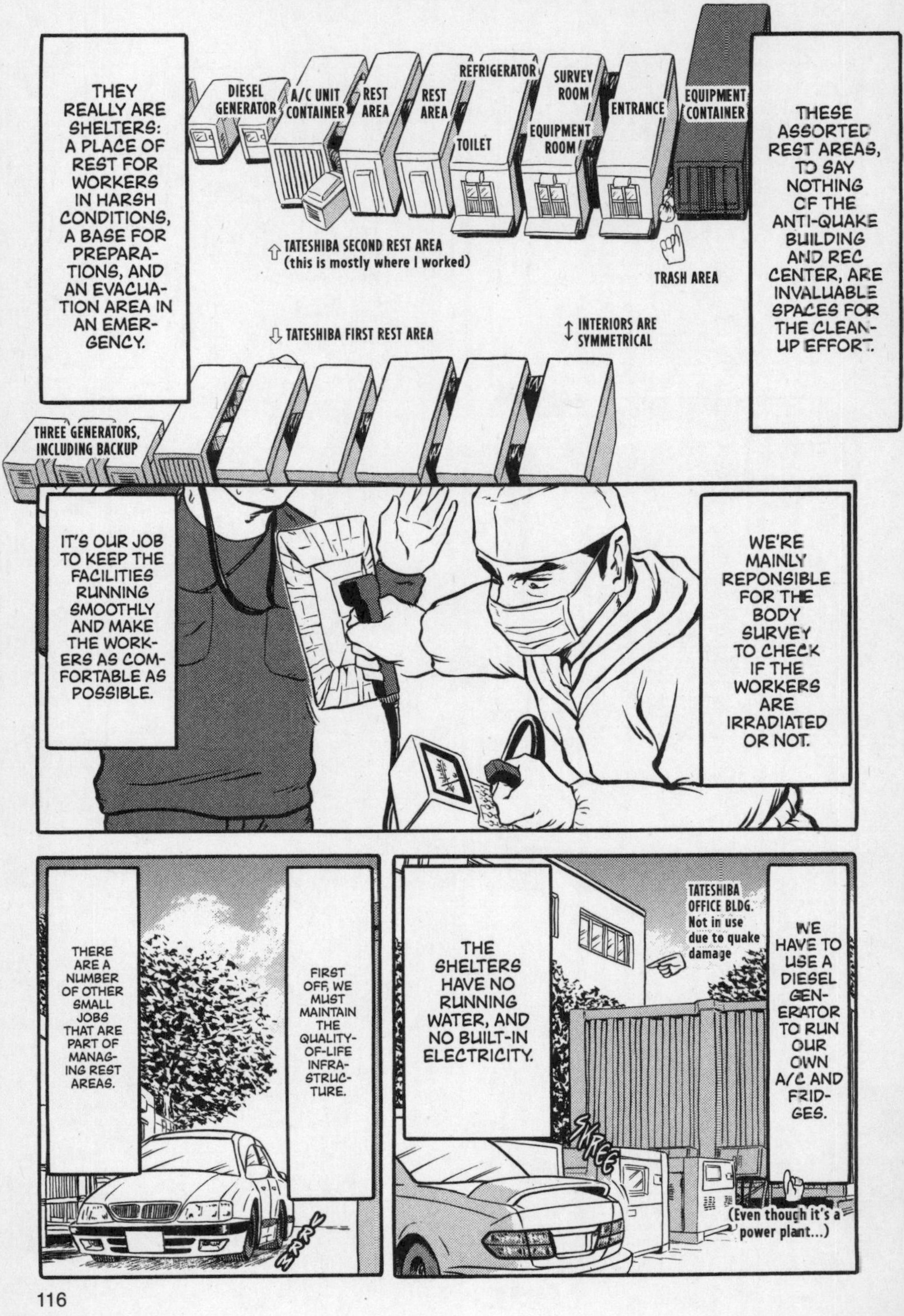

THEY REALLY ARE SHELTERS: A PLACE OF REST FOR WORKERS IN HARSH CONDITIONS, A BASE FOR PREPARATIONS, AND AN EVACUATION AREA IN AN EMERGENCY.

DIESEL GENERATOR

A/C UNIT CONTAINER

REST AREA

REST AREA

REFRIGERATOR

TOILET

SURVEY ROOM

EQUIPMENT ROOM

ENTRANCE

EQUIPMENT CONTAINER

THESE ASSORTED REST AREAS, TO SAY NOTHING OF THE ANTI-QUAKE BUILDING AND REC CENTER, ARE INVALUABLE SPACES FOR THE CLEAN-UP EFFORT.

↑ TATESHIBA SECOND REST AREA
(this is mostly where I worked)

TRASH AREA

⇩ TATESHIBA FIRST REST AREA

↑ INTERIORS ARE SYMMETRICAL

THREE GENERATORS, INCLUDING BACKUP

IT'S OUR JOB TO KEEP THE FACILITIES RUNNING SMOOTHLY AND MAKE THE WORKERS AS COMFORTABLE AS POSSIBLE.

WE'RE MAINLY REPONSIBLE FOR THE BODY SURVEY TO CHECK IF THE WORKERS ARE IRRADIATED OR NOT.

THERE ARE A NUMBER OF OTHER SMALL JOBS THAT ARE PART OF MANAGING REST AREAS.

FIRST OFF, WE MUST MAINTAIN THE QUALITY-OF-LIFE INFRASTRUCTURE.

THE SHELTERS HAVE NO RUNNING WATER, AND NO BUILT-IN ELECTRICITY.

TATESHIBA OFFICE BLDG. Not in use due to quake damage

WE HAVE TO USE A DIESEL GENERATOR TO RUN OUR OWN A/C AND FRIDGES.

(Even though it's a power plant...)

HERE WE GO.
SO THE FIRST TASK WHEN WE ARRIVE IS TO START THE GENERATOR ENGINE.
KCHAK
DRUNN
THEN WE TURN ON THE AIR CONDITIONER.
VWEE
IT HAS A POWERFUL FILTER THAT CLEANS UP THE OUTSIDE AIR, WHICH IS WHY WE CAN TAKE OUR MASKS OFF INSIDE THE REST AREA.
VWOHHH
THE ROLE OF THE REST AREA IS TO PROVIDE A SPACE WHERE WE CAN TAKE OUR MASKS OFF AND FEEL COMFORTABLE.
LET'S GET THE WATER INSIDE.
THE TATESHIBA EMPLOYEES ACTUALLY SHOW UP AROUND SEVEN O'CLOCK.
AIR GOOD!
ENGINE GOOD!
WE NEED TO GET THE STRUCTURE READY TO OPEN AND SERVE ITS CONSTITUENTS.
WHEN I GOT THIS JOB, THEY SAID...
THINK OF THE REST AREA DUTIES AS SERVICE SECTOR WORK.
THE WORKERS THAT COME THERE ARE YOUR CUSTOMERS. PLEASE CONDUCT YOURSELVES AS IF YOU WERE ENGAGING IN CUSTOMER SERVICE.

Primary subcontractor

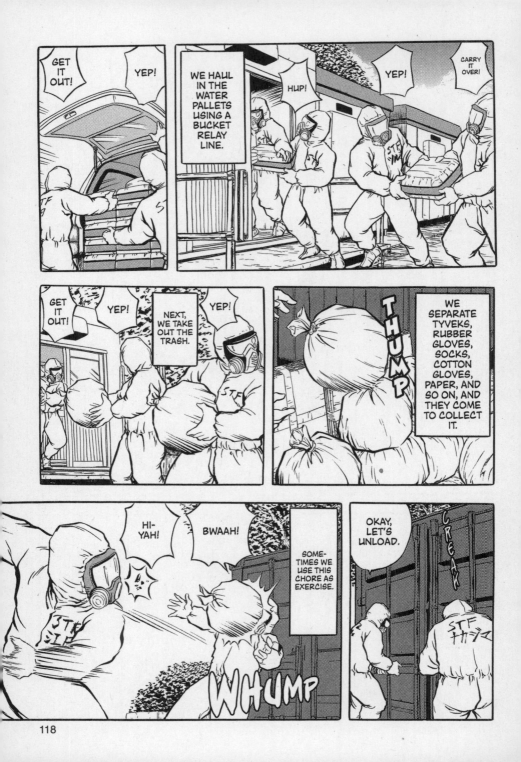

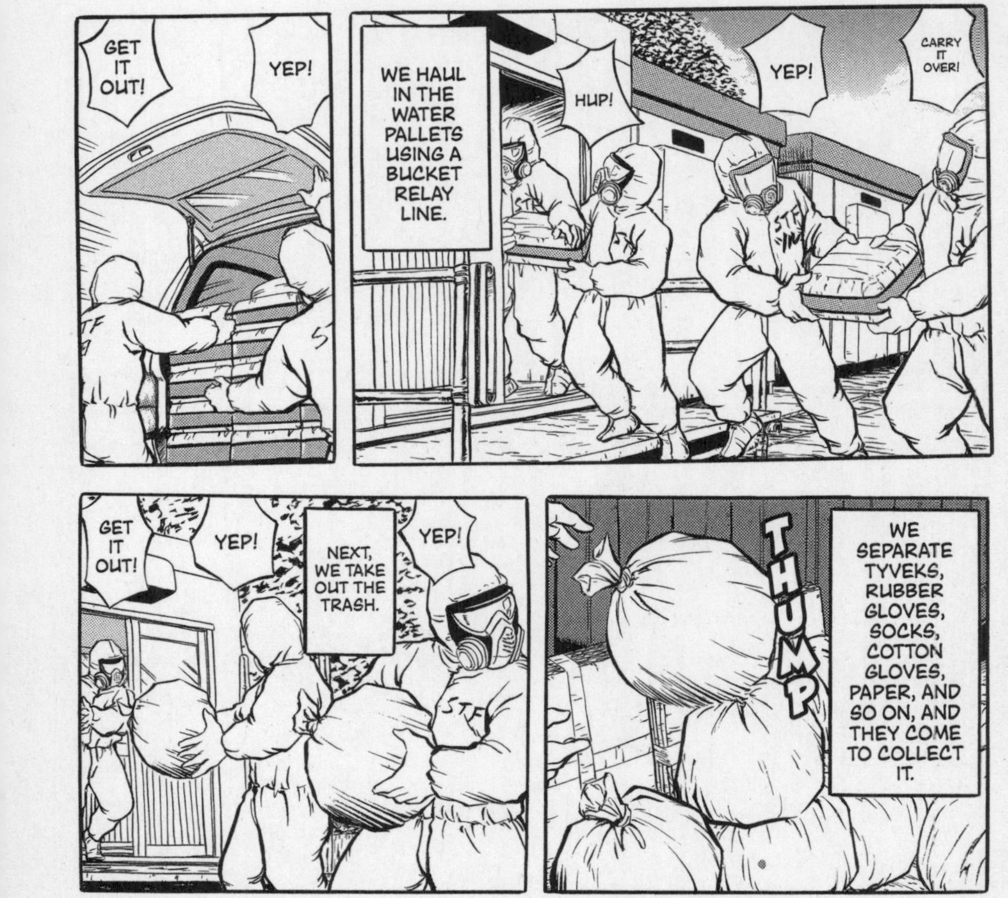
GET IT OUT!
YEP!
WE HAUL IN THE WATER PALLETS USING A BUCKET RELAY LINE.
HUP!
YEP!
CARRY IT OVER!
GET IT OUT!
YEP!
NEXT, WE TAKE OUT THE TRASH.
YEP!
THUMP
WE SEPARATE TYVEKS, RUBBER GLOVES, SOCKS, COTTON GLOVES, PAPER, AND SO ON, AND THEY COME TO COLLECT IT.
HI-YAH!
BWAAH!
SOME-TIMES WE USE THIS CHORE AS EXERCISE.
WHUMP
OKAY, LET'S UNLOAD.
CREAK

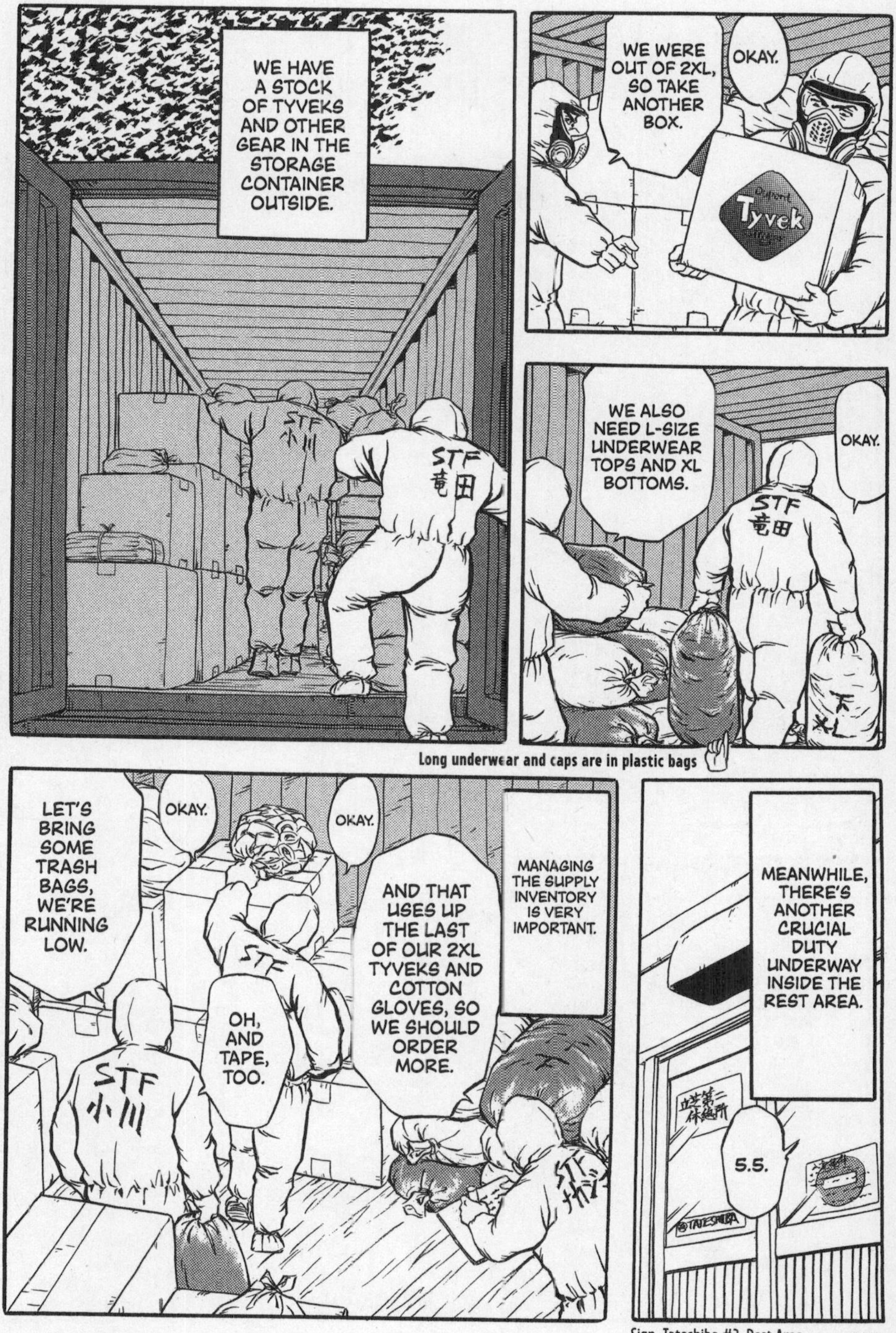

Long underwear and caps are in plastic bags

Sign: Tateshiba #2, Rest Area

Taking numbers in all directions

MEASURING THE RADIATION LEVELS.

THAT'S A 4.0.

GOT IT.

WE USE SURVEY METERS TO MEASURE THE ATMOSPHERIC RADIATION AT A FEW PLACES IN THE BUILDING.

SMEAR FILTERS WILL WIPE UP ANY CONTAMINATION ON THE FLOOR.

Fold here

WIPE

WIPE

We measure the filter in here

A DUST SAMPLER WILL HELP US COLLECT AIRBORNE DUST.

By Ichi-F standards, of course

THEN IT GETS MEASURED IN A SPECIAL DEVICE WITH A GEIGER-MÜLLER (GM) TUBE.

Put sample here

Geiger counter (GM tube)

BY THE WAY, THE REST AREA READINGS DIFFER DEPENDING ON THE SPOT, BUT GENERALLY BETWEEN 3.0 AND 5.5 MICROSIEVERTS, AND WE DON'T GET OUTLIER READINGS ON SMEARS OR DUST. IT'S A CLEAN LOW-RAD ENVIRONMENT.

WE MARK THESE DOWN ON A CHECK SHEET EVERY DAY AND SEND IT TO TEPCO.

Heating water too

NATURALLY, WE HAVE MORE MUNDANE CLEANING TO DO, AS WELL AS ORGANIZING SUPPLIES AND MAKING THINGS RUN PROPERLY.

3L

Cooling the new water bottles

Tyvek

Radiation-absorbing sheets come in stacks that must be separated one-by-one

THE OTHER LIFELINE FOR THIS REST AREA IS THE TASK OF REFUELING.
IT INVOLVES HEAVY LIFTING OUTDOORS AND LOTS OF SWEAT, SO WE NEED TO CHANGE INTO OUR WORK UNDERWEAR FOR THIS.
THEY SAY, TONGUE-N-CHEEK, THAT "CHANGING CLOTHES IS YOUR JOB AT A NUCLEAR PLANT."
WELL, I CERTAINLY REMEMBER DOING A WHOLE LOT OF THAT DURING MY TIME AT ICHI-F.

Sign: Covers Sign: Socks Sign: Cotton Gloves Sign: Rubber Gloves

綿手
ゴム手
右
AND IT'S NOT JUST UNDERWEAR—THERE'S TYVEKS, GLOVES, SOCKS, CAPS, SHOE COVERS...
OUR TOP PRIORITY AS A REST AREA IS TO HAVE ENOUGH OF THESE SUPPLIES TO SERVE AS A STAGING AREA TO HEAD TO WORK.

Box: R Box: L

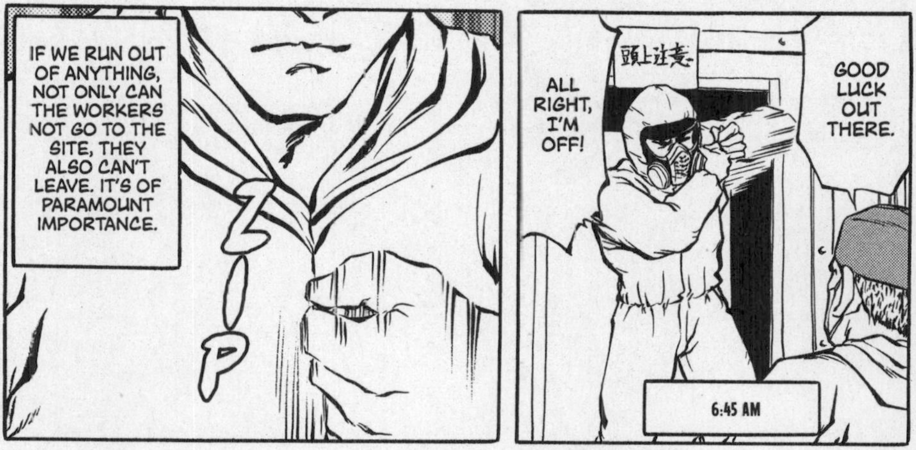
IF WE RUN OUT OF ANYTHING, NOT ONLY CAN THE WORKERS NOT GO TO THE SITE, THEY ALSO CAN'T LEAVE. IT'S OF PARAMOUNT IMPORTANCE.
ZIP
ALL RIGHT, I'M OFF!
GOOD LUCK OUT THERE.
6:45 AM

Sign: Watch your head

CONTRACTOR OFFICE BLDG.
(Unused due to quake damage)
PREFAB STOREHOUSE
FIRST, I'VE GOT TO GET THE FUEL CONTAINERS FROM THE STOREHOUSE OF THE MASTER CONTRACTOR, TOYO ENEX.
STF 竜田
WE KEEP THE CONTAINERS HERE BECAUSE THERE ARE TEN OF THEM, AND THERE'S NO STORAGE SPACE FOR HAZARDOUS MATERIALS IN THE REST AREA.
18-LITER CONTAINERS
You have to struggle with two, because carrying one takes too long
GONK
ONCE ALL TEN ARE PACKED UP, INCLUDING THE EMPTIES FROM THE DAY BEFORE, WE HEAD BACK.
The base of the fuel can hose acts as a flathead screwdriver
THERE ARE TWO GENERATORS FOR EACH REST AREA. ONE IS FOR THE FREEZER AND FRIDGE, SO IT'S WORKING 24 HOURS A DAY.
STF 竜田
PSHHHT
SWIK
SWIK
Vent port

IT HASN'T BEEN FUELED SINCE MIDDAY YESTERDAY, SO IT TAKES THREE WHOLE 18-LITER CANISTERS.

PSHHHH

BLUB BLUB

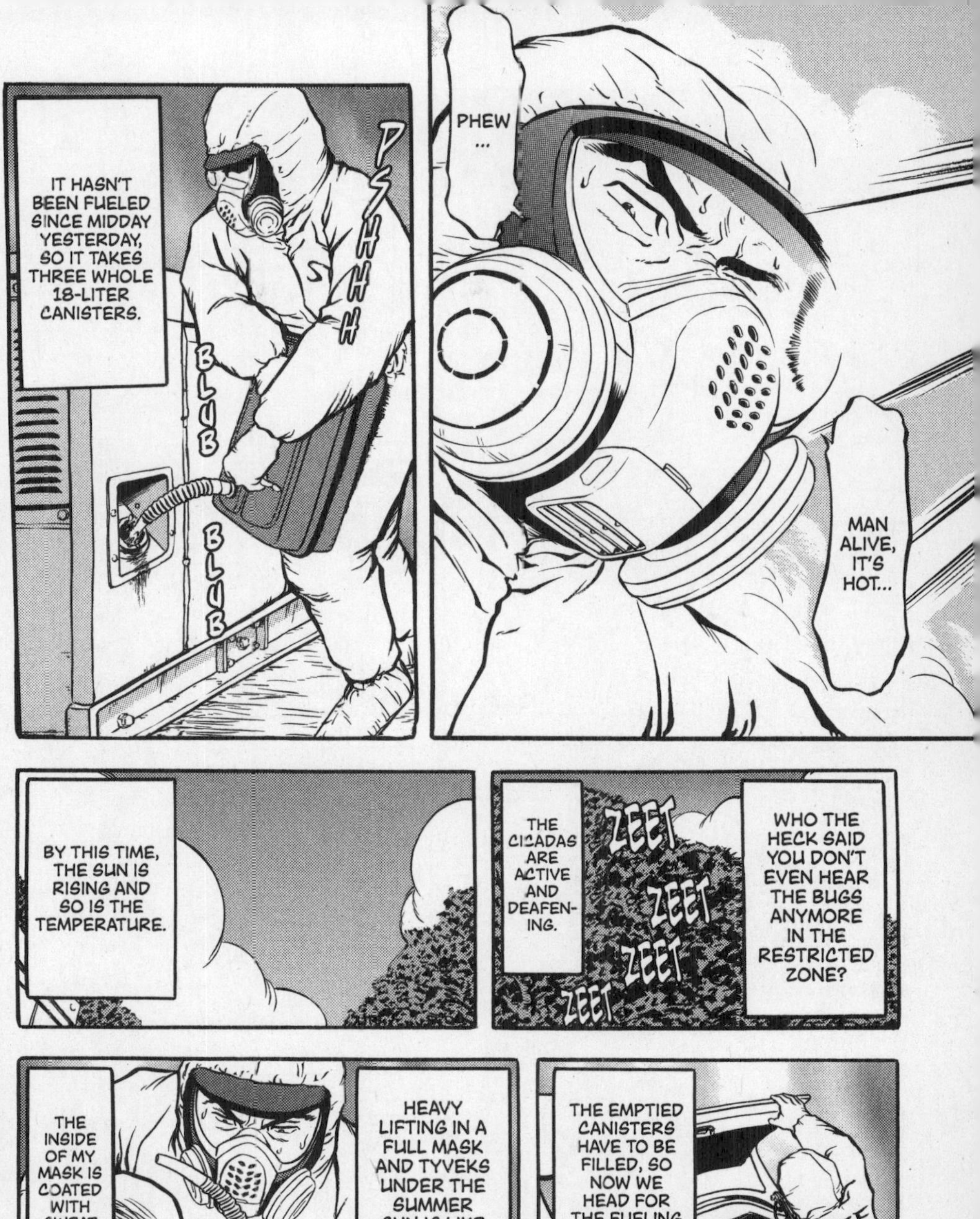

PHEW ...

MAN ALIVE, IT'S HOT...

BY THIS TIME, THE SUN IS RISING AND SO IS THE TEMPERATURE.

THE CICADAS ARE ACTIVE AND DEAFENING.

ZEET
ZEET
ZEET
ZEET

WHO THE HECK SAID YOU DON'T EVEN HEAR THE BUGS ANYMORE IN THE RESTRICTED ZONE?

THE INSIDE OF MY MASK IS COATED WITH SWEAT NOW.

HEAVY LIFTING IN A FULL MASK AND TYVEKS UNDER THE SUMMER SUN IS LIKE WEIGHT TRAINING INSIDE A SAUNA.

THE EMPTIED CANISTERS HAVE TO BE FILLED, SO NOW WE HEAD FOR THE FUELING STATION.

STF
竜田

SURE THING!
I'VE GOT TEN TODAY.
Helmet has a wide brim to stave off the sun
THE ICHI-F GAS STATION IS OPEN VERY EARLY.
WEL-COME!
GOOD MORNING.
STAY SAFE!
SEE YOU!
VRMMMM
YOU MARK DOWN THE COMPANY CODE AND AMOUNT.
THERE'S NO CASH AT ICHI-F. EVERY-THING IS ON A TAB.
DDT
SSD
STF
NOT AS TOUGH AS STANDING OUT IN THE SUN ALL DAY LIKE YOU! BEST OF LUCK WITH THAT.
THAT'S A TOUGH JOB!
IT ONLY TAKES ABOUT THIRTY MINUTES, BUT THE REFUELING TASK IS THE TOUGHEST OF ANY AT THE REST AREA.
IT REALLY FEELS LIKE HARD LABOR...
BUT AS A MATTER OF FACT, I PRE-FERRED THE PHYSICAL ASPECT OF THE WORK.
GRAH!
NOW THAT THEY'RE FULL, THEY GO BACK TO THE STORE-HOUSE.

BACK FROM FUELING, AND IT'S ABOUT TIME FOR THE TATESHIBA WORKERS TO ARRIVE.
I'M BACK ...
7:30 AM
STF 竜田
GOOD MORN-ING.
YOU'RE ALL DIRTY. GET CHANGED!
MR. AKASHI IS AN EMERGENCY MEDIC TATESHIBA ASSIGNED TO THE REST AREA. A REASSURING PRESENCE.
TATESHIBA
明石
FROM HYOGO (57)
Wall Sign: Tops
GAAAH!
I SWEAT ALL THROUGH THE TYVEK, SO I HAVE TO CHANGE UNDER-WEAR, TOO.
上
下
AT THE TIME, UNDERWEAR AND CAPS WERE DISPOSABLE, BUT AT NEARBY 2-F, THEY'VE BEEN REUSING THE CLOTHING SINCE THEIR LAUNDRY FACILITIES CAME BACK.
Hamper: Bottoms, tops
OH.
HERE THEY ARE.
TAP TAP
THE BUS FROM J-VILLAGE IS HERE, DROPPING OFF LOADS OF TATESHIBA WORKERS.
MORNIN'.
PUT YOUR MASKS IN HERE.

THREE AT A TIME.

SHUT THE OUTER DOOR.

THE ENTRANCE WAY IS A DOUBLE-DOOR SYSTEM.

THE INTERIOR HAS A HIGH AIR PRESSURE THANKS TO THE A/C. THIS ENSURES THAT THE OUTSIDE AIR CANNOT LEAK IN THROUGH THE DOORS. IT FEELS LIKE BEING IN A DOMED STADIUM.

THERE'S ALWAYS A CERTAIN AMOUNT OF AIRFLOW, FROM THE VENT IN THE BACK OF THE REST AREA ROOM TO THE EXHAUST NEAR THE DOORS.

They have replacements for the allergic

THE NEWLY-ARRIVED WORKERS GET THEIR WORK GEAR.

AND ANOTHER TYVEK...

NON-ALLERGENIC RUBBER, PLEASE.

HERE YOU GO.

THEN THERE ARE FINAL MEETINGS...

WE'RE GOING HERE TODAY.

OKAY.

GET YOUR FLUIDS NOW.

GEARING UP...

Leak check

PFFP

A cooling vest

AND THEY HEAD FOR THE SITES.

SHALL WE GO?

READY!

HAVE YOU GOT YOUR APD AND GLASS BADGE?

I SURE DO!

IT FEELS SILLY FOR BOTH SIDES TO DO THIS LAST CONFIRMATION. BUT IT'S MANDATORY, EVER SINCE SOME SHADY SUBCONTRACTORS TRIED TO HIDE THEIR DOSIMETERS TO GET AROUND THE EXPOSURE LIMITS.

LATER, IN 2013, THEY STARTED USING SUITS WITH CLEAR PATCHES ON THE CHEST, WHICH MADE THE PHYSICAL TOUCH-CHECK UNNECESSARY.
OKAY GUYS, LET'S PUT IN SOME GOOD WORK OUT THERE! TAKE CARE.
GOOD MORNING.
WHEN THERE ARE FOLKS COMING AND GOING AT THE SAME TIME, THE ENTRANCE GETS JAMMED.
MORNIN'!
GOOD MORNING.
CLICK
CLICK
CLICK
40 PEOPLE IS THE MAXIMUM YOU CAN FIT INTO A REST AREA AT ONE TIME.
BUT BETWEEN SHOWING UP IN THE MORNING AND COMING BACK AFTER THE SHIFT, NOT TO MENTION MULTIPLE TEAMS, THE ACTUAL NUMBER OF BODIES GOING THROUGH IN A DAY IS MORE LIKE TWO OR THREE HUNDRED.
THERE ARE WAVES IN THE FLOW OF PEOPLE.
ARE WE LIGHTER NOW?
LET'S USE THIS TIME, THEN.
YO.
Number of guests is obvious from counting the shoes in the cubby
9:00 AM
I'LL EAT LUNCH FIRST.
WE USE THE DOWNTIME TO TAKE TURNS EATING.
GO RIGHT AHEAD.
IT'S ONLY 9, BUT WE GOT UP SO EARLY, WE'LL BE HUNGRY BY NOW.

Sign: Watch your head

Doing a head count

Sign: Watch your head Sign: Cotton gloves

Sign (mirrored): Tateshiba #2 Rest Area

CHAPTER 4 - END

TATESHIBA SECOND REST AREA LAYOUT MAP

Please use this for reference when reading.

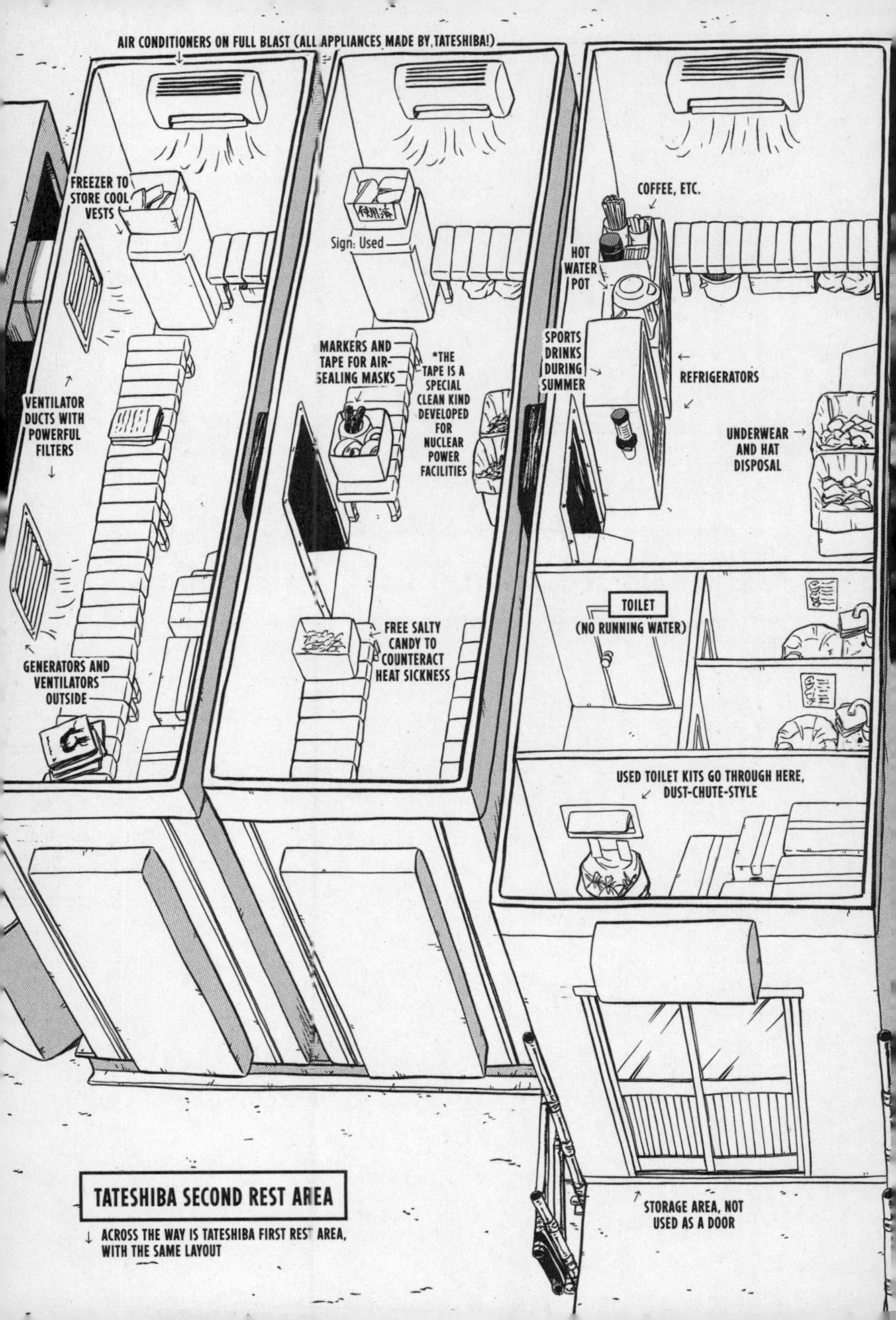
AIR CONDITIONERS ON FULL BLAST (ALL APPLIANCES MADE BY TATESHIBA!)
FREEZER TO STORE COOL VESTS
VENTILATOR DUCTS WITH POWERFUL FILTERS
GENERATORS AND VENTILATORS OUTSIDE
Sign: Used
MARKERS AND TAPE FOR AIR-SEALING MASKS
*THE TAPE IS A SPECIAL CLEAN KIND DEVELOPED FOR NUCLEAR POWER FACILITIES
FREE SALTY CANDY TO COUNTERACT HEAT SICKNESS
COFFEE, ETC.
HOT WATER POT
SPORTS DRINKS DURING SUMMER
REFRIGERATORS
UNDERWEAR AND HAT DISPOSAL
TOILET
(NO RUNNING WATER)
USED TOILET KITS GO THROUGH HERE, DUST-CHUTE-STYLE
STORAGE AREA, NOT USED AS A DOOR
TATESHIBA SECOND REST AREA
↓ ACROSS THE WAY IS TATESHIBA FIRST REST AREA, WITH THE SAME LAYOUT

ENTRANCE BUILDING
NO A/C HERE
SUPPLY STORAGE CONTAINER
CLEANING VACUUM
Wall signs: L/R
SURVEY ROOM
VARIOUS MEASURING DEVICES
ENTRANCE
ONE-WAY ONLY
DISCARD RUBBER GLOVES, TYVEKS, ETC.
DUST SAMPLER
Wall signs: Bottoms/Tops
下
上
DISCARDED TYVEKS REALLY PILE UP
STICKY MATS TO CATCH SPRAYED PARTICLES OF RADIOACTIVE MATERIAL
DOUBLE DOORS
ONE-WAY ONLY
EXIT
EQUIPMENT DISTRIBUTION
SHOE CUBBIES
EXHAUST VENT (AIR IS ONE-WAY TOO)
DOUBLE DOORS
TATESHIBA
NOT USED AS A DOOR
FRONT (AND ONLY) DOORWAY

RADIATION CONTROL HANDBOOK

A BOOKLET ISSUED TO THOSE WORKING IN RADIATION CONTROL ZONES, SUCH AS NUCLEAR POWER FACILITIES. IT CONTAINS A RECORD OF ONE'S RADIATION EXAM, SAFETY EDUCATION, WORK PERIOD, AND EMPLOYER, AS WELL AS ONE'S EXPOSURE HISTORY. IT'S THE SAME SIZE AS A DEPOSIT BOOK FROM A BANK. LIKE DEPOSITS, EXPOSURE AMOUNTS ADD UP OVER TIME, ONLY WITHOUT THE WITHDRAWALS AND INTEREST. THEY'RE ISSUED TO INDIVIDUAL WORKERS, BUT IN ORDER TO RECORD THE MONTHLY EXPOSURE AMOUNT AS MEASURED BY ONE'S GLASS BADGE, THE PRIMARY CONTRACTOR HOLDS ONTO THE HANDBOOK, ONLY RETURNING IT WHEN ONE QUITS THEIR SERVICE.

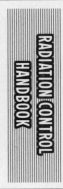

THE WORKER ID AND BARCODE MUST BE HANDED IN, SO THE ONLY RECORD OF ONE'S WORK THERE IS THIS HANDBOOK. INCIDENTALLY, THE WORKER ID CONTAINS A HOLOGRAM, SO IT CAN'T BE COUNTERFEITED WITH A COLOR COPIER.

PLEASE CLOSE THE DOOR.
OKAY, THREE AT A TIME.
JULY 2012, TEPCO FUKUSHIMA DAIICHI NUCLEAR POWER PLANT, TATESHIBA (FICTIONAL NAME) REST AREA
SO HOT!
LET US IN AL-READY!
BWAAH...
WE'RE BAAACK ...
GOOD WORK OUT THERE.
KOHHHH
RATTLE RATTLE
CHAPTER 5:
FUKUSHIMA SUMMERTIME BLUES (PART 2)

It's a Tateshiba rule to clean returning masks with wet wipes

Sign: Rubber Gloves Sign: Tyvek Sign: Socks

Sign: Watch your head Sign: Watch your head

Sign: Cotton gloves

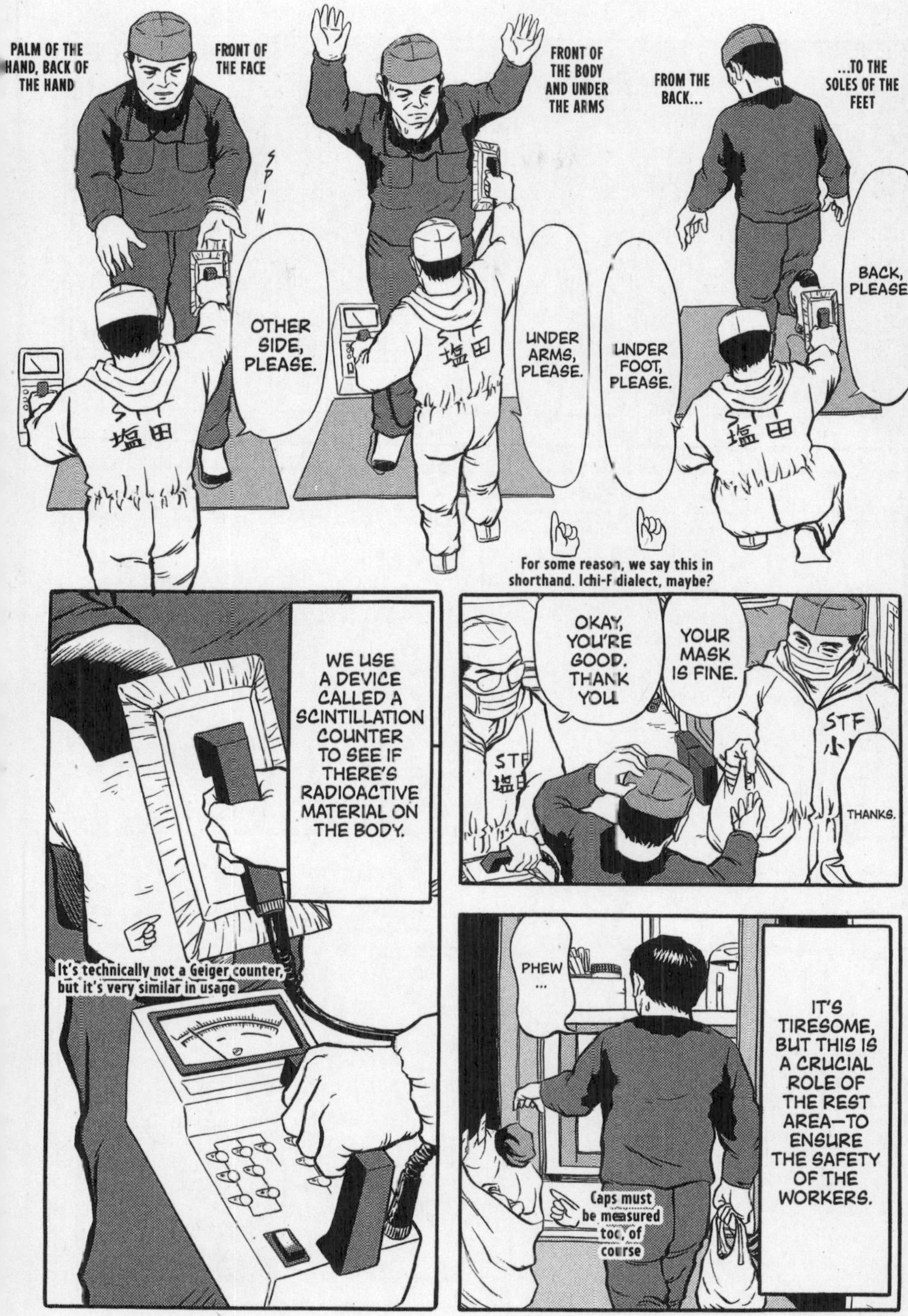

PALM OF THE HAND, BACK OF THE HAND

FRONT OF THE FACE

FRONT OF THE BODY AND UNDER THE ARMS

FROM THE BACK...

...TO THE SOLES OF THE FEET

SPIN

OTHER SIDE, PLEASE.

UNDER ARMS, PLEASE.

UNDER FOOT, PLEASE.

BACK, PLEASE.

塩田

塩田

塩田

For some reason, we say this in shorthand. Ichi-F dialect, maybe?

WE USE A DEVICE CALLED A SCINTILLATION COUNTER TO SEE IF THERE'S RADIOACTIVE MATERIAL ON THE BODY.

It's technically not a Geiger counter, but it's very similar in usage

OKAY, YOU'RE GOOD. THANK YOU!

YOUR MASK IS FINE.

STF

STF 小

STF 塩田

THANKS.

PHEW...

Caps must be measured too, of course

IT'S TIRESOME, BUT THIS IS A CRUCIAL ROLE OF THE REST AREA—TO ENSURE THE SAFETY OF THE WORKERS.

MAN, THAT WAS HOT.
PWOP
Pull this cord
THE SPORTS DRINK HERE...
PSHHHHH

We called this "Pocari," but I don't know if the contents are actually that product. It tasted the same, though.

...THE FRIDGE THAT CHILLS THE WATER BOTTLES...
AHHH! NICE AND COLD!
...AND THE FREEZER FOR THE COLD PACKS IN THE COOL VESTS MUST HAVE POWER, SO ONE OF THE GENERATORS IS ALWAYS RUNNING.

Box: Used freezing packs

THANKS TO THIS FRIDGE...
ALL RIGHT, I'LL TAKE MY LUNCH NOW.
OKAY.
...WE REST AREA WORKERS GET TO CHILL OUR FOOD AND DRINKS. IT'S A NICE PERK OF THE JOB.
CHRRR

Carton: Cafe Au Lait

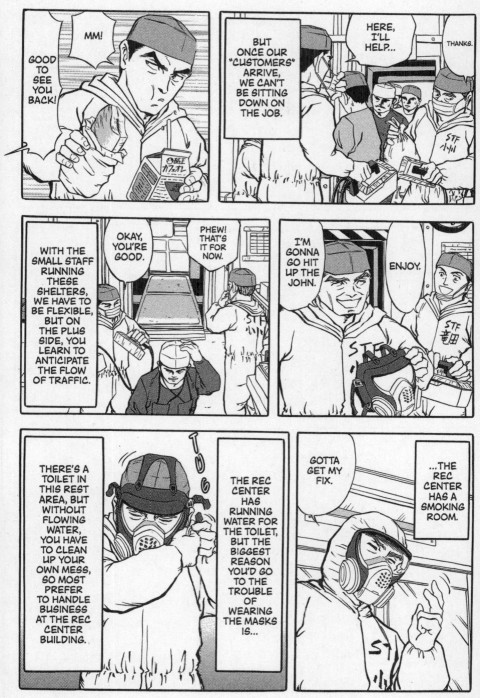

MM!
GOOD TO SEE YOU BACK!
BUT ONCE OUR "CUSTOMERS" ARRIVE, WE CAN'T BE SITTING DOWN ON THE JOB.
HERE, I'LL HELP...
THANKS.
WITH THE SMALL STAFF RUNNING THESE SHELTERS, WE HAVE TO BE FLEXIBLE, BUT ON THE PLUS SIDE, YOU LEARN TO ANTICIPATE THE FLOW OF TRAFFIC.
OKAY, YOU'RE GOOD.
PHEW! THAT'S IT FOR NOW.
I'M GONNA GO HIT UP THE JOHN.
ENJOY.
THERE'S A TOILET IN THIS REST AREA, BUT WITHOUT FLOWING WATER, YOU HAVE TO CLEAN UP YOUR OWN MESS, SO MOST PREFER TO HANDLE BUSINESS AT THE REC CENTER BUILDING.
TUG
THE REC CENTER HAS RUNNING WATER FOR THE TOILET, BUT THE BIGGEST REASON YOU'D GO TO THE TROUBLE OF WEARING THE MASKS IS...
GOTTA GET MY FIX.
...THE REC CENTER HAS A SMOKING ROOM.

THEY'RE ABOUT TO COME FOR THIS. PUT IT DOWN IN THE ENTRANCE.
OKAY.
10:00 AM
THERE'S ALSO ORDER SHEETS FOR EQUIPMENT AND HEALTH CHECKSHEETS FOR REST AREA WORKERS.
TOYO ENEX, THE MASTER CONTRACTOR, COMES TO COLLECT THE EXPOSURE REPORT AND DUST/SMEAR SAMPLES.
FOR THE HEALTH SHEET, YOU MUST MEASURE YOUR BLOOD PRESSURE EVERY DAY, AS WELL AS WHEN YOU REFILLED ON FLUID AND SODIUM IN A PARTICULAR HOUR.
BUT OF COURSE, YOU DON'T HAVE THE TIME TO CHECK EVERY SINGLE HOUR...
I THINK IT WAS LIKE THIS.
...SO MOST JUST JOT DOWN FROM MEMORY AT THE END OF THE DAY. BOTH SIDES UNDERSTAND THAT THIS CAN ONLY BE SO PRECISE.
AS LONG AS THE PROCESS MAKES YOU AWARE OF HEAT SAFETY, IT'S DOING THE JOB, IN MY OPINION.
HERE THEY ARE.
TAP TAP
HERE YOU GO.
PUT THIS UP, PLEASE.
THEY BRING NOTICES, TOO.
SURE THING.
AT THE EXIT OF THE EQUIPMENT ROOM.

Bags: Tateshiba Rest Area

Sign (upside down): Check once more APD is equipped!

Underwear and caps get laundered at 2-F for reuse

They place it directly in the container

TOILET MAN-AGE-MENT.
KCHAK
WHOA ...!
THEY DID IT AGAIN ...
WHAT'S WRONG ?
WELL, AT LEAST THEY PUT THE BAG DOWN FIRST ...
UGH, JUST SITTING RIGHT THERE ...
Self-censored
JUST MAKE SURE YOU REMIND ANYONE WHO USES THIS.
WE KEEP WARNING THEM...
THE SHELTERS DON'T HAVE WATER OR SEWAGE PIPES, SO WE USE DISASTER KITS.
Yellow plastic bag goes over the seat
Spread a sawdust-like absorber inside (has a sterilizing scent-killing effect)
One packet for pee, one each before and after you poo
A special string ties up the edge of the bag when done
Tied off with those cable ties
Through the dust chute to the outside
A collection bag is taped to the wall under the outside of the chute to catch the bags
* (Ultra-vital) After use, always remember to set up a yellow bag for the next person to use!

Sign: When you're done, set up the next bag!

WE TEACH PEOPLE THE SYSTEM WHEN THEY FIRST COME, AND THERE'S A DIAGRAM POSTED WITH INSTRUCTIONS ON IT.
使用後は次の袋をセット!
THE WORST IS WHEN PEOPLE JUST GO STRAIGHT IN THE BOWL WITHOUT A BAG...
BUT IF IT HAPPENS, EITHER WE OR THESE GUYS HAVE TO CLEAN IT UP.
TOMORROW, THEN!
THANKS, AS ALWAYS.
STF 竜田
THAT'S A TOUGH JOB...
THAT COMPANY SCOOPS UP ALL THE LOW-COST DUTIES.
STF 竜田
STF 玉名
HIGH-EXPOSURE JOBS COST A LOT, BUT THE SPECIALIZED WORK GOES TO GENERAL CONTRACTORS OR NUCLEAR COMPANIES, SO THE JUICY JOBS DON'T TRICKLE DOWN.
AT ICHI-F, THERE'S MORE TOUGH CHEAP JOBS THAN THERE ARE HIGH-EXPOSURE, WELL-PAID ONES.
JUST THE THOUGHT OF DOING SECURITY, FUELING, OR VEHICLE SURVEY OUT IN THE HEAT MAKES ME WANT TO DIE.
STF
STF

Sign: Socks

PEOPLE OUTSIDE SEEM TO THINK THAT IF YOU WORK AT ICHI-F, YOU'RE LIKE A HERO DRAMATICALLY FIGHTING AGAINST MASSIVE EXPOSURE IN HIGH-DANGER CONDITIONS.
BUT IT TURNS OUT THE MAJORITY OF US ARE DOING GRUNT WORK LIKE THIS.
BUT IF WE DIDN'T HAVE PEOPLE TO DO THESE JOBS, ICHI-F WOULDN'T BE RUNNING.
MR. AKASHI ...
NO MATTER HOW LOW AND UGLY THE WORK...
...ANYONE WORKING HERE HAS A RIGHT TO BE PROUD.
...
YOU'RE RIGHT.
11:00 AM

Hard to remove

CLIK
CLIK
WELCOME BACK.
UGH ...
BUT STILL, WORKING IN THIS SUMMER HEAT IS A SPECIAL KIND OF TORTURE.
AAH!
PSHAAAA
BLOOOP
IN FACT, SOME PEOPLES' GLOVES ARE SO FULL OF SWEAT...
PSHAAAAA
...THAT IT AUDIBLY SPILLS INTO THE BAG WHEN THEY DUMP THEM.
THE SWEAT THAT BUILDS UP IN THE GLOVES SPRAYS OUT AND HITS YOU IN THE FACE SOMETIMES. THIS WORKPLACE IS LITERALLY COVERED IN MALE SWEAT.
OH, S-SORRY.
IT'S OKAY... JUST GOES TO SHOW HOW HARD YOU'VE BEEN WORKING.

It's not even as cool as that sounds

Sign: Watch your head
WHEN A TEAM RETURNS, THE FLOOR IS ALL WET.
AS THE TEMPERATURE RISES, SO DOES OUR USAGE OF KIM TOWELS...
Kim Towel: the paper towels favored by nuclear facilities
MR. AKASHI, COME QUICK!
OH?!
Tateshiba medical staff
WHAT IS IT?
HE'S NOT FEELING WELL.
WHAT'S THE MATTER?
I'M FEELING KIND OF DIZZY...
SHVR SHVR
TREMBLING FINGERS. HIGH TEMPERATURE.
CAN YOU HELP ME?
LET'S SET DOWN THE BED.
RATTLE
RATTLE
I'LL GO GET A PUNCH-COOL AND SOME OS-1.

YOU'VE GOT HEAT-STROKE. SET HIM DOWN.

ELEVATED TEMPERATURE, TREMBLING EXTREMITIES, DEHYDRATION DUE TO SWEAT, DIZZINESS, HEADACHES, NAUSEA.

HERE WE GO.

THE SYMPTOMS MIGHT NOT BE BAD ENOUGH TO REPORT TO TEPCO, BUT WORKING EVERY DAY IN THE MIDSUMMER HEAT WILL CAUSE SOME WORKERS TO BREAK DOWN.

WHAM

Punch-Cool: Cooling pack that activates by impact

DRINK UP.

BLUB BLUB

This fluid replenishment solution works better than the sports drink (supposedly) when you're dehydrated

NESTLE THAT PACK INTO HIS PIT.

OKAY.

Bottle: Oral Fluid Replenishment OS-1

HOW YA FEEL?
I'M... A BIT BETTER NOW.
KEEP FANNING HIM FOR A BIT.
OKAY.
HEAT SICKNESS CAN BE FATAL IF IT GETS BAD ENOUGH. IT'S A MORE IMMINENT THREAT THAN RADIATION.
HOW IS HE?
HE'LL BE FINE, I THINK.
CAN'T BLAME HIM, WITH THIS HEAT AND ALL THE GEAR WE WEAR.
THAT'S RIGHT. EVEN 30 MINUTES CAN BE ENOUGH TO KNOCK YOU OUT, IF IT'S BAD ENOUGH.
TAP TAP
COME ON IN!
11:30 AM
WATCH YOUR STEP.
HEYA!
BUT EVEN WITH THESE DIFFICULT CONDITIONS, THERE ARE TEAMS THAT GO OUT FOR SHIFTS TWO OR THREE TIMES A DAY.

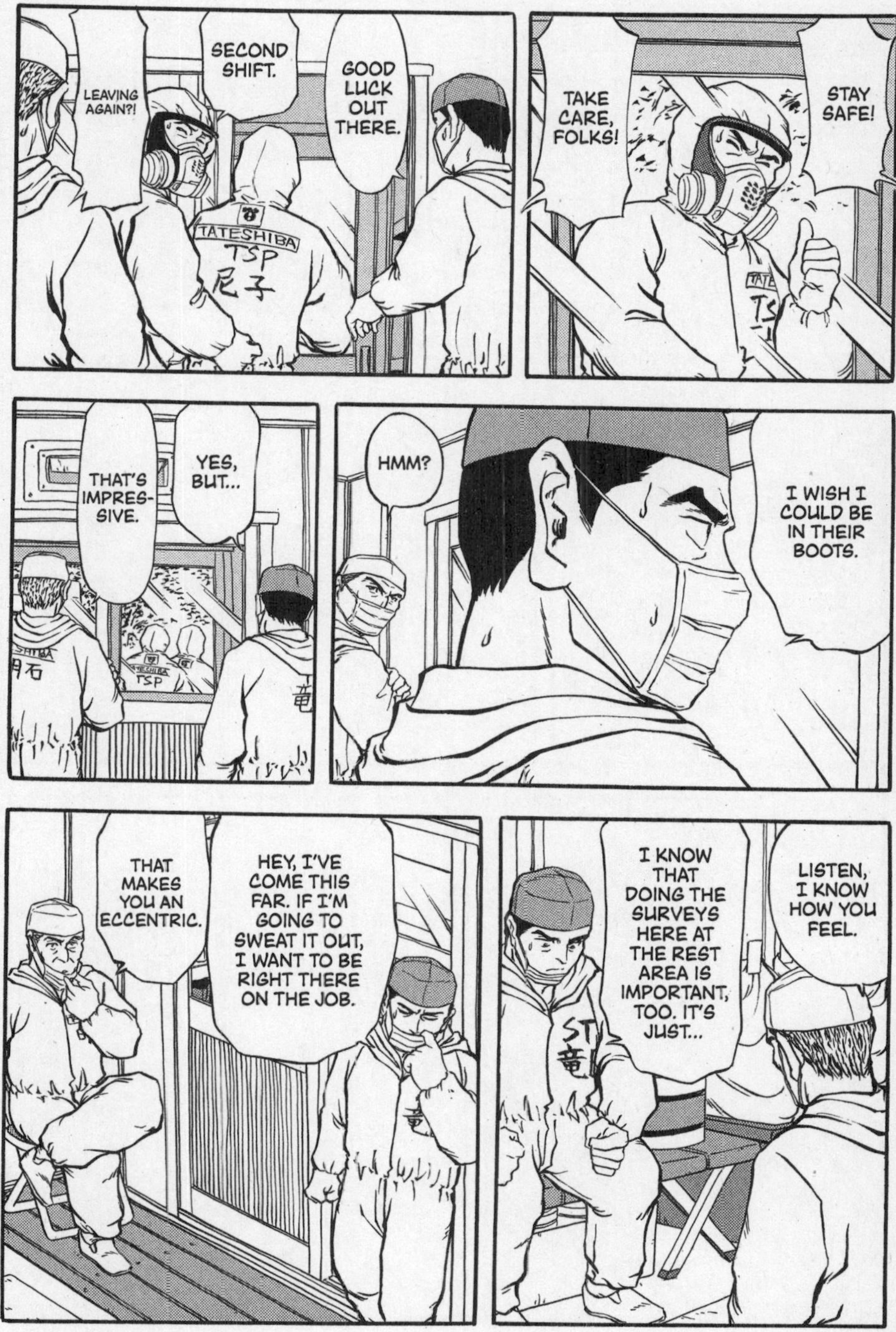

147

Being in the SDF meant he had many licenses (large vehicle, EMT, etc.)

IF I HAD THE LEVELS LEFT, I'D WANT TO GO OUT THERE, TOO.
MR. AKASHI IS A FORMER SDF OFFICER. AFTER HE RETIRED FROM THE FORCE, HE GOT COMMISSIONED BY TATESHIBA...
...AND HE WAS IN CHARGE OF DELIVERING MATERIALS TO ICHI-F RIGHT AFTER THE ACCIDENT.
HE WAS REASSIGNED TO BE THE REST AREA MEDICAL OFFICER BECAUSE HE WAS REACHING HIS EXPOSURE LIMIT.
TATESHIB
明石
SDF: (Japan) Self-Defense Forces
YOU AREN'T SCARED OF WORKING ON-SITE?
WELL, WHAT ABOUT YOU?
DEPENDS ON THE RAD LEVELS.
EXACTLY. ALL YOU REALLY NEED IS THE DATA. THAT ELIMINATES THE FEAR OF THE UNKNOWN.
TATESH
PLUS, I HEAR THEY PAY BETTER FOR HIGHER EXPOSURE.
AND SOME FOOLS ARE ATTRACTED TO THE MONEY, I SUPPOSE.
EVERYONE HAS THEIR REASONS FOR BEING HERE. AND THE JOB WOULDN'T GET DONE IF NOT FOR FOOLS LIKE US.
YES, I SUPPOSE JUST VOLUNTEERING TO COME WORK AT A PLACE LIKE THIS MAKES US FOOLS...

IF I'M GOING TO BE A FOOL, I AT LEAST WANT TO GET OUT THERE AND TIGHTEN A BOLT OR TWO.
INDEED. I KNOW HOW YOU FEEL...
...BUT PROTECTING THIS SPACE IS OUR DUTY.
THIS IS OUR BATTLE-FIELD.
IF THERE'S ONE THING WE CAN'T AFFORD, IT'S CASUALTIES.
YES, SIR.
STF
BUT EVEN AS I WAITED AT THE REAR...
...I COULDN'T HELP BUT IMAGINE WHAT IT WOULD BE LIKE AT THE FRONT LINE.

GOOD WORK OUT THERE.
THANKS!
AS THE TEAMS FINISH WORK AND GO BACK HOME...
...AND FEWER AND FEWER GROUPS GO OUT FOR THEIR SHIFTS...
ALL RIGHT, I'LL BE BACK!
...WE START TO PREPARE TO CLOSE THE BUSINESS.
12:15 PM
VRMM
THE MOST IMPORTANT STEP BEFORE YOU LEAVE IS REFUELING.
WE HAUL OUT A FEW FULL CONTAINERS FROM THE MORNING.
THIS WILL REPLACE WHAT WE USED TODAY.
IT'S ESPECIALLY CRUCIAL FOR THE ALWAYS-ON GENERATOR. YOU FEEL NERVOUS ABOUT LEAVING UNLESS IT'S TOPPED OFF.
TSHHHH
WE'RE STANDING INSIDE A POWER PLANT! WHY IS THIS NECESSARY?!
THE CONDITIONS OUTSIDE ARE EVEN WORSE NOW THAN THEY WERE IN THE MORNING.

It's so hot, you get irrationally angry (though it is important to procure stable power soon)

THE SPENT CONTAINERS GO BACK TO THE STOREHOUSE.
STF 竜田
THE FUELING STATION IS CLOSED BY NOW.
NOW I HEAD TO VEHICLE SURVEY.
STF 竜田
Placing the contamination testing permit in a visible spot
NORMALLY THIS GETS DONE WHEN EVERYONE IS GOING HOME, BUT AT THIS POINT, YOU COULD "SHORTCUT" THE SYSTEM BY RUNNING THE TEST AHEAD OF TIME, WHEN WE HAD ABOUT TWO HOURS OF DOWNTIME.
OKAY, YOU'RE GOOD.
WHAP
MAGNETIC CERTIFICATE
LATER, WHEN THEY SHRANK THE RESTRICTED ZONE, THEY CRACKED DOWN AND FORCED VEHICLES TO GO FROM SURVEY DIRECTLY OUT OF THE PLANT, SO THIS SHORTCUT NO LONGER WORKS.
Certificate: Measurement complete
I'M BACK NOW.
AHA, PERFECT.
ONCE BACK FROM FUELING AND SURVEYING, THE TATESHIBA WORKERS ARE STARTING TO LEAVE.
12:45 PM
ALL RIGHT, LET'S DO THIS!
NOW THE TRUE COMPETITION BEGINS.

ROCK, PAPER, SCISSORS!

Sometimes we play other games

YES! I WON!

ROCK, PAPER...

WE'RE SETTLING WHO HAS TO RETURN THE APDs.

AHH! I LOST!

THANKS, PAL!

CLANK

CLANK

YOU CAN RETURN APDs ALL AT ONCE, SO ONE UNLUCKY SOUL GETS TO GO BACK TO THE ANTI-QUAKE BUILDING.

ALL RIGHT, I'LL BE BACK.

MAN, HE SUCKS AT THAT GAME.

THE REST OF US CLEAN UP AND RE-STOCK.

10 TYVEKS.

4 RUBBER GLOVES.

A BUNCH TODAY, TOO.

WE MUST REMEMBER TO COUNT UP THE SEPARATED BAGS OF DISCARDED SUPPLIES.

Report: Radiation Management (For 2012) Name: Kazuto Tatsuta Workplace, Work detail Tateshiba Rest Area, Survey duty

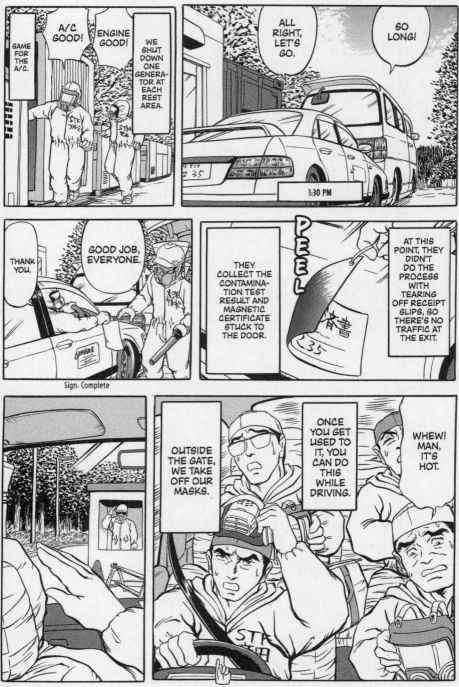

Sign: Complete

Don't do this at home, kids

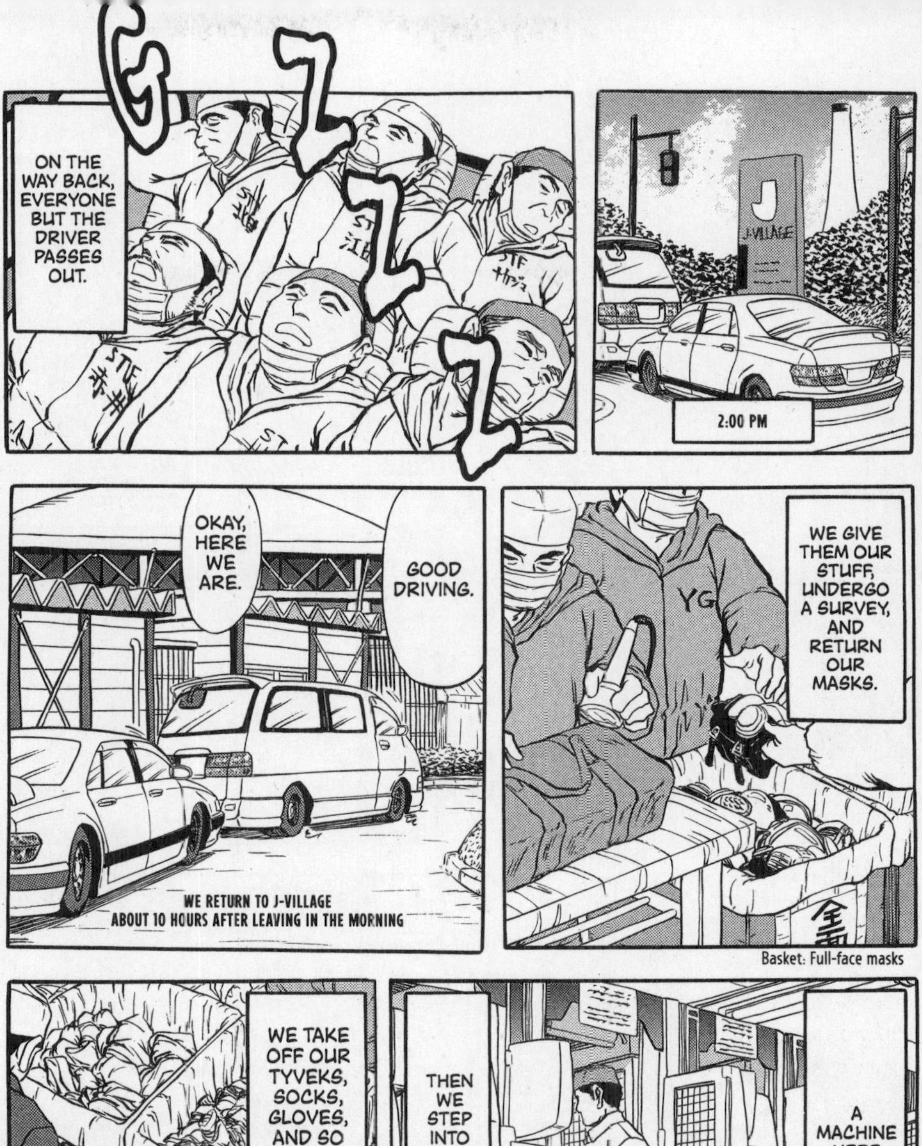
ON THE WAY BACK, EVERYONE BUT THE DRIVER PASSES OUT.
GZZZ
2:00 PM
J-VILLAGE
OKAY, HERE WE ARE.
GOOD DRIVING.
WE RETURN TO J-VILLAGE ABOUT 10 HOURS AFTER LEAVING IN THE MORNING
WE GIVE THEM OUR STUFF, UNDERGO A SURVEY, AND RETURN OUR MASKS.
WE TAKE OFF OUR TYVEKS, SOCKS, GLOVES, AND SO ON.
THEN WE STEP INTO THIS GATE-TYPE SURVEY DEVICE.
3
A MACHINE HERE DOES THE JOB THAT WE HAVE TO DO BY HAND AT ICHI-F.

Basket: Full-face masks

Sign: Socks

Overhead unit comes down
NWEEEE
YOU STAND IN THIS POSITION FOR 10 SECONDS.
The whole surface is sensors
Put your hands in here
KCHAK
IF IT DOESN'T PICK UP ANYTHING, YOU CAN LEAVE OUT THE OTHER WAY.
SOME HOSPITALS HAVE TYPES OF THIS DEVICE THAT MEASURE INTERNAL RADIATION EXPOSURE, BUT UNLIKE A WBC (WHOLE-BODY COUNTER), THIS ONLY MEASURES SURFACE CONTAMINATION. IT DOES NOT ACTUALLY GIVE INTERNAL READINGS.
WHEN THE SURVEY IS DONE, YOU CAN RETRIEVE YOUR STUFF...
AND NOW WE SPLIT UP.
OKAY, GOOD WORK, EVERY-ONE.
THANKS, YOU GUYS.
HOWEVER, THERE'S ONE MORE CHECKPOINT AFTER THIS NOW.
BEEP
VWAAA
J-Village Exit Receipt
Worker ID: xxxxxx
Pass Time: 2012/07/xx/14:15
Caps go in here
Sign: We appreciate your hard work

SCAN YOUR WORKER ID BARCODE AND IT PRINTS OUT A RECEIPT MARKING THE TIME YOU PUNCHED OUT.
J-Village Exit Receipt
Worker ID: xxxxxx
Pass Time: 2012/07/xx/14:15
Pass Location: JV
Thank you for your work.
Take care on your way home.
ヾ(●⌒▽⌒●)ノ♪
SINCE SOME SUBCONTRACTORS WERE PUTTING THEIR EMPLOYEES THROUGH EXTREMELY LONG SHIFTS, THEY STARTED KEEPING TRACK OF NOT JUST THE APD RETURN TIME, BUT ALSO WHEN WE LEFT THE RESTRICTED ZONE. THAT WAY THEY COULD MORE FIRMLY OVERSEE WORK CONDITIONS.
For some reason, they print a little face emoji —(≧∀≦)—!
AN APD'S ALARM WILL GO OFF BEFORE IT REACHES 10 HOURS OF ACTIVATION TIME, BUT SOME SUBCONTRACTORS MASTERED THE SHADY ART OF RETURNING IT AND BORROWING A NEW ONE TO GET AROUND THIS.
SO LONG, GUYS!
YOU GOING FOR DRINKS AGAIN TODAY?
YOU BET!
UNFORTUNATELY(?) THE COMPANY I WORKED FOR WAS NOT THIS SKETCHY, SO I DON'T KNOW EXACTLY HOW THEY PULLED THESE SHENANIGANS OFF, BUT TO THE COMPANIES THAT TAKE THIS SERIOUSLY, IT'S A PAIN IN THE ASS.
AND THE MOST FRUSTRATING PART IS THAT IT'S ONLY THE STORIES ABOUT THE BAD BEHAVIOR THAT GET PICKED UP AND SPREAD AROUND BY THE MEDIA.
OKAY, LET'S GO. ANOTHER CRAMPED CAR FULL OF FIVE MEN.
2:20 PM
MWOOF
CLICK
UGH ...!

We take a different car back from the one we drove to and from Ichi-F

I THOUGHT THE SUMMER IN TOHOKU WOULD BE COOL.

TSUBAME 21

SO WE HAVE TO SUFFER LIKE THIS UNTIL THE FALL?

INSTEAD, THE SUMMER OF 2012 WAS THE HOTTEST I'VE EVER SUFFERED.

パチンコ スロット

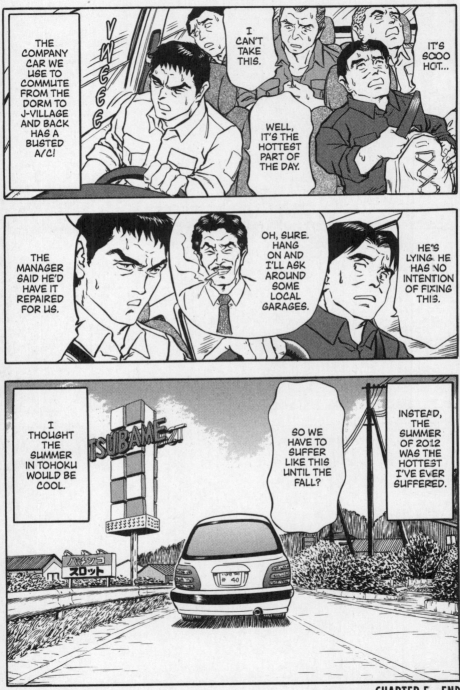

Sign: Pachinko Slots

CHAPTER 5 - END

JOBAN LINE, TOMIOKA STATION

RIGHT NOW THIS TRAIN STATION IS OPEN AGAIN, BUT IT WAS OFF-LIMITS UNTIL MARCH 31, 2013, SO THE EFFECTS OF THE EARTHQUAKE ARE STILL QUITE VISIBLE. THE STATION BUILDING WAS WASHED AWAY BY THE TSUNAMI, AND WEEDS COVER THE TRACKS. THE ROADS HAVE BEEN CLEARED BECAUSE PEOPLE ARE ALLOWED TO TEMPORARILY RETURN HOME, BUT THE STORES AND HOTELS AROUND THE STATION ARE STILL IN A DESTROYED STATE. THE TOWN OF TOMIOKA, LIKE OTHERS, IS STILL STUCK IN TIME SINCE MARCH 2011.

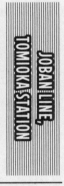

AT PRESENT, TOMIOKA STATION AT LEAST HAS A TEMPORARY BATHROOM, UNLIKE TATSUTA WHEN THE AUTHOR FIRST VISITED. TATSUTA BELIEVES THIS WAS SET UP BECAUSE OF THE NUMBER OF PEOPLE COMING TO VIEW THE QUAKE DEVASTATION.

Sign: Café Renoir

WELL, LET'S SEE...
PEOPLE OFTEN ASK ME, "WAS IT SCARY?" BUT...
...AND THAT'S WHAT I'D SAY.
I SEE. THANK YOU.
2014, TOKYO
ON TO THE NEXT QUES-TION.
HOW DID YOU FEEL WHEN YOU FIRST VISITED DAIICHI AND J-VILLAGE, MR. TATSUTA?
I ALWAYS GET ASKED, "WHAT DID YOU FEEL WHEN YOU FIRST WENT TO JV OR 1-F?" BUT IT'S NOT A QUESTION THAT I CAN ANSWER WITH A SIMPLE SOUNDBITE.
CHAPTER 6: FIRST TIME IN ICHI-F
SINCE I CAME BACK FROM ICHI-F AND BEGAN PUBLISHING THIS COMIC, I'VE HAD A NUMBER OF MEDIA INTERVIEWS, WHICH ARE DEFINITELY NOT MY FORTE.

Sheet: Newspaper Public Page

Of course, I do my best to answer it for the interview

Sign: Café Renoir

SINCE THERE ARE STILL MANY THINGS I HAVEN'T DEPICTED YET, I'LL GO BACK AND TALK ABOUT MY FIRST TRIP INTO ICHI-F.
THIS WAS AT THE START OF JUNE 2012, A THREE-DAY TRAINING PERIOD THAT WAS PART OF REGISTRATION AND CERTIFICATION TO WORK THERE.
THIS COURSE, SEPARATED INTO a EDUCATION AND b EDUCATION, WAS MY FIRST VISIT TO JV.
"a" and "b" are lowercase, for some reason
THE FIRST DAY WAS THE "RADIATION MANAGEMENT EDUCATION" DAY. EVERYONE GOING TO A NUCLEAR PLANT HAS TO TAKE THIS.
THUMP
THUMP
THUMP
Worker from Kuromori Construction's Iwaki Office
THUMP
THIS IS JV.
OOOH.
WE'RE FINALLY HERE!
WHAT YOU'RE STANDING ON NOW WASN'T ORIGINALLY A PARKING LOT, BUT A GRASS FIELD.
WHOA ...
ZSH

Sign: Watch for cows

*Picture is apparently from the Uzbekistan match on June 6, 2009

Banner: Do your best with courage and hope, for the sake of a brighter future for Japan! Please understand how grateful we all are!
Saitama City Tsuchiai Middle School 1-8

Small banner: To all the workers at Fukushima Daiichi
THANK YOU
Do your best today

Top Sign: To all the workers at Fukushima Daiichi

Heart: "heart"

Vertical Sign: Onominami Middle School

Booklet: Radiation Safety Training "a" Education

OKAY, EVERYONE. WE'VE GOT A LONG DAY, SO LET'S GET THROUGH IT.

THE INSTRUCTOR IS NOT FROM TEPCO, BUT ONE OF THE CLEANUP-AFFILIATED COMPANIES.

ALL THE STUDENTS ARE MIDDLE-AGED MEN OR OLDER.

THERE'S AN UNSPOKEN UNDERSTANDING THAT "WE'RE ALL JUST HERE BECAUSE IT'S REQUIRED BY LAW."

IT'S SO RELAXED AND LAZY HERE. I FEEL LIKE I'M BACK IN DRIVER'S ED.

YOU'RE RIGHT, THOUGH.

SHH!

HOWEVER, THERE IS A TEST AT THE END OF EACH COURSE, SO I DID LISTEN INTENTLY.

WE START FROM THE TOPIC OF ALPHA AND BETA RAYS.

THE MORNING "a" COURSE COVERS BASIC INFORMATION ON RADIATION. THE AFTERNOON "b" COURSE IS MORE PRACTICAL INFORMATION ON THE RESTRICTED ZONE AND ENTRY/EXIT PROCEDURES.

WE'RE ALL JUST GRUMPY OLD MEN WHO HAVEN'T STUDIED HARD AT ANYTHING SINCE WE LEFT SCHOOL (IF WE EVER STUDIED IN THE FIRST PLACE).
THE POST-LUNCH CLASS WAS ESPECIALLY SLEEP-INDUCING.
UGH ...
THE ONE THING THAT ROUSED US...
ALL RIGHT, PLEASE TAKE A MASK FROM ONE OF THESE BOXES.
...WAS TRYING ON MASKS, THE ONLY PRACTICAL PORTION OF THE LESSON.
SO THIS IS WHAT THEY'RE LIKE!
IF THEY SMELL BAD, USE A WET WIPE TO CLEAN THEM OFF.
I FIGURED THEY'D BE A BIT MORE STUFFY THAN THIS.
BUT IT DOES KINDA SMELL A BIT.
POOF
AND NOW YOU BREATHE IN TO MAKE SURE IT STICKS TO YOUR FACE, RIGHT?

First time trying the air leak check

THERE WERE OTHER EXPLANATIONS ABOUT EQUIPMENT AND STUFF...

...BUT THEY WERE ALL BASED ON PRE-ICHI-F DISASTER STANDARDS.

Normally red and blue. It's like a superhero outfit, very cool!

BUT THINGS ARE CURRENTLY DIFFERENT AT ICHI-F, SO JUST CONSIDER THESE A GENERAL GUIDELINE.

THE INSTRUCTOR HAD TO MAKE A DISCLAIMER.

OTHER POWER PLANTS ARE ONE THING, BUT THEY SHOULD REALLY GIVE THE INCOMING ICHI-F WORKERS LESSONS BASED ON THE ACTUAL CONDITIONS AND EXPOSURE LEVELS WE'LL BE FACING.

THIS MIGHT HAVE CHANGED SINCE I TOOK THE COURSE. (I ONLY HAD TO UNDERGO TRAINING THE ONE TIME.)

OKAY, YOU PASS.

THANK YOU.

THAT'S IT FOR THE a AND b COURSES.

ANYWAY, WE ALL PASSED THE FINAL TEST WITH FLYING COLORS. (IN FACT, THEY DON'T FAIL ANYONE.)

AH, I'M TIRED!

WELL, WE DON'T NEED TO STUDY TOMORROW, AT LEAST.

THE NEXT DAY WILL BE OUR WORKER REGISTRATION AND WBC.*

I won't repeat any questions, since they reuse them, but they're super easy, so if you're going to take the test, don't worry!

*Whole-body counter

Metal plates

Artificial turf

Just sit still for two minutes wearing only a shirt

*Count per minute: The number of ionization (radiation) events detected, which gets converted to sieverts or becquerels. Also called "count."

Circle: (Certified)

Sheet: Whole-Body Counter Results; Location: Tokyo Electric WBC Center; Company: Toyo Enex; Name: Kazuto Tatsuta; Count Rate: 1205 cpm(NET)

I learned the answer to this through personal experience—look forward to that scene!

Badge: 1-F Plant
Shibahama Technol Fukushima
Tatsuta, Kazuto

See Chapter 3

Gray Dosimeter: Tatsuta, Kazuto

Everything goes around your neck (plus license, for the driver)

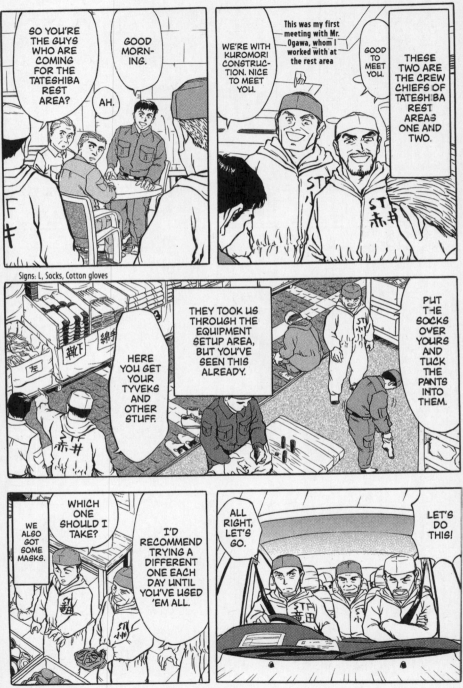

SO YOU'RE THE GUYS WHO ARE COMING FOR THE TATESHIBA REST AREA?
AH.
GOOD MORNING.
WE'RE WITH KUROMORI CONSTRUCTION. NICE TO MEET YOU.
This was my first meeting with Mr. Ogawa, whom I worked with at the rest area
GOOD TO MEET YOU.
THESE TWO ARE THE CREW CHIEFS OF TATESHIBA REST AREAS ONE AND TWO.
Signs: L, Socks, Cotton gloves
HERE YOU GET YOUR TYVEKS AND OTHER STUFF.
THEY TOOK US THROUGH THE EQUIPMENT SETUP AREA, BUT YOU'VE SEEN THIS ALREADY.
PUT THE SOCKS OVER YOURS AND TUCK THE PANTS INTO THEM.
WE ALSO GOT SOME MASKS.
WHICH ONE SHOULD I TAKE?
I'D RECOMMEND TRYING A DIFFERENT ONE EACH DAY UNTIL YOU'VE USED 'EM ALL.
ALL RIGHT, LET'S GO.
LET'S DO THIS!

ALL THE TRAFFIC LIGHTS ARE BLINKING YELLOW ...
ONLY HERE, ALONG ROUTE 6. THE REST ARE JUST PLAIN OFF.
YEAH... THERE'S NOBODY WALKING AROUND ...
NARAHA

In June 2012, everything past JV was the restricted zone, but later in August, they opened up the town.

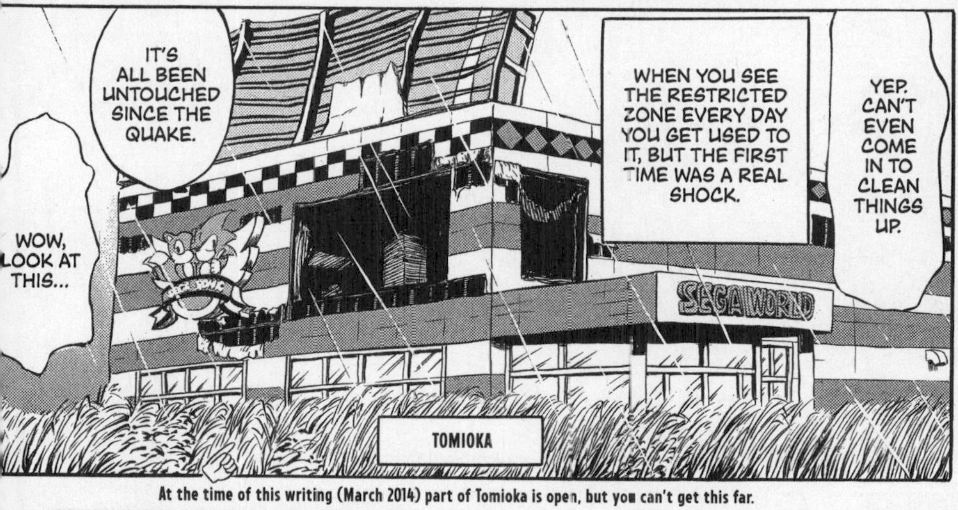

WOW, LOOK AT THIS...
IT'S ALL BEEN UNTOUCHED SINCE THE QUAKE.
SEGA WORLD
WHEN YOU SEE THE RESTRICTED ZONE EVERY DAY YOU GET USED TO IT, BUT THE FIRST TIME WAS A REAL SHOCK.
YEP. CAN'T EVEN COME IN TO CLEAN THINGS UP.
TOMIOKA

At the time of this writing (March 2014) part of Tomioka is open, but you can't get this far.

IN FACT, MR. OGAWA HERE IS AN EVACUEE. HIS HOME WAS WASHED AWAY BY THE TSUNAMI.
TRUST ME, THERE ARE SPOTS FAR WORSE THAN THIS.

MANY OF THE ICHI-F WORKERS ARE AMONG THOSE WHO HAVE BEEN AFFECTED.

IT'S SURPRISING HOW MANY PEOPLE GET TICKETED.

THE LIGHTS AROUND HERE AREN'T ON AT ALL.

WATCH OUT YA DON'T JUST CRUISE THROUGH 'EM, THOUGH. THE COPS DRIVE THROUGH HERE, TOO.

OKUMA

WE PUT ON OUR FULL MASKS BEFORE GOING INTO ICHI-F, BUT DUE TO THE RAIN, IT WASN'T AS HORRIBLY MUGGY AS IT WOULD GET LATER.

WERE YOU AFRAID YOUR FIRST TIME GOING IN?

AHA! WE'RE FINALLY HERE!

I GET THIS QUESTION A LOT, BUT IN OUR CASE, IT WAS MORE OF A SENSE OF SATISFACTION THAT WE'D FINALLY MADE IT AFTER SUCH A LONG WAIT.

The tanks of waste water

AT THIS POINT, THE ACCUMULATION OF SO MUCH CONTAMINATED WATER WASN'T SUCH A BIG PROBLEM YET.
LOOK AT ALL THOSE TANKS.
SO THAT WAS THE CHILDISH EXTENT OF MY THOUGHTS.
THERE'S NO ROOM FOR NERVES OR PATHOS WHEN THE CAR IS FULL OF RAUCOUS LAUGHTER.
RIGHT? SO LET US GIVE TANKS.
IF YOU EVER SAY A JOKE THAT BAD AGAIN, I'LL TOSS YOU INTO ONE OF 'EM!!
HA HA HA HA
0.8 mSv daily dose
AT THE ANTI-QUAKE BUILDING, WE GET AN APD FOR THE FIRST TIME.
JUST TELL THEM POINT-EIGHT.
YES, SIR.
Don't know what that means yet
BEEP
HERE YOU GO, POINT-EIGHT. STAY SAFE.
THANKS.
THEN WE VISITED OUR WORKPLACE, THE REST AREA.
OOH.
THIS IS THE TATESHIBA REST AREA.
TATESHIBA WAS OFF WORK THAT DAY, SO THERE WERE NO WORKERS INSIDE THE STRUCTURE.

YOU'LL LEARN ABOUT THE ACTUAL WORK ON-THE-JOB STARTING TOMORROW.
OKAY.
FOR BEING ALL MEN, THIS PLACE IS SURPRISINGLY TIDY.
ONCE THE CLEANUP EFFORTS WERE UNDERWAY, ICHI-F HAD BEEN DILIGENTLY CLEANED FOR SAFETY PURPOSES.

I assumed there would be a bunch of pubes all over the floor (sometimes there are)

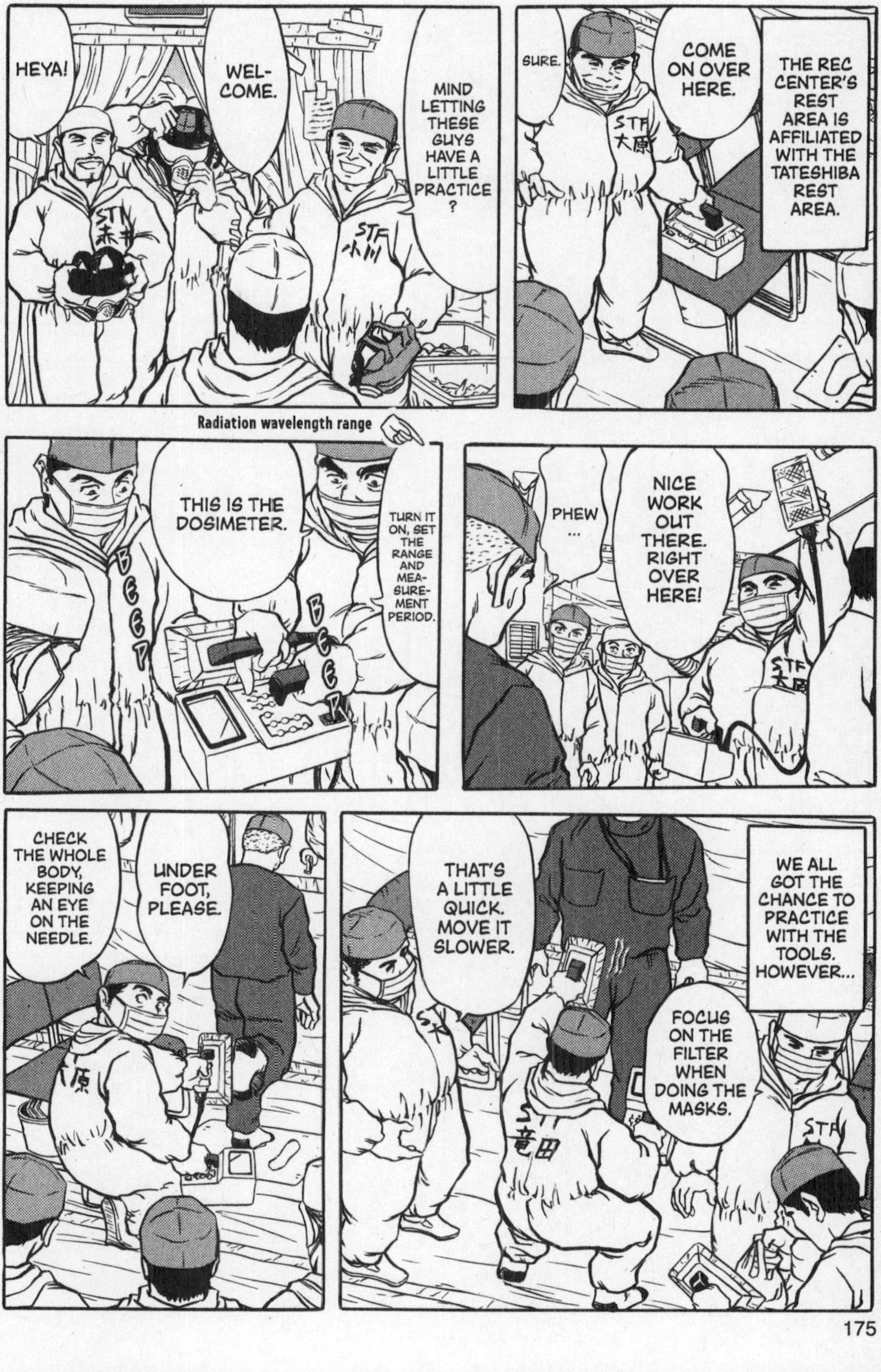

Radiation wavelength range

It's always buzzing a bit
HMM ...
THE REC CENTER GETS LOTS OF LOW-EXPOSURE WORKERS.
The higher the range gets, the less sensitive the reaction
I'M NOT GETTING ANYONE WITH ANY CONTAMI-NATION.
MAYBE YOU HAVE THE RANGE SET TOO HIGH?
OH?
STF
竜田
HANG ON, THEN. I'LL SHOW YOU WHAT A POSITIVE RESULT LOOKS LIKE.
WHAT DOES HE MEAN?
I DUNNO.
DID WE TOUCH A WRONG NERVE?
WE'D HEARD RUMORS THAT THEY PURPOSEFULLY LEFT THE RANGE WIDE OR OTHERWISE TWEAKED THE MACHINES, SO I DECIDED TO ASK.
STF
竜田
HERE, TRY THIS!
BOOM
Boots from a high-exposure site
LET SE
OH...
BWEEE
WHOA!

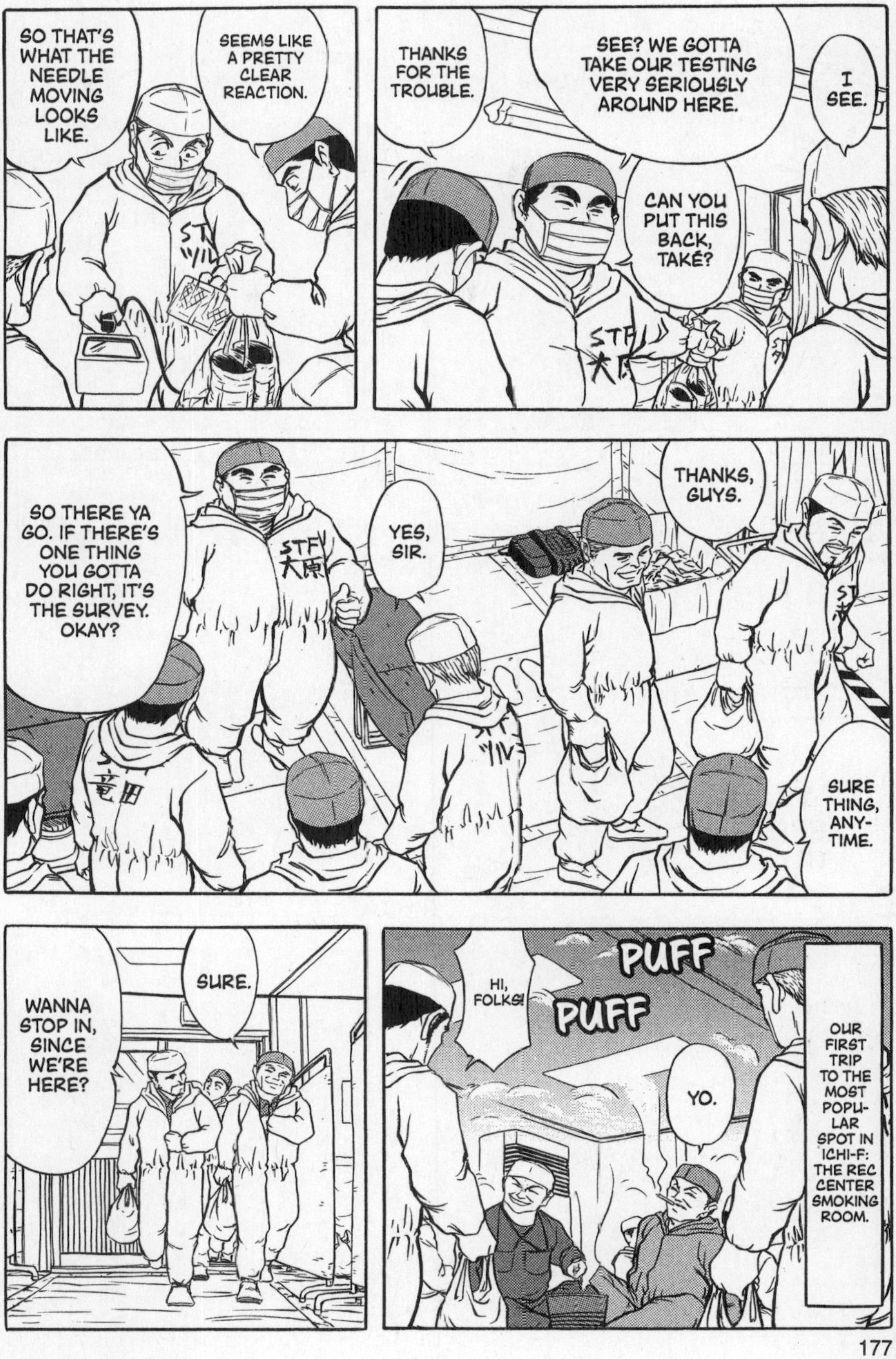

177

WHOA...ALL I SEE IS YELLOW.
HOW'S YOUR LITTLE GUY DOIN'?
SEEIN' PLENTY OF ACTION, TRUST ME!
HAH! LIAR!
WORD AROUND ONAHAMA SAYS YOU CAN'T GET IT UP ANYMORE!
BWA HA HA HA
THE TOPIC OF CONVER-SATION IS ALMOST ALWAYS EITHER GAMBLING OR DIRTY JOKES.
IT'S PEACEFUL IN HERE.
IT SURE IS.
IT SEEMS ...
... NORMAL, EVEN.
PERHAPS THIS SIGHT OUGHT TO BE MY ANSWER WHENEVER I GET ASKED THE QUESTION, "WHAT DO YOU REMEMBER MOST ABOUT YOUR FIRST DAY AT ICHI-F?"
OF COURSE, I HAD MY DOUBTS AND ANXIETIES BEFORE I GOT HERE, AND IF IT LOOKED REALLY BAD, I WAS PREPARED TO HIGHTAIL IT BACK HOME.
BUT SEEING NORMAL GUYS LAUGHING ABOUT NORMAL TOPICS LIKE THIS COMPLETELY ERASED MY DOUBTS.

OF COURSE, IT PROBABLY HELPS THAT I CAME IN A FULL YEAR AFTER THE CLEANUP STARTED, AND THINGS SETTLED DOWN A BIT...
Y'KNOW THE ONE THING I DON'T LIKE? THAT ONE KID FROM THE MASTER CONTRACTOR.
THE REAL WISE GUY, YEAH?
...
HE BARELY EVER SHOWS UP TO LOOK FOR HIMSELF, BUT HE GIVES US ALL THESE CRAZY ORDERS.
AND SOMEHOW, HE GETS PAID THE BIG MONEY. WAY MORE THAN US, AT LEAST.
OF COURSE, WHEN PEOPLE GATHER, THEY AIR THEIR GRIEVANCES.
ONE O' THESE DAYS I'M GONNA DRAG HIM TO A REAL HOTSPOT AND WATCH HIM SQUIRM!
THAT PART OF IT ALSO STRUCK ME AS TYPICAL OF ANY OTHER WORK-PLACE.
IT'S VERY OBVIOUS WHEN YOU THINK ABOUT IT, BUT ONCE I SAW IT WITH MY OWN EYES, I REALIZED JUST HOW BIG THE GAP WAS BETWEEN REALITY AND THE IMAGINED SITUATION FROM THE OUTSIDE.
ALL RIGHT.
LET'S HEAD BACK.
SURE THING.
IN MOST CASES, THE CONDITIONS AT ICHI-F WERE A PLEASANT SURPRISE TO ME. (WHICH PROBABLY TELLS YOU HOW MUCH THE BAD IMAGE IS SPREADING OUT OF CONTROL...)

I DON'T INTEND TO PORTRAY ICHI-F AS A SAFE AND PLEASANT WORKPLACE, OF COURSE.

I DOUBT THERE ARE MANY PLACES IN THE WORLD THAT REQUIRE AS MUCH TEDIOUS PREPARATION, AND THAT CAN BE SO DEADLY.

ANTI-QUAKE BUILDING FIRST.

OKAY.

WHICH IS PRECISELY WHY WE WORK HERE: TO MAKE THE CONDITIONS SAFER.

WE RETURNED OUR APDS AND GOT OUR FIRST LEVELS RECEIPT.

THANKS FOR YOUR HARD WORK.

JUST 0.02 MSV? THAT'S SO LOW.

WE ALL GOT THE SAME NUMBER.

AT LAST, I TRULY FELT LIKE I HAD BECOME AN ICHI-F WORKER.

THEN...

ALL RIGHT, LET'S GO.

AH.

WHAT IS IT?

LOOK...

HMM?

LOOK HOW CLOSE IT IS...
THAT? THAT'S THE STACK FOR UNITS 1 AND 2.
YOU SCARED?
A BIT...
I WANNA GO SEE IT!
Normal reaction
Idiot
WILL WE GET TO?
WELL, YOU MIGHT GET A CLOSER LOOK SOMETIME. LET'S HEAD BACK FOR TODAY.
CLICK
OH...
HEY, ISN'T THIS MASAYUKI YUHARA?
The pavement is slick / with the falling rain...

*The Unit 1-2 stack contains some extremely high radiation levels at its base. It's very dangerous.

I KNOW THIS. THIS WAS A HUGE HIT!

Like drops of silver / down my cheek...

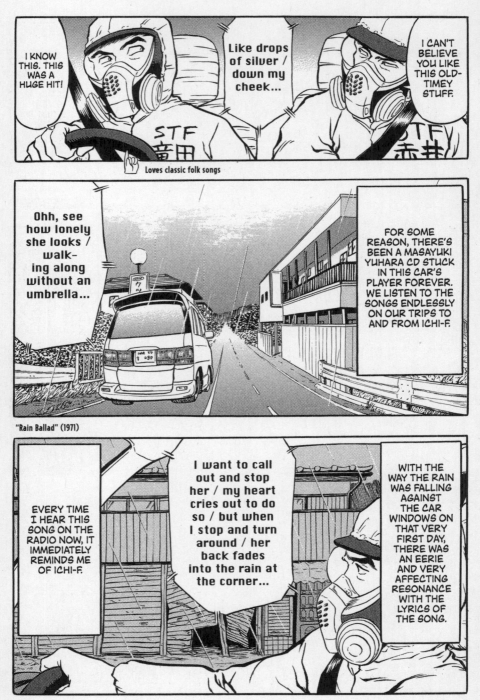

I CAN'T BELIEVE YOU LIKE THIS OLD-TIMEY STUFF.

Loves classic folk songs

Ohh, see how lonely she looks / walk-ing along without an umbrella...

FOR SOME REASON, THERE'S BEEN A MASAYUKI YUHARA CD STUCK IN THIS CAR'S PLAYER FOREVER. WE LISTEN TO THE SONGS ENDLESSLY ON OUR TRIPS TO AND FROM ICHI-F.

"Rain Ballad" (1971)

EVERY TIME I HEAR THIS SONG ON THE RADIO NOW, IT IMMEDIATELY REMINDS ME OF ICHI-F.

I want to call out and stop her / my heart cries out to do so / but when I stop and turn around / her back fades into the rain at the corner...

WITH THE WAY THE RAIN WAS FALLING AGAINST THE CAR WINDOWS ON THAT VERY FIRST DAY, THERE WAS AN EERIE AND VERY AFFECTING RESONANCE WITH THE LYRICS OF THE SONG.

The rain has quenched the fire / that burned in my young heart / at the sight of your name-less face...
SO THE IMPRESSION I WAS LEFT WITH AFTER MY FIRST DAY AT ICHI-F IS VERY CLOSELY TIED TO THE AMBIENCE CREATED BY THE RAIN AND THIS SORROWFUL SONG.
A memory of the distant past...
...AND THAT'S WHAT I'D SAY.
THANK YOU VERY MUCH.
BEEP
I THINK I CAN PUT TOGETHER A VERY GOOD ARTICLE OUT OF THIS.
I'M VERY GLAD TO HAVE BEEN A HELP.

AS I LOOK UP AT THE SPARKLING LIGHTS OF TOKYO AT NIGHT, GLEAMING IN THE RAIN, I THINK BACK TO THE PLACE THAT GENERATED ALL OF THAT ELECTRICITY.
ALONG WITH THAT SONG.
A MEMORY OF THE DISTANT PAST...
...EXCEPT THAT IT'S NOT THE PAST. THE WORK CONTINUES TODAY.
The container over Unit 4 in 2014. They're extracting fuel now!

CHAPTER 6 - END

LATE JUNE 2012
KUROMORI CONSTRUCTION, IWAKI OFFICE
An apartment near the train station
HEY, GENTLEMEN.
WE'RE BACK, SIR!
OKAY, I'LL HAND OVER YOUR PAY. LET'S DO THIS ONE AT A TIME.
OKAY.
KUROMORI'S PAY GETS TOTALED AT THE END OF THE MONTH AND PAID OUT AT THE END OF THE FOLLOWING MONTH.
SO THIS IS OUR MONEY FROM MAY.
IN OTHER WORDS, THIS IS OUR FIRST SALARY IN FUKUSHIMA.
HERE YOU GO. FILL OUT THE RECEIPT.
THANK YOU, SIR.
I CALCULATED IT ALREADY, SO I KNEW THIS WAS COMING, BUT...
WE WERE ON STANDBY ALL THROUGH MAY, EXCEPT FOR A FEW DAYS HELPING AT A NORMAL CONSTRUCTION SITE.

Thankfully, they did cut us a deal on housing. Thanks! ♡

Sheet: Kazuto Tatsuta (May)
Koriyama: Housing = 12,000, Meals = 9,100
Iwaki: Housing 8d (500) = 4,000, Meals 6 (350) = 2,100

Receipt: May 2012 Paycheck Receipt, Kazuto Tatsuta, Kuromori Construction

Columns: Work Shifts; Base Pay; Other Pay; Employment Insurance; Total Minus Cost

He still writes the receipt

He managed to get more work days, so he wound up with a bit more pay

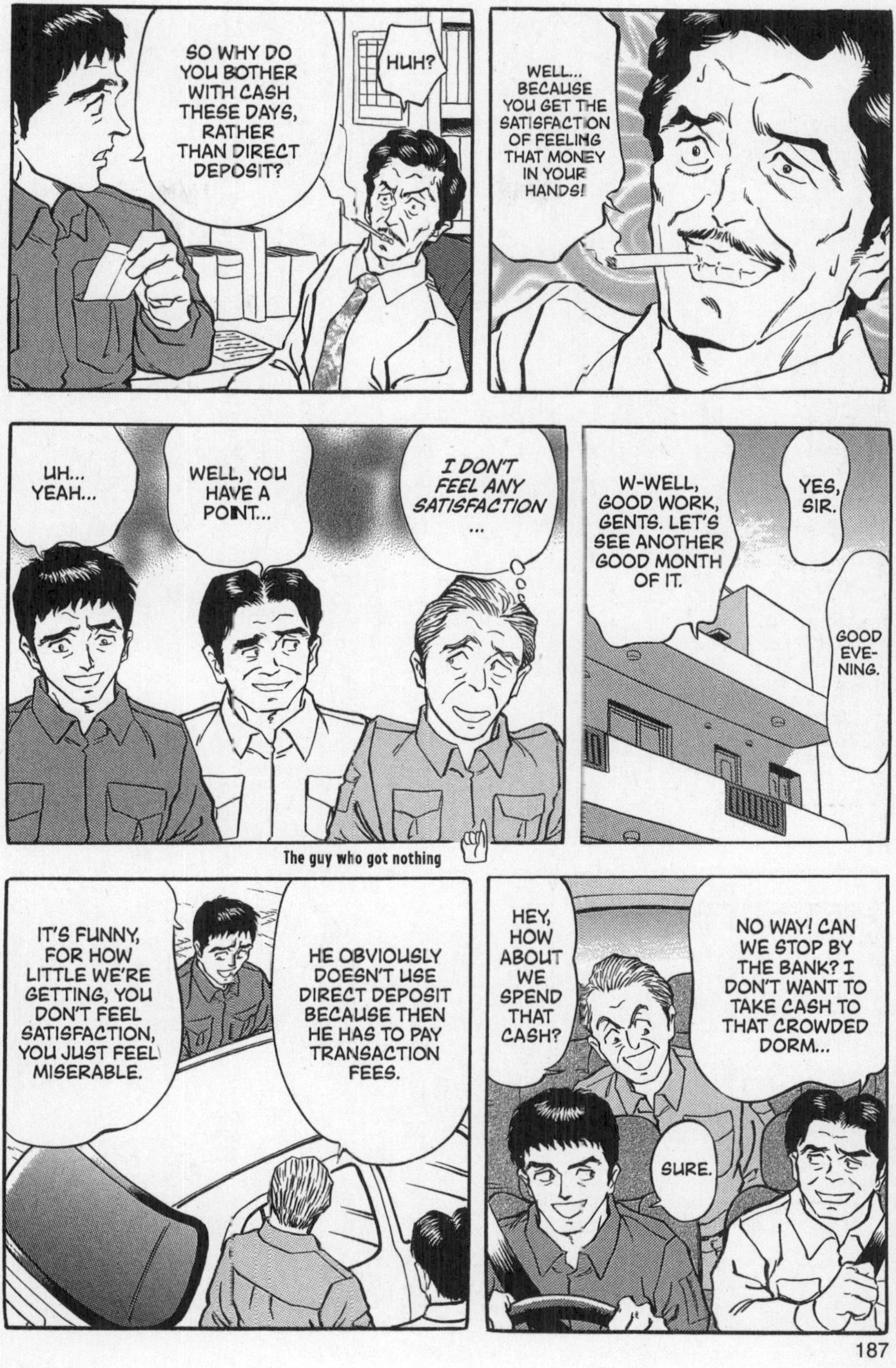

The guy who got nothing

Sign: Toho Bank

IN A HOUSE WITH OVER TEN COMPLETE STRANGERS AND NO LOCKERS, IT TAKES A BOLD MAN TO LEAVE HIS VALUABLES BEHIND.
東邦銀行
P
IF ONLY HE'D JUST DEPOSITED THEM FOR US. IT'S JUST AN EXTRA HASSLE FOR US.
TRUE, I WOULDN'T WANT TO LEAVE A FEW 10,000-YEN BILLS UNSUPERVISED IN THAT PLACE.

I wouldn't

He wouldn't

BUT WE DID JUST GET PAID, SO...
SHALL WE HIT THE TOWN?
ALL YOU DID WAS BORROW MONEY ...
ALL RIGHT, HOP IN! I'LL GO AND MULTIPLY MY CASH AT THE RACETRACK!
AND IF YOU WIN, I'LL GET TO EAT YAKINIKU.
THIS IS WHAT HAPPENS WHEN YOU GIVE CASH TO GUYS LIKE US.

Sign: Hang in there, Iwaki!!

SO YOU SEE, WE'RE NOT ONLY HELPING THE CLEAN-UP EFFORT, WE'RE ALSO STIMULATING THE LOCAL ECONOMY.
がんばっぺ!!
いわき
THAT MAKES IT SOUND BETTER, DOESN'T IT?

TRANSLATION NOTES, PART 1

MAKOTO HIRATA, PAGE 60

A fugitive of the infamous Aum Shinrikyo cult that was responsible for the sarin gas attack on a Tokyo subway in 1995. While nearly 200 members of the cult have been apprehended and brought to trial, a trio managed to stay at large for many years, and were often featured on wanted posters nationwide. One of the three, Hirata, caused a stir when he turned himself in to police on New Year's Eve 2011, just minutes before 2012 began.

AFTER THE ZONE RECONFIGURATION, WHEN KAZUTO TATSUTA FIRST VISITED THE STATION, THERE WERE STILL WANTED POSTERS UP FOR AUM SHINRIKYO'S MAKOTO HIRATA. THIS WAS MANY MONTHS AFTER HE HAD ALREADY BEEN APPREHENDED, SO IT FELT LIKE TIME HAD STOPPED AT THE STATION.

BUT... WHY?
WELL, I FIGURED THAT I COULD TAKE ON A JOB THAT WILL HELP THOSE AFFECTED BY THE DISASTER...
PLUS THE PAY IS GOOD.

THE "MONEY" SIGN, PAGE 83

You may notice that some of the characters make a little circle with their thumb and forefinger when discussing financial matters. This is the colloquial Japanese sign for money, the equivalent of rubbing one's fingers together. It's implicitly understood; in these cases the characters don't explicitly say "money" in the original Japanese, but merely refer to it as "this" in reference to the hand gesture (e.g. "my job's going to make me a lot of *this!*").

GOLDEN WEEK, PAGE 87

A customary vacation week in the first week of May, due to the cluster of a number of official holidays, including Constitution Memorial Day, Children's Day, and the Emperor's Birthday for Emperor Showa (who reigned from 1926-1989). Because the holidays are so close, the custom of going ahead and taking the entire week made Golden Week become a de facto weeklong holiday for many businesses.

It's almost Golden Week, a weeklong holiday in the spring

AND FINALLY, MORE THAN A YEAR AFTER THE DISASTER, AND TEN MONTHS SINCE I STARTED LOOKING FOR ONE OF THESE JOBS...
Can you come to Koriyama over the holiday ahead?
I've got a job clearing wreckage at the plant, 20,000 yen a day.
Ship your stuff to this address.
THIS ACTUALLY SOUNDS PRETTY SOLID!

PACHINKO, PAGE 101

A uniquely Japanese form of gambling that is similar to playing a vertical pinball machine, only using much smaller balls that are closer to ball bearings. Many modern pachinko machines are actually "pachi-slots" that function as slot machines when the balls are guided to trigger spots that then spin the slots. The payout is more balls; these balls are then exchanged for a relatively meaningless trinket that can *then* be exchanged for cash at a nearby storefront run by the pachinko parlor (in all but name), thus circumventing the anti-gambling laws.

Iwaki's bicycle racetrack was a base for disaster supplies, but as of June 2011, it was open again.

POCARI, PAGE 136

A popular, everpresent sports beverage in Japan, known by the slightly alarming name (to English speakers) "Pocari Sweat." The cloudy white drink, which is said to replenish electrolytes, has a very mild citrus flavor and somewhat resembles a lighter, watery Gatorade.

We called this "Pocari," but I don't know if the contents are actually that product. It tasted the same, though.

ICHI-F

ICHI-F

CHAPTER 7

High-exposure and sensitive areas are off-limits, of course.

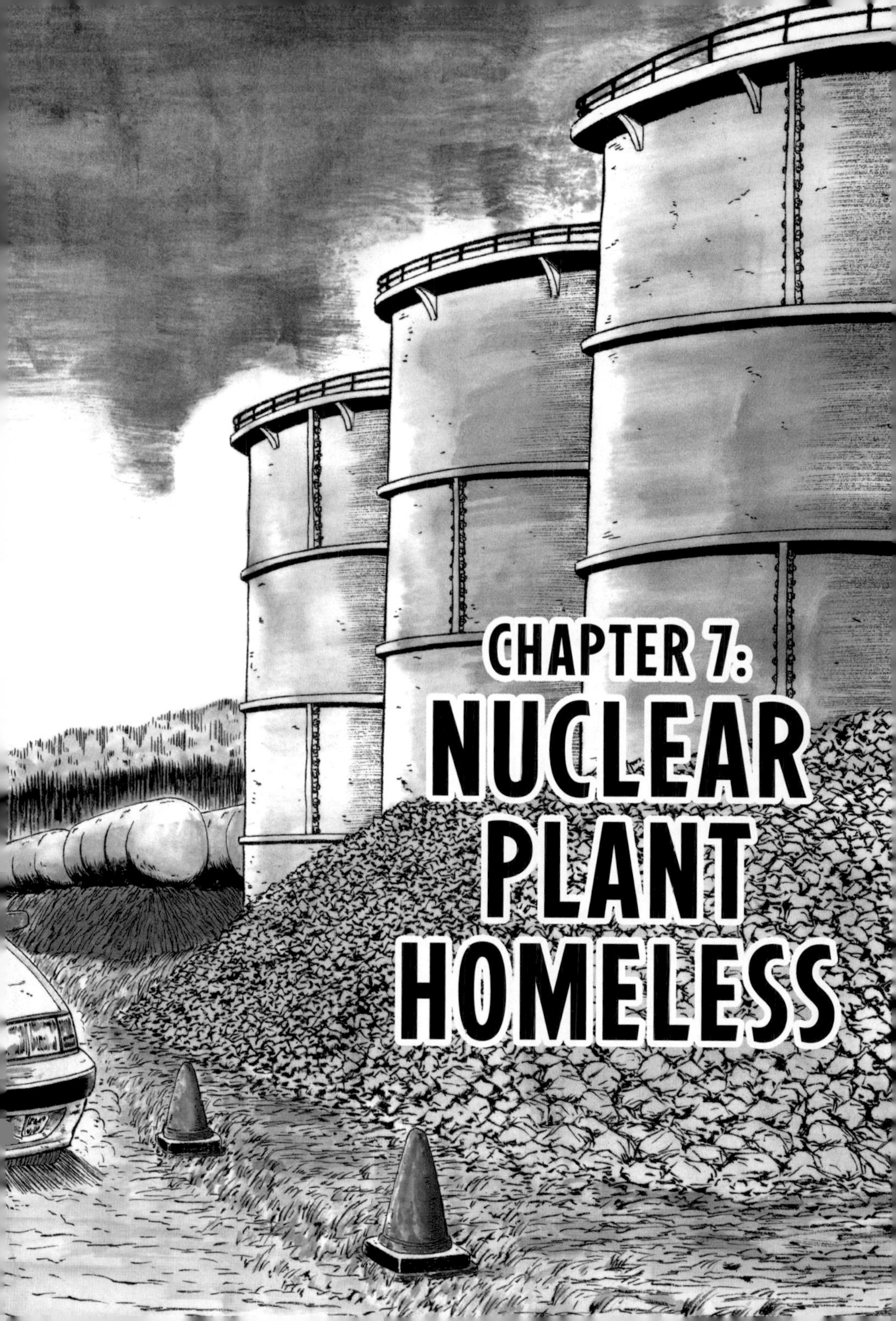
CHAPTER 7:
NUCLEAR PLANT HOMELESS

OOOH, THAT YELLOW THING IS GONE NOW.
Primary Containment Vessel (PCV) lid
Only Reactor Pressure Vessel (RPV) is left
AS THE REMOVAL OF DEBRIS CONTINUED AT UNIT 4, THEY WERE ABLE TO USE A CRANE TO PULL OUT THE CONTAINMENT LID ON AUGUST 10TH, LEAVING ONLY THE PRESSURE VESSEL (RPV) LID LEFT.
UNIT 4 WAS UNDER INSPECTION AT THE TIME OF THE DISASTER, SO THE LID OF THE CONTAINMENT BUILDING AND PRESSURE VESSEL WERE REMOVED AND PLACED ON THE OPERATING FLOOR (WITH THE SPENT FUEL POOL).
IT WAS SUCH A VISIBLE LANDMARK THAT ITS REMOVAL REALLY GIVES YOU A SENSE OF PROGRESS.

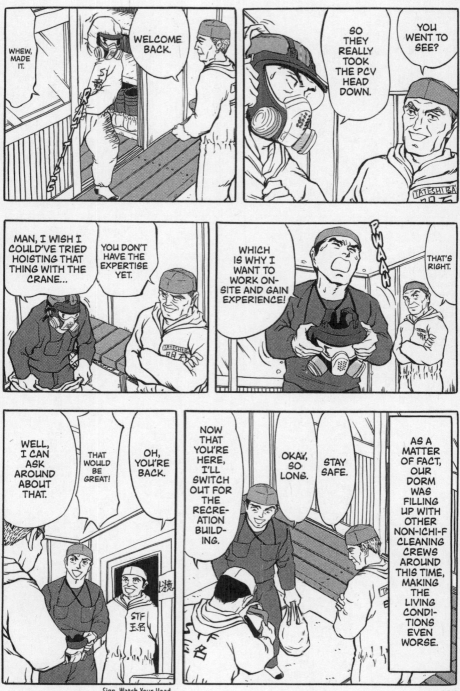

Sign: Watch Your Head

WITHOUT THE TIME TO RELAX AND DO YOUR BUSINESS IN THE MORNING, THE FLUSHING TOILET AT THE REC BUILDING WAS A GODSEND TO US.
SOMETIMES IT FEELS LIKE WE'RE COMING TO ICHI-F JUST TO TAKE A CRAP.
I WANT OUT OF THAT DORM SO BAD.
YES, REALLY, WHAT *ARE* YOU DOING HERE?
THERE WERE OTHER ISSUES ASIDE FROM THE BATH-ROOM.
WHOSE IS THIS?
YOUR LAUNDRY'S DONE.
LOOK WHAT MY LIFE'S COME TO: PUTTING AWAY STRANGERS' UNDERWEAR...
AND NO ROOM TO DRY...
LAUNDRY, CLEANING, TAKING OUT TRASH, THE NIGHTTIME SNORING, TEETHGRINDING, MUTTERING...THEN THERE'S THE FIGHT FOR FRIDGE SPACE, TV CHANNEL RIGHTS...
CREAK-CREAK-CREAK-CREAK! YOU HEAR IT CLEAR AS DAY.
I'VE NEVER ACTUALLY HEARD TEETH-GRINDING LIKE THAT BEFORE.
I THINK IT'S THAT ONE GUY IN DECON-TAMINA-TION...
...EVERY IMAGINABLE SOURCE OF STRESS IS AMPLIFIED. IF SOMETHING DIDN'T CHANGE, SOMEONE WAS GOING TO LOSE IT AND EXPLODE.

AND THEN, OF COURSE, THERE WAS THE LOW PAY.
43,000 YEN...
I KNEW IT WOULD BE ***BAD***, BUT MAN—IT'S BAD.
AND I GOT ZILCH.
WE STARTED GETTING PAID AT LAST IN LATE JUNE, BUT IT GOT CANCELED OUT BY OUR PRIOR DEBT, LEAVING US WITH ALMOST NOTHING.
ALL RIGHT, I'M GETTING THE HELL OUT OF THERE!
ENOUGH OF THAT DORM AND COMP-ANY!
AROUND AUGUST, WE FINALLY CAUGHT UP WITH OUR ADVANCES AND HAD A LITTLE SOME-THING TO WORK WITH.
SO WE START-ED LOOK-ING FOR OTHER JOBS AROUND ICHI-F.
GOT ANY GOOD WORK OR RENTAL LEADS?
HMM.
IF THAT'S WHAT YOU WANT, I KNOW THE PRESI-DENT OF A COMPANY YOU COULD TALK TO.
WE GOT SOME HITS FROM VARI-OUS FOLKS ...
WELL, I GOT WORK BOTH AT ICHI-F AND ELSEWHERE, BUT IF YOU LEAVE THAT COMPANY, YOU WON'T HAVE A ROOF OVER YOUR HEADS.
AND WE DON'T HAVE ANY HOUSING ON HAND...
...BUT BASICALLY ALL THE SMALL OR MIDSIZED SUBCON-TRACTORS AROUND IWAKI WERE COMMUTE-ONLY, WITH NO SOLUTIONS FOR LODGING.

SO FIRST COMES HOUSING ...
AH, NOPE. YOU WON'T FIND ANY APARTMENTS IN IWAKI RIGHT NOW.
I WAS AFRAID OF THAT.
BACK THEN (AND NOW), IT WAS EXTREMELY DIFFICULT TO FIND A PLACE IN IWAKI.
RESIDENTS OF IWAKI WHO LOST THEIR HOMES IN THE QUAKE AND TSUNAMI HAD TO FIND OTHER SHELTER.
MOST OF THE PEOPLE FORCED TO EVACUATE DUE TO THE ICHI-F ACCIDENT CAME TO IWAKI.
MANY RESIDENTS OF ADJACENT TOWNS LIKE HIRONO DECIDED TO PACK UP AND MOVE.
AND THEN YOU HAVE A FLOOD OF OUTSIDE WORKERS LIKE US, COMING IN FROM ALL OVER THE NATION.
THERE'S JUST NOT ENOUGH HOUSING FOR ALL OF THEM, ESPECIALLY RENTALS.
AND EVEN WORSE FOR US...
SOME PLACES EXPLICITLY TURN DOWN ALL WORKERS.
IT CAN'T BE HELPED THAT A SHORT-TERM, UNSTABLE TENANT LIKE A CLEANUP WORKER ISN'T AS PREFERABLE AS A PROPER LONG-TERM RESIDENT.
I SEE ...
BUT THE WORST PART IS THAT SOME OF THE LANDLORDS ARE AFRAID THAT THE PEOPLE WORKING AT ICHI-F AND SIMILAR AREAS WILL ACTUALLY CONTAMINATE THEIR PROPERTY.

OTHER BUSI- NESSES REFUSED ICHI-F WORKERS, TOO.
WHEN I WAS LOOKING FOR A NEW CAR TO REPLACE MY CURRENT COMPANY VEHICLE, I WAS TOLD...
I'M AFRAID WE'RE NOT RENTING VEHICLES TO ANY- ONE TRAVEL- ING TO ICHI-F.
ACTUALLY, WE CAN'T DRIVE IT ALL THE WAY THERE. AND THE VEHICLES GET TESTED AT J-VILLAGE ...
Sign: Car Rental Lease
BUT SOME PEOPLE DO SAY THAT THERE'S A GREATER- THAN- ZERO CHANCE OF CONTAM- INATION, SO...
I DON'T THINK ABOUT IT AT ALL ON A REGULAR BASIS, BUT EXPERIENCES LIKE THIS ARE A HARSH REMINDER THAT SOME SEE US AS DIRTY, TAINTED.
IT'S TIMES LIKE THIS THAT I WISH THERE WAS MORE COMMON KNOWLEDGE OF RADI- ATION AND RADIO- ACTIVE MATERIAL.
EVEN A YEAR AFTER THE ACCI- DENT, PEOPLE ACT LIKE THIS IN NEARBY IWAKI.
WHEN I MEN- TIONED THIS TO A CO- WORKER FROM IWAKI...
I CAN'T BELIEVE THAT. IT'S UNFORGIV- ABLE.
I'M NOT GOING TO PULL THE "WE'RE DOING THIS FOR FUKUSHIMA" CARD, BUT...
YEAH, I'M TRYING TO MAKE A GOOD LIVING, BUT EVEN STILL, THIS IS PRETTY SAD.
...

THEN DON'T WORRY ABOUT IT! WORK, HOUSING, CAR—I'LL TAKE OF ALL OF IT FOR YA!
HE WAS THE TYPE WHO EXHIBITED LEADERSHIP AS A YOUNG DELINQUENT, SO DESPITE BEING YOUNGER THAN US, HE HAD A CHARISMATIC AND CARING NATURE.
ARE YOU SURE?
I'VE GOT CONNECTIONS.
MEN LIKE THAT TEND TO KNOW PEOPLE.
GOT ANY DECENT CARS, BOSS?
OH! WELCOME.
IF YOU HAVE ANY CHEAP SECOND-HAND STATION WAGONS, THAT WOULD BE GREAT.
SURE DO.

HOW ABOUT THIS ONE?
I'LL LET IT GO FOR 100,000 YEN.
WOW, WHAT A LE-MON.
SHUDD-UP.
THIS MIGHT WORK, THOUGH ...
SO WHAT ARE YOU GONNA DO WITH THIS THING?
WELL, IF I CAN'T FIND A PLACE TO LIVE, I FIGURE AT LEAST I'VE GOT SPACE IN HERE.
ARE YOU SERIOUS ?!
JV'S OPEN 24 HOURS A DAY AND IT'S GOT BATHROOMS. FOR BATHING, THERE'S THE YUMOTO HOT SPRINGS.
IF I CAN GET A HIGH-EXPOSURE JOB, I CAN GO INTO DEBT...
THIS IS ACTUALLY WHAT I WAS PLANNING AT THE TIME.
YOU'RE REAL DUMB, PAL! I LIKE YOU.
ER, THANKS? IF I NEED YOUR HELP, I'LL BE BACK.
THERE'S NO NEED TO DO ALL THAT! WE CAN FIND A HOUSE!
WHAT ABOUT THIS?!

There are some hidden spots that cost just 100 yen that only locals know about. The water's amazing!

Sadly, I never ended up needing his help

CLINK...
WHOA ...
AND THIS IS 13,000 A MONTH ...?
NO WONDER IT'S SO INSANELY CHEAP.
HEY, IT'S A FIXER-UPPER.
YES, A LITTLE WORK MIGHT DO THE TRICK...
BUT WE'LL NEED A CAR-PEN-TER...
SO AUGUST CONSISTED OF WORK AT ICHI-F STARTING IN THE EARLY MORNING, THEN HOUSE-HUNTING IN THE AFTERNOON.
THIS ONE LOOKS ...
...LIKE IT USED TO BE A BAR, MAYBE?
HEY, LET'S RUN OUR OWN ESTABLISH-MENT!
In the mood
TAKE IT SERIOUSLY.
WHY ARE YOU HERE IN FUKU-SHIMA?
SOME OTHER LOCAL WORKERS HELPED GET US IN TOUCH WITH OTHER PLACES, WHICH WAS GREATLY APPRECIATED, BUT...
THIS ONE NEEDS A LOT OF WORK, TOO.
TRUE. AND THE BATH IS BROKEN AS WELL.
...ALL OF THEM NEEDED MAJOR REPAIRS, AND AT THE TIME, IWAKI HAD A SHORTAGE OF HANDYMEN AND CONTRACTORS.

MANY REPAIRS ARE NEEDED DUE TO QUAKE DAMAGE, AND NOW THERE'S A HUGE WAVE OF NEW HOME CONSTRUCTION.
I'VE HEARD THAT SOME PEOPLE ARE ON A YEAR-LONG WAITING LIST FOR ROOF REPAIRS.
I GUESS WE SHOULD HAVE SEEN THIS COMING.
IF THEY WERE IDEAL FOR LIVING, THEY'D BE RENTED OUT ALREADY.
IT'LL BE A LONG FIGHT ...
There are still places in Iwaki with tarp sheets over their roofs
AS FOR NEW JOBS, ALL THE COMPANIES WE HEARD FROM SAID...
WELL, IF YOU CAN JUST HANG ON A LITTLE WHILE, I'LL CONTACT YOU WHEN WE GET A GOOD LEAD.
OKAY...
SO THERE WAS NO PROGRESS ON THAT FRONT, AND WHEN WE WENT TO OUR BOSS...
WE'RE THINKING OF QUITTING SOON...
CAN YOU JUST WAIT A BIT? I NEED TO FIND REPLACEMENTS.
Can't leave until we have a place to live, so timing is crucial
DON'T WORRY, WE DON'T INTEND TO JUST WALK OUT ON OUR JOBS.
JUST MAKE IT QUICK, PLEASE.
OOOH, THIS ONE'S STILL LISTED. (EVEN THOUGH THERE'S NO WAY THEY ACTUALLY HAVE A JOB TO DO.)
I COLLECTED INFORMATION AT THE LOCAL HELLO WORK AGENCY.
Already know most of these businesses

I'M BACK.
HOW'D IT GO?
OUR OWN KUROMORI CONSTRUCTION HAS A LISTING: 20,000 YEN A DAY, JUST LIKE WHEN WE JOINED UP.
AGAIN?
AND THEY AIN'T GOT NO JOBS PAY NG THAT MUCH.
MAYBE THEY'RE GOING TO GATHER A BUNCH OF PEOPLE AND KEEP THEM ON STANDBY AT THIS DORM AGAIN.
YOU MEAN LIKE ME?
Guy who got gathered up and kept on standby
I FEEL BAD FOR YOU.
AT ANY RATE, SUBCONTRACTORS NEED TO HAVE PEOPLE ON HAND SO THEY CAN BE READY TO START WORK AS SOON AS A JOB COMES IN.
AW, DANG ...
SO PEOPLE KEPT FLOODING IN.
WE'VE GOT THREE NEW FACES STARTING TODAY.
AGAIN ?!
WE'RE ALREADY FULL ...
SO WHAT ARE YOUR JOBS?
THEY SAID IT WAS DECONTAMINATION, BUT WE HAVE TO WAIT A WHILE.
THAT FIGURES ...

LISTEN, TAKE OUR ADVICE: LEAVE AS SOON AS YOU CAN.
YOU DON'T KNOW WHEN WORK WILL START, AND IT WON'T PAY WHAT THEY LURED YOU HERE WITH.
I SEE ...
IT SOUNDS CRUEL, BUT HALF OF IT WAS AN ATTEMPT TO BE HELPFUL.
THE OTHER HALF WAS TRYING TO PROTECT AGAINST OUR OWN MISERY DUE TO OVER-CROWD-ING.
AS A MATTER OF FACT, WE WERE COM-PLETELY STRESSED OUT NOW.
IF ANYONE ELSE MOVES IN, I'M LEAVING.
OKAY, LOUD AND CLEAR.
THE LOOK ON HIS FACE SAID, "I'D LIKE TO SEE YOU TRY."
HE PROBABLY ASSUMES THAT IT'S IMPOSSIBLE FOR A LABORER TO GET A ROOM ON HIS OWN IN AN UNFAMILIAR CITY.
AND IN IWAKI TODAY, IT'LL PRACTI-CALLY TAKE A MIRACLE. STILL...
AT THIS POINT, WE JUST HAD TO USE WILLPOWER.
DON'T COUNT US OUT!

HMM ...
HOW ABOUT THIS ONE?
BUT STILL, WE HAD LITTLE LUCK.
NONE OF US COULD PAY RENT ON HIS OWN, SO OUR DECISION HAD TO BE UNANIMOUS.
YOU'RE RIGHT ...
NO, I THINK WE SHOULD RECONSIDER THIS ONE.
IN THIS CASE, I'M WILLING TO LOWER MY STANDARDS ...
JUST ABOUT THE TIME THAT I WAS RESIGNING MYSELF TO LIVING OUT OF A CAR...
S-SORRY, I KNOW IT'S TOUGH.
ARE YOU GUYS KIDDING ME? MAKE UP YOUR MINDS ALREADY!
THIS IS MY WIFE.
I'M SORRY ABOUT HIM. I HEAR HE'S BEEN SHOWING YOU AROUND ALL THESE DUMPS.
H-HELLO. YOUR HUSBAND'S REALLY BEEN GOING OUT ON A LIMB FOR US, MA'AM.
WHAT A LOOKER!
SHE'S TOO GOOD FOR HIM.
HOW ABOUT THIS ONE? I'M FRIENDS WITH THE LANDLORD HERE.
TURNS OUT, SHE WAS EVEN MORE HELPFUL AND CHARIS- MATIC THAN HE WAS.

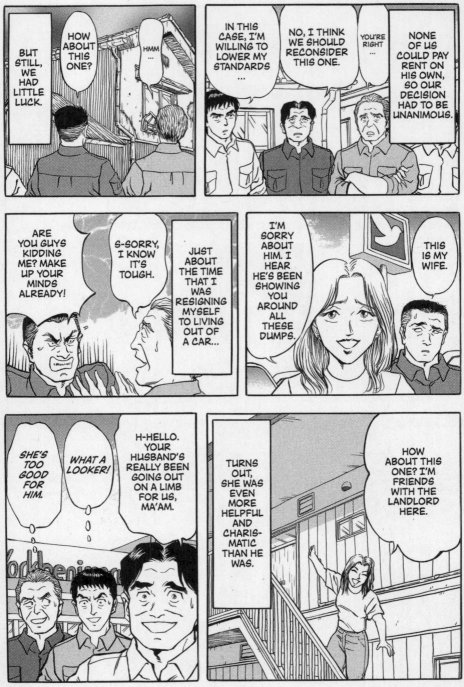

Two bedrooms (120 and 80 sq. feet), separate bath and toilet

HEY, HOW ABOUT THIS...
IT'S 30,000 YEN A MONTH, AND SINCE I KNOW THEM, NO EXTRA DEPOSITS NECES-SARY.
NOT BAD... (I FEEL LIKE THE FLOOR IS TILTED, THOUGH.)
YEAH. (THIS IS A MIRACU-LOUS FIND.)
IT'S NICE. (IF THERE'S A QUAKE, WE'LL JUST DEAL WITH IT.)
WE'LL TAKE IT!
THANK YOU VERY MUCH!
GLAD TO HELP!
GRIN
NOW THAT WE'VE SETTLED THE BUSINESS, LET'S GET SOMETHING TO EAT!
FRIED PORK CUT-LET!
BUT WE DON'T HAVE THE MONEY FOR...
IT'S ON ME!
HUH?
WE CAN'T ACCEPT THAT! NOT AFTER YOU JUST SWUNG US SUCH A NICE DEAL...

GET ALL THE EXTRA RICE, MISO SOUP, AND CABBAGE YOU WANT.
THANK YOU SO MUCH.
BUT WHY ARE YOU GOING OUT ON A LIMB SO FAR FOR US?
WELL, YOU CAME FROM SO FAR AWAY TO WORK HERE. I CAN'T STAND THE THOUGHT OF YOU LEAVING WITH A BAD TASTE IN YOUR MOUTH.
WE DON'T WANT ANYONE THINKING THE PEOPLE OF FUKUSHIMA ARE COLD AND UNCARING.
EVEN THOUGH IT WAS JUST AN ORDINARY CHAIN RESTAURANT, I VIVIDLY REMEMBER THIS PORK CUTLET BEING THE BEST I'VE EVER EATEN.
OH... WE'VE ALREADY LEARNED THAT VERY WELL.
FUKU-SHIMA IS SUCH A COM-PASSION-ATE PLACE.

THE FIRST STEP TO FINDING A GOOD PLACE TO LIVE WAS TO CULTIVATE PERSONAL RELATIONSHIPS.
MORE RICE!
熟成とんかつ
熟成とんかつ
MORE CABBAGE, PLEASE!
IT WAS THROUGH MEETING MANY KINDS OF PEOPLE THAT WE SURVIVED IN FUKUSHIMA.

Sign & Banner: Ripe Tonkatsu

THE NEXT DAY, IT WAS BACK TO WORKING AT ICHI-F, SIGNING THE LEASE, MOVING...
Mr. Tsurumi was our representative, as the eldest
YOU DON'T USUALLY SIGN YOUR FORMS HERE, HUH?
HEY, WHATEVER GETS THE JOB DONE. LIFE'S FUNNY!
WE GOT OUR APPLIANCES USED.
WOW, THIS IS A CHEAP LAUNDRY MACHINE!
WE NEED A FRIDGE, TOO.

Signing the landlord's lease at the shopping mall lobby

THERE'S NO SCREEN ON THIS WINDOW.
IF WE HAFTA CALL A WINDOW INSTALLER, THAT'LL COST A LOT.
JUST DO THIS!
OKAY!
BASH

H-HEY, WHAT ARE YOU DOING?!
IF WE JUST BUY A SCREEN, WE CAN ATTACH IT TO THE FRAME OF THE PAPER DOOR WITH BIG STAPLES!
RIP
RIP
OH, I GET IT!
IT'S WEIRD, BUT IT'LL WORK!
RIP
WHAP
WHAP
WHAP
This is fun!
WE'VE FOUND AN APARTMENT, SO WE'RE LEAVING THE DORM.
REALLY? YOU DID?!
WE APPRECIATE ALL THE HELP.
...
THEY CLEARLY DIDN'T THINK THAT WE'D EVER SUCCEED IN LEAVING.
FEELS LIKE WE FINALLY GOT ONE OVER ON THEM!
SO AROUND LATE AUGUST, THREE MEN FROM THEIR LATE 40s TO 50s...
...BEGAN LIVING TOGETHER IN AN APARTMENT WITH SLOPING FLOORS, NO SLIDING PAPER-SCREEN DOOR, AND NO CURTAINS. (BUT WE DID HAVE A SCREEN!)
Visible from outside (especially at night)

WITH A PLACE TO LIVE SECURED, NEXT WAS A NEW JOB.
WORK SITE?
VEHICLE SURVEY.
WHEN THE TATESHIBA REST AREA WAS OFF FOR A DAY, WE WOULD GO TO THE RECREATION BUILDING TO HELP OUT.
STF
ツル
EVEN THERE ...
WOW, THAT'S WHAT THEY QUOTED TO GET YA HERE?
Most are stunned
STF
植田
YES, AND IT'S WHY WE WANT TO QUIT THIS JOB.
SEE IF YOU CAN GET US IN WITH YOU.
HMM.
STF
竜田
STF
ツル
IT'S NOT THAT EASY. THERE'S AN UNSPOKEN RULE THAT YOU DON'T HEADHUNT OTHERS AT THE SAME REST AREA.
There's a gentleman's agreement about this
I'D HEARD THE RUMORS THAT IT WASN'T ALLOWED TO MOVE BETWEEN COMPANIES IN THE SAME SUBCONTRACTING CHAIN.
STF
植田
BUT...I SUPPOSE I CAN ASK AROUND.
WE REALLY APPRECIATE IT.
BUT THAT WASN'T GOING TO GET US DOWN.
STF
竜田

WORKERS OF VARIOUS STRIPES COME TO THE REC BUILDING.
MAN, IT'S HOT!
NICE WORK OUT THERE.
WORK SITE?
FUEL-ING STA-TION.
HMM ...
THAT VOICE...
IS THAT YOU, ONO?!
I SEE YOU ALL THE TIME!
HUH?
OH...
YOU'RE TATSUTA!!

HEY, IT'S THE TATSUTA WHO SHOWS UP EVERY MORNING!
OHH!
IT'S YOU!
I'VE NEVER SEEN YOUR FACE BEFORE!
IT'S NICE TO FINALLY MEET YOU! (IN A MANNER OF SPEAKING)
STF
WE ALWAYS SEE EACH OTHER WEARING FULL MASKS, SO WE DON'T ACTUALLY GET TO SEE EACH OTHERS' FACES. (WHAT ARE WE, MASKED WRESTLERS?)
YOU'RE MORE HANDSOME THAN I FIGURED!
NO WAY! YOU'RE SO SUAVE!
YOU MAKE AC-QUAIN-TANCES IN WEIRD WAYS AT ICHI-F.
BY THIS TIME, THE SUMMER WAS SLOWLY NEARING ITS END.
WE MIRACULOUSLY ESCAPED THE DORM, BUT OUR SEARCH FOR A BETTER JOB WAS GOING NOWHERE. ESPECIALLY MY PERSONAL REQUEST, WHICH WAS FOR A HIGH-EXPOSURE WORK SITE.
I'M SURE MY GO-BETWEEN WAS BEING CAU-TIOUS...
PARDON ME, MR. TATSUTA.
YES?
STF

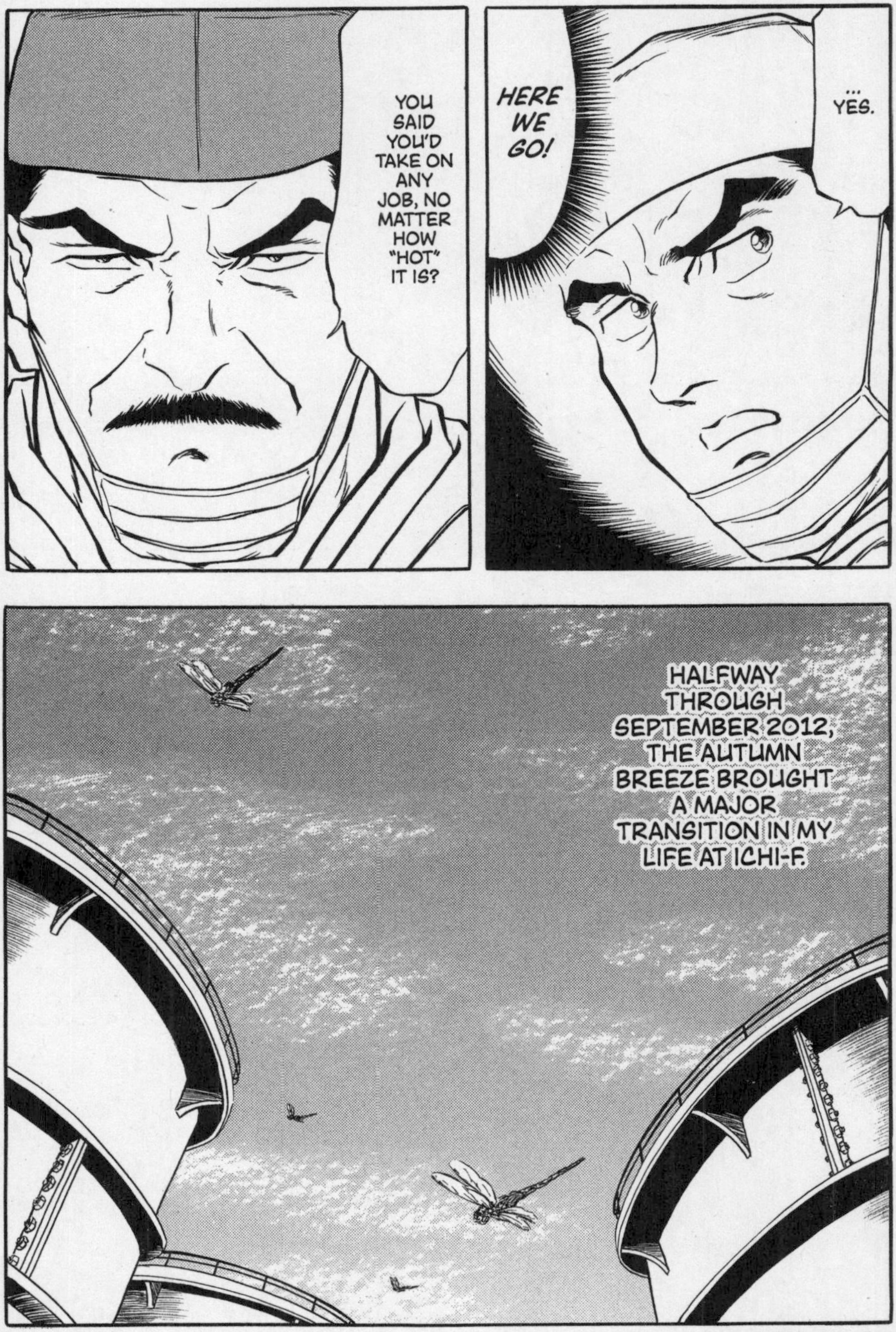
YOU SAID YOU'D TAKE ON ANY JOB, NO MATTER HOW "HOT" IT IS?
...YES.
HERE WE GO!
HALFWAY THROUGH SEPTEMBER 2012, THE AUTUMN BREEZE BROUGHT A MAJOR TRANSITION IN MY LIFE AT ICHI-F.

CHAPTER 7 - END

SEPTEMBER 2012 — COMPANY RECREATION BLDG.
NICE WORK OUT THERE TODAY.
WORK SITE?
AREA C.
During Tateshiba Rest Area off-days, we work at the rec center
DID YOU HEAR ABOUT THE UNIT 3 CRANE? IT COLLAPSED.
WOW, REALLY?!
THAT'S WHAT THEY'RE SAYING.
ALL THE UNIT 3 WORK IS CANCELLED FOR TODAY.
OH, MAN ...

WHAT IF IT'S A HUGE DISASTER ...?
CHAPTER 8:
TROUPE ICHI-F
UNDER FOOT, PLEASE.
I CAN'T GET MY MIND OFF IT!
OKAY, NOW'S A GOOD TIME...
I'M GOING TO GO FUEL UP FOR TATESHIBA!
OH .. STAY SAFE.

VRMMM
EVEN WHEN NO ONE'S THERE, THE TATESHIBA REST AREA GENERATOR IS RUNNING, SO SOMEONE HAS TO GO FROM THE REC BUILDING TO REFUEL IT.
KRK
SCREEEE
BUT BEFORE THAT...
?
RRRK
THERE'S NOTHING WRONG WITH THE CRANE... SO WHAT WAS THAT STORY ABOUT?
IT'S TRUE THEY'RE NOT WORKING HERE, THOUGH.
IN THIS SENSE, EVEN IN ICHI-F, BAD INFORMATION CAN MAKE ITS WAY AROUND.

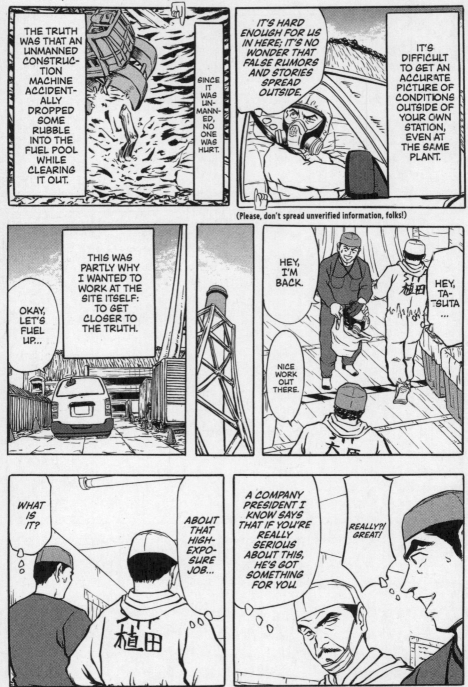

THE TRUTH WAS THAT AN UNMANNED CONSTRUCTION MACHINE ACCIDENTALLY DROPPED SOME RUBBLE INTO THE FUEL POOL WHILE CLEARING IT OUT.

SINCE IT WAS UNMANNED, NO ONE WAS HURT.

IT'S HARD ENOUGH FOR US IN HERE; IT'S NO WONDER THAT FALSE RUMORS AND STORIES SPREAD OUTSIDE.

IT'S DIFFICULT TO GET AN ACCURATE PICTURE OF CONDITIONS OUTSIDE OF YOUR OWN STATION, EVEN AT THE SAME PLANT.

(Please, don't spread unverified information, folks!)

THIS WAS PARTLY WHY I WANTED TO WORK AT THE SITE ITSELF: TO GET CLOSER TO THE TRUTH.

OKAY, LET'S FUEL UP...

HEY, I'M BACK.

NICE WORK OUT THERE.

HEY, TATSUTA...

WHAT IS IT?

ABOUT THAT HIGH-EXPOSURE JOB...

A COMPANY PRESIDENT I KNOW SAYS THAT IF YOU'RE REALLY SERIOUS ABOUT THIS, HE'S GOT SOMETHING FOR YOU.

REALLY?! GREAT!

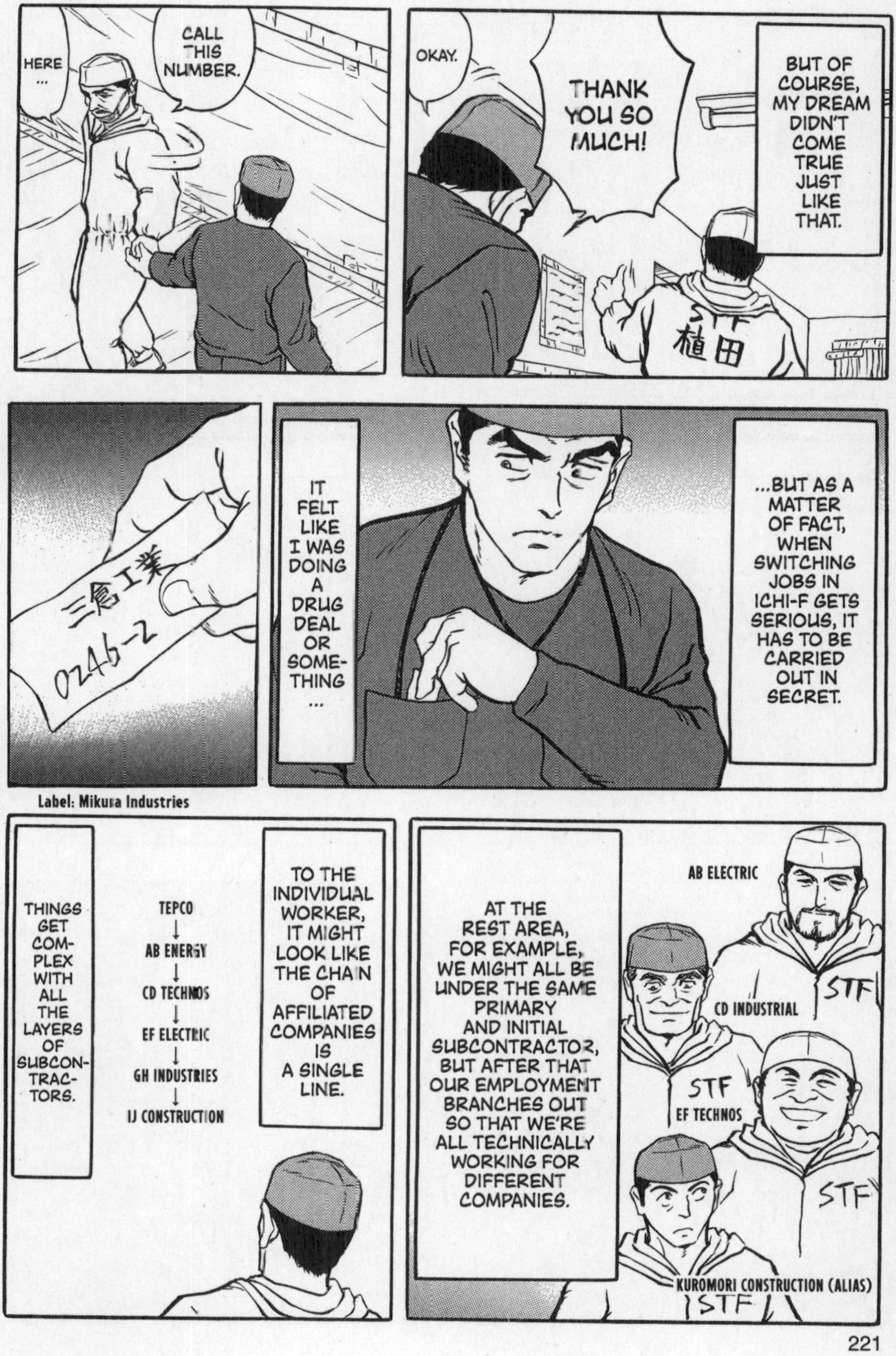
CALL THIS NUMBER.
HERE ...
OKAY.
THANK YOU SO MUCH!
BUT OF COURSE, MY DREAM DIDN'T COME TRUE JUST LIKE THAT.
STF 植田
三倉工業
0246-2
IT FELT LIKE I WAS DOING A DRUG DEAL OR SOME-THING ...
...BUT AS A MATTER OF FACT, WHEN SWITCHING JOBS IN ICHI-F GETS SERIOUS, IT HAS TO BE CARRIED OUT IN SECRET.
Label: Mikura Industries
THINGS GET COM-PLEX WITH ALL THE LAYERS OF SUBCON-TRAC-TORS.
TEPCO
↓
AB ENERGY
↓
CD TECHNOS
↓
EF ELECTRIC
↓
GH INDUSTRIES
↓
IJ CONSTRUCTION
TO THE INDIVIDUAL WORKER, IT MIGHT LOOK LIKE THE CHAIN OF AFFILIATED COMPANIES IS A SINGLE LINE.
AT THE REST AREA, FOR EXAMPLE, WE MIGHT ALL BE UNDER THE SAME PRIMARY AND INITIAL SUBCONTRACTOR, BUT AFTER THAT OUR EMPLOYMENT BRANCHES OUT SO THAT WE'RE ALL TECHNICALLY WORKING FOR DIFFERENT COMPANIES.
AB ELECTRIC
STF
CD INDUSTRIAL
STF
EF TECHNOS
STF
KUROMORI CONSTRUCTION (ALIAS)
STF

*Delegating work to lower companies
AND THESE BUSINESSES AREN'T NECESSARILY AT THE SAME POINT IN THE CHAIN—SOME ARE CLOSER TO THE TOP.
AB ELECTRIC (TERTIARY SUBCON.) TAKE-HOME DAILY PAY ¥16,000
THIS IS WHY SOME PEOPLE GET PAID AS MUCH AS TWICE AS OTHERS DOING THE SAME JOB.
KUROMORI CONSTRUCTION (SENARY SUBCON.) TAKE-HOME DAILY PAY ¥8,000
This is just an example!
AND AS FOR THE INTERMEDIATE BUSINESSES...
OKAY, WE'LL PASS* THIS ON FOR 15,000 YEN.
IN THAT CASE, 10,000 YEN.
I CAN ONLY PAY 8,000.
KUROMORI COULDN'T MUSCLE ITS WAY HIGHER, PROBABLY BECAUSE THEY WERE BASED FURTHER AWAY IN KORIYAMA, NOT IWAKI.
THEY DON'T SUBCONTRACT EVERYTHING; SOMETIMES THEY ORDER WORKERS FROM BELOW TO FILL OUT DUTIES THAT THE COMPANY'S OWN WORKFORCE CAN'T COVER.
YOU THREE, GO.
OKAY.
SOME COMPANY OWNERS ARE ACTUAL WORKERS ON THE JOB, THEMSELVES.
In this case, he not only gets the middleman fees, but his own earnings
BY WORKING ON THE JOB, THEY CAN MAKE CONNECTIONS.
I'VE GOT THIS JOB COMING IN. YOU GOT ANYONE YOU CAN SEND MY WAY?
WE'RE ALL FULL, BUT I CAN ASK AROUND.
NOW IF YOU PASS ON AN EXTRA, SEPARATE JOB...
HOW MANY MEN CAN YOU GET FOR ME?
LET'S SEE...
...AND TAKE IT *UP* THE CHAIN TO YOUR PARENT COMPANY INSTEAD...

IN THIS EXAMPLE, XX INDUSTRIES IS THE QUATERNARY SUBCONTRACTOR AND YY CONSTRUCTION IS THE QUINARY AT WORKSITE A, WHILE THEIR PLACES IN THE CHAIN ARE REVERSED AT WORKSITE B.
...YOU WILL FIND THAT THE SAME COMPANY CAN BE BOTH ABOVE AND BELOW YOU IN DIFFERENT WORK ASSIGNMENTS. (WITH WAGES SCOOPED OUT APPROPRIATELY, OF COURSE.)
Site A
QUATERNARY ¥20,000
QUINARY ¥15,000
SENARY ¥10,000
TAKES OUT ¥5,000
TAKES OUT ¥5,000
XX INDUSTRIES
YY CONSTRUCTION
TAKES OUT ¥6,000
TAKES OUT ¥6,000
SENARY ¥10,000
QUINARY ¥16,000
QUATERNARY ¥22,000
Site B
IN THIS SENSE, EACH COMPANY KIND OF JUST GOES WITH THE FLOW, WITH THE LOWEST RUNG ON THE JOB IN CHARGE OF SUPPLYING THE ACTUAL LABOR.
BY THE TIME YOU GET TO THE BOTTOM LEVEL, MOST OF THE PAY IS ESSENTIALLY ABOUT THE SAME.
SO THERE'S ALWAYS RECRUITING HAPPENING ON THE DOWN LOW TO DRUM UP NUMBERS.
WANNA WORK WITH US?
UHH ...
GIVEN THE COMPLICATED TANGLE OF PERSONAL RELATIONSHIPS, CROSSING THE LINE AND REVEALING THAT YOU'RE PLOTTING TO SNEAK PEOPLE AROUND BEHIND OTHERS' BACKS WILL GET YOU KICKED OUT OF THE AREA, I FOUND OUT.
THEREFORE, ALL TALK OF TRANSFERRING JOBS AT ICHI-F IS DONE IN SECRET, LIKE YOU'RE MAKING A DRUG DEAL.
TONIGHT... THE USUAL SPOT.
GOT IT.

THE SIMPLE FACT OF THE MATTER IS THAT YOU CAN'T GET ACTUAL WORKERS AT ICHI-F WITHOUT KNOWING THE LOCALS.
This explains why I had so much trouble breaking in through Hello Work
PEOPLE MIGHT THINK THAT THE MANY-LAYERED SUBCONTRACTING SYSTEM IS PROBLEMATIC, BUT IT'S HOW WE MAINTAIN THE CLEANUP EFFORTS. IT ENSURES LOCAL HIRING AND PROPS UP THE ECONOMY HERE.
THAT'S NOT TO SUGGEST THAT THE SYSTEM IS IDEAL, BUT YOU CAN SAY THAT ABOUT ALMOST ANY PLACE IN JAPAN. (IT'S JUST THAT THERE ARE TOO MANY LEVELS AT ICHI-F...)
HI, MY NAME'S TATSUTA. I GOT YOUR INFORMATION FROM MR. UEDA.
SO ALL THAT WE LOW-LEVEL WORKERS CAN HOPE TO DO IS MOVE ONE COMPANY UP THE CHAIN.
YOU SAID YOU'LL WORK ANY-WHERE?
THAT'S RIGHT.
WE HAVE EASIER ASSIGN-MENTS IN SAFER LOCA-TIONS.
NO, I WOULD PREFER HIGH-EXPOSURE, HIGH-PAY.
THAT MAKES YOU QUITE DIFFERENT FROM THE OTHERS.
IT DOES?
WELL, THAT'S FINE. I'LL CALL YOU IF SOMETHING COMES IN. WE'LL BE ABOUT TERTIARY IN THE CHAIN.

HOPE TO HEAR FROM YOU, SIR!

AT THE TIME, I THOUGHT THIS COMPANY WAS THE ONE FOR ME.

BUT THERE WAS NO GUARANTEE THAT I WOULD GET A JOB.

WE'RE GOING TO MEET WITH THE MANAGER OF XY INDUSTRIAL TODAY.

WE INDIVIDUALLY BARGAINED WITH VARIOUS COMPANIES, AND WOULD GO AND MEET WITH THEM AS A GROUP IF NECESSARY.

We answered in the affirmative to every one, just in case.

SOMETIMES IT WAS AT A RESTAURANT, SOMETIMES IT WAS IN THE PARKING LOT OF A CONVENIENCE STORE.

IF YOU COME WORK FOR US, WE CAN PAY YOU A BIT MORE THAN THAT.

WE'RE LOOKING FORWARD TO IT.

WE HAD MANY SUCH QUIET MEETINGS WITH PRESIDENTS AND MANAGERS AT SMALLER SUBCONTRACTORS...

...BUT THINGS MOVE FAST AT ICHI-F, SO IT WASN'T POSSIBLE TO GAUGE THE PROPER MOMENT TO TRANSFER.

WELL THEN...

I'LL BRING YOU IN ONCE WE GET A CONTRACT, SO MAKE SURE YOU HAVE THINGS SET UP TO LEAVE YOUR CURRENT JOB.

HOW ARE WE SUPPOSED TO QUIT OUR CURRENT WORK IF WE DON'T HAVE THE NEXT ONE LINED UP YET?

THE LAST THING WE WANT TO DEAL WITH IS UNEMPLOYMENT.

BUT I SEIZED THE INITIATIVE.
I'M GOING TO QUIT BY THE END OF SEPTEMBER.
UH... RIGHT...
I HAD NO GUARANTEE OF FINDING A NEW JOB...
...BUT I UNDERSTOOD THAT AS LONG AS I GAVE THEM NOTICE OF AT LEAST TWO WEEKS, THE COMPANY COULD NOT LEGALLY KEEP ME THERE.
YOU SURE?
I'LL LAND ON MY FEET.
I WAS ALSO OPTIMISTIC THAT NOW THAT I HAD A PLACE TO LIVE, A SHORT STINT WITHOUT A JOB WOULDN'T KILL ME.
BUT MY COMPANIONS, WHO JUST WANTED TO TRANSFER TO ANOTHER MANAGEMENT POSITION IN ICHI-F...
WHAT ABOUT YOU GUYS?
WE'LL HANG ON ANOTHER MONTH OR SO...
...COULDN'T JUST UP AND QUIT LIKE ME.
Avoiding high-exposure sites so they can continue working longer.
AND AFTER THAT?
MAYBE I'LL PACK UP AND GO BACK HOME.
THEY HAD TO BE VAGUE SO AS NOT TO REVEAL THEIR INTENTIONS.

IN OTHER WORDS, WE WERE PUTTING ON A BIT OF AN ACT TO ALL PARTIES AROUND US AS WE NEGOTIATED A CHANGE OF SCENERY.
AND YOU?
I'M NEARLY READY TO RETIRE ...
SPEAKING OF ACTING, HERE'S ANOTHER STORY.
EVERY-ONE, GATHER 'ROUND!
YES, SIR!
THIS ALSO HAP-PENED IN SEP-TEMBER.
WE'VE GOT WORD THAT TEPCO'S COMING FOR A MORNING INSPECTION NEXT WEEK.
OHH.
BUT WHY NOW?
STF 竜田
STF 江田
STF 赤井
STF 小川
THEY'RE TOURING ALL STATIONS TO ENSURE THAT WE'RE FOLLOWING TBMKY PROCE-DURES.
I SEE ...

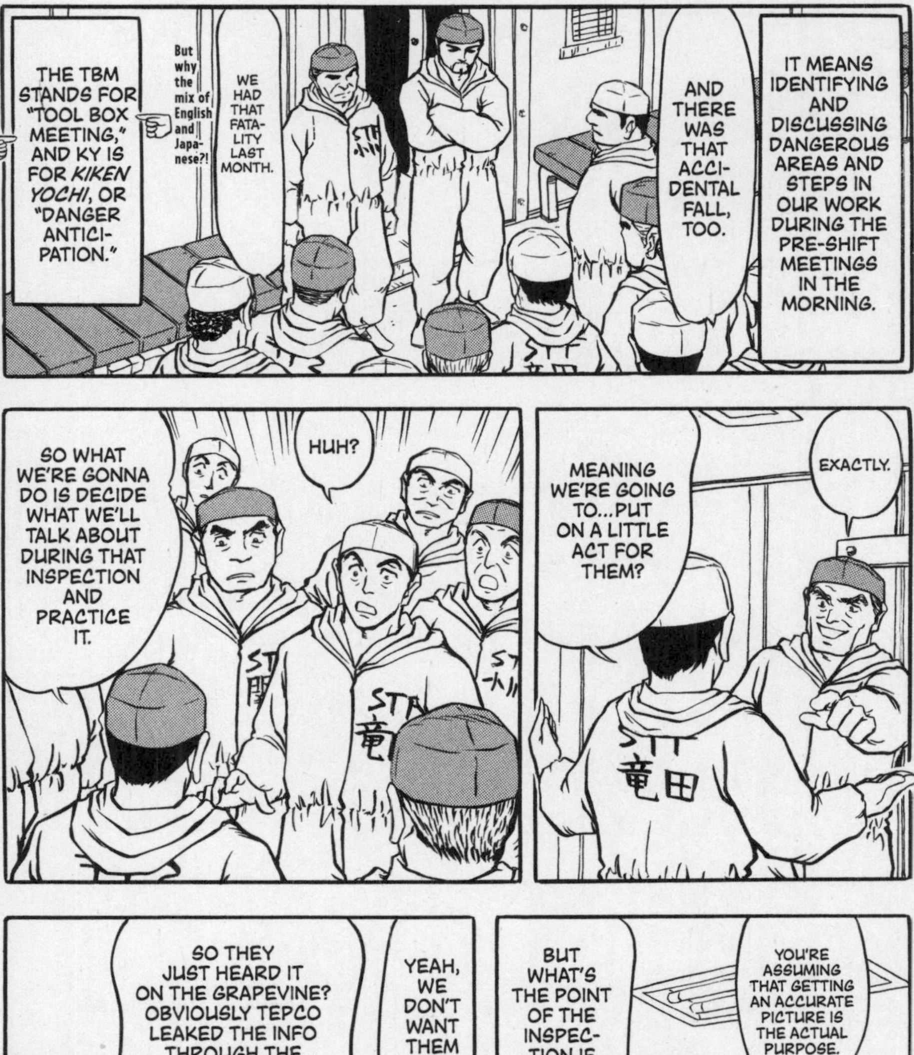

THE TBM STANDS FOR "TOOL BOX MEETING," AND KY IS FOR *KIKEN YOCHI*, OR "DANGER ANTICIPATION."
But why the mix of English and Japanese?!
WE HAD THAT FATALITY LAST MONTH.
AND THERE WAS THAT ACCIDENTAL FALL, TOO.
IT MEANS IDENTIFYING AND DISCUSSING DANGEROUS AREAS AND STEPS IN OUR WORK DURING THE PRE-SHIFT MEETINGS IN THE MORNING.
SO WHAT WE'RE GONNA DO IS DECIDE WHAT WE'LL TALK ABOUT DURING THAT INSPECTION AND PRACTICE IT.
HUH?
MEANING WE'RE GOING TO...PUT ON A LITTLE ACT FOR THEM?
EXACTLY.
SO THEY JUST HEARD IT ON THE GRAPEVINE? OBVIOUSLY TEPCO LEAKED THE INFO THROUGH THE MASTER CONTRACTOR TO MAKE SURE WE'RE PREPARED.
YEAH, WE DON'T WANT THEM SHOWING UP OUTTA THE BLUE.
BUT WHAT'S THE POINT OF THE INSPECTION IF IT'S NOT A SURPRISE?
YOU'RE ASSUMING THAT GETTING AN ACCURATE PICTURE IS THE ACTUAL PURPOSE.

It's supposed to be like we're sitting around on toolboxes

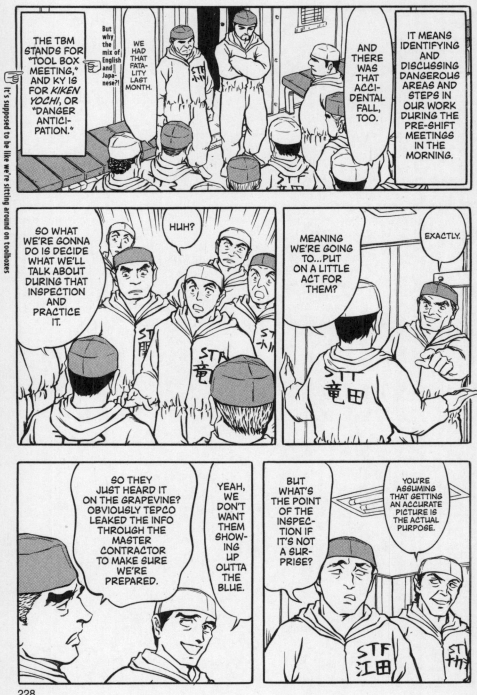

OKAY, ENOUGH OF THE CONSPIRACY THEORIES. LET'S FIGURE OUT OUR LINES!
ALL RIGHT!
FIRST, LET'S LIST ALL THE DANGER AREAS. WHO'S GOT ONE?
ME.
TA-TSUTA.
I NEARLY JAMMED MY FINGER IN THE ENTRANCE DOOR-WAY.
YOU IDIOT...OKAY, FINE. HOW DO WE DEAL WITH THAT?
WE CALL OUT WHEN OPENING OR CLOS-ING IT.
THAT SOUNDS ABOUT RIGHT. WHAT ELSE?
ME.
SOME OF OUR WORKERS HAVE NEARLY SLIPPED ON THE SWEAT ON THE FLOOR.
HOW DO WE DEAL WITH THAT?
JUST HAVE TO WIPE IT OFF CON-STANTLY.
THIS IS KINDA... FUN.
WE FIGURED OUT WHO WOULD SAY WHAT, AND IN WHAT ORDER. WITH THAT SCRIPT IN HAND, WE PRACTICED THE CHAR-ADE A FEW TIMES.

Very relieved that it worked

YES, IT WAS ALL ONE BIG FARCE THAT WE PUT ON.
STAY SAFE!
THANKS!
TEPCO
BUT WE *DID* ENACT MANY OF THE SAFETY RECOMMENDATIONS WE RAISED.
IT'S A LITTLE THING, BUT A HEIGHTENED FOCUS ON WORKPLACE SAFETY MADE THE SILLINESS WORTH IT, I THINK.
STRIPED TAPE
Sign: Watch your head
ON TOP OF THAT, PART OF THE REASON WE COULD LAUGH ABOUT THIS IS THE FACT THAT THE REST AREA IS ONE OF THE SAFEST PLACES HERE, RELATIVELY SPEAKING.
頭上注意
OKAY, TODAY'S SITE IS...
STF
HERE AND HERE! THEY'RE HOTSPOTS, SO STAY CLEAR!
GOT IT!
THE SAFETY-PREPAREDNESS OF THE TEAMS GOING TO ACTUAL DANGER ZONES IS DEADLY SERIOUS.
YOU'D BETTER LISTEN UP, OR I'LL WHUP YOU UPSIDE YOUR HEADS!
WE'RE SORRY, SIR!
YIKES...
THAT'S THE KIND OF TENSE, SERIOUS WORK I WANT TO TRY OUT.

NOT TO SUGGEST THAT THE PRAISE OUR TEPCO GUEST GAVE US EMBOLDENED US, BUT WE CONTINUED OUR CLEVER ACTING AS WE MANAGED OUR JOB NEGOTIATIONS.
PLEASE FIND SOMETHING QUICKLY. I CAN'T MAKE ENDS MEET.
OH, I SEE...
IN THAT CASE, I'LL GET SOMETHING READY FOR YOU SO THAT YOU CAN SWITCH IN AS SOON AS YOU QUIT.
THE TRANSFER WAS STARTING TO SOUND MORE REALISTIC.
EVENTUALLY, IT GOT TO THE END OF THE MONTH, THE DAY OF MY REMOVAL.*
THANKS FOR EVERYTHING YOU'VE DONE FOR ME.
SO YOU'RE HEADING IN WITH THE HIGH-EXPOSURE TEAM, HUH?
WELL, NOTHING'S FINAL.
YOU'RE AN ODD ONE, I'LL GIVE YA THAT.

*Removal = leaving a job in the radiation management zone

IF THEY STILL HAD KAMIKAZE FIGHTERS, YOU'D BE THE FIRST TO SIGN UP. AM I WRONG?
AHH... MAYBE YOU'RE RIGHT ABOUT THAT.
WHAT ABOUT YOU, MR. AKASHI?
ME?
WELL, I GUESS WE'RE BOTH IDIOTS WHO ACTUALLY WANT TO BE ON THE FRONT LINE.

Mr. Akashi was a former SDF soldier who joined Tateshiba after discharge. Right after the Ichi-F accident, he got an assignment transporting materials to the site. (See Chapter 5)

BUT EVEN THE "FRONT LINE" HERE AT ICHI-F DOESN'T INVOLVE ANY KIND OF SUICIDE RUNS.
TRUE, BUT THAT DOESN'T MEAN YOU DON'T NEED TO BE CAREFUL.
YES, SIR.
WELL, STAY SAFE!
STAY SAFE!
I WENT TO PAY MY RE-SPECTS AT THE REC CEN-TER.
I'M GETTING MY REMO-VAL TODAY. THANKS FOR EVERY-THING.
I SEE. TAKE CARE.
BUT I'LL BE RIGHT BACK HERE!
TO GET MEASURED THIS TIME!
AHHH.
WELL, WE'LL BE HERE FOR YA.
SEE YOU THEN!
I WASN'T SURE THAT I'D ACTUALLY BE BACK RIGHT AWAY.
BUT AT THIS POINT, I FELT MORE EXCITEMENT TOWARD MY NEXT JOB THAN ANY WORRY ABOUT THE FUTURE.

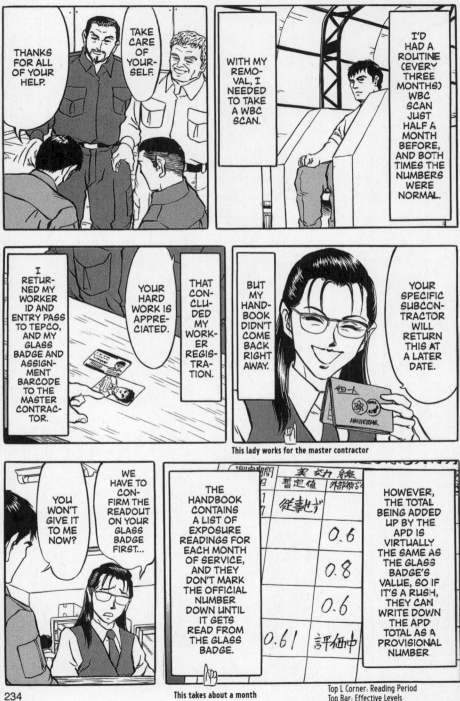

This lady works for the master contractor

HOWEVER, THE TOTAL BEING ADDED UP BY THE APD IS VIRTUALLY THE SAME AS THE GLASS BADGE'S VALUE, SO IF IT'S A RUSH, THEY CAN WRITE DOWN THE APD TOTAL AS A PROVISIONAL NUMBER

THE HANDBOOK CONTAINS A LIST OF EXPOSURE READINGS FOR EACH MONTH OF SERVICE, AND THEY DON'T MARK THE OFFICIAL NUMBER DOWN UNTIL IT GETS READ FROM THE GLASS BADGE.

測定期間	実効線量	
	暫定値	外部被ばく
	従事せず	
		0.6
		0.8
		0.6
	0.61	評価中

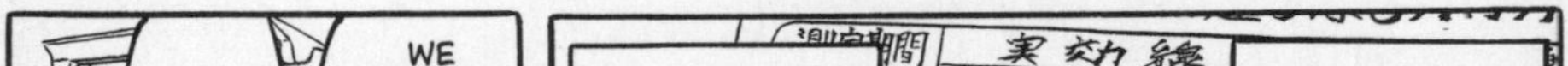

This takes about a month

Top L Corner: Reading Period
Top Bar: Effective Levels
L Column: Provisional Level, Pre-service
R Column: External Exposure, In assessment

I'LL NEED MY HANDBOOK FOR THE NEXT JOB, SO IT'S UNNERVING NOT TO HAVE IT IN MY POSSESSION, BUT AT LEAST THIS MEANS PARTING WAYS WITH KUROMORI CONSTRUCTION.
THANK YOU FOR EVERY-THING.
ER... YEAH...
WE BUTTED HEADS DUE TO OUR PERSONAL NEEDS ON MULTIPLE OCCASIONS, BUT I HAVE TO ADMIT THAT THIS COM-PANY WAS ALSO VICTIMIZED BY THE MULTI-LAYERED SUBCON-TRACTING SYSTEM.
WELL, TAKE CARE OF YOURSELF OUT THERE.
AFTER ALL IS SAID AND DONE, I DON'T HATE THEM—I'M GRATE-FUL TO THEM.
THANK YOU, SIR.
I FEEL KIND OF BAD THAT I'VE DEPICTED THEM AS VILLAINS IN THIS BOOK.
SO WHAT HAPP-ENS NOW?
GOOD QUES-TION.
MAYBE WE SHOULD GO VISIT UP NORTH.
THE DISA-STER AREA?
YES.

I WON'T HAVE A BETTER OPPORTUNITY THAN THIS ONE.

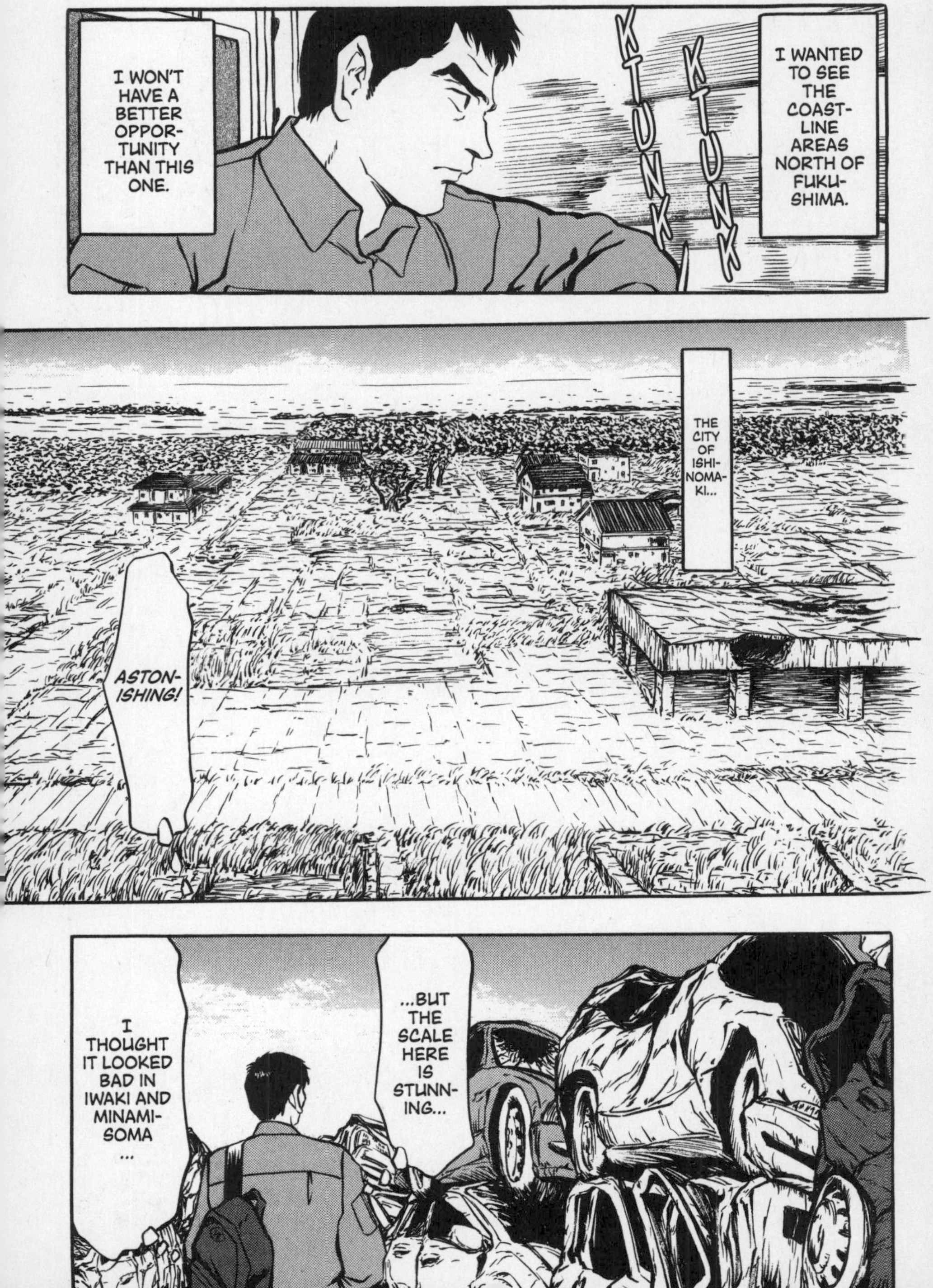

I WANTED TO SEE THE COAST-LINE AREAS NORTH OF FUKU-SHIMA.

KTUNK KTUNK

THE CITY OF ISHI-NOMA-KI...

ASTON-ISHING!

I THOUGHT IT LOOKED BAD IN IWAKI AND MINAMI-SOMA...

...BUT THE SCALE HERE IS STUNN-ING...

I TOOK A TRAIN AND A CONNECTING BUS FROM SENDAI TO ISHINO-MAKI.
A YEAR AND A HALF LATER, AND THERE'S STILL JUST A MOUN-TAIN OF RUBBLE ...
I WAS LEFT HUMBLED BY THE UNIMAGINABLE DESTRUCTION OF THE TSUNAMI, AND THAT WAS ONLY WHAT I COULD SEE WITHIN WALKING DISTANCE OF THE STATION.
IN FUKUSHIMA, IT'S EASY TO ZOOM IN ON WHAT'S HAPPENING AT ICHI-F...
...BUT THE REAL DISASTER HERE WAS THE TSUNAMI ITSELF...
HM ?
BEEP BEEP...
Ah, Mr. Tatsuta! We've got a job offer. Can you come in tomorrow?
TATSUTA SPEAK-ING.

TO-MOR-ROW?!

Yes, just come to the office. I'll see you then.

I WAS HOPING TO LOOK AROUND A BIT MORE WHILE I HAD THE CHANCE, BUT ALAS.

ANOTHER LAST-MINUTE CALL...BUT IT'S WHAT I WANTED.

Used to things being sudden

!

TA-TSUTA SPEAK-ING!

BEEP BEEP...

Sign: Ishinomaki

I hear you've been removed. Your handbook came back to the office.

OH.

THANK YOU, SIR!

BUT I MUST APOLOGIZE— IVE TAKEN A JOB ON-SITE WITH A DIFFERENT COMPANY ...

Huh?

Ah, I see... That's too bad. Well, we've got your handbook, so come on in and get it.

YES, SIR. THANK YOU.

I STILL FEEL VERY SORRY ABOUT LEAVING THE COMPANY THAT OFFERED ME A JOB AND GOT BACK MY RADIATION CONTROL HANDBOOK, BUT IT WAS THE BEST CHOICE FOR ME.
HERE YOU GO.
I'M SO SORRY! I'M SO SORRY.
BUT NOW MY HANDBOOK IS BACK.
HERE'S YOUR CONTRACT.
I OFFICIALLY SIGNED WITH MY NEW COMPANY.
LET'S SEE...
THERE WAS ANOTHER RADIATION EXAM AND WBC TEST.
YOU'LL JUST FEEL A LITTLE PINCH ...
AAAH!
I TOOK NEW PICTURES AND GOT A NEW WORKER ID AND ENTRY PASS.
東菱電工福島支社
THEN THE MASTER CONTRACTOR OF *THIS* WORK SENT ME A NEW GLASS BADGE AND ASSIGNMENT BARCODE.

Sign: Tobishi Denko Fukushima

THOSE WHO HAVE ALREADY TAKEN THE a AND b EDUCATION COURSES DON'T NEED TO VISIT THE LECTURE HALL AGAIN, BUT I DID HAVE TO TAKE A LESSON IN "SPECIALIZED RADIATION CONTROL" AT THE MASTER CONTRACTOR'S OFFICE DUE TO THE DANGEROUS ASSIGNMENT.
UNLIKE THE THINGS I LEARNED BEFORE, THIS WAS A PRACTICAL COURSE GOING OVER THE EQUIPMENT AND PROCEDURES WE WOULD USE RIGHT AT THE WORK SITE.

You feel more nervous with a small group

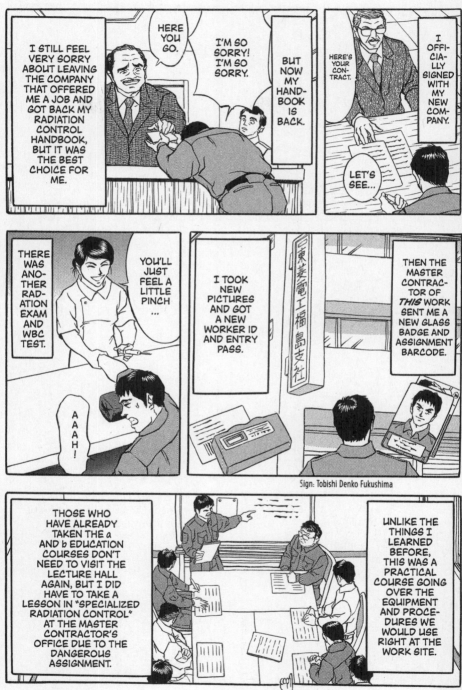

IN PRACTICE, THIS WAS MORE LIKE A TUTORIAL AND PLANNING MEETING ABOUT THE JOB, AND TRANSITIONED PROMPTLY INTO A PRE-WORK CONFERENCE.
THIS WAS WHERE THE MEMBERS OF THE WORK SITE FIRST MET.
THERE WERE SEVERAL DAYS OF CAREFUL PREPARATIONS AFTER THIS...
...UNTIL WE FINALLY SET FOOT ON THE SITE WHILE HAULING IN OUR EQUIPMENT.
IT WAS LESS THAN TEN DAYS SINCE MY REMOVAL, BUT OVER FOUR MONTHS SINCE I HAD FIRST VISITED ICHI-F.
AT LAST, I WAS BACK IN ICHI-F ...
...AS A PROPER WORKER THIS TIME.
I MADE IT.
AT LAST, I'M HERE ...
TDF
竜田

CHAPTER 8 - END

HAMAKAZE SHOPPING DISTRICT

THE PEOPLE FROM THE SHOPPING DISTRICT OF HISANOHAMA WERE DEVASTATED BY THE GREAT EAST JAPAN EARTHQUAKE, AND THEY OPENED UP A TEMPORARY LOCATION ON THE GROUNDS OF HISANOHAMA FIRST ELEMENTARY SCHOOL AS OF SEPTEMBER 3RD, 2011. IT'S NICE TO HEAR THE SHOPKEEPERS' ENERGETIC VOICES WHEN YOU STOP BY. THERE'S A NUMBER OF BUSINESSES, FROM SALONS TO BARS TO FISHMARKETS, AS WELL AS A SALES OUTLET FOR PHOTOS AND DVDS OF THE DISASTER DAMAGE.

ON HIS WAY HOME FROM WORK, KAZUTO TATSUTA WOULD OCCASIONALLY STOP HERE AND DINE ON RAMEN OR POTSTICKERS NEAR THE ENTRANCE. IT'S ONE OF HIS FAVORITE PLACES TO VISIT IN IWAKI.

OCTOBER 2012
THIS IS THE FIRST TIME I SET FOOT INSIDE THE REACTOR BUILDINGS OF ICHI-F, WHILE HAULING EQUIPMENT FOR OUR PIPE CONSTRUCTION.
TDF 竜田
LET'S GET GOIN'.
ALL RIGHT.
TDF 竜田
CHAPTER 9:
CAREER EXPOSURE
IT WAS THE RADIOACTIVE WASTE DISPOSAL BUILDING ADJACENT TO THE UNIT 3 REACTOR BUILDING.
TDF

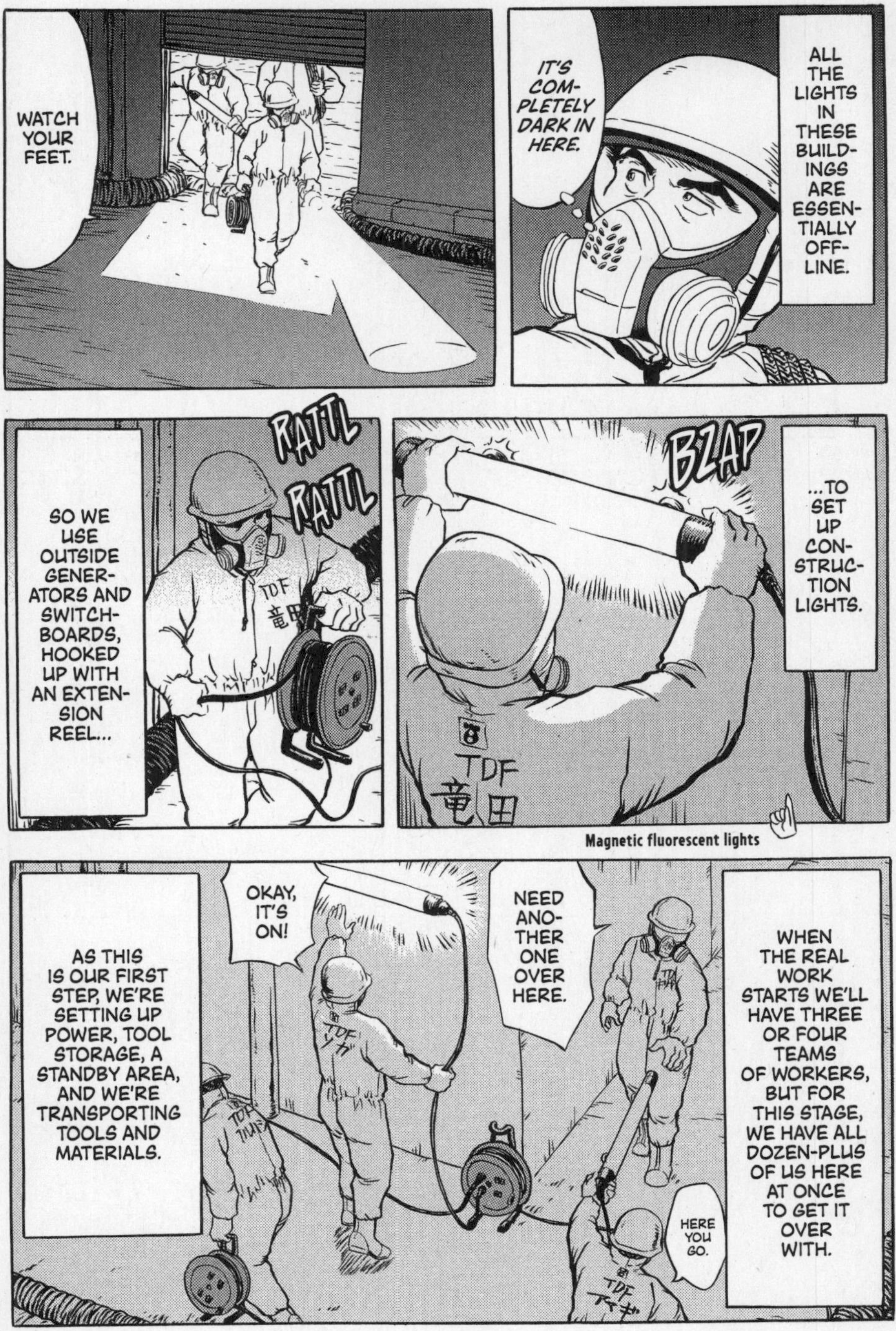
WATCH YOUR FEET.
IT'S COMPLETELY DARK IN HERE.
ALL THE LIGHTS IN THESE BUILDINGS ARE ESSENTIALLY OFF-LINE.
RATTL RATTL
SO WE USE OUTSIDE GENERATORS AND SWITCHBOARDS, HOOKED UP WITH AN EXTENSION REEL...
TDF
竜田
BZAP
...TO SET UP CONSTRUCTION LIGHTS.
TDF
竜田
Magnetic fluorescent lights
AS THIS IS OUR FIRST STEP, WE'RE SETTING UP POWER, TOOL STORAGE, A STANDBY AREA, AND WE'RE TRANSPORTING TOOLS AND MATERIALS.
OKAY, IT'S ON!
NEED ANOTHER ONE OVER HERE.
WHEN THE REAL WORK STARTS WE'LL HAVE THREE OR FOUR TEAMS OF WORKERS, BUT FOR THIS STAGE, WE HAVE ALL DOZEN-PLUS OF US HERE AT ONCE TO GET IT OVER WITH.
HERE YOU GO.

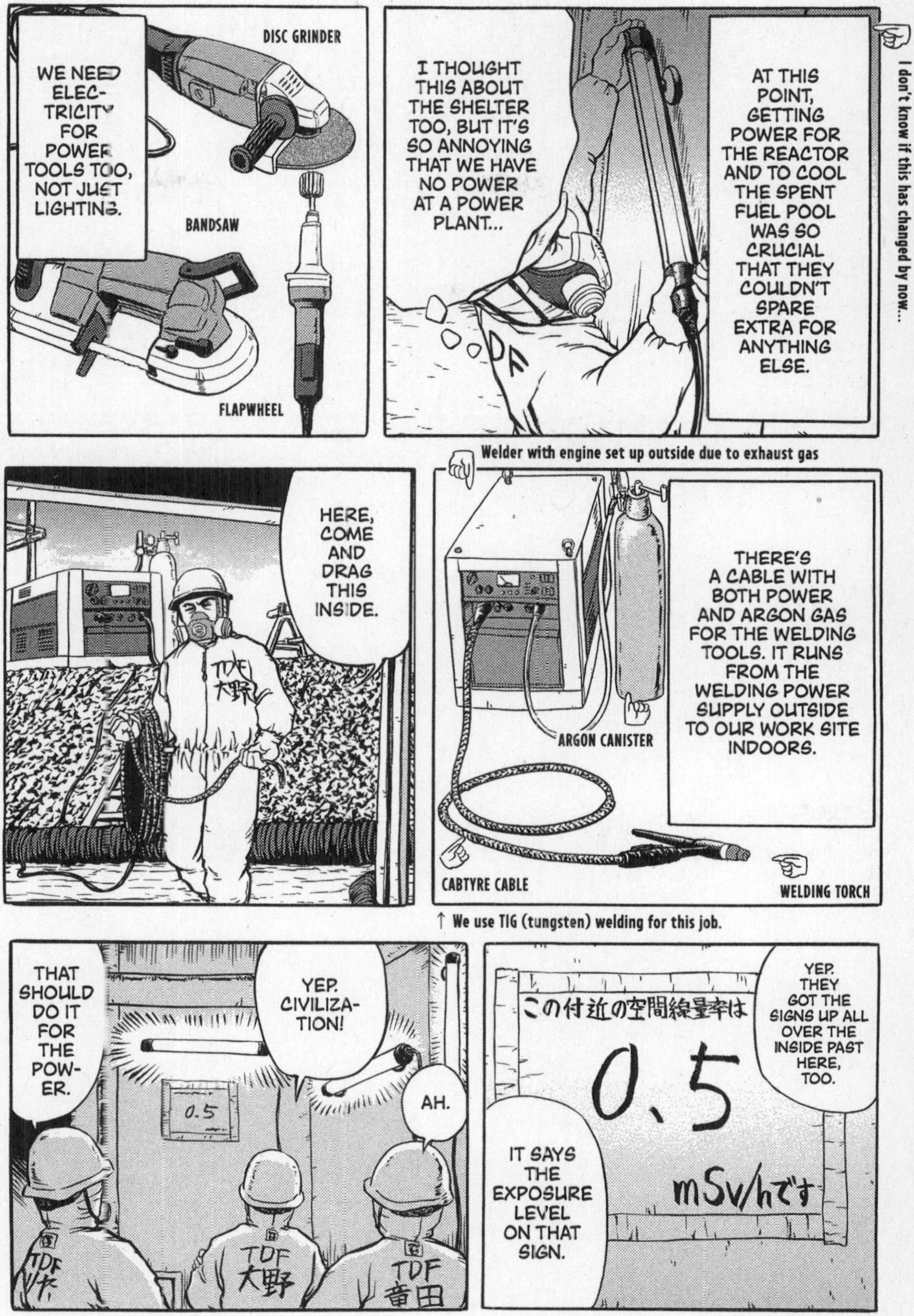
WE NEED ELEC-TRICITY FOR POWER TOOLS TOO, NOT JUST LIGHTING.
DISC GRINDER
BANDSAW
FLAPWHEEL
I THOUGHT THIS ABOUT THE SHELTER TOO, BUT IT'S SO ANNOYING THAT WE HAVE NO POWER AT A POWER PLANT...
AT THIS POINT, GETTING POWER FOR THE REACTOR AND TO COOL THE SPENT FUEL POOL WAS SO CRUCIAL THAT THEY COULDN'T SPARE EXTRA FOR ANYTHING ELSE.
I don't know if this has changed by now...
Welder with engine set up outside due to exhaust gas
HERE, COME AND DRAG THIS INSIDE.
TDF 大野
THERE'S A CABLE WITH BOTH POWER AND ARGON GAS FOR THE WELDING TOOLS. IT RUNS FROM THE WELDING POWER SUPPLY OUTSIDE TO OUR WORK SITE INDOORS.
ARGON CANISTER
CABTYRE CABLE
WELDING TORCH
↑ We use TIG (tungsten) welding for this job.
THAT SHOULD DO IT FOR THE POW-ER.
YEP. CIVILIZA-TION!
AH.
0.5
TDF 大野
TDF 竜田
YEP. THEY GOT THE SIGNS UP ALL OVER THE INSIDE PAST HERE, TOO.
この付近の空間線量率は
0.5
mSv/hです
IT SAYS THE EXPOSURE LEVEL ON THAT SIGN.
Sign: The atmospheric radiation here is 0.5 mSv/h

*Team member who measures radiation
OUTSIDE: 0.8
0.4
0.2
0.5
0.8
1.0
0.3
1.5
0.8
0.5
THE RADIATION NUMBERS ARE VERY DIFFERENT DEPENDING ON WHERE YOU STAND.
THE LEVELS ARE HIGHER AROUND THE PIPES THAT TRANSPORT HIGHLY-CONTAMINATED WASTE WATER, BUT THEY GET LOWER WITH A WALL IN BETWEEN.
THAT'S WHY, BEFORE WE START WORKING, TOOL STORAGE AND STANDBY LOCATIONS ARE SELECTED BASED ON TEPCO'S SURVEY MAP AND THE DATA COLLECTED BY OUR COMPANY'S MONITOR.*
THIS PRIOR PREPARATION IS VERY CRUCIAL, SO LET'S GO BACK IN TIME A BIT.
THIS SPOT HERE RUNS QUITE HOT, SO WHEN YOU NEED TO GO ON STANDBY AT THE SITE, GO HERE INSTEAD.
THERE'S LOTS OF STUFF TO DO BEFORE WORK, SUCH AS CONFIRMING RADIATION LEVELS, WORKFLOW, INSPECTING TOOLS, AND SO ON.
THIS IS ONE OF THE PARTS WE'LL BE ATTACHING ON THIS JOB.
YOU HAVE TO FIT THEM TOGETHER LIKE THIS, SO IN ORDER TO CUT DOWN ON THE ACTUAL ON-SITE TIME REQUIRED, YOU'RE GOING TO DO PREFAB, STARTING TOMORROW.
PREFAB? WE'RE GOING TO BUILD... PREFAB HOUSING?
DON'T BE AN IDIOT. WHY WOULD WE BUILD HOUSES?

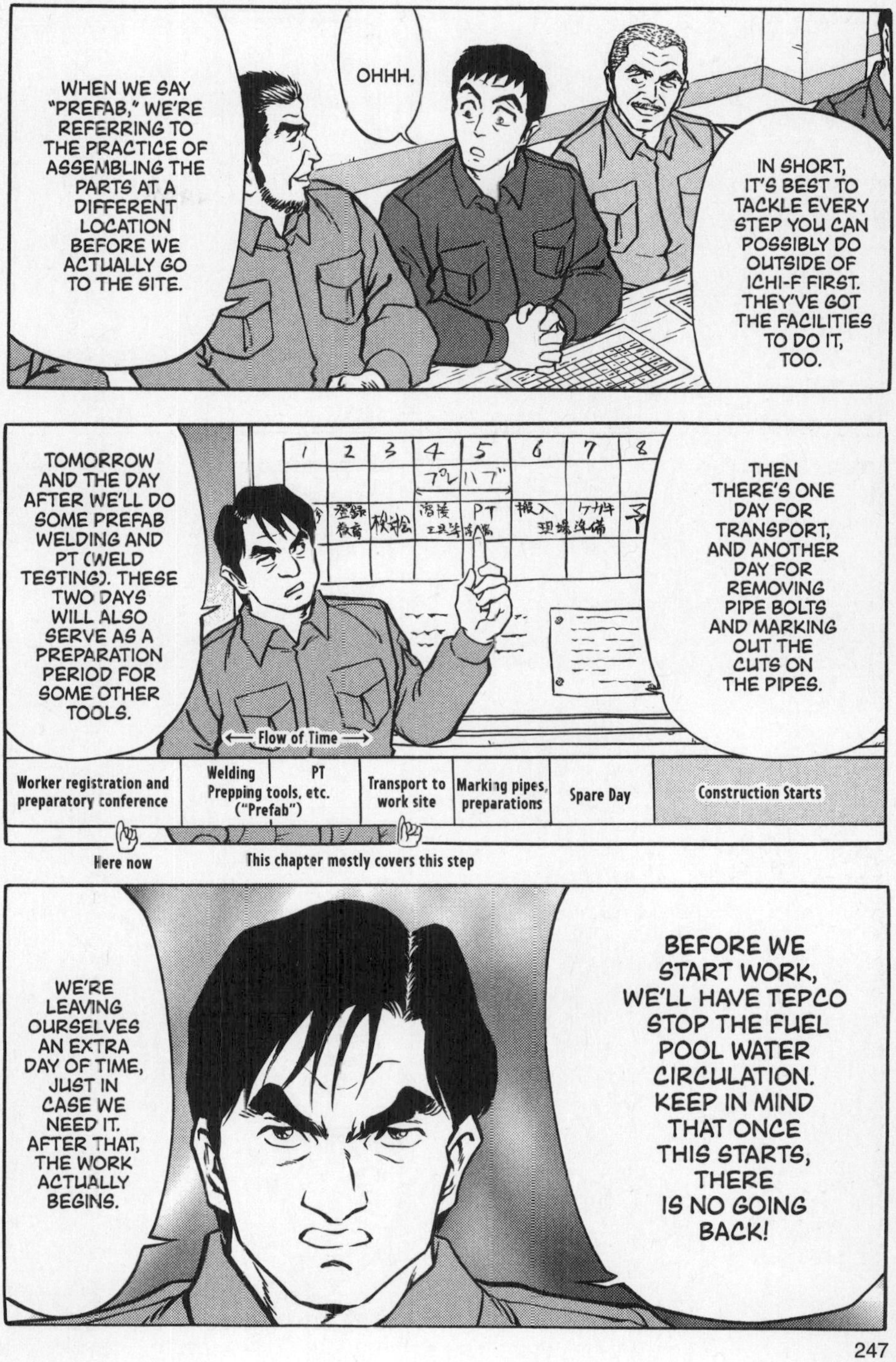
WHEN WE SAY "PREFAB," WE'RE REFERRING TO THE PRACTICE OF ASSEMBLING THE PARTS AT A DIFFERENT LOCATION BEFORE WE ACTUALLY GO TO THE SITE.
OHHH.
IN SHORT, IT'S BEST TO TACKLE EVERY STEP YOU CAN POSSIBLY DO OUTSIDE OF ICHI-F FIRST. THEY'VE GOT THE FACILITIES TO DO IT, TOO.
TOMORROW AND THE DAY AFTER WE'LL DO SOME PREFAB WELDING AND PT (WELD TESTING). THESE TWO DAYS WILL ALSO SERVE AS A PREPARATION PERIOD FOR SOME OTHER TOOLS.
THEN THERE'S ONE DAY FOR TRANSPORT, AND ANOTHER DAY FOR REMOVING PIPE BOLTS AND MARKING OUT THE CUTS ON THE PIPES.
1 2 3 4 5 6 7 8
← Flow of Time →
Worker registration and preparatory conference
Welding
PT
Prepping tools, etc.
("Prefab")
Transport to work site
Marking pipes, preparations
Spare Day
Construction Starts
Here now
This chapter mostly covers this step
WE'RE LEAVING OURSELVES AN EXTRA DAY OF TIME, JUST IN CASE WE NEED IT. AFTER THAT, THE WORK ACTUALLY BEGINS.
BEFORE WE START WORK, WE'LL HAVE TEPCO STOP THE FUEL POOL WATER CIRCULATION. KEEP IN MIND THAT ONCE THIS STARTS, THERE IS NO GOING BACK!

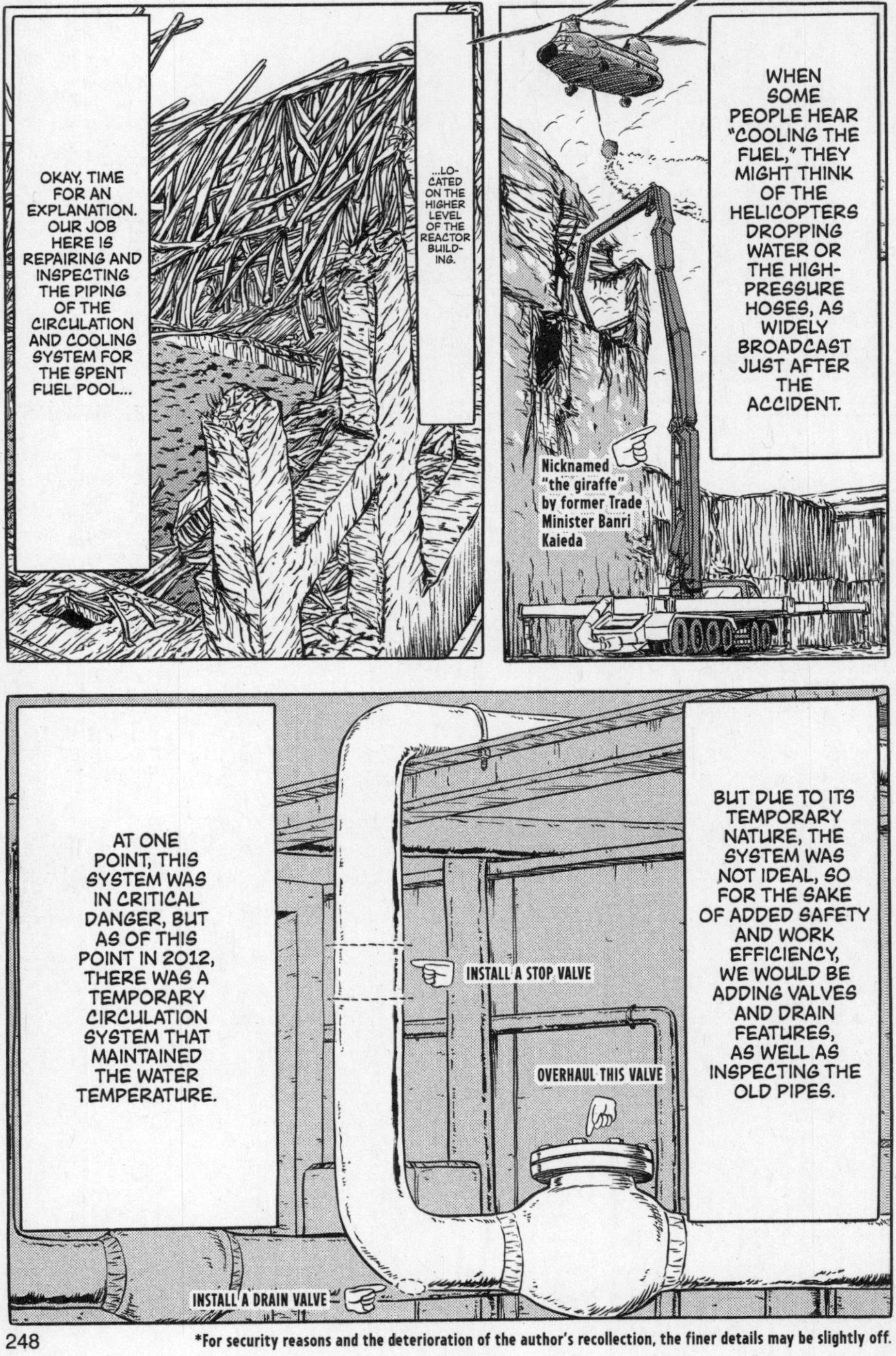
OKAY, TIME FOR AN EXPLANATION. OUR JOB HERE IS REPAIRING AND INSPECTING THE PIPING OF THE CIRCULATION AND COOLING SYSTEM FOR THE SPENT FUEL POOL...
...LOCATED ON THE HIGHER LEVEL OF THE REACTOR BUILDING.
WHEN SOME PEOPLE HEAR "COOLING THE FUEL," THEY MIGHT THINK OF THE HELICOPTERS DROPPING WATER OR THE HIGH-PRESSURE HOSES, AS WIDELY BROADCAST JUST AFTER THE ACCIDENT.
Nicknamed "the giraffe" by former Trade Minister Banri Kaieda
AT ONE POINT, THIS SYSTEM WAS IN CRITICAL DANGER, BUT AS OF THIS POINT IN 2012, THERE WAS A TEMPORARY CIRCULATION SYSTEM THAT MAINTAINED THE WATER TEMPERATURE.
BUT DUE TO ITS TEMPORARY NATURE, THE SYSTEM WAS NOT IDEAL, SO FOR THE SAKE OF ADDED SAFETY AND WORK EFFICIENCY, WE WOULD BE ADDING VALVES AND DRAIN FEATURES, AS WELL AS INSPECTING THE OLD PIPES.
INSTALL A STOP VALVE
OVERHAUL THIS VALVE
INSTALL A DRAIN VALVE

*For security reasons and the deterioration of the author's recollection, the finer details may be slightly off.

NATURALLY, WE CAN'T WORK ON THE PIPES IF THERE'S WATER RUNNING THROUGH THEM.
SO DURING THE SIX OR SO DAYS THAT THIS JOB LASTS, THE COOLING CIRCULATION TO THE SPENT FUEL POOL MUST BE STOPPED, AND THE WATER DRAINED FROM THE PIPES.
But not the water in the pool itself
This water is contaminated and needs to be collected, although it's not as bad as the reactor cooling water
IN OTHER WORDS, DURING CONSTRUCTION IT WILL HAVE THE SAME LACK OF COOLING THAT IT DID FOLLOWING THE ACCIDENT.
THIS MIGHT SOUND ALARMING TO YOU.
BUT UNLIKE AFTER THE ACCIDENT, THE WATER LEVEL OF THE POOL IS STABLE NOW, AND THE HEAT OF THE FUEL BREAKING DOWN IS LOWER, SO THERE AREN'T THE SAME TEMPERATURE SPIKES.
THAT DOESN'T MEAN THAT IT'S PERFECTLY SAFE TO KEEP THE COOLING SYSTEM OFF, OF COURSE, SO WE ABSOLUTELY MUST COMPLETE THE JOB ON SCHEDULE.
6
7
8
9
10
11
12
13
14
Construction Period
Transport
Marking
Spare
Pipe-cutting
Installing flanges
First pass welding
First pass PT
Second/final passes
Final PT, install valves
Cooling stopped
SO WE CAREFULLY PUT THE ITINERARY TOGETHER AND MAKE SURE WE'RE COMPLETELY PREPARED FOR EACH STEP.

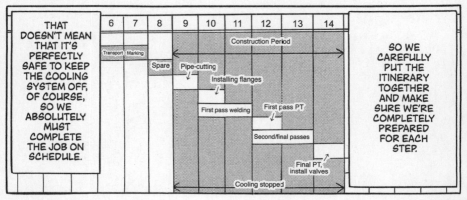

Sign: Tobishi Denko Fukushima Branch

THE DAY AFTER OUR INITIAL EXAMS IS PREFAB WORK.
東菱電工福島支社
MASTER CONTRAC-TOR'S WAREHOUSE IN IWAKI
OKAY, FLIP THAT SWITCH.
YES, SIR.
TSEEEEEE
Don't ever look directly at it!
WHOAAA ...

WE USE A METHOD CALLED TIG WELDING ON THE PIPES FOR ITS PRECISION.
WOW, IT'S SO CLEAN ...
THIS IS ON ANOTHER LEVEL FROM THE ARC WELDING I LEARNED DURING THE TRAINING COURSES.
BEFORE I CAME TO FUKUSHIMA, I EARNED QUALIFICATIONS IN VARIOUS SUBJECTS TO GIVE MYSELF A HIRING EDGE, LIKE HEAVY VEHICLES, CRANE OPERATION, GAS WELDING, AND ARC WELDING.
Me
OOH.
YOU GOT TALENT, PAL.
REALLY? THANKS.
SO I LEARNED TO APPRECIATE THE DIFFERENCE BETWEEN GOOD AND BAD WELDING, IN MY OWN AMATEUR WAY.
TWING
OKAY, RUB OFF THE SLAG NOW.
GOTCHA.
KRSHK
KRSHK
OOOOH ...
Having fun learning arc welding in Tokyo

The wave-like welding mark is called the "bead," and it's how you can tell the quality of the weld.

IT'S BEAUTIFUL!
THIS BEAD IS A WORK OF ART!!
OF COURSE, IT'S NOT FAIR TO COMPARE ARC WELDING OF THICK METAL PARTS TO THE PRECISION TIG WELDING OF PIPES.
BUT I COULDN'T HELP BUT MARVEL AT THE SKILL OF A TRUE PROFESSIONAL.
THEY MUST HAVE TRUE MASTERS OF THE CRAFT AT ICHI-F.
OKAY, LET'S PUT DOWN ANOTHER LAYER.
RIGHT!
FOR PARTS THAT REQUIRE EXTREME TOUGHNESS, A WELD MUST BE DONE IN SEVERAL LAYERS.
KWEEEE

THE PROCESS OF WELDING ACTUALLY INVOLVES MANY STEPS, WHICH IS WHY IT'S SO IMPORTANT THAT WE TAKE CARE OF EVERYTHING WE CAN BEFOREHAND, GIVEN OUR LIMITED TIME TO WORK IN ICHI-F.
WE FINISHED UP THE FIRST DAY OF PREFAB, SO THE NEXT DAY WILL BE CHECKING THE WELDS.
Sign: Tobishi Denko Fukushima

HERE YOU ARE, MR. ISOHARA.
THANK YOU.
THIS IS THE PENE-TRANT TESTING, OR PT STAGE, WHERE WE CHECK FOR THE PRE-SENCE OF TINY CRACKS IN THE WELDED AREA.
YOUR WORK IS AS GOOD AS EVER, MR. ONO.
CAN YOU ASSIST ME IN THE PT WORK, TATSUTA?
YES, SIR. I'LL DO WHATEVER YOU NEED.
PT IN-VOLVES SPREAD-ING A RED PENE-TRANT LIQUID ONTO THE WELD, THEN WIPING IT OFF.
NEXT, YOU SPRAY A WHITE POWDER ONTO IT. IF THERE ARE ANY CRACKS, THE RED WILL COME UP TO THE SURFACE WHERE YOU CAN SEE IT.
PSHT

I'M NOT SEEING ANYTHING.
JUST A FAINT BIT OF PINK.
IF THERE'S ANY DAMAGE, IT WILL BE CLEAR, BRIGHT RED.
OF COURSE, IT'S UNLIKELY THAT THERE WILL BE ANY CRACKS, GIVEN MR. ONO'S SKILL, BUT WE CANNOT AFFORD TO BE LAX ABOUT QUALITY CONTROL.
NOW WIPE IT CLEAN AGAIN.
OKAY.
YOU CAN TELL A COMPANY THAT DOES CRUCIAL CONSTRUCTION WORK TAKES THINGS SERIOUSLY.
WIPE
THEIR STANDARDS ARE VERY STRICT.
ALL RIGHT, PT IS FINISHED!
LET'S LOAD UP OUR MATERIALS FOR TRANSPORT.
YES, SIR.
AFTER OUR TWO-DAY PREFAB AND PREPARING ALL OF OUR EQUIPMENT, IT WAS FINALLY TIME TO TRANSPORT IT INTO THE BUILDING—THE SCENE THAT LED OFF THIS CHAPTER.

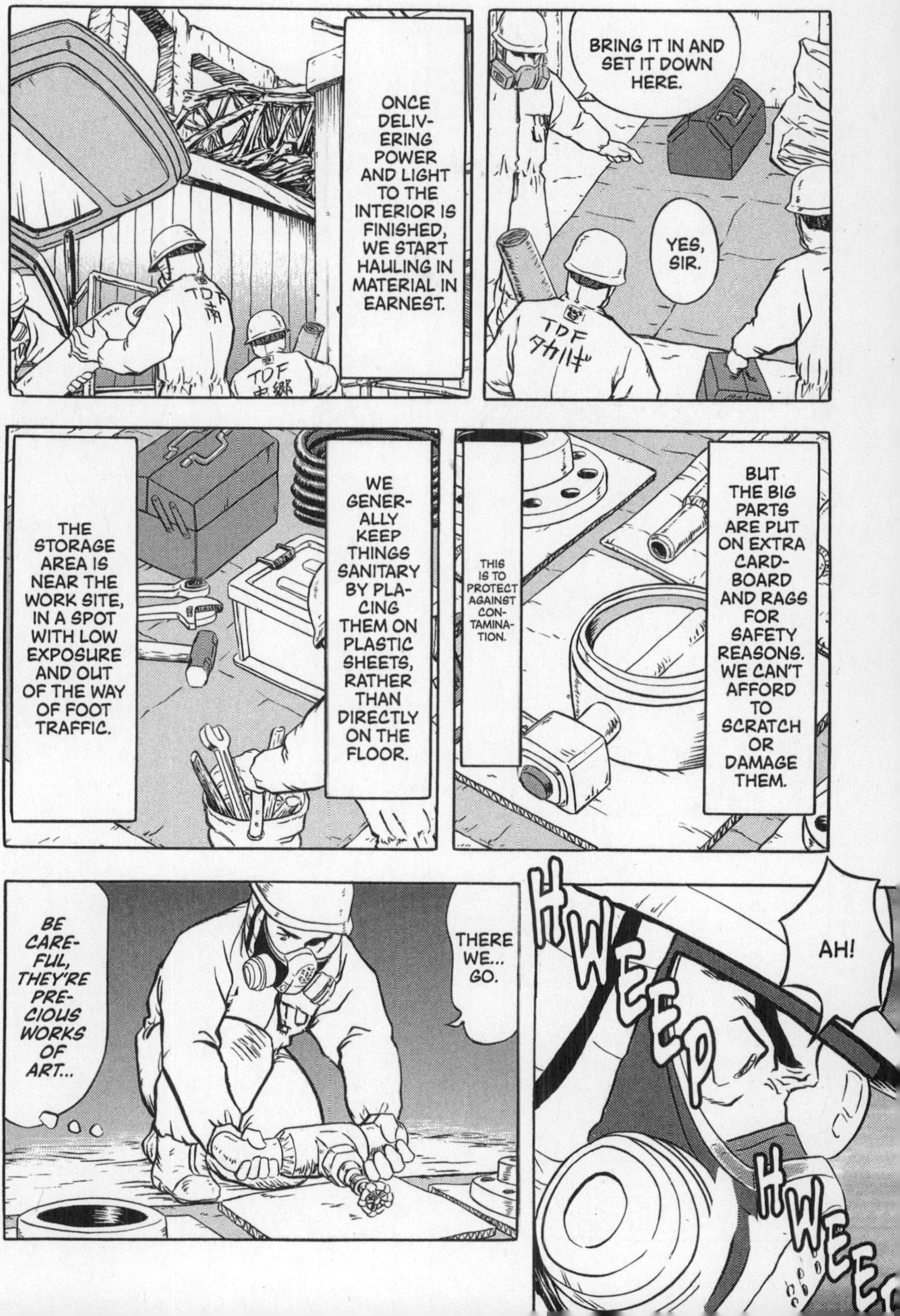
ONCE DELIVERING POWER AND LIGHT TO THE INTERIOR IS FINISHED, WE START HAULING IN MATERIAL IN EARNEST.
BRING IT IN AND SET IT DOWN HERE.
YES, SIR.
THE STORAGE AREA IS NEAR THE WORK SITE, IN A SPOT WITH LOW EXPOSURE AND OUT OF THE WAY OF FOOT TRAFFIC.
WE GENERALLY KEEP THINGS SANITARY BY PLACING THEM ON PLASTIC SHEETS, RATHER THAN DIRECTLY ON THE FLOOR.
THIS IS TO PROTECT AGAINST CONTAMINATION.
BUT THE BIG PARTS ARE PUT ON EXTRA CARDBOARD AND RAGS FOR SAFETY REASONS. WE CAN'T AFFORD TO SCRATCH OR DAMAGE THEM.
BE CAREFUL, THEY'RE PRECIOUS WORKS OF ART...
THERE WE... GO.
HWEEP
AH!

WHOA... I'VE NEVER HEARD MY OWN DEVICE GO OFF.
OH YEAH? HOW'S IT FEEL?
KIND OF EXCITING, ACTUALLY. LIKE I'VE FINALLY COME FAR ENOUGH FOR THIS THING TO COME IN HANDY!
YOU REALLY ARE CRAZY.
HWEEP
HWEEP
AAH!
YOUR FIRST TIME TOO, IZUMI?
YES.
THAT SCARED ME ...
WELL, IT SHOULD.
Since it's 0.8 mSv total, it will go off every 0.16 received
I GUESS WITH THIS HIGH A NUMBER, IT'S BOUND TO GO OFF EVEN-TUALLY.
0.5
ACTU-ALLY, THIS IS ONE OF THE COOLER SPOTS.
Even outside the buildings, there are places with about 1 mSv/h
OUR NUMBER FOR THE DAY IS POINT-EIGHT, SO OF COURSE IT'LL BEEP.
AS YOU MAY REMEM-BER, THE APD (ACTIVE PERSONAL DOSI-METER) IS SET SO THAT ITS ALARM GOES OFF AS IT REACHES EVERY FIFTH OF THE DAILY SET TOTAL.

SO GET BACK TO WORK, BEFORE IT BEEPS AGAIN!
YES, SIR!
I HAD THE SAME NUMBER AT THE REST AREA, 0.8 MSV, AND MY APD HAD NEVER GONE OFF ONCE WHEN I WAS THERE.
IT GIVES ME THE CHILLS TO THINK I'M HERE...
OUR SHIFT TODAY WAS SHORT, SO I WAS STILL SET AT 0.8, BUT ONCE WE GOT STARTED FOR REAL, IT WOULD BE 1.8 MSV.
0.21 mSv
THERE'S A LIMIT TO AN INDIVIDUAL WORKER'S YEARLY ALLOWED RADIATION LEVELS, SO THE WORK PLAN NEEDS TO ELIMINATE ANY UNNECESSARY EXPOSURE.
IS THERE STILL MORE?
THE REST IS EASY.
THAT'S WHY WE BRING IN EVERYONE TO DO SIMPLE STUFF LIKE TRANSPORTING EQUIPMENT, SO WE CAN GET IT OVER WITH QUICKLY.

Depending on the place and work, some have even higher numbers. Or so I hear.

It's just under 20 mSv for almost all the companies

WHAT DO YOU MEAN, "EASY"?
IT'S THE HEAVIEST THING!
Bandsaw
HUP!
URGH!
IS SOMETHING WRONG?
N... NO...
WHAT WAS THAT ...?
OWW, MY HEAD HURTS ...
THROB
THROB
DOES THAT MEAN ...
...I TIGHTENED THE STRAPS ON MY MASK TOO TIGHT?!

WEIRD. I'VE BEEN PUTTING ON THESE MASKS FOR FOUR MONTHS.
IT WAS FAMILIAR ENOUGH THAT I SHOULD'VE BEEN COMPLETELY AWARE OF HOW TIGHT TO FASTEN MY MASK.
TDF
竜田
AND IT'S A BEGINNER'S MISTAKE TO PULL IT ON TOO TIGHT OUT OF FEAR OF INHALATION.*
KTUNK
AFTER I TALKED BIG GAME ABOUT BEING EXCITED TO DO A HIGH-EXPOSURE JOB...
...AM I ACTUALLY TERRIFIED, DEEP DOWN?!

*Inhaling irradiated particles of dust

OH, RIGHT. I HAVE TWO TYVEKS ON, SO I CAN'T ACTUALLY REACH THE INNER BANDS TO LOOSEN THEM.
SCRATCH
SCRATCH
GEEZ, THIS IS HELL...
?
TDF
竜田

We remove the first layer to not take any contamination back with us
ALL RIGHT, THAT'S EVERYTHING.
LET'S HEAD BACK.
WHEW!
TDF 竜田
TDF 大野
TAKE OFF YER OUTER TYVEK RIGHT HERE.
FWAP
ZWIP
AND THE GLOVES GO IN HERE
We set up these dumping bags on the first day
THERE WE GO...
WHOOPS, HOLD ON.
TDF 木戸
DO YOUR BEST TO PEEL OVER THE DIRTY TYVEK YOU'RE REMOVING.
YOU WANT TO ROLL UP ANY CONTAMINATED MATERIAL INSIDE OF IT.
Your mom scolded you for undressing this way as a kid, but here it's the right way!
AND BE CAREFUL WHEN YOU TAKE YOUR FEET OUT. DO NOT STEP ON THE FLOOR! IT'LL GET YOU DIRTY ALL AT ONCE.
YIKES ...
URP
URP
TDF 大野
IT'S A PAIN JUST GETTING IN AND OUT OF HERE.
REMEMBER, ALL THE EXTRA LAYERS ARE IMPORTANT TO KEEPING YOU CLEAN AND SAFE.
TDF 泉
TDF 大野
We do discard the socks too, though

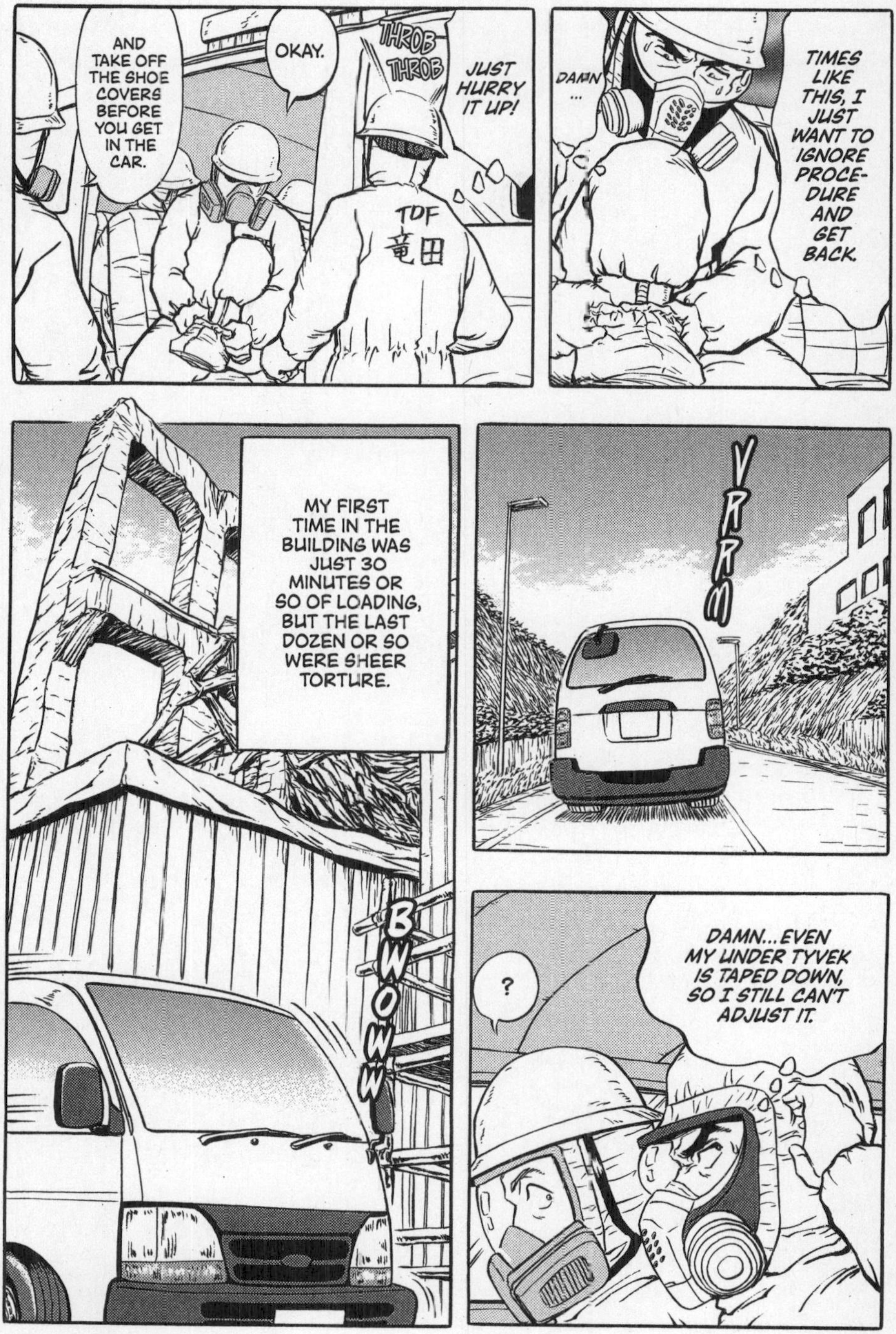
AND TAKE OFF THE SHOE COVERS BEFORE YOU GET IN THE CAR.
OKAY.
THROB THROB
JUST HURRY IT UP!
TDF 竜田
DAMN...
TIMES LIKE THIS, I JUST WANT TO IGNORE PROCEDURE AND GET BACK.
MY FIRST TIME IN THE BUILDING WAS JUST 30 MINUTES OR SO OF LOADING, BUT THE LAST DOZEN OR SO WERE SHEER TORTURE.
BWOWW
VRRM
?
DAMN... EVEN MY UNDER TYVEK IS TAPED DOWN, SO I STILL CAN'T ADJUST IT.

WHAT'S THE MATT- ER?
N-NO- THING...
I'M TOO EMBARR- ASSED TO ADMIT THAT I HAVE A HEADACHE FROM TIGHTENING MY MASK TOO MUCH.

Always disclose any physical issues!

MY RADIATION EXPOSURE FOR THAT DAY WAS 0.36 MSV.
===Personal Readout===
ID No.: xxxxxxx
APD No.: xxxxx
WID: xxxxx
Start: 2012/10/xx 10:05
End: 2012/10/xx 11:50
---Gamma Dose (mSv
Session: 0.36
---Beta Dose (mSv)---
Session: 0.0
---Active Time---
Session:
Print Date:
/xx/11:50:25
JUST 30 MINUTES OF WORK GAVE ME A DOSAGE A FULL DIGIT HIGHER THAN A DAY AT THE SHELTER.
NO MATTER HOW MUCH YOU UNDER- STAND AND PROPERLY ESTIMATE THE DANGERS OF YOUR DESTINATION IN YOUR HEAD, YOUR HEART AND BODY ARE MORE HONEST.
AAAAAGH!
MY FIRST TRIP INSIDE THE BUILDING WAS A VERY BITTER EXPER- IENCE.

Eight hours in the rest area gave me 0.03 mSv at the most

CHAPTER 9 - END

IWAKI, OCTOBER 2012
BEE-BEEP
BEE-BEEP
OH... GOOD MORNING.
MORNING.
BEEP...
4:45 AM
I SWITCHED TO A NEW ASSIGNMENT, BUT MY ROOMMATES ARE STILL WORKING SURVEY AT THE REST AREA.
YOU DON'T HAVE TO GET UP NOW.
NO, I'VE SLEPT ENOUGH.
WELL, WE'RE HEADING OFF, THEN.
STAY SAFE!
Nothing to do at night, so I sleep early
The rest area has to prepare to open, so they leave earlier
THERE'S A BIT OF TIME BEFORE I NEED TO LEAVE, BUT GOING BACK TO SLEEP IS DANGEROUS, SO THIS IS WHEN I ENJOY SOME COFFEE BEFORE DAWN.
Crappy instant stuff
NOW THAT I'VE MOVED TO CONSTRUCTION WORK INSTEAD OF MANAGERIAL DUTIES, MY DAILY SCHEDULE IS A BIT DIFFERENT.

CHAPTER 10:
N-1 ROUTE TO 1-F

THE PICKUP SPOT IS THIS LOCAL SUPERMARKET.

OOH, HELL OF A SUNRISE TODAY.

WITHOUT ANOTHER MEANS OF COMMUTING, I HAVE TO CATCH A COMPANY CAR TO WORK.

HERE THEY ARE.

VRRM

5:45 AM

HOP IN!

GOOD MORNING, GENTLEMEN.

IT'S A CARPOOL OF WORKERS FOR THE SAME SUBCONTRACTOR, HEADING TO J-VILLAGE.

N-1
MOR-NIN'!
HOP IN!
WE PICK UP A FEW MORE ALONG THE WAY.
N-1
N-1
THERE'S A PARKING LOT FOR A MAJOR PACHINKO PARLOR THAT WE OFTEN USE AS A MEETING LOCATION.
SINCE THEY OFTEN STOPPED IN TO PLAY SOME BIG ROUNDS OF PACHINKO, THE OWNERS WERE MORE THAN HAPPY TO LET US TAKE UP SPOTS THERE.
THERE WERE A NUMBER OF WORKERS WHO WOULD PARK THEIR OWN CARS HERE AND HITCH A RIDE IN THE COMPANY VEHICLE.
MOR-NING.

(I'm only assuming this.)

At this time, it was the newest machine out

FIRST ORDER OF BUSINESS IS YESTERDAY'S RESULTS.
WHICH ONE DIDJA PLAY?
I WAS PLUM OUTTA LUCK YESTERDAY.
ULTRAMAN TARO.
OH YEAH, WHEN YOU GET GOING, THAT ONE LASTS FOREVER.
ALONG THE WAY, WE STOP TO GET LUNCHES FOR LATER.
SHALL I HEAT THIS UP FOR YOU?
I'M NOT EATIN' IT YET!
BEEP
WHICH WAY ARE WE TAKIN' TODAY?
ROUTE 6 WILL ALREADY BE PACKED, SO LET'S TAKE SANROKU INSTEAD, SHALL WE?
EITHER WAY, IT'LL BE JAMMED.
PARDON ME ...
WHAT IS IT, TATSUTA?
YOU'RE TALKING ABOUT ROUTE 35, RIGHT?
県道
35
BUT *SANROKU* MEANS "36." WHY DO YOU CALL IT THAT?

TRUST ME, WE KNOW OUR NUMBERS.

IT AIN'T THE NUMBER. WE MEAN "SANROKU," THE WORD FOR THE FOOT OF A MOUNTAIN, LIKE WHERE WE'RE HEADING.

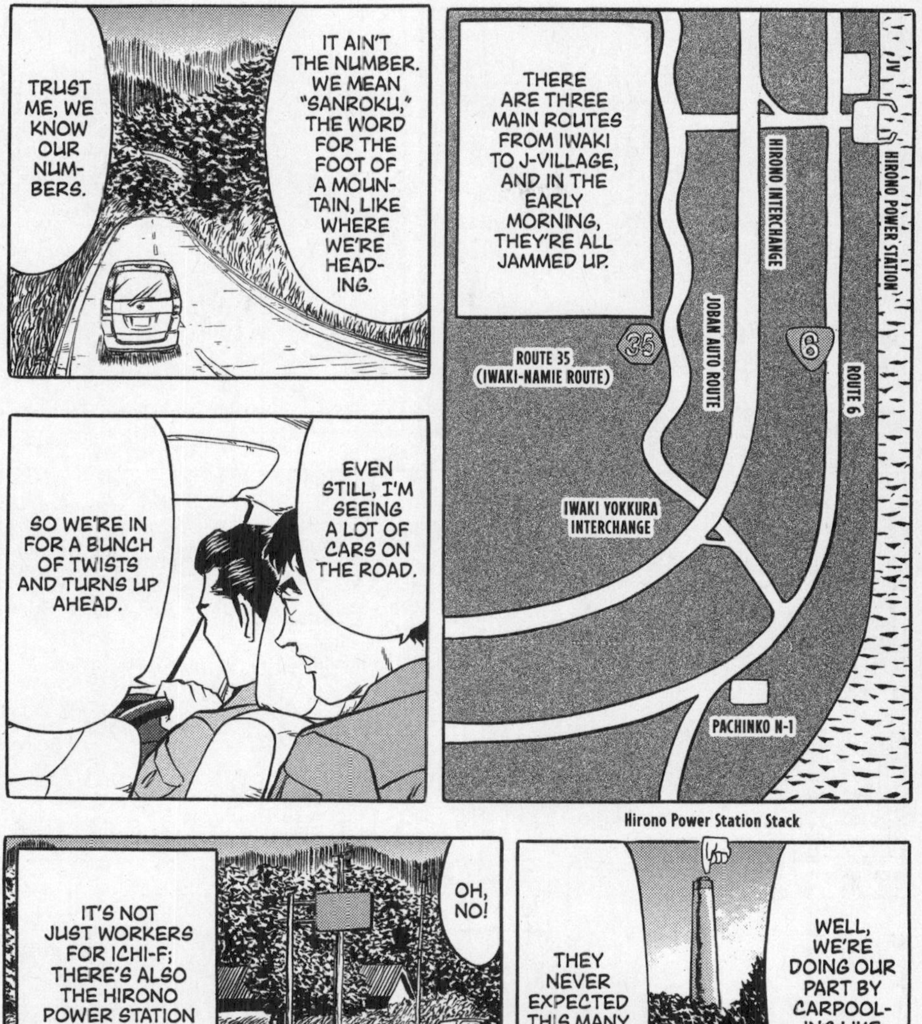

THERE ARE THREE MAIN ROUTES FROM IWAKI TO J-VILLAGE, AND IN THE EARLY MORNING, THEY'RE ALL JAMMED UP.

HIRONO POWER STATION

HIRONO INTERCHANGE

JOBAN AUTO ROUTE

ROUTE 6

ROUTE 35 (IWAKI-NAMIE ROUTE)

35

6

IWAKI YOKKURA INTERCHANGE

PACHINKO N-1

SO WE'RE IN FOR A BUNCH OF TWISTS AND TURNS UP AHEAD.

EVEN STILL, I'M SEEING A LOT OF CARS ON THE ROAD.

Hirono Power Station Stack

IT'S NOT JUST WORKERS FOR ICHI-F; THERE'S ALSO THE HIRONO POWER STATION AND OTHER CLEANUP WORKERS. THE RESULTING TRAFFIC IS WAY MORE THAN THIS LITTLE TOWN WAS MEANT TO HANDLE.

6:40 AM

OH, NO!

THEY NEVER EXPECTED THIS MANY PEOPLE TO EVER BE HERE ON A REGULAR BASIS.

WELL, WE'RE DOING OUR PART BY CARPOOLING LIKE THIS.

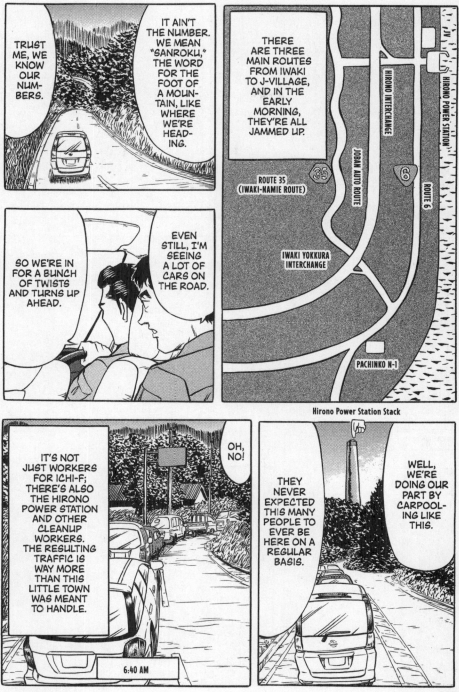

*See Chapter 8.

AT JV, WE DO OUR TBMKY.*
LET'S DO OUR BEST TO MINIMIZE THE DANGER!
THERE'S A GYM AND POOL ON THE JV CAMPUS, SO A FEW OF THE MASTER CONTRACTORS USE THEM AS CHANGING AREAS.

Sign: Miyoshi Sweets

IN THE VAN, WE PASS THROUGH THE FAMILIAR DESOLATE RESTRICTED ZONE ON THE WAY TO ICHI-F.
7:30 AM
AT LEAST HERE THE LIGHTS ARE ON, EVEN IF THEY'RE JUST BLINKING YELLOW.
OKUMA

OH, THAT'S RIGHT. THEY'RE OFF UP AHEAD...
YEP.
I SUPPOSE IT MEANS WE MIGHT BE ABLE TO MOVE BACK HERE EVENTUALLY...
MR. SAKAMOTO'S HOME IS AROUND HERE, SO THE STATE OF THE LIGHTS IS A SIGN OF HOPE THAT HE MIGHT ONE DAY BE ABLE TO LIVE THERE AGAIN.
カマタ

Building: Kamata

IN FACT, THE OPERATION OF THE TRAFFIC LIGHTS PROBABLY HAD NOTHING TO DO WITH THE LIKELIHOOD OF RETURNING. STILL, I FELT LIKE I CAUGHT A GLIMPSE INTO THE MENTALITY OF THOSE FORCED TO EVACUATE FROM THEIR HOMES.
AT THE TIME I WRITE THIS (AUGUST 2014) ALL THE LIGHTS ON ROUTE 6 ARE ON.
SO I BELIEVE THAT EVERY-ONE WILL BE ABLE TO RETURN SOME-DAY!

In September 2014, it became possible to drive through here without a pass.

AS ALWAYS, WHEN WE GET TO ICHI-F, OUR FIRST STEP IS BORROWING AN APD.
1.8, PLEASE.
HERE YOU GO. STAY SAFE.
8:00 AM

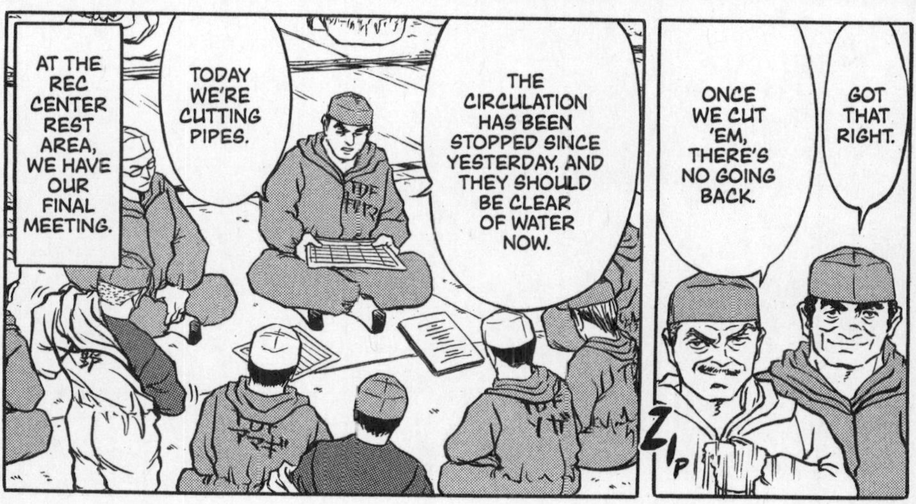
AT THE REC CENTER REST AREA, WE HAVE OUR FINAL MEETING.
TODAY WE'RE CUTTING PIPES.
THE CIRCULATION HAS BEEN STOPPED SINCE YESTERDAY, AND THEY SHOULD BE CLEAR OF WATER NOW.
ONCE WE CUT 'EM, THERE'S NO GOING BACK.
GOT THAT RIGHT.
ZIP

I THINK WE CAN DO THIS WITH THREE TEAMS ON ONE-HOUR SHIFTS.
TDF 大野
TDF 竜田
TDF キリヤマ
ONO, YOU'RE TEAM 1.
SAKA-MOTO, TEAM 2.
GOT IT.
YAMA-SHITA, TEAM 3.
YES.
TDF 坂元
EACH OF YOU, SELECT AN ASSISTANT AND A MONITOR.
THERE'S ALSO AN INSPECTION TEAM AND OTHER COMPANIES IN THERE. PAY CLOSE ATTENTION TO GENERAL SAFETY.
WHEN YOU'RE CUTTING PIPE AND SHOOTING SPARKS, PUT DOWN A FIREPROOF SHEET AND KEEP ANY INFLAMMABLES AT A SAFE DISTANCE.
AW-RIGHT, LET'S GO!
PFFT
OKAY!
STAY SAFE!
TODAY IT'S A THREE-MAN TEAM: VETERAN WORKER, ASSISTANT (ME), AND MONITOR.

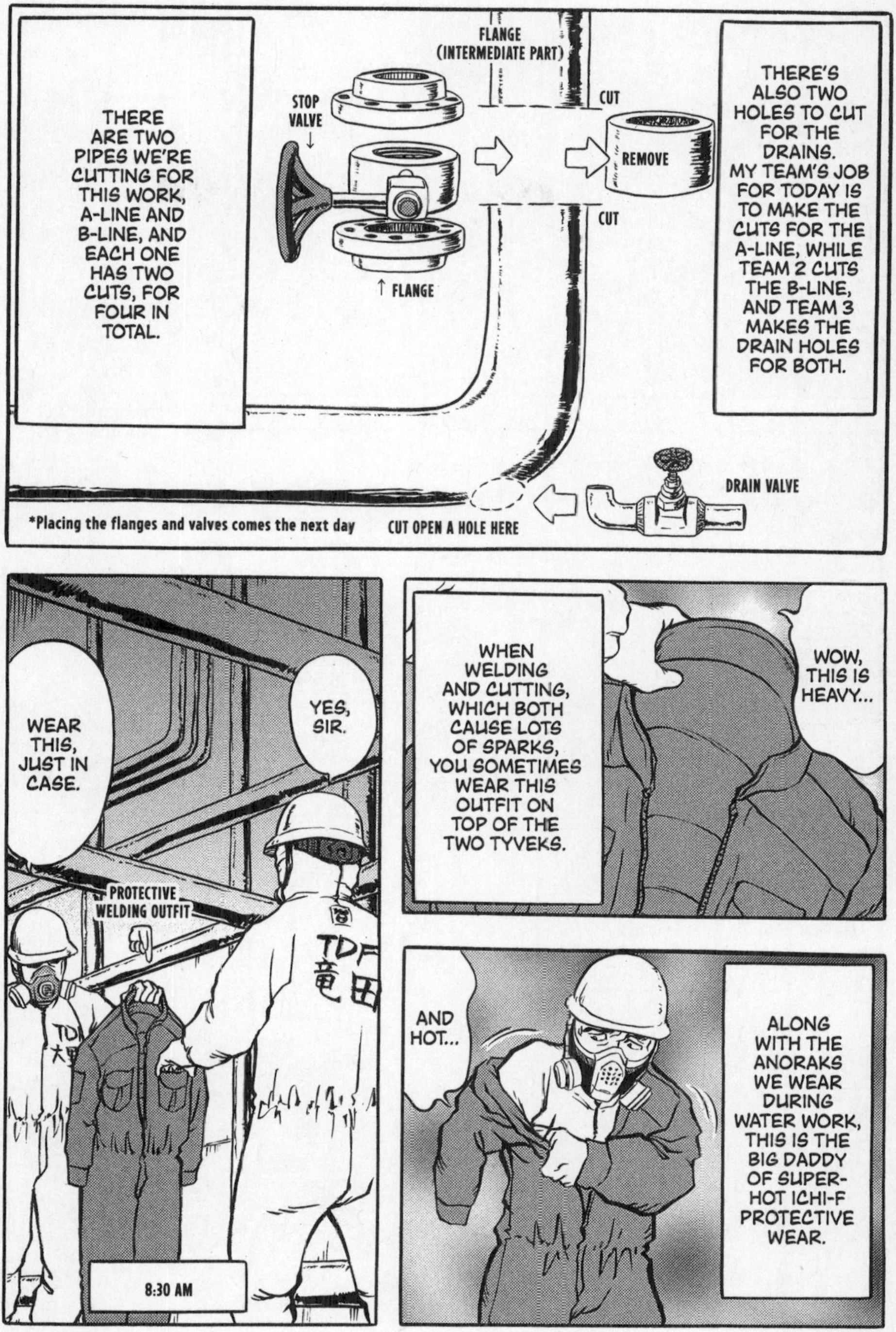

THERE ARE TWO PIPES WE'RE CUTTING FOR THIS WORK, A-LINE AND B-LINE, AND EACH ONE HAS TWO CUTS, FOR FOUR IN TOTAL.

FLANGE (INTERMEDIATE PART)

STOP VALVE

CUT

REMOVE

CUT

↑ FLANGE

THERE'S ALSO TWO HOLES TO CUT FOR THE DRAINS. MY TEAM'S JOB FOR TODAY IS TO MAKE THE CUTS FOR THE A-LINE, WHILE TEAM 2 CUTS THE B-LINE, AND TEAM 3 MAKES THE DRAIN HOLES FOR BOTH.

DRAIN VALVE

*Placing the flanges and valves comes the next day CUT OPEN A HOLE HERE

WEAR THIS, JUST IN CASE.

YES, SIR.

PROTECTIVE WELDING OUTFIT

8:30 AM

WHEN WELDING AND CUTTING, WHICH BOTH CAUSE LOTS OF SPARKS, YOU SOMETIMES WEAR THIS OUTFIT ON TOP OF THE TWO TYVEKS.

WOW, THIS IS HEAVY...

AND HOT...

ALONG WITH THE ANORAKS WE WEAR DURING WATER WORK, THIS IS THE BIG DADDY OF SUPER-HOT ICHI-F PROTECTIVE WEAR.

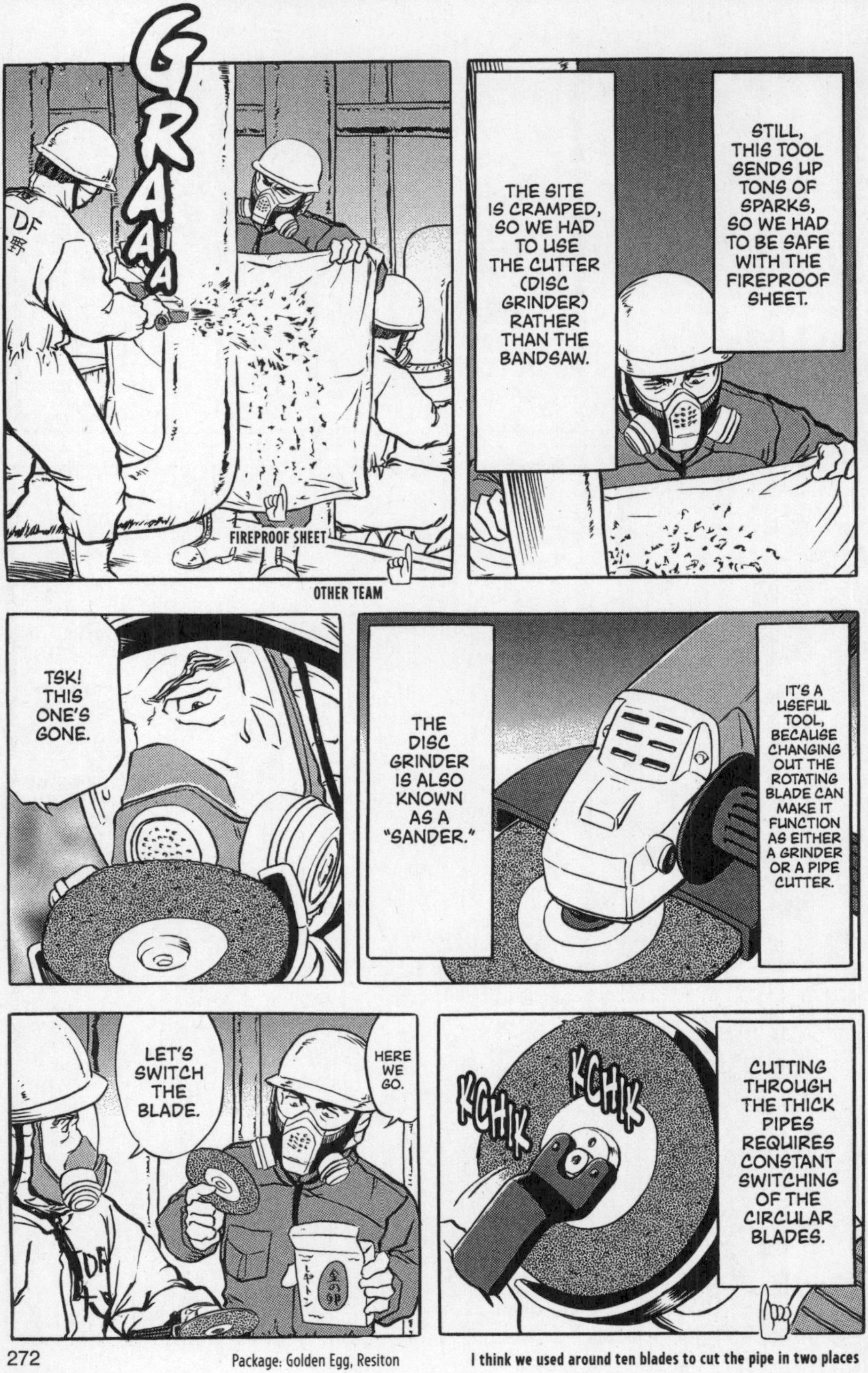
GRAAA
FIREPROOF SHEET
OTHER TEAM
THE SITE IS CRAMPED, SO WE HAD TO USE THE CUTTER (DISC GRINDER) RATHER THAN THE BANDSAW.
STILL, THIS TOOL SENDS UP TONS OF SPARKS, SO WE HAD TO BE SAFE WITH THE FIREPROOF SHEET.
TSK! THIS ONE'S GONE.
THE DISC GRINDER IS ALSO KNOWN AS A "SANDER."
IT'S A USEFUL TOOL, BECAUSE CHANGING OUT THE ROTATING BLADE CAN MAKE IT FUNCTION AS EITHER A GRINDER OR A PIPE CUTTER.
LET'S SWITCH THE BLADE.
HERE WE GO.
KCHIK
KCHIK
CUTTING THROUGH THE THICK PIPES REQUIRES CONSTANT SWITCHING OF THE CIRCULAR BLADES.

Package: Golden Egg, Resiton

I think we used around ten blades to cut the pipe in two places

DAMN, I WANT TO CUT THE PIPE, TOO!

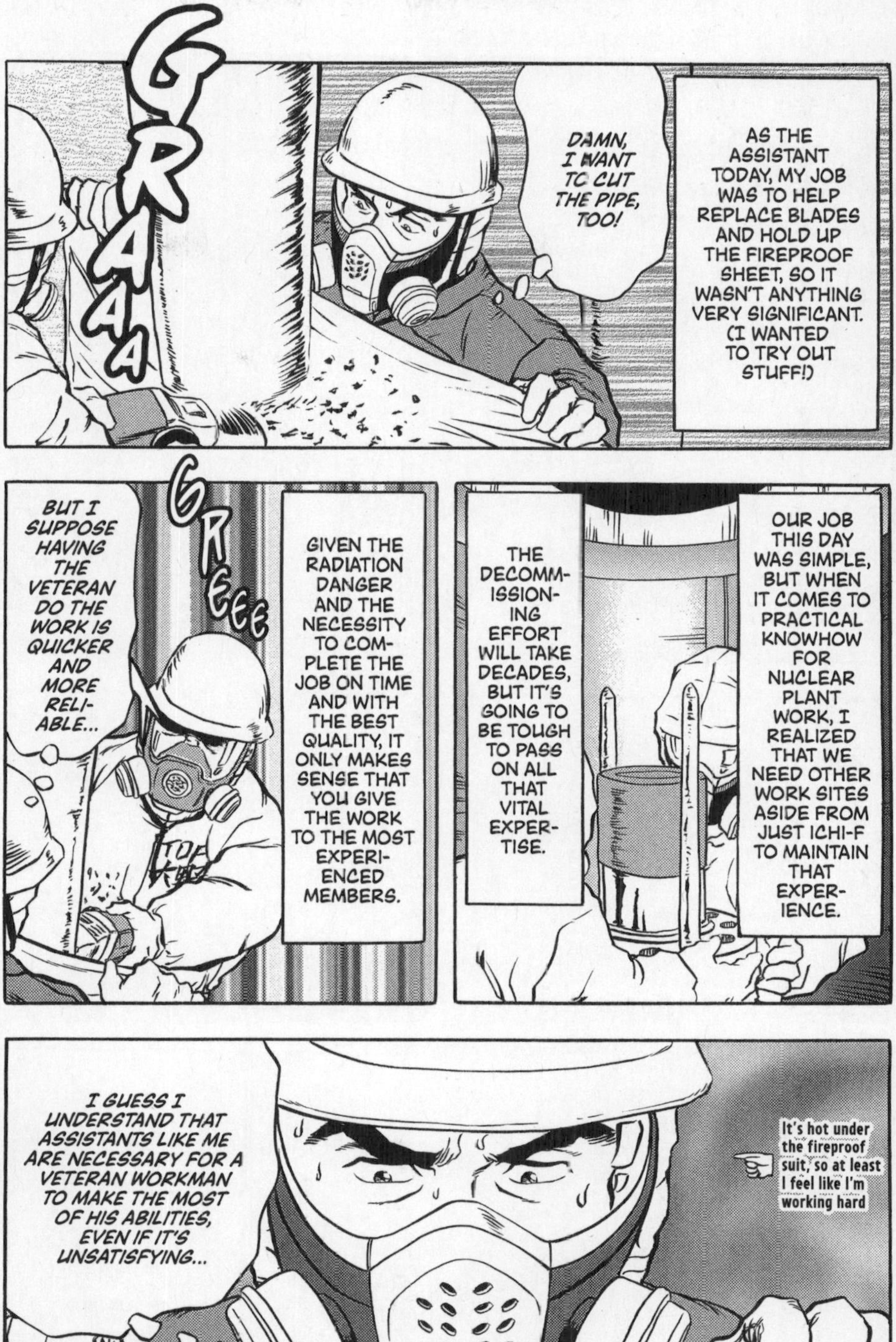

AS THE ASSISTANT TODAY, MY JOB WAS TO HELP REPLACE BLADES AND HOLD UP THE FIREPROOF SHEET, SO IT WASN'T ANYTHING VERY SIGNIFICANT. (I WANTED TO TRY OUT STUFF!)

BUT I SUPPOSE HAVING THE VETERAN DO THE WORK IS QUICKER AND MORE RELIABLE...

GIVEN THE RADIATION DANGER AND THE NECESSITY TO COMPLETE THE JOB ON TIME AND WITH THE BEST QUALITY, IT ONLY MAKES SENSE THAT YOU GIVE THE WORK TO THE MOST EXPERIENCED MEMBERS.

THE DECOMMISSIONING EFFORT WILL TAKE DECADES, BUT IT'S GOING TO BE TOUGH TO PASS ON ALL THAT VITAL EXPERTISE.

OUR JOB THIS DAY WAS SIMPLE, BUT WHEN IT COMES TO PRACTICAL KNOWHOW FOR NUCLEAR PLANT WORK, I REALIZED THAT WE NEED OTHER WORK SITES ASIDE FROM JUST ICHI-F TO MAINTAIN THAT EXPERIENCE.

I GUESS I UNDERSTAND THAT ASSISTANTS LIKE ME ARE NECESSARY FOR A VETERAN WORKMAN TO MAKE THE MOST OF HIS ABILITIES, EVEN IF IT'S UNSATISFYING...

It's hot under the fireproof suit, so at least I feel like I'm working hard

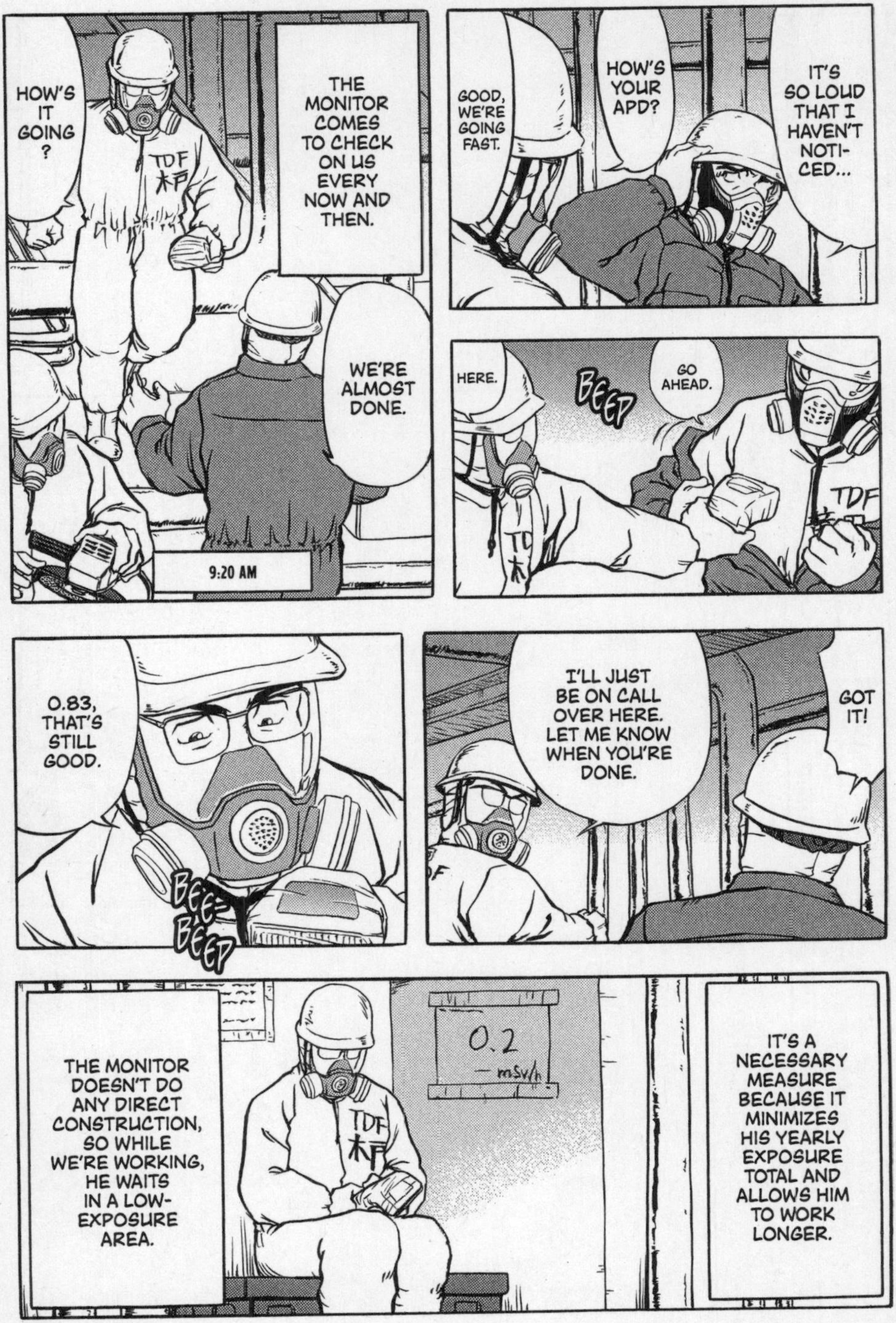

274

GRNNG
THERE, GOT IT!
TAKE THAT OUT TO THE ENTRANCE, AND I'LL PUT THE TOOLS AT THE NEXT SPOT.
RIGHT!
WHOA ...
THE INSIDE OF THE PIPE IS COATED WITH SLUDGE.
This is typically pretty irradiated
YEAH, THAT'S GOOD.
I THINK WE'LL MANAGE TO FINISH THE DAY'S QUOTA AT THIS RATE.
NICE WORK, GUYS.
WE'RE ALL DONE.
SO HOT!
TDF
WE SWITCHED OFF WITH TEAM 2 OUTSIDE THE REC CENTER.
YOU CAN GET THROUGH IT IN AN HOUR.
ALL RIGHT.
IF YOU RUN OUT OF REPLACEMENT BLADES, THERE ARE MORE AT THE TOOL STORAGE AREA.
GOT IT.
9:30 AM

*Rad-waste Building

YOU ALL RIGHT?
AIN'T THAT A LITTLE TOO MUCH?
MY BODY'S JUST FINE, IT'S MY QUOTA I'M WORRIED ABOUT.
IN THE REC CENTER, YOU ONLY GET 0.01 MSV A DAY, SO A WHOLE MILLISIEVERT IS A SHOCK TO THEM.
It's usually the lower-exposure workers who report here, too
WELL, TAKE CARE OUT THERE.
THANKS FOR THE CONCERN!
↓ The monitor got about 0.5 mSv
I'M BACK.
HEY, SIT DOWN AND RELAX!
HOW MUCH WAS IT?
THE MONITOR HAS TO MARK DOWN EVERYONE'S NUMBERS EACH DAY.
High-exposure workers must report this to TEPCO
1.02.
1.03 FOR ME.
Our numbers are similar because we were in the same place all day
TIME FOR LUNCH!
IT'S NOT YET TEN O'CLOCK, BUT I GOT UP EARLY AND JUST FINISHED MY WORK SHIFT, SO I'M STARVING.
9:50 AM
DANG, IT'S PRACTICALLY ROOM TEMP. STILL, TASTES GOOD.
We had a fridge during the Tateshiba Rest Area days

Carton: Rakuou Cafe Au Lait

I'VE FEATURED THIS BEVERAGE MULTIPLE TIMES IN THIS COMIC, AND GOT SOME ENTHUSIASTIC COMMENTS ABOUT IT.
MANY SIZE OPTIONS
酪王 カフェオレ
1000ml
500ml
300ml
200ml
There's also "high cafe au lait" with more coffee
RAKUOU CAFE AU LAIT IS A PROUD STAPLE OF FUKUSHIMA LIFE.
IT'S GOT A GOOD DAIRY SMOOTHNESS AND THE RIGHT LEVEL OF SWEETNESS, BUT BECAUSE IT'S MOSTLY DISTRIBUTED WITHIN FUKUSHIMA PREFECTURE, IT DOESN'T HAVE MUCH RECOGNITION NATIONWIDE.
GOTTA LOVE THE SMOOTH MOUTHFEEL, REFRESHING AFTERTASTE, AND RICH COFFEE SCENT...
As far as Tokyo goes, I've seen it on sale at the Shinjuku and Akiharabara JR stations, as well as the Fukushima goods shop in Nihonbashi and Yaesu.
BUT AS ATTENTION IS DRAWN TO FUKUSHIMA PRODUCTS IN THE WAKE OF THE DISASTER, THERE ARE MORE AND MORE FANS POPPING UP. IT'S BECOME A SYMBOL OF THE AREA'S REFUSAL TO BE A VICTIM.
AS A FAN OF THE DRINK, I'M ROOTING FOR THEM ALL THE WAY!
Package for national distribution
Fans gathered in Akihabara, 2013
BUT I ALSO GOT TONS OF LETTERS FROM FANS OF OTHER BRANDS!
DRAW BEKO-NO-CHICHI TOO!
EVERYONE WHO LIVES IN IWAKI DRINKS KIMURA MILK!
HOW ABOUT FUKU-CHAN CAFE AU LAIT?
MATSUNAGA ICE CREAM TREATS!
I'M SORRY, I'M SORRY.
FUKUSHIMA IS A DAIRY-RICH PREFECTURE, AND THERE ARE SO MANY DAIRY PRODUCTS I CAN'T POSSIBLY INTRODUCE THEM ALL.
Aizu Chuo Dairy "Aizu's Beko-no-Chichi"
Fukushima Dairy "Fuku-chan Cafe Au Lait"
べこの乳
手造り アイス まんじゅう
べこの乳発 会津の雪
Kimura Milk Plant "Kimura Pasteurized Cafe Au Lait"
AFTER THE ACCIDENT, THERE WERE CRUEL RUMORS THAT THEY WERE MIXING IN DAIRY FROM OTHER AREAS TO REDUCE RADIATION LEVELS. IN GENERAL, THERE'S BEEN A LOT OF UNFAIR STEREOTYPING OF THE FOOD SAFETY FROM THIS REGION. THE FACT THAT THEIR DAIRY INDUSTRY HAS REBOUNDED SO FIRMLY IS A TESTAMENT TO THE HARD WORK OF THE DAIRY FARMERS AND THE COMPANIES' STRICT QUALITY CONTROL. I'M MOVED BY THEIR EFFORTS!
Matsunaga Dairy "Ice Cream Buns"
"Beko-no-Chichi Snow of Aizu" Yogurt

SORRY ABOUT GETTING SIDETRACKED THERE. ANYWAY, ONCE I EAT LUNCH, I TAKE A NAP. WE CAN'T GO HOME UNTIL TEAMS 2 AND 3 FINISH ANYWAY, SO THERE'S NOTHING TO DO BUT SLEEP.
ONE HOUR OF ACTUAL WORK WITH A TWO-HOUR NAP, AND IT'S 20,000 YEN A DAY? THIS JOB IS PARADISE!
ZZZZZ
STILL, THERE'S LOTS OF PREP TIME AND GEARING UP, PLUS THE SALARY IS HIGH DUE TO THE DANGERS INVOLVED.
PLUS, I CAN ONLY WORK AT THE AMOUNT OF RADIATION I RECEIVED TODAY FOR 20 DAYS A YEAR, SO IT'S NOT EXACTLY THAT LUCRATIVE IN THE LONG RUN.
BUT SOME-ONE'S GOT TO DO IT.
WE'RE BACK! TEAM 3'S ALL DONE.
WEL-COME BACK.
TODAY'S MISSION IS COM-PLETE.
LET'S GET GOING, THEN.
11:50 AM

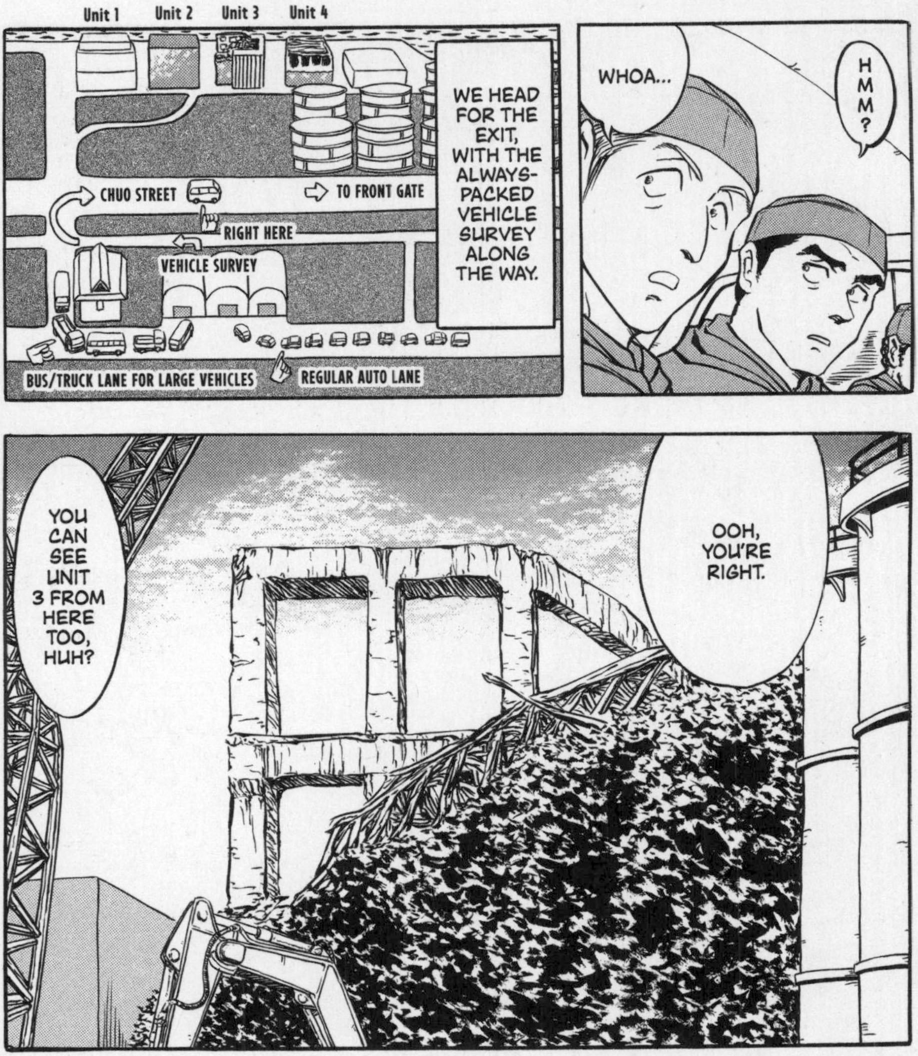
Unit 1
Unit 2
Unit 3
Unit 4
CHUO STREET
TO FRONT GATE
RIGHT HERE
VEHICLE SURVEY
BUS/TRUCK LANE FOR LARGE VEHICLES
REGULAR AUTO LANE
WE HEAD FOR THE EXIT, WITH THE ALWAYS-PACKED VEHICLE SURVEY ALONG THE WAY.
WHOA...
HMM?
YOU CAN SEE UNIT 3 FROM HERE TOO, HUH?
OOH, YOU'RE RIGHT.
ONCE THEY CLEAR THE UPPER RUBBLE, IT WON'T BE VISIBLE FROM HERE.
IT'S A DIFFERENT ANGLE FROM USUAL, SO THE SIGHT IS NOVEL.
相馬焼
BACK THROUGH THE RE-STRICTED ZONE TO JV.

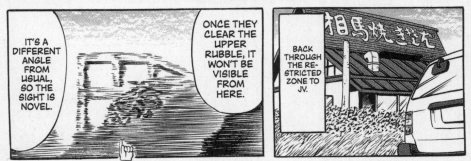

The higher wreckage has been taken away, so you can't see it from Chuo St. anymore

Roof: Somayaki Pottery

Sign: Thank you for your work

We split up into different directions, so the traffic isn't as bad

The old name for the JR Iwaki Station

WHERE YA GOIN'?
I THOUGHT I'D VISIT THE BATH-HOUSE ON THE WAY HOME.
OUR APART-MENT ONLY HAD A SHOWER.
EXCUSE ME, CAN YOU DROP ME OFF AT TAIRA STATION?
YEAH, SURE.
仲の湯
↑2F 入口
防犯連絡所
THE BATH? IT'S NOT OPEN YET, IS IT?
ACTUALLY, IT OPENS RIGHT AT TWO O'CLOCK.
THANKS FOR THE RIDE.
WELL, SO LONG...
IT SEEMS LIKE A PRETTY LUXURI-OUS DAY, BUT THE SAD THING IS THAT YOU CAN'T ACTUALLY WORK LIKE THIS FOR VERY LONG AT ICHI-F
PHEWWW!
AND SO I END MY WORK-DAY BY BEING THE VERY FIRST GUY INTO THE BATH.
2:10 PM

Sign: Nakanoyu, entrance on second floor

Vertical Sign: Crime-Prevention Office

Strange location - on the second floor of a mixed-use building

CHAPTER 10 - END

JOBAN LINE, TATSUTA STATION

EARLIER IN THE BOOK IT WAS SAID THAT THIS STATION WAS OUT OF SERVICE, BUT AS OF JUNE 1ST, 2014, THE HIRONO-TATSUTA LINE WAS OPEN AGAIN. TOMIOKA STATION, WHICH IS THE NEXT ONE TO THE NORTH, IS STILL CLOSED, SO FOR THE MOMENT, TATSUTA STATION IS THE END OF THE NORTHBOUND LINE FROM IWAKI, THOUGH IT WILL BE OPEN ALL THE WAY TO TOMIOKA STATION BY 2017. CITIZENS ARE FREE TO WALK THROUGH THE AREA AROUND THE STATION TO HELP PREPARE FOR THE REPEAL OF THE RESTRICTED ZONE, BUT STAYING OVERNIGHT IS STILL FORBIDDEN.

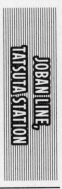

THE AUTHOR VISITED AT THE END OF 2014 AND FOUND THAT THE VENDING MACHINES OUTSIDE THE STATION HAD POWER AGAIN, AND SOME CONTAINED BEVERAGES THAT AREN'T SOLD ANYMORE. AND YET, THE POSTAL BOX OUT FRONT IS STILL COVERED WITH SHEETS.

I WORKED AT ICHI-F FROM JUNE TO DECEMBER 2012.
竜田一人
福島第一原子力発電所労働記（1）
All my inking is done with a fine-point brush
THE FOLLOWING YEAR, I TOOK ON A PEN NAME AND BEGAN TO DEPICT MY EXPERIENCES IN COMIC FORM, AS A "MASKED AUTHOR."
Technically, it was my nuclear plant work where I wore the masks!
AS A MATTER OF FACT...
立芝 WWE/UFC タツタ
VWOM
SKREE
THE PRIMARY REASON TO HIDE MY IDENTITY WAS TO NOT CAUSE TROUBLE FOR THE COMPANIES AND PEOPLE I WORKED WITH.
IT WAS A GOOD THING I DID.
CREAK
CHK
BUT I ALSO DID IT BECAUSE I WANTED THE ABILITY TO CONTINUE WORKING AT ICHI-F.

CHAPTER 11:
THE WORKER WITH A GUITAR
WOW... THEY REALLY DID FLATTEN IT DOWN!

I WAS ALSO WORKING AT ICHI-F THIS YEAR, 2014.
*THIS IS THE EXTERIOR OF THE UNIT 3 REACTOR BUILDING AS OF 2014.
TS TATESHIBA
WWE/UFC
タツタ

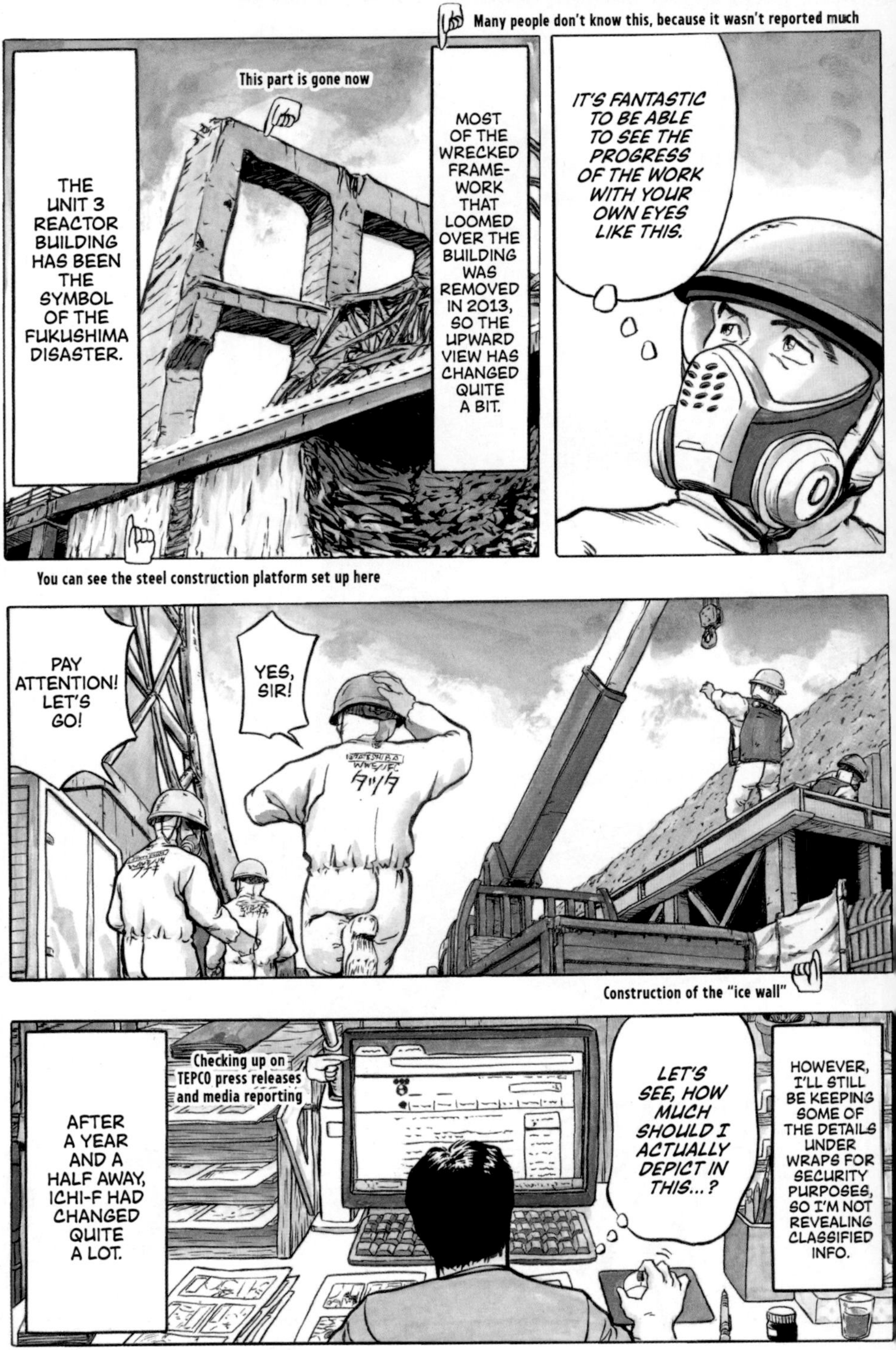

Many people don't know this, because it wasn't reported much
This part is gone now
THE UNIT 3 REACTOR BUILDING HAS BEEN THE SYMBOL OF THE FUKUSHIMA DISASTER.
MOST OF THE WRECKED FRAME-WORK THAT LOOMED OVER THE BUILDING WAS REMOVED IN 2013, SO THE UPWARD VIEW HAS CHANGED QUITE A BIT.
IT'S FANTASTIC TO BE ABLE TO SEE THE PROGRESS OF THE WORK WITH YOUR OWN EYES LIKE THIS.
You can see the steel construction platform set up here
PAY ATTENTION! LET'S GO!
YES, SIR!
Construction of the "ice wall"
AFTER A YEAR AND A HALF AWAY, ICHI-F HAD CHANGED QUITE A LOT.
Checking up on TEPCO press releases and media reporting
LET'S SEE, HOW MUCH SHOULD I ACTUALLY DEPICT IN THIS...?
HOWEVER, I'LL STILL BE KEEPING SOME OF THE DETAILS UNDER WRAPS FOR SECURITY PURPOSES, SO I'M NOT REVEALING CLASSIFIED INFO.

Using Twitter to avoid doing work

OOH, I GOT A DM.

Nice to meet you! Thanks for reading my comic. I'm very pleased that it's meeting the approval of a local citizen.

AS A MATTER OF FACT, THIS ISN'T THE FIRST TIME WE'VE MET...

CLICK

CLICK

From a friend in real life

Nice to meet you! Sorry about DMing you out of the blue. I was surprised to see pictures of my area on your account. Can't wait for more Iwaki pics!

OH.

NATURALLY, I'VE KEPT THE FACT THAT I'M DRAWING THIS COMIC A SECRET FROM ALL MY LOCAL ACQUAINTANCES, NOT TO MENTION MY ICHI-F ASSOCIATES.

I HAVE TO ADMIT, HIDING MY IDENTITY FROM PEOPLE I ACTUALLY KNOW AND LIKE...

...IS A VERY PAINFUL THING AT TIMES...

WITH MY INCREASED PRESENCE ON THE INTERNET, THIS MEANS I FEEL MORE AND MORE GUILTY ABOUT WHAT I'M DOING.

Button: Send Message

AFTER MY FIRST VOLUME CAME OUT...

I read your manga!

OH, YOU KNEW IT WAS ME?

...ONE OF THE GUYS WHO WORKED WITH ME AT THE REST AREA FIGURED IT OUT.

THERE ARE PROBABLY OTHERS AROUND ME WHO HAVE FIGURED IT OUT.
IF TEPCO OR THE CONTRACTORS WERE REALLY, TRULY INTERESTED, THEY WOULD BE ABLE TO ROOT ME OUT WITH NO TROUBLE.
IN A FEW CASES, I ALSO REVEALED IT MYSELF.
I'm sorry, I used you as a model in my story.
REALLY?

Former roommate (since we might live together again)

AND DESPITE LETTING MANY SUBCONTRACTORS KNOW THAT I WANTED TO WORK AT ICHI-F AGAIN, THE FACT THAT I HAD NO LEADS FOR A YEAR AND A HALF WAS TROUBLING ME.
I've got a job for you. Are you in?
I'M IN, I'M IN!
THAT WAS THE PART THAT WORRIED ME THE MOST ABOUT GOING BACK TO WORK AT ICHI-F.

I wondered if there was a "Do Not Hire" poster going around with my face on it...

ARE YOU MR. TATSUTA? COME IN THE BACK SO WE CAN TALK...
HUH?
WHAT IF THEY'RE JUST SETTING ME UP?
I'LL BE TAKING AN ID PHOTO. READY?
SO EVEN WHEN I FINALLY DID HEAR BACK ON A PROMISING LEAD AND FOUND MYSELF IN J-VILLAGE AGAIN DOING WORKER REGISTRATION...

There are female employees at J-Village too

I EXILE THEE FROM ICHI-F!
YES, MY LORD!
OUT-OF-CONTROL IMAGINATION
...I WAS WORRYING MYSELF TO DEATH UNTIL I FINALLY GOT MY ENTRY PASS.
HERE YOU GO.
タツタカズト
竜田 一人
Covered with a plastic layer to make copying harder!
SO WHEN I GOT USHERED RIGHT THROUGH THE PROCESS, IT ALL FELT RATHER SILLY.
THANK YOU.

Also thinking that it would make for good story material

Badge: Tokyo Electric WID (1-F) Tatsuta, Kazuto

WELL, THAT MAKES SENSE. AS LONG AS I'M NOT DEPICTING ANYTHING THAT COULD JEOPARDIZE THE SECURITY OF THE OPERATION, IT SHOULDN'T BE A PROBLEM.
I SUPPOSE THERE'S NO REASON A HUGE COMPANY LIKE TEPCO WOULD FEEL THE NEED TO EXPOSE A SINGLE LITTLE MAN LIKE ME.

THAT DOESN'T MEAN I INTEND TO REVEAL MY IDENTITY, BUT IT AT LEAST RELAXED SOME OF THE APPREHENSION I'D BUILT UP OVER TIME.
I SUPPOSE I CAN DRAW MORE PERSONAL STORIES OUTSIDE OF ICHI-F, THEN.
IT'LL PROBABLY REVEAL ME TO MY FRIENDS IN IWAKI, BUT IT WOULD BE SILLY TO KEEP THAT A SECRET FOREVER.
SOME EVENTS OUTSIDE OF MY WORK DURING THIS STINT AT ICHI-F WERE VERY MEMORABLE, SO I'D LIKE TO TAKE THIS OPPORTUNITY TO DEPICT THEM.

WE DON'T CARE WHAT YOU WERE DOING IN YOUR PRIVATE TIME! REPORT ON THE SHOCKING TRUTHS OF THE NUCLEAR INDUSTRY!
I'M SORRY, I'M SORRY.
SOME MIGHT DESIRE A MORE INCISIVE LOOK, BUT I HOPE YOU'LL ACCEPT THIS STORY AS A GLIMPSE INTO THE AREAS THE DISASTER AFFECTED.
ANYWAY, EVEN ICHI-F WORKERS LIKE TO HIT THE TOWN AT NIGHT AND GO DRINKING.
Nakanoyu, the bathhouse I visited after work
IN THEIR OFF-HOURS, THE WORKERS LIKE THEIR BOOZE, GAMBLING, AND WOMEN.
鎌倉御殿
アイドル
ASIDE FROM THESE VICES, MANY OF US ENJOY HEALTHIER PURSUITS LIKE FISHING, MOTORCYCLES, AND SURFING.
AS FOR ME, I LIKE TO PLAY THE GUITAR (BADLY) AND SING.
Trying to make myself look better
WHEN I GET BACK TO IWAKI AFTER A DAY AT ICHI-F, THERE ARE TWO PLACES I ALWAYS WANT TO VISIT.
ONE IS A LIVE-MUSIC BAR I GOT TO KNOW TWO YEARS AGO.
BAR QUEEN
I'LL START THIS CHAPTER HERE.

Superhuman acoustic fingerpicking

They always judge the new guys

The flower of life / between the crests / of the waves... ♪
RAHH
NO WAY, HE'S SINGING TRADITIONAL *ENKA* SONGS?!
WAY TO GO!
AT PLACES LIKE THIS, VIRTUALLY EVERYONE PLAYS GUITAR, PERFORMING FOLK OR ROCK COVERS, OR THEIR OWN ORIGINAL SONGS.
Between my brother and I... ♪
BUT I LOVE ENKA AND OLD-FASHIONED TRADI-TIONALS.
HEY, THAT WAS GREAT! (EXCEPT FOR THE GUITAR-PLAYING.)
THANKS.

Sign: Welcome to music city Koriyama, Vienna of the Northeast

ALL RIGHT, SING ALONG! HEY-HEY-HO!
BY LEADING OFF WITH THIS, I WAS LUCKY ENOUGH TO EARN THE LOCAL MUSIC COMMUNITY'S APPROVAL AND MAKE SOME FRIENDS OUTSIDE OF WORK. IT'S WHY I REALLY WANTED TO COME BACK.
HEY-HEY-HO!
UNTIL I ACTUALLY VISITED FUKUSHIMA, I NEVER REALIZED WHAT A MUSICALLY-ACTIVE AREA IT WAS. THERE ARE AMATEUR MUSICIANS EVERYWHERE.
♪ようこそ♪
楽都
東北のウィーン
郡山

The "Vienna" part is most definitely self-appointed...

THE STUDENT CHORUS HERE WINS NATIONAL COMPETITIONS NEARLY EVERY YEAR.
IN THE FALL, TOWNS HERE AND THERE HOLD OUTDOOR MUSICAL EVENTS WHERE MUSIC ACTS PERFORM ON THE STREET.
OUTDOOR CONCERT IN IWAKI

There's also "Koriyama Outdoor Sound Stage," "Kitakata Sound on the Town Concerts," etc.

THEY'VE GOT AS MUCH MUSIC AND PASSION FOR IT AS TOKYO!
IN FACT, THEY'RE EVEN MORE ENTHUSIASTIC!
NOW THAT I'VE MADE MY TRIUMPHANT RETURN TO IWAKI'S EXCITING MUSIC SCENE, THERE'S ONE OTHER PLACE I'VE GOT TO VISIT AGAIN...
I'M BACK, IWAKI!
WOOOO!!

IT'S JUST ONE OF MANY TEMPORARY HOUSING BUILDINGS AROUND IWAKI.
ひまわり

Sign: Futaba Town Support Center Himawari

GOOD AFTER-NOON.
HELLO.
UHM, AND YOU ARE?
I CAME HERE ONCE TO SING, TWO YEARS AGO. I WAS HOPING THAT I MIGHT BE ABLE TO DO THAT AGAIN.
I CAN'T BLAME HIM FOR NOT RECOGNIZING ME.
双葉町サポートセンター
ひまわり

I'm using a falsified name for this place

EVEN BEFORE THE DISASTER, I HAD A PRACTICE OF VISITING RETIREMENT HOMES TO CHEER UP THE ELDERLY.
YOU WANNA VOLUNTEER? SHINKAWA HERE WILL SHOW YOU AROUND THE GOOD SPOTS.
YOU SING ENKA WITH THE GUITAR? NICE!
TWO YEARS AGO, WHEN I TOLD KUROMORI CONSTRUCTION THAT I WANTED TO SING FOR THE ELDERLY IN TEMPORARY HOUSING, ONE OF THE EMPLOYEES INVOLVED IN VOLUNTEER WORK ESCORTED ME AROUND A BIT.

"Midaregami" (Disheveled Hair)

MY GOODNESS.
WELL, I'LL BE.
THE THREAD OF LOVE / THAT CANNOT REACH YOU
TANGLES AROUND MY HEART / AND DRAWS OUT THE TEARS
THERE IS A STONE TRIBUTE TO THE SONG BENEATH THE LIGHTHOUSE THAT PLAYS THE TUNE WHENEVER IT SENSES SOMEONE WALKING NEARBY. IT'S A VITAL PILGRIMAGE SPOT FOR FANS.
I'VE FINALLY MADE IT HERE ...
Groupie who visited this site as soon as he got to Iwaki
THE LIGHTHOUSE WAS DAMAGED IN THE EARTHQUAKE, AND AS OF 2012, WHEN I VISITED IT, THE BUILDING ITSELF WAS OFF-LIMITS FOR SAFETY REASONS.
SHINE YOUR LIGHT / ON MY HIDDEN SENTIMENT
DON'T LET ME BE / LONELY TONIGHT
THE TWO TOWNS ON EITHER SIDE OF THE LIGHTHOUSE, TOYOMA AND USUISO, WERE TERRIBLY RAVAGED BY THE TSUNAMI.
NEXT UP IS ANOTHER FUKUSHIMA SONG: WAVE YOUR HANDKERCHIEF / OUT THE LOCOMOTIVE WINDOW...
...AND THE GIRL IN THE FIELD / THROWS A FLOWER BOUQUET... ♪

Atsuo Okamoto's "Kogen Ressha wa Yuku" (The Highlands Train Rides On)
A hit song of 1954 about the Numajiri Railroad Line, written by Toshio Oka and composed by Yuji Koseki, both from Fukushima.

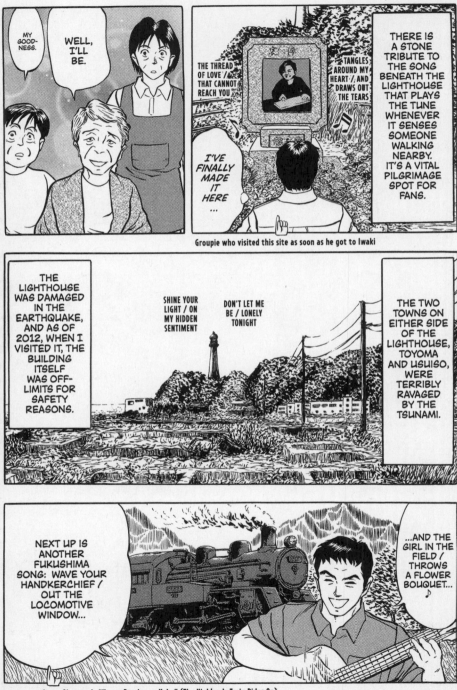

GOT ANY RE-QUESTS? I'LL PLAY 'EM!
YOU NEVER HEAR ANYONE SING THOSE OLD SONGS ANYMORE.
WOW, THAT SURE TOOK ME BACK!
LAH, LA-LA-LAAA!
ALL TOGETHER NOW!
LAH-LAH-LAH-LAH-LAH! HERE WE GO...

♪ OH NO, YOU DON'T / OH NO, YOU DON'T...
NOW DO A KIYOSHI HIKAWA SONG! ♡
♪ SHAKEN AND SHOOK / BY THE WAVE OF THE WAVES...
PLAY "KAERI-BUNE (RETURN SHIP)"!
THE THING ABOUT CLASSICS IS THAT THEY TRANSCEND THE BARRIERS OF TIME AND PLACE.

Now I'm just a slave to their whims

WHICH IS WHY I WANTED TO GET BACK HERE SO BAD, NOW THAT I'M AT ICHI-F AGAIN.
IT'S A DIFFICULT SPOT TO REACH WITHOUT A CAR, SO I WASN'T ABLE TO RETURN, TWO YEARS AGO.
I'M SORRY, FOLKS. I REALLY AM.
YEAH, YOU SAID YOU'D BE RIGHT BACK HERE!
YA KNOW, I THINK I REMEMBER SEEIN' YOU BEFORE.

Thankfully, I got a cheap used car

RETURNING TO WORK AT ICHI-F AND SINGING HERE AS A DRIFTING TROUBADOUR ...
...WERE TWO DEEP DESIRES THAT OCCUPIED AN EQUAL SPACE IN MY HEART.
I WAS HAPPY TO ACHIEVE THEM BOTH...
THANK YOU SO MUCH.
COME AGAIN, WON'T YOU?
...BUT I COULDN'T HELP BUT WONDER ABOUT THE HARD REALITY.
THANK YOU, LADIES. I HOPE SO.
WHEN CAN YOU COME AGAIN?
GOOD QUESTION. I'D LIKE TO VISIT AT LEAST ONCE MORE WHILE I'M HERE.
WE DON'T GET AS MANY VOLUNTEERS AROUND HERE AS WE DID BEFORE.
OUR SCHEDULE'S ALWAYS OPEN.

HE WAS RIGHT; THE EVENT SCHEDULE HAD BEEN PACKED BEFORE, BUT NOW THERE WAS NOTHING GOING ON.
行事予定表
サギに注意!
IT'S TIMES LIKE THIS, WHEN THE EFFECTS OF THE DISASTER ARE "WEATHERED OVER" AND OLD, THAT THINGS CAN BE THE MOST PAINFUL AND LONELY.

Calendar: Event Schedule

Sign: Watch out for scams!

OH, THAT? IN THE TOHOKU AREA WE CELEBRATE TANABATA BY THE OLD CALENDAR, SO IT MIGHT SEEM LATE TO YOU FOLKS FROM AROUND TOKYO.
HANG ON...
I HEAR ABOUT ELDERLY RESIDENTS DYING ALONE IN THE TEMPORARY HOUSING.
WELL, IT'S BEEN THREE YEARS NOW. I EXPECT IT WILL GET EVEN WORSE.
...
WELL, IT'S ALWAYS ON EVERYONE'S MIND...
NO, I NOTICED...
ふるさとに早く帰れますように
TWO YEARS LATER, AND THE WISHES THEY WRITE DOWN FOR THE HOLIDAY HAVEN'T CHANGED A BIT...
...IT'S THE SAME WISHES THEY WERE WRITING TWO YEARS AGO...

It's well after July 7th now

Prayer: To go back home as soon as possible

WHILE IT'S TRUE THAT THE WORK AT ICHI-F IS PROCEEDING BIT BY BIT, THAT'S ONLY SO MUCH...
THE HARD WORK OF THE LABORERS AT ICHI-F IS IMPROVING THE SITUATION, BUT THAT'S A SEPARATE MATTER FROM THE LOCALS' ABILITY TO RETURN TO THEIR HOMES.

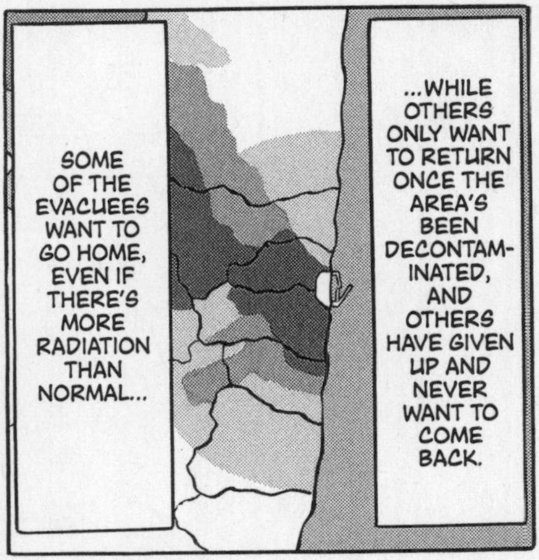
SOME OF THE EVACUEES WANT TO GO HOME, EVEN IF THERE'S MORE RADIATION THAN NORMAL...
...WHILE OTHERS ONLY WANT TO RETURN ONCE THE AREA'S BEEN DECONTAMINATED, AND OTHERS HAVE GIVEN UP AND NEVER WANT TO COME BACK.

I ONLY HOPE WE CAN MAKE THESE WISHES COME TRUE AS SOON AS POSSIBLE...
いつか必ず双葉に帰れますように
双葉は負けない!
健康で長生き
彼氏がほしい♡

Top L: Futaba will never give in! Top center: To one day return to Futaba
Bottom L: I want a boyfriend ♡ Bottom R: A long, healthy life

THERE ARE PROBABLY A NUMBER OF AREAS THAT WOULD BE SAFE ENOUGH TO GO BACK TO RIGHT NOW, BASED ON CURRENT EXPOSURE.
OF COURSE, THE REPAIRS TO DAMAGED INFRA-STRUC-TURE ARE ANOTHER MATTER.
Packing up irradiated mud and plants during decontamination

WOULDN'T IT BE ALL RIGHT FOR THOSE WHO RECOGNIZE THE RISKS TO RETURN TO THEIR HOMES NOW?
READING THESE, I WISHED FOR A MORE FLEXIBLE POLICY TOWARD RETURNEES, ESPECIALLY THE ELDERLY.
ARE YOU... ALL RIGHT?
OH... S-SORRY, IT'S NOTHING. THANK YOU FOR EVERYTHING.
THANKS FOR HAVING ME! I HAD A LOT OF FUN.
THANKS FOR COMING BY. SEE YOU AGAIN.
I'M TOTALLY AWARE THAT THIS VOLUNTEERING IS NOTHING MORE THAN SATISFYING A PERSONAL DESIRE.
JUST SINGING A FEW SONGS ISN'T THE SAME THING AS TRULY BRINGING RELIEF TO THE HEARTS OF THE DISASTER VICTIMS.

I'm only doing it because I enjoy it when people like my singing

I'M JUST HERE AS A CONSTRUCTION WORKER OVER THE PERIOD OF MY JOB.
LIKE ANY OTHER OUTSIDER, I'LL PACK MY BAGS AND GO BACK TO TOKYO WHEN MY CONTRACT IS UP.
STILL, I'M SURE I'LL FIND A WAY TO STAY INVOLVED WITH THIS REGION.
IF POSSIBLE, I'LL DO IT UNTIL THE DAY THAT EVERYONE CAN GO BACK TO WHERE THEY WANT TO LIVE.
I'M HOME!
I ended up visiting one more time during this employment period

CHAPTER 11 - END

BAR QUEEN

A LIVE MUSIC RESTAURANT/BAR NEAR IWAKI STATION, FEATURING PRO MUSICIANS IN A WIDE VARIETY OF GENRES. TATSUTA'S APPEARANCE HERE WAS ON AN "OPEN MIC" NIGHT, WHERE ANYONE IS FREE TO SIGN UP TO PERFORM. THE HOTEL IN THIS BUILDING HOUSES MANY 1-F WORKERS WHO COME DOWN TO QUEEN TO DRINK.

INCIDENTALLY, THE OWNER, ISAO KATO, A READER OF *ICHI-F,* RECOGNIZED TATSUTA'S IDENTITY IMMEDIATELY WHEN HE READ THE SCENE OF HIS "KYODAI-BUNE" PERFORMANCE.

CHAPTER 12:
HERO INTERVIEW
ONCE THIS COMIC GOT SERIALIZED, I STARTED DOING INTERVIEWS WITH VARIOUS MEDIA OUTLETS.
MOST OF THE JOURNALISTS TOOK MY ANSWERS CAREFULLY AND SERIOUSLY, BUT A FEW OF THEM WERE A BIT KOOKIER... I FIGURE I'LL GO OVER THIS ASPECT NOW.
講
談
社
Sign: Kodansha
THE FIRST QUESTION IS ALWAYS...
WHY FUKUSHIMA DAIICHI? WHY DRAW A MANGA?
AND MY ANSWER IS...
OH, JUST A LOT OF COINCIDENCES LINING UP.
Extremely abbreviated
IF YOU REALLY WANT THAT STUFF, YOU CAN GO FIND THE ARTICLES THEMSELVES.
Thanks to an early-to-bed, early-to-rise schedule
ANOTHER FREQUENT QUESTION IS...
AND HOW IS YOUR HEALTH?
... WHICH IS A SURPRISE TO ME.
Looking extremely worried
ACTUALLY, I'VE GOT MORE ENERGY NOW THAN I DID BEFORE GOING TO FUKUSHIMA.
OF COURSE, I APPRECIATE THE CONCERN FOR MY SAFETY.
BUT SOMETIMES IT MAKES ME MAD, BECAUSE THEY'RE ASSUMING THAT GOING TO ICHI-F MEANS YOU *MUST* BE GETTING SICK.

*Tatsuta was working at Ichi-F again while he was drawing this material, so Chapters 12 and 13 are short-format

I've been saying this since Tokyo got the Olympics, but no one put it in their articles

*The governor of Fukushima Prefecture has requested the Olympic Flame as well. If it does come true, the cleanup should be much further along by then. I want to run with it!

YOU'VE NEVER SEEN ME BEFORE THIS!
MAYBE I'VE LOOKED LIKE THIS ALL ALONG!!
N-NO, I ASSURE YOU...
AT THIS POINT, I WAS GETTING CLOSE TO MY BREAKING POINT.
SOME OTHER INTERVIEWERS BETRAYED THE ANGLE OF THEIR PUBLICATION EARLY.
WOW, THERE ARE THAT MANY LAYERS OF SUBCONTRACTING...?
THIS PAPER HAD EXPERTISE ON LABOR ISSUES.
BROUGHT IN UNDER FALSE ADVERTISEMENTS AND EXPLOITED...
I CAN'T BELIEVE YOU WERE ABLE TO BEAR IT.
WELL, I ENJOYED IT IN ITS OWN WAY!
BUT THAT'S BECAUSE YOU'RE SO STRONG AND HEARTY.
MOST NORMAL PEOPLE CAN'T HANDLE SUCH STRESS...
ACTUALLY, ALL THE PEOPLE WORKING THERE ARE PRETTY MUCH NORMAL GUYS.
OH, REALLY! SO YOU'RE SAYING THAT IT'S ALL *ORDINARY* PEOPLE WHO ARE FORCED TO ENDURE SUCH DANGEROUS AND NEGLIGENT EXPOSURE CONDITIONS!

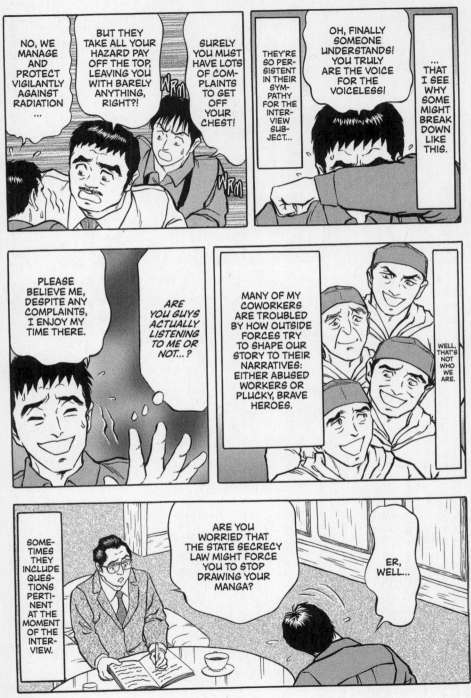

SURELY YOU MUST HAVE LOTS OF COMPLAINTS TO GET OFF YOUR CHEST!
BUT THEY TAKE ALL YOUR HAZARD PAY OFF THE TOP, LEAVING YOU WITH BARELY ANYTHING, RIGHT?!
WRM
WRM
NO, WE MANAGE AND PROTECT VIGILANTLY AGAINST RADIATION ...
THEY'RE SO PERSISTENT IN THEIR SYMPATHY FOR THE INTERVIEW SUBJECT...
OH, FINALLY SOMEONE UNDERSTANDS! YOU TRULY ARE THE VOICE FOR THE VOICELESS!
... THAT I SEE WHY SOME MIGHT BREAK DOWN LIKE THIS.
PLEASE BELIEVE ME, DESPITE ANY COMPLAINTS, I ENJOY MY TIME THERE.
ARE YOU GUYS ACTUALLY LISTENING TO ME OR NOT...?
MANY OF MY COWORKERS ARE TROUBLED BY HOW OUTSIDE FORCES TRY TO SHAPE OUR STORY TO THEIR NARRATIVES: EITHER ABUSED WORKERS OR PLUCKY, BRAVE HEROES.
WELL, THAT'S NOT WHO WE ARE.
SOMETIMES THEY INCLUDE QUESTIONS PERTINENT AT THE MOMENT OF THE INTERVIEW.
ARE YOU WORRIED THAT THE STATE SECRECY LAW MIGHT FORCE YOU TO STOP DRAWING YOUR MANGA?
ER, WELL...

I DON'T THINK I'VE EVER CONSIDERED IT.

I'VE ONLY DRAWN THINGS THAT ANYONE WOULD FIND OUT ONCE THEY GET THERE. EVEN THE ENTRY PROCEDURES AND THE APD AND EQUIPMENT STUFF.

I SEE...

VERY INTERESTING. BY THE WAY...

THE MOST SHOCKING THING TO ME IN ALL OF THESE INTERVIEWS IS THIS NEXT QUESTION.

WHAT'S AN APD?

YOU READERS ARE PROBABLY FAMILIAR WITH THESE BY NOW, AND CERTAINLY ANYONE INTERESTED IN NUCLEAR PLANTS AND RADIATION WILL KNOW THEM.

APD

THEY'RE VITAL ITEMS FOR ANY NUCLEAR WORKER THAT MEASURE PERSONAL RADIATION EXPOSURE.

GLASS BADGE DOSIMETER

OH, BOY... WHERE TO BEGIN...?

YOUR NEWSPAPER'S BEEN WRITING TONS OF ARTICLES ABOUT THESE PLANTS! (AT LEAST READ MY COMIC FIRST!)

(*｀Д´)」

CHAPTER 12 - END

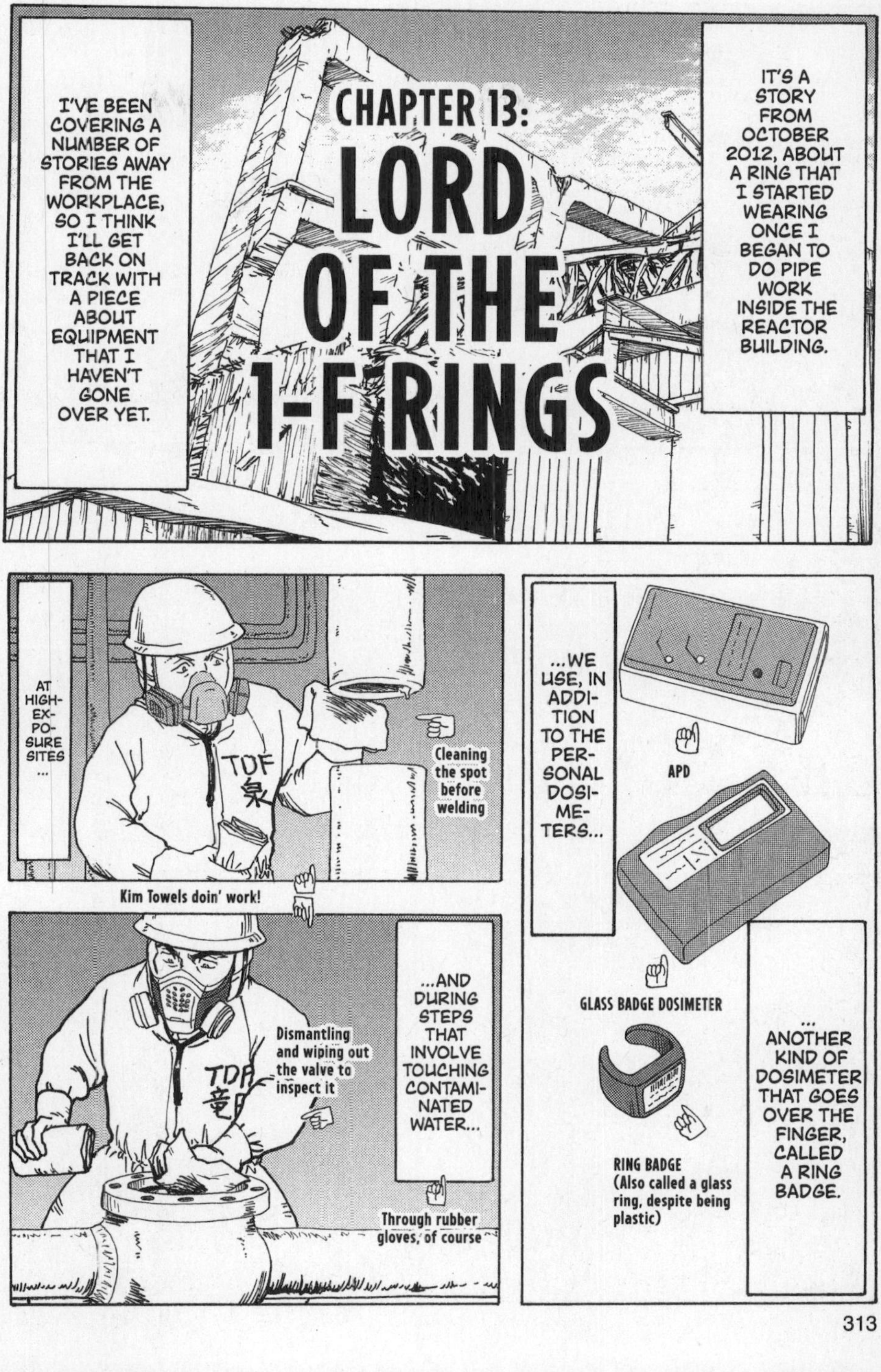
CHAPTER 13:
LORD OF THE 1-F RINGS
I'VE BEEN COVERING A NUMBER OF STORIES AWAY FROM THE WORKPLACE, SO I THINK I'LL GET BACK ON TRACK WITH A PIECE ABOUT EQUIPMENT THAT I HAVEN'T GONE OVER YET.
IT'S A STORY FROM OCTOBER 2012, ABOUT A RING THAT I STARTED WEARING ONCE I BEGAN TO DO PIPE WORK INSIDE THE REACTOR BUILDING.
AT HIGH-EXPOSURE SITES...
Cleaning the spot before welding
TDF
Kim Towels doin' work!
...AND DURING STEPS THAT INVOLVE TOUCHING CONTAMINATED WATER...
Dismantling and wiping out the valve to inspect it
TDF
Through rubber gloves, of course
...WE USE, IN ADDITION TO THE PERSONAL DOSIMETERS...
APD
GLASS BADGE DOSIMETER
RING BADGE (Also called a glass ring, despite being plastic)
...ANOTHER KIND OF DOSIMETER THAT GOES OVER THE FINGER, CALLED A RING BADGE.

*Technically, it's the barium-137 that cesium-137 decays into that emits gamma rays. If you're curious about this stuff, I encourage you to research for yourself!

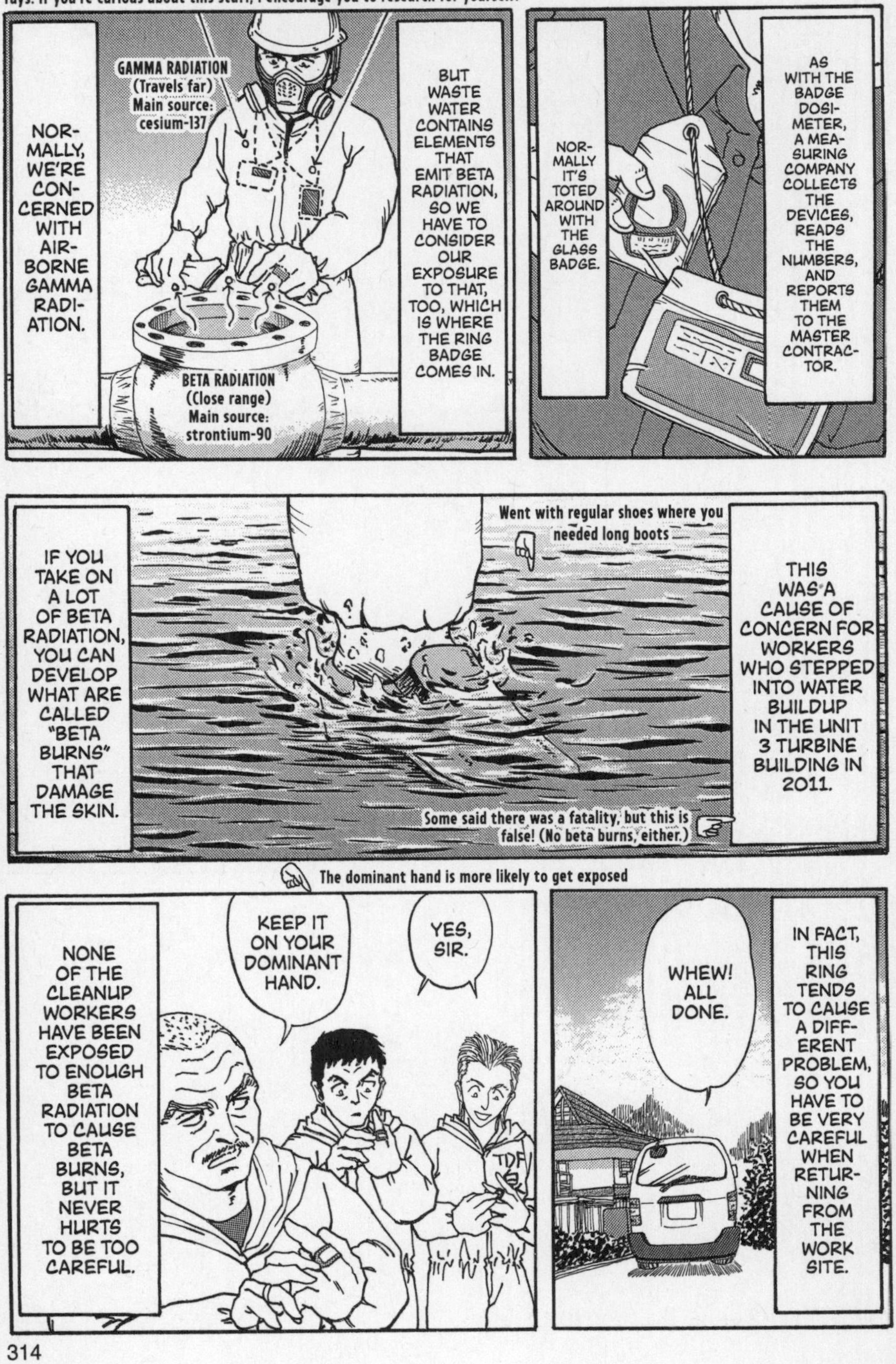

NORMALLY, WE'RE CONCERNED WITH AIRBORNE GAMMA RADIATION.
GAMMA RADIATION (Travels far) Main source: cesium-137
BETA RADIATION (Close range) Main source: strontium-90
BUT WASTE WATER CONTAINS ELEMENTS THAT EMIT BETA RADIATION, SO WE HAVE TO CONSIDER OUR EXPOSURE TO THAT, TOO, WHICH IS WHERE THE RING BADGE COMES IN.
NORMALLY IT'S TOTED AROUND WITH THE GLASS BADGE.
AS WITH THE BADGE DOSIMETER, A MEASURING COMPANY COLLECTS THE DEVICES, READS THE NUMBERS, AND REPORTS THEM TO THE MASTER CONTRACTOR.
IF YOU TAKE ON A LOT OF BETA RADIATION, YOU CAN DEVELOP WHAT ARE CALLED "BETA BURNS" THAT DAMAGE THE SKIN.
Went with regular shoes where you needed long boots
THIS WAS A CAUSE OF CONCERN FOR WORKERS WHO STEPPED INTO WATER BUILDUP IN THE UNIT 3 TURBINE BUILDING IN 2011.
Some said there was a fatality, but this is false! (No beta burns, either.)
The dominant hand is more likely to get exposed
NONE OF THE CLEANUP WORKERS HAVE BEEN EXPOSED TO ENOUGH BETA RADIATION TO CAUSE BETA BURNS, BUT IT NEVER HURTS TO BE TOO CAREFUL.
KEEP IT ON YOUR DOMINANT HAND.
YES, SIR.
TDF
WHEW! ALL DONE.
IN FACT, THIS RING TENDS TO CAUSE A DIFFERENT PROBLEM, SO YOU HAVE TO BE VERY CAREFUL WHEN RETURNING FROM THE WORK SITE.

MAN, EVEN IN OCTOBER, THIS GEAR IS TOO HOT!

AHHH...

GET... OFF...

The bottom layer (cotton) gloves are sweaty and hard to remove

NICE WORK, GUYS.

THANKS.

GOOD WORK OUT THERE.

OKAY, GO AHEAD.

HMM?

IZUMI, WHAT HAPPENED TO YOUR RING BADGE?

UH.

WHAT?

DID YOU NOT PUT IT ON?

NO, I HAD IT ON WHEN WE LEFT...

OH BOY, YOU'VE DONE IT NOW.

WAIT ON THAT TRASH!
HMM?
NOT AGAIN!
KSHUF
KSHUF
STF
THERE'S A RING BADGE IN HERE SOMEWHERE.
SOMETIMES THE RING SLIPS OFF WITH THE GLOVES WHEN YOU REMOVE THEM.
SEARCH! FIND IT, OR WE HAVE TO SUBMIT PAPERWORK!
OH NO...
IT'S SO COMMON THAT NOWADAYS THE CONTRACTORS WILL ATTACH IT TO A WRISTBAND WITH STRING TO PREVENT YOU FROM LOSING IT.
VELCRO
ATTACHED TO STRING
FOUND IT!
THANK GOODNESS.
GREAT, WHAT DO WE DO ABOUT THIS NOW?
SORRY, SORRY! WE'LL CLEAN IT UP.
DON'T WORRY, WE'LL HANDLE IT.
WHATCHA DOIN' OVER HERE?
STF

CHAPTER 13 - END

BECAUSE I WENT TO ICHI-F FROM TIME TO TIME DURING 2014, MY FOCUS HAS SWITCHED AROUND TO JUMBLED TOPICS. PLEASE FORGIVE MY LACK OF CONTINUITY; WE'RE ALMOST THROUGH IT.
AS A LITTLE BIT OF A PRESENT, I THINK I'LL INTRODUCE SOME OF THE LITTLE THINGS I'VE NOTICED AROUND THE PLANT RECENTLY.
HEY, NICE WORK OUT THERE!
CHAPTER 14:
(GET YOUR KICKS ON) ROUTE 6!
Anti-Earthquake Building
OOH! ♪
WHEW, THAT WAS A HELL OF A WORK ASSIGN-MENT TODAY...
WEL-COME BACK.
Don't ask about this yet

WOW, WHAT A LOOKER! ♡
ESPECIALLY IN THIS ENVIRONMENT. ☆
AT VERY RARE INTERVALS, YOU SEE WOMEN IN ICHI-F.
GOOD POINT. IT'S BASICALLY ALL MEN HERE.
SERIOUSLY.
WHAT IS THIS, AN ALL-BOYS' SCHOOL?
BUT MOST OF THEM WERE FOREIGN MEDIA, AND ABOVE A CERTAIN AGE.
BUT NOWADAYS...
WE'RE BACK!
THERE YOU ARE.
WE JUST SAW A REAL BABE BACK THERE.
YEAH, SHE'S WITH THE MEDIA. MORE OF THEM NOWADAYS.
...THE DOMESTIC MEDIA SENDS IN MORE REPORTERS WHO ARE FEMALE.

Young and attractive ones, too!

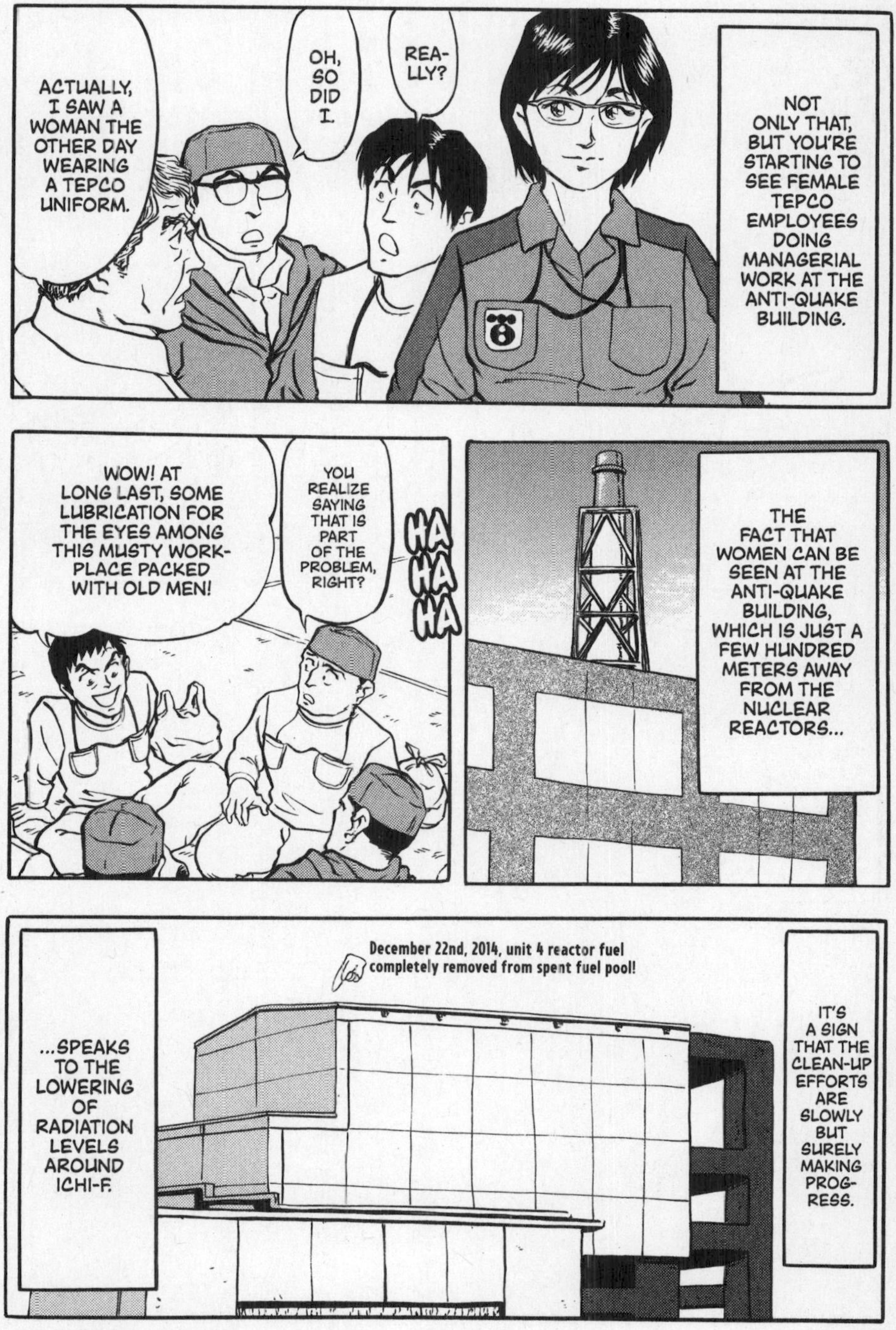
ACTUALLY, I SAW A WOMAN THE OTHER DAY WEARING A TEPCO UNIFORM.
OH, SO DID I.
REALLY?
NOT ONLY THAT, BUT YOU'RE STARTING TO SEE FEMALE TEPCO EMPLOYEES DOING MANAGERIAL WORK AT THE ANTI-QUAKE BUILDING.
WOW! AT LONG LAST, SOME LUBRICATION FOR THE EYES AMONG THIS MUSTY WORKPLACE PACKED WITH OLD MEN!
YOU REALIZE SAYING THAT IS PART OF THE PROBLEM, RIGHT?
HA HA HA
THE FACT THAT WOMEN CAN BE SEEN AT THE ANTI-QUAKE BUILDING, WHICH IS JUST A FEW HUNDRED METERS AWAY FROM THE NUCLEAR REACTORS...
...SPEAKS TO THE LOWERING OF RADIATION LEVELS AROUND ICHI-F.
December 22nd, 2014, unit 4 reactor fuel completely removed from spent fuel pool!
IT'S A SIGN THAT THE CLEAN-UP EFFORTS ARE SLOWLY BUT SURELY MAKING PROGRESS.

There are signs like this all over

Sign: Radiation Levels Microsieverts/hour 0.19 μSv/h in this area

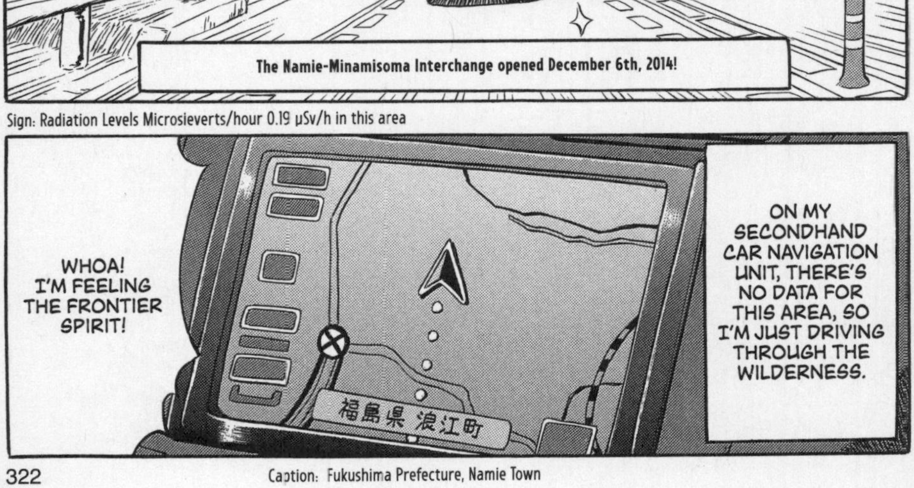

Caption: Fukushima Prefecture, Namie Town

IN A WAY, IT FEELS LIKE THIS FORMER RESTRICTED ZONE REGION IS THE FINAL FRONTIER FOR MODERN JAPAN'S CONSTRUCTION AND DEVELOPMENT.

IT WAS A TERRIBLE DISASTER THAT CAUSED IT, BUT YOU CAN REALLY FEEL THE FRONTIER SOUL IN THE PEOPLE TAKING PART IN THE RENOVATION AND RECLAMATION OF THE LAND.

WHAT I'D LIKE TO GO OVER IN DEPTH THIS TIME IS THE REOPENING OF OUR WORK COMMUTE: ROUTE 6, RUNNING NORTH AND SOUTH FROM IWAKI TO SENDAI, THE MAIN ARTERY OF THE COASTAL TRAFFIC OF FUKUSHIMA.

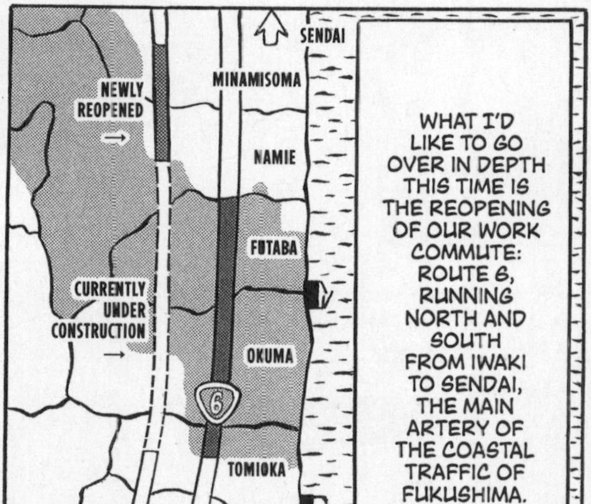

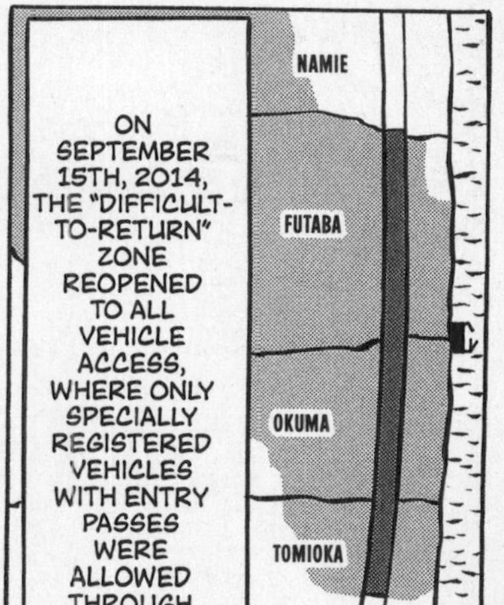

ON SEPTEMBER 15TH, 2014, THE "DIFFICULT-TO-RETURN" ZONE REOPENED TO ALL VEHICLE ACCESS, WHERE ONLY SPECIALLY REGISTERED VEHICLES WITH ENTRY PASSES WERE ALLOWED THROUGH BEFORE.

NEWLY REOPENED

CURRENTLY UNDER CONSTRUCTION

SENDAI

MINAMISOMA

NAMIE

FUTABA

OKUMA

TOMIOKA

JOBAN EXPRESSWAY

NARAHA

J-VILLAGE

TOKYO

HIRONO

IWAKI

MAP LEGEND: DIFFICULT-TO-RETURN ZONE

NAMIE

FUTABA

OKUMA

TOMIOKA

NARAHA

PREVIOUSLY OFF-LIMITS

WHEN YOU COULDN'T DRIVE THROUGH HERE, THE DETOUR FROM IWAKI TO MINAMISOMA TOOK A GOOD THREE HOURS, WHETHER THROUGH THE MOUNTAIN ROADS OR THE HIGHWAYS.

VERY NARROW

WHOAAA!

FROZEN OVER

MOUNTAIN ROAD

I TRIED TO DRIVE WHAT I THOUGHT WAS THE SHORTEST ROUTE IN WINTER 2012, AND NEARLY DIED IN THE ATTEMPT.

Very dangerous for inexperienced drivers, even with 4WD snow tires

WITH ROUTE 6 ("ROKKOKU") OPEN AGAIN, THE TRIP IS AN HOUR AND A HALF. TRAFFIC HAS RETURNED TO THE FLAT STREETS ALONG THE COAST.

仙台 303

Now you see plates from other prefectures like Sendai, where there were none before

I'M CERTAIN THAT REOPENING TRAFFIC BETWEEN NORTH AND SOUTH WILL HAVE A MASSIVE EFFECT ON THE RECOVERY OF THE DISASTER AREAS.

This is what the people in Ibaraki and Fukushima call it

ON A FALL DAY JUST AFTER THE ROAD OPENED ...

6 ROUTE

...I DROVE UP ROUTE 6 TO MINAMI-SOMA.

HAVING BEEN LIVING IN IWAKI, THIS IS AN AREA THAT WAS ALWAYS CLOSE, BUT SO FAR AWAY.

MINAMISOMA ROADSIDE STATION

NOW I COULD PICK UP THINGS I'D ONLY HEARD ABOUT.
HERE'S YOUR ORDER.
THANK YOU.
AT LAST, I GET TO TRY...
...A "SHIMITEN"!
THIS IS AMAZING!
A SHIMITEN IS A TYPE OF PRESERVED RICE CAKE COATED WITH DONUT BATTER AND FRIED.
THINK OF IT LIKE A CORN DOG VERSION OF A RICE CAKE
THIS IS A LOCAL DELICACY OF MINAMISOMA, CRISPY ON THE OUTSIDE AND CHEWY INSIDE, WITH A RICH FLAVOR.
IT'S SO GREAT THAT I CAN ALREADY GET FROM IWAKI TO MINAMISOMA AND EAT THIS INCREDIBLE TREAT...
NOT ONLY WAS THE REDUCTION IN TRIP TIME A WELCOME SURPRISE, THE REOPENING OF ROUTE 6 HAPPENED MUCH SOONER THAN I EXPECTED IT WOULD.

Sign: Shimiten: Konohata

Package: Shimiten

Gate: No Entry

Sign: No Entry

Carton: Matsunaga Coffee

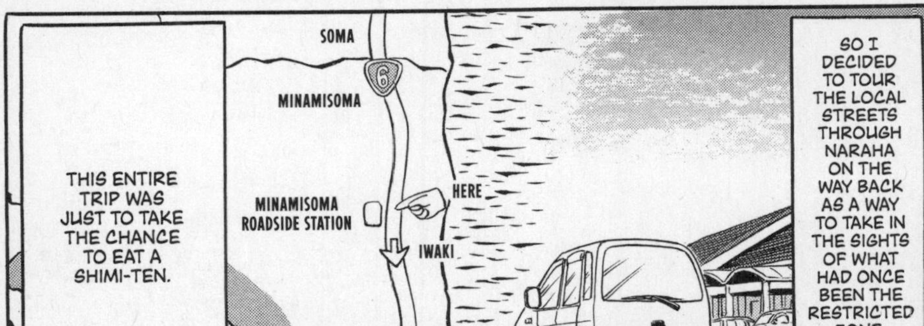

ROKUMANGOKU
ODAKA DISTRICT, MINAMISOMA
EVEN IN LATE 2014, THERE ARE RUINED BUILDINGS FROM THE TSUNAMI STANDING AROUND.
IT MUST HAVE BEEN AWFUL AROUND HERE, TOO...
(SEE PG.96)
BUT THE MOUNTAINS OF WRECKAGE AND RUINED VEHICLES IN MINAMISOMA TWO YEARS AGO...
MAY 2012
OCTOBER 2014
...ARE PRETTY MUCH ENTIRELY CLEANED UP, A SIGN OF PROGRESS FOR THE RECOVERY EFFORT.

ON THE SIDE STREETS, SOME OF THE SIGNS ARE DIFFER-ENT.
獣と衝突
They put a sticker over it to update it
AROUND 2012 THEY ALL SAID "CATTLE COLLISIONS," BUT NOW MANY SAY "ANIMAL" OR "BOAR."
THE CATTLE HAVE ALL BEEN BROUGHT UNDER CONTROL, SO BOARS ARE THE BIG THING NOW.

Sign: Animal/ Collision Warning

WHEN YOU GET TO NAMIE, LARGE GATES AND FENCES CATCH THE EYE AT THE TOWN BORDER.
THERE ARE TRAFFIC OFFICERS STATIONED AT ALL THE MAJOR INTER-SECTIONS. KEEP UP THE GOOD WORK, FELLAS!
This huge wedding chapel is a landmark
THE SECURITY PRESENCE GROWS AT THE BORDER BETWEEN NAMIE AND FUTABA.
BEFORE, THERE WAS A CHECK-POINT HERE TO KEEP CIVILIAN CARS OUT.
There's police around here, so watch out. (For what?)

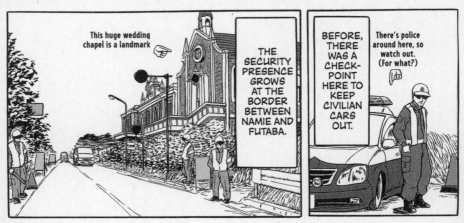

Sign: Difficult-to-Return Zone (including high-exposure areas) beyond this point

Sign: Warning - motorcycles, motorized scooters, light autos, and pedestrians may not proceed

Sign: Don't open the irradiated highway!

THE CABINET'S NUCLEAR DISASTER COUNTER-MEASURES OFFICE RECOM-MENDS KEEPING YOUR CAR WINDOWS SHUT WHEN PASSING THROUGH.
THAT MAKES PEOPLE AFRAID THAT THEY MIGHT PICK UP RADIOACTIVE MATERIAL WHILE ON THIS ROAD.
VWEEE
WHOOPS, WASN'T PAYING ATTEN-TION.
SHWIK
WELL, TWO YEARS AGO ...
2012
I'LL ADMIT THIS NOW, SINCE I DON'T THINK WE'LL GET INTO TROUBLE, BUT WE WOULD ROLL DOWN THE WINDOWS WHEN SMOKING IN THE CAR.
VWEEE
PUFF PUFF
HEY, ROLL DOWN THE WIN-DOW!
AND THAT CAR WENT TO ICHI-F EVERY-DAY, AND NEVER GOT HELD UP IN VEHICLE SURVEY.
DESPITE THIS PRACTICE, WE NEVER ONCE GOT FLAGGED FOR ANY KIND OF INTERNAL EXPO-SURE ON TESTS.
THIS IS JUST MY PERSO-NAL OPINION, THOUGH.
IF IT WAS THAT SAFE TWO YEARS AGO, THEN I'D IMAGINE THE DANGER IS EVEN SLIGHTER NOW, WITH ALL THE DECONTAM-INATION EFFORTS AND ROAD-WORK GOING ON.
PLEASE, RELAX AND ENJOY YOUR DRIVE THROUGH THE AREA.
JUST REMEM-BER TO FOLLOW THE RULES!

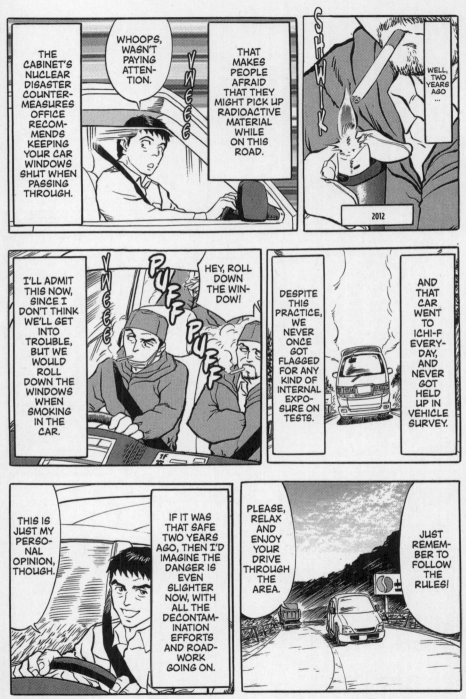

AFTER ALL OF THAT, WE GO THROUGH FUTABA AND TURN RIGHT (TO THE WEST) TOWARD FUTABA STATION, WHICH IS STILL ON LOCKDOWN.
THIS IS WHERE YOU SEE THIS STREET SIGN WHICH HAS RECENTLY BECOME FAMOUS.

Sign: Nuclear energy for a brighter future

Please keep your eyes on the road!

Vertical Sign: Futaba Town Market

原子力郷土の発展豊かな未来
A LITTLE FURTHER DOWN ON THE LEFT (EAST) IS THIS SIGN IN FRONT OF THE FUTABA TOWN HALL.

Sign: Local prosperity and a rich future with nuclear energy

Sign: Naraha
Energy Welfare City
A rich town created by nature and science

Sign: Nuclear energy, gentle on the earth
Okuma Town, gentle on people

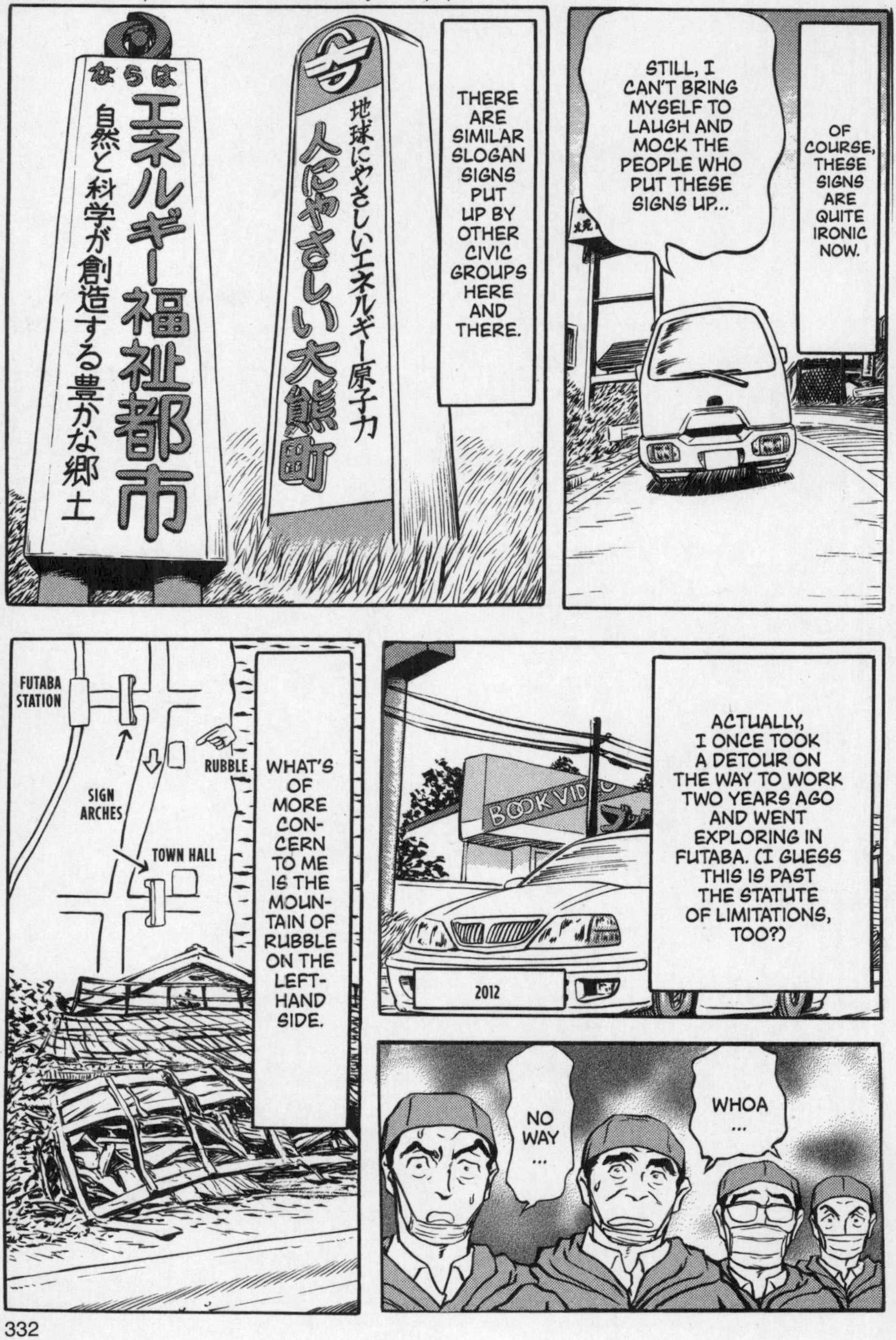

OF COURSE, THESE SIGNS ARE QUITE IRONIC NOW.
STILL, I CAN'T BRING MYSELF TO LAUGH AND MOCK THE PEOPLE WHO PUT THESE SIGNS UP...
ならは
エネルギー福祉都市
自然と科学が創造する豊かな郷土
地球にやさしいエネルギー原子力
人にやさしい大熊町
THERE ARE SIMILAR SLOGAN SIGNS PUT UP BY OTHER CIVIC GROUPS HERE AND THERE.
ACTUALLY, I ONCE TOOK A DETOUR ON THE WAY TO WORK TWO YEARS AGO AND WENT EXPLORING IN FUTABA. (I GUESS THIS IS PAST THE STATUTE OF LIMITATIONS, TOO?)
2012
WHOA ...
NO WAY ...
WHAT'S OF MORE CONCERN TO ME IS THE MOUNTAIN OF RUBBLE ON THE LEFT-HAND SIDE.
FUTABA STATION
RUBBLE
SIGN ARCHES
TOWN HALL

Sign: Pachinko University

Sign: Warning
Slow Down

People like to take photos here, but you're not allowed to stop and get out!

IT'S THE ONE PLACE YOU CAN SEE THE ICHI-F EXHAUST STACKS AND THE SWARM OF CRANES...
...ON THE ROUTE FROM ROUTE 6 TO THE NUCLEAR PLANT.
Noticing upon a fresh look
THERE'S MORE CRANES THERE NOW.
福島第一
原子力発電所
BUT EVEN MORE EYE-CATCHING THAN THE SMOKE-STACKS IS...
The paint is fading but the logo design is great!
...THIS SIGN!
原子力運送

Sign: Fukushima Daiichi Nuclear Power Plant

Sign: Nuclear Shipping

SADLY, THIS PARTICULAR COMPANY WAS ALREADY OUT OF BUSINESS BEFORE THE QUAKE, WHEN CONSTRUCTION FELL OFF FOLLOWING THE BUILDING OF 1-F AND 2-F.
I REALLY LIKE THIS SIGN.
Totally sincere, not ironic
1-F IS THIS WAY
IT'S FRESH AND NEW TO SEE IT FROM A DIFFERENT ANGLE.
BEFORE LONG, WE'RE AT THE INTER-SECTION WHERE WE NORMALLY TURN TO GO TO THE PLANT.
ON SECOND GLANCE, THERE ARE OTHER THINGS DIFFERENT FROM TWO YEARS AGO.
UP AHEAD, IT'S ALL FAMI-LIAR.
MOST STRIKING TO ME WAS THE ADDITION OF FENCES AROUND THE RESIDENCES ON EITHER SIDE OF THE STREET.
IT'S ALL VERY IMPOSING...
IT'S A SAD REMINDER THAT NOW THAT PEOPLE ARE ALLOWED TO PASS THROUGH, CRIME AGAINST UNOCCUPIED PROPERTY WILL INCREASE.

AS FOR THE NEARBY FIELDS, THE YELLOW CARPETS OF GOLDENROD HAVE BEEN HALF-REPLACED BY THE SILVER STALKS OF SUSUKI GRASS.
THIS VIEW SEEMS A LITTLE BIT MORE REAL THAN WHEN THE WHOLE FIELD WAS JUST STUNNING YELLOW...

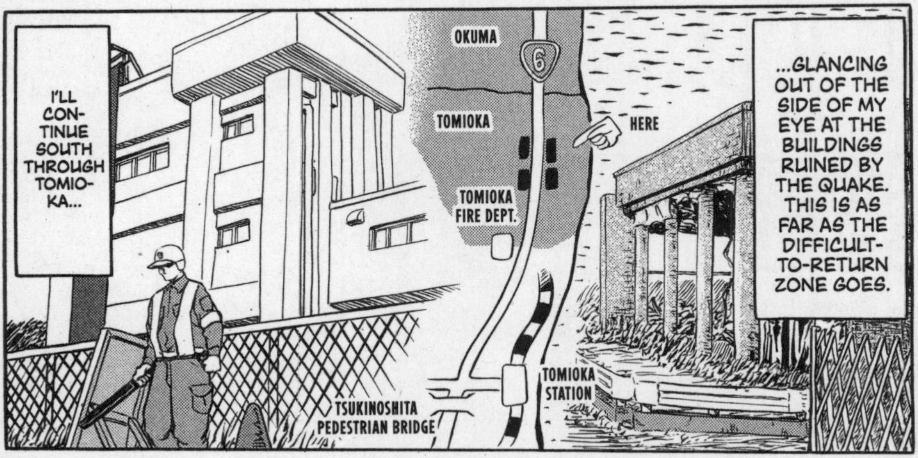
I'LL CONTINUE SOUTH THROUGH TOMIOKA...
OKUMA
6
TOMIOKA
HERE
TOMIOKA FIRE DEPT.
TOMIOKA STATION
TSUKINOSHITA PEDESTRIAN BRIDGE
...GLANCING OUT OF THE SIDE OF MY EYE AT THE BUILDINGS RUINED BY THE QUAKE. THIS IS AS FAR AS THE DIFFICULT-TO-RETURN ZONE GOES.

Sign: Tomioka will never give up!

UP AHEAD, WE TURN LEFT AT THE LIGHT WHERE THE BIG BANNER HANGS FROM THE PEDESTRIAN BRIDGE...
富岡は負けん!
月の下
Tsukinoshita

 Tsukinoshita means "under the moon." Along with "Yonomori" (Night Forest), Tomioka has some cool location names!

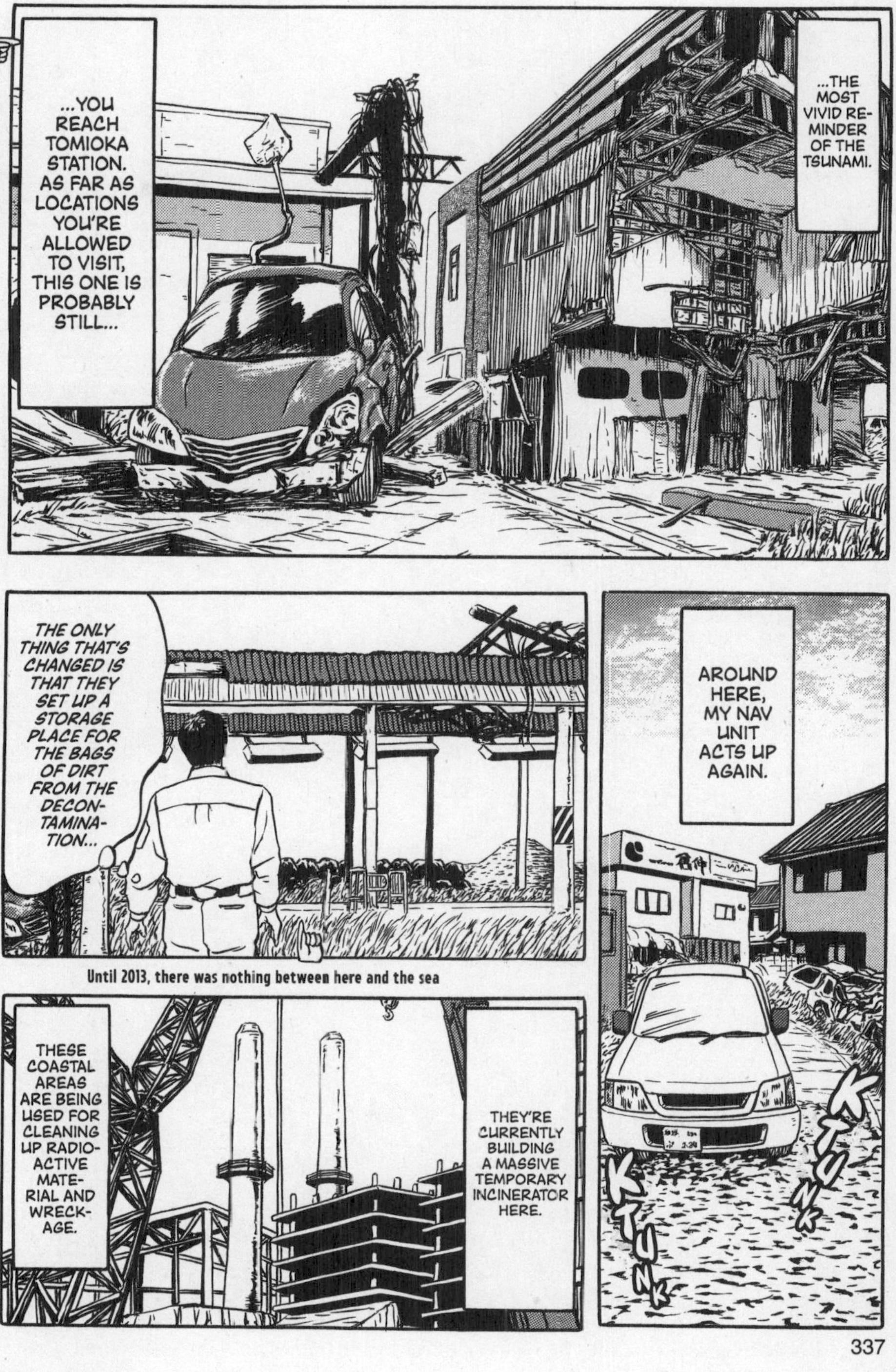

...YOU REACH TOMIOKA STATION. AS FAR AS LOCATIONS YOU'RE ALLOWED TO VISIT, THIS ONE IS PROBABLY STILL...
...THE MOST VIVID RE-MINDER OF THE TSUNAMI.
THE ONLY THING THAT'S CHANGED IS THAT THEY SET UP A STORAGE PLACE FOR THE BAGS OF DIRT FROM THE DECON-TAMINA-TION...
AROUND HERE, MY NAV UNIT ACTS UP AGAIN.
THESE COASTAL AREAS ARE BEING USED FOR CLEANING UP RADIO-ACTIVE MATE-RIAL AND WRECK-AGE.
THEY'RE CURRENTLY BUILDING A MASSIVE TEMPORARY INCINERATOR HERE.
KTUNK
KTUNK

They finally started cleaning it up in late 2014

Until 2013, there was nothing between here and the sea

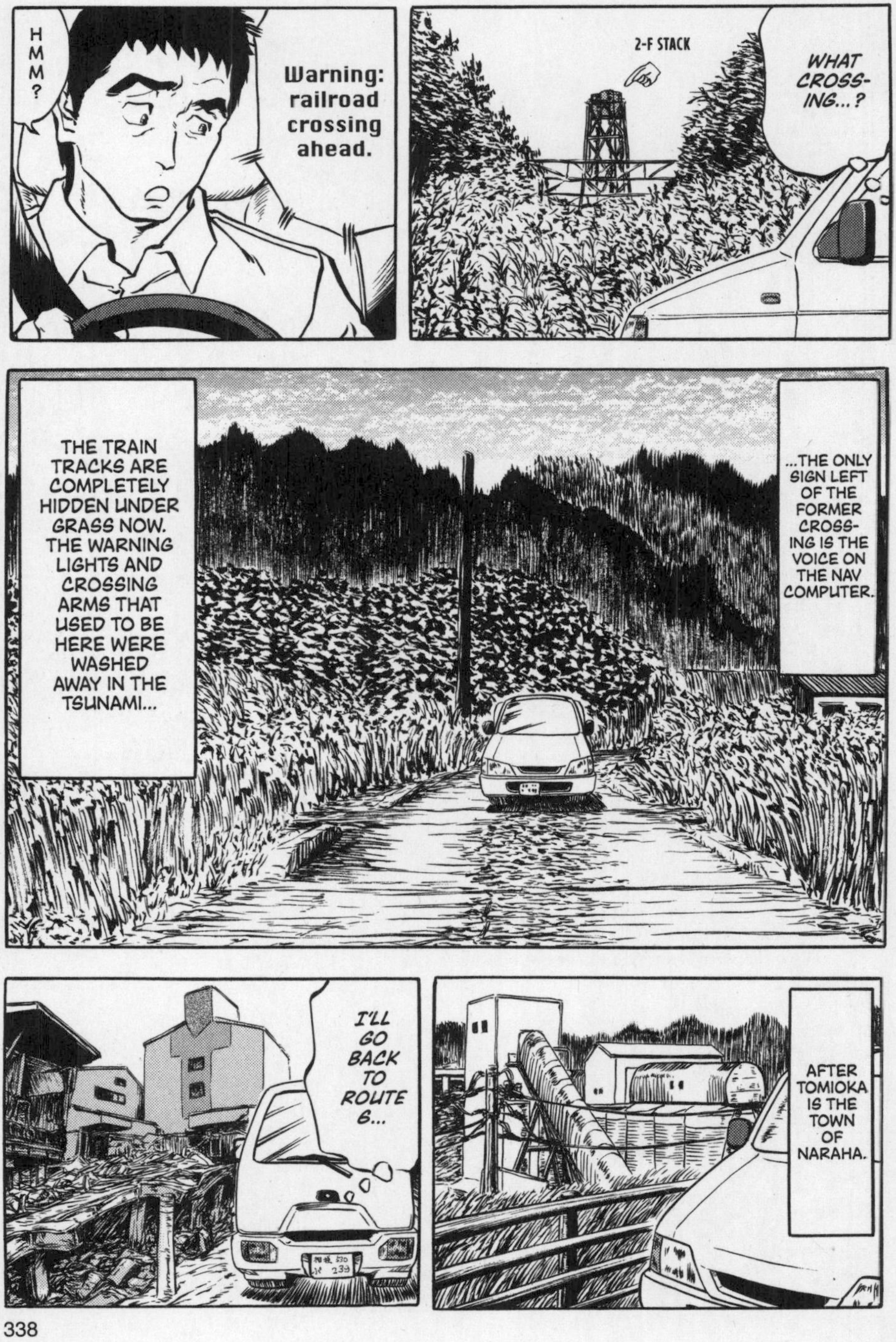
HMM?
Warning: railroad crossing ahead.
2-F STACK
WHAT CROSSING...?
THE TRAIN TRACKS ARE COMPLETELY HIDDEN UNDER GRASS NOW. THE WARNING LIGHTS AND CROSSING ARMS THAT USED TO BE HERE WERE WASHED AWAY IN THE TSUNAMI...
...THE ONLY SIGN LEFT OF THE FORMER CROSSING IS THE VOICE ON THE NAV COMPUTER.
I'LL GO BACK TO ROUTE 6...
AFTER TOMIOKA IS THE TOWN OF NARAHA.

Gray Sign: Oraho-tei Top Sign: Eat Here!! Take Home!! This Is Your Stop

THERE'S A TEMPORARY MARKET AREA IN THE PARKING LOT OF THE TOWN HALL.

Two restaurants

All kinds of food

RESIDENTS PREPARING TO RETURN HOME AND DECONTAMINATION WORKERS CAN EAT LUNCH OR DO SHOPPING HERE.

Smiley Sign: Také-chan Cafeteria White Vertical Sign: Your Stop Mall Bathrooms, too

THE TWO SPECIALTIES HERE ARE THE CHIVES-AND-LIVER STIR FRY AT TAKÉ-CHAN CAFETERIA AND THE CITRUS SOFT SERVE AT ORAHO-TEI.

THEY'RE BOTH DELICIOUS!

WE'RE ALMOST AT THE END OF MY FORMER RESTRICTED-ZONE TOUR.

HIRONO POWER STATION SMOKESTACKS

BUT BEFORE WE FINISH, I WANT TO SHOW OFF TWO THINGS THAT STRUCK ME THIS FALL.

WHAT ARE THOSE BANNERS?

HMM?

Banner: Lots for Sale
Naraha Town

SO... THEY'RE SELL-ING LAND?
WITH THE EVACUATION ORDER ABOUT TO LIFT, THE TOWN IS PREPARING TO SELL HOMES.
分譲中
楢葉町
I FEEL THEIR UNBREAKABLE SPIRIT!
BUT YOU CAN SEE THE INTENTION OF THE PEOPLE TO RETURN AND LIVE HERE!
分
Wants to live here someday
分譲中
楢葉町
WHOA ...!
THERE WAS ANOTHER SIGHT THAT LODGED ITSELF DEEP IN MY HEART.

THE UNATTENDED FIELDS WERE FULL OF BLOOMING COSMOS FLOWERS.

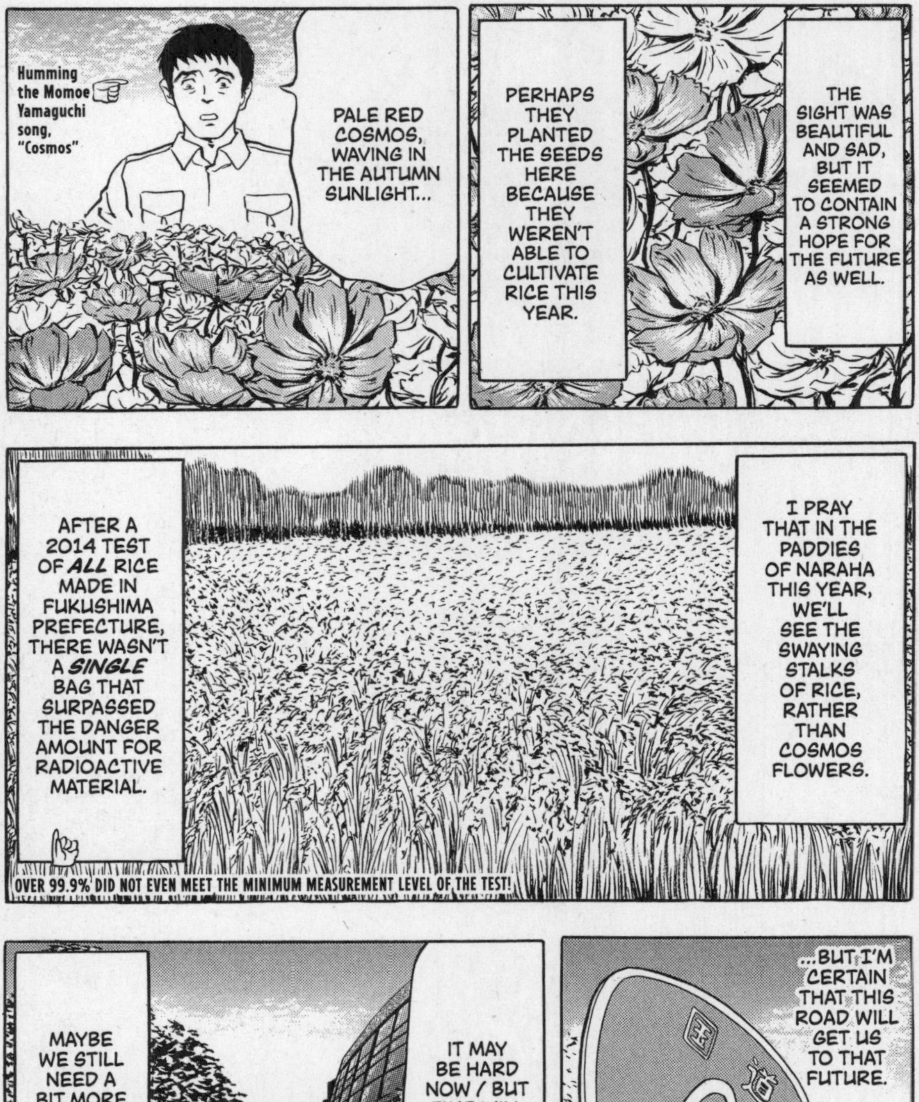
Humming the Momoe Yamaguchi song, "Cosmos"
PALE RED COSMOS, WAVING IN THE AUTUMN SUNLIGHT...
PERHAPS THEY PLANTED THE SEEDS HERE BECAUSE THEY WEREN'T ABLE TO CULTIVATE RICE THIS YEAR.
THE SIGHT WAS BEAUTIFUL AND SAD, BUT IT SEEMED TO CONTAIN A STRONG HOPE FOR THE FUTURE AS WELL.
AFTER A 2014 TEST OF ALL RICE MADE IN FUKUSHIMA PREFECTURE, THERE WASN'T A SINGLE BAG THAT SURPASSED THE DANGER AMOUNT FOR RADIOACTIVE MATERIAL.
OVER 99.9% DID NOT EVEN MEET THE MINIMUM MEASUREMENT LEVEL OF THE TEST!
I PRAY THAT IN THE PADDIES OF NARAHA THIS YEAR, WE'LL SEE THE SWAYING STALKS OF RICE, RATHER THAN COSMOS FLOWERS.
MAYBE WE STILL NEED A BIT MORE TIME BEFORE WE CAN LAUGH ABOUT ALL OF THIS...
IT MAY BE HARD NOW / BUT TIME WILL MAKE US LAUGH IT OFF...♪
6
ROUTE
...BUT I'M CERTAIN THAT THIS ROAD WILL GET US TO THAT FUTURE.

CHAPTER 14 - END

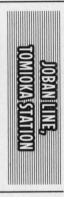

JOBAN LINE, TOMIOKA STATION

WHILE SERVICE HAS RESUMED TO ADJACENT TATSUTA STATION, THE RECOVERY EFFORTS AROUND TOMIOKA STATION ARE NOT VERY FAR ALONG. AS SHOWN IN THE PREVIOUS CHAPTER, THE TRACKS ARE COVERED IN GRASS AND WEEDS, AND YOU CAN'T SEE THE CROSSING. THANKFULLY, THE CLEARING OF WRECKAGE BEGAN IN LATE 2014. WE'RE LOOKING FORWARD TO THE EVENTUAL RECOVERY.

IN LATE 2014, WHEN I WENT BACK TO WORK AT ICHI-F, I FOCUSED ON LITTLE DIVERSIONS AND SIDE STORIES, RATHER THAN MY MAIN NARRATIVE.
SO AT THIS POINT, I'D LIKE TO PUT A CAP ON THE ACCOUNT OF MY 2012 WORK STINT.
CHAPTER 15:
"I'LL BE BACK."
OCTOBER 2012

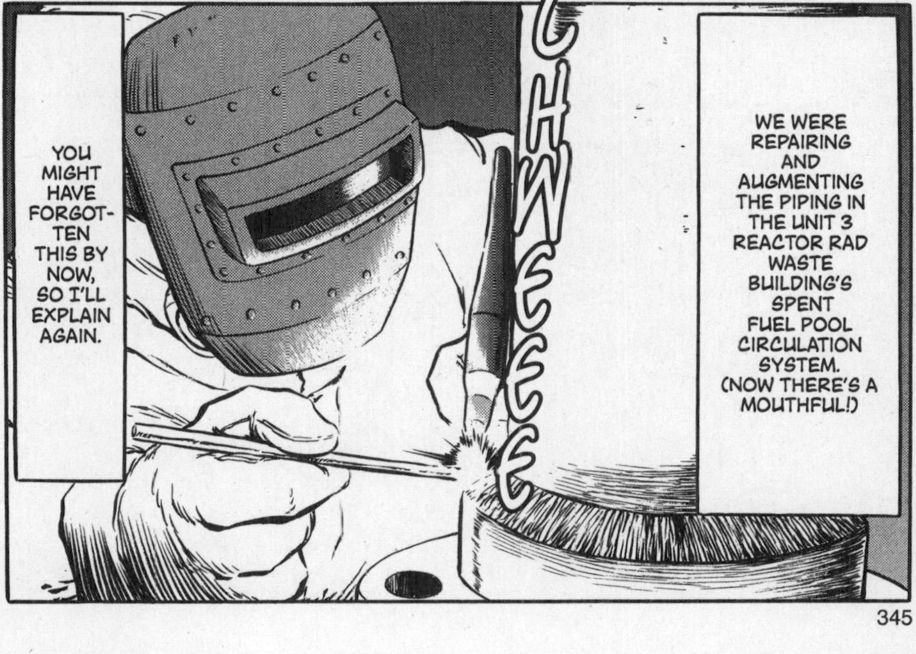
YOU MIGHT HAVE FORGOT-TEN THIS BY NOW, SO I'LL EXPLAIN AGAIN.
CHWEEEE
WE WERE REPAIRING AND AUGMENTING THE PIPING IN THE UNIT 3 REACTOR RAD WASTE BUILDING'S SPENT FUEL POOL CIRCULATION SYSTEM. (NOW THERE'S A MOUTHFUL!)

TODAY'S JOB IS WELDING ON THE FLANGE, A PART FOR THE STOP VALVE.

WELD HERE

STOP VALVE

FLANGE

FLANGE

WELD HERE

BUT...

...

CHWEEE

NOTHIN' TO DO...

NOPE.

0.2 mSv/h

YOU CAN'T HELP IT. SOME STEPS JUST HAVE TO BE LEFT TO THE VETERANS.

CHWEEE

KEEE

WHEN THE WELDING IS HAPPENING IN EARNEST, THE ASSISTANT'S JOB IS TO PREPARE THE WORK AND CLEAN UP AFTERWARD.

YOU'RE RIGHT.

SO, AS THE ASSISTANT, I FIND MYSELF WITH LITTLE TO DO ON DAYS LIKE THIS.

Sign: The atmospheric radiation here is 0.2 mSv/h

WE HAVE TO AVOID ANY UNNECESSARY RADIATION EXPOSURE, IN ORDER TO MAXIMIZE THE AMOUNT OF WORK WE CAN DO.
WAITING IS PART OF THE JOB.
THE (RADIATION) MONITOR USUALLY MAKES THIS HIS STANDBY LOCATION.
WHEN THERE'S NOTHING TO DO, YOU STAY AT A LOW-EXPOSURE SPOT.
この場所の線量当量率
0.2 mSv/h
ANOTHER DAY SAFELY IN THE BOOKS.
COMING!
HEY, I'M DONE!
0.2
TDF 竜田
TDF 木戸
HERE YA GO.
NICE WORK.
TDF 大野
TDF 木戸
TDF 竜田

It's the monitor's job to collect discarded Tyveks and waste material

"Did you finish the welding?" "What was your exposure?" "0.3 mSv"

WE'RE BACK!
HI AGAIN.
YOU ROLL ON THAT FINAL PASS?
YEP, JUST SQUEEZED IT IN.
HOW MUCH?
POINT-THREE.

*Inspecting the welds

SO THAT MEANS TOMORROW IS PT,* WITH TEPCO PRESENT.
CORRECT. WE'RE CALLING OUR GUESTS IN AT NINE.

OUR "GUESTS" FROM TEPCO ATTEND THE INSPECTION OF VITAL WORK AREAS.
WE OFTEN CALL EMPLOYEES OF HIGH-RANKING BUSINESSES (UPPER CONTRACTORS, MASTER CONTRACTORS) "GUESTS."
東京電力

Suit: TEPCO

THAT'S ANOTHER DAY DOWN.
OKAY, LET'S GO.
FOR BETTER OR FOR WORSE, DECOMMISSIONING A PLANT IS A BUSINESS.

I'M HOME ...
WEL-COME BACK.
FINISH THE WELD-ING?
YOU BET WE DID!
HAVE THEY RE-SUMED COOL-ING, THEN?
NO, THAT'LL ONLY HAPPEN ONCE WE PASS INSPECTION TOMORROW AND ATTACH THE VALVE.
DURING THIS PROCESS, THE COOL-ING SYSTEM FOR THE SPENT FUEL POOL IS TURNED OFF.
THE THOUGHT OF IT BEING OFF...
KABOOM
... MIGHT ALARM THOSE WHO RE-MEM-BER THE ACCI-DENT IT-SELF.
ALSO, IN MARCH 2013, A RAT WANDERED INTO THE POWER PANEL AND SHORTED OUT THE POOL'S COOLING SYSTEM.
COOLING WAS RESTORED THE NEXT DAY AND NOTHING CAME OF IT, BUT THEY MADE A BIG DEAL OUT OF IT, AS I RECALL.
WUP WUP WUP
FSHHHHH

The cause of the hydrogen explosion was the loss of power to the reactor cooler, not the fuel pool

APPARENTLY IT'S RATHER COMMON FOR THE POOL'S COOLING CIRCULATION TO BE SHUT DOWN FOR A FEW DAYS AT A TIME FOR CONSTRUCTION.
OHH.
I'M SURPRISED THAT'S NOT BETTER KNOWN, ESPECIALLY AMONG FOLKS WORKING HERE.
RATHER THAN JUST REACTING VISCERALLY TO THE PHRASE "COOLING SHUTDOWN," I HOPE THAT YOU CAN ACCEPT THE INFORMATION WHEN PLACED IN THE CONTEXT OF THE ACTUAL CONDITIONS AND WORKFLOW.
福島第
<1. 原子炉および原子炉格
号機
1号機
2号機
3号機
<2. 使用済燃料プールの状況
号機 冷却方法
1号機 循環冷却システム
2号機 循環冷却システム 運転中
3号機 循環冷却システム 運転中
4号機 循環冷却システム 運転中 25.5℃
循環冷却システム 運転中 35.6℃
FOR THE RECORD, THIS JOB STOPPED THE CIRCULATION FOR ABOUT FIVE DAYS, AND THE WATER TEMPERATURE ROSE 10 DEGREES CELSIUS.
WHAT WAS YOUR LEVEL TODAY?
POINT-FIVE.
GREAT! SO YOU DIDN'T GO THAT HIGH.
I WAS JUST HANGING OUT IN THE COOLER SPOTS.
BUT COMPARED TO US...
0.01 mSv
...THAT'S FIFTY TIMES HIGHER!
I DON'T KNOW, YOU JUST GET NUMB TO THE NUMBERS.
EVEN THE LARGEST NUMBER STOPS HAVING MEANING IF YOU EXPERIENCE IT THE SAME WAY EVERY DAY.

The data is updated every day on TEPCO's website

Fukushima Daiichi <1. Nuclear Reactor Conditions (units 1-3). <2. Spent Fuel Pool Conditions (Unit No., Cooling Method, Status).
Unit 1, Circulating Cooling System, Functioning; Unit 2, Circulating Cooling System, Functioning, 25.5 C
Unit 3, Circulating Cooling System, Functioning, 35.6 C; Unit 4, Circulating Cooling System, Functioning, 7.2 C

BUT IT'S NOT LIKE TAKING ON 20 MILLISIEVERTS IS GOING TO MAKE A DIFFERENCE TO YOU.
THAT'S TRUE, BUT THE YEARLY LIMIT'S AN ISSUE...
GOOD POINT. ONCE THIS JOB IS OVER, I'LL ONLY HAVE LIKE 10 LEFT TO GO.
THE DESIGNATED YEARLY RADIATION EXPOSURE LIMIT FOR NUCLEAR WORKERS IS 50 MILLISIEVERTS, AND 100 MSV OVER FIVE YEARS. BUT MOST COMPANIES IMPOSE A LIMIT OF NO MORE THAN 20 MSV, WHICH MAKES 100 OVER FIVE YEARS.
Badge: Tatsuta, Kazuto
THEY'RE PLANNING A SIMILAR PROJECT IN DECEMBER, SO I'LL DO THAT TO ROUND OUT MY LIMIT.
SO YOU WON'T LAST THROUGH MARCH.
SHOULDN'T YOU JUST CONTINUE AT THE REST AREA INSTEAD?
AS I'VE NOTED BEFORE, WHEN YOU HIT YOUR LIMIT, IT DOESN'T GET RESET UNTIL APRIL 1ST. SO YOU'RE LOCKED OUT OF ICHI-F UNTIL THEN.
It sounds arbitrary, but you've got to draw a line at some point
WE'RE GETTING BETTER PAY NOW THAT WE'VE SWITCHED COMPANIES.
Still working in a shelter, but transferring subcontractors got them an extra one or two thousand yen a day
IF YOU WORK WITH US, YOU CAN EASILY GET BY.
THANKS FOR THE CONSIDERATION, BUT THIS IS WHAT I CAME HERE TO DO.
PLUS THE MONEY IS BETTER!

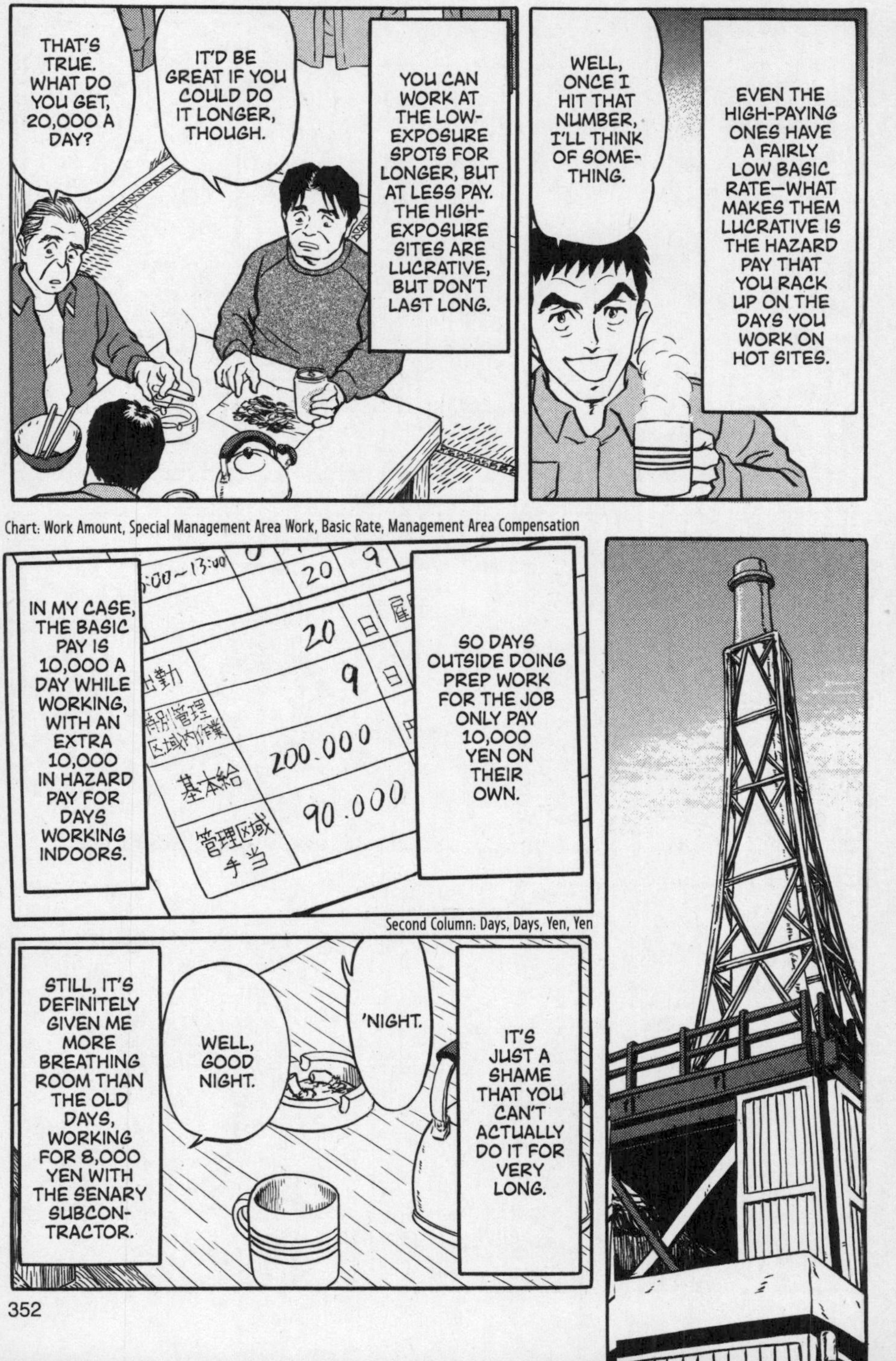
THAT'S TRUE. WHAT DO YOU GET, 20,000 A DAY?
IT'D BE GREAT IF YOU COULD DO IT LONGER, THOUGH.
YOU CAN WORK AT THE LOW-EXPOSURE SPOTS FOR LONGER, BUT AT LESS PAY. THE HIGH-EXPOSURE SITES ARE LUCRATIVE, BUT DON'T LAST LONG.
WELL, ONCE I HIT THAT NUMBER, I'LL THINK OF SOME-THING.
EVEN THE HIGH-PAYING ONES HAVE A FAIRLY LOW BASIC RATE—WHAT MAKES THEM LUCRATIVE IS THE HAZARD PAY THAT YOU RACK UP ON THE DAYS YOU WORK ON HOT SITES.
Chart: Work Amount, Special Management Area Work, Basic Rate, Management Area Compensation
IN MY CASE, THE BASIC PAY IS 10,000 A DAY WHILE WORKING, WITH AN EXTRA 10,000 IN HAZARD PAY FOR DAYS WORKING INDOORS.
20
9
200.000
90.000
SO DAYS OUTSIDE DOING PREP WORK FOR THE JOB ONLY PAY 10,000 YEN ON THEIR OWN.
Second Column: Days, Days, Yen, Yen
STILL, IT'S DEFINITELY GIVEN ME MORE BREATHING ROOM THAN THE OLD DAYS, WORKING FOR 8,000 YEN WITH THE SENARY SUBCON-TRACTOR.
WELL, GOOD NIGHT.
'NIGHT.
IT'S JUST A SHAME THAT YOU CAN'T ACTUALLY DO IT FOR VERY LONG.

THE NEXT DAY IS THE PT STAGE WITH TEPCO PRE-SENT.
AFTER PASSING INSPEC-TION, WE ATTACH THE VALVE.
You tighten it on with bolts
THEN THEY START UP THE WATER SYSTEM TO TEST THE SEAL.
0.8 mSv exposure that day
SO I GUESS WE DON'T GET TO SEE THEM TURN IT ON.
0.9 mSv exposure
HEY, IT'S A SHIFT SYSTEM, WE CAN'T DO ANYTHING ABOUT IT. BUT IT DOES FEEL LESS FULFILLING, DOESN'T IT?
Already done for the day with high enough exposure that they have to hang back
THE WORK CONTINUES ON, REGARDLESS OF HOW ANY INDIVIDUAL FEELS.
ALL RIGHT, LET'S SLAP IT ON.
THE NEXT DAY WE RUSTPROOF THE METAL.
GWOHH...
I CAN HEAR WHAT SOUNDS LIKE A PUMP, SO THERE MUST BE WATER PASSING THROUGH HERE.

WHOOPS.
SPLATCH
HMMM... I DON'T LIKE HOW I BOTCHED THIS SPOT. IT'S UGLY.
HEY, QUIT WASTIN' TIME OVER THERE!
IT'S JUST RUST-PROOFING, IT AIN'T MEANT TO LOOK PRETTY. IT'S MORE IMPORTANT THAT YOU DO IT QUICK SO YOU DON'T TAKE ANY EXTRA RADIATION.
YES, SIR.
BESIDES, WE'RE JUST GONNA TEAR IT DOWN EVENTUALLY.
YEAH ...
THAT'S TRUE...
NO MATTER HOW MUCH YOU FOCUS ON THE EXECU-TION...
...OUR ULTI-MATE PUR-POSE HERE IS TO TEAR DOWN THIS FACILITY.

THE ONLY THING YA GOTTA TAKE YOUR TIME ON IS ASSURING THE PRODUCT QUALITY.
IT'S CRUCIAL HERE.
...YES, SIR!
THAT'S RIGHT.
EVEN IF ALL OF THIS IS ULTIMATELY MEANT TO BE TORN DOWN, DOING THE JOB RIGHT AND PROPERLY IS THE ONLY WAY TO ENSURE WE GET TO THE GOAL OF DECOMMISS-IONING THIS PLANT.
IT'S NOT AT ALL A BACKWARDS PROCESS; I'VE SEEN THE FORWARD-LOOKING SPIRIT OF ALL THOSE WORKING AT ICHI-F TO ACHIEVE THE RENOVATION AND REBIRTH OF THIS AREA.
WE JUST DON'T TALK ABOUT IT...

ALONG WITH THE RUST-COATING, WE REATTACH AND TIGHTEN THE PIPE FIXTURES TO FINISH THE JOB.
TDF 泉
Even the new guy is a reliable hand by the end of it
TODAY'S LEVEL: 0.8 mSv
NEXT DAY IS RETRIEVING TOOLS AND CLEANING UP THE WORKSITE.
TDF 竜田
TODAY'S LEVEL: 0.3 mSv
ALL RIGHT, WE ALL LOADED?
WHAM
YEP! GOOD WORK, ALL.
UMM... DO YOU MIND TAKING OVER THE DRIVING FOR ME?
REALLY? SURE... WHAT'S UP, MR. TATSUTA?
TDF 竜田
WELL...
MY MASK IS ALL FOGGED UP.

YIKES! THAT SOUNDS BAD.
I REALLY APPRECIATE IT.
WHAT HAPPENED?
IT'S AN AIR LEAK.
WHEN FULL-FACE MASKS GET A LEAK, IT OFTEN FOGS UP INSIDE.
It also happens when there's a big temperature difference
NEARLY ALL LEAKS ARE CAUSED BY NOT TIGHTENING THE BANDS ENOUGH.
The others are loose filters or faulty masks
I GUESS I WAS TOO CAUTIOUS AGAINST NOT GIVING MYSELF A HEADACHE...
MY FIRST DAY ON THIS JOB, I GOT A HEADACHE FROM PULLING IT TOO TIGHT...
I GUESS I WAS FEELING TOO RELAXED WITH THIS BEING THE LAST DAY...
...AND ON THE LAST DAY, I GOT A LEAK FOR BEING TOO LOOSE.
SO THIS STORY COMES TO A (LITERALLY) LOOSE END...
...BUT THAT WAS BASICALLY THE END TO THIS JOB.

SEE CHAP. 9

WITH THE WORK OUT OF THE WAY ...
TAIRA NEIGHBORHOOD OF IWAKI
...IT'S TIME FOR A PARTY.
TO A JOB WELL DONE!
CHEEEERS!!
THERE'S OVER A DOZEN PEOPLE PRESENT, FROM THE WORK CHIEF AND MANAGING DIRECTOR OF THE MASTER CONTRACTOR, TO THE PRESIDENT OF THE PRIMARY SUBCONTRACTOR, TO THE WORKERS LIKE ME.
YOUR EFFORTS GOT IT ALL DONE ON SCHE-DULE.
IT WASN'T ME, IT WAS THE MEN DOING THE WORK.
SOMETIMES THIS TURNS INTO REFLEC-TION ON WHAT WE COULD DO BETTER, BUT MOSTLY IT'S JUST A NORMAL CHANCE TO DRINK AND MAKE MERRY.

Top: Today's Specials

IT WAS HERE THAT I FIRST GOT TO TRY...
OH.
日のおすすめ
冷奴・
メヒカリ唐揚げ・
うに貝焼・・
WHAT'S THAT? MEHI-KARI?
DO YOU SUPPOSE I COULD ORDER ONE OF THESE?

List: Shell-cooked urchin, Fried mehikari, Chilled tofu

At the market I saw some from Aichi, west of Tokyo!

Package: Mehikari from Onahama

LATER, THEY FOUND THAT MEHI-KARI DID NOT TEST POSITIVE FOR RADI-ATION, AND THEY ADDED IT TO THE LIST OF SPECIES TO BE TEST-FISHED.
NOW YOU CAN GET THEM FROM FUKUSHIMA (ONAHAMA, FOR EXAMPLE) AT THE MARKET—IN SMALL QUANTITIES.
THE ONE I ATE ON THIS OCCA-SION WASN'T LOCAL, BUT IT WAS LONG-AWAITED.
I GOT TO SAVOR THE TRUE SENSE OF PLACE I EARNED BY BEING HERE.

After-party at a karaoke bar

I DON'T BE-LIEVE THAT MY PRE-SENCE HERE HAS CAUSED SOME PRO-FOUND CHANGE ...
BETWEEN THE CRESTS OF THE WAVES... ♪
BUT THERE IS SOME-THING PARTICU-LARLY SATISFYING ABOUT FINISHING UP A HARD JOB WITH ALL OF THESE PEOPLE.

Card: TEPCO WID (1-F)

WHEN AN INDIVI-DUAL WORK ORDER IS COMPLETE, YOU GET DIS-CHARGED AND YOUR WORKER ID IS DEACTI-VATED.
THEN YOU RETURN YOUR ID, YOUR ASSIGN-MENT BAR-CODE, AND YOUR GLASS BADGE, AND AS USUAL...
... IT'S TIME FOR THE WBC.
HERE ARE YOUR RE-SULTS.
THANKS.

ID: Tatsuta, Kazuto

Top Sheet: 10/2/2012, Tokyo Electric WBC Center, Kazuto Tatsuta 1925 cpm

Bottom Sheet: Kazuto Tatsuta, 1682 cpm

YOU MEAN THAT TEPCO DOCTORS THE MACHINES TO SPIT OUT LOWER NUMBERS?
YEAH, EXACTLY. SO THAT THE WORKERS' EXPOSURE LOOKS BETTER...
THAT'S RIGHT, I HEARD THAT TOO...
IT WAS A STORY ABOUT SOMEONE WHOSE WHOLE-BODY COUNT WAS FINE WHEN MEASURED AT J-VILLAGE, BUT TURNED OUT TO BE WAY HIGHER AT A DIFFERENT NUCLEAR PLANT, WHICH PREVENTED HIM FROM WORKING THERE.
BEEP!
BEEP!
This is my imagination - WBCs don't have alarms
SOUNDS INTRIGUING! MAYBE I'LL GO AND FIND OUT FOR MYSELF.
AND HOW YA GONNA DO THAT?
Sign: Tokiwa Hospital
A FEW DAYS LATER
I WENT TO A LOCAL HOSPITAL IN IWAKI AND PAID OUT OF POCKET TO TAKE THEIR WBC TEST.
It cost about 5,000 yen!
RIGHT THIS WAY, MR. TATSUTA.
THANK YOU.

The standing model is considered to be more reliable, relatively speaking.

OOOH, THIS IS NEAT!

THE RESULT...

WE DID NOT PICK UP ANY READINGS OF CESIUM, MR. TATSUTA.

I DIDN'T THINK SO.

IF THERE ARE NO PEAKS HERE, HERE, AND HERE, THAT MEANS THERE'S BASICALLY NO RADIOACTIVE CESIUM.

HE EVEN DID A SPECTRAL ANALYSIS FOR ME.

AND THE PEAK ON THE RIGHT IS POTASSIUM.

Studied up a bit

You have to change outfits in case there's any radioactive material or your clothes (at JV, you just remove your top)

TURNS OUT RUMORS ARE JUST RUMORS.

OH... HUH!

GOOD FOR YOU, MR. HUMAN GUINEA PIG!

AT THE END OF THIS JOB IN OCTOBER, I RETURNED TO TOKYO FOR A BIT.

AFTER A MONTH AWAY, I THEN REPORTED BACK TO ICHI-F IN DECEMBER FOR ANOTHER JOB.

OF COURSE, I TOOK ANOTHER WBC TEST BEFORE THAT JOB...

...AND MY NUMBERS WERE HIGHER THAN WHEN I LEFT ICHI-F IN OCTOBER.

LOOKS LIKE I WAS ACTUALLY GETTING MORE INTERNAL RADIATION BACK IN TOKYO THAN I WAS WORKING AT ICHI-F!

REALLY?!

THIS IS PROBABLY NOT THE CASE, BUT MORE A SIGN OF HOW MUCH THESE VALUES CAN FLUCTUATE.

Circle: (Certified)

It doesn't become an issue until you reach five digits

I KNOW I'M BEATING A DEAD HORSE HERE, BUT WHAT WE'RE REALLY CONCERNED ABOUT ISN'T INTERNAL RADIATION, BUT OUR EXTERNAL RADIATION EXPOSURE REACHING CERTAIN MANDATED LIMITS.

THE PROJECT IN DECEMBER ENDED SAFELY, BUT AT THE END OF IT MY RADIATION EXPOSURE TOTAL FOR THE YEAR WAS OVER 18 MILLISIEVERTS.

OF THAT TOTAL, 2.6 MSV WERE FROM WORKING AT THE REST AREA.

I'M GOING TO HEAD BACK HOME UNTIL THE SPRING.

WELL, TAKE CARE.

COME BACK WHENEVER YOU WANT.

8.3 MSV WERE FROM THE OCTOBER JOB.

WELL, THAT'S ABOUT WHAT WE EXPECTED.

EVERYONE'S NEARLY AT THE LIMIT NOW.

7.6 MSV WERE FROM DECEMBER.

I HAD NO GUAR-AN-TEE OF WHEN MY RE-TURN WOULD BE...
BELIEVE ME, I'LL BE BACK!
WE'LL BE WAIT-ING!
PLEASE CALL ME AGAIN IF YOU GET ANY GOOD CONTRACTS STARTING IN THE SPRING.
WE CERTAINLY WILL.
18.5 MSV WERE WHAT I WAS EXPOSED TO AT ICHI-F OVER THE COURSE OF 2012.

The next time I came here, this (the upper floor wreckage of the Unit 3 Building) wouldn't be here

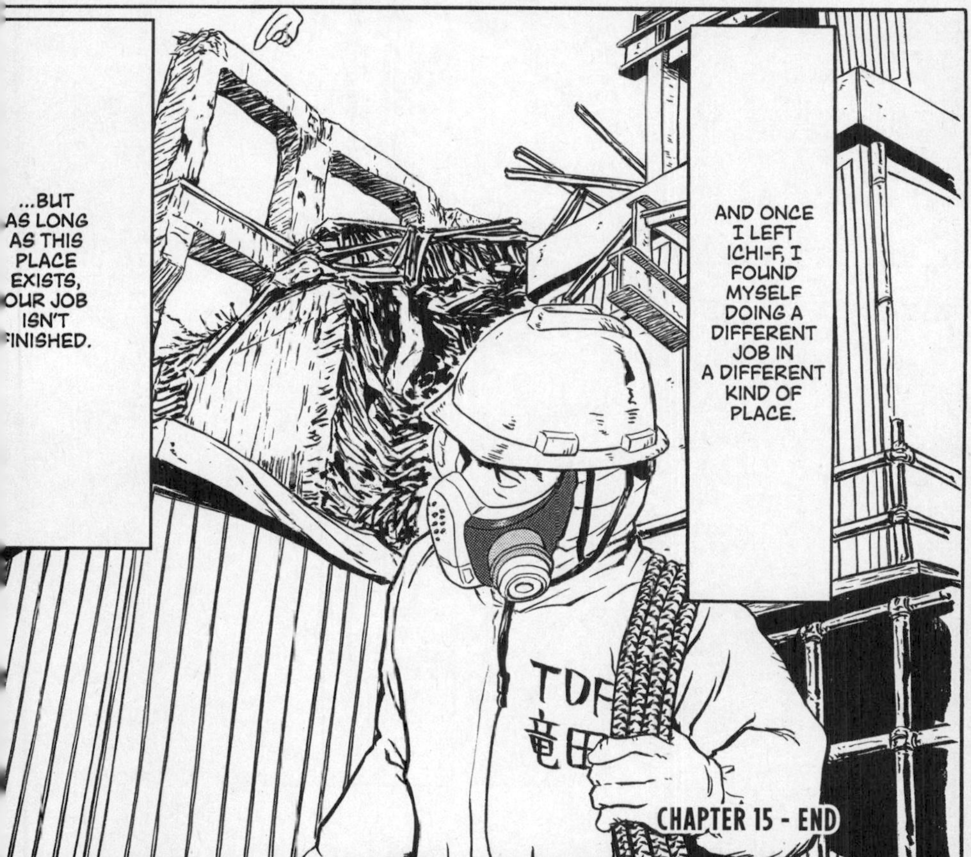
AND ONCE I LEFT ICHI-F, I FOUND MYSELF DOING A DIFFERENT JOB IN A DIFFERENT KIND OF PLACE.
...BUT AS LONG AS THIS PLACE EXISTS, OUR JOB ISN'T FINISHED.
TDF
竜田
CHAPTER 15 - END

The following is an extra piece drawn for the May 19th, 2014 issue of *Shukan Gendai* (Modern Weekly).

IN A BUILDING AT ICHI-F, 2012
THE TEAM IS AT WORK IN FULL HEAVY GEAR.
EXTRA STORY 2:
EXTRACTION DIFFICULTIES
MR. TATSUTA ...
SOMETIMES NATURE OVERRIDES OUR BEST EFFORTS TO IGNORE IT.
WHAT'S THE MATTER, IZUMI?
Some rest areas have an all-you-can-drink policy to prevent overheating
I...I REALLY NEED TO PEE...
WHAT ?!
DIDN'T YOU TAKE CARE OF THAT BACK AT THE SHELTER?!
I DID, BUT I DRANK TOO MUCH OF THAT SPORTS DRINK...
I'M SORRY, MR. ONO, BUT I NEED TO ESCORT IZUMI TO THE TOILET...
ARE YOU KIDDING?!
TDF 大野
I'M SORRY ...
TDF 竜田
WELL, ALL RIGHT—JUST MAKE IT QUICK.
WE WILL!
TDF 竜田

OKAY, FIRST YOU TAKE A TYVEK OFF.
YES, SIR.
AND THE GLOVES.
We wear two layers in high-contamination environments
PUT SOME SHOE COVERS ON BEFORE GETTING IN THE CAR.
YES, SIR.
Absolutely no riding with contaminated shoes!
MAN, I DON'T WANT TO HAVE TO TAKE ANOTHER SURVEY.
VRMMM
DON'T WORRY, I'LL TAKE YOU TO THE BEST SPOT.
THERE ARE FLUSH TOILETS IN THE ANTI-QUAKE BUILDING AND COMPANY REC BUILDING...
...BUT TO GET IN THERE, YOU HAVE TO REMOVE ALL EQUIPMENT AND UNDERGO A FULL DECONTAMINATION SURVEY.
It can easily take most of an hour during busy periods
HERE WE ARE.
ISN'T THIS TATESHIBA ...?
THERE ARE VERY FEW TOILETS YOU CAN USE AT ICHI-F IN YOUR TYVEK FROM BEING ON-SITE.
VRMM
TATESHIBA SITE PREP. FACILITY (AKA: DIY building)
THIS IS ONE OF THOSE VALUABLE HIDDEN SPOTS.

AHH, THANK GOD...
ZIIIP
KSHUF KSHUF
WHOA, WAIT A MINUTE!
WH-WHAT IS IT NOW?
YOU SHOULD TAKE OFF YOUR OTHER SET OF RUBBER GLOVES.
We wear cotton gloves first, then two pairs of rubber gloves
WHAT IF THERE'S A WHOLE BUNCH OF RADIO-ACTIVE GUNK ON THESE GLOVES?
WHAT DO YOU THINK'S GONNA HAPPEN TO YOUR JOHNSON AFTER YOU TOUCH IT?
This is extremely unlikely, since we wear two pairs on the job for this very purpose!
OH ...
IF IT GETS A HIT IN SURVEY, THEY'LL TAKE YOU TO A SEPARATE ROOM FOR DECONTAM-INATION.
I'VE NEVER SEEN IT MYSELF, BUT IF WORD GETS AROUND THAT SOME GUY SHOWED POSITIVE ON HIS GROIN, I HAVE NO DOUBT HE'LL BE FAMOUS BEFORE LONG.
FWOP
WHAT ABOUT THE COTTON GLOVES ?
UP TO YOU.
BUT I BET IT'S BEST NOT TO GO BARE-HANDED AROUND HERE.

Sign: If you pee, you must flush the urinal!!!!
You don't flush, you don't pee!!

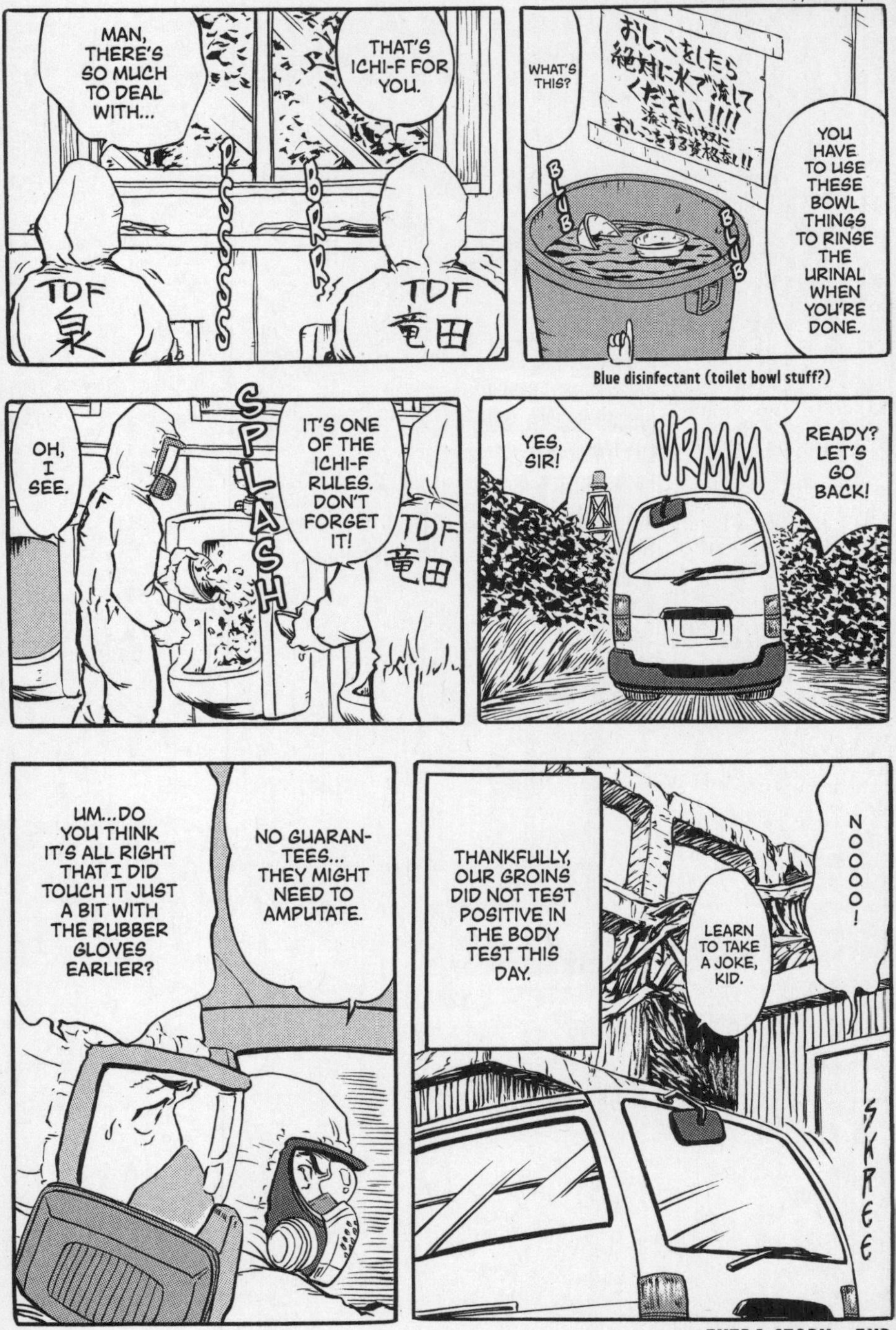

Blue disinfectant (toilet bowl stuff?)

EXTRA STORY - END

MEHIKARI

THE NAME (MEANING "EYE-LIGHT") COMES FROM THEIR LARGE, GLOWING GREEN EYES. THE MEHIKARI CAUGHT AROUND IWAKI ARE ESPECIALLY FATTY AND DELICIOUS, MAKING THEM HIGHLY PRIZED AT THE FISH MARKET. THERE WAS NO FISHING HAPPENING IN IWAKI AFTER THE EARTHQUAKE UNTIL A TEST WAS DONE ON OCTOBER 18TH, 2013, TWO YEARS AND SEVEN MONTHS LATER. THEY PULLED UP EIGHT TYPES OF FISH, INCLUDING MEHIKARI.

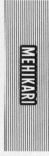

MEHIKARI IS FANTASTICALLY GOOD WHEN FRIED. ITS IDEAL SEASON IS THE COLD MONTHS, FROM NOVEMBER TO FEBRUARY.

The following is an extra piece drawn for the August 22nd, 2014 issue of *Friday*.

GREETINGS, READERS OF *FRIDAY*. I'M TATSUTA, AUTHOR OF THIS COMIC ABOUT WORKING AT FUKUSHIMA DAIICHI. SINCE THIS IS BEING RUN IN A DIFFERENT MAGAZINE THAN USUAL, ENJOY THIS LITTLE SECRET STORY OF THE CONDITIONS HERE.
THERE ARE PEOPLE OF MANY BACKGROUNDS AT ICHI-F; SOME RUMORS SAY, "THEY'RE SHIPPING IN ALL KINDS OF YAKUZA TO WORK THERE!" WHAT HAVE I SEEN FOR MYSELF? WELL...
EXTRA STORY 3:
A MAN'S BACK
We have to wear our own boxers/briefs!
OKAY, YOU'RE GOOD TO GO.
WHEW! HOT ONE OUT THERE.
THE UNDERGARMENTS WE WEAR ON THE JOB ARE PROVIDED BY TEPCO AND GET COLLECTED AFTER USE.
Sign: Caps
HEY, HOW'S IT GOIN'? WHERE YOU WORKIN' NOW?
INDOOR PIPING. HOW 'BOUT YOU?
WELDING THE TANKS. MAN, IT'S HOT WORK...

THAT IS STUNNING.
HELL OF A PIECE.
SO LONG.
CATCH YOU LATER.
ARE YOU FRIENDS WITH THAT GUY, MR. ONO?
HEH...YOU SAW THE TATTOO AND THOUGHT HE WAS A YAKUZA?
ER, WELL ...
HE'S A FORMER FISHERMAN.
THEY HAVE A PRACTICE AROUND HERE OF GETTING BIG TATTOOS, SO IF THEIR BODIES WASH UP, THEY CAN BE IDENTIFIED.
OH, I SEE ...
OTHER BLUE-COLLAR TYPES GET TATTOOS TOO, LIKE SCAFFOLDING WORKERS.
YOU WORK AROUND JOBS LIKE THIS, YOU'LL SEE SOME TATTOOS.
NOW THAT YOU MENTION IT, I'VE SEEN A NUMBER OF YOUNGER FORMER DELINQUENTS WITH TATTOOS HERE AND THERE IN ICHI-F.

AND I'M SURE THERE ARE, IN FACT, SOME EX-YAKUZA IN HERE.
BUT YOU'RE SAYING THAT JUST HAVING A TRADITIONAL TATTOO ISN'T PROOF THAT YOU'RE A YAKUZA.
THAT CERTAINLY PUTS A NEW PERSPECTIVE ON THOSE "SCANDALOUS" EXPOSÉS WITH HIDDEN-CAMERA PICTURES OF TATTOOED MEN SUPPOSEDLY TAKEN AT A SHELTER IN ICHI-F.
BESIDES, IF THEY WERE REAL YAKUZA, THEY WOULDN'T BE ACTUALLY GETTING DIRTY ON THE JOB, THEY'D JUST RUN SOME MIDDLEMAN TAKE-THE-MONEY-AND-RUN SCHEME.
YEAH, THAT MAKES SENSE!
HA HA HA
THAT'S A PROB-LEM OF ITS OWN, THOUGH...
ALL RIGHT, I GOTTA CHANGE.
MR. TATSU-TA...
HMM?
I DON'T THINK I'VE EVER SEEN MR. ONO'S BACK...
NOW THAT YOU MEN-TION IT...
GIVEN HOW IMPOSING HE IS, I WOULDN'T BE SURPRISED AT ANYTHING HE MIGHT BE SPOR-TING...
SWISH
SWISH...
THAT'S TRUE...

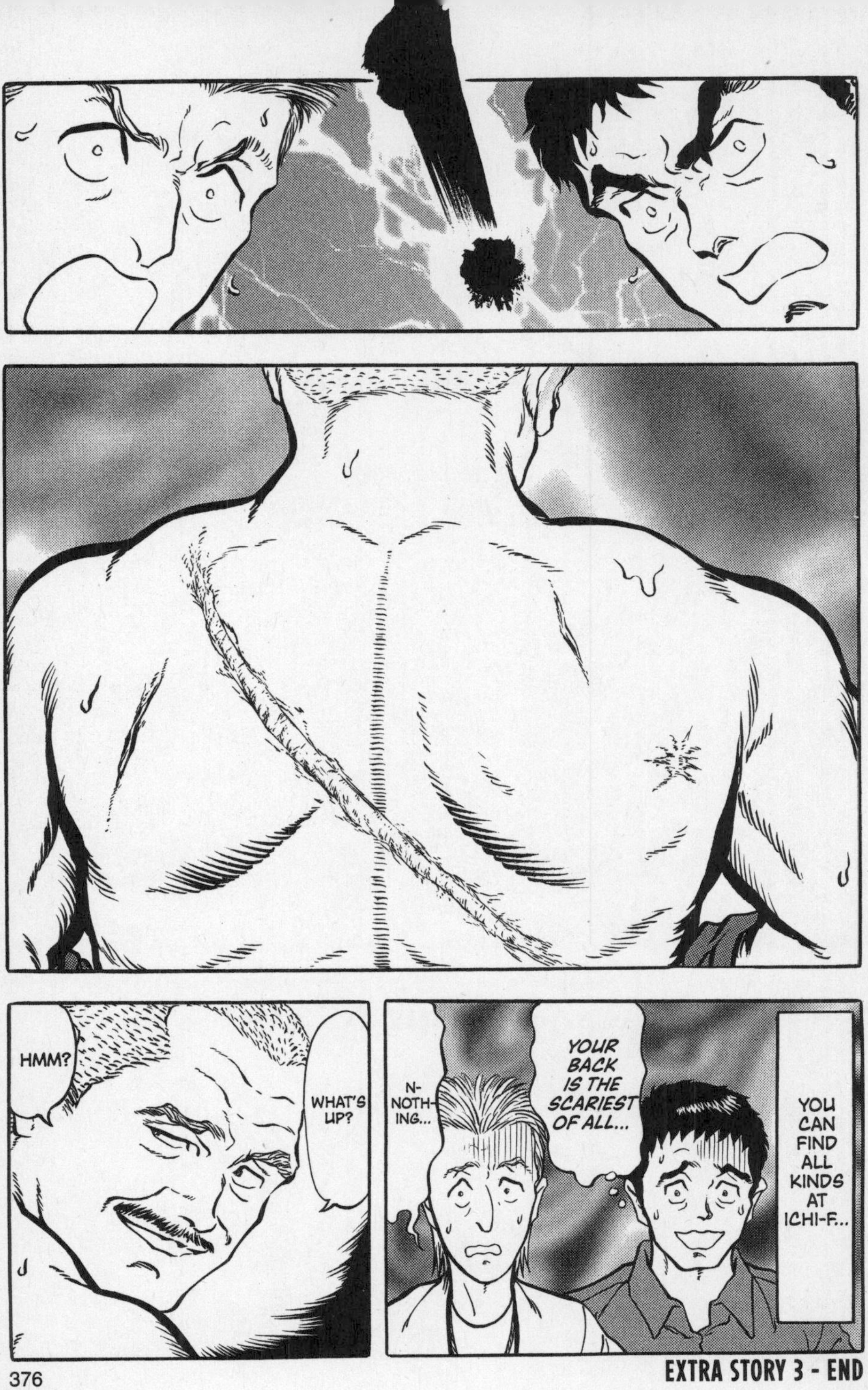

YOU CAN FIND ALL KINDS AT ICHI-F...
YOUR BACK IS THE SCARIEST OF ALL...
N-NOTHING...
WHAT'S UP?
HMM?

EXTRA STORY 3 - END

TRANSLATION NOTES, PART 2

***ENKA*, PAGE 294**

A kind of sentimental, soulful music that rose to prominence in the first few decades after WWII. Although some of the performance and instrumental elements of *enka* are Western in nature, the melodies, subject matter, and singing style are rooted in more traditional Japanese folk music. Performers often wear kimonos, and the songs tend to be about lost love, close bonds, and lonely, righteous suffering. The singing style of *enka* involves long, drawn-out notes delivered with a nasal vibrato that may seem strange to first-time listeners. As musical styles evolved throughout the late 20th century, *enka* came to be considered "old-fashioned," but it remains a popular and iconic style of Japanese music.

TANABATA, PAGE 301

A summer festival holiday that literally means "evening of the seventh." It is meant to honor the meeting of lovers Orihime and Hikoboshi, two gods who are represented in the night sky by the stars Vega and Altair. The lovers' paths only cross on the seventh day of the seventh month. Due to the differences in calendars over the years, certain regions of Japan celebrate Tanabata on different days (this is true of certain other holidays as well). The Tohoku (northeast Japan) region celebrates it in August, rather than July. In addition to the usual summer festival activities, Tanabata is characterized by the writing of wishes on strips of paper called *tanzaku* that are attached to bamboo trees.

STATE SECRECY LAW, PAGE 310

A 2013 act proposed by the cabinet of Prime Minister Shinzo Abe and passed by the National Diet. It prohibits and punishes the release of information that the state considers relevant to national defense. This includes such topics as defense systems, foreign affairs, counterintelligence operations, and anti-terrorism efforts.

ICHI-F

ICHI-F

CHAPTER 16: LET IT GO

HIGH-SPEED BUS FROM IWAKI TO TOKYO
DECEMBER 2012
東京駅
AS I HEADED BACK TO THE CAPITAL FROM FUKUSHIMA, MY WORK PERIOD CONCLUDED...
...THE IMAGES OF THE NUCLEAR PLANT AND DISASTER AREAS OF THE LAST SIX MONTHS PLAYED ACROSS MY EYELIDS.
1.5

IT WAS ONLY HALF A YEAR, YET I EXPERIENCED SO MANY VIVID THINGS...
AND NOW THAT I'VE SEEN THEM...

...I'VE GOT TO DRAW THEM FOR YOU.

NO ONE ASKED ME TO DO IT, AND THERE WASN'T ANY REASON I HAD TO DRAW THEM.

BUT WHEN I WENT FROM THE EMPTY RE-STRICTED ZONE AND TSUNAMI DAMAGE...

...TO THE DAZZLING NIGHT SKY OF TOKYO...

...I COULDN'T POSSIBLY KEEP DOWN THE RISING DESIRE WITHIN MYSELF TO SHOW THESE THINGS TO PEOPLE.

I DON'T INTEND TO MAKE THIS SPECIFICALLY ABOUT THE DISCREP-ANCIES BETWEEN TOKYO AND FUKUSHIMA.

BUT BEING FROM THE TOKYO AREA, IT'S PROBABLY UNAVOID-ABLE.

Headline: Plutonium Headline: Worker Dies Abandoned by TEPCO Headline: Fukushima Mutations Abound

ANYWAY HAVING SEEN THE DIFFERENCE BETWEEN THE REAL FUKUSHIMA AND ITS IMAGE THROUGHOUT THE REST OF THE COUNTRY...
WOW, ALL THE STUFF IN THIS RAG IS B.S.!
RIGHT?
..I WANTED TO LEAVE MY EXPERIENCES BEHIND AS A RECORD OF SORTS.

I WAS ALREADY AN (UNSUCCESSFUL) ARTIST BY TRADE...
...SO IF I WAS GOING TO TELL MY STORY, THE COMIC FORMAT WOULD BE THE WAY.
DARVISH 11
Mostly cheapo convenience store mags: True stories, sports, documentaries...

Mag: Charismatic Cabaret Girl Spills Her Secrets

I DIDN'T GO TO FUKUSHIMA WITH THE INTENTION OF MAKING A MANGA ABOUT IT...
OOOH, THIS WOULD MAKE A GOOD STORY.
BUT ON THE OTHER HAND, I CAN'T SAY THAT I WENT TO WORK THERE WITHOUT ANY INTEREST IN DRAWING IT, EITHER.
THERE'S A MEANING IN HAVING MANY DIFFERENT PEOPLE RECORD THEIR EXPERIENCE IN MANY DIFFERENT WAYS, IN MY OPINION.
AND AT THIS POINT, I BET I'M THE ONLY ONE WHO WILL DRAW IT IN A COMIC.
STF 竜田
STF

Always on the hunt for material by nature

Which I could only stretch out by living with my folks

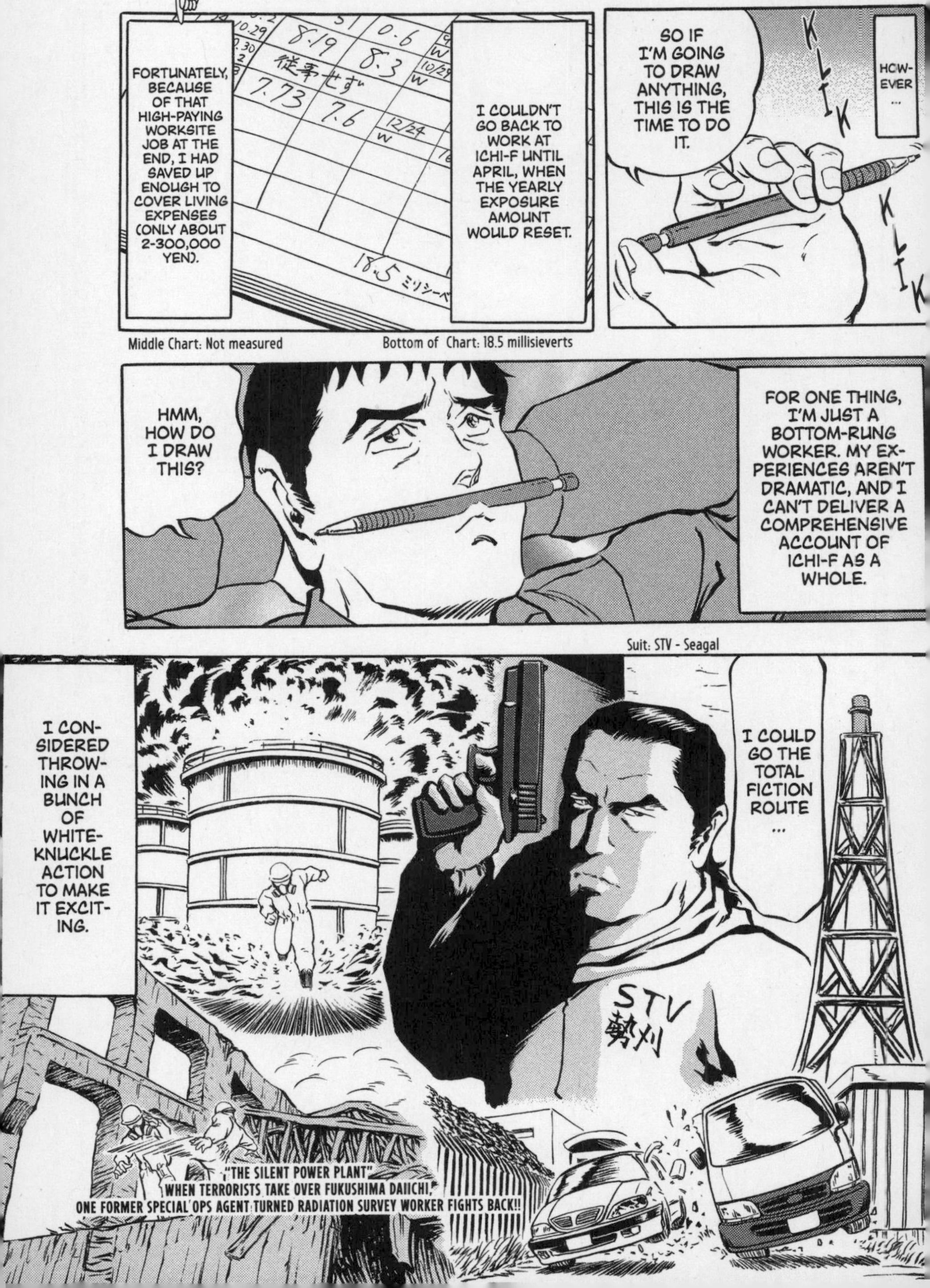

HOW-EVER ...
SO IF I'M GOING TO DRAW ANYTHING, THIS IS THE TIME TO DO IT.
KLIK
KLIK
FORTUNATELY, BECAUSE OF THAT HIGH-PAYING WORKSITE JOB AT THE END, I HAD SAVED UP ENOUGH TO COVER LIVING EXPENSES (ONLY ABOUT 2-300,000 YEN).
I COULDN'T GO BACK TO WORK AT ICHI-F UNTIL APRIL, WHEN THE YEARLY EXPOSURE AMOUNT WOULD RESET.
従事せず
18.5 ミリシーベ
Middle Chart: Not measured
Bottom of Chart: 18.5 millisieverts
FOR ONE THING, I'M JUST A BOTTOM-RUNG WORKER. MY EXPERIENCES AREN'T DRAMATIC, AND I CAN'T DELIVER A COMPREHENSIVE ACCOUNT OF ICHI-F AS A WHOLE.
HMM, HOW DO I DRAW THIS?
Suit: STV - Seagal
I COULD GO THE TOTAL FICTION ROUTE ...
I CONSIDERED THROWING IN A BUNCH OF WHITE-KNUCKLE ACTION TO MAKE IT EXCITING.
STV 勢刈
"THE SILENT POWER PLANT"
WHEN TERRORISTS TAKE OVER FUKUSHIMA DAIICHI,
ONE FORMER SPECIAL OPS AGENT TURNED RADIATION SURVEY WORKER FIGHTS BACK!!

BUT IF I EXAGGERATE THINGS, THAT PUTS ME IN THE SAME BOAT AS THE ONES STIRRING PEOPLE UP WITH BAD INFO.
TOSS
SO ULTIMATELY I COULDN'T DRAW ANYTHING I DIDN'T SEE.
IN FACT, THE TOTAL LACK OF SENSATIONAL MEDIA BAIT...
...OR OTHER DRAMATIC EVENTS WHILE I WAS THERE SEEMED FRESH AND NOVEL TO ME.
THE LACK OF THRILLING, JUICY MATERIAL IS EXACTLY WHAT HAPPENED TO ME AT ICHI-F, AND IT OCCURRED TO ME THAT THIS WAS THE "HIDDEN TRUTH" THAT THE MEDIA NEVER REPORTS.
LET IT GOOOO LET IT GOOOO CAN'T HOLD IT BACK ANYMORE... ♪
I KNEW LOTS OF PEOPLE HAD TO BE CURIOUS ABOUT WHAT IT WAS LIKE THERE, SO I DREW UP THE FIRST CHAPTER AS AN INTRODUCTORY TOUR...
I HAD NO CONTRACT OR PLACE TO PUBLISH IT, AND THE "GUIDE TO ICHI-F" I DREW WITH MINIMAL INFO ENDED UP BEING THE RATHER RANDOM LENGTH OF 37 PAGES.
IS ANYONE EVEN GOING TO BE INTERESTED IN PRINTING THIS?
ACTUALLY, IT WAS JUST IN DRAFT* FORM ...

Sorry, this part is a lie. The song wasn't out yet

*A rough outline/storyboard before actually drawing the finished product

I EVEN HAD AN OFFER FROM A MAJOR PUBLISHER TO EXPAND IT INTO BOOK FORM.
NICE TO MEET YOU.
I'M WITH XYZ INTERNATIONAL.
I BROUGHT IT TO A FRIEND OF MINE IN EDITORIAL PRODUCTION.
LISTEN, I'VE GOT THIS PROJECT GOING...
WOW, REALLY?! I'VE GOT TO SEE THIS!
I NEED TO JUST TAKE IT TO A MAGAZINE LIKE EVERYONE ELSE.
I DIDN'T THINK I'D GET TO GO STRAIGHT TO A BOOK, ANYWAY.
神保町駅 Jimbōchō Sta.
APRIL 2013
THAT'S TOO BAD.
Sounds like the plan hit a rough patch.
IN THE END, THE PROJECT FELL THROUGH...
DO YOU THINK THIS IS BEST SUITED TO THE COMIC FORMAT?
ERR...
MY FIRST DESTINATION WAS NOT THE EVENTUAL PUBLISHER *MORNING*, BUT A RIVAL MAG.
HMM...

I SUPPOSE YOU'RE RIGHT. THERE'S SO MUCH TEXT AND NOT MUCH EXCITEMENT.

THE YOUNG EDITOR DID NOT TAKE TO IT.

IF YOU EVER DRAW SOMETHING ELSE, PLEASE BRING IT IN.

The classic turned-down phrases

SURE THING. SEE YOU THEN!

Too spiteful to just go back home

AND HE DIDN'T EVEN GIVE ME HIS CARD. TALK ABOUT STRIKING OUT!

I'LL GIVE THE NEXT PLACE A SHOT.

Hello, Morning Editorial Office.

HI, I WORK AT FUKUSHIMA DAIICHI NUCLEAR POWER PLANT, AND I DREW A MANGA ABOUT IT.

Would rather try everything in one outing

Slight exaggeration

WHAT, REALLY?!

I'm here in Tokyo from Fukushima. Do you think you could take a look at it?

YES, IT WAS A VERY UNDERHANDED MEANS OF GETTING HIM TO SEE IT. I WAS DOING WHATEVER I COULD TO GET A MEETING THAT VERY DAY.

Today's tough. What about the day after tomorrow?

OKAY, PERFECT. I'LL SEE YOU THEN!

Gave in right away

Definitely lying now

WEIRD. HE SAID HE WAS HERE FROM FUKUSHIMA. WHERE'S HE STAYING?
WHAT'S UP?
CLICK
OH, A WORKER AT FUKUSHIMA DAIICHI WANTED ME TO LOOK AT HIS MANGA.
OOOH.
THE MANGA ITSELF MIGHT NOT BE GREAT, BUT IT'S TOTALLY WORTH HEARING WHAT HE HAS TO SAY, I BET.
WELL, I'LL BE ...
Surprised at how "passable" the work is
COME ON. YOU'VE GOT TO BE A PRO ALREADY.
OH, NO. JUST AN AMATEUR DABBLER.
Why am I hiding this?
PARTLY, THIS WAS A WEIRD STRATEGY OF MINE TO MAKE THE IMPACT OF THE PIECE GREATER BY MAKING HIM THINK AN AMATEUR WORKER DREW IT.
TDF 竜田
When it got published, I redrew these pages in color, but they were originally b/w
THE OTHER PART OF ME JUST WANTED HIM TO VIEW THE WORK OBJECTIVELY WITHOUT CONSIDERING MY OWN PAST AS PART OF IT.

I'LL BE HONEST: THIS IS A TOUGH ONE. IT'S A DELICATE SUBJECT, AND AT A HIGH PAGE COUNT.
WE MIGHT HAVE A BETTER CHANCE IF WE SUBMIT TO AN AMATEUR CONTEST AND GET IT APPRAISED BY JUDGES.
THIS IS A SURE-FIRE HIT, I JUST CAN'T TELL HIM YET.
IF YOU WIN THE CONTEST, WE'LL RUN IT FOR SURE. THE RESULTS ARE ANNOUNCED IN OCTOBER.
REALLY? OCTOBER ...
Going to try elsewhere if not accepted on the spot
SO I'LL JUST HOLD ONTO THIS MANGA FOR YOU ...
NO WAY AM I LETTING THIS GET AWAY!
ER... GEE, THANKS.
I RAN OUT OF MY CASH BUFFER, AND HAD TO TAKE QUICK JOBS TO MAKE ENDS MEET.
WELL, SHOOT. I GUESS THERE'S NO QUICK CASH IN THIS EITHER WAY.
THE MONTHS PASSED INTO SUMMER.
AFTER APRIL, WHEN MY EXPOSURE TOTAL WAS RESET FOR THE YEAR, I DIDN'T GET ANY IMMEDIATE LEADS BACK TO ICHI-F.
AND THERE'S NOTHING PROMISING THROUGH HELLO WORK.
I know all the sketchy places to ignore by now

I'm not blessed with the skill to do two things at once, unfortunately!
YOU'RE PASSING THROUGH THE SELECTION STAGE OF THE CONTEST QUICKLY, SO GET READY TO DRAW A FOLLOW-UP.
OKAY ...
BUT IT'S HARD TO DO THAT WHILE WORKING A JOB...
CLINK
CLANK
WEL-COME!
AND WHAT DO I DO FOR A SEQUEL? I CAN'T JUST DO MORE TOURS OF THE PLANT.
WHAT IF I MAKE EVERYONE LOOK TINY AND CUTE LIKE THIS?
WAIT! THAT'S IT!
CARTOONY ICHI-F
This got rejected, but you can see shades of it in Chapter 2
GIVEN THE SERIOUS TOPIC, THIS MIGHT BE A BIT TOO FRIVOLOUS OF A LOOK...
Common-sense opinion
HMM, I GUESS YOU'RE RIGHT...
Just wants to make it as light and ap-proachable as possible
I CON-TINUED ON WITH THIS TRIAL-AND-ERROR INTO THE FALL...
It's all over! You've won!
REALLY ?!

BEING THE SELF-INTERESTED TYPE, I QUIT MY PART-TIME JOB AND STARTED ON MORE COMICS IN EARNEST.
ALL RIGHT! NOW I'VE GOT A MEANS TO PAY THE BILLS!
BUT THE FUR-THER I GOT...
HMM, HOW FAR HAS THE WORK GONE BY NOW?
...THE MORE CURIOUS I WAS ABOUT THE STATE OF THINGS AND MY FRIENDS BACK THERE.
I WONDER WHAT EV-ERYONE'S UP TO NOW...
AND YET I'M STILL NOT GET-TING ANY CALLS BACK FROM FU-KUSHIMA...
THE THING IS, I DON'T EVEN KNOW IF THIS FOLLOW-UP WILL GO ANYWHERE. IT DEPENDS ON HOW THE FIRST ONE'S RECEIVED.
Realizing I could be unemployed again
...UNTIL OCTO-BER 3RD, 2013: MY FIRST CHAP-TER RAN IN THE MAGA-ZINE.
I WAS STILL IN LIMBO AS BOTH A MANGA ARTIST AND A DECOM-MISSION WORKER ...
TO MY RELIEF, MANY PEO-PLE WANT-ED TO READ MORE.
UH, OKAY...
It's crazy over here! Get cracking on the next one!
THANK-FULLY, THE FEED-BACK WAS HUGE.

Homesick, despite being home

Magazine: *Morning*

RRRR
ALL RIGHT, NOW I CAN FOCUS ON THIS FOR A WHILE.
WITH MY COMIC NOW SERIALIZED, I WAS LOCKED IN WITH DEADLINES. AND JUST THEN...
RRR
着信中
OXI工業
ISN'T THIS...?
WHOA!
RRRR
HELLO?
MR. TATSUTA! WE'VE GOT A JOB LINED UP, CAN YOU COME IN NEXT WEEK?
NEXT WEEK?!
Yep. See you then!
WHAT DO I DO? I'VE BEEN WAITING AGES FOR THIS CALL...
I REALLY WANT TO GO BACK TO ICHI-F...

Phone: Incoming OXI Ind.

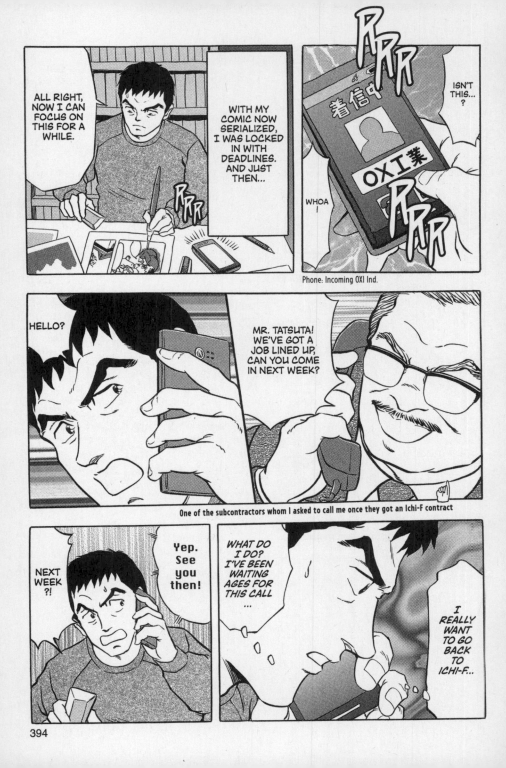

One of the subcontractors whom I asked to call me once they got an Ichi-F contract

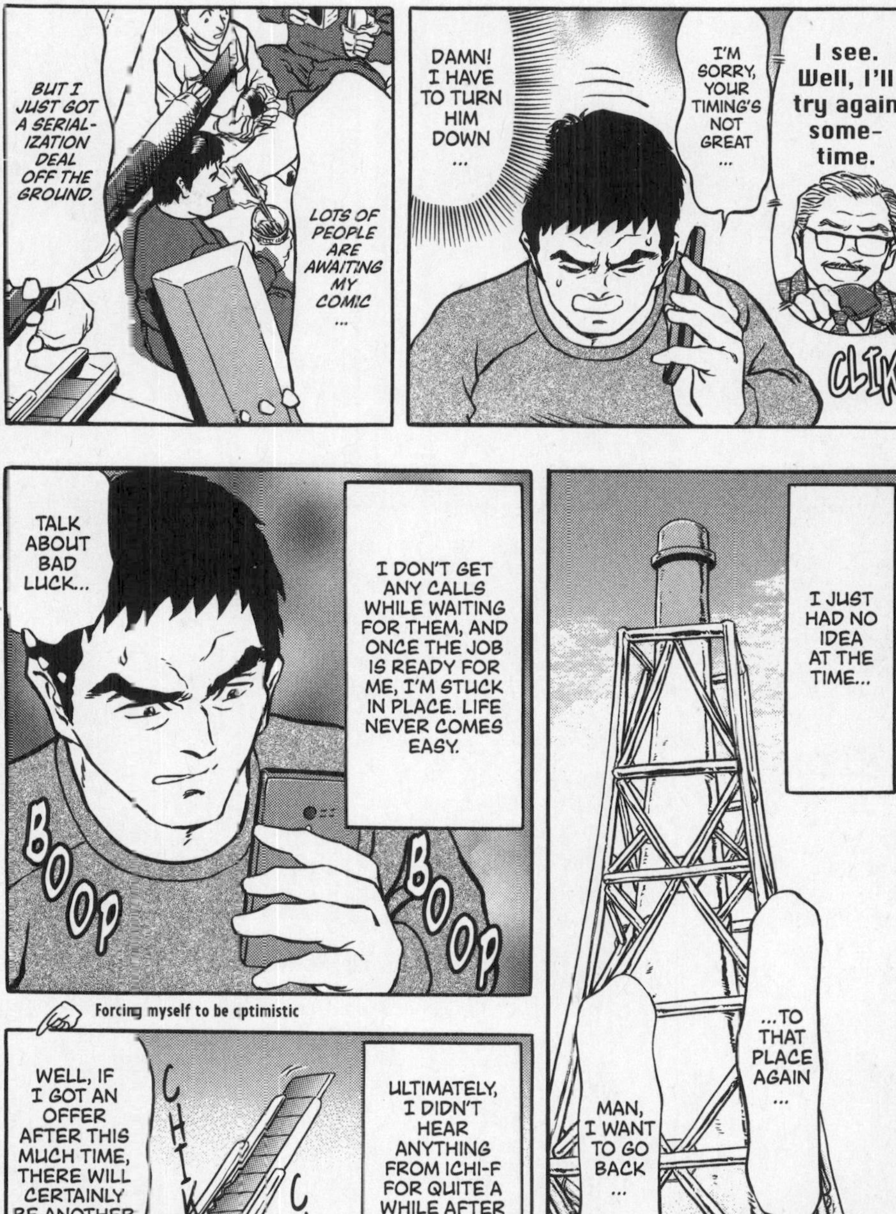
BUT I JUST GOT A SERIALIZATION DEAL OFF THE GROUND.
LOTS OF PEOPLE ARE AWAITING MY COMIC ...
DAMN! I HAVE TO TURN HIM DOWN ...
I'M SORRY, YOUR TIMING'S NOT GREAT ...
I see. Well, I'll try again sometime.
CLIK
TALK ABOUT BAD LUCK...
I DON'T GET ANY CALLS WHILE WAITING FOR THEM, AND ONCE THE JOB IS READY FOR ME, I'M STUCK IN PLACE. LIFE NEVER COMES EASY.
BOOP
BOOP
Forcing myself to be cptimistic
WELL, IF I GOT AN OFFER AFTER THIS MUCH TIME, THERE WILL CERTAINLY BE ANOTHER ONE.
CHIK
CHIK
ULTIMATELY, I DIDN'T HEAR ANYTHING FROM ICHI-F FOR QUITE A WHILE AFTER I TURNED THIS OFFER DOWN.
I JUST HAD NO IDEA AT THE TIME...
MAN, I WANT TO GO BACK ...
...TO THAT PLACE AGAIN ...

CHAPTER 16 - END

SEPTEMBER 2013
WE'LL GO BACK TO JUST BEFORE THE ISSUE OF MORNING WITH THE FIRST CHAPTER OF *ICHI-F* IN IT.
AT A TOKYO-AREA CAFÉ PRIVATE ROOM
茶 喫茶 ルノワール
Sign: Café Renoir
I WAS DOING A SHOOT WITH A PHOTO WEEKLY FROM THE SAME PUBLISHER AS *MORNING*.
MY NAME'S TATSUTA. NICE TO MEET YOU.
MY *MORNING* EDITOR
WE WORK FOR THE SAME COMPANY.
PHOTO MAG EDITOR
THANKS FOR MEETING WITH US TODAY.
WRITER
IT'S GOOD TO MEET YOU.
CAMERAMAN
Dressed in uniform for effect
AS A MATTER OF FACT, I HAD A SECRET WEAPON ON HAND.
I'M SORRY, I'M JUST AN ORDINARY LABORER, SO I DON'T HAVE BUSINESS CARDS.
I BOUGHT IT TO HELP HIDE MY IDENTITY.

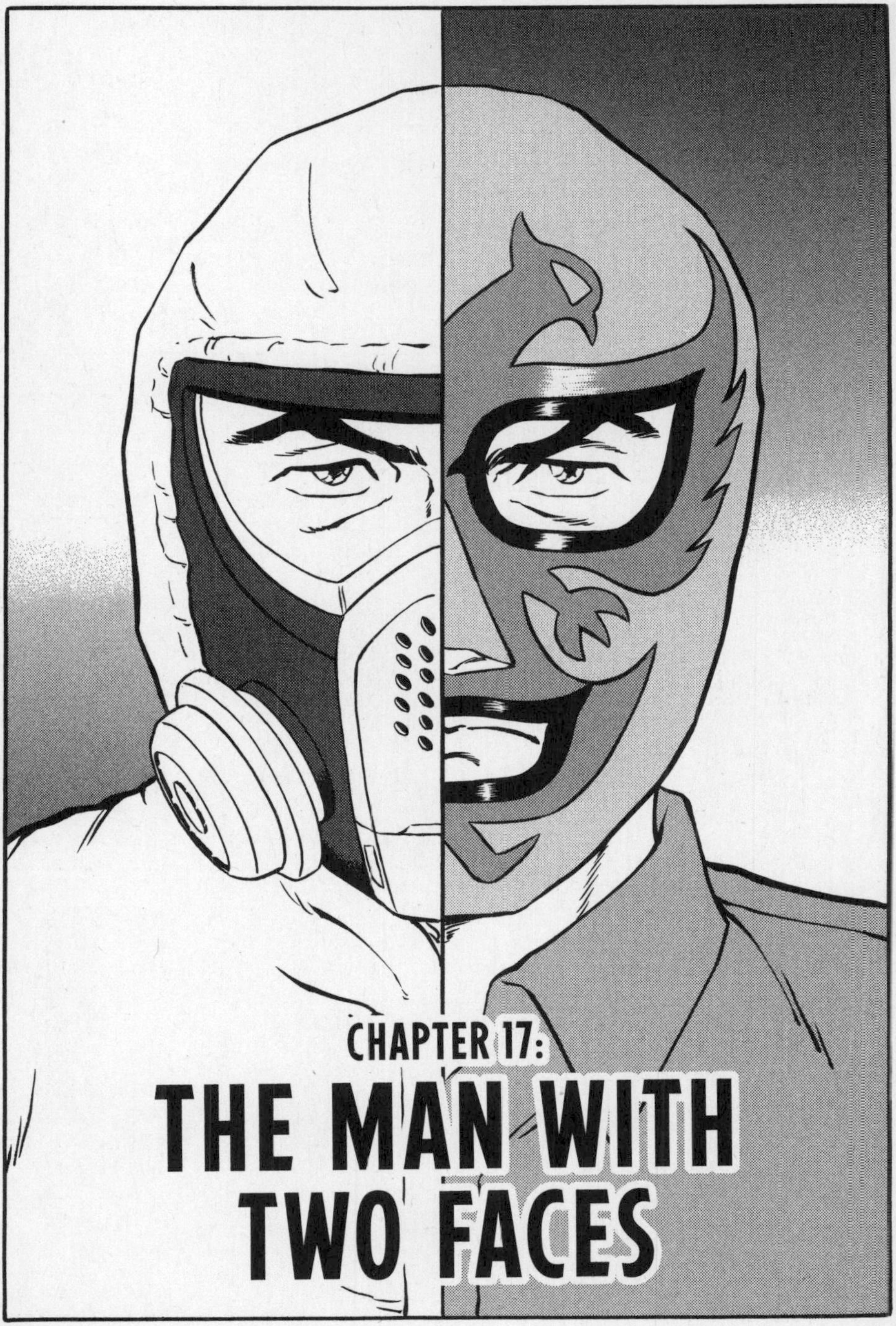
CHAPTER 17:
THE MAN WITH TWO FACES

We're going to get into wrestling for a bit. Non-fans, please stick through it!

Screen: Mask Catalog, Estrella, Pro wrestling masks

The design was different back when he would multiply (Right?)

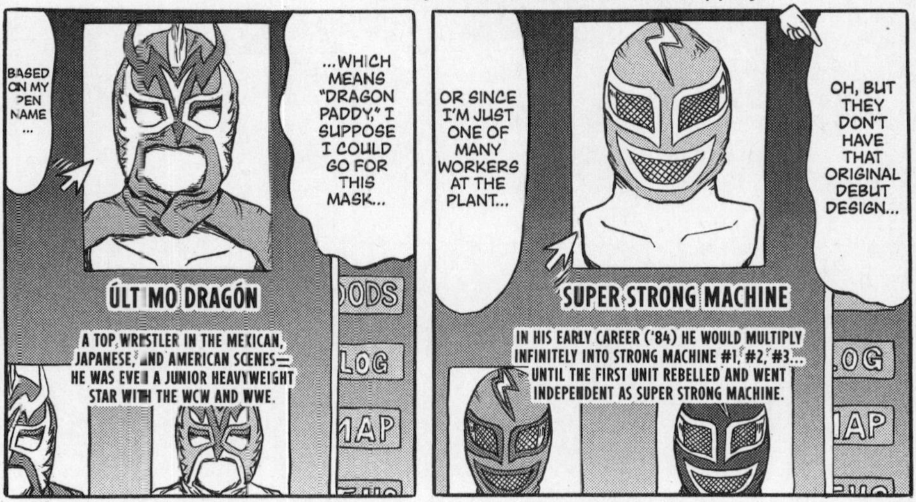

DOS CARAS IS A MEXICAN WRESTLER—*DOS* MEANS "TWO," AND *CARAS* MEANS "FACES."
SO OUT OF RESPECT FOR THE "MAN WITH TWO FACES," AS A WRESTLING FAN, I DECIDED THIS WAS BEST, EVEN THOUGH I KNEW IT WAS A STRETCH.
Self-praise
His brother is Mil Mascaras, the "man of a thousand masks."
I ACCEPTED THE MEDIA OFFER ONLY IF I COULD HIDE MY FACE.
SO... WHY FU-KUSHIMA?
These questions are refreshing the first time, not so much the millionth time
GOOD QUESTION... I ACTUALLY WASN'T LOOKING AT ICHI-F SPECIFICALLY AT THE BEGINNING...
The more I answered it, the more my answer firmed up
I WAS AFRAID THAT THEY WOULDN'T ACTUALLY COMPLY WITH THIS REQUEST.
OKAY, PHOTO TIME.
RUSTLE
RUSTLE
NO FACES, RIGHT?
YES, PLEASE. SORRY ABOUT THE TROUBLE.

IF YOU USED THIS TO COVER YOUR FACE, THAT WOULD BE THE PERFECT IMAGE.
GARDEN-VARIETY ITEMS
ALSO, IF YOU COULD WEAR THIS SUIT...
ERR ...
I DON'T KNOW ABOUT THOSE ...
FULL MASKS AND PROTECTIVE CLOTHING ARE JUST LIKE A UNIFORM FOR US.
I DON'T MEAN TO PRETEND THEY'RE SACRED, BUT I FEEL LIKE IT WOULD BE A DISSERVICE TO THE PEOPLE WORKING THERE IF I'M PUTTING THEM ON HERE.
PLUS, CIVILIANS ALSO WEAR PROTECTIVE CLOTHING WHEN GOING IN OR OUT OF THE RESTRICTED ZONE.
CONSID-ERING THE FEEL-INGS OF THOSE FORCED TO EVACU-ATE...
...I HAVE TO ADMIT I'M RELUCTANT TO SLAP ON THE PROTECTIVE OUTFIT WHERE IT'S NOT NECESSARY.
SHH
ON A SIMILAR NOTE, OVERUSE OF THE NUCLEAR RADIATION SYMBOL WEAKENS ITS WARNING VALUE, SO BE JUDICIOUS, PLEASE!
← This one

SO I'LL WEAR *THIS*.

WHOA!

DOS CARAS!

One in four or five recognizes the mask

WELL, THIS IS GONNA LOOK REAL DUMB NOW!

YOU SURE?

A bit offended

CLICK CLICK

Doing the "checking pages" pose

PEOPLE MIGHT THINK I WAS JOKING AROUND, AND IT'S TRUE THAT I THOUGHT IT WAS A BIT SILLY.

BUT GIVEN THAT I REFUSED TO WEAR THE SUIT, THIS WAS MY SERIOUS ANSWER TO THE ISSUE OF HIDING MY IDENTITY.

OKAY, LET'S GET NO MASK THIS TIME.

WE ALSO TOOK SOME NON-MASKED PHOTOS AND WRAPPED IT UP.

AS LONG AS IT'S FROM THE NECK DOWN.

WHEN THE MAGAZINE CAME OUT, THEY USED THE NECK-DOWN PHOTOS.

Covering my name on the radiation management handbook with my finger

I'M SURE THE MAGAZINE PEOPLE ALSO CONSIDERED A WRESTLING MASK TO BE INAPPROPRIATE FOR THE CONTENT.

*The Mexican style of pro wrestling, meaning "free fighting." Luchadors work ordinary jobs by day and put on masks to wrestle in secret by night.

THE OFFICE DID GET ONE CALL.
Hey, you the editor of Ichi-F?
YES, I AM...
In the comic, I had this as "Kuromori Construction," but he guessed the real name in one!
WHAT IS THIS? A COMPLAINT?
PARDON ME, MAY I ASK WHO'S SPEAKING?
Well, I can't tell ya that...
BUT THIS "TATSUTA" FELLA DRAWIN' THE SERIES HAD TO BE WORKIN' FOR XYZ.
IT'S TOTALLY OBVIOUS JUST BY SEEIN' THE SHELTER LAYOUT.
WHOA...HE'S RIGHT. THIS IS LEGIT. MAYBE I CAN FIND OUT HOW MUCH HE KNOWS.
OH, I SEE. WELL, IF YOU KNOW THAT MUCH, YOU MUST KNOW HIS NAME TOO, I PRESUME?
Nope, not his name yet...
SO YOU DON'T!
But if I feel like it, I can crack the case.

AND... WHAT ARE YOU CALLING ABOUT?
Just wanted to let ya know that the higher-ups are watchin' ya.
WATCH-ING, YOU SAY?
"HIGHER-UPS," HUH? SO THIS GUY MUST BE WITH A SUBCONTRACTOR.
The major plant construction company running the rest area
So that you don't draw any funny business.
WHAT DO YOU MEAN BY "FUNNY BUSINESS"? HAS THERE BEEN ANY "FUNNY BUSINESS" IN ICHI-F THUS FAR?
Not that I've seen yet...
But there's parts and tools involved with "Tateshiba" and their power plant patents ...
And there's security concerns about showin' stuff...
THE HIGHER-UPS ARE ON PINS-AND-NEEDLES ABOUT THIS STUFF, WORRYIN' THAT TEPCO'S GONNA CRACK DOWN ON US.
IF THEY LOOK INTO WHOEVER'S DRAWIN' THIS, THEY'LL FIND OUT IN A SNAP.
AND IF THAT HAPPENS, THIS TATSUTA FELLA AIN'T GONNA HAVE A JOB IN THE TATESHIBA SYSTEM NO MORE.

...AND THAT'S WHAT HE SAID. SO I GUESS THE GUYS THERE CAN TELL.
WELL, SURE, OF COURSE THEY CAN.
BUT MR. TATSUTA, HOW DO YOU KNOW ABOUT THAT PATENTED STUFF?
WHAT DO YOU MEAN? YOU THINK AN ORDINARY SHELTER MANAGEMENT GUY KNOWS ABOUT PATENTED TECH?
FIRST OF ALL, I'VE NEVER HAD ANY INTENTION OF DRAWING SECURITY CHECKPOINT STUFF.
WELL, IN THAT CASE, I GUESS WE'RE PROBABLY IN THE CLEAR?
BUT EVEN IF I DON'T INTEND TO LET OUT ANY SENSITIVE INFORMATION, THAT CAN HAPPEN BY ACCIDENT.
TO BE HONEST, I'M GRATEFUL THAT SOMEONE ELSE ON THE SCENE IS READING THE COMIC.
BUT THEY'RE PLACING WAY TOO MUCH STOCK IN A BOTTOM-RUNG GUY LIKE ME.
THERE'S ALWAYS BEEN A PART OF ME THAT FEELS GUILTY ABOUT "BETRAYING" MY FELLOW WORKERS BY DEPICTING THEIR SECRETS FOR THE PUBLIC.

SO I COULDN'T HELP BUT BE WORRIED THAT I HADN'T HEARD FROM ICHI-F FOR OVER A YEAR SINCE LEAVING.
STILL NO CALLS ...
WHILE THAT WAS GOING ON, THE FIRST COL-LECTED VOLUME CAME OUT.
I DID MORE INTER-VIEWS THAN I EVER HAD IN MY LIFE.
APRIL 2014
A FRE-QUENT QUES-TION WAS...
WHAT DO YOU PLAN TO DO NEXT?
WELL, I'LL CONTINUE DRAWING, OF COURSE...
...BUT I'D ALSO LIKE TO GO BACK TO ICHI-F TO WORK.
People who haven't heard me say this before usually look shocked
AHH. WOULD YOU BE DOING RE-SEARCH WHILE YOU'RE THERE?
NO, NOT FOR MY COMIC'S SAKE.
IT'S JUST A SIMPLE DESIRE TO GO THERE AND WORK.
HONESTLY, I CONSIDER MYSELF A CON-STRUCTION WORKER BEFORE A COMIC ARTIST.

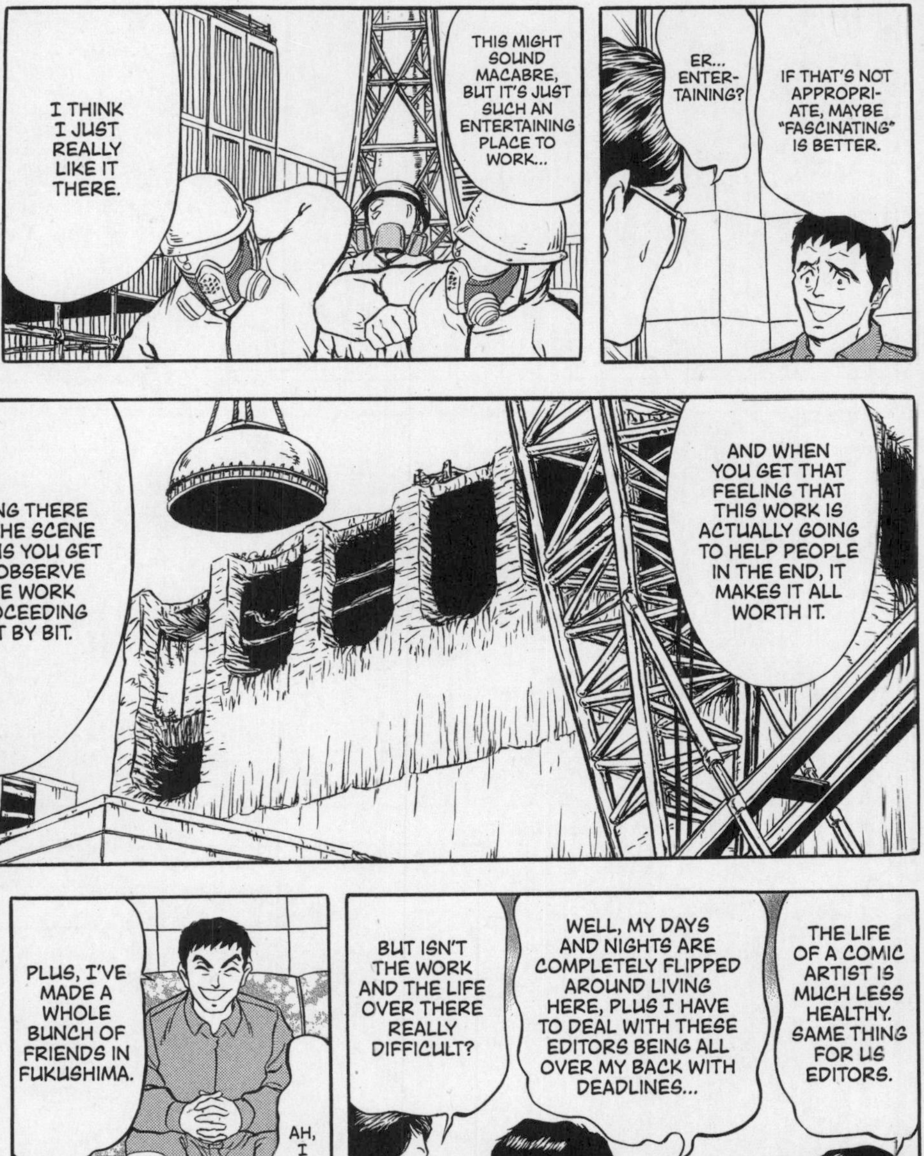
I THINK I JUST REALLY LIKE IT THERE.
THIS MIGHT SOUND MACABRE, BUT IT'S JUST SUCH AN ENTERTAINING PLACE TO WORK...
ER... ENTER-TAINING?
IF THAT'S NOT APPROPRI-ATE, MAYBE "FASCINATING" IS BETTER.
BEING THERE ON THE SCENE MEANS YOU GET TO OBSERVE THE WORK PROCEEDING BIT BY BIT.
AND WHEN YOU GET THAT FEELING THAT THIS WORK IS ACTUALLY GOING TO HELP PEOPLE IN THE END, IT MAKES IT ALL WORTH IT.
PLUS, I'VE MADE A WHOLE BUNCH OF FRIENDS IN FUKUSHIMA.
AH, I SEE ...
BUT ISN'T THE WORK AND THE LIFE OVER THERE REALLY DIFFICULT?
WELL, MY DAYS AND NIGHTS ARE COMPLETELY FLIPPED AROUND LIVING HERE, PLUS I HAVE TO DEAL WITH THESE EDITORS BEING ALL OVER MY BACK WITH DEADLINES...
THE LIFE OF A COMIC ARTIST IS MUCH LESS HEALTHY. SAME THING FOR US EDITORS.

HA HA, I SEE. THANK YOU BOTH.
NO, THANK YOU!
olleHelo
WHEW!
During "press tours" I would do two days of 6-7 interviews each
NICE WORK TODAY.
We're both bushed by the end
BUT YOU KNOW, IF YOU NEVER GET TO GO BACK THERE TO WORK...
...THEY'RE GOING TO THINK, "HE'S ALL TALK, NO WALK."
I REALIZE THAT'S AN IRONIC COMMENT COMING FROM THE GUY DEMANDING THAT YOU DRAW.
TRUE, AFTER ALL MY COMMENTS ABOUT WANTING TO WORK THERE, IT MAKES ME LOOK DUMB IF I NEVER DO.
Board: [obscured] Bookstore, Kazuto Tatsuta
HAVE YOU HEARD ANYTHING FROM FUKUSHIMA?
書店様
竜田一
NOT A WORD...
IT'S BEEN A YEAR AND A HALF SINCE I LEFT ICHI-F. THEY MUST HAVE FOUND ME OUT AND BANNED ME...
WELL, I SUPPOSE IT'S MY FAULT TO BEGIN WITH.

An autograph for a bookstore to display

RATHER THAN CELEBRATING MY VERY FIRST COLLECTED VOLUME OF COMICS ON SALE...
UGH, MAYBE I SHOULDN'T HAVE DRAWN THIS SERIES AFTER ALL...
JUNE 2014
...I WAS MORE PREOCCUPIED WITH ANXIETY, FEELING I COULD NEVER GO BACK TO WORKING AT ICHI-F. THEY WERE UNCOMFORTABLE DAYS.
Look, I know you're worried, but focus on what you've got going on here! Draw, draw, draw!
YES, I KNOW, I'M SORRY.
IT'S JUST HARD TO DO WHEN I'M FREAKING OUT THAT THIS IS THE VERY CAUSE OF MY LACK OF CALLS...
HMM?
RRRR
WHOA!!
RRRR
信中
田町工業

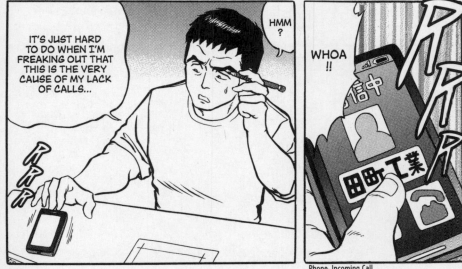

Phone: Incoming Call
Tamachi Industrial

Mr. Tatsuta, can you show up here next week?
AHA—(°∀°)—!!
I CAN, I CAN! NEXT WEEK?
I DON'T KNOW ALL THE DETAILS YET, BUT WE'RE ABOUT TO GET A MONTHLONG CONSTRUCTION GIG.
GOT IT! I'LL FREE UP MY SCHEDULE TO MAKE THE TRIP
Good to hear!
...AND FOR THAT REASON, I'D LIKE TO TAKE A BREAK FROM THE SERIES...
WELL, YOU GOT THE FIRST BOOK OUT, SO I GUESS YOU'RE OFF THE HOOK.

IT'S GOOD NEWS THOUGH, RIGHT? YOU DIDN'T GET SHUT OUT AFTER ALL!
BUT I CAN'T REST EASY UNTIL I'M OFFICIALLY REGISTERED AGAIN.
AND YOU'RE GOING STARTING NEXT WEEK?
THE THING IS, YOU NEVER KNOW WHEN WORK WILL ACTUALLY START AT ICHI-F, SAME AS IT WAS BEFORE...
LOTS OF NUCLEAR PLANT JOBS GET PUT TOGETHER REAL QUICK.
YOU MENTIONED THAT IT'S HARD TO MAKE PLANS, BUT IT'S REALLY ANNOYING WHEN YOU'VE GOT ME AT THE WHIMS OF THAT PROCESS TOO!
RIGHT?
Used to it
W-WELL...SEE IF YOU CAN WORK ON SOME STORYBOARDS WHILE YOU'RE WAITING.
YOU BET!
Carefree without the deadlines
CON-STRUCTION PLANS AT ICHI-F MUST BE APPROVED BY THE NRA.*
THE SUB-CONTRAC-TORS HAVE TO GATHER PEOPLE.
AND IT OFTEN REQUIRES CAREFUL CO-ORDINATION WITH OTHER PROCESSES THAT ARE HAP-PENING AT THE SAME TIME. SO IT'S VERY RARE FOR THINGS TO JUST SPRING INTO MOTION.
Sometimes you have to wait for this job to finish before you can work nearby

*Nuclear Regulation Authority

Mentally I'm in worker mode, so I can't think about manga

THE FOL-LOWING WEEK, I HEARD NOTH-ING.
GREAT, THE FAMED STANDBY HELL AGAIN?
THEY STILL HAVEN'T CALLED? ARE YOU MAKING STORYBOARD PROGRESS?
NOTHING ON EITHER FRONT, I'M AFRAID...
IN THAT CASE, LET'S AT LEAST DO SOME PRESS. WE'VE GOT AN OFFER RIGHT NOW.
Sure, I can do that.
SOME-HOW IT'S JULY 2014 ALREADY.
SO WE USED THE DOWN-TIME TO DO AN INTER-VIEW.
GLAD TO BE HERE TODAY.
Tired of putting on the uniform - done with the image and it's too hot!
OUR SPECIAL ISSUE IS ON THE NEWEST 3D* JOBS.
SO I WAS HOPING TO HEAR ABOUT THE 3Ds OF FUKUSHIMA DAIICHI.
UHHH ...
I DON'T KNOW WHAT TO SAY...

*The 3Ds are "Dirty, Dangerous, and Demanding" blue-collar jobs. In Japanese these are the 3Ks, for "Kitanai, Kiken, Kitsui."

ACTUALLY, WITH THE HIGH LEVELS OF RADIATION, YOU'RE LIMITED TO SHORT WORK TIMES, SO IT'S NOT THAT DEMANDING.
AND THE REST AREAS AND BATHROOMS ARE NICE AND CLEAN.
Right after the accident in 2011, it was different
AS FAR AS THE DANGER, AS LONG AS YOU USE YOUR EQUIPMENT PROPERLY, IT'S JUST LIKE ANY OTHER CON-STRUCTION JOB...
SO IF I HAD TO COME UP WITH A RE-PLACEMENT TERM...
WELL, WHAT'S THE WORST PART? YOU CAN'T "SCRATCH" YOUR NOSE WHEN IT ITCHES.
YES, EXACTLY!
AND THOSE FULL-FACE MASKS "STINK"!
They get cleaned so it's usually okay, but once in a while you get a bomb
AND WHAT'S THE LAST ONE?
LET'S SEE... THE WANTED ADS ARE "SKETCHY"! THERE YOU GO: 3S!
This is a stretch
GOING THROUGH HELLO WORK IS EXACTLY AS I DEPICTED IN THE COMIC. SOME WORKERS JUST UP AND LEFT IN THE MIDDLE OF THE NIGHT.
I'VE HEARD DOZENS OF STORIES FROM GUYS WHO FOUND OUT THAT THE JOB OFFER WAS COMPLETELY DIFFERENT FROM WHAT WAS ADVER-TISED.

AS A MATTER OF FACT, I'VE GOT AN UPCOMING JOB OFFER...
BUT YOU'VE BEEN WAITING FOR NEARLY A MONTH. YOU COULD HAVE DRAWN A FULL CHAPTER BY NOW.
I'M SORRY, I'M SORRY!
THANK YOU, GUYS.
SURE THING.
AND RIGHT AFTER WE WRAPPED UP...
IT'S TRUE, THE "SYSTEM" FOR "SETTING UP" WORK IS "STRESSFUL."
Still thinking up S-words
OH!
RRRR
READY TO TAKE YOUR RADIATION EXAM TOMORROW, MR. TATSUTA?
TOMOR-ROW ?!

ALL OF A SUDDEN, HUH?
SO I'M GOING TO GET MY TEST TOMORROW.
We'll be waiting.
ALL RIGHT, GOT IT! TOMORROW!
IT WAS NEARLY A MONTH SINCE I GOT THE OFFER, AND OVER A YEAR AND A HALF SINCE I'D LAST BEEN THERE.
"SUDDEN" IS ANOTHER S-WORD FOR ICHI-F.
SUNSHINE IWAKI
BUT IN JULY 2014, I WAS HEADING BACK TO ICHI-F.
TO PUT ON MY *OTHER* MASK AGAIN.

CHAPTER 17 - END

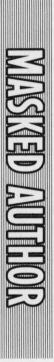

MASKED AUTHOR

WHILE FICTIONAL NAMES HAVE BEEN USED FOR COMPANIES AND INDIVIDUALS, TATSUTA ALWAYS HAD CONCERN THAT THOSE CLOSE TO THE SITUATION WOULD FIGURE IT OUT IF THEY READ THE COMIC. SO WHEN TATSUTA FOUND WORK AGAIN AT ICHI-F IN 2014, BOTH HE AND HIS EDITOR WERE RELIEVED. INCIDENTALLY, SINCE FINISHING HIS DEPICTION OF THE 2014 WORK STINT, TATSUTA HAS NOT RECEIVED ANY CALLS ABOUT NEW JOBS THERE.

JULY 2014, HOSPITAL IN IWAKI
I TOOK A RADIATION EXAM FOR MY FOURTH VISIT TO ICHI-F, THE FIRST IN A YEAR AND A HALF.
YOU'VE GOT NO PROBLEMS, MR. TATSUTA.
BLOOD TEST RESULTS
YOUR NUMBERS ARE GOOD.
THANKS.
HERE'S YOUR RESULT FORM.
AND I'LL NEED A RECEIPT FOR TAMACHI INDUSTRIAL.
IT'S ONLY AFTER THIS STEP THAT IT FINALLY SINKS IN THAT YOU'LL BE WORKING AT ICHI-F.
OF COURSE ...
...I DON'T ACTUALLY KNOW WHAT THAT WORK WILL BE AT THIS POINT...
VMMM

JOBAN JOINT POWER PLANT (cool smokestacks!)

CHAPTER 18:
CLOSE ENCOUNTERS

THEY JUST SAY "COME HERE," AND I HAVE TO JUMP...

CAN YOU MAKE IT?

I'LL BE THERE!

BUT I CAN'T DO IT FOR TOO LONG... (I HAVE THIS SECRET MANGA TO DRAW.)

IT'S A FAIRLY HIGH-EXPOSURE SPOT, SO IT SHOULD LAST ABOUT A MONTH.

Oh, that's perfect. What are we doing?

UM...

I heard it involved clearing wreckage inside Unit 3.
OOOH!
WE'LL GET YOU 20,000 YEN PER DAY.
Thank you so much.
AND NOW THAT I'M ACTUALLY HERE...
WHEN I WAS WORKING THERE IN 2012, IT WASN'T IN THE REACTOR BUILDING, BUT THE RELATIVELY COOL (LOW-RADIATION) WASTE BUILDING
REACTOR BUILDING (IN 2012)
DOES "INSIDE UNIT 3" MEAN THE ACTUAL REACTOR BUILDING? PEOPLE CAN'T EVEN GET IN THERE...
RAD/WASTE BUILDING
YES, I'D LIKE TO GO IN THERE...
...BUT ISN'T 20,000 A DAY A BIT ON THE CHEAP SIDE FOR THAT?
田町工業
I GUESS I'LL FIND OUT WHEN I GET THERE.
HELLO, IT'S NICE TO SEE YOU AGAIN...

Sign: Tamachi Industrial

Many of them are trying to get cash fast

UH, WHAT ABOUT HOUSING...?
WE'LL BRING YOU IN NEXT WEEK.
SO I JUST HAVE TO GO BACK HOME TODAY?
WE'LL BE MEETING UP AT THE DORM NEXT WEEK.
IT'S IN HITA-CHI.
FUTABA
OKUMA
TOMIOKA
NARAHA
HIRONO
1-F
2-F
JV
IWAKI
JOBAN EXPRESSWAY
6
TAMACHI INDUSTRIAL OFFICE IN DOWNTOWN IWAKI
FUKUSHIMA PREFECTURE
IBARAKI PREFECTURE
KITAIBARAKI
TAKAHAGI
TAMACHI INDUSTRIAL HITACHI DORM
HITACHI
WOW, HITA-CHI?
IWAKI IS OVER 40 KM FROM ICHI-F, AND HITACHI IS 50 KM FURTHER SOUTH FROM THERE.
MOST OF THE RESTRICTED ZONE RESIDENTS HAVEN'T BEGUN TO RETURN HOME YET, WHILE THE NUMBER OF WORKERS INCREASES. IWAKI HAS LONG BEEN OVER CAPACITY.
ARE YOU KIDDING ME? I'M LIVING DOWN IN IBARAKI?
GUESS THERE'S NO CHOICE ...
MORE THAN A FEW ICHI-F WORKERS COMMUTE BY CROSSING PREFECTURES FROM NORTHERN IBARAKI NOW.

Street Signs: Uchigomidaisakai

Kind of looking forward to Ibaraki

WHAT? HITA-CHI?
THAT'S RIGHT ...
WELL, IT'S TRUE THAT IT'S BASICALLY IMPOSSIBLE TO RENT A NEW PLACE IN IWAKI NOW.
THAT'S WHAT I FIGURED. SO IF IT'S BAD ENOUGH, I WAS HOPING TO MOVE BACK IN WITH YOU AGAIN, IF THAT'S ALL RIGHT.
SINCE I MADE THE TRIP, I FIGURED I WOULD MEET A FAMILIAR FACE.
THAT'S QUITE ALL RIGHT. IT'S JUST ME THERE NOW.
Former roommate - quite tanned now!
SO I HEAR THAT MR. TAMANA MOVED BACK TO KUMAMOTO.
TATESHIBA CLOSED DOWN THAT REST AREA, SO EVERYONE ELSE HAS BEEN SCATTERED ELSEWHERE.
OTHER FORMER ROOMMATES
NOW I'M DOING DECON-TAMINA-TION OUTSIDE THE PLANT.
A LOT OF STUFF CAN HAPPEN TO A PERSON IN A YEAR AND A HALF, HUH?

WELCOME BACK!
IT'S REALLY GREAT TO BE BACK HERE, AFTER ALL THAT!
HAVE A GOOD EVE-NING.
THANKS FOR THE RIDE.
MR. TSURUMI LOOKS HEALTHIER THAN WHEN HE WAS AT ICHI-F.
You don't even get tan in the summer at Ichi-F due to the heavy masks
I SUPPOSE IT MUST BE BECAUSE HE'S GETTING LOTS OF FRESH AIR OUTSIDE.
WHEN YOU THINK ABOUT IT, WORKING AT ICHI-F MIGHT ACTUALLY BE BETTER FOR YOUR SKIN...
IT SAYS I GET A SOLO ROOM AT A BUSINESS HOTEL. AND NO HOUSING COST, EITHER? WHAT'S THE CATCH?
SO THE NEXT WEEK, I MADE THE TRIP BACK TO THE PLACE WHERE THE COMPANY DORM WAS.

Sign: Ripe Pork Cutlet

Sign: Hitachi Center

IS... THIS IT? IS THIS PLACE IN BUSINESS?
Sign: Hotel New Hitachi

HI THERE!
GOOD MORNING.
THUMP
IS THIS PLACE OUT OF BUSINESS...?
YEP. BOUGHT THE BUILDING ON AUCTION AFTER THEY WENT BANKRUPT.
CREAK
AH, I SEE. SO IT'S NOT A FUNCTIONING HOTEL.
AND WE'VE ONLY GOT POWER AND WATER, NO GAS. SO THERE'S NO HOT WATER.
CREAK
CREAK
SO FOOD AND BATHS WILL BE ON US, THEN.
They went out of business before the disaster

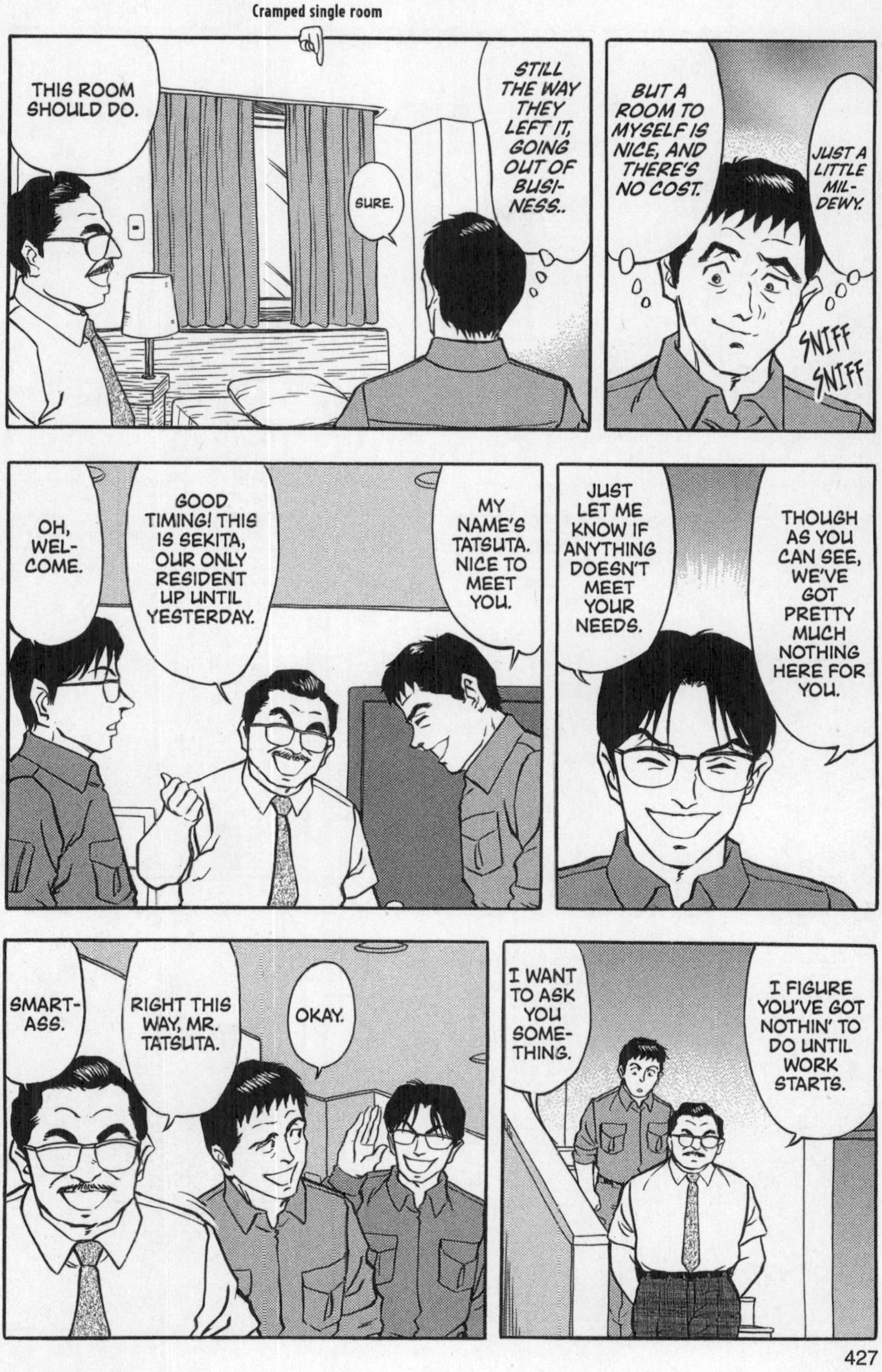

Cramped single room

WOW, THIS LOOKS LIKE...
A FORMER BAR IN THE BASEMENT!
I WAS THINKIN' WE COULD MAKE THIS THE DINING HALL AND HAVE EVERYONE EAT HERE.
BUT FIRST, I NEED THIS WALLPAPER HERE FIXED UP.
I DON'T NEED TO CALL A HANDYMAN 'CUZ I AIN'T OPENIN' THIS UP FOR BUSINESS.
BAMBOO SCRAPER
JUST SLAP SOME GLUE ON THIS SCRAPER...
OFFICE GLUE
...AND FILL IN THE SPOTS WHERE IT'S COMIN' OFF THE WALL.
Being enclosed underground means the humidity and mold is out of control
THEN FLATTEN IT DOWN WITH THE ROLLER.
ROLL
THAT'S USUALLY ENOUGH TO GET IT FLUSH AGAIN.
ROLL
AH, I SEE.
I CAN PAY YOU FOR THE LABOR UNTIL THE JOB STARTS. LET'S SAY, 8,000 YEN A DAY.
DEAL?
SURE! I'LL DO IT!
Seems easy enough and decent pay, so I'm in

Depending on the contract terms, companies might pay a certain percentage of salary as a standby payment while you're waiting. If not, some of them find odd jobs like this for you to do. My first subcontractor, Kuromori Construction, sent us on civil engineering jobs.

BUT HOW LONG WILL I BE ON STANDBY?

WELL, THAT DEPENDS ON THE PAPERWORK FROM THE MASTER CONTRACTOR AND THE PROGRESS OF THE PLANNING STAGES.

I SUPPOSE YOU'LL PROBABLY DO THE INSTRUCTION COURSE BY THE END OF THE WEEK.

OH, RIGHT! SPEAK-ING OF THE WORK...

WHAT ARE WE ACTUALLY DOING?

AH, GOOD QUES-TION!

So stunned by the housing situation that I forgot to ask

Unit 1 Reactor Bldg

YOU'LL BE AN ASSIS-TANT.

YOU'RE INSPECTING THE INTE-RIOR OF THE UNIT 1 REACTOR BUILDING.

Unit 3 Reactor Bldg

SO IT'S UNIT 1, NOT UNIT 3?

UNHAPPY ?

NOT AT ALL! I'M JUST RELIEVED TO GET THE CHANCE TO WORK THERE!

WELL, KEEP IT UP WITH THE WALL-PAPER, AND YOU'LL BE THERE SOON.

SO I SPENT MY DAYS PRETENDING TO BE AN UPHOLSTERER AS I WAITED.
AND... WHAT AM I DOING HERE, AGAIN...?
Starting to doubt myself
SINCE THERE'S NO WATER HEATER, I TRAVEL TO A NEARBY HOT SPRING ON DAY TRIPS...
TO BE HONEST, THIS IS BETTER!
...AND VISIT THE COIN LAUNDRY FOR CLOTHES.
CAN'T COOK EITHER, SO I HAVE TO EAT OUT OR BUY INSTANT LUNCHES.
AND I WENT TO A PUBLIC BATH, SO IT DOESN'T SEEM THAT BAD AT ALL.
BUT HEY, I COULDN'T COOK FOR MYSELF TWO YEARS AGO, EITHER.
TV doesn't work. And it's a CRT!
AS USUAL, I HAD THE ANXIETY OF NOT KNOWING WHEN WORK WOULD START HANGING OVER MY HEAD...
THIS IS ACTUALLY KIND OF FUN.
...BUT I WAS MANAGING TO ENJOY MY STANDBY PERIOD.
It only lasted three days
FWIP
AHH, PERFECT! ♡
Getting good at it

NICE WORK!
TAKE A BREAK.
OH, THANK YOU.
IT'S LOOKING MUCH BETTER IN HERE.
WELL, THERE'S NOTHING I CAN DO ABOUT THE MOLD, I'M AFRAID.
CAN'T HELP THAT, IT'S BEEN UN-TOUCHED FOR YEARS.
ANYWAY, YOUR INSTRUCTION COURSE STARTS TOMORROW.
ALL RIGHT!
FINALLY...
BUT I'M GLAD TO KNOW THAT I FINISHED SPRUCING THIS PLACE UP FIRST.
Oddly satisfied with myself
THE NEXT DAY WAS THE PRIMARY SUBCON-TRAC-TOR'S INSTRUC-TION.
WE SPENT ONE DAY AT THEIR HIRONO OFFICE AND ONE AT THE NI-F (2-F) OFFICE.
ALL OF IT WAS PRACTICAL INFORMA-TION ABOUT CURRENT EQUIPMENT AND SAFETY GUIDELINES.

A collection of subcontractor workers, as well as employees of the primary subcontractor making their first Ichi-F trip

THE NI-F OFFICE GETS USED FOR WORK COMMUNICATION AND MEETINGS OFTEN...
...SO I GOT A NI-F ID TOO.
Comes in a laminated case
NATURALLY, AS NI-F WAS SAFE FROM THE DISASTER, THERE'S NO PROTECTIVE CLOTHING NEEDED.
WOW, IT'S SO PEACEFUL HERE!
YOU EVEN SEE PEOPLE JOGGING.
I TRIED VISITING THE CAFETERIA.
My young coworker Yotsuzawa
Delicious pork cutlet curry
AND, OF COURSE, THERE ARE VENDING MACHINES.
KTUNK
Machine: Rakuou Dairy
THERE'S NO MONEY AT ICHI-F: NO CAFETERIA, NO STORES, NO MACHINES.
IT'S REALLY A DIFFERENT EXPERIENCE WHERE THE MONEY ECONOMY WORKS.
It's cold! What a delight!
BUT THEY'RE WORKING TOWARD OPENING A MAJOR SHELTER AREA AND CAFETERIA THERE SOON.
I'M SO EXCITED!
Under construction in 2014

AT LAST, THE ICHI-F REGISTRATION DAY.
IN ADDITION TO THE USUAL WBC TEST AT J-VILLAGE ...
The numbers are fine - if there's any change, it's within the margin of error
THIS TIME, THERE WAS A NEW SYSTEM: VEIN AUTHENTICATION.
STICK YOUR FINGER IN HERE.
OOH, NEW SECURITY STEPS?
THAT WAS NERVE-WRACKING THOUGH ...
AS I MENTIONED BEFORE, I DIDN'T SUFFER ANY IDENTITY-RELATED CENSURE FROM TEPCO ITSELF. REGISTRATION ENDED SMOOTHLY.
THE NEXT MORNING WAS MY FIRST TRIP TO ICHI-F.
ETC専用
4:00 AM
IT'S STILL DARK OUT...
IT TAKES A FULL HOUR ON THE FREEWAY JUST TO REACH THE HIRONO INTERCHANGE WHERE YOU FIND JV.
HOW CAN IT BE SO FAR AWAY?
Sign: ETC Vehicles

My co-resident Sekita is also doing this job

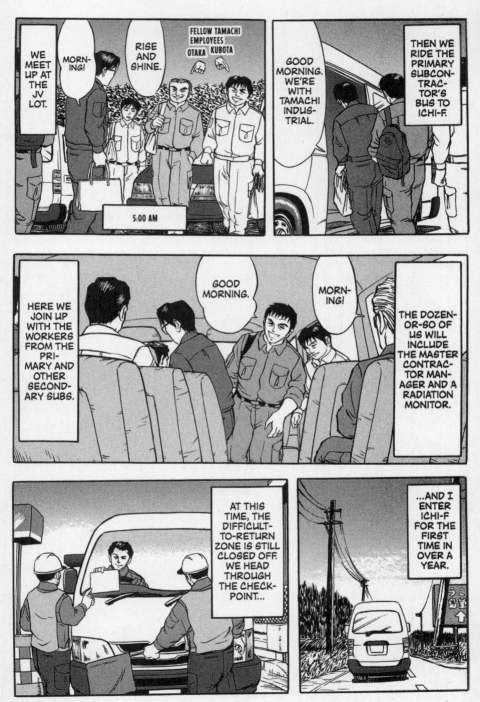

WE MEET UP AT THE JV LOT.
MORN-ING!
RISE AND SHINE.
FELLOW TAMACHI EMPLOYEES
OTAKA
KUBOTA
5:00 AM
GOOD MORNING. WE'RE WITH TAMACHI INDUS-TRIAL.
THEN WE RIDE THE PRIMARY SUBCON-TRAC-TOR'S BUS TO ICHI-F.
HERE WE JOIN UP WITH THE WORKERS FROM THE PRI-MARY AND OTHER SECOND-ARY SUBS.
GOOD MORNING.
MORN-ING!
THE DOZEN-OR-SO OF US WILL INCLUDE THE MASTER CONTRAC-TOR MAN-AGER AND A RADIATION MONITOR.
AT THIS TIME, THE DIFFICULT-TO-RETURN ZONE IS STILL CLOSED OFF. WE HEAD THROUGH THE CHECK-POINT...
...AND I ENTER ICHI-F FOR THE FIRST TIME IN OVER A YEAR.

FUKUSHIMA DAIICHI NUCLEAR POWER PLANT, ENTRY FACILITY
SO THIS IS THE NEW ENTRY FACILITY, HUH?

WE LEAVE THE CAR AT THE PARKING LOT. THIS IS STILL OUT-SIDE ICHI-F GROUNDS.
5:30 AM
ASIDE FROM A FEW CARGO VEHICLES, ALL EXTERIOR COMMUTER VEHICLES AND INTERIOR VEHICLES ARE KEPT STRICTLY SEPARATE.

These get surveyed too, of course

YOU CAN COME THIS FAR WITH NORMAL CLOTHES AND NO MASK.
WHEN WE WERE WORKING IN 2012, YOU HAD TO PUT ON A TYVEK AT J-VILLAGE, AND WE HAD TO PUT ON OUR FULL MASKS DURING THE TRIP.
THE LOOK OF COM-MUTERS TO ICHI-F HAS CHANGED MUCH IN A FEW YEARS.

In 2011, you had to put the mask on at JV!

The vein authentication test from JV gets repeated here

You have to show inside your bags

Sign: Certify

We're in this category

You must have cotton gloves and surgical mask here

You pull yours right out of the charging hold

Touch panel (very unresponsive!)

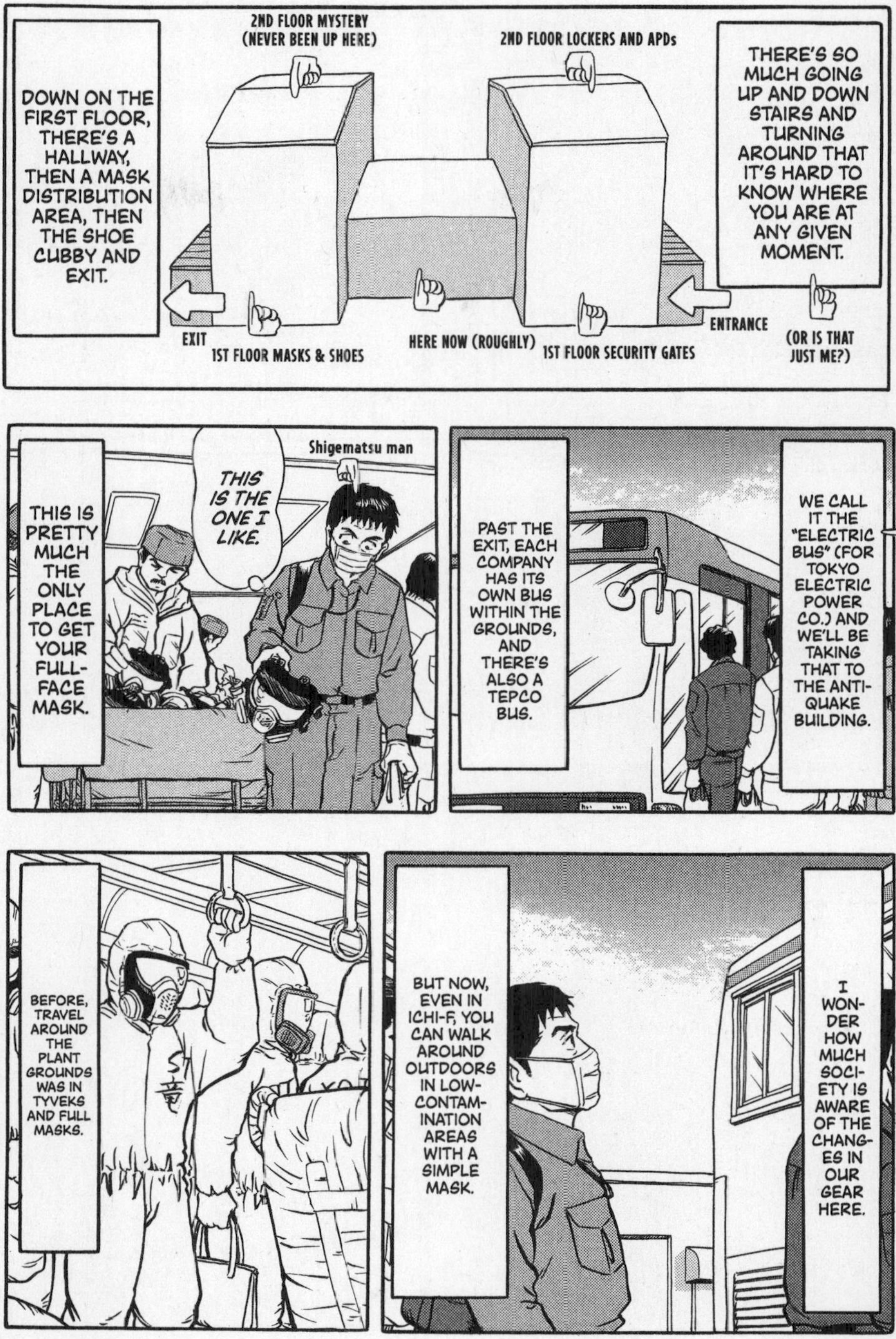
DOWN ON THE FIRST FLOOR, THERE'S A HALLWAY, THEN A MASK DISTRIBUTION AREA, THEN THE SHOE CUBBY AND EXIT.
2ND FLOOR MYSTERY (NEVER BEEN UP HERE)
2ND FLOOR LOCKERS AND APDs
THERE'S SO MUCH GOING UP AND DOWN STAIRS AND TURNING AROUND THAT IT'S HARD TO KNOW WHERE YOU ARE AT ANY GIVEN MOMENT.
(OR IS THAT JUST ME?)
ENTRANCE
1ST FLOOR SECURITY GATES
HERE NOW (ROUGHLY)
1ST FLOOR MASKS & SHOES
EXIT
THIS IS PRETTY MUCH THE ONLY PLACE TO GET YOUR FULL-FACE MASK.
THIS IS THE ONE I LIKE.
Shigematsu man
PAST THE EXIT, EACH COMPANY HAS ITS OWN BUS WITHIN THE GROUNDS, AND THERE'S ALSO A TEPCO BUS.
WE CALL IT THE "ELECTRIC BUS" (FOR TOKYO ELECTRIC POWER CO.) AND WE'LL BE TAKING THAT TO THE ANTI-QUAKE BUILDING.
Not actually electric
BEFORE, TRAVEL AROUND THE PLANT GROUNDS WAS IN TYVEKS AND FULL MASKS.
BUT NOW, EVEN IN ICHI-F, YOU CAN WALK AROUND OUTDOORS IN LOW-CONTAMINATION AREAS WITH A SIMPLE MASK.
I WONDER HOW MUCH SOCIETY IS AWARE OF THE CHANGES IN OUR GEAR HERE.

FIRST TIME IN ICHI-F IN A YEAR AND A HALF.
I'M FINALLY BACK.
IT'S A TEN-MINUTE TRIP BY BUS TO THE ANTI-QUAKE BUILDING.
OOH, THERE'S THE REC CENTER!
I FELT A STRANGE KIND OF NOSTALGIA.
I HOPE EVERYONE'S DOING WELL...
IN FACT, I WONDER IF ANYONE I KNEW IS EVEN HERE ANYMORE.
BUT THIS ISN'T A MEMORIAL TOUR.
I'M ABOUT TO HAVE A CLOSE ENCOUNTER WITH THE UNKNOWN.
THE REACTOR BUILDING AWAITS.

CHAPTER 18 - END

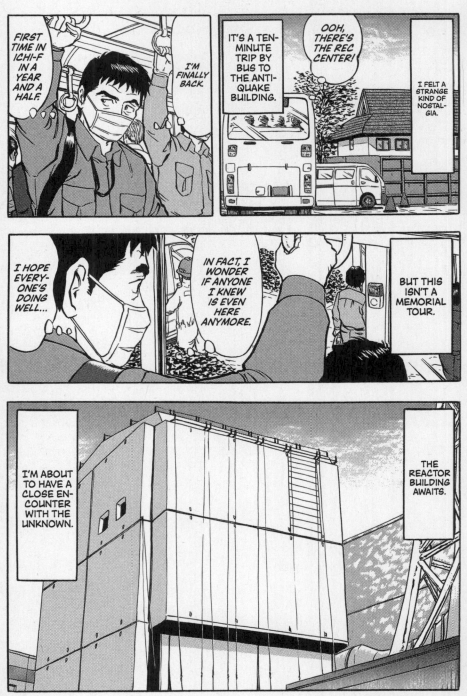

THIS IS YOUR STOP MALL

THIS TEMPORARY MALL IN FRONT OF THE NARAHA TOWN HALL ALONG ROUTE 6, MADE UP OF BUSINESSES THAT HAD TO EVACUATE FROM NARAHA, OPENED UP ON JULY 31ST, 2014. IT'S ABOUT 15 KILOMETERS SOUTH OF ICHI-F. AS DEPICTED IN CHAPTER 14, TATSUTA'S FAVORITES ARE TAKÉ-CHAN CAFETERIA'S CHIVES-AND-LIVER STIR FRY AND ORAHO-TEI'S CITRUS SOFT SERVE.

CLEANUP AND ICHI-F WORKERS AND RESIDENTS PREPARING TO RETURN CAN MAKE THIS "THEIR STOP." (BY THE WAY, THE EVACUATION ORDER FOR NARAHA WAS LIFTED ON SEPTEMBER 5TH, 2015.)

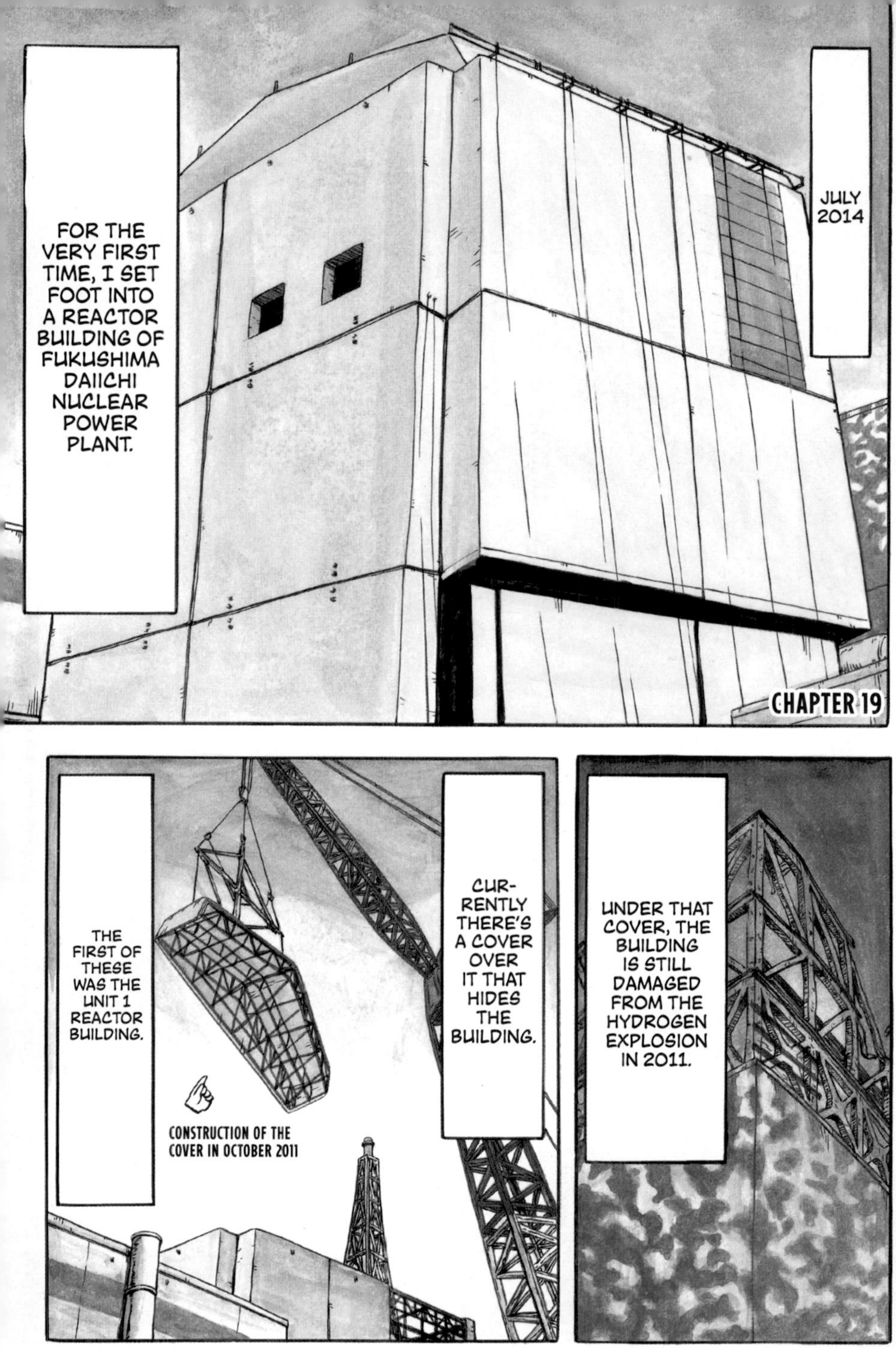
JULY 2014
FOR THE VERY FIRST TIME, I SET FOOT INTO A REACTOR BUILDING OF FUKUSHIMA DAIICHI NUCLEAR POWER PLANT.
CHAPTER 19
THE FIRST OF THESE WAS THE UNIT 1 REACTOR BUILDING.
CONSTRUCTION OF THE COVER IN OCTOBER 2011
CUR-RENTLY THERE'S A COVER OVER IT THAT HIDES THE BUILDING.
UNDER THAT COVER, THE BUILDING IS STILL DAMAGED FROM THE HYDROGEN EXPLOSION IN 2011.

CHAPTER 19:
BRB, WORKING @ REACTOR BLDG

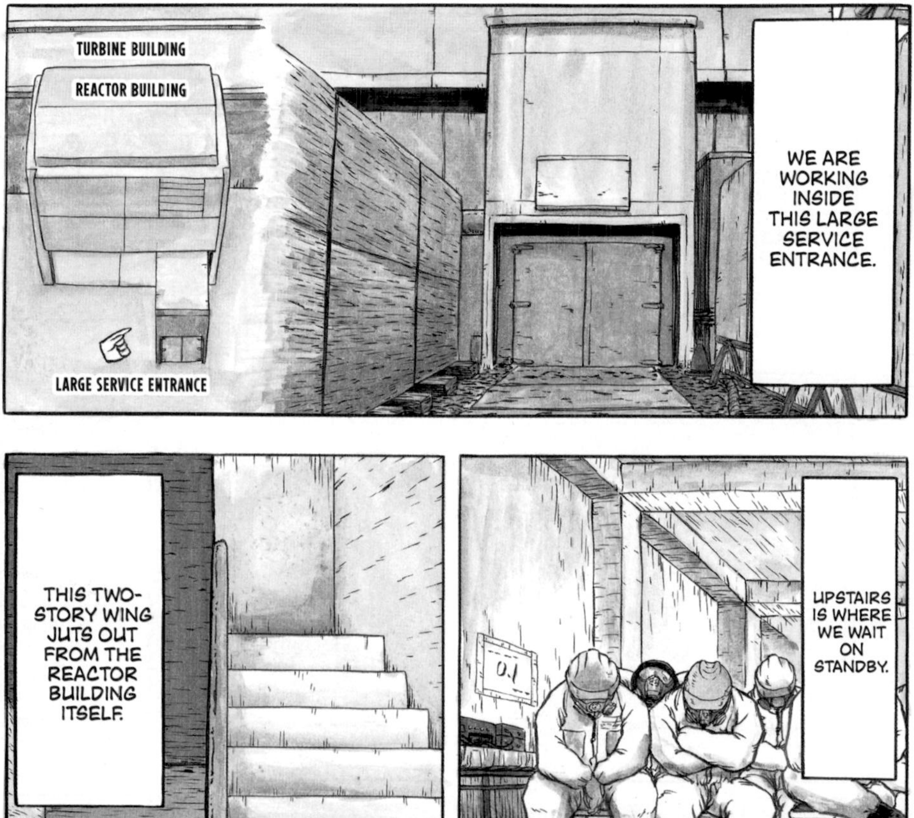
TURBINE BUILDING
REACTOR BUILDING
LARGE SERVICE ENTRANCE
WE ARE WORKING INSIDE THIS LARGE SERVICE ENTRANCE.
THIS TWO-STORY WING JUTS OUT FROM THE REACTOR BUILDING ITSELF.
UPSTAIRS IS WHERE WE WAIT ON STANDBY.
ZZZ ...
SNORR
TATESHIBA
WE OFTEN TAKE NAPS HERE.

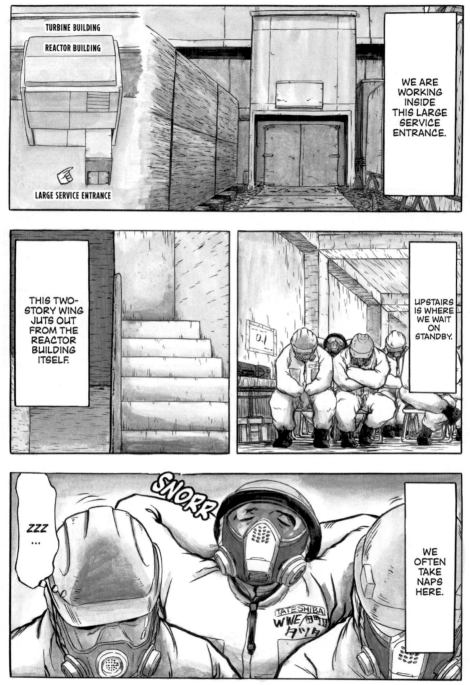

*Sign: The atmospheric radiation here is 0.1 mSv/h

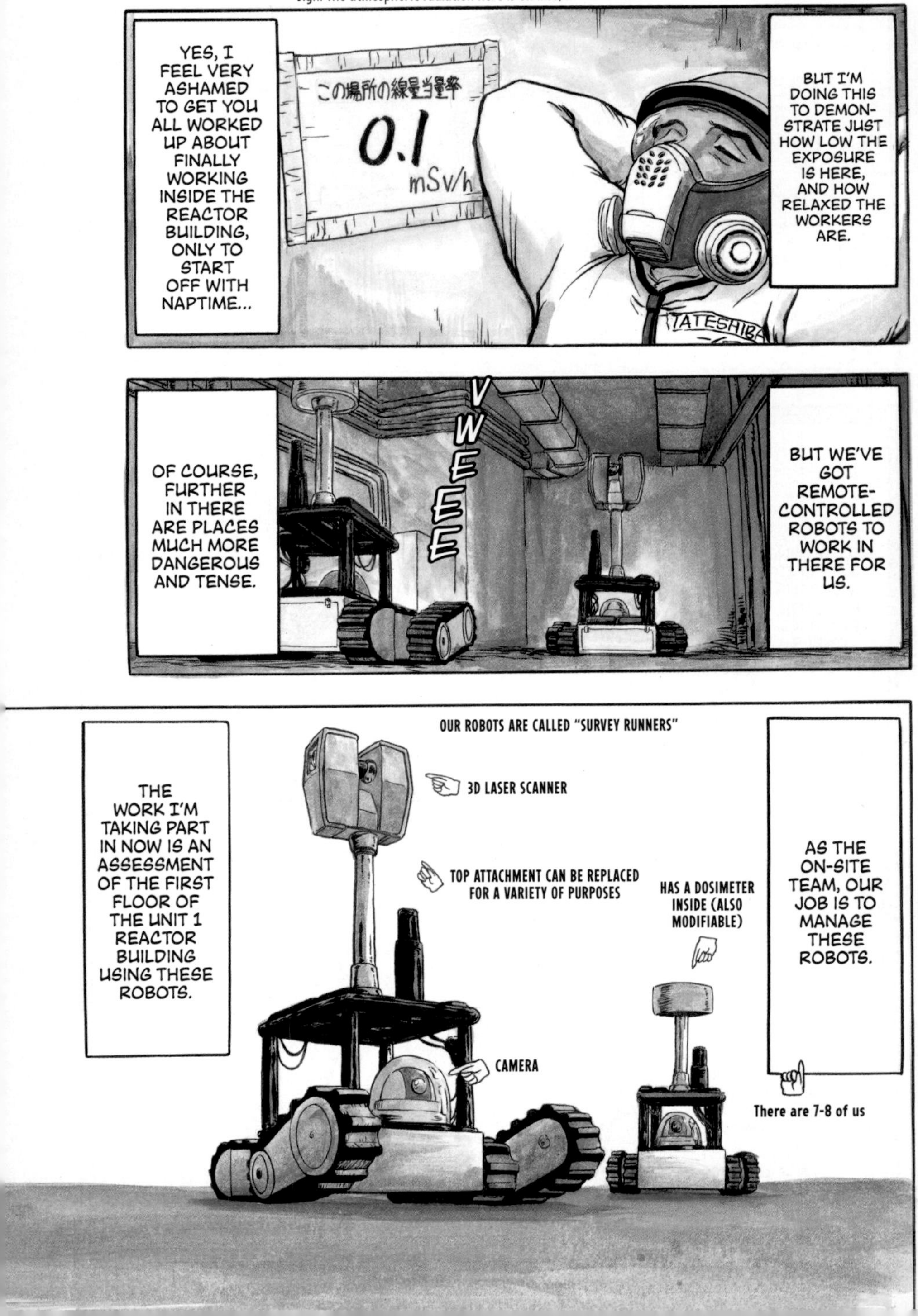

YES, I FEEL VERY ASHAMED TO GET YOU ALL WORKED UP ABOUT FINALLY WORKING INSIDE THE REACTOR BUILDING, ONLY TO START OFF WITH NAPTIME...
この場所の線量当量率
0.1
mSv/h
TATESHIBA
BUT I'M DOING THIS TO DEMON-STRATE JUST HOW LOW THE EXPOSURE IS HERE, AND HOW RELAXED THE WORKERS ARE.
OF COURSE, FURTHER IN THERE ARE PLACES MUCH MORE DANGEROUS AND TENSE.
VWEEE
BUT WE'VE GOT REMOTE-CONTROLLED ROBOTS TO WORK IN THERE FOR US.
THE WORK I'M TAKING PART IN NOW IS AN ASSESSMENT OF THE FIRST FLOOR OF THE UNIT 1 REACTOR BUILDING USING THESE ROBOTS.
OUR ROBOTS ARE CALLED "SURVEY RUNNERS"
3D LASER SCANNER
TOP ATTACHMENT CAN BE REPLACED FOR A VARIETY OF PURPOSES
HAS A DOSIMETER INSIDE (ALSO MODIFIABLE)
CAMERA
AS THE ON-SITE TEAM, OUR JOB IS TO MANAGE THESE ROBOTS.
There are 7-8 of us

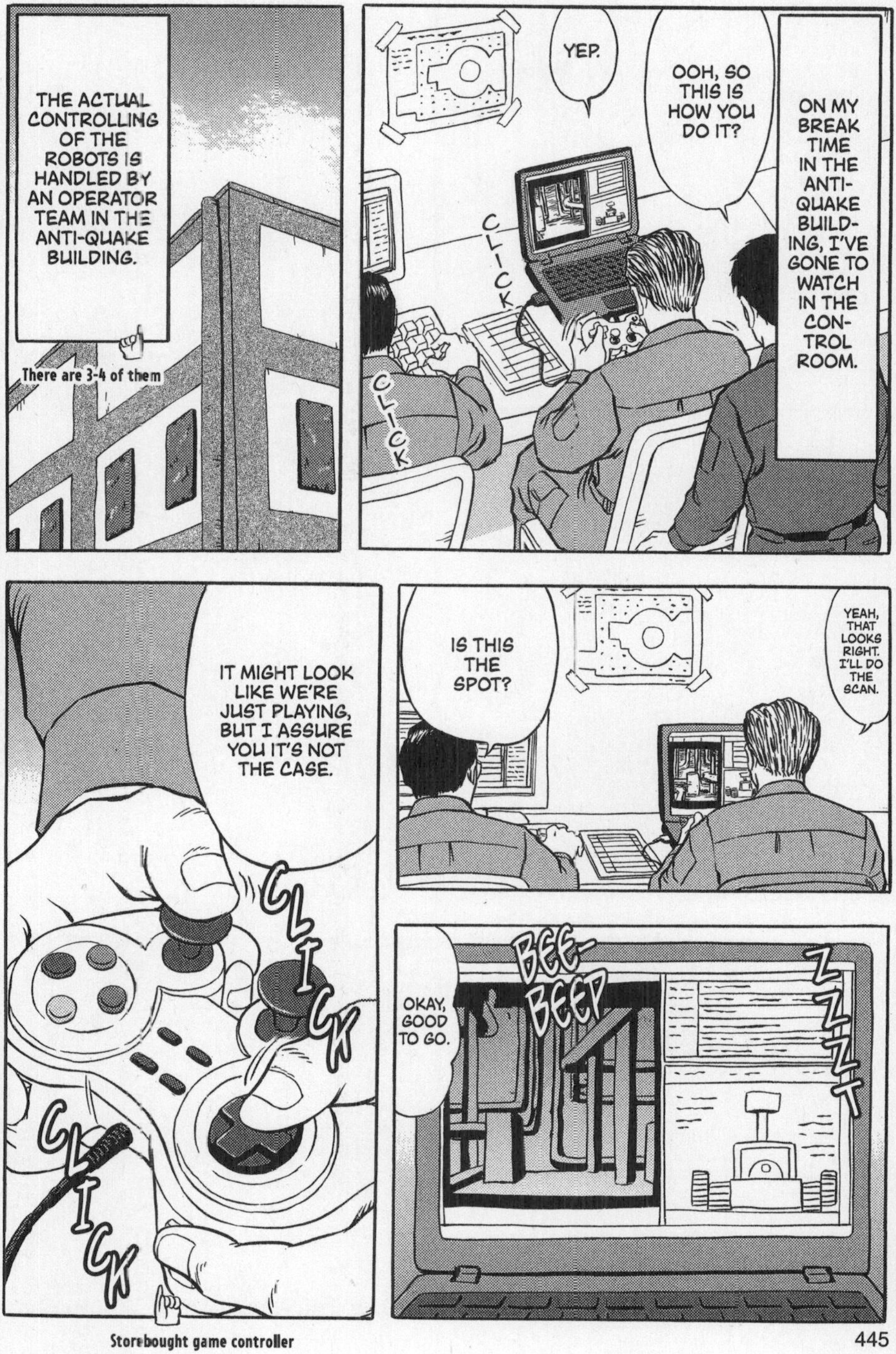

THE ACTUAL CONTROLLING OF THE ROBOTS IS HANDLED BY AN OPERATOR TEAM IN THE ANTI-QUAKE BUILDING.

There are 3-4 of them

YEP.

OOH, SO THIS IS HOW YOU DO IT?

ON MY BREAK TIME IN THE ANTI-QUAKE BUILDING, I'VE GONE TO WATCH IN THE CONTROL ROOM.

CLICK

CLICK

IT MIGHT LOOK LIKE WE'RE JUST PLAYING, BUT I ASSURE YOU IT'S NOT THE CASE.

IS THIS THE SPOT?

YEAH, THAT LOOKS RIGHT. I'LL DO THE SCAN.

CLICK

CLICK

OKAY, GOOD TO GO.

BEE-BEEP

ZZZT

Store-bought game controller

WHAT IS THE PURPOSE OF THIS, YOU ASK? WELL, BY DOING 3D SCANS, THEY'RE PUTTING TOGETHER A COMPUTER MODEL OF THE BUILDING.
IT'S NECES-SARY TO HAVE PRECISE MEASURE-MENT DATA FOR FUTURE DECOMMIS-SION WORK.

The computer can compile and assemble the laser scanning

OKAY, NEXT.
THIS LOOKS FUN!
I THINK WE CAN GET THROUGH THREE MORE SPOTS TODAY.
CLICK
CLICK
計測地点MA
OUR DUTY FOR THIS JOB IS TO SPEND A WEEK PERFORMING A FEW DOZEN SCANS AROUND THE REACTOR BUILDING GROUND FLOOR.

Just thinks it's grown men playing video games

SURE, WE MIGHT JUST BE SERVANTS TO THESE ROBOTS, BUT I'M OVERJOYED, GETTING TO SURVEY UNIT 1.
TWO YEARS EAR-LIER...
...WHEN I WAS WORKING AT THE REST SHELTER OF THE TATESHIBA COMPANY IN SUMMER 2012...
I'M BACK ...
NICE WORK OUT THERE!

WORK SITE?

UNIT 1.

CAN'T HELP THAT; IT'S MY FIRST TRIP IN THERE.

YUP, YOU'VE GOT A HIT ON YOUR FILTER.

INDOOR INVESTIGATION OF UNIT 1 WAS JUST STARTING.

IS IT THAT CRAZY IN THERE?

ACTUALLY, I DON'T KNOW YET.

DAMN, I WANT TO GO AND SEE!

AT THE TIME, THEY WERE SENDING IN THEIR MOST EXPERIENCED SURVEYERS.

Stronger kind

AND NOW THE SURVEYING AND DECONTAMINATION HAS GOTTEN TO THE POINT WHERE I'M IN THERE TAKING NAPS.

AND AT THE TIME, THEY WERE USING CHARCOAL FILTERS.

DUST FILTER

TATE SHIBA WWE 田町家 タツタ

IT'S BEEN THREE YEARS AND FOUR MONTHS FROM THE ACCIDENT TO NOW, JULY 2014.

I JUST WANT TO THANK ALL OF THOSE WORKERS WHO GOT US HERE THROUGH THEIR RADIATION CLEANING AND ENVIRONMENTAL IMPROVEMENTS! (THOUGH NATURAL DECAY PLAYED A PART, TOO.)

TATESHIBA WWE田町家 タツタ

But still going back to sleep

We put them on this stand when not in use

WELL, I DON'T WANT YOU THINKING ALL I DO IS SIT AROUND AND NAP, SO LET'S SHOW OFF WHAT WE REALLY DO HERE.
READY...
...AND GO!
BEFORE WE CAN SEND THE ROBOT IN, THERE ARE PREPARATORY STEPS.
TATESHIBA
WWE

Takes hard work to lower it down (about 40 kg (90 lbs)?)

THE ROBOTS WE USE GO TWO TO A TEAM.
COMM LIGHT IS GOOD.
DOSIMETER GOOD.
ATTACHING SCANNER.
BATTERY GOOD!
CHECK YOU'RE GETTING THE SIGNAL.
YOU MIGHT BE WONDERING, WHY TWO ROBOTS?
TATESHIBA
TATESHIBA

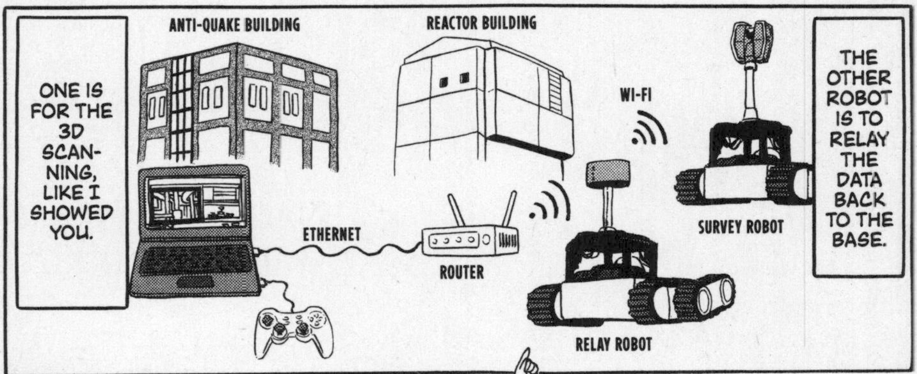
ONE IS FOR THE 3D SCANNING, LIKE I SHOWED YOU.
ANTI-QUAKE BUILDING
REACTOR BUILDING
WI-FI
ETHERNET
ROUTER
RELAY ROBOT
SURVEY ROBOT
THE OTHER ROBOT IS TO RELAY THE DATA BACK TO THE BASE.

Also monitors conditions and radiation

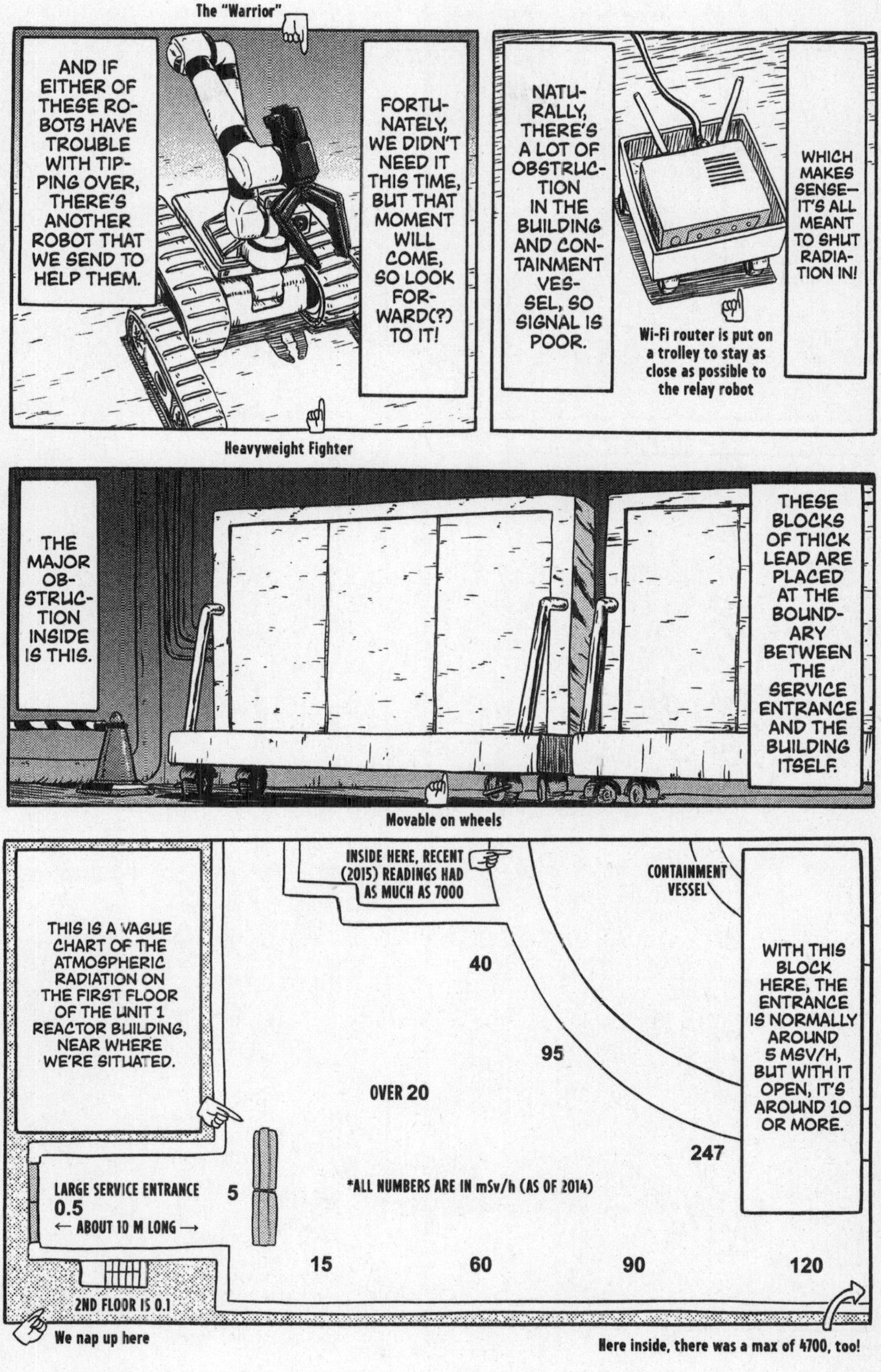
The "Warrior"
AND IF EITHER OF THESE ROBOTS HAVE TROUBLE WITH TIPPING OVER, THERE'S ANOTHER ROBOT THAT WE SEND TO HELP THEM.
FORTUNATELY, WE DIDN'T NEED IT THIS TIME, BUT THAT MOMENT WILL COME, SO LOOK FORWARD(?) TO IT!
Heavyweight Fighter
NATURALLY, THERE'S A LOT OF OBSTRUCTION IN THE BUILDING AND CONTAINMENT VESSEL, SO SIGNAL IS POOR.
WHICH MAKES SENSE— IT'S ALL MEANT TO SHUT RADIATION IN!
Wi-Fi router is put on a trolley to stay as close as possible to the relay robot
THE MAJOR OBSTRUCTION INSIDE IS THIS.
THESE BLOCKS OF THICK LEAD ARE PLACED AT THE BOUNDARY BETWEEN THE SERVICE ENTRANCE AND THE BUILDING ITSELF.
Movable on wheels
THIS IS A VAGUE CHART OF THE ATMOSPHERIC RADIATION ON THE FIRST FLOOR OF THE UNIT 1 REACTOR BUILDING, NEAR WHERE WE'RE SITUATED.
INSIDE HERE, RECENT (2015) READINGS HAD AS MUCH AS 7000
CONTAINMENT VESSEL
WITH THIS BLOCK HERE, THE ENTRANCE IS NORMALLY AROUND 5 MSV/H, BUT WITH IT OPEN, IT'S AROUND 10 OR MORE.
40
95
OVER 20
247
LARGE SERVICE ENTRANCE
0.5
← ABOUT 10 M LONG →
5
*ALL NUMBERS ARE IN mSv/h (AS OF 2014)
15
60
90
120
2ND FLOOR IS 0.1
We nap up here
Here inside, there was a max of 4700, too!

There are other work teams going in and out, so sometimes you see hoses and cables that serve some unknown purpose

WE OPENED THEM UP TO SEND IN THE ROBOTS YESTERDAY.

WE'VE GOT TWO RADIATION SHIELDS.

THEY'RE NOT CONNECTED, SO WE CAN JUST PULL ONE AWAY.

WE DO A SERIOUS MORNING PLANNING MEETING.

THAT CABLE'S GOING TO BE TROUBLE.

SOMEONE'S GOTTA TAKE CARE OF THAT.

BEFORE WE ACT, WE CHECK OUT THE AREA.

WE'LL PULL IT THIS WAY

Beyond the shields it's over 10 mSv/h

OKAY, LET'S HEAD BACK!

THE EXPOSURE IS PRETTY HIGH HERE, SO WE CAN'T WASTE ANY TIME.

WE DO ONE MORE MEETING, AND THEN ...

I'LL LIFT THE CABLE OUT OF THE WAY (SINCE IT SEEMS EASY).

JUST LIFT IT! NO PULLING!

... TIME TO WORK!

OKAY, GO!!

DON'T RUSH IT!

MOVE, MOVE!

WHAT ARE WE, THE ARMY?

HRRGG

IF YOU EVER WANTED TO SEE OLD GUYS PUT SOME JUICE INTO THEIR STEP, THIS IS THE TIME!

ALL RIGHT! NOW DRAW IT BACK!

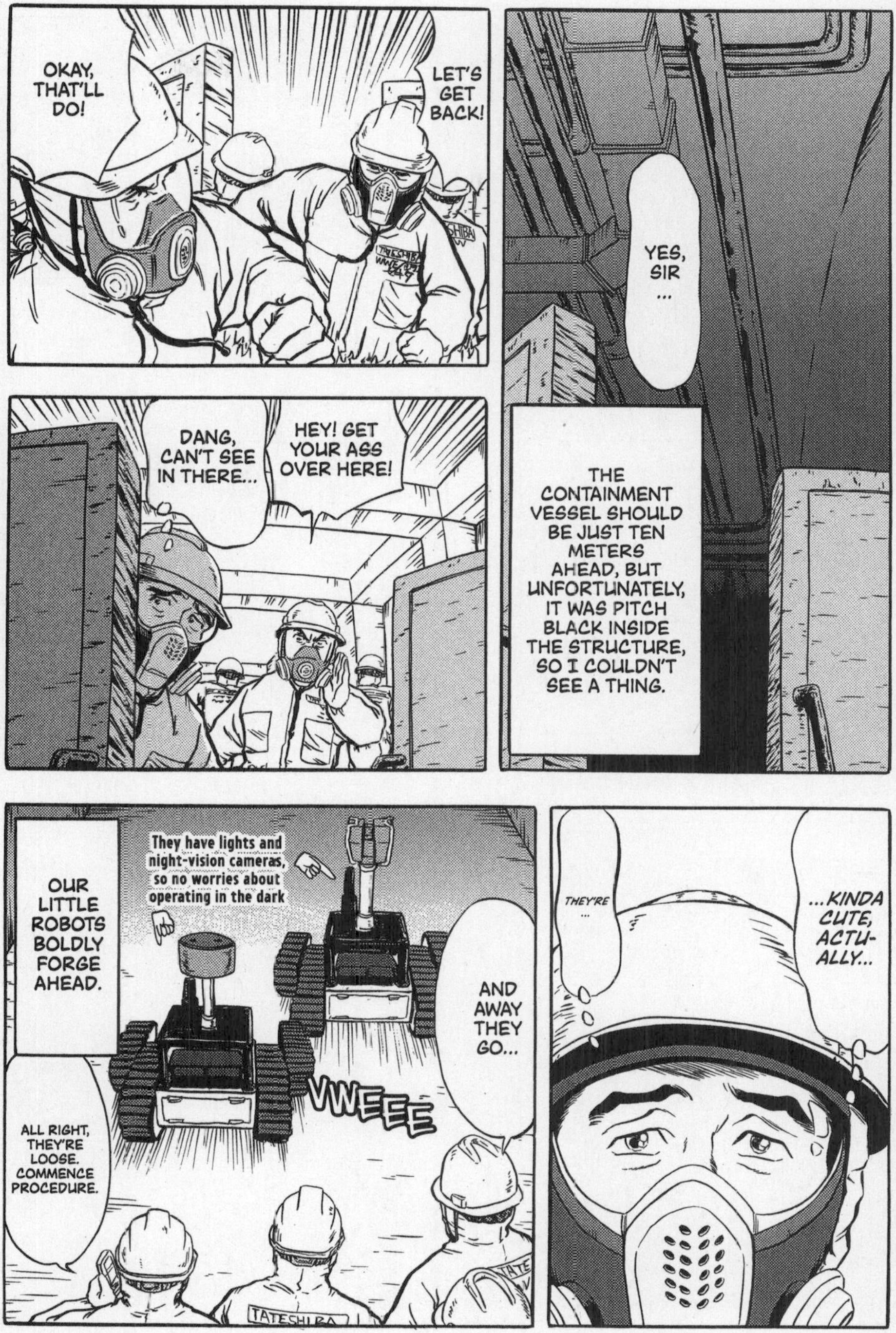
OKAY, THAT'LL DO!
LET'S GET BACK!
YES, SIR ...
HEY! GET YOUR ASS OVER HERE!
DANG, CAN'T SEE IN THERE...
THE CONTAINMENT VESSEL SHOULD BE JUST TEN METERS AHEAD, BUT UNFORTUNATELY, IT WAS PITCH BLACK INSIDE THE STRUCTURE, SO I COULDN'T SEE A THING.
OUR LITTLE ROBOTS BOLDLY FORGE AHEAD.
They have lights and night-vision cameras, so no worries about operating in the dark
AND AWAY THEY GO...
VWEEE
ALL RIGHT, THEY'RE LOOSE. COMMENCE PROCEDURE.
THEY'RE ...
...KINDA CUTE, ACTU-ALLY...

ONCE THE ROBOTS ARE AWAY, THERE'S REALLY NOTHING TO DO.
WE EITHER STAY AT THE SCENE OR GO BACK TO THE ANTI-QUAKE BUILDING.
TRAFFIC JAM
IT'S ONE THING IF YOU HAVE TO WAIT OVER TWO HOURS, BUT FOR JUST ONE...
...MOST WORKERS DON'T WANT TO GO THROUGH THE HASSLE OF THE SURVEY AND CHANGING AT THE ANTI-EARTHQUAKE BUILDING.
PLUS, TWO YEARS AGO THERE WERE ABOUT 3,000 WORKERS A DAY, BUT NOW IT'S MORE LIKE 7,000.
DEPENDING ON THE TIME OF DAY, THERE MIGHT NOT EVEN BE ROOM TO SIT.
WE ALL WANT TO AVOID RADIATION EXPOSURE, BUT IF IT'S JUST 0.1 MSV FOR A SINGLE HOUR, I UNDERSTAND PREFERRING TO JUST WAIT ON THE WORK SITE.
We're not just waiting, we also recharge batteries and stuff
PLUS, IT'S SURPRISINGLY COOL INSIDE THE REACTOR BUILDING!
The concrete walls are thick
IT DEPENDS ON THE WEATHER OF THE DAY, BUT IT'S AMAZING THAT I'M WEARING A FULL MASK IN JULY AND FEEL COMFORTABLE...

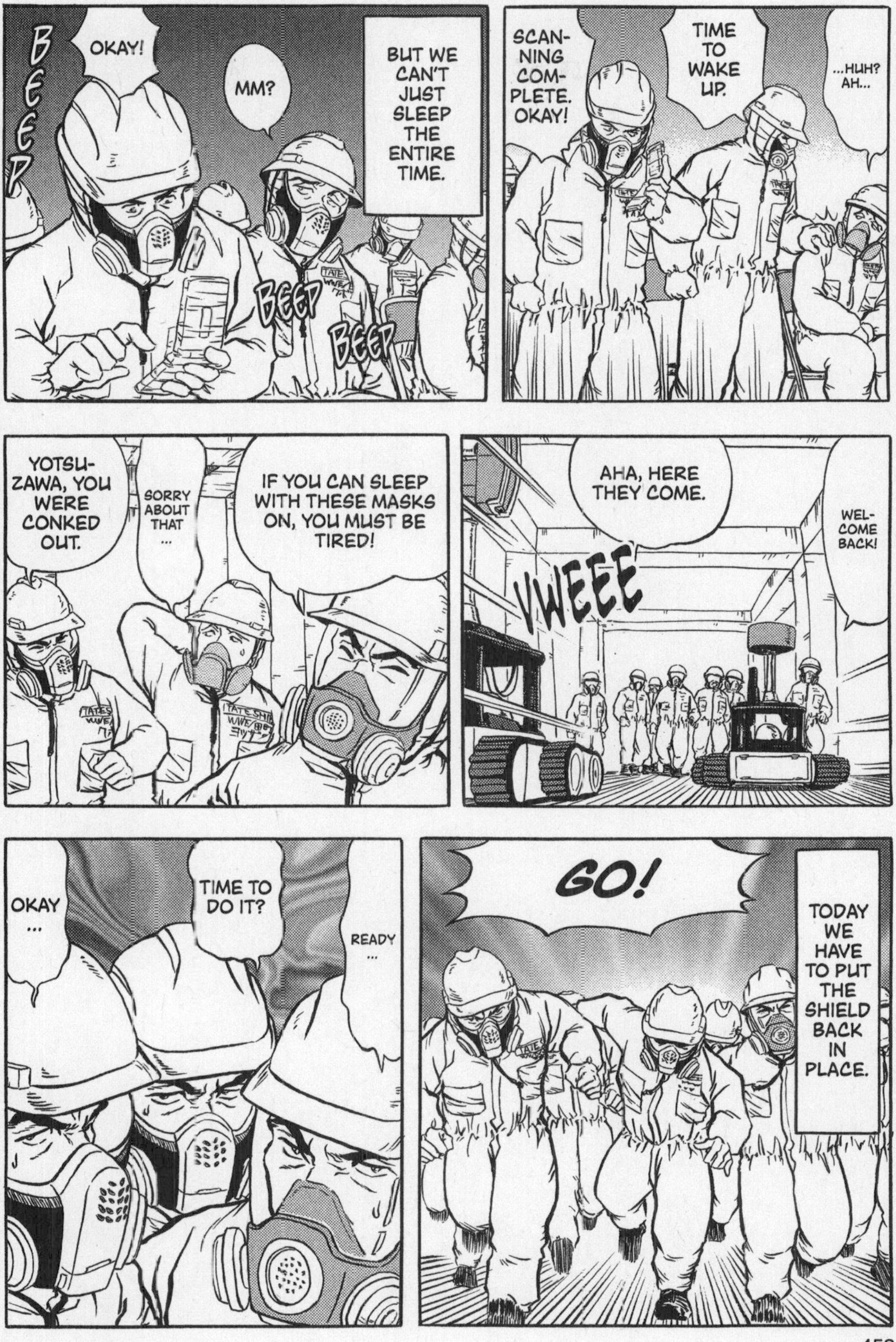
BEEP
OKAY!
MM?
BUT WE CAN'T JUST SLEEP THE ENTIRE TIME.
BEEP
BEEP
SCAN-NING COM-PLETE. OKAY!
TIME TO WAKE UP.
...HUH? AH...
YOTSU-ZAWA, YOU WERE CONKED OUT.
SORRY ABOUT THAT ...
IF YOU CAN SLEEP WITH THESE MASKS ON, YOU MUST BE TIRED!
AHA, HERE THEY COME.
WEL-COME BACK!
VWEEE
OKAY ...
TIME TO DO IT?
READY ...
GO!
TODAY WE HAVE TO PUT THE SHIELD BACK IN PLACE.

OKAY, PUSH!
WASTE TIME AND WE'LL RACK UP EXTRA NUMBERS!
MOOOOVE!
HRRGG
WE GET IT, WE GET IT.
THERE YOU GO! GET INTO IT!

He's just enjoying himself

LET'S GO!
YEAH!
HUFF
WHEW! WE MADE GOOD TIME TODAY, I BET.
HUFF
WHAT KIND OF SPORT ARE WE PLAYING?
WHEEZE
WHEEZE
THIS IS HARD LABOR FOR OLDER GUYS!
HUFF
IT'S NO BIG DEAL TO HANG AROUND LOW-EXPOSURE AREAS, BUT YOU REALLY NEED TO MINIMIZE THE TIME IN THE HOTSPOTS.
IF WE CAN MOVE THAT QUICK...
...THEN WE'VE STILL GOT IT!
HUFF
THAT'S THE KEY TO WORKING A LONG TIME AT ICHI-F.

i.e. the "caterpillar" treads

Wet wipes

First alarm (my limit today was 2.0 mSv, so it's at 0.4 right now)

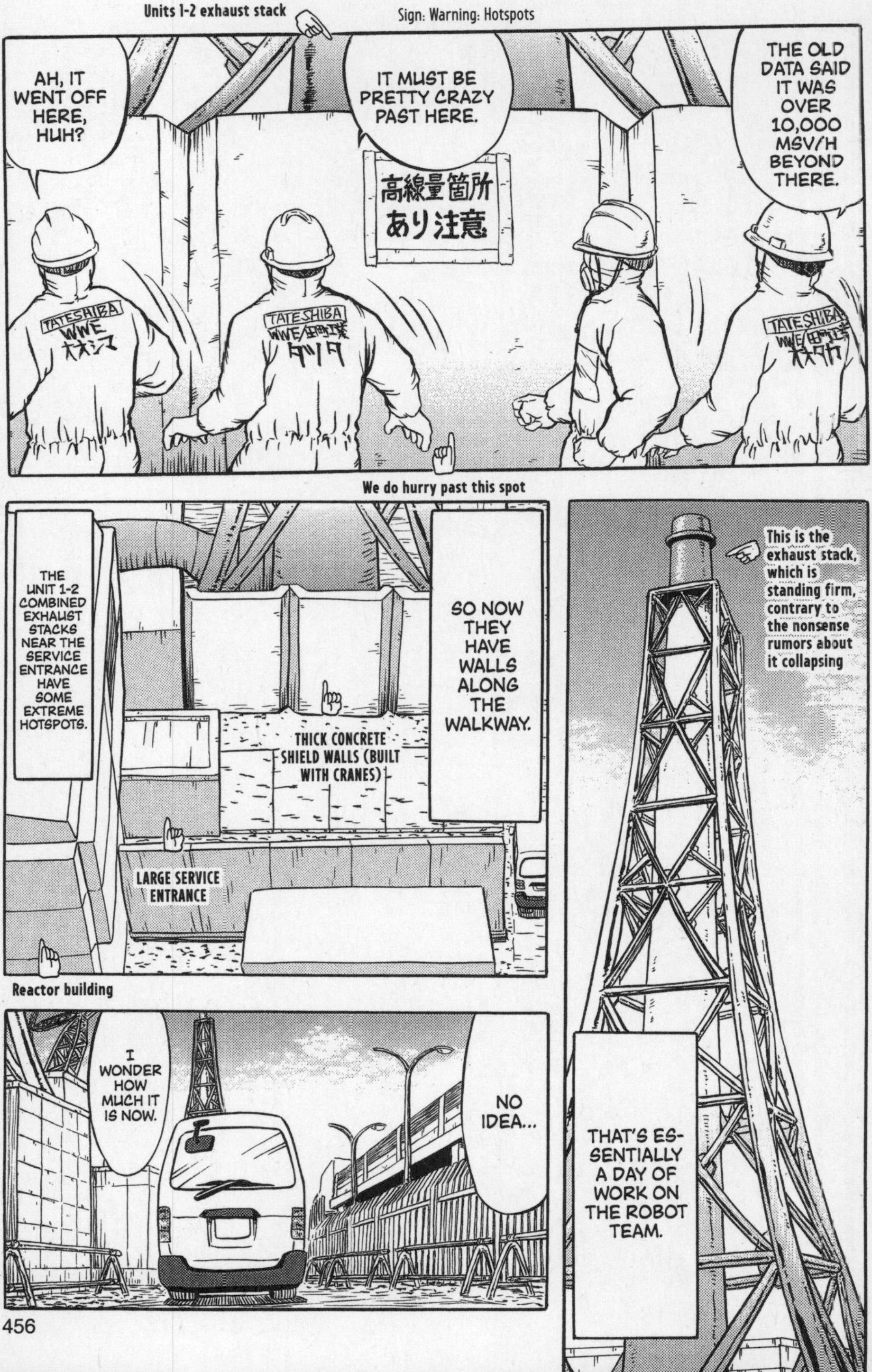

Units 1-2 exhaust stack

Sign: Warning: Hotspots

AH, IT WENT OFF HERE, HUH?

IT MUST BE PRETTY CRAZY PAST HERE.

高線量箇所 あり注意

THE OLD DATA SAID IT WAS OVER 10,000 MSV/H BEYOND THERE.

TATESHIBA WWE オオシズ

TATESHIBA WWE 白井事業 タシツ

TATESHIBA WWE 白井事業 オスツ

We do hurry past this spot

THE UNIT 1-2 COMBINED EXHAUST STACKS NEAR THE SERVICE ENTRANCE HAVE SOME EXTREME HOTSPOTS.

SO NOW THEY HAVE WALLS ALONG THE WALKWAY.

THICK CONCRETE SHIELD WALLS (BUILT WITH CRANES)

LARGE SERVICE ENTRANCE

This is the exhaust stack, which is standing firm, contrary to the nonsense rumors about it collapsing

Reactor building

I WONDER HOW MUCH IT IS NOW.

NO IDEA...

THAT'S ES-SENTIALLY A DAY OF WORK ON THE ROBOT TEAM.

WE CHANGE AT THE ANTI-QUAKE BUILDING, THEN TAKE THE BUS TO THE ENTRY FACILITY.
10:00 AM
THE EXTRA TANKS AND PARKING LOTS HAVE WIPED OUT A LOT OF GREEN HERE.
THERE'S A LOT LESS GREEN-ERY...
THERE'S ALSO BEEN A LOT OF WORK EXPANDING GROUND FACING TO CUT DOWN ON UNDER-GROUND WATER SEEPAGE.
Roadsides and slopes used to be covered with grass, now paved over with asphalt and mortar spray
THE ICHI-F CAMPUS IS LOOKING MORE AND MORE DRY AND DESOLATE.
I'M SURE IT'S TO MINI-MIZE RA-DIATION AND THE SPREAD OF DUST...
...BUT IT'S A BIT SAD.
My personal record two years ago was 1.5 mSv in a day
I HAD 0.41 MSV TO-DAY.
I TURN IN MY MASK AND APD, TAKE A CONTAMI-NATION TEST, AND LEAVE.

Once again, this is not actually electric

The primary subcontractors stop at the office in Ni-F, but we lower subcontractors usually get to go home right away

Picked up at a mini-mart in Hirono

Same

Top Sign: Horizon Kamine

*We leave about 4:00 AM (see Chapter 18)

Sign: Restaurant Café

A hot spring utilizing the exhaust heat from the Hitachi City trash furnace

I HAVE ONE MORE JOB, THOUGH ...
ACTUALLY, I'VE GOT SOMETHING MORE IMPORTANT TO DO THAN RELAX IN THE BATH...
SO YOU'LL BE ABLE TO DRAW UP STORYBOARDS WHILE YOU'RE THERE, RIGHT?
YES, OF COURSE! I'LL E-MAIL THEM TO YOU WHEN I'M DONE WITH THEM.

They had put out my first collected volume and advertised the second as "coming this fall!"

WELL, IT'S EASY TO MAKE GUARAN-TEES...
...BUT THE TRUTH IS, SINCE COMING HERE I'VE BEEN IN TOTAL WORKER MODE. I CAN'T EVEN GET INTO THE COMIC MINDSET.
CLIK
WELL, NO USE TOR-TURING MY-SELF. GOT AN EARLY MORNING TOMOR-ROW...

(This is around when I was drawing Chapters 9 and 10)

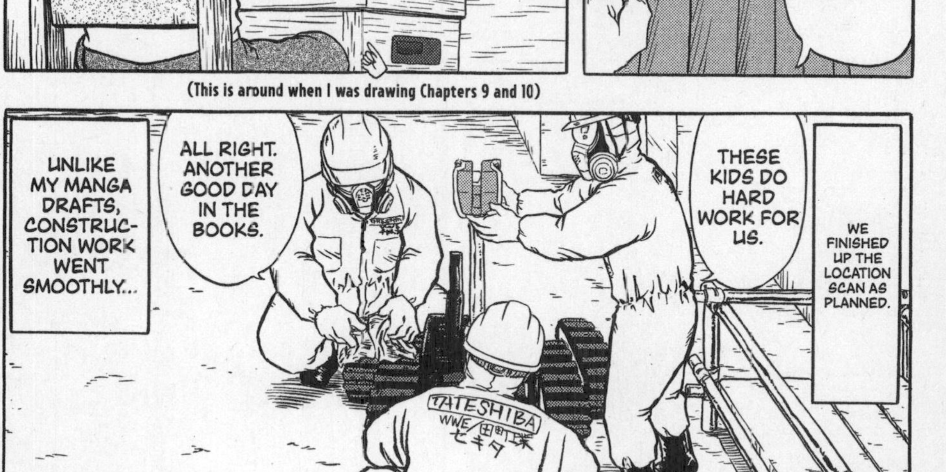
UNLIKE MY MANGA DRAFTS, CONSTRUC-TION WORK WENT SMOOTHLY...
ALL RIGHT. ANOTHER GOOD DAY IN THE BOOKS.
THESE KIDS DO HARD WORK FOR US.
WE FINISHED UP THE LOCATION SCAN AS PLANNED.
TATESHIBA

I WON'T BOTHER TO DEPICT WHERE THE STORAGE LOCATION IS.
I DOUBT ANYONE'S GOING TO WANT TO STEAL A CON-TAMINATED ROBOT LIKE THIS, EXPENSIVE OR NOT.
IT'S A GOOD THING WE DIDN'T NEED THE WARRIOR.
THE ROBOTS GO BACK INTO STORAGE FOR A BIT.
It rolls onto the truck lift on its own
I'LL EVEN DO UPHOL-STERY FOR YA!
CALL ME AGAIN ANY-TIME.
HA HA, SOUNDS GOOD.
IT'S A SHAME IT WAS SO SHORT, YOU DIDN'T GET TO EARN THAT MUCH.
THANKS FOR EVERY-THING.
I WENT BACK HOME BEFORE THE END OF JULY.
IN THE END, I SPENT EIGHT DAYS WORK-ING AND RACKED UP TWO MILLI-SIEVERTS.
OH, CRAP... BUT I HAVEN'T DONE ANY STORY-BOARDS YET...
東京 141km
Tokyo
THAT WAS WAY LESS RADIATION THAN I EXPECTED, SO I CAN STILL WORK ANOTHER FULL JOB THIS YEAR.

CHAPTER 19 - END

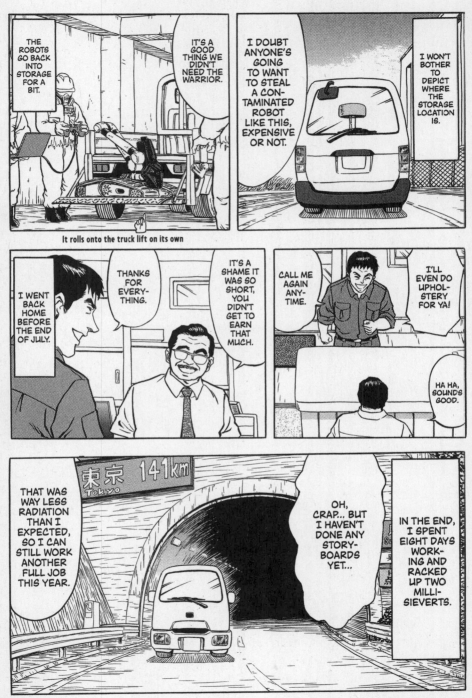

PORT YOTSUKURA ROADSIDE STATION

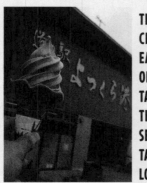

THIS STOP TEMPORARILY CLOSED UP AFTER THE EARTHQUAKE AND REOPENED ON AUGUST 11TH, 2012. TATSUTA'S FAVORITE HERE IS THE SUNSHINE TOMATO SOFT SERVE. IT'S AN ACQUIRED TASTE THAT USES ONLY LOCALLY-GROWN TOMATOES.

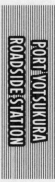

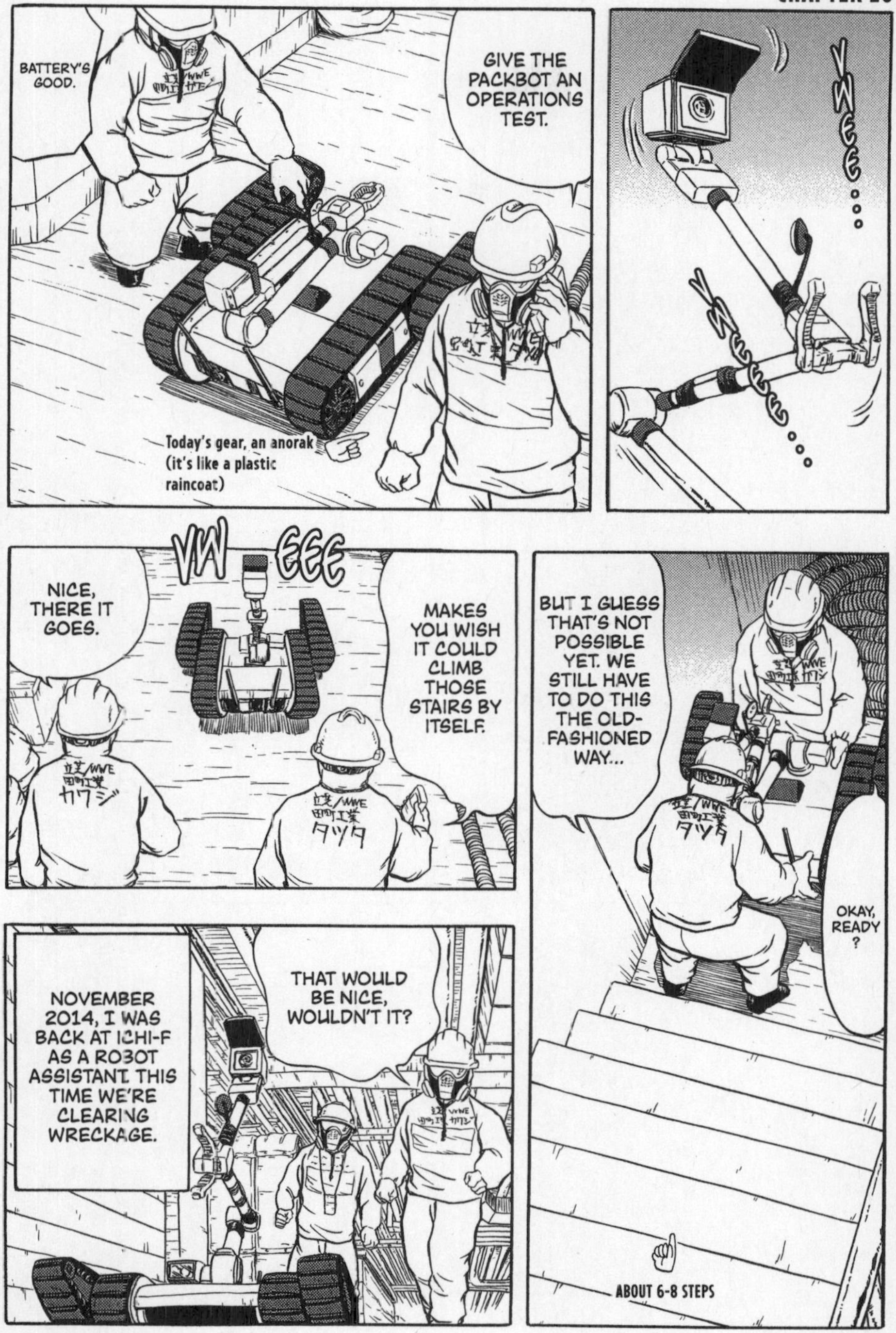

GIVE THE PACKBOT AN OPERATIONS TEST.

BATTERY'S GOOD.

Today's gear, an anorak (it's like a plastic raincoat)

VWEEE...

NICE, THERE IT GOES.

VW EEE

MAKES YOU WISH IT COULD CLIMB THOSE STAIRS BY ITSELF.

BUT I GUESS THAT'S NOT POSSIBLE YET. WE STILL HAVE TO DO THIS THE OLD-FASHIONED WAY...

OKAY, READY?

NOVEMBER 2014, I WAS BACK AT ICHI-F AS A ROBOT ASSISTANT THIS TIME WE'RE CLEARING WRECKAGE.

THAT WOULD BE NICE, WOULDN'T IT?

ABOUT 6-8 STEPS

CHAPTER 20: PINING FOR A SOLUTION

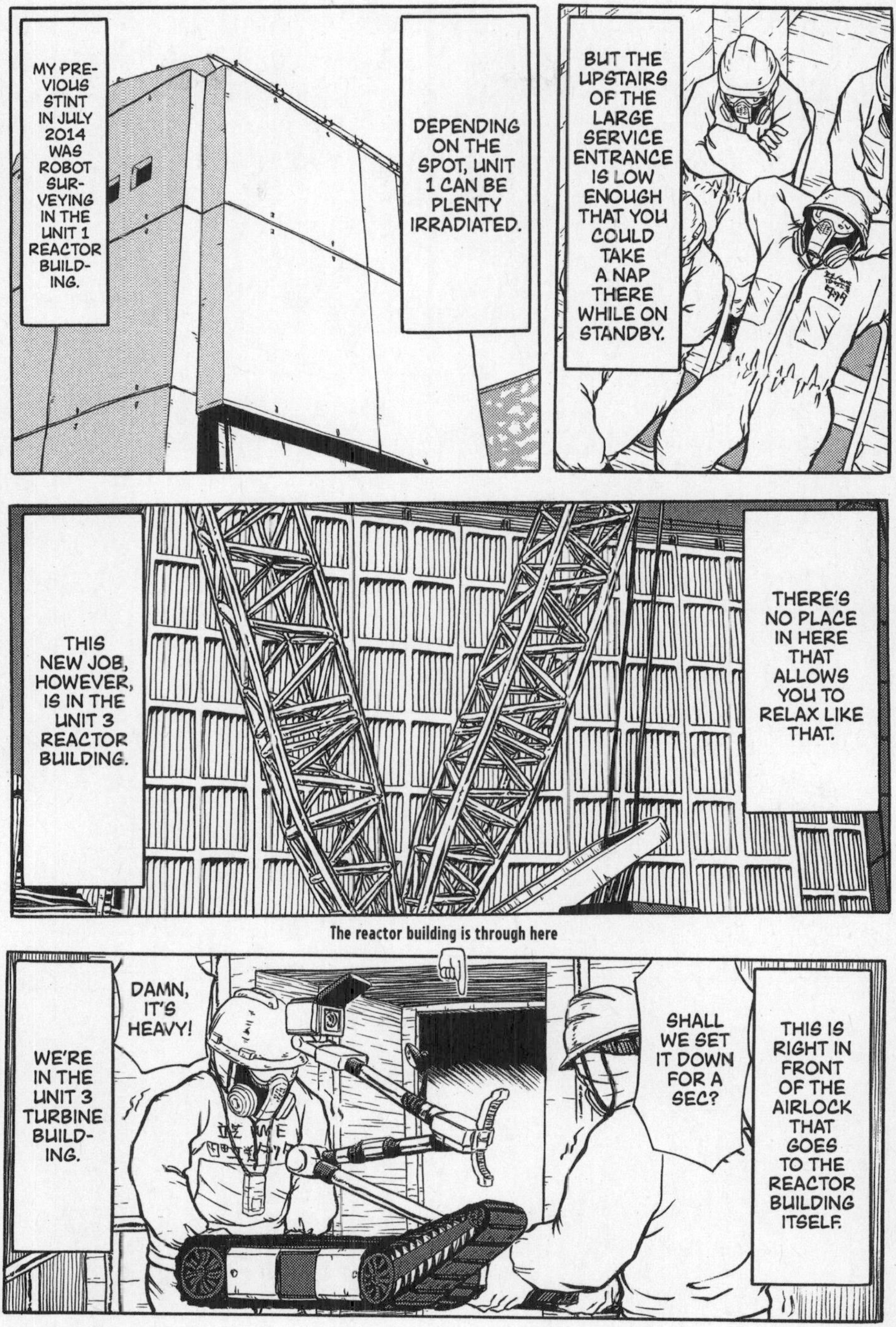
MY PRE-VIOUS STINT IN JULY 2014 WAS ROBOT SUR-VEYING IN THE UNIT 1 REACTOR BUILD-ING.
DEPENDING ON THE SPOT, UNIT 1 CAN BE PLENTY IRRADIATED.
BUT THE UPSTAIRS OF THE LARGE SERVICE ENTRANCE IS LOW ENOUGH THAT YOU COULD TAKE A NAP THERE WHILE ON STANDBY.
THIS NEW JOB, HOWEVER, IS IN THE UNIT 3 REACTOR BUILDING.
THERE'S NO PLACE IN HERE THAT ALLOWS YOU TO RELAX LIKE THAT.
The reactor building is through here
WE'RE IN THE UNIT 3 TURBINE BUILD-ING.
DAMN, IT'S HEAVY!
SHALL WE SET IT DOWN FOR A SEC?
THIS IS RIGHT IN FRONT OF THE AIRLOCK THAT GOES TO THE REACTOR BUILDING ITSELF.

There are spots over 10 mSv/h, especially perpendicular to the opening, so we always dart to the side

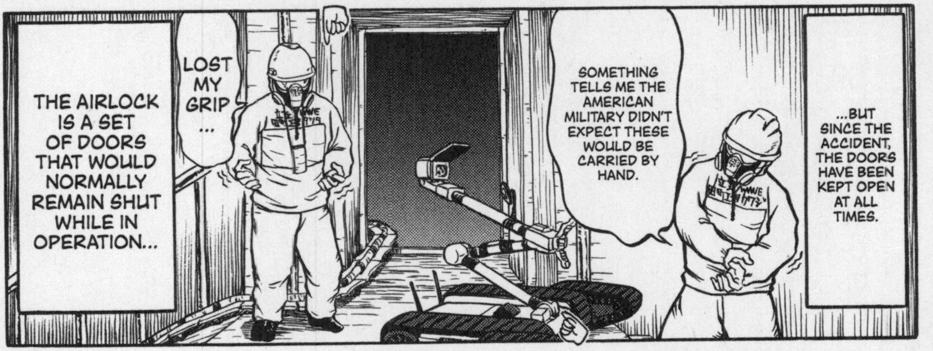

It's only about 20 kg (45 lbs), but there are no easy handles to grasp

THERE ARE TWO KINDS OF ROBOTS FOR THIS ASSIGNMENT, BOTH MADE BY THE SAME AMERICAN MILITARY CONTRACTOR.

THIS IS "PACKBOT," THE MONITORING/COMMUNICATION ROBOT WE'RE CARRYING NOW

MIRROR (DOSIMETER READOUT IS FIXED WITH TAPE SO IT'S ALWAYS VISIBLE IN THE CAMERA)

CAMERA

THIS PART CAN GRAB OBJECTS

DOSIMETER (ALSO AFFIXED)

THE OTHER ONE IS THE "WARRIOR," THE REMOVAL ROBOT THAT I MENTIONED LAST TIME

THE FINE DETAILS ARE MILITARY SECRETS, I GUESS.

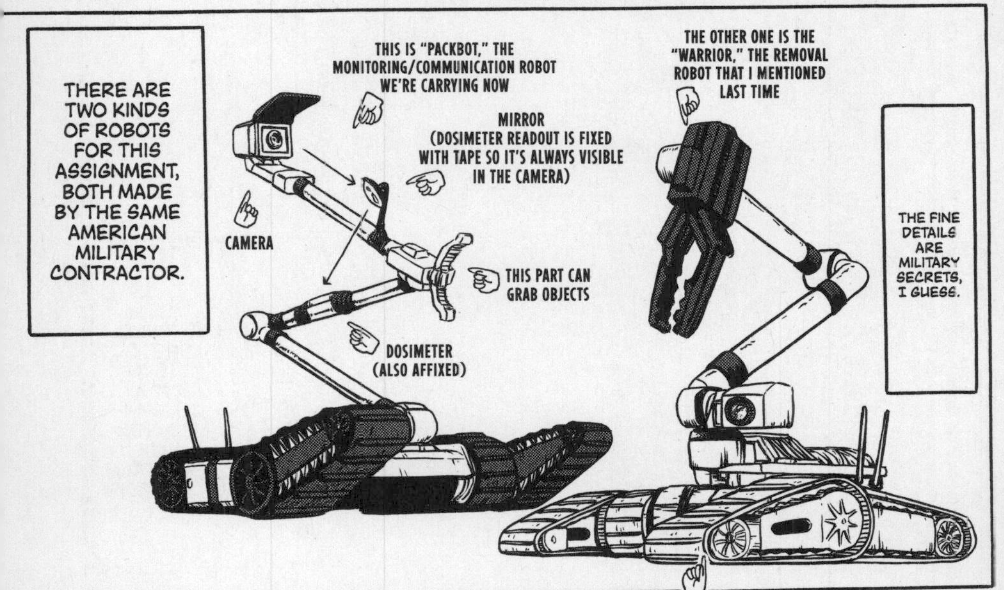

This one's about 70 kg (155 lbs), so it can't be carried by people

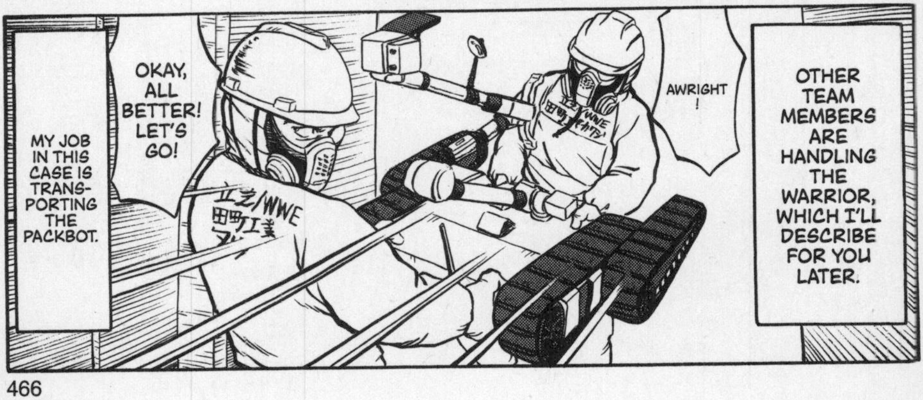

AND SET IT DOWN!

STAIRS AND STEPS THIS SHALLOW PROBABLY AREN'T OUT OF THE REALM OF POSSIBILITY FOR THE PACKBOT TO CLEAR ON ITS OWN...

...BUT HAULING IT IS FASTER.

It's over 10 mSv/h this way

*The exposure is different depending on whether you're near the back or the entrance side, holding the robot

It's around 3-4 mSv/h here

AND NOW RETREAT!

THE AMOUNT OF TIME WE SPEND IN THE REACTOR BUILDING IS JUST TEN SECONDS!

EEP!

THERE'S ANOTHER THING WE HAUL IN HERE.

THERE'S A RESIN HOSE TO HOLD ALL THE CABLES (ABOUT 50M LONG)

IT'S WHAT WE CALL THE "AP CART" WITH THE WI-FI ROUTER FOR REMOTE CONTROL.

HANDLE FOR PACKBOT TO GRAB

ON ROLLERS

AP = Access Point

AT UNIT 1, WE COULD JUST LEAVE IT NEAR THE ENTRANCE, BUT THE SIGNAL IS BAD IN UNIT 3.

SO PACKBOT HAS TO PULL IT ALONG ON ITS OWN.

We set it down here

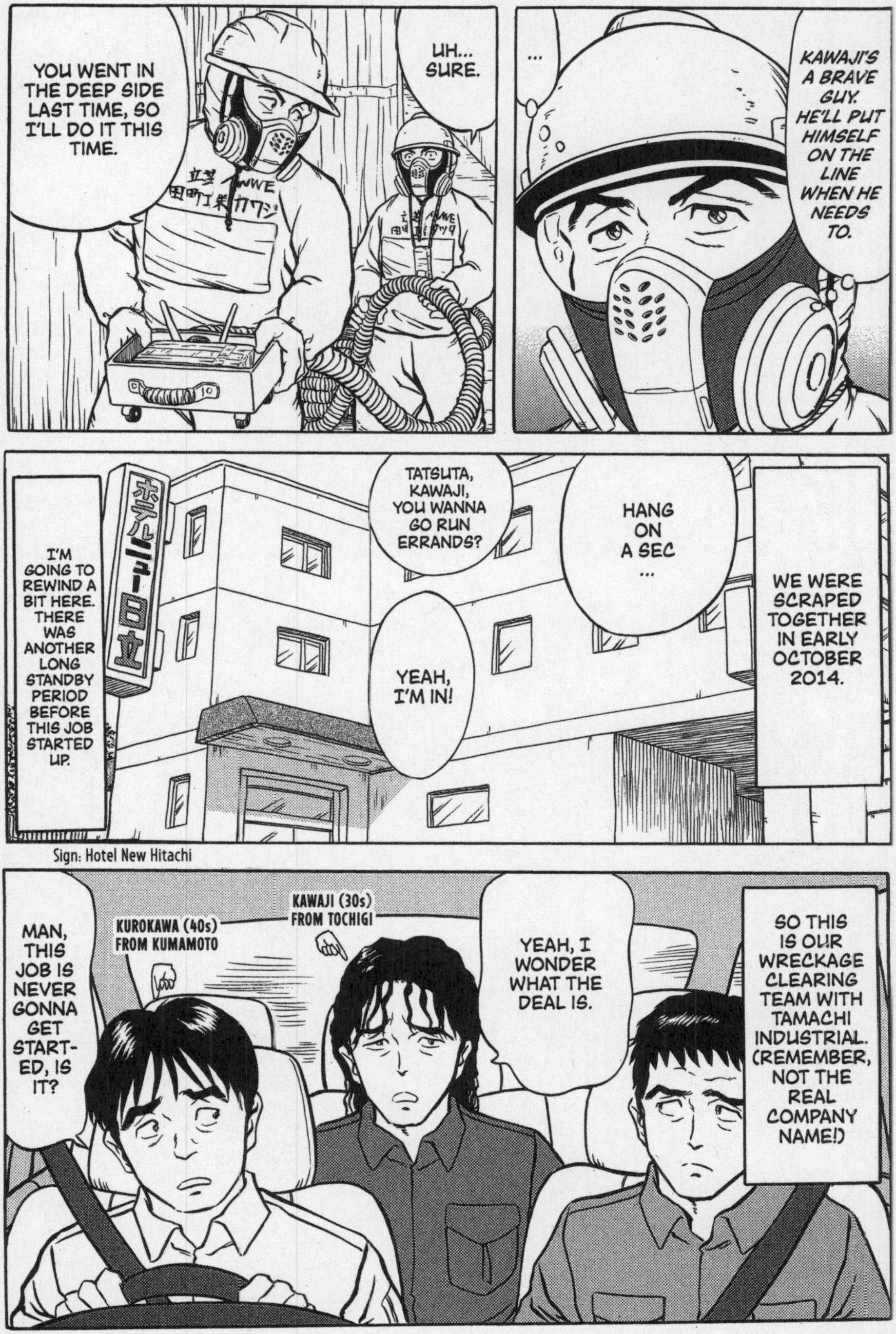
YOU WENT IN THE DEEP SIDE LAST TIME, SO I'LL DO IT THIS TIME.
UH... SURE.
...
KAWAJI'S A BRAVE GUY. HE'LL PUT HIMSELF ON THE LINE WHEN HE NEEDS TO.
I'M GOING TO REWIND A BIT HERE. THERE WAS ANOTHER LONG STANDBY PERIOD BEFORE THIS JOB STARTED UP.
TATSUTA, KAWAJI, YOU WANNA GO RUN ERRANDS?
YEAH, I'M IN!
HANG ON A SEC ...
WE WERE SCRAPED TOGETHER IN EARLY OCTOBER 2014.
MAN, THIS JOB IS NEVER GONNA GET START- ED, IS IT?
KUROKAWA (40s) FROM KUMAMOTO
KAWAJI (30s) FROM TOCHIGI
YEAH, I WONDER WHAT THE DEAL IS.
SO THIS IS OUR WRECKAGE CLEARING TEAM WITH TAMACHI INDUSTRIAL. (REMEMBER, NOT THE REAL COMPANY NAME!)
Sign: Hotel New Hitachi

THIS WAS THEIR FIRST RODEO AT ICHI-F, SO AS THE VETERAN OF THE GROUP, I BECAME THE DE FACTO LEADER.

DON'T GET HASTY, FELLAS. THIS IS JUST HOW IT WORKS.

BUT WE'RE NOT HERE TO WORK AT THE POWER STATION.

They were getting jobs at Hirono and Hitachinaka power stations while we were waiting

I MEAN, I APPRECIATE THE CHANCE TO EARN A DAILY WAGE, BUT STILL ...

As the team leader, I got an extra 2,000 yen a day - up to 22,000 now!

YEAH, THAT'S TRUE. I WAS SURE WORRIED THE FIRST TIME I CAME.

I WONDERED IF I'D EVER ACTUALLY WORK AT ICHI-F.

There's a limit to the number of people the part-time job needs, so I didn't get to go

DON'T WORRY, IT'LL START SOON ENOUGH.

BUT I THOUGHT I WAS GOING TO HAUL IN THE CASH OVER A SHORT-TERM JOB...

WELL, THAT TURNED OUT TO BE A DUD.

Honestly, I do not recommend coming to Ichi-F for this purpose

AT THIS RATE, I'M STARTING TO LOSE FAITH IN THE WHOLE ICHI-F OPERATION...

HOW DO I KNOW IT'S SAFE THERE ?

I MEAN ...

OH, DON'T WORRY ABOUT THAT. THEY TAKE RADIATION MANAGE-MENT VERY SERIOUSLY.

WELL, I'VE TAKEN A TON OF WBC TESTS AND NEVER HAD A BAD READING.

BUT THERE'S NOT JUST EXTERNAL EXPOSURE, THERE'S INTERNAL EXPOSURE, TOO.

HUH? IS HE ONE OF THOSE TYPES...?

THE THYROID CANCER WASN'T CAUSED BY THE NUCLEAR ACCIDENT, IT'S JUST A GENERAL OCCURRENCE THAT THEY'RE DISCOVERING MORE OFTEN NOW.

THAT MIGHT BE FINE FOR AN ADULT...

...BUT YOU HEAR ABOUT AN INCREASE IN FUKUSHIMA CHILDREN WITH THYROID CANCER, AND...

THIS MIGHT BE OLD NEWS TO YOU, BUT THYROID CANCER IS SOMETHING THAT MANY, MANY PEOPLE HAVE, AND THE VAST MAJORITY NEVER EXPERIENCE ANY ADVERSE EFFECTS.

BUT BECAUSE IT WAS MANDATED THAT ALL CHILDREN IN FUKUSHIMA MUST BE TESTED AFTER THE ACCIDENT, THEY STARTED COUNTING UP CASES THAT WOULD NORMALLY NEVER BE DISCOVERED.

TO COMPARE THESE NUMBERS, THE MINISTRY OF THE ENVIRONMENT DID TESTS IN AOMORI, NAGASAKI AND YAMANASHI, AND FOUND THE DIFFERENCE IN THE RATE OF THYROID ABNORMALITIES TO BE NEGLIGIBLE.

甲状腺がん遺伝子変異
チェルノブイリと別型

AND AFTER STUDYING THE GENETIC MUTATIONS IN THE CHILDREN'S CANCER CELLS, THEY WERE DIFFERENT FROM THOSE OBSERVED AFTER THE CHERNOBYL ACCIDENT.

Article: Genetic mutation in thyroid cancer cells differs from Chernobyl's

WELL, I WANT TO SEE IT FOR MYSELF. PLUS, I NEED THE MONEY.

HONESTLY, IF YOU'RE THAT WORRIED, I WOULDN'T RECOMMEND FORCING YOURSELF TO WORK AT ICHI-F.

BUT STILL, A JOB IS A JOB, AND YOU'VE GOT TO DO IT.

MAYBE SEEING HOW IT'S RUN WILL CHANGE YOUR MIND.

PERSON-ALLY, WHICH-EVER SIDE IS RIGHT, I DON'T INTEND TO RAISE A FUSS.

SPOKEN LIKE A STOIC FORMER SDF SOLDIER, MR. KUROKAWA!

AS IT TURNED OUT, I NEEDN'T HAVE WORRIED.

THAT MAKES ME WONDER, ONCE WE'RE ON THE SCENE, WILL KAWAJI MANAGE TO DO THE WORK PROPERLY...?

HAH!

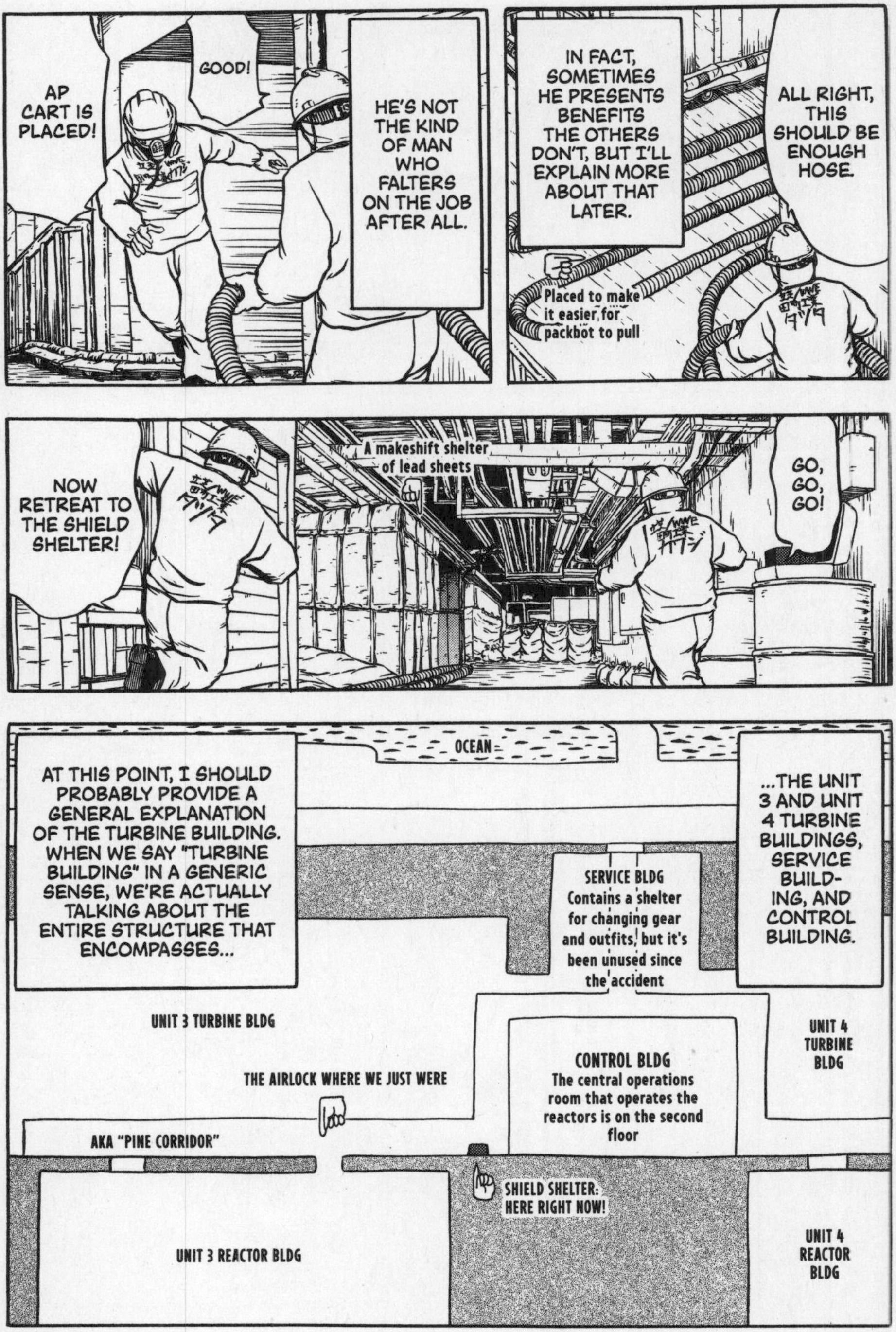
AP CART IS PLACED!
GOOD!
HE'S NOT THE KIND OF MAN WHO FALTERS ON THE JOB AFTER ALL.
IN FACT, SOMETIMES HE PRESENTS BENEFITS THE OTHERS DON'T, BUT I'LL EXPLAIN MORE ABOUT THAT LATER.
ALL RIGHT, THIS SHOULD BE ENOUGH HOSE.
Placed to make it easier for packbot to pull
NOW RETREAT TO THE SHIELD SHELTER!
A makeshift shelter of lead sheets
GO, GO, GO!
AT THIS POINT, I SHOULD PROBABLY PROVIDE A GENERAL EXPLANATION OF THE TURBINE BUILDING. WHEN WE SAY "TURBINE BUILDING" IN A GENERIC SENSE, WE'RE ACTUALLY TALKING ABOUT THE ENTIRE STRUCTURE THAT ENCOMPASSES...
OCEAN
...THE UNIT 3 AND UNIT 4 TURBINE BUILDINGS, SERVICE BUILD-ING, AND CONTROL BUILDING.
SERVICE BLDG
Contains a shelter for changing gear and outfits, but it's been unused since the accident
UNIT 3 TURBINE BLDG
UNIT 4 TURBINE BLDG
CONTROL BLDG
The central operations room that operates the reactors is on the second floor
THE AIRLOCK WHERE WE JUST WERE
AKA "PINE CORRIDOR"
SHIELD SHELTER: HERE RIGHT NOW!
UNIT 3 REACTOR BLDG
UNIT 4 REACTOR BLDG

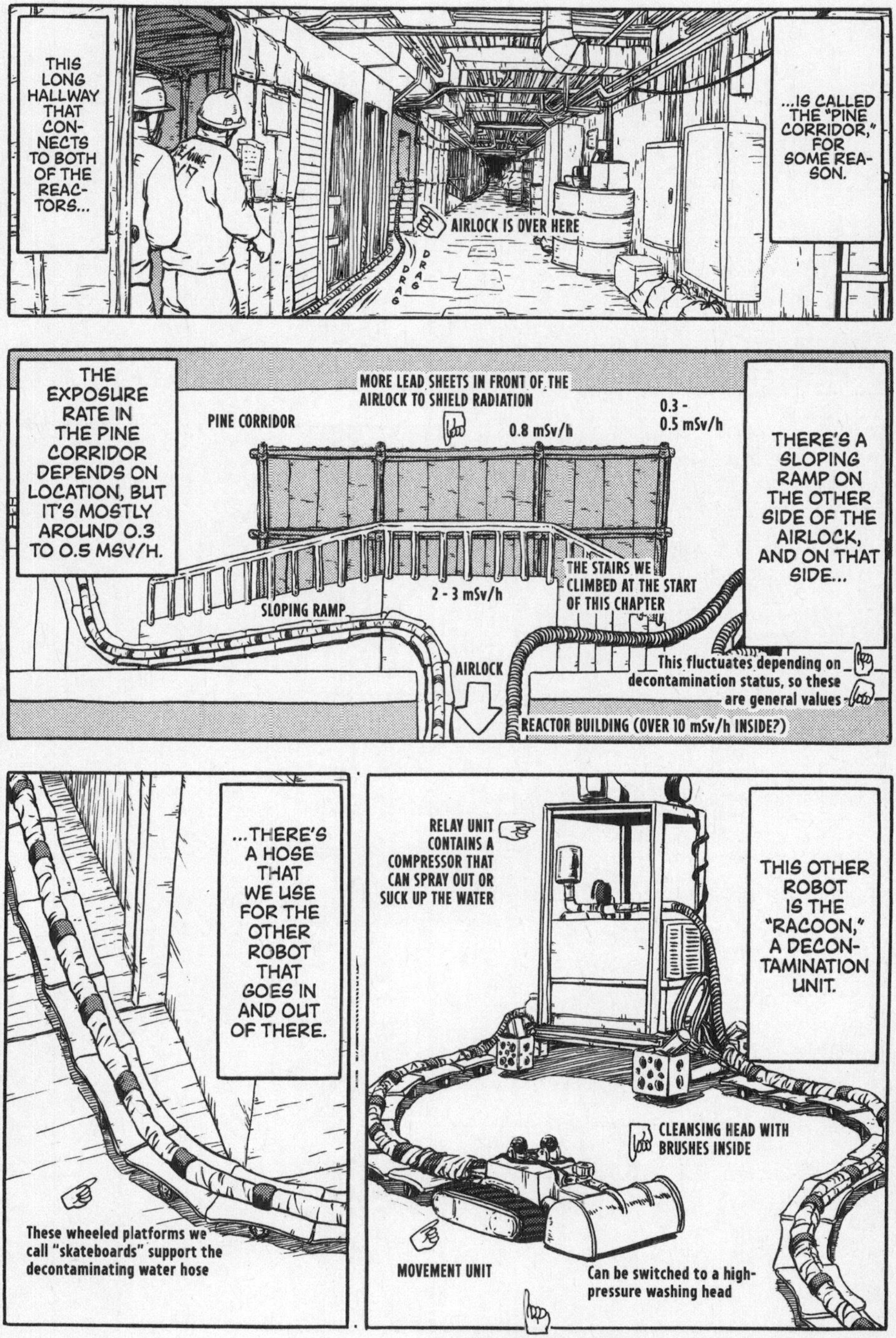
THIS LONG HALLWAY THAT CONNECTS TO BOTH OF THE REACTORS...
AIRLOCK IS OVER HERE
DRAG DRAG
...IS CALLED THE "PINE CORRIDOR," FOR SOME REASON.
THE EXPOSURE RATE IN THE PINE CORRIDOR DEPENDS ON LOCATION, BUT IT'S MOSTLY AROUND 0.3 TO 0.5 MSV/H.
MORE LEAD SHEETS IN FRONT OF THE AIRLOCK TO SHIELD RADIATION
PINE CORRIDOR
0.8 mSv/h
0.3 - 0.5 mSv/h
THE STAIRS WE CLIMBED AT THE START OF THIS CHAPTER
2 - 3 mSv/h
SLOPING RAMP
AIRLOCK
REACTOR BUILDING (OVER 10 mSv/h INSIDE?)
This fluctuates depending on decontamination status, so these are general values
THERE'S A SLOPING RAMP ON THE OTHER SIDE OF THE AIRLOCK, AND ON THAT SIDE...
...THERE'S A HOSE THAT WE USE FOR THE OTHER ROBOT THAT GOES IN AND OUT OF THERE.
These wheeled platforms we call "skateboards" support the decontaminating water hose
THIS OTHER ROBOT IS THE "RACOON," A DECONTAMINATION UNIT.
RELAY UNIT CONTAINS A COMPRESSOR THAT CAN SPRAY OUT OR SUCK UP THE WATER
CLEANSING HEAD WITH BRUSHES INSIDE
MOVEMENT UNIT
Can be switched to a high-pressure washing head

THE DECONTAMINATION TEAM THAT COMES IN AFTER US USES THIS ONE

THIS GUY DOES THE LAUDABLE DUTY OF REDUCING RADIATION...
DRAG
DRAG
SKATEBOARDS
...BUT THE SKATEBOARD HOSE HOGS UP ALL THE RAMP, SO THE PACKBOT HAS TO USE THE STAIRS.
BEE-BEE-BEEP
HELLO?
OH, NO!
IT'S STUCK? I'LL GET IT.
IF THE HOSE GETS STUCK ON A CORNER, THE OPERATOR'S ROOM IN THE ANTI-QUAKE BUILDING WILL CALL US.
I'LL GO!
NO, THIS ONE'S MY TURN!
DASH
STRANGELY ENOUGH, EVERYONE WANTS TO AVOID EXTRA RADIATION EXPOSURE, BUT WE ALSO WANT TO BE THE FIRST ONE IN THERE.
WHAT IS THIS FEELING, ANYWAY?
I'M ASSUMING IT COMES FROM COMPASSION FOR OUR TEAMMATES.
BUT PART OF ME WONDERS IF THERE'S SOME MALE PRIDE AT STAKE, TOO...

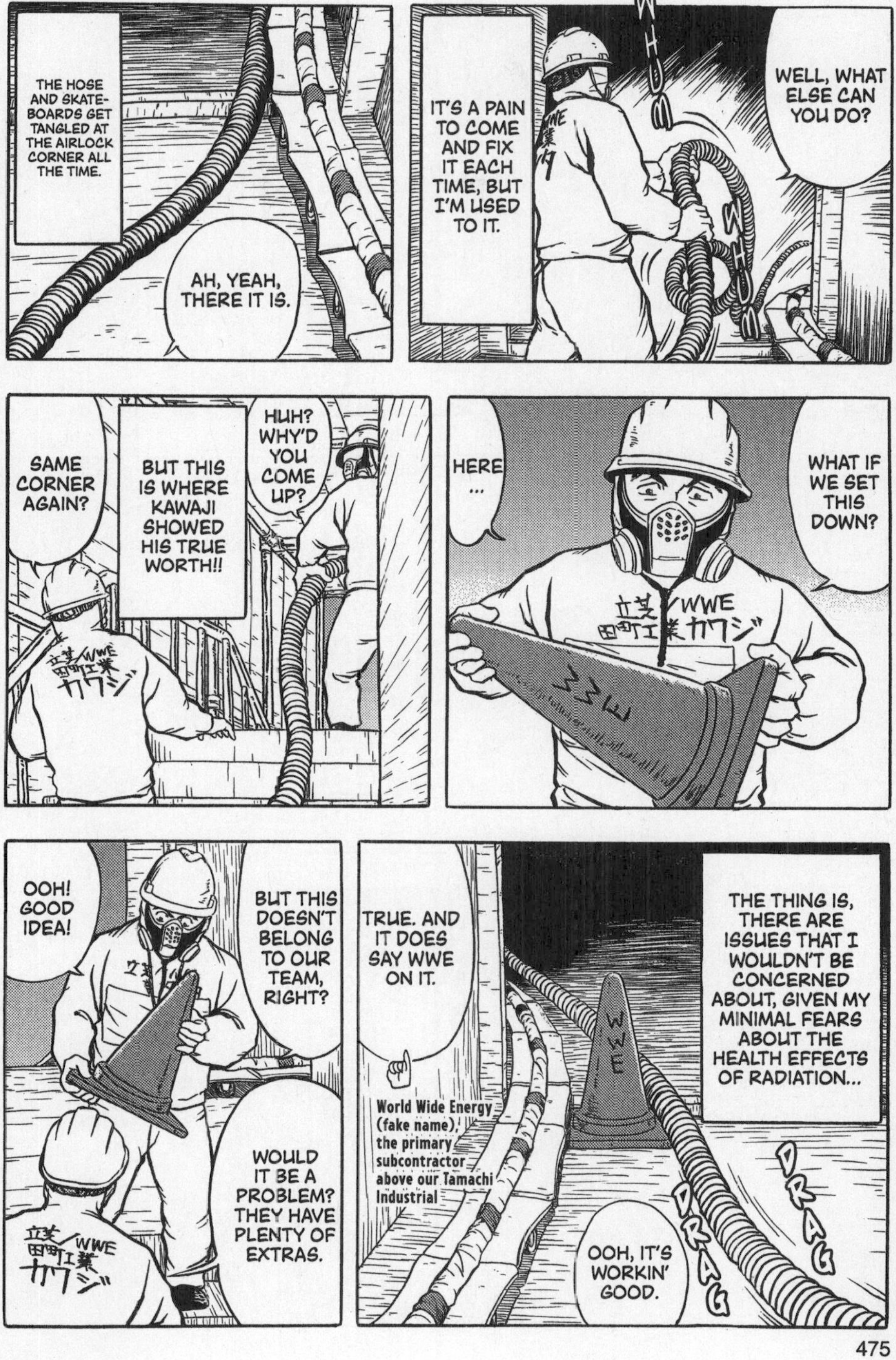
THE HOSE AND SKATE-BOARDS GET TANGLED AT THE AIRLOCK CORNER ALL THE TIME.
AH, YEAH, THERE IT IS.
IT'S A PAIN TO COME AND FIX IT EACH TIME, BUT I'M USED TO IT.
WHUM
WHUM
WELL, WHAT ELSE CAN YOU DO?
SAME CORNER AGAIN?
BUT THIS IS WHERE KAWAJI SHOWED HIS TRUE WORTH!!
HUH? WHY'D YOU COME UP?
HERE...
WHAT IF WE SET THIS DOWN?
WWE
OOH! GOOD IDEA!
BUT THIS DOESN'T BELONG TO OUR TEAM, RIGHT?
WOULD IT BE A PROBLEM? THEY HAVE PLENTY OF EXTRAS.
TRUE. AND IT DOES SAY WWE ON IT.
World Wide Energy (fake name), the primary subcontractor above our Tamachi Industrial
THE THING IS, THERE ARE ISSUES THAT I WOULDN'T BE CONCERNED ABOUT, GIVEN MY MINIMAL FEARS ABOUT THE HEALTH EFFECTS OF RADIATION...
WWE
OOH, IT'S WORKIN' GOOD.
DRAG
DRAG

...BUT THOSE WHO ARE MORE WARY OF EXPOSURE THINK CAREFULLY ABOUT IMPROVEMENTS THAT ULTIMATELY HELP ALL OF US.

I THINK THIS MIGHT WORK.

WE SHOULD DO THAT AT THE START TOMORROW.

EVEN THOUGH I RATTLE ON ALL THE TIME ABOUT HOW MINIMIZING EXPOSURE IS IMPORTANT TO INCREASE THE NUMBER OF DAYS YOU CAN WORK, I HAD TO ADMIT THAT THIS OPENED MY EYES TO HOW RESIGNED I WAS ABOUT THE CURRENT STATE OF THINGS.

AND IT LEFT A MARK ON ME ABOUT HIS MERITS.

HE WILLINGLY NOMINATES HIMSELF TO GO INTO THE DANGEROUS SPOTS.

MAYBE HAVING A BIT OF FEAR IS ACTUALLY THE BEST THING FOR YOU.

BEE- BEE- BEEP

WE'RE DONE PULLING IT CLEAR. GO AHEAD!

ALL RIGHT!

HEY, HERE WE ARE.

AHA, GOOD TIMING.

THE WARRIOR-HAULING DUO RETURNS.

OUR JOB IS ESSENTIALLY TRANSPORTING THE ROBOT IN.

EVERYTHING OKAY?

THINGS SPED UP PARTWAY.

THE DECONTAMINATION TEAM THEN PULLS IT BACK OUT.

USED OUR NEW SECRET WEAPON!

SECRET WEAP-ON?

SHIRAIWA FROM IWAKI, ONE OF THE NON-TAMACHI MEMBERS

THE FOUR OF US ARE THE MAIN ROBOT-HAULING TEAM THIS TIME AROUND.

MORE LIKE *CUT* THEM OFF.

CH-CHUK

WEARING TYVEK UNDERNEATH

IT'S FINE, SINCE THEY'RE DISPOSABLE ANYWAY.

I'LL EXPLAIN WHEN WE GET BACK.

LET'S TAKE THESE OFF!

SHA-KING

CH-CHUK

TAKING OFF YOUR OUTER LAYER WHEN YOU LEAVE HAP-PENS AT ALL WORK SITES.

MAN, I'M EX-HAUSTED TODAY.

HOPE-FULLY IT'LL ALL WORK OUT.

THAT'S THE END OF THE DAY...

AND IT'S NOT EVEN MORNING YET.

YEP, THIS JOB IS A NIGHT SHIFT.

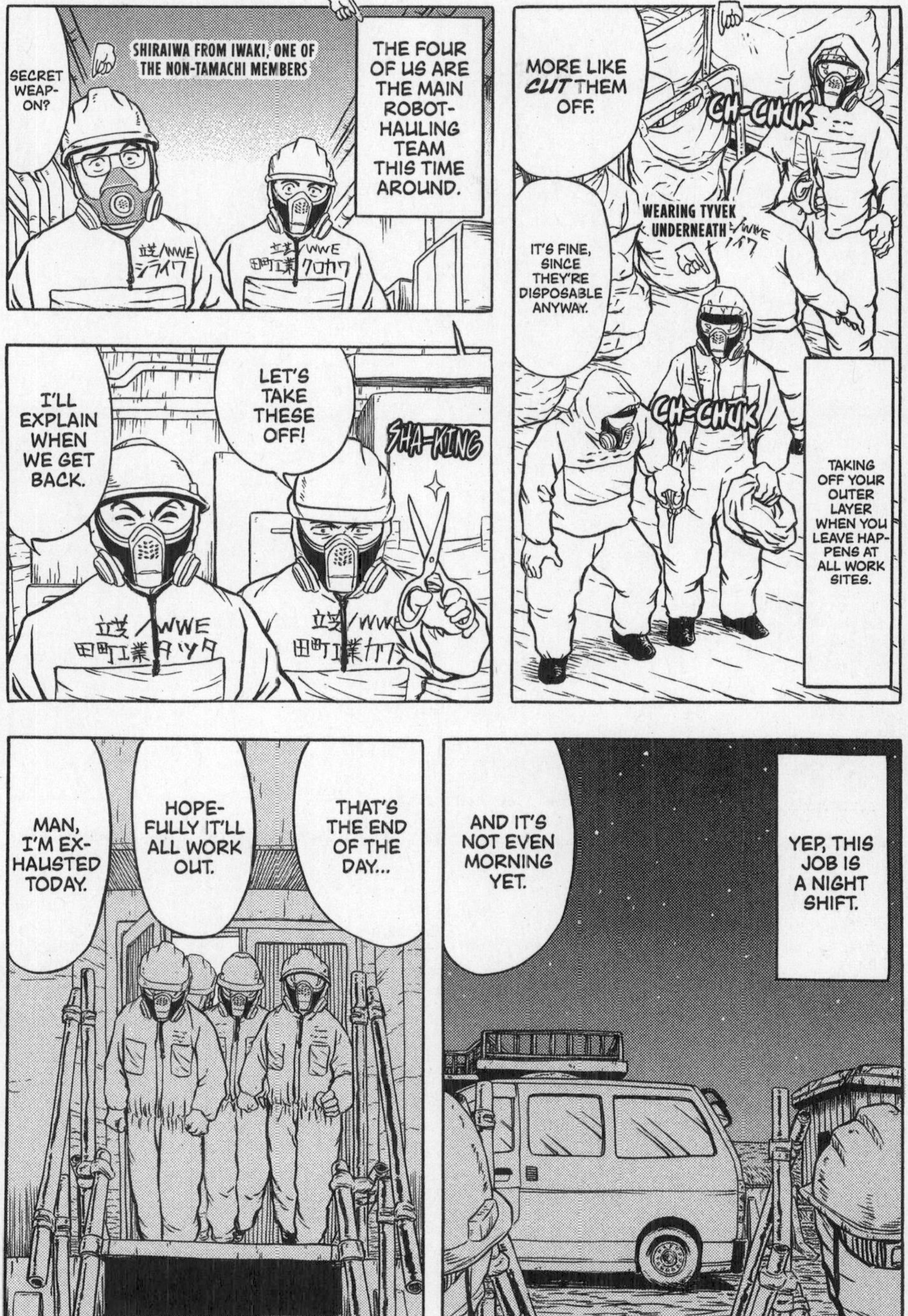

I'M USED TO LATE SHIFTS FROM WORKING ON THE SHIP.
I CAN'T EVEN TELL WHEN I SHOULD BE GOING TO BED...
I'M DEAD TIRED ...
WE LEAVE HITACHI AT 12:30 AM.
Former Naval SDF
WE REACH THE JV PARKING LOT AT 2:00, THEN HEAD FOR ICHI-F.
We take the primary subcontractors car from JV
WE'RE INSIDE ICHI-F BY 2:30 OR 3:00.
AFTER GEARING UP, WE LEAVE FOR THE SITE BEFORE 4:00.
IF ALL GOES WELL, WE FIN-ISH UP AT THE SITE AROUND 5:00 AND RETURN TO THE ANTI-QUAKE BUILD-ING.
I SEE / NOT A SOUL / ON THE WHARF / AT NIIIIIGHT ♪
1-F Port
OUR DAY'S WORK IS OVER BEFORE WE EVEN SEE THE SUNRISE.

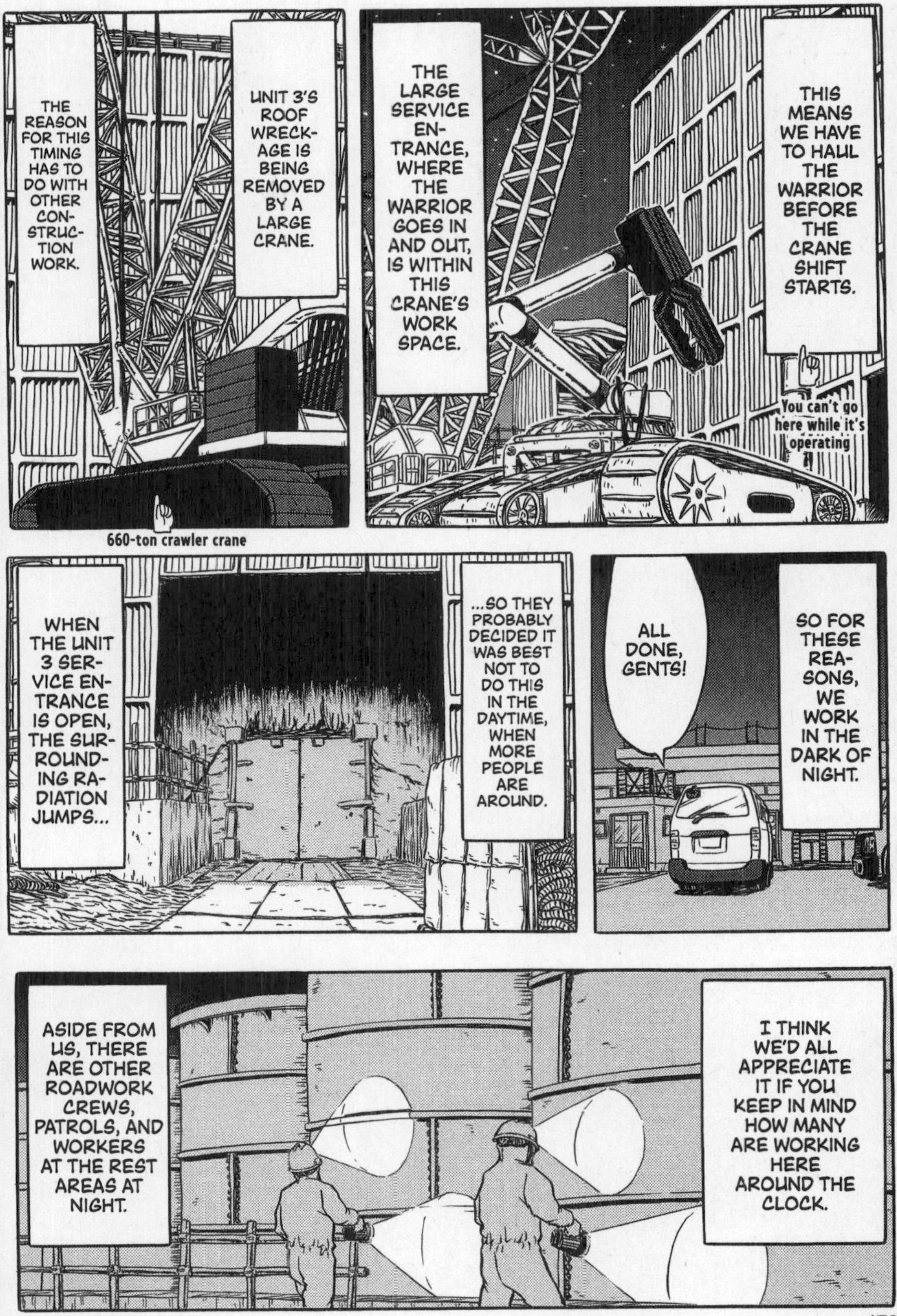

THE REASON FOR THIS TIMING HAS TO DO WITH OTHER CONSTRUCTION WORK.

UNIT 3'S ROOF WRECKAGE IS BEING REMOVED BY A LARGE CRANE.

660-ton crawler crane

THE LARGE SERVICE ENTRANCE, WHERE THE WARRIOR GOES IN AND OUT, IS WITHIN THIS CRANE'S WORK SPACE.

THIS MEANS WE HAVE TO HAUL THE WARRIOR BEFORE THE CRANE SHIFT STARTS.

You can't go here while it's operating

WHEN THE UNIT 3 SERVICE ENTRANCE IS OPEN, THE SURROUNDING RADIATION JUMPS...

...SO THEY PROBABLY DECIDED IT WAS BEST NOT TO DO THIS IN THE DAYTIME, WHEN MORE PEOPLE ARE AROUND.

ALL DONE, GENTS!

SO FOR THESE REASONS, WE WORK IN THE DARK OF NIGHT.

ASIDE FROM US, THERE ARE OTHER ROADWORK CREWS, PATROLS, AND WORKERS AT THE REST AREAS AT NIGHT.

I THINK WE'D ALL APPRECIATE IT IF YOU KEEP IN MIND HOW MANY ARE WORKING HERE AROUND THE CLOCK.

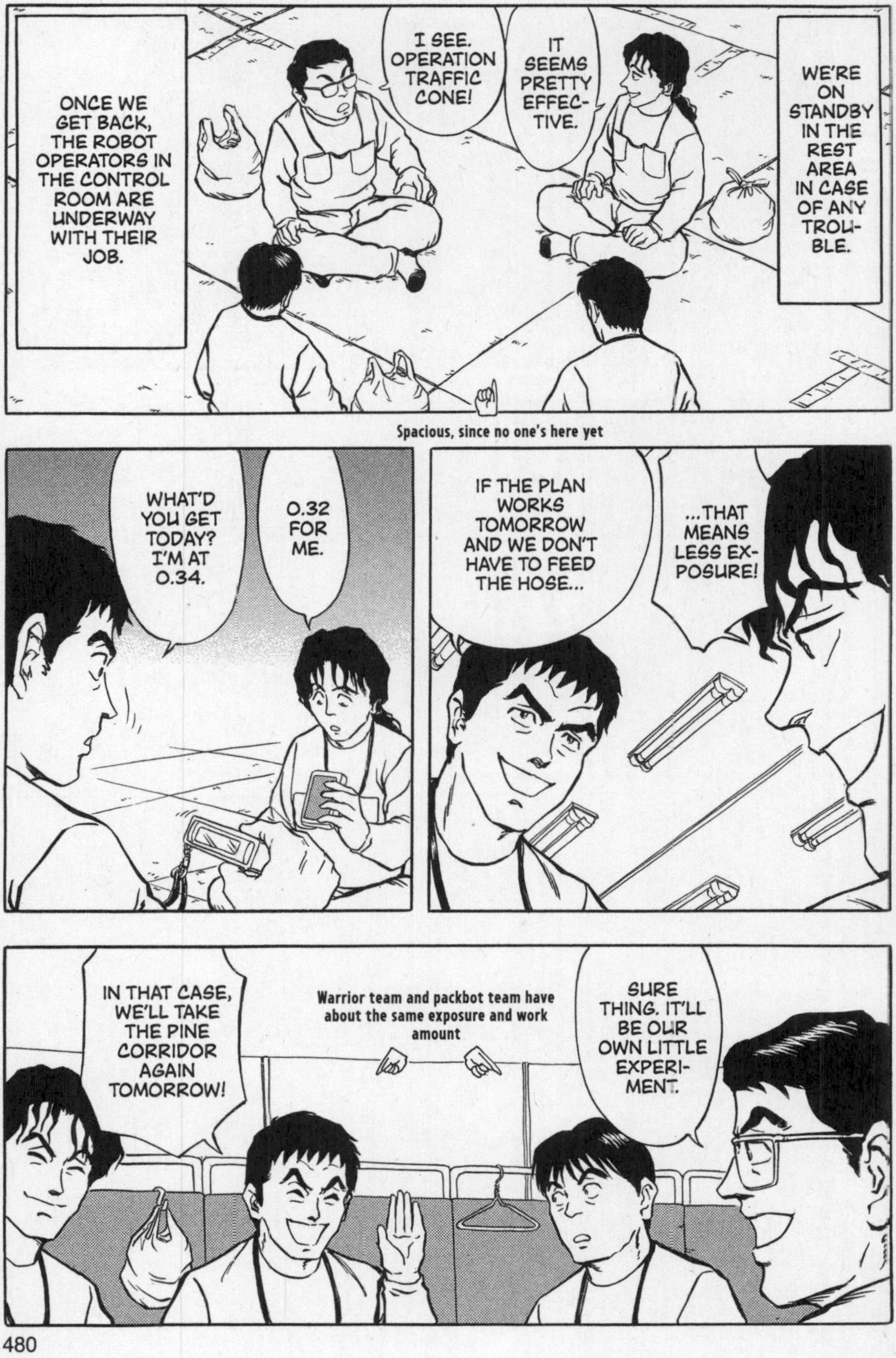
ONCE WE GET BACK, THE ROBOT OPERATORS IN THE CONTROL ROOM ARE UNDERWAY WITH THEIR JOB.
I SEE. OPERATION TRAFFIC CONE!
IT SEEMS PRETTY EFFECTIVE.
WE'RE ON STANDBY IN THE REST AREA IN CASE OF ANY TROUBLE.
Spacious, since no one's here yet
WHAT'D YOU GET TODAY? I'M AT 0.34.
0.32 FOR ME.
IF THE PLAN WORKS TOMORROW AND WE DON'T HAVE TO FEED THE HOSE...
...THAT MEANS LESS EXPOSURE!
IN THAT CASE, WE'LL TAKE THE PINE CORRIDOR AGAIN TOMORROW!
Warrior team and packbot team have about the same exposure and work amount
SURE THING. IT'LL BE OUR OWN LITTLE EXPERIMENT.

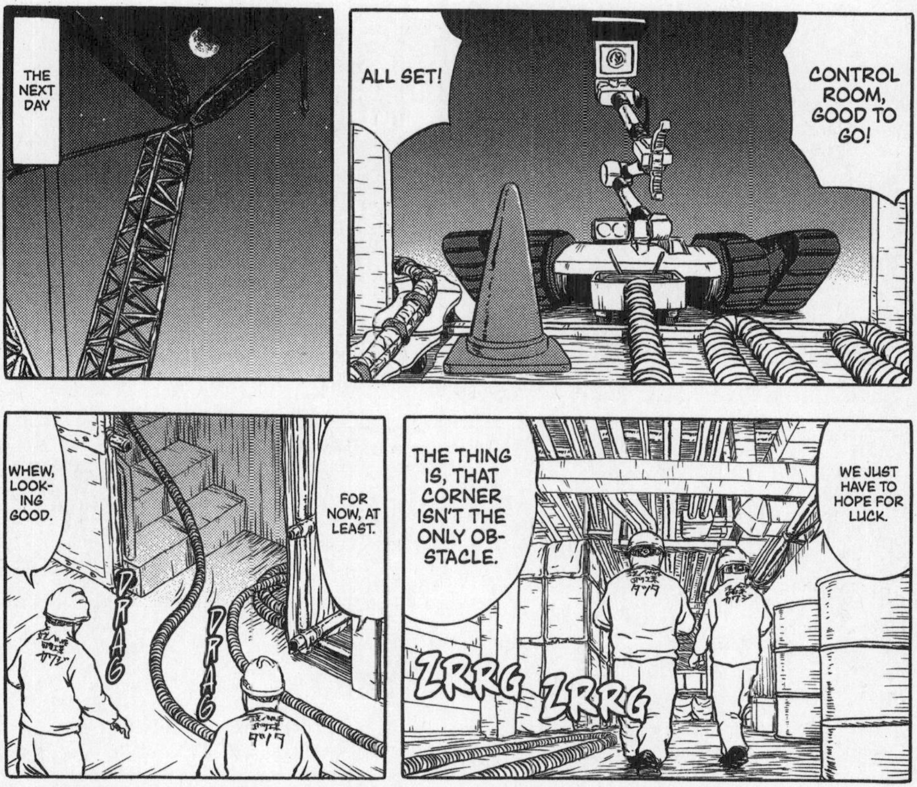
THE NEXT DAY
ALL SET!
CONTROL ROOM, GOOD TO GO!
WHEW, LOOK-ING GOOD.
FOR NOW, AT LEAST.
DRAG
DRAG
THE THING IS, THAT CORNER ISN'T THE ONLY OB-STACLE.
WE JUST HAVE TO HOPE FOR LUCK.
ZRRG ZRRG

When the phone rings too early, it's usually because it got stuck somewhere

BEE-BEE-BEEP
YES?
UH-OH, TROUBLE?
HOSE IS FULLY DEPLOYED!
ALL RIGHT, GOOD TO HEAR!
WOO-HOO! THAT WAS FAST!

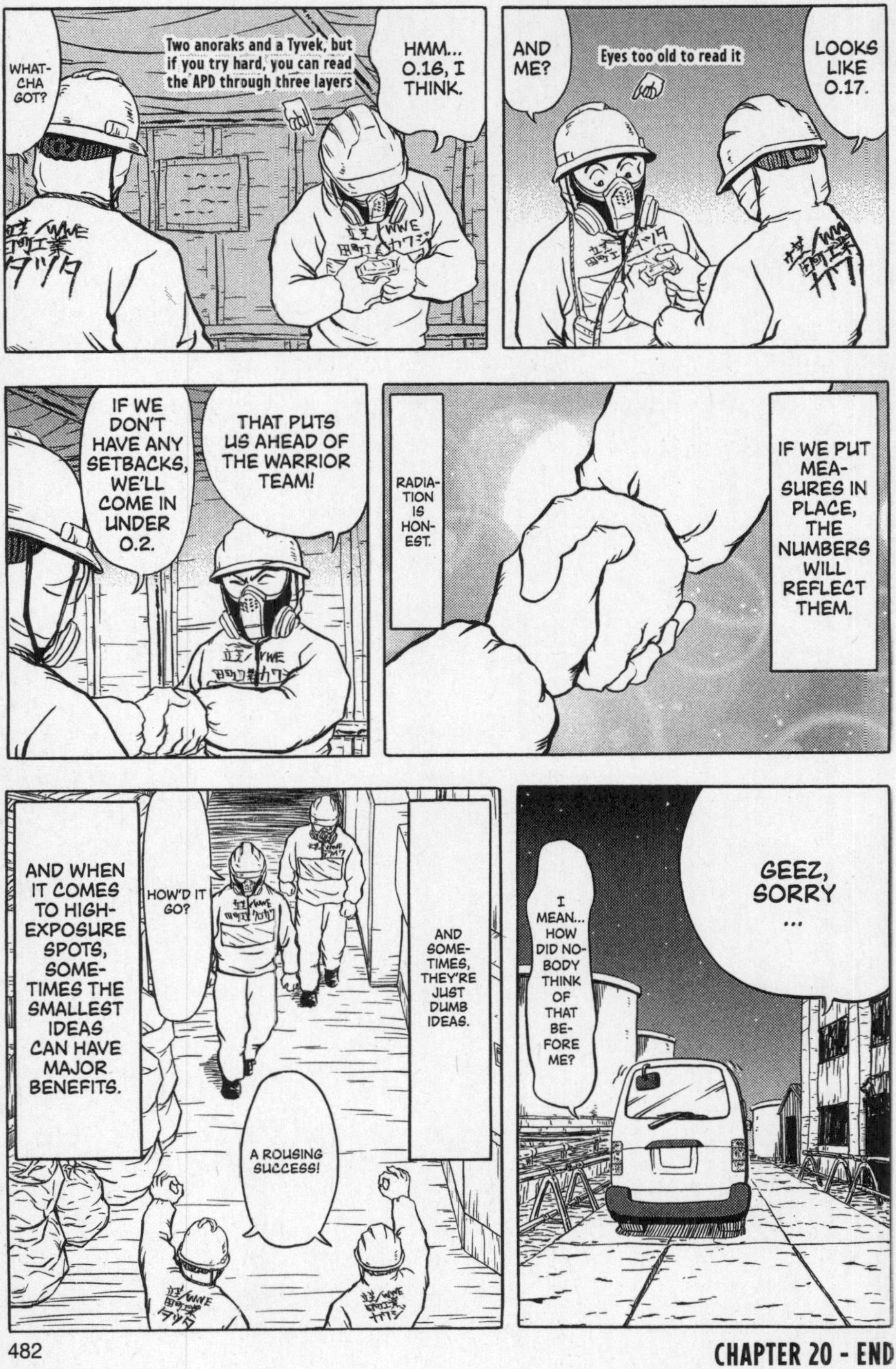

CHAPTER 20 - END

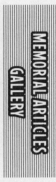

MEMORIAL ARTICLES GALLERY

THIS FACILITY TAKES ITEMS FOUND DURING THE TSUNAMI WRECKAGE CLEANUP EFFORTS SUCH AS PHOTOS AND ALBUMS. IT'S IN THE TOWN OF NAMIE NORTH OF ICHI-F, ON THE OCEAN SIDE OF ROUTE 6. YOU DON'T NEED TO BE A RESIDENT TO BROWSE, SO TATSUTA VISITED A FEW TIMES AFTER ROUTE 6 REOPENED. IT ALSO HAS ITEMS LIKE STUFFED ANIMALS AND GUITARS.

CHAPTER 21

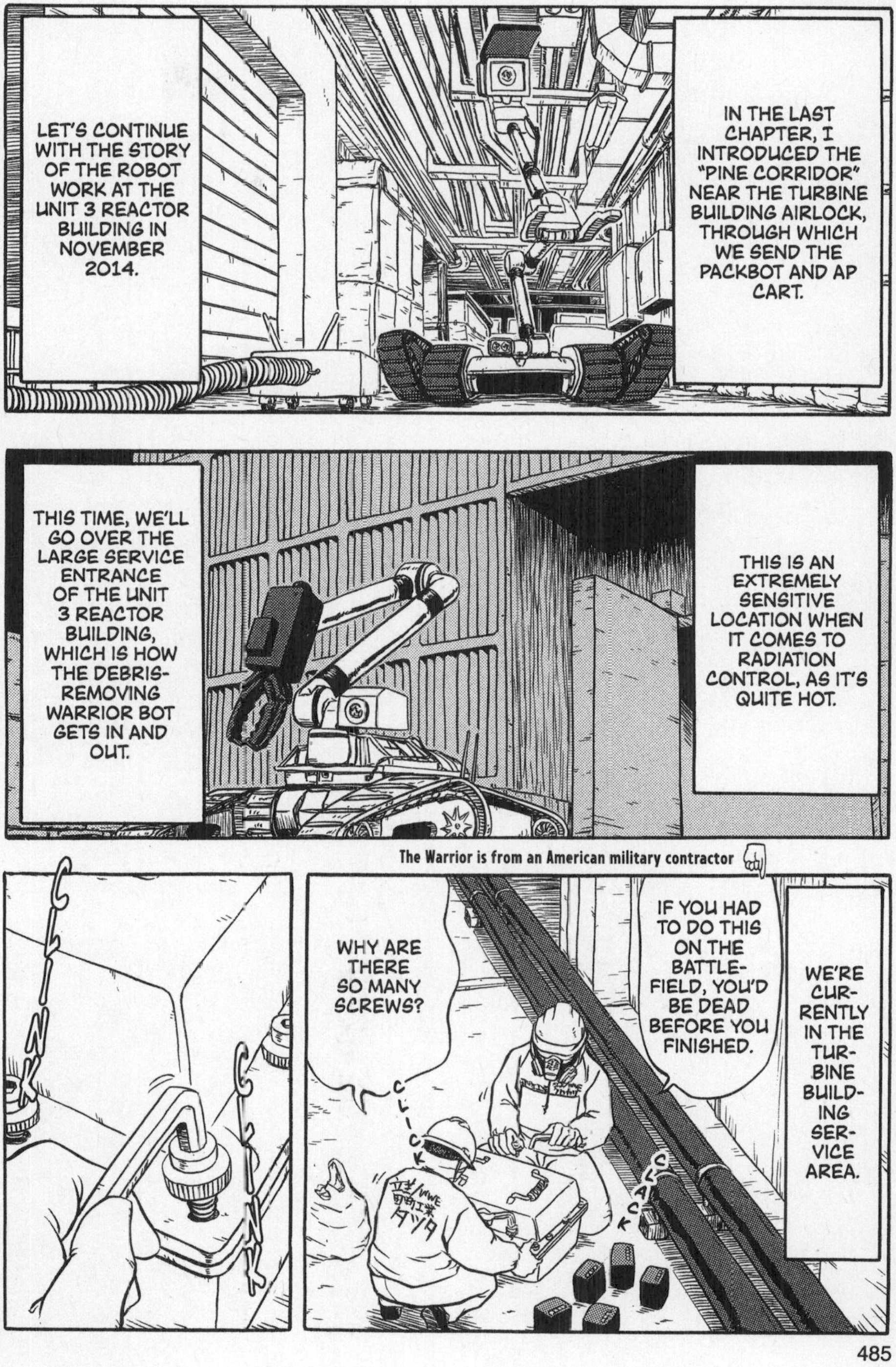

LET'S CONTINUE WITH THE STORY OF THE ROBOT WORK AT THE UNIT 3 REACTOR BUILDING IN NOVEMBER 2014.
IN THE LAST CHAPTER, I INTRODUCED THE "PINE CORRIDOR" NEAR THE TURBINE BUILDING AIRLOCK, THROUGH WHICH WE SEND THE PACKBOT AND AP CART.
THIS TIME, WE'LL GO OVER THE LARGE SERVICE ENTRANCE OF THE UNIT 3 REACTOR BUILDING, WHICH IS HOW THE DEBRIS-REMOVING WARRIOR BOT GETS IN AND OUT.
THIS IS AN EXTREMELY SENSITIVE LOCATION WHEN IT COMES TO RADIATION CONTROL, AS IT'S QUITE HOT.
The Warrior is from an American military contractor
CLINK
CLINK
WE'RE CURRENTLY IN THE TURBINE BUILDING SERVICE AREA.
WHY ARE THERE SO MANY SCREWS?
IF YOU HAD TO DO THIS ON THE BATTLEFIELD, YOU'D BE DEAD BEFORE YOU FINISHED.
CLICK
CLACK

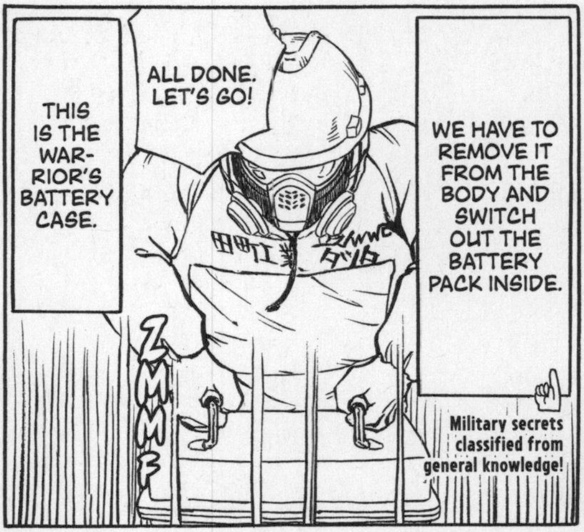
THIS IS THE WARRIOR'S BATTERY CASE.
ALL DONE. LET'S GO!
WE HAVE TO REMOVE IT FROM THE BODY AND SWITCH OUT THE BATTERY PACK INSIDE.
ZMMMF
Military secrets classified from general knowledge!

DAMN, THIS IS HEAVY...
0.05
THIS STEP TAKES OVER TEN MINUTES, SO WE HAVE TO DO IT IN A LOW-EXPOSURE AREA.

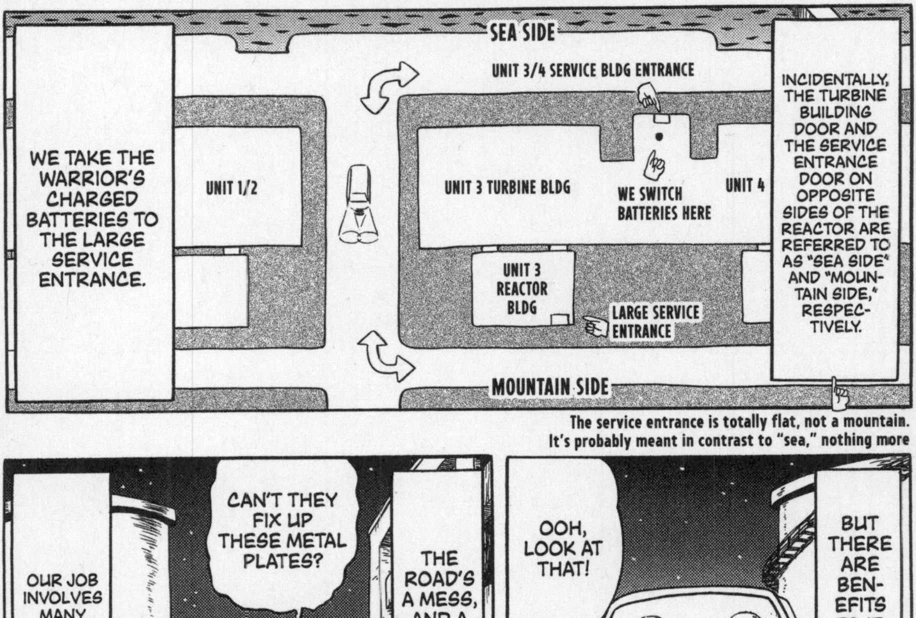
WE TAKE THE WARRIOR'S CHARGED BATTERIES TO THE LARGE SERVICE ENTRANCE.
SEA SIDE
UNIT 3/4 SERVICE BLDG ENTRANCE
UNIT 1/2
UNIT 3 TURBINE BLDG
WE SWITCH BATTERIES HERE
UNIT 4
UNIT 3 REACTOR BLDG
LARGE SERVICE ENTRANCE
MOUNTAIN SIDE
INCIDENTALLY, THE TURBINE BUILDING DOOR AND THE SERVICE ENTRANCE DOOR ON OPPOSITE SIDES OF THE REACTOR ARE REFERRED TO AS "SEA SIDE" AND "MOUNTAIN SIDE," RESPECTIVELY.

The service entrance is totally flat, not a mountain.
It's probably meant in contrast to "sea," nothing more

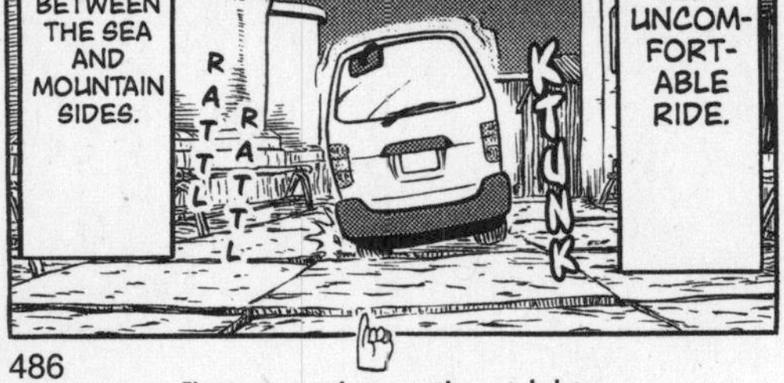
OUR JOB INVOLVES MANY TRIPS BETWEEN THE SEA AND MOUNTAIN SIDES.
CAN'T THEY FIX UP THESE METAL PLATES?
THE ROAD'S A MESS, AND A VERY UNCOMFORTABLE RIDE.
RATTL
RATTL
KTUNK

OOH, LOOK AT THAT!
BUT THERE ARE BENEFITS TO IT, TOO.

There are gaps between the metal plates

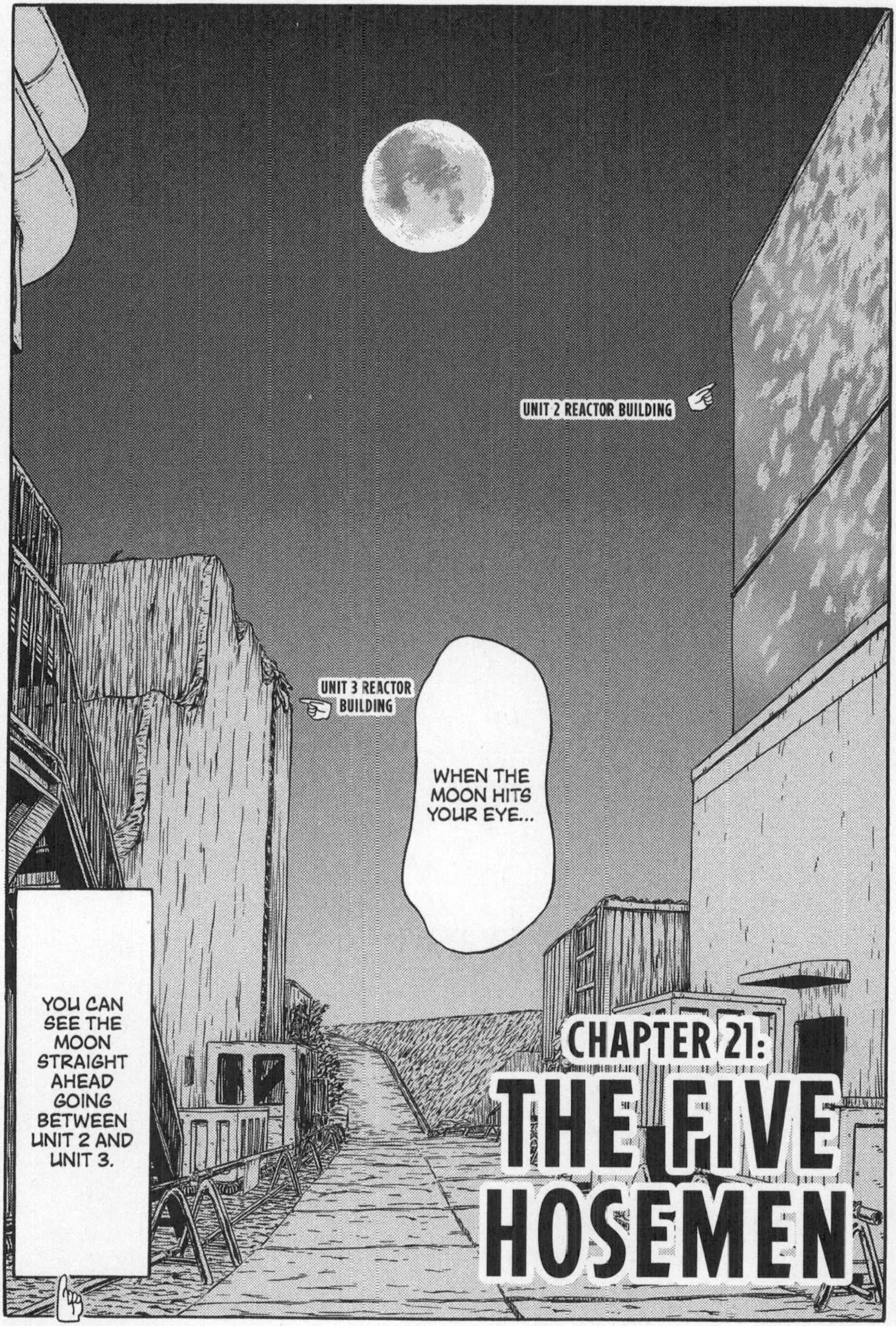

Depends on phase of the moon, time, and weather

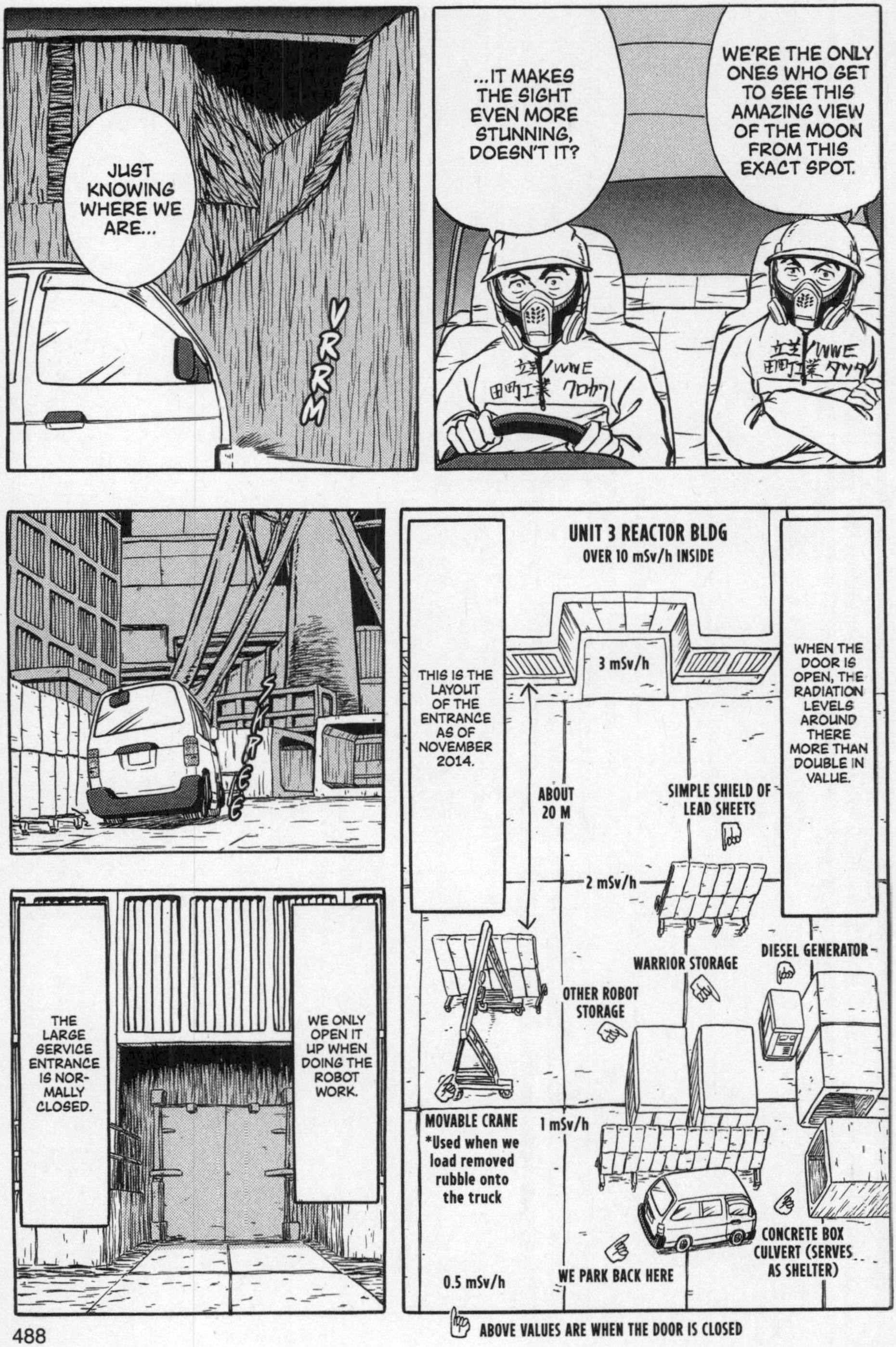

ABOVE VALUES ARE WHEN THE DOOR IS CLOSED

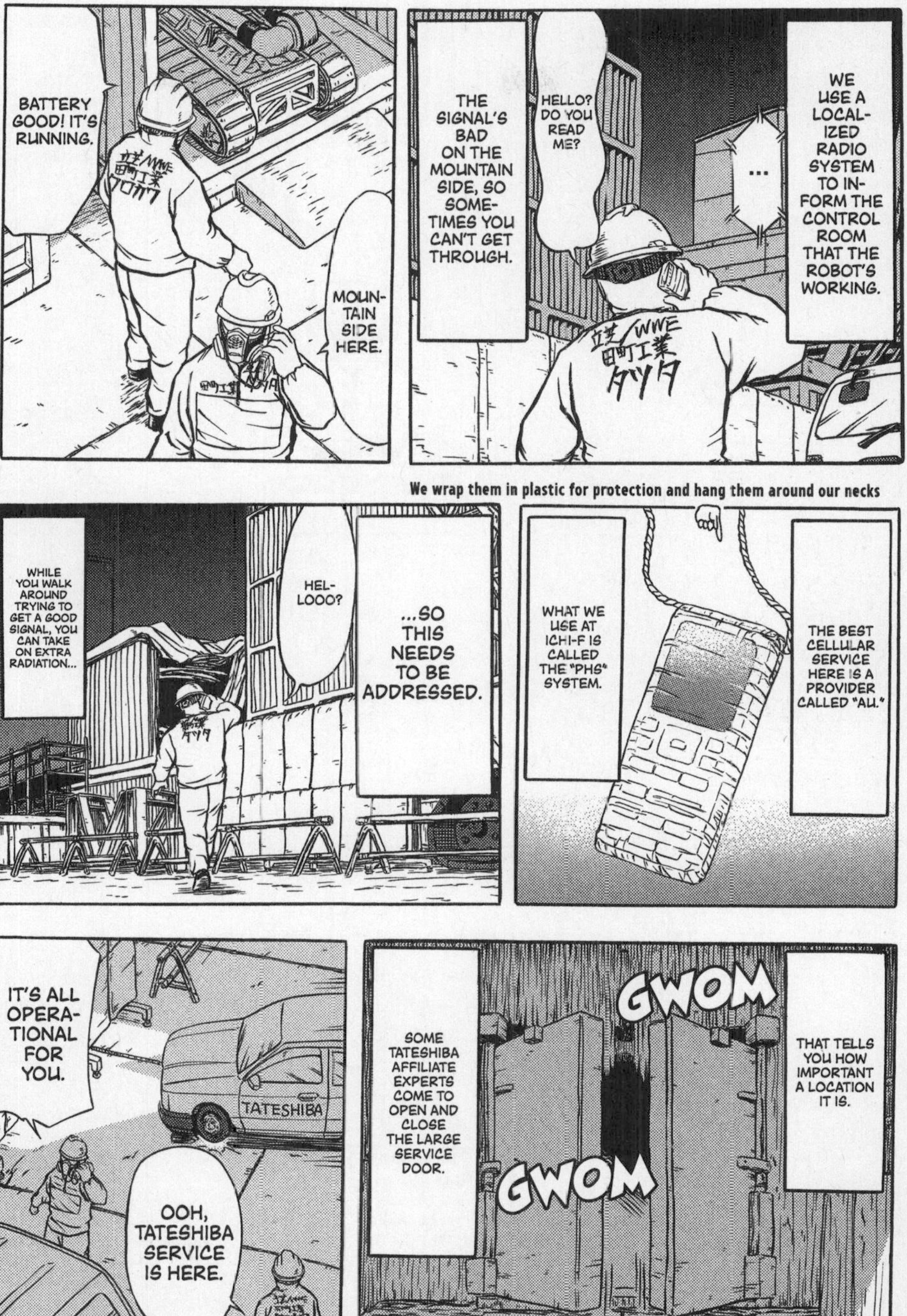

BATTERY GOOD! IT'S RUNNING.
MOUN-TAIN SIDE HERE.
THE SIGNAL'S BAD ON THE MOUNTAIN SIDE, SO SOME-TIMES YOU CAN'T GET THROUGH.
HELLO? DO YOU READ ME?
...
WE USE A LOCAL-IZED RADIO SYSTEM TO IN-FORM THE CONTROL ROOM THAT THE ROBOT'S WORKING.
We wrap them in plastic for protection and hang them around our necks
WHILE YOU WALK AROUND TRYING TO GET A GOOD SIGNAL, YOU CAN TAKE ON EXTRA RADIATION...
HEL-LOOO?
...SO THIS NEEDS TO BE ADDRESSED.
WHAT WE USE AT ICHI-F IS CALLED THE "PHS" SYSTEM.
THE BEST CELLULAR SERVICE HERE IS A PROVIDER CALLED "AU."
IT'S ALL OPERA-TIONAL FOR YOU.
TATESHIBA
OOH, TATESHIBA SERVICE IS HERE.
SOME TATESHIBA AFFILIATE EXPERTS COME TO OPEN AND CLOSE THE LARGE SERVICE DOOR.
GWOM
GWOM
THAT TELLS YOU HOW IMPORTANT A LOCATION IT IS.

Electric-powered

WE'LL MEET UP WITH THE SEA SIDE TEAM AND HEAD BACK TO THE ANTI-QUAKE BUILDING.
ONCE IT'S OPEN, WE GOTTA BOUNCE.
AFTER STARTING UP THE ROBOT, THE OPERATORS IN THE CONTROL ROOM TAKE OVER.
THE WARRIOR CAN GO THROUGH THE SERVICE ENTRANCE ON ITS OWN.
THE PACKBOT GOES IN FROM THE SEA SIDE, AND THEY BOTH MEET UP INSIDE THE REACTOR BUILDING. THE WARRIOR THEN BEGINS ITS RUBBLE CLEANUP PROCESS.
WARRIOR
Warrior has a camera too; the more eyes, the safer the work process
CAMERA
PACKBOT
CAMERA
THE PACKBOT IS LIKE AN ASSISTANT—IT PULLS ALONG THE AP CART TRANSMITTING THEIR DATA, AND KEEPS AN EYE ON THE WARRIOR'S SURROUNDINGS.
JUST A BIT LEFT!
ALL RIGHT, GOT IT.
WOW, YOU'RE GOOD AT THAT.
Came to watch, since there's nothing else to do in the break room
IT'S ALL DOWN TO EXPERI-ENCE, REALLY.

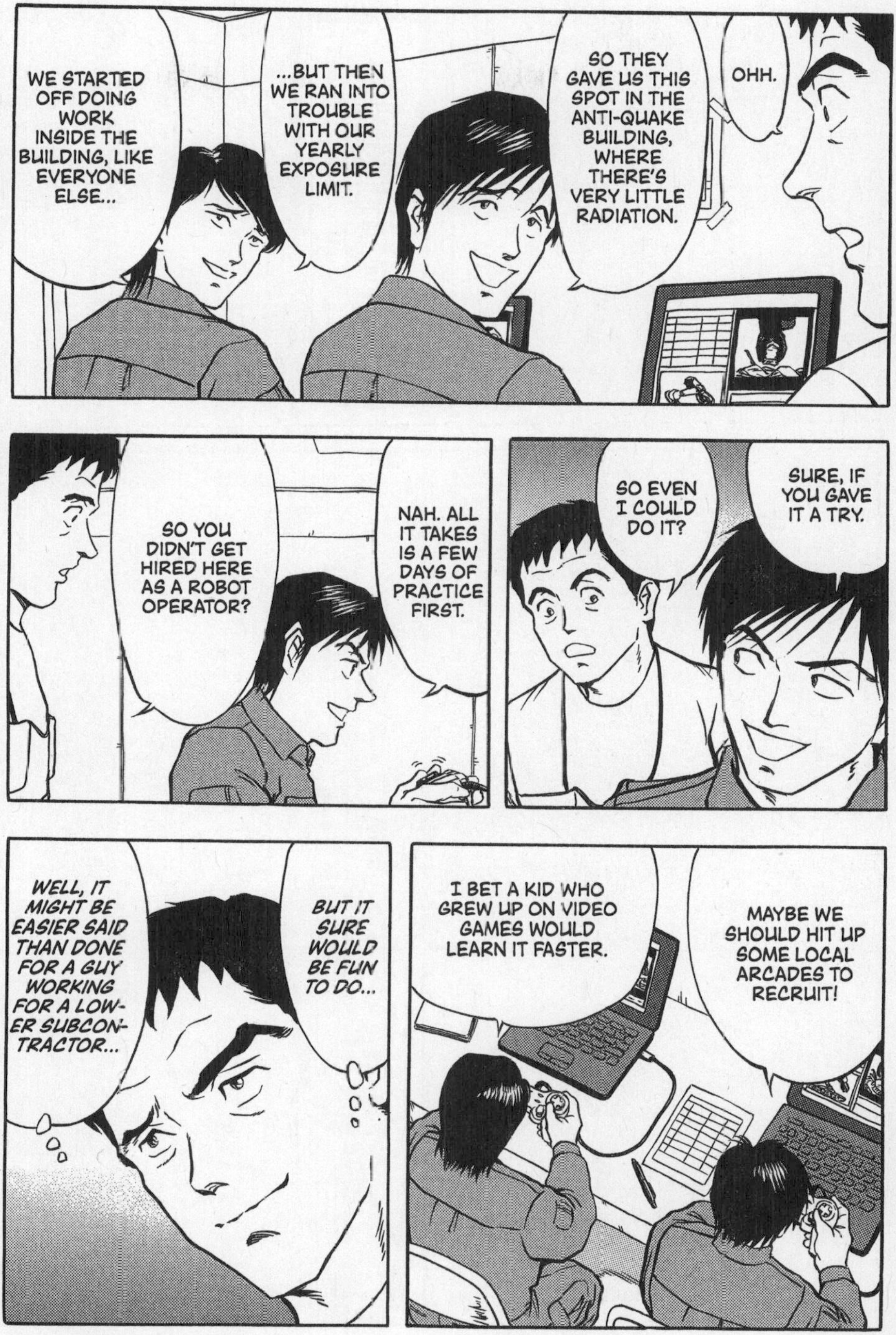
WE STARTED OFF DOING WORK INSIDE THE BUILDING, LIKE EVERYONE ELSE...
...BUT THEN WE RAN INTO TROUBLE WITH OUR YEARLY EXPOSURE LIMIT.
SO THEY GAVE US THIS SPOT IN THE ANTI-QUAKE BUILDING, WHERE THERE'S VERY LITTLE RADIATION.
OHH.
SO YOU DIDN'T GET HIRED HERE AS A ROBOT OPERATOR?
NAH. ALL IT TAKES IS A FEW DAYS OF PRACTICE FIRST.
SO EVEN I COULD DO IT?
SURE, IF YOU GAVE IT A TRY.
WELL, IT MIGHT BE EASIER SAID THAN DONE FOR A GUY WORKING FOR A LOWER SUBCONTRACTOR...
BUT IT SURE WOULD BE FUN TO DO...
I BET A KID WHO GREW UP ON VIDEO GAMES WOULD LEARN IT FASTER.
MAYBE WE SHOULD HIT UP SOME LOCAL ARCADES TO RECRUIT!

APRIL 2015: UNIT 1 REACTOR CONTAINMENT VESSEL INVESTIGATION ROBOT
BUT THE THING IS, THE PROCEDURES NEEDED FOR RUBBLE CLEANUP AND DECONTAMINATION HAVE BEEN ESTABLISHED FOR A WHILE, SO BASICALLY ANYONE CAN DO THIS STUFF WITH A LITTLE PRACTICE FIRST.
PIPE-DUCKING CONFIGURATION
IT TRANSFORMS!!
STAIR-CLIMBING CONFIGURATION
I'M GUESSING THAT WHEN THEY START INVESTIGATING INSIDE THE CONTAINMENT VESSEL ITSELF, THEY'LL HAVE TO USE HIGHLY-TRAINED ENGINEERS WITH ACE PILOT SKILLS.
BUT ULTI-MATELY, THIS IS HOW YOU CONTROL THEM.
IN ESSENCE, USING EXISTING CIVILIAN PRODUCTS IS QUICKER, BOTH FOR PRODUCTION AND TRAINING.
STILL, USING A GAME CONT-ROLLER IN THIS NICE SAFE ROOM...
...MAKES YOU FEEL GUILTY TOWARD THE GUYS OUT THERE ON THE SCENE.
Ordinary storebought controller
DON'T BE SILLY. YOU'VE ALREADY TAKEN YOUR RADIATION—THAT'S WHY YOU'RE IN HERE!
I KNOW, BUT STILL...
REGARDLESS OF HOW MUCH EXPOSURE SOMEONE'S TAKEN ALREADY, THERE'S ALWAYS A FEELING OF COMPASSION FOR THOSE HEADING TO THE HIGH-RAD HOTSPOTS.
OKAY, ON TO THE NEXT SPOT...
VWEEE
THAT'S BECAUSE EVERYONE UNDER-STANDS THE FRUSTRA-TION AND TRICKINESS OF MANAG-ING THAT REMAINING EXPOSURE.

EVERY COMPANY STRUGGLES TO MAN-AGE ITS EMPLOYEES' EXPOSURE LEVELS.
NEXT DAY, 2:30 AM
ENTRY FACILITY REST AREA
GOOD MORNING, EVERYONE. TODAY WE'RE JOINED BY SECTION CHIEF MITA FROM WWE'S MAIN TOKYO OFFICE.
I'M MITA. NICE TO MEET YOU.
NICE TO MEET YOU, SIR.
SO THEY'RE FINALLY SENDING A MANAGER FROM THE MAIN OFFICE TO THE SCENE, HUH?
WELL, ALL OF US WORKING LOCALLY ARE BASICALLY AT OUR LIMIT FOR THE YEAR.
I DON'T KNOW, IT'LL BE HARD TO TELL THE SECTION CHIEF, "PICK UP THAT HOSE AND RUN!"
DON'T BE SHY ABOUT THAT. I'M HERE TO DO THE WORK WITH YOU!
DOES THAT MEAN THE DEPARTMENT CHIEF AND GENERAL MANAGER WILL BE HERE NEXT?
IF THEY DO COME, WE'LL RUN 'EM RAGGED!
HA HA HA HA HA HA
ALL JOKES ASIDE, WE'LL BE LOADING THE PACKBOT VIA THE MOUNTAIN SIDE AS WELL, STARTING TODAY.
THAT WILL INCREASE OUR EXPOSURE, WHICH IS WHY WE'VE CALLED FOR THIS EXTRA HELP.
DEADLY SERIOUS

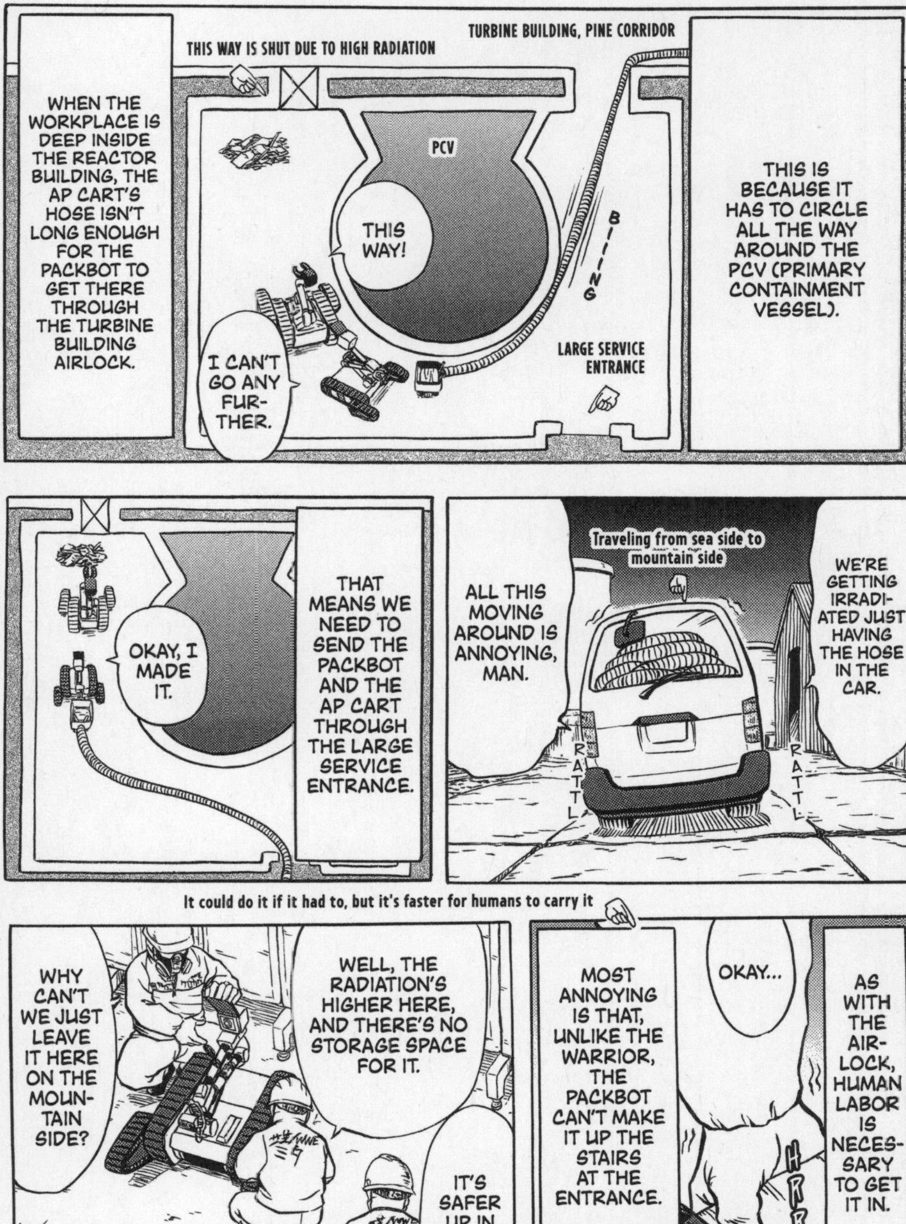

WHEN THE WORKPLACE IS DEEP INSIDE THE REACTOR BUILDING, THE AP CART'S HOSE ISN'T LONG ENOUGH FOR THE PACKBOT TO GET THERE THROUGH THE TURBINE BUILDING AIRLOCK.
THIS WAY IS SHUT DUE TO HIGH RADIATION
TURBINE BUILDING, PINE CORRIDOR
PCV
THIS WAY!
I CAN'T GO ANY FURTHER.
BIIING
LARGE SERVICE ENTRANCE
THIS IS BECAUSE IT HAS TO CIRCLE ALL THE WAY AROUND THE PCV (PRIMARY CONTAINMENT VESSEL).
OKAY, I MADE IT.
THAT MEANS WE NEED TO SEND THE PACKBOT AND THE AP CART THROUGH THE LARGE SERVICE ENTRANCE.
Traveling from sea side to mountain side
ALL THIS MOVING AROUND IS ANNOYING, MAN.
WE'RE GETTING IRRADIATED JUST HAVING THE HOSE IN THE CAR.
RATTL
RATTL
It could do it if it had to, but it's faster for humans to carry it
WHY CAN'T WE JUST LEAVE IT HERE ON THE MOUNTAIN SIDE?
WELL, THE RADIATION'S HIGHER HERE, AND THERE'S NO STORAGE SPACE FOR IT.
IT'S SAFER UP IN THE PINE CORRIDOR.
MOST ANNOYING IS THAT, UNLIKE THE WARRIOR, THE PACKBOT CAN'T MAKE IT UP THE STAIRS AT THE ENTRANCE.
OKAY...
AS WITH THE AIRLOCK, HUMAN LABOR IS NECESSARY TO GET IT IN.
HRRG

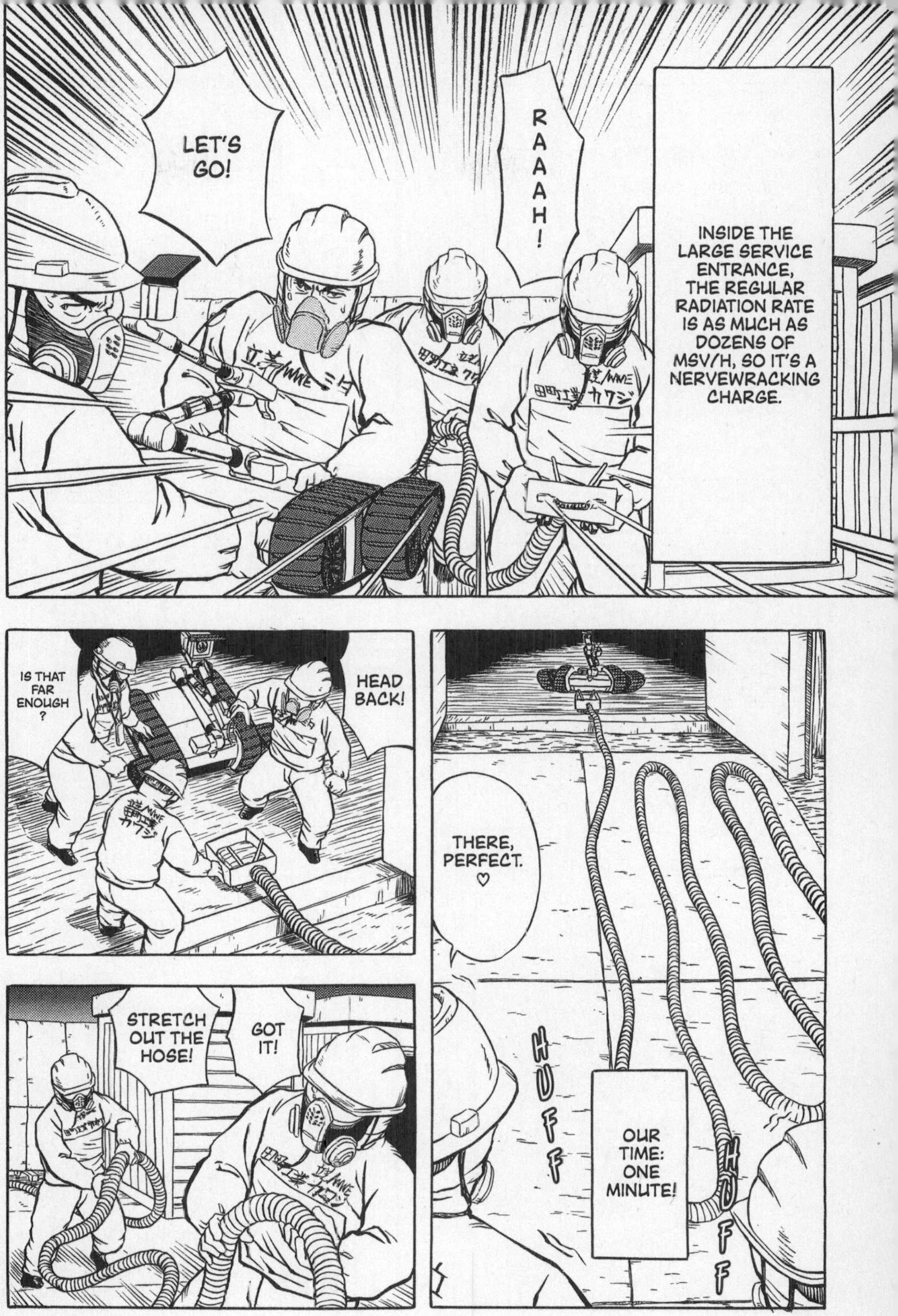

RAAAAH!
LET'S GO!
INSIDE THE LARGE SERVICE ENTRANCE, THE REGULAR RADIATION RATE IS AS MUCH AS DOZENS OF MSV/H, SO IT'S A NERVEWRACKING CHARGE.
HEAD BACK!
IS THAT FAR ENOUGH?
THERE, PERFECT. ♡
GOT IT!
STRETCH OUT THE HOSE!
OUR TIME: ONE MINUTE!
HUFF
HUFF

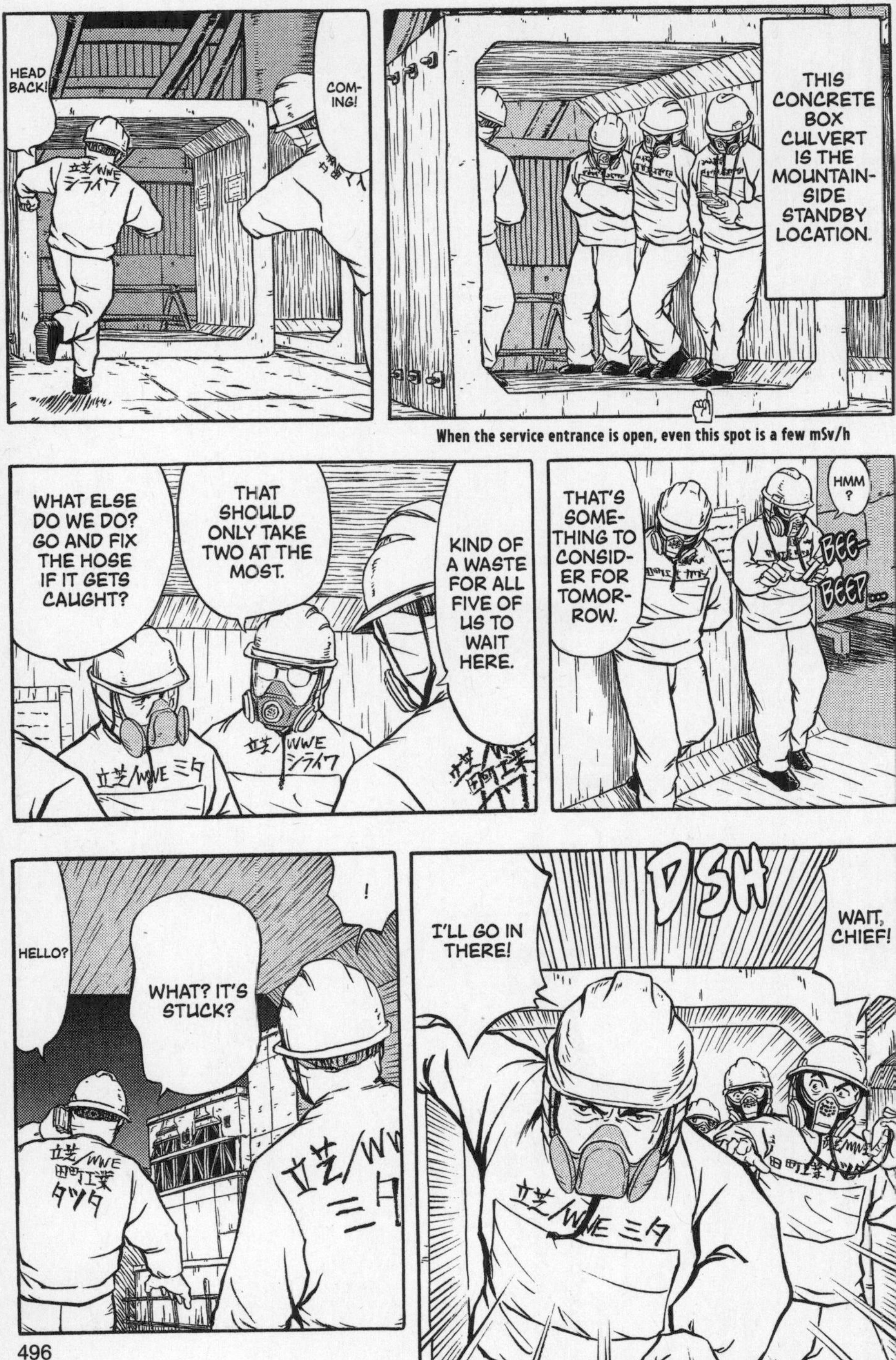

When the service entrance is open, even this spot is a few mSv/h

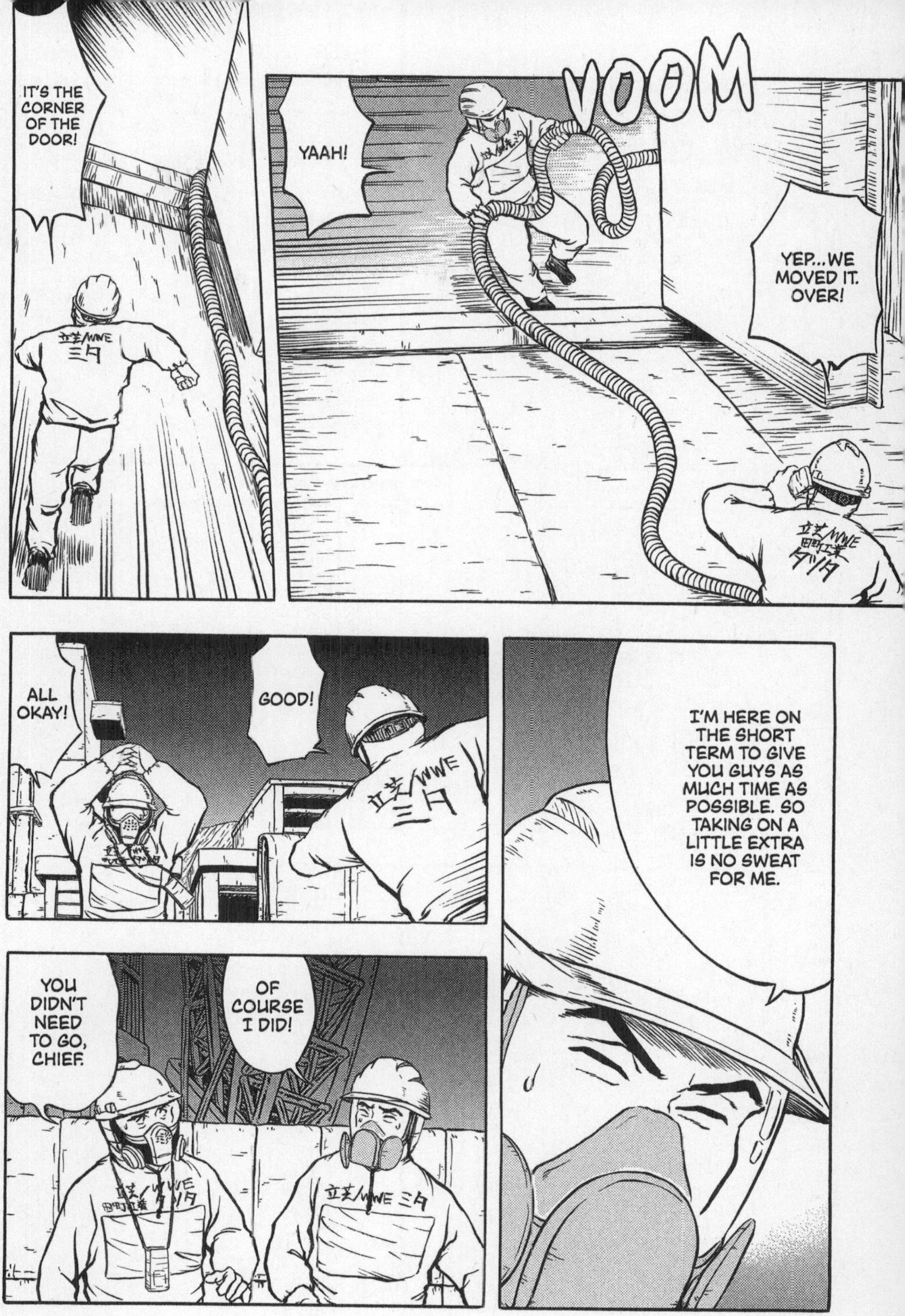
YEP...WE MOVED IT. OVER!
VOOM
YAAH!
IT'S THE CORNER OF THE DOOR!
GOOD!
ALL OKAY!
YOU DIDN'T NEED TO GO, CHIEF.
OF COURSE I DID!
I'M HERE ON THE SHORT TERM TO GIVE YOU GUYS AS MUCH TIME AS POSSIBLE. SO TAKING ON A LITTLE EXTRA IS NO SWEAT FOR ME.

BEE-BEEP...
WOW, CHIEF...
AH, YES? GREAT, SO IT'S ALL INSIDE NOW!
PERFECT.
THE ANNOYING THING IS THAT WE HAVE TO COME BACK LATER.
THAT'S THE END OF THE TRANSPORT STAGE. WE HEAD BACK TO THE SHELTER.
AFTER THE RUBBLE CLEARING, WE PULL OUT THE BOTS AND ROLL UP THE AP CART AND HOSE UNDER A BLUE TARP SHEET.
FWAP
I'M TELLING YOU, NO ONE'S GONNA STEAL AN IRRADIATED ROBOT LIKE THIS.
THE PACKBOT GOES INTO THE WWE STORAGE.
Location hidden because it's a high-precision device
THE NEXT DAY
OKAY, IT'S DOWN!
GET BACK!
WE DETERMINED THAT ONLY TWO WERE NEEDED ON STANDBY AFTER HAULING THE BOT IN.
SO LONG.
SEE YOU IN A BIT, THEN!
SO THE OTHER THREE HEADED BACK TO THE ANTI-QUAKE BUILDING TO MINIMIZE OUR LEVELS.

Borrowed another car

SHALL WE GO, TOO?

THE CHIEF AND I STAYED BEHIND.

Lost at rock-paper-scissors

By request

OUR STANDBY LOCATION IS ATOP A HILL OVER 200 METERS AWAY, WHERE IT'S SAFE.

UNITS 1-2

UNITS 3-4

THE HILL USED TO BE CALLED YACHO-NO-MORI, THE "WILD BIRD FOREST," BUT NOW IT'S JUST TANKS.

UPHILL

UNIT 3 LARGE SERVICE ENTRANCE

IT'S LESS THAN 0.02 MSV/H HERE.

WAIT HERE

FORMER YACHO-NO-MORI

ONCE THE ROBOT IS ALL THE WAY IN, WORK GOES SMOO-THLY.

NOTHIN' TO DO NOW.

ON THIS DAY, WE HAD AN HOUR TO WAIT AFTER HAULING THEM.

SIGH ...

THE LACK OF ANY PRESSING TASKS IS A SIGN THE WORK IS GOING WELL.

I KNOW ...

BUT THEY COULD ALSO LET US GO BA...AH!

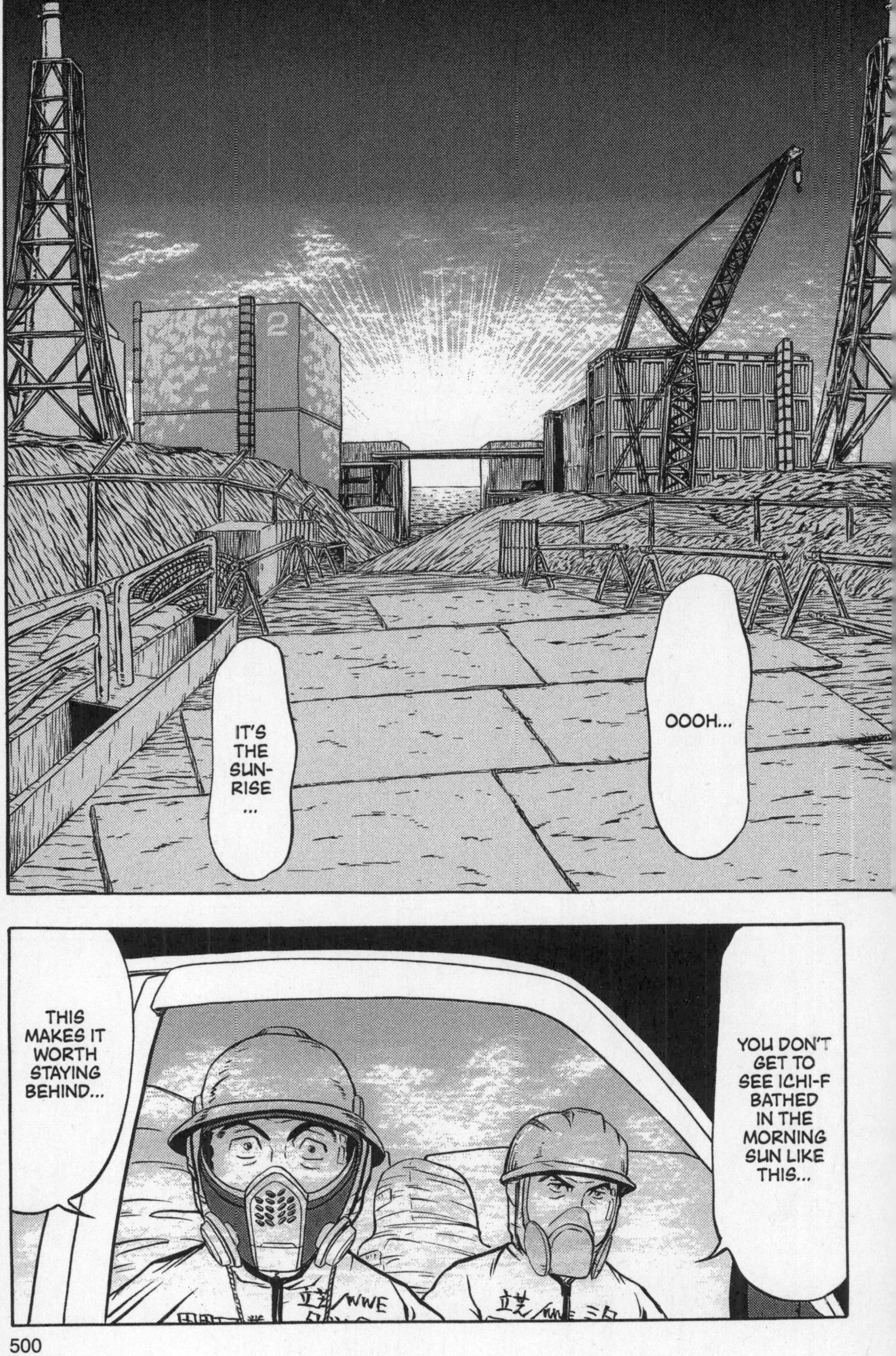
OOOH...
IT'S THE SUN-RISE...
YOU DON'T GET TO SEE ICHI-F BATHED IN THE MORNING SUN LIKE THIS...
THIS MAKES IT WORTH STAYING BEHIND...

SOMETIMES WORKING THE NIGHT SHIFT AT ICHI-F IS COOL.
NOTHING BAD HAPPENED, SO WE DIDN'T NEED TO RUSH BACK.

Wait one hour at a 1 mSv/h spot and you do indeed end up with 1 mSv

A clerk comes over immediately

Taken to a separate room
AH, HERE IT IS.
THE ANNOYING ENEMY THAT IS CONTAMINATION.
TAKE OFF YOUR SOCK.
YEP, STILL A BIT THERE.
Records are taken
YOU'VE GOT BODY CONTAMINATION. WORK SITE?
UNIT 3 REACTOR.
IT SHOULD COME OFF IF YOU WIPE IT.
THANKS.
Wet tissues
EVEN THE TINIEST BIT OF RADIOACTIVE CONTAMINATION MEANS CLEANING OFF AND PAPERWORK.
OKAY, YOU'RE GOOD.
IT DIDN'T TURN UP AT THE ANTI-QUAKE BUILDING. AND I CHANGED MY SOCKS, TOO.
IT PROBABLY POPPED UP ON YOUR SHOES ON THE WAY HERE, THEN.
GOOD GRIEF...
WE HAVE TO WEAR "DIRTY SHOES" FROM THE ANTI-QUAKE BUILDING, WHERE THEY'RE REUSED FROM ON-SITE WORK.

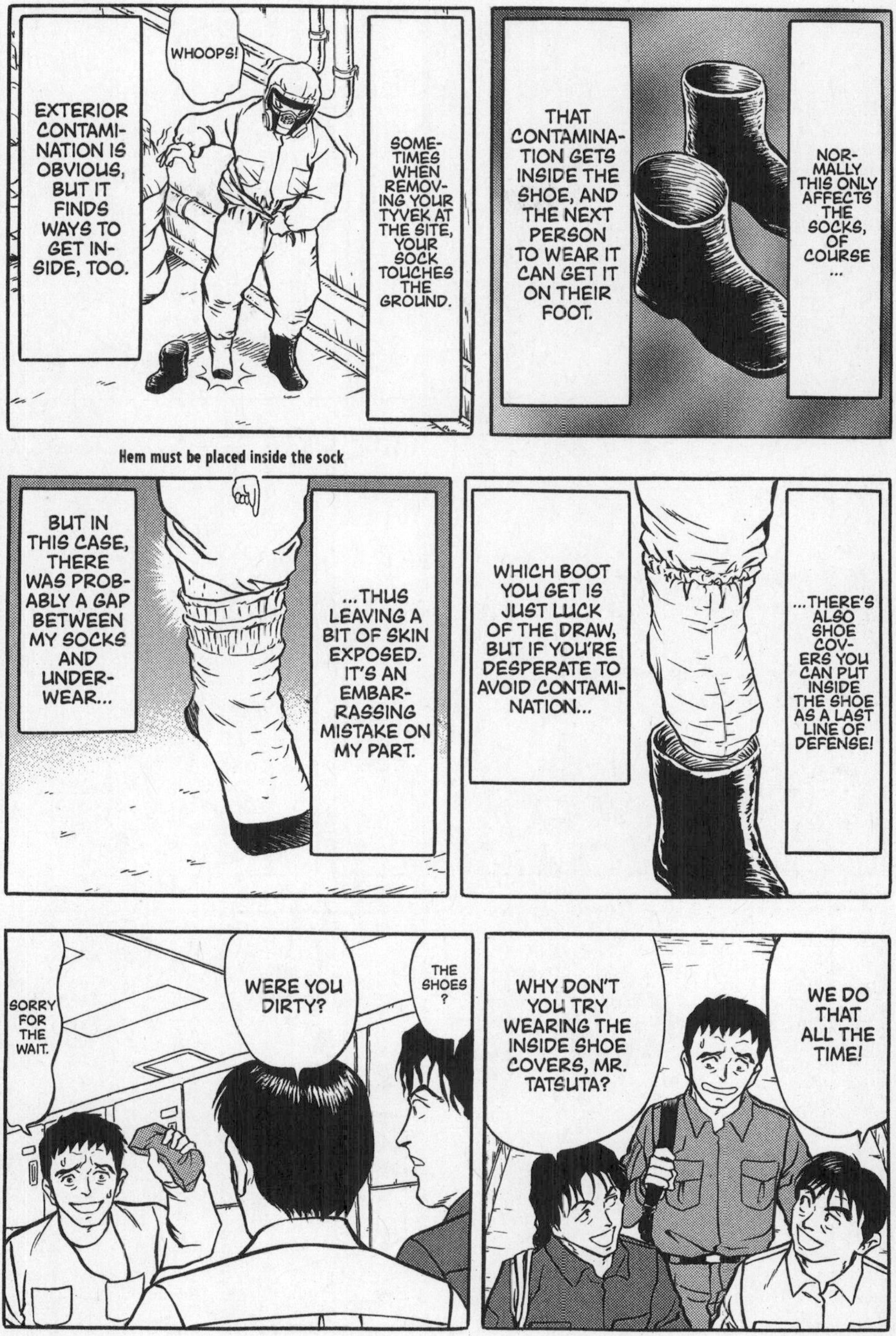
WHOOPS!
EXTERIOR CONTAMINATION IS OBVIOUS, BUT IT FINDS WAYS TO GET INSIDE, TOO.
SOMETIMES WHEN REMOVING YOUR TYVEK AT THE SITE, YOUR SOCK TOUCHES THE GROUND.
THAT CONTAMINATION GETS INSIDE THE SHOE, AND THE NEXT PERSON TO WEAR IT CAN GET IT ON THEIR FOOT.
NORMALLY THIS ONLY AFFECTS THE SOCKS, OF COURSE ...
Hem must be placed inside the sock
BUT IN THIS CASE, THERE WAS PROBABLY A GAP BETWEEN MY SOCKS AND UNDERWEAR...
...THUS LEAVING A BIT OF SKIN EXPOSED. IT'S AN EMBARRASSING MISTAKE ON MY PART.
WHICH BOOT YOU GET IS JUST LUCK OF THE DRAW, BUT IF YOU'RE DESPERATE TO AVOID CONTAMINATION...
...THERE'S ALSO SHOE COVERS YOU CAN PUT INSIDE THE SHOE AS A LAST LINE OF DEFENSE!
SORRY FOR THE WAIT.
WERE YOU DIRTY?
THE SHOES?
WHY DON'T YOU TRY WEARING THE INSIDE SHOE COVERS, MR. TATSUTA?
WE DO THAT ALL THE TIME!

ALL RIGHT, GUYS. YOU GOT ME...
WHATEVER HAPPENED TO AN ABUNDANCE OF CAUTION?
YOU DON'T LIKE THEM BECAUSE IT'S HARDER TO WALK IN THEM, RIGHT?
19 広野
KEEP IT TOGETHER, MR. TATSUTA. YOU'RE OUR TEAM LEADER!
SORRY, SORRY...
JOBAN EXPRESSWAY, YOTSUKURA PARKING AREA
YIPPEE!
AS AN APOLOGY FOR THE WAIT, I'LL BUY YOU A FRIED MEHIKARI MEAL.
よつくら亭
OOOH, THE MEHIKARI HERE ARE HUGE!
YOU SHOULD TRY GETTING CONTAMINATED AGAIN SOMETIME.
TRUST ME, AFTER THIS, I'LL BE WEARING THOSE SHOE LINERS...

Sign: 19 Hirono

Sign: Yotsukura-tei

CHAPTER 21 - END

YUJI KOSEKI

A RENOWNED COMPOSER FROM FUKUSHIMA PREFECTURE. HE WAS ACTIVE BEFORE, DURING, AND AFTER WWII, AND WROTE MANY FAMOUS PIECES LIKE THE "OLYMPIC MARCH" FOR THE OPENING CEREMONIES OF THE 1964 TOKYO OLYMPICS, AND THE THEME FOR THE SUMMER KOSHIEN HIGH SCHOOL BASEBALL TOURNAMENT. TATSUTA'S REPERTOIRE OF OLD TUNES INCLUDES MANY OF HIS SONGS, ESPECIALLY "NIGHT OF THE IOMANTE." IN CHAPTER 11, HE DEPICTED A PERFORMANCE OF KOSEKI'S "THE HIGHLANDS TRAIN RIDES ON" AT A TEMPORARY HOUSING DEVELOPMENT.

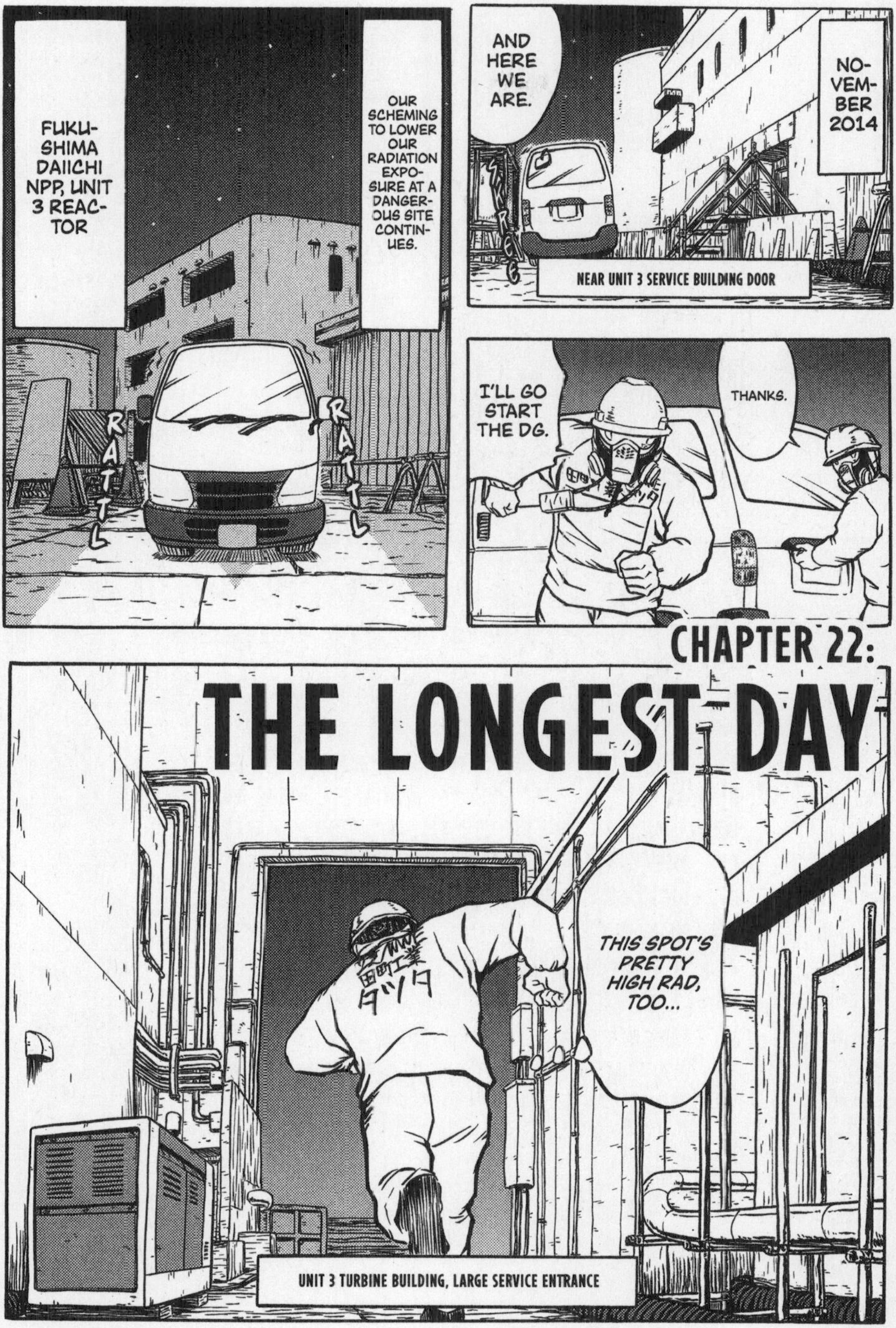
NOVEMBER 2014
AND HERE WE ARE.
SKREE
NEAR UNIT 3 SERVICE BUILDING DOOR
OUR SCHEMING TO LOWER OUR RADIATION EXPOSURE AT A DANGEROUS SITE CONTINUES.
FUKUSHIMA DAIICHI NPP, UNIT 3 REACTOR
RATTL
RATTL
THANKS.
I'LL GO START THE DG.
CHAPTER 22:
THE LONGEST DAY
THIS SPOT'S PRETTY HIGH RAD, TOO...
UNIT 3 TURBINE BUILDING, LARGE SERVICE ENTRANCE

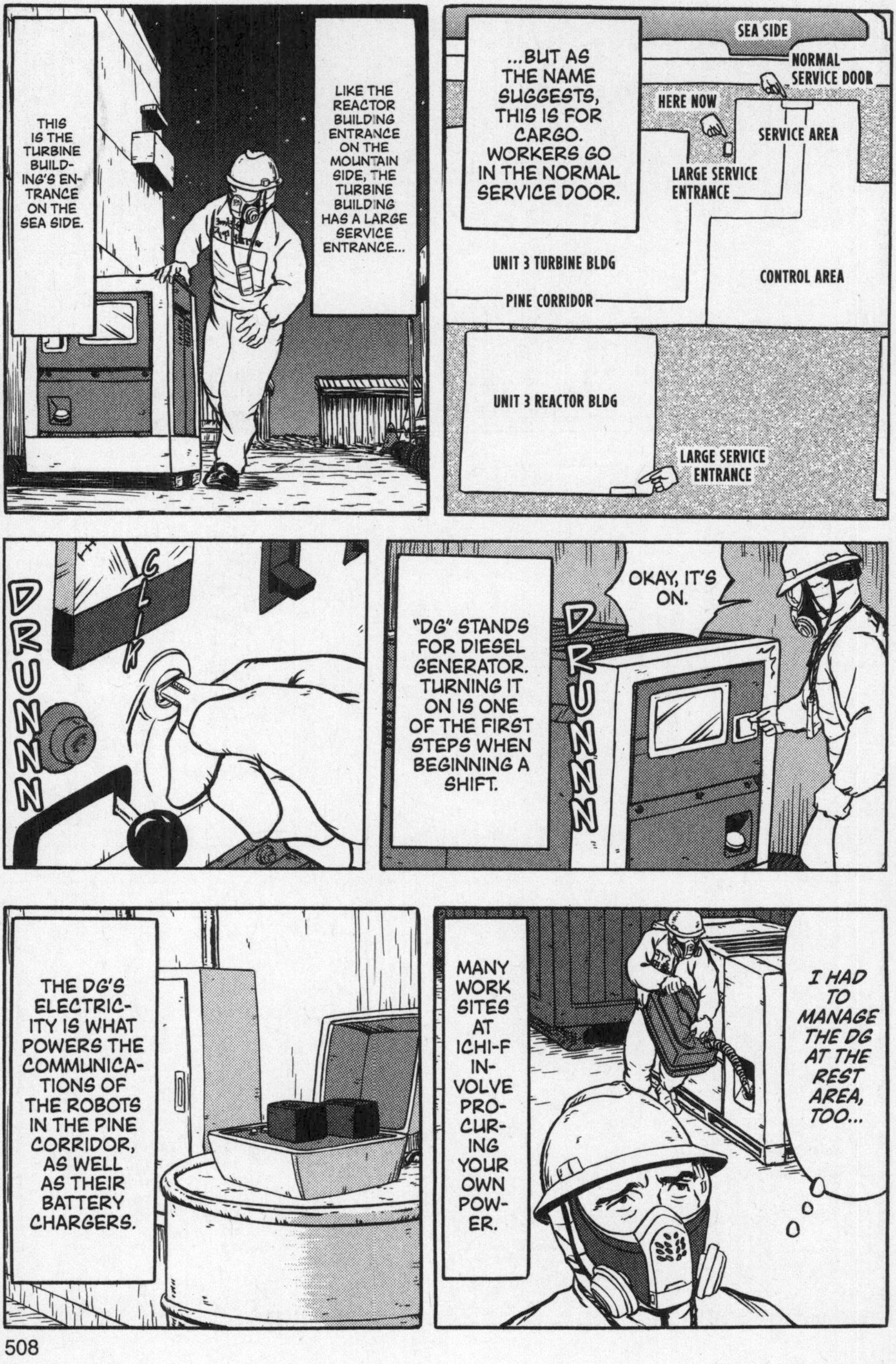
THIS IS THE TURBINE BUILDING'S ENTRANCE ON THE SEA SIDE.
LIKE THE REACTOR BUILDING ENTRANCE ON THE MOUNTAIN SIDE, THE TURBINE BUILDING HAS A LARGE SERVICE ENTRANCE...
...BUT AS THE NAME SUGGESTS, THIS IS FOR CARGO. WORKERS GO IN THE NORMAL SERVICE DOOR.
SEA SIDE
NORMAL SERVICE DOOR
HERE NOW
SERVICE AREA
LARGE SERVICE ENTRANCE
UNIT 3 TURBINE BLDG
CONTROL AREA
PINE CORRIDOR
UNIT 3 REACTOR BLDG
LARGE SERVICE ENTRANCE
DRUNNN
CLIK
"DG" STANDS FOR DIESEL GENERATOR. TURNING IT ON IS ONE OF THE FIRST STEPS WHEN BEGINNING A SHIFT.
OKAY, IT'S ON.
DRUNNN
THE DG'S ELECTRICITY IS WHAT POWERS THE COMMUNICATIONS OF THE ROBOTS IN THE PINE CORRIDOR, AS WELL AS THEIR BATTERY CHARGERS.
MANY WORK SITES AT ICHI-F INVOLVE PROCURING YOUR OWN POWER.
I HAD TO MANAGE THE DG AT THE REST AREA, TOO...

BUT THIS IS NO TIME FOR MEMORIES.
OH, CRAP ...
THE RADIATION IS FAIRLY HIGH AROUND HERE.
DSH
THE UNIT 3 SERVICE ENTRANCES ARE A PAIN, ON BOTH THE MOUNTAIN AND SEA SIDES.
CREAK
AT UNIT 1 I COULD TAKE A NAP INSIDE!
DG IS GOOD!
SHALL WE GO, THEN?
HOLD THIS...
HMMM ...
HOSE (TIED UP)
PACKBOT
AP CART
AS SHOWN LAST CHAPTER, THIS IS THE DAY WE MOVED THE PACKBOT FROM THE SEA SIDE TO THE MOUNTAIN SIDE ENTRANCE.
LET'S GO!
RAAAH!
HELLO?
!
WHAT? IT'S STUCK?
AT THE TIME, I MENTIONED THAT WE CHANGED OUR STANDBY LOCATION TO REDUCE RADIATION EXPOSURE, BUT NOW I'LL DESCRIBE ANOTHER SUCH MEASURE WE TOOK TO INCREASE SAFETY.

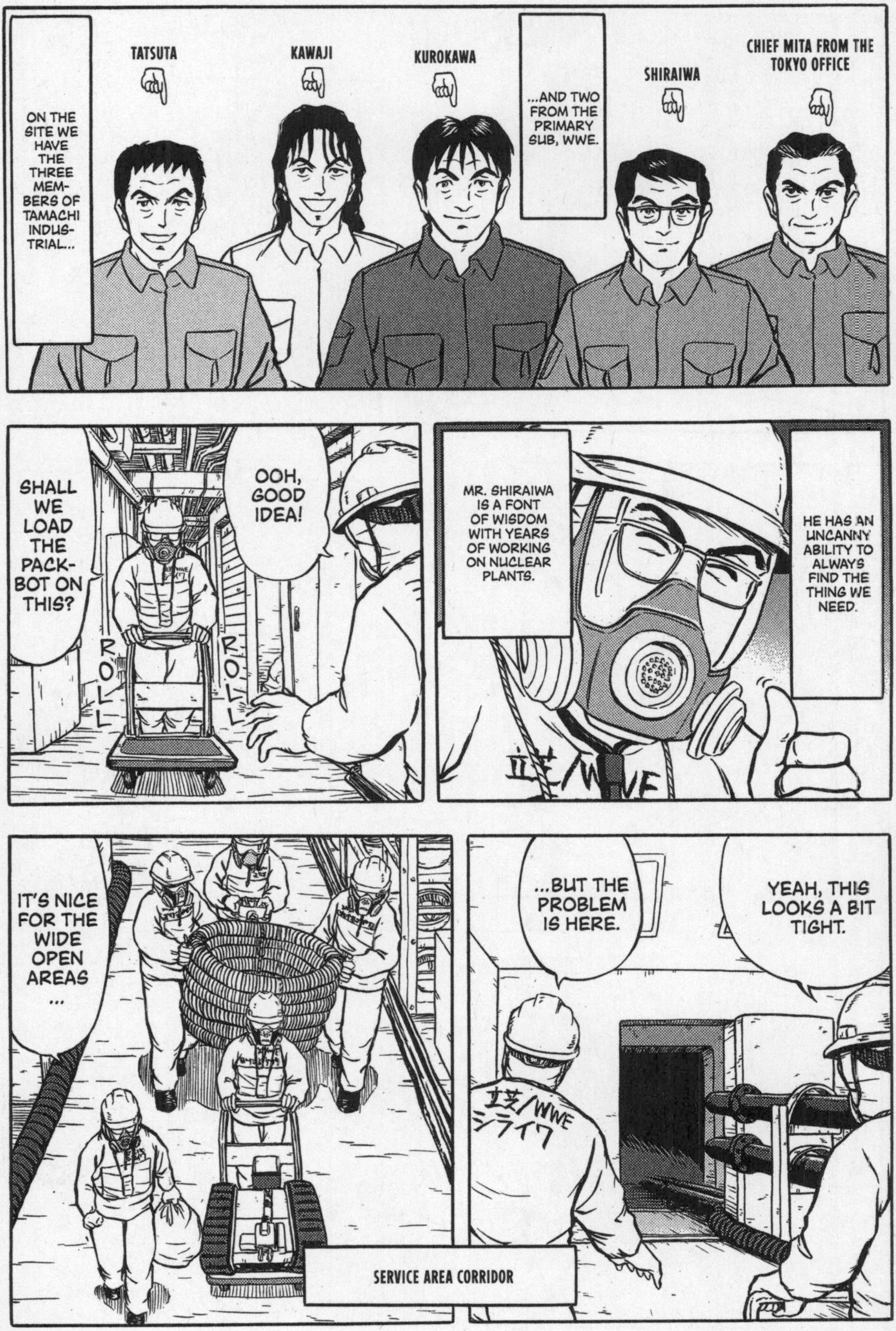
ON THE SITE WE HAVE THE THREE MEMBERS OF TAMACHI INDUSTRIAL...
TATSUTA
KAWAJI
KUROKAWA
...AND TWO FROM THE PRIMARY SUB, WWE.
SHIRAIWA
CHIEF MITA FROM THE TOKYO OFFICE
SHALL WE LOAD THE PACKBOT ON THIS?
ROLL
ROLL
OOH, GOOD IDEA!
MR. SHIRAIWA IS A FONT OF WISDOM WITH YEARS OF WORKING ON NUCLEAR PLANTS.
HE HAS AN UNCANNY ABILITY TO ALWAYS FIND THE THING WE NEED.
IT'S NICE FOR THE WIDE OPEN AREAS...
SERVICE AREA CORRIDOR
...BUT THE PROBLEM IS HERE.
YEAH, THIS LOOKS A BIT TIGHT.
WWE
シライワ

THANKS TO THE PIPING AND OTHER THINGS BUILT AFTER THE ACCIDENT TO FACILITATE CLEANUP, SOME SPOTS ARE MORE CRAMPED THAN BEFORE.

NOPE, NOT GONNA WORK.

GAKK

WHAT ABOUT SIDEWAYS?

THIS SHOULD WORK.

HOLDING IT LIKE THIS IS JUST BAKING IN RADIATION.

THE CATERPILLAR TREADS ARE CONTAMINATED FROM ROLLING ON THE GROUND.

Might as well be pressing it against the APD

EVEN WORSE IS THE HOSE.

I TOLD YOU, IT WON'T WORK.

WE DIDN'T NEED TO TRY TO KNOW THAT.

SPLIT IT INTO TWO.

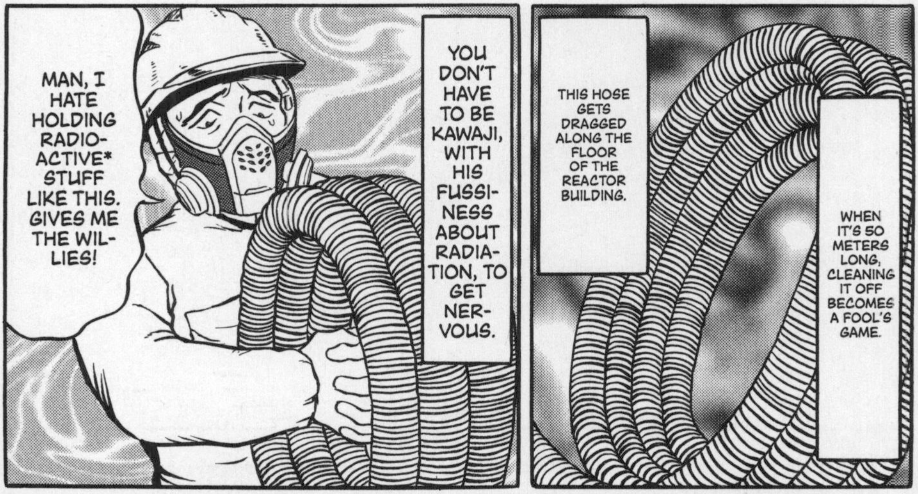
MAN, I HATE HOLDING RADIO-ACTIVE* STUFF LIKE THIS. GIVES ME THE WIL-LIES!
YOU DON'T HAVE TO BE KAWAJI, WITH HIS FUSSI-NESS ABOUT RADIA-TION, TO GET NER-VOUS.
THIS HOSE GETS DRAGGED ALONG THE FLOOR OF THE REACTOR BUILDING.
WHEN IT'S 50 METERS LONG, CLEANING IT OFF BECOMES A FOOL'S GAME.

*In our lingo, we often call highly-contaminated things "radioactive," because it seems like they might as well be a source of radiation.

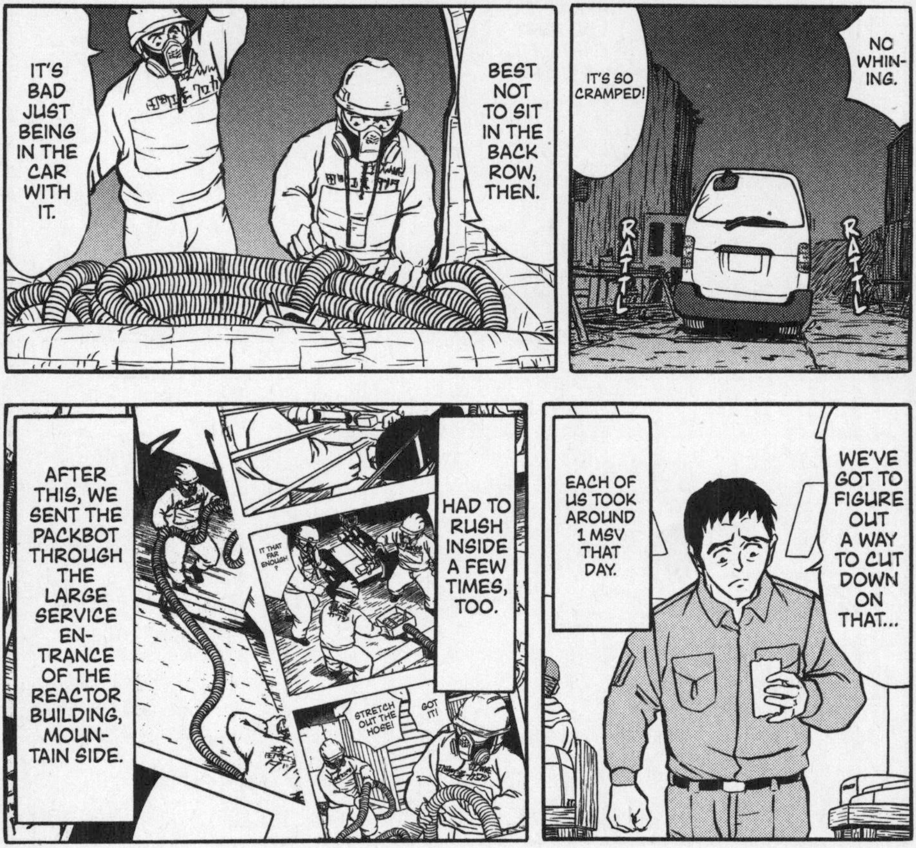
IT'S BAD JUST BEING IN THE CAR WITH IT.
BEST NOT TO SIT IN THE BACK ROW, THEN.
IT'S SO CRAMPED!
NO WHIN-ING.
RATTL
RATTL
AFTER THIS, WE SENT THE PACKBOT THROUGH THE LARGE SERVICE EN-TRANCE OF THE REACTOR BUILDING, MOUN-TAIN SIDE.
IT THAT FAR ENOUGH ?
HAD TO RUSH INSIDE A FEW TIMES, TOO.
STRETCH OUT THE HOSE!
GOT IT!
EACH OF US TOOK AROUND 1 MSV THAT DAY.
WE'VE GOT TO FIGURE OUT A WAY TO CUT DOWN ON THAT...

Unomisaki Hot Spring in Hitachi
HMM, IT'S A TOUGH NUT TO CRACK ...
I HAD ONE OTHER PROBLEM ON MY MIND.
GOTTA GET BACK TO THAT OTHER WORK ...
WHEN I CAME TO WORK IN OCTOBER...
...SO I'M AFRAID I'LL BE BUSY THERE FOR A WHILE.
HMM ...
WELL, IN PRINCIPLE I DON'T MIND YOU GOING, SINCE IT'S GOING TO GENERATE MORE MATERIAL FOR US TO PUBLISH...
...BUT IT DOES HURT THAT THE SERIALIZATION PACE WILL SLOW DOWN FOR IT.
THE LAST TIME (JULY), YOU DIDN'T ACTUALLY PUT TOGETHER ANY STORYBOARDS, DID YOU?
I'M SORRY... BUT IF I CAN'T DO LONGER STORYBOARDS, I MIGHT BE ABLE TO FULLY DRAW AND INK SOME SHORT PIECES.
Trying to bargain out of it

ACTUALLY, IT MIGHT BE INTERESTING TO HAVE YOU DRAW UP FINISHED MATERIAL WHILE DOING THE DECOMMISSIONING WORK.
RIGHT? AND I HAVE MY OWN ROOM, SO I COULD PROBABLY MANAGE IT.
BUT ONCE I ACTUALLY TRIED DRAWING...
DANG! THE TABLE'S TOO SMALL!
No room for an inkpot
I CAN'T DRAW WITH A BRUSH LIKE I USUALLY DO.
WELL, I'LL TRY IT WITH THE AUTOGRAPH PEN.
THIS DID NOT FOOL THE PRO'S EYES.
WHAT DID YOU DRAW THIS WITH? IT'S NOT YOUR USUAL LINEWORK.
Sorry, sorry!
Chapter 13
BUT IN THIS COMIC'S CASE, YOU COULD SAY THAT THE LOOK OF THE ART CHANGING WITH THE CIRCUMSTANCES IS PART OF THE CHARM...?
WE'LL GO WITH IT THIS TIME, BUT I'D RATHER YOU CAME BACK AND DID IT PROPERLY FOR THE NEXT CHAPTER.

So how much longer do you think your stint will last there?
THROUGH THE END OF NO-VEMBER, I THINK ...
At first you just said it'd be a month!
I'M SORRY, I'M SORRY.
IT'S BEEN NEARLY TWO MONTHS BY THIS POINT.
IF YOU DON'T COME BACK SOON, IT'S GOING TO BE TOO LONG OF A HIATUS FOR THE SERIAL-IZATION.
AND WE NEED TO PUT OUT THE SECOND VOLUME SOON.
I GET THE SITUA-TION.
I CAN'T JUST SIT BACK AND ENJOY THE WORK LIFE HERE...
TO BE HONEST, THOUGH, I WANT TO HEAD HOME KNOWING I WORKED RIGHT TO MY EXPOSURE LIMIT...
立芝/WWE
田町工業
タツタ

Volume 1 had a notice saying "Coming in the fall!"

Open-air bath with a gorgeous ocean view

THE NEXT DAY, WHEN THE CHIEF AND I RETURNED FROM BEING ON STANDBY FOR THE ROBOTS...
HERE WE ARE!
WEL-COME BACK.
...MR. SHIRAIWA HAD A NEW PLAN.
THE THREE OF US WERE JUST THINK-ING ABOUT HOW TO RETURN THE PACKBOT TO THE SEA SIDE TO-MORROW.
WE'RE TIRED OF CARRY-ING THAT CONTAMI-NATED STUFF THROUGH THOSE TIGHT DOORS, RIGHT?
IT'S A LONG DISTANCE TO GO.
AND HEAVY.
TRUE.
IF I'M BEING HONEST, YES, I'M TIRED OF IT.
THEN ...
WHAT IF WE USE THIS ?
WHAT'S THAT?
THE SPOT WHERE WE TURN ON THE DG?

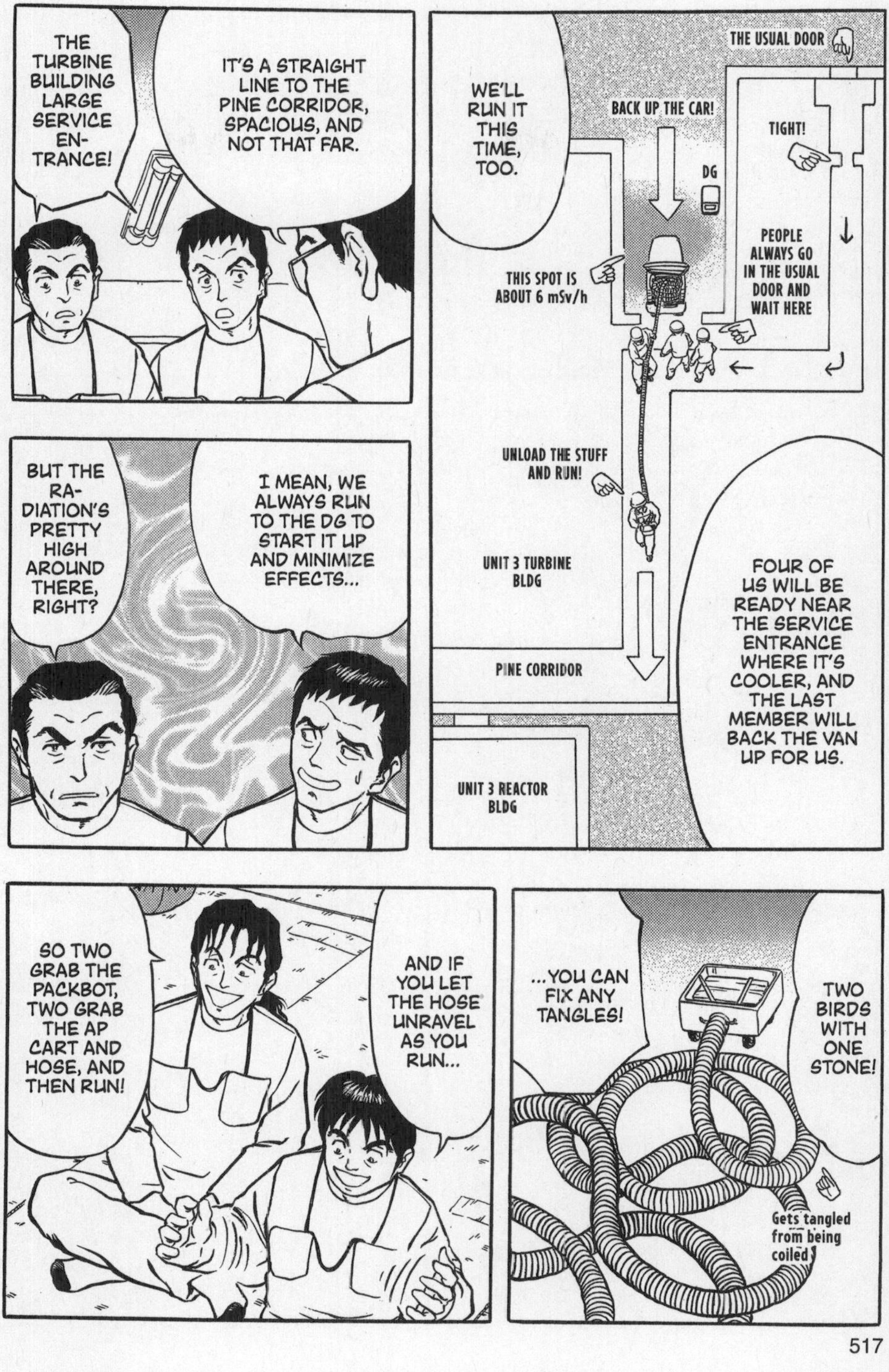

THE TURBINE BUILDING LARGE SERVICE ENTRANCE!

IT'S A STRAIGHT LINE TO THE PINE CORRIDOR, SPACIOUS, AND NOT THAT FAR.

BUT THE RADIATION'S PRETTY HIGH AROUND THERE, RIGHT?

I MEAN, WE ALWAYS RUN TO THE DG TO START IT UP AND MINIMIZE EFFECTS...

WE'LL RUN IT THIS TIME, TOO.

THE USUAL DOOR

BACK UP THE CAR!

DG

TIGHT!

THIS SPOT IS ABOUT 6 mSv/h

PEOPLE ALWAYS GO IN THE USUAL DOOR AND WAIT HERE

UNLOAD THE STUFF AND RUN!

UNIT 3 TURBINE BLDG

PINE CORRIDOR

UNIT 3 REACTOR BLDG

FOUR OF US WILL BE READY NEAR THE SERVICE ENTRANCE WHERE IT'S COOLER, AND THE LAST MEMBER WILL BACK THE VAN UP FOR US.

SO TWO GRAB THE PACKBOT, TWO GRAB THE AP CART AND HOSE, AND THEN RUN!

AND IF YOU LET THE HOSE UNRAVEL AS YOU RUN...

...YOU CAN FIX ANY TANGLES!

TWO BIRDS WITH ONE STONE!

Gets tangled from being coiled

I'LL ADMIT, IT'S A GAMBLE.

SHORT TIME IN A HOT SPOT VERSUS LONG TIME IN A COOL SPOT.

CARRYING THE HOSE AND TREADS, YOU'RE GETTING YOUR RADIATION EITHER WAY.

I THINK IT'S WORTH ATTEMPTING.

THEN WE'LL TRY IT TOMORROW!

WE'LL CALL IT "OPERATION DG"!

DOES IT EVEN NEED A NAME THAT COOL?

AT THE WORST, THE DRIVER WILL GET A NICE BIG DOSE SITTING RIGHT AT THE SERVICE ENTRANCE HOTSPOT.

SUCKS FOR WHOEVER IS THE DRIVER!

THE NEXT DAY, WE SWITCH TO THE SEA SIDE ENTRANCE.

ALL LOADED UP!

SLAM!

ROBOT WORK FINISHED, 7:00 AM

AND LET'S GET GOING...

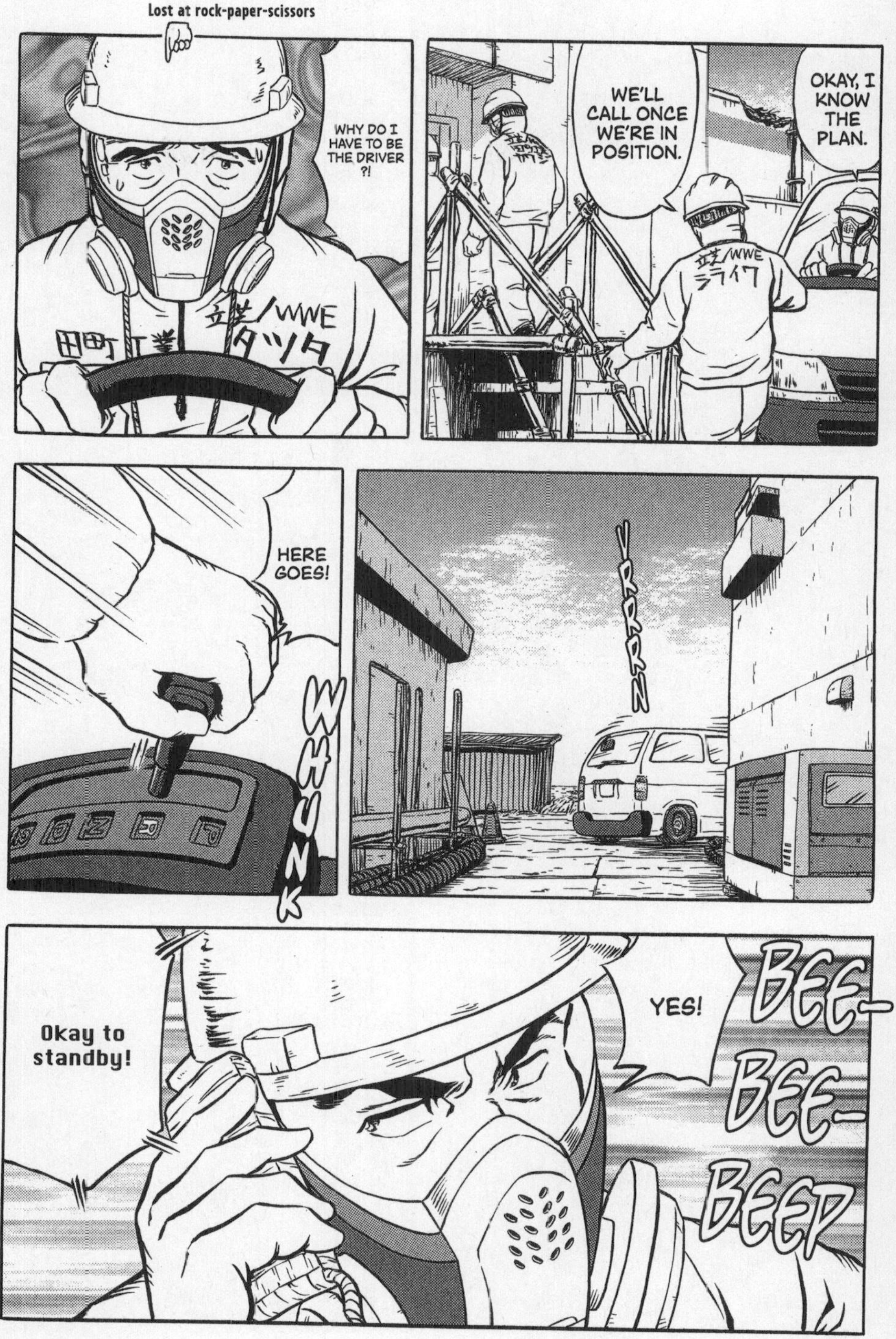

Lost at rock-paper-scissors

GRAAAAH
GO!
ALL RIGHT, UNLOAD!
WATCH YOUR STEP, CHIEF!
RAAAAH!
GOOD!
WE GOT THE PACK-BOT!
AW GEEZ, IT'S STILL OPEN...
VRRRM
NO TIME TO CLOSE IT FIRST.

WELL?
ALL DONE!
立芝/WWE
田町工業
タツタ
IT WORKED PERFECT. WE GOT OUT THE KINKS, TOO!
THAT WAS QUICK.
NOW THE QUESTION IS, WHAT WILL OUR NUMBERS BE AFTER THIS?
ESPECIALLY FOR THE DRIVER.
OH SURE, SINGLE ME OUT!
HOW MUCH DID YOU HAVE?
0.5, ACTUALLY.
GREAT! WE HALVED IT!
OF COURSE, THERE ARE MANY FACTORS OF EXPOSURE, SO WE CAN'T SAY FOR SURE...
All exposure levels were less than half what they were two days ago
BUT I THINK WE CAN SAY...

OPERA-TION DG IS A SUC-CESS!
WITH-OUT A DOUBT!
DAP
THANKS FOR YOUR HELP, CHIEF MITA.
NOT AT ALL. YOU PUT YOURSELF ON THE LINE.
OH, IS TODAY THE END?
SORRY I COULDN'T HELP OUT LONGER.
DON'T BE SILLY, YOU WERE A GREAT BOON TO US!
WE'D LOVE TO HAVE YOU HERE ALL THE TIME!
AND I'D LOVE TO BE HERE, BUT WORK CALLS IN THE TOKYO OFFICE...
WE COULD HOLD YOU HOSTAGE IN THE HITACHI DORM.
GOOD IDEA!
PLEASE, ANYTHING BUT THAT...
I WANTED TO STAY WORKING AT ICHI-F FOREVER TOO, BUT ...

I GUESS I CAN'T AVOID THAT.
ALL THINGS MUST COME TO AN END.
I'M SORRY, SIR. I'VE GOT TO GET GOING BACK NOW.
I SEE. THANK YOU.
Sign: Tamachi Industrial
I FEEL BAD, BECAUSE I'VE STILL GOT WIGGLE ROOM IN MY EXPO-SURE CAP.
AND YA CAN'T JUST PASS IT ON TO SOMEONE ELSE!
I'LL CALL YOU AGAIN NEXT YEAR IF I GET ANYTHING.
THANK YOU, SIR.
CON-GRATS ON A GOOD YEAR OF WORK!
WE'VE STILL GOT A BIT OF TIME LEFT BEFORE WE'RE DONE.
SORRY TO LEAVE YOU EARLY, GUYS.
HUH?
HERE, TAKE THIS.
THEY BROUGHT A BACKUP FOR ME ...

THIS IS HOW EXPERIENCE GETS PASSED ON...
JUST MAKE SURE YOU TELL THE NEXT GROUP AFTER US.
AH, I SEE. ALL THE LITTLE THINGS YOU DO ADD UP!
THE TRANSFER OF DUTIES IS SERIOUS.
ZRRG ZRRG
THE OTHER MEMBERS LEFT IN DECEMBER...
Lucky saps got to go all the way to their radiation limit
...BUT I'M SURE SOMEONE IS CONTROLLING THOSE ROBOTS AT ICHI-F AT THIS VERY MOMENT.
WITH EVEN MORE IMPROVEMENTS, TIPS, AND TRICKS BY NOW.
MY EXPOSURE TOTAL FOR THIS MONTH OF LABOR WAS ABOUT 9 MSV. TOTALED UP WITH MY STINT IN JULY, MY SUM FOR THE YEAR WAS 11 MSV.
I COULDA GONE ANOTHER 9 MSV...
THAT ACCUMULATION OF KNOWLEDGE IS A CRUCIAL BUT UNKNOWN PILLAR OF THE DECOMMISSION WORK.

CHAPTER 22 - END

HOT SPRINGS

AS WE'LL TOUCH ON IN THE SPECIAL EPILOGUE, THERE ARE MANY HOT SPRINGS AROUND ICHI-F, AND TATSUTA MADE THEM A FREQUENT STOP ON HIS WAY BACK FROM A SHIFT. SOME FAVORITES THAT DIDN'T MAKE IT INTO THE STORY ARE KANIARAI HOT SPRING IN YOTSUKURA, WHICH REOPENED IN JULY 2013, SAHAKO-NO-YU IN THE YUMOTO NEIGHBORHOOD, AND THE NEARBY PUBLIC BATHHOUSE JONOYU.

BLUB
BLUB
SO THIS IS THE FAMOUS MIYAGI POTATO STEW?
YOU BET.
IN YAMAGATA, THEY MAKE IT WITH BEEF AND SOY SAUCE, BUT HERE WE USE PORK AND MISO.
Mistake many from Tokyo area make
ISHINO-MAKI CITY, MIYAGI — NOVEMBER 2014
ISN'T THAT JUST TONJIRU PORK SOUP?
They always take offense
SAY THAT AGAIN, AND I'LL WHUP YOU UPSIDE TH' HEAD!
I GOT TO TAKE PART IN A POTATO STEW EVENT FOR A TEMPO-RARY HOUSING LOCATION.
IT WAS HELD AT A REGIONAL TOWN BUILDING. AS I UNDERSTOOD IT, THEY'RE USUALLY DONE AROUND CAMPFIRES IN A DRY RIVER BED.
I'D LIKE TO POUND THE RICE MOCHI!
OOH!
IT WAS JUST A FUN VOL-UNTEER EVENT.

Sign: Resident Center

THERE!
HRRRG ...
WHAT'S WRONG? YOU'RE LOOKIN' UNSTEADY!
CHAPTER 23:
I'LL BE BACK!

Referring to the packbot

ALL RIGHT! WITNESS THE METTLE OF A PLANT WORKER!
SPLAT
THERE WE GO!
THE HELL'S THAT?
JUST SWING IT!
FWUD
SORRY, I'VE NEVER HELD UP ANYTHING HEAVIER THAN A NUCLEAR REACTOR INSPECTION ROBOT BEFORE...
FWUD
THE HEAD VOLUNTEER IS FROM TOKYO.
IT'S GOOD EXERCISE, ISN'T IT?
THERE!
HMF!
SPLAT
I HAVEN'T DONE MOCHI POUNDING SINCE I WAS A KID.
I GOT THE INVITATION RIGHT AT A TIME WHEN I WAS ON BREAK FROM ICHI-F.
WE MET AS FELLOW MUSICIANS.
LET'S GET THIS CONCERT STARTED!

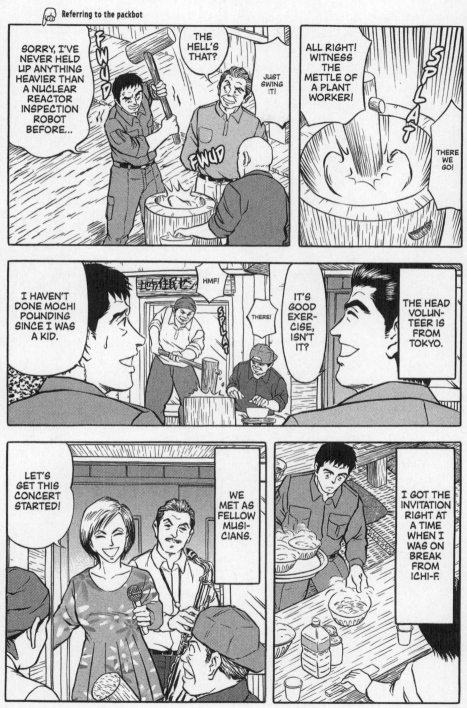

STEW, MOCHI, AND MUSIC. WE GOT A MIX OF RESIDENTS AT THE TEMPORARY HOUSING DEVELOPMENT...
...PLUS LOCALS FROM ADJA-CENT RE-GIONS.
IS THAT WHY YOU RENTED OUT THIS LOCAL HALL INSTEAD OF HOLDING IT AT THE HOUSING PROJECT, SO THAT WE COULD BRING IN NEARBY RESIDENTS, TOO?
WELL, IT'S TRUE THAT THIS PLACE IS A LOT BIGGER THAN THE TEMPORARY HOUSING AREA...
BUT IT SEEMS LIKE THOSE BEING REHOUSED HAVE FEW CHANCES TO MINGLE WITH RESIDENTS, AND VICE VERSA.
I THOUGHT IT WOULD BE A GOOD CHANCE TO LOOSEN UP.
AH, GOOD POINT. I'VE HEARD ABOUT FRICTION BETWEEN EVACUEES AND LOCALS IN IWAKI, TOO.
IT'S MADE EXTRA COMPLICAT-ED IN THE CASE OF NUCLEAR EVACUEES, SINCE THERE'S COMPEN-SATION MONEY INVOLVED, TOO.

2012 graffitti on Iwaki's town hall reading "Go home, radioactive mutants"

STILL, IT'S NOT JUST THE EVACUEES WHO ARE VICTIMS OF THE DISASTER, IT'S THOSE AROUND THEM WHO WELCOME THEM IN AS WELL—JUST TO DIFFERENT DEGREES.
YES. IT'S EASY TO FORGET THAT...
I THINK I'LL PLAY A SONG NOW.
THAT'S THE SPIRIT!
CLAP
CLAP
CLAP
"LOVERS IN YURA-KUCHO"!
YOUR WISH IS MY COM-MAND!
AS I'VE MENTIONED BEFORE, I DO OLD-FASHIONED SONGS.
IN ADDI-TION TO MUSICIANS, THERE WERE VOLUNTEER CHIRO-PRACTORS OFFERING SERVICES.
AND WITH A KARA-OKE EVENT THROWN IN TO BOOT, IT WAS A VERY LIVELY DAY.

I'M AFRAID THIS IS IT FOR TODAY, EVERY-ONE...
...BUT THERE'S A PHRASE THAT I ALWAYS WONDER IF I SHOULD SAY OR NOT AT THE END. AND THAT IS...
"I'LL BE BACK."
THE PROBLEM WITH THIS IS THAT IT ASSUMES YOU'LL STILL BE LIVING HERE IN THIS TEMPORARY HOUSING ...
DON'T BE FOOLISH! COME ON RIGHT BACK!
YOU'RE SURE?
OF COURSE!
THEY AIN'T GONNA SORT EVERYTHING OUT THAT QUICK—EVEN IF WE DO WANNA GET OUTTA HERE!
BESIDES, WE CAN STILL COME TOGETHER, EVEN WHEN WE'RE OUT OF THE HOUSING PROJECT.
WHILE THE LENGTH-ENING OF THE TEM-PORARY HOUSING CRISIS IS A SERIOUS ISSUE, IT ALSO CREATES PERSONAL BONDS LIKE THESE.
THANK YOU SO MUCH!

Sign: Resident Center

IN MARCH 2015, FOUR YEARS AFTER THE EARTH-QUAKE...
...THERE WERE ABOUT 80,000 PEOPLE IN TEMPORARY HOUSING IN THE THREE PREFECTURES AFFECTED (IWATE, MIYAGI, FUKUSHIMA). THE TOTAL NUMBER OF DISPLACED IS ABOUT 220,000.
FACED WITH A NUMBER THAT CAN'T POSSIBLY GO DOWN TO ZERO ALL AT ONCE, THERE ARE PEOPLE OUT THERE...
THANKS FOR COMING OUT TODAY.
I HAD FUN.
...WHO DON'T GET ANGRY OR SELF-PITYING, BUT CONTINUE ON WITH THEIR LIVES, DETERMINED TO FIND WHATEVER IT IS THEY CAN DO.
EVEN IF THAT'S NOTHING MORE THAN SELF-SATIS-FACTION IN THE END.
SINCE I'M HERE, I MIGHT AS WELL PAY A VISIT...
THE NEXT DAY...

THIS IS THE CITY OF ISHI-NOMAKI IN NO-VEMBER 2014.
WOW...
IT MIGHT LOOK LIKE A SIMPLE PLOT OF EMPTY LAND...
I DON'T BE-LIEVE IT...
...BUT IT WAS ONCE AN ENORMOUS PILE OF RUBBLE.
A YEAR AND A HALF LATER, AND THERE'S STILL JUST A MOUN-TAIN OF RUBBLE ...
THEY CLEANED IT ALL UP...

See Chapter 8

Also from Chapter 8

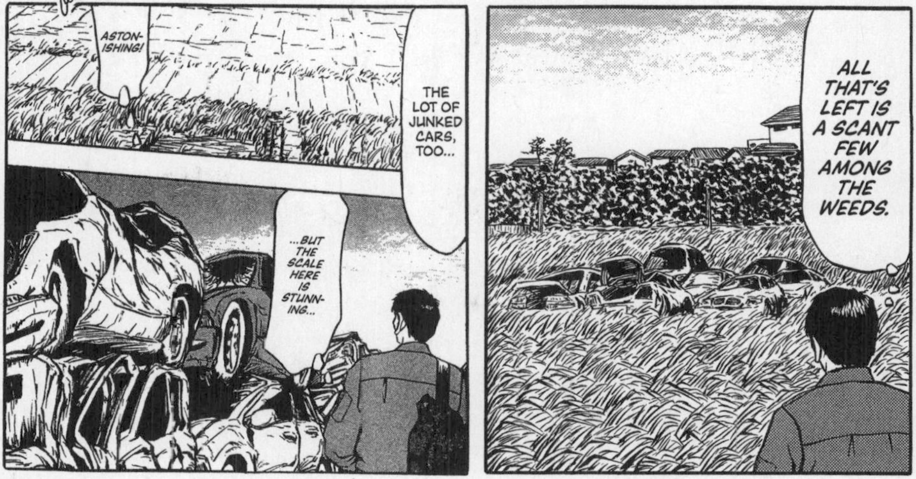
ASTONISHING!
THE LOT OF JUNKED CARS, TOO...
...BUT THE SCALE HERE IS STUNNING...
ALL THAT'S LEFT IS A SCANT FEW AMONG THE WEEDS.

THE WORK HAS ADVANCED IN SOME PLACES, AND GONE NOWHERE IN OTHERS. SOME SPOTS ARE DIFFERENT, SOME THE SAME.
OKAWA ELEMENTARY SCHOOL, ISHINOMAKI
(Under debate whether to preserve as disaster monument)

THE DISASTER REGION ISN'T JUST A BIG MONOLITH—CONDITIONS AND PROGRESS ARE DIFFERENT EVERY PLACE YOU LOOK.
ENOSHIMA WELFARE HALL, ONAGAWA
(Demolished in January 2015)

THERE'S CONSTRUCTION ALL OVER THE PLACE.
ONAGAWA, NOVEMBER 2014
ENOSHIMA WELFARE HALL

VWAAA
JUST STAY SAFE, FOLKS.
YIKES!
BETWEEN THE NEW PROTECTIVE TIDE WALLS AND THE REGRADING OF LAND, THE WHOLE PACIFIC COASTLINE OF THE TOHOKU REGION LOOKS LIKE ONE GIANT CONSTRUCTION SCENE.

AS A MATTER OF FACT, RIGHT AROUND THIS TIME, THERE WAS A CASUALTY-CAUSING ACCIDENT AT ICHI-F, AND WORK STOPPED FOR A FEW DAYS WHILE THEY SORTED IT OUT.
AND I SHOULD GET BACK TO THE SITE...

WHEN AN ACCIDENT OCCURS AT ICHI-F, ALL WORK IS HALTED...
...SO THEY CAN INVESTIGATE THE CAUSE AND ENSURE CONDITIONS ARE SAFE ENOUGH TO PROCEED. THAT GOES FOR EVERYTHING, NOT JUST THE PRECISE AREA WHERE THE ACCIDENT HAPPENED.
NATURALLY, THEY MUST ENSURE THE SAFETY OF THE WORK.
立入禁止
BUT THE EFFECTS OF THE WORK STOPPAGE MANIFEST IN MANY WAYS.
ALREADY-SCHEDULED WORK BECOMES MUCH HARDER TO DO ON TIME.
HURRY!
YOU CAN IMAGINE THAT, IN SOME CASES, THEY ASK THE IMPOSSIBLE OF THE WORK TEAMS.
AND FOR THE WORKERS, GETTING A FEW EXTRA DAYS OFF ISN'T ALWAYS A BONUS.
WE GET PAID BY THE DAY, AFTER ALL.
I DON'T KNOW HOW THINGS ARE FOR SALARIED EMPLOYEES AT MAJOR CONTRACTORS, BUT FOR US SUBCONTRACTORS DOWN THE LINE, ONE FEWER DAY WORKING IS ONE FEWER DAY'S INCOME.
DAMN, NOT ANOTHER WORK STOPPAGE.
HAVEN'T MADE BEANS THIS MONTH.
WHEN THE COMPANY ORDERS YOU NOT TO WORK, SOME WILL PAY YOU A STANDBY STIPEND, BUT HOW MUCH COMPLETELY DEPENDS ON THE COMPANY.

Sign: No Entry

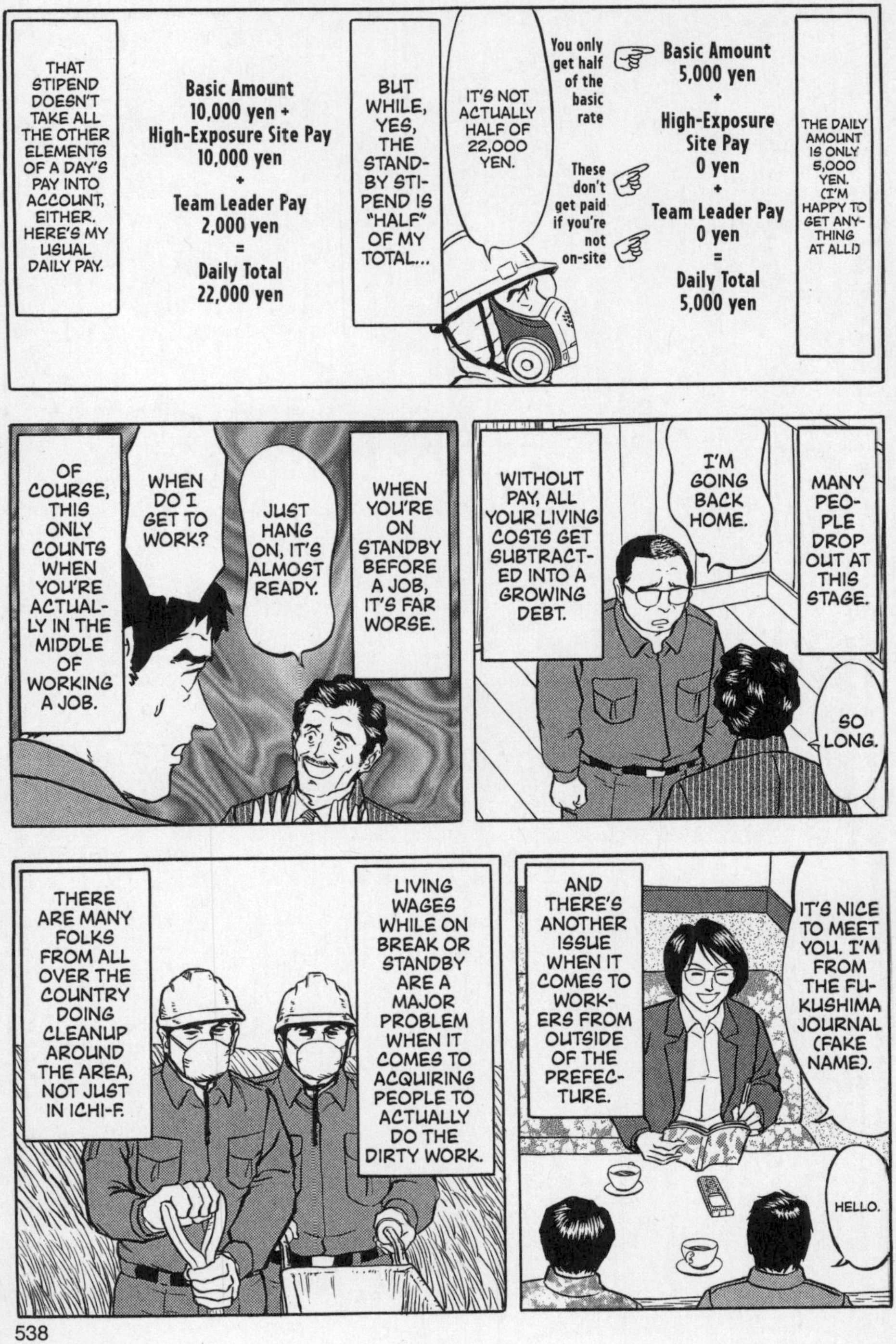
THAT STIPEND DOESN'T TAKE ALL THE OTHER ELEMENTS OF A DAY'S PAY INTO ACCOUNT, EITHER. HERE'S MY USUAL DAILY PAY.
Basic Amount 10,000 yen + High-Exposure Site Pay 10,000 yen + Team Leader Pay 2,000 yen = Daily Total 22,000 yen
BUT WHILE, YES, THE STANDBY STIPEND IS "HALF" OF MY TOTAL...
IT'S NOT ACTUALLY HALF OF 22,000 YEN.
You only get half of the basic rate
These don't get paid if you're not on-site
Basic Amount 5,000 yen + High-Exposure Site Pay 0 yen + Team Leader Pay 0 yen = Daily Total 5,000 yen
THE DAILY AMOUNT IS ONLY 5,000 YEN. (I'M HAPPY TO GET ANYTHING AT ALL!)
OF COURSE, THIS ONLY COUNTS WHEN YOU'RE ACTUALLY IN THE MIDDLE OF WORKING A JOB.
WHEN DO I GET TO WORK?
JUST HANG ON, IT'S ALMOST READY.
WHEN YOU'RE ON STANDBY BEFORE A JOB, IT'S FAR WORSE.
WITHOUT PAY, ALL YOUR LIVING COSTS GET SUBTRACTED INTO A GROWING DEBT.
I'M GOING BACK HOME.
MANY PEOPLE DROP OUT AT THIS STAGE.
SO LONG.
THERE ARE MANY FOLKS FROM ALL OVER THE COUNTRY DOING CLEANUP AROUND THE AREA, NOT JUST IN ICHI-F.
LIVING WAGES WHILE ON BREAK OR STANDBY ARE A MAJOR PROBLEM WHEN IT COMES TO ACQUIRING PEOPLE TO ACTUALLY DO THE DIRTY WORK.
AND THERE'S ANOTHER ISSUE WHEN IT COMES TO WORKERS FROM OUTSIDE OF THE PREFECTURE.
IT'S NICE TO MEET YOU. I'M FROM THE FUKUSHIMA JOURNAL (FAKE NAME).
HELLO.

Many of them just rent out normal houses

WHEN I DID AN INTER-VIEW WITH A WRITER FROM A LOCAL PAPER...
AS A MATTER OF FACT, ACROSS FROM MY PARENTS' HOME IN FUKUSHIMA, THEY'VE GOT A DOZEN OR SO MEN LIVING IN ONE HOUSE...
TO MY SURPRISE, IT TURNED OUT THEY WERE ALL INVOLVED IN THE DECONTAMINATION PROCESS.
AH, YES. IT IS A LITTLE EERIE SEEING SO MANY OLDER MEN PACKED LIKE SARDINES INTO A HOUSE LIKE THAT, ISN'T IT?
Did that himself
THAT'S RIGHT. I MEAN, I'M GRATEFUL THEY'RE HERE FOR THE BENEFIT OF FUKUSHIMA, BUT...
I KNOW WHAT YOU MEAN. THEY'RE NOT ALWAYS THE BEST-BEHAVED MEN.
I'VE HEARD THAT SOME GET INTO TROUBLE WITH LOUD DRUNKEN-NESS AND FIGHTING.
IN FACT, THE LOCAL CRIME BULLETIN OF OUR PAPER HAS WORKERS LISTED NEARLY EVERY DAY FOR LITTLE THINGS LIKE FIGHTING AND THEFT...
除染作業員
万引きで逮捕
IT'S A PROB-LEM ...
IT'S FUNNY, I NEVER USED TO LOCK MY DOOR WHEN I WENT OUT, BUT NOW I'VE STARTED GETTING INTO THE HABIT.
I'M ACTUALLY MORE AMAZED THAT IT WAS PEACEFUL ENOUGH YOU DIDN'T IN THE FIRST PLACE.

Paper: Decontamination worker arrested for shoplifting

I SUPPOSE IT'S UNAVOIDABLE THAT WHEN TOTAL STRANGERS SUDDENLY ENTER THE COMMUNITY ...
...THE RESULT IS SOME CONFUSION AND UNEASE.
YES, I UNDERSTAND HOW IT GOES. BUT IT'S THE SAME FOR THOSE COMING IN.
IT'S HARD TO FEEL COM-FORT-ABLE UNTIL YOU'RE SETTLED IN.
THE EARTHQUAKE AND THE ICHI-F ACCIDENT ABRUPTLY TIED TOGETHER PEOPLE WHO HAD NO PREVIOUS CONNECTION TO EACH OTHER:
NUCLEAR PLANT AND DECONTAMINA-TION WORKERS AND THE LOCAL RESIDENTS AROUND THEM—AS WELL AS EVACUEES AND THOSE IN THE AREAS WHERE THEY WOUND UP.
EVERYONE IS JUST BLINDLY FEELING AROUND THEM...
...TO FIND WAYS TO DEAL WITH A DISTANCE THAT JUST GOT MUCH CLOSER.
I KNOW IT'S NOT MY PLACE TO SAY...
THE VAST MAJORITY OF THE WORKERS ARE SERIOUS, HARDWORKING MEN, SO PLEASE HAVE PATIENCE AND UNDERSTANDING WITH THEM.
ER... OF COURSE ...

IT'S SAID THAT THE PEOPLE OF FUKUSHIMA TEND TO BE PASSIVE COMMUNICATORS.

I HAPPEN TO BE ON THE SHY SIDE, MYSELF.

IT WAS OFTEN QUITE SCARY TO BE ENTERING A WORLD OF COMPLETE STRANGERS.

BUT AS WITH ANYWHERE ELSE, ONCE I MADE THE LEAP...

...I LEARNED THEY WERE ALL NORMAL, JUST LIKE ME.

A MASKED CONCERT IN FUKUSHIMA, 2015

AND NOW THAT I'VE MADE FRIENDS...

...I'VE STARTED VISITING FUKUSHIMA MORE OFTEN, NOT JUST FOR WORK AND COMIC BOOKS.

I HARDLY HAD ANY PERSONAL CONNECTION TO FUKUSHIMA BEFORE THE DISASTER.
Phenomenon where the snow pack on Mt. Azuma-Kofuji looks like a rabbit, signaling the approach of spring
OOOH, A SNOW RABBIT.
AND NOW IT'S SOMETHING LIKE A SECOND HOMETOWN TO ME.

郡山駅
MY FIRST VISIT WAS IN MAY 2012.
I STARTED WORK AT ICHI-F IN JUNE.

Sign: Koriyama Station

I WENT FROM WORKING AT THE SHELTER TO DOING INDOOR PIPE WORK.
I HAD TO LEAVE WHEN I REACHED MY YEARLY LIMIT.

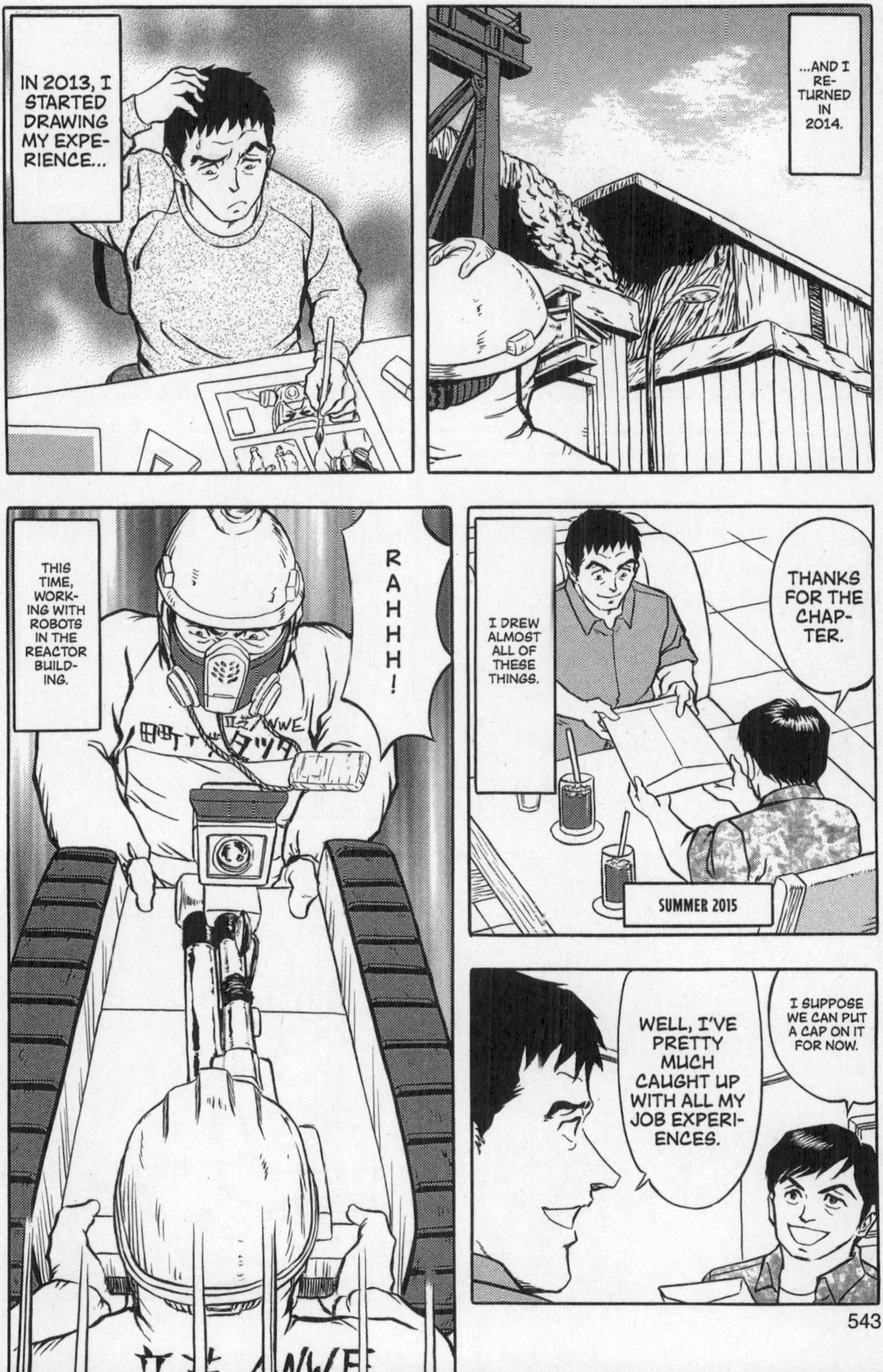
IN 2013, I STARTED DRAWING MY EXPE-RIENCE...
...AND I RE-TURNED IN 2014.
THIS TIME, WORK-ING WITH ROBOTS IN THE REACTOR BUILD-ING.
RAHHH!
I DREW ALMOST ALL OF THESE THINGS.
THANKS FOR THE CHAP-TER.
SUMMER 2015
I SUPPOSE WE CAN PUT A CAP ON IT FOR NOW.
WELL, I'VE PRETTY MUCH CAUGHT UP WITH ALL MY JOB EXPERI-ENCES.

THAT'S A GOOD IDEA. NO POINT STRETCHING IT OUT.

SO MY STORY WILL TAKE A HIATUS FOR NOW.

IF I EVER GET TO WORK AT ICHI-F OR COME ACROSS ANY INTERESTING STORIES, PERHAPS WE SHALL MEET AGAIN.

ALL YOU SUBCONTRACTORS, I'M AWAITING YOUR JOBS!

IN SEPTEMBER 2015, AS I'M DRAWING THIS, IT'S BEEN FOUR AND A HALF YEARS...

...SINCE THE GREAT EAST JAPAN EARTHQUAKE, AS WE CALL IT HERE. AND OVER THREE YEARS SINCE I FIRST GOT INVOLVED IN FUKUSHIMA.

BUT WHILE A WHOLE BUNCH OF OTHER THINGS HAVE CHANGED ...

THE ENCHANTING SIGHT OF HIRONO POWER STATION'S EXHAUST STACK RISING ABOVE THE COASTAL MIST STAYS THE SAME.

WHEN I STARTED WORK, THERE WAS A POLICE CHECKPOINT AT THE INTERSECTION NEXT TO J-VILLAGE.
JUST ABOUT ANYTHING WITHIN 20 KM OF ICHI-F WAS AN OFF-LIMITS PROTECTED ZONE.

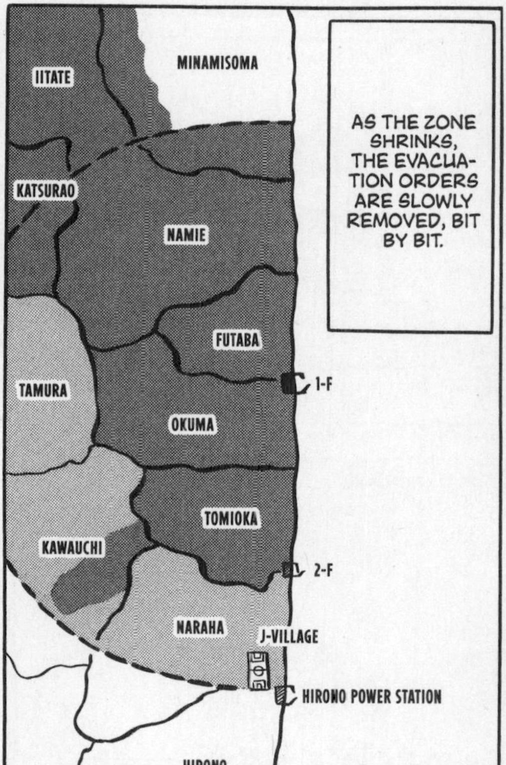
MINAMISOMA
IITATE
KATSURAO
NAMIE
FUTABA
TAMURA
1-F
OKUMA
TOMIOKA
KAWAUCHI
2-F
NARAHA
J-VILLAGE
HIRONO POWER STATION
HIRONO
IWAKI
Legend: Within 20 km
Legend: No longer under evacuation
Legend: Evacuation zones as of Sept. 2015
AS THE ZONE SHRINKS, THE EVACUATION ORDERS ARE SLOWLY REMOVED, BIT BY BIT.

Renovation Memorial Ceremony

楢葉町復興祈
こころ,つなぐならは
THE EVACUATION ORDER OF NARAHA WAS LIFTED THIS YEAR ON SEPTEMBER 5TH.

Top Sign: Naraha Town Renovation

Banner: Naraha, Connecting Hearts

THE LOTS FOR SALE, WHICH I SHOWED YOU BEFORE ...
分譲中
楢葉町
SO... THEY'RE SELLING LAND?
BUT YOU CAN SEE THE INTENTION OF THE PEOPLE TO RETURN AND LIVE HERE.

See Chapter 14

...NOW FEATURE NEW BUILDINGS UNDER CONSTRUCTION.
OOOH!

YOU STILL SEE THOSE BLACK BAGS OF CONTAMINATED DIRT AND PROTECTIVE GREEN SHEETS...
...BUT THERE ARE ALSO MORE AND MORE FIELDS AND PADDIES REPLANTED.

AND THE ENTIRETY OF ROUTE 6 AND THE JOBAN EXPRESSWAY ARE OPEN NOW.
JOBAN EXPRESSWAY, MINAMISOMA-KASHIMA REST STATION "SEDETTE KASHIMA"
THEY'VE OPENED NEW SERVICE AREAS ALONG THE WAY, BRINGING CROWDS AND LIVELINESS TO THE HOLIDAY AND VACATION SEASONS.

Sign: Tatsuta Station

AFTER THE ROADS, THERE'S RAIL. TO THE SOUTH (TOKYO) DIRECTION OF ICHI-F, THE CLOSEST YOU COULD GET ON THE JR JOBAN LINE...
...WAS HIRONO.

竜田駅
WHEN I VISITED IN 2012, STATIONS OUT OF ORDER WERE COVERED IN WEEDS AND ABANDONED.

BUT IN JUNE 2014, THE HIRONO-TATSUTA STRETCH REOPENED.
竜田駅
TATSUTA STATION
SORRY FOR TAKING YOUR NAME WITHOUT PERMISSION.
ON THE NORTHERN (SENDAI) SIDE OF ICHI-F, THEY'RE ALSO RESTORING SERVICE FROM HARANOMACHI-SOMA AND HAMAYOSHIDA-WATARI.

AS FOR WHAT'S LEFT, TOMIOKA STATION, THE NEXT ONE AFTER TATSUTA...
...WAS STILL AS DEVASTATED AS IT WAS BY THE TSUNAMI, AS OF 2014.

RADIOACTIVE MATERIAL DISPOSAL FACILITY
THEY TORE DOWN THE STATION IN 2015, WITH PLANS TO REBUILD AND REOPEN THE LINE TO TATSUTA BY MARCH 2018.
THE CLOSED AREAS NORTH OF NAMIE STATION SHOULD BE REOPENED BY SPRING OF 2017.
CLOSER TO ICHI-F, THERE ARE NO PLANS SET IN STONE YET FOR THE TOMIOKA-NAMIE CORRIDOR, BUT I'M CERTAIN THAT SERVICE WILL BE FULLY RESTORED IN THE NEAR FUTURE.
HITACHI E657 SERIES EXPRESS, SUPER COOL!
RATHER THAN GIVING CREDENCE TO THE BOILERPLATE "NO PATH TO THE FUTURE," "SLUGGISH RECOVERY" NARRATIVES...
...WHY NOT LEND AN EYE TO THOSE AREAS WHICH ARE RECOVERING, SLOWLY BUT SURELY?

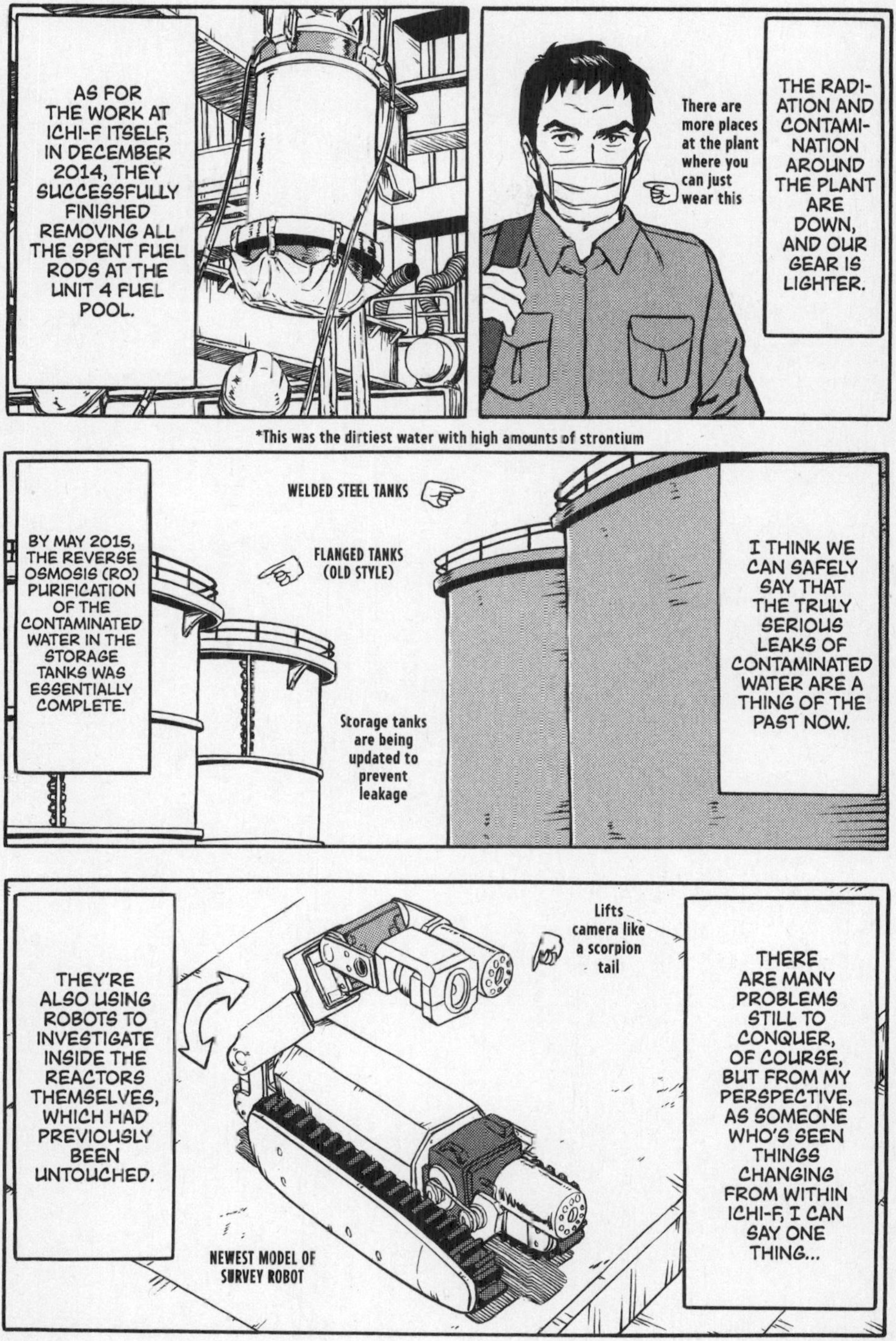
AS FOR THE WORK AT ICHI-F ITSELF, IN DECEMBER 2014, THEY SUCCESSFULLY FINISHED REMOVING ALL THE SPENT FUEL RODS AT THE UNIT 4 FUEL POOL.
There are more places at the plant where you can just wear this
THE RADIATION AND CONTAMINATION AROUND THE PLANT ARE DOWN, AND OUR GEAR IS LIGHTER.
*This was the dirtiest water with high amounts of strontium
BY MAY 2015, THE REVERSE OSMOSIS (RO) PURIFICATION OF THE CONTAMINATED WATER IN THE STORAGE TANKS WAS ESSENTIALLY COMPLETE.
WELDED STEEL TANKS
FLANGED TANKS (OLD STYLE)
Storage tanks are being updated to prevent leakage
I THINK WE CAN SAFELY SAY THAT THE TRULY SERIOUS LEAKS OF CONTAMINATED WATER ARE A THING OF THE PAST NOW.
THEY'RE ALSO USING ROBOTS TO INVESTIGATE INSIDE THE REACTORS THEMSELVES, WHICH HAD PREVIOUSLY BEEN UNTOUCHED.
Lifts camera like a scorpion tail
NEWEST MODEL OF SURVEY ROBOT
THERE ARE MANY PROBLEMS STILL TO CONQUER, OF COURSE, BUT FROM MY PERSPECTIVE, AS SOMEONE WHO'S SEEN THINGS CHANGING FROM WITHIN ICHI-F, I CAN SAY ONE THING...

IF THIS MINDSET CAN SPREAD, THEN I BELIEVE THE RECOVERY OF THE ENTIRE TOHOKU REGION, NOT JUST FUKUSHIMA, WILL BECOME THAT MUCH SMOOTHER.
NOTHING WILL HAPPEN THAT CAN BE WORSE THAN WHAT ALREADY HAPPENED.
IN TRUTH, WE ALL CAN'T WAIT UNTIL THE WORK AT ICHI-F COMES TO AN END, BUT SINCE THAT'S GOING TO TAKE A WHILE LONGER, I'LL JUST LEAVE YOU WITH THESE WORDS.
竜田駅
TATSUTA STATION
I'LL BE BACK!

CHAPTER 23 - END

ICHI-F

END

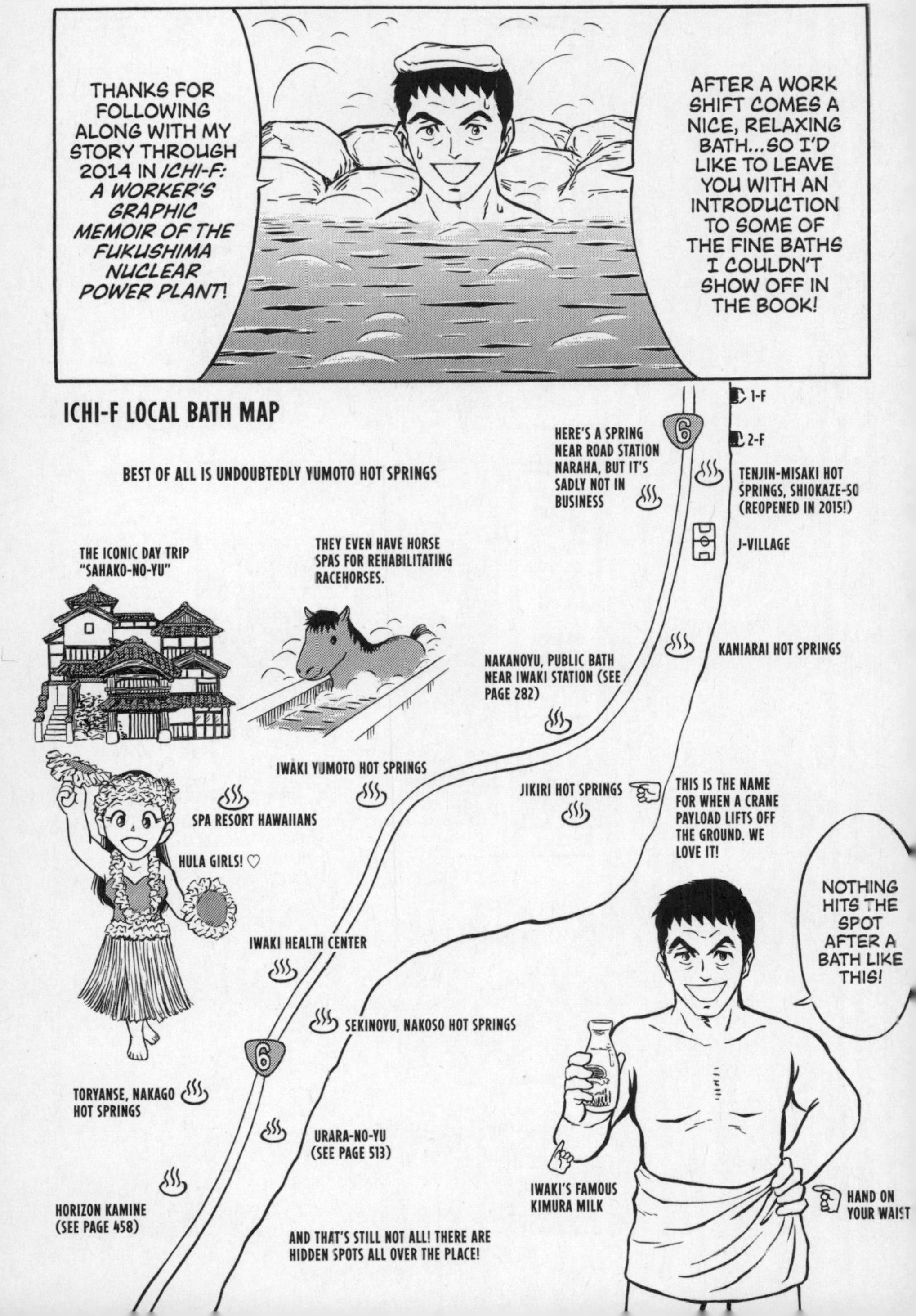

THANKS FOR FOLLOWING ALONG WITH MY STORY THROUGH 2014 IN *ICHI-F: A WORKER'S GRAPHIC MEMOIR OF THE FUKUSHIMA NUCLEAR POWER PLANT!*

AFTER A WORK SHIFT COMES A NICE, RELAXING BATH...SO I'D LIKE TO LEAVE YOU WITH AN INTRODUCTION TO SOME OF THE FINE BATHS I COULDN'T SHOW OFF IN THE BOOK!

ICHI-F LOCAL BATH MAP

BEST OF ALL IS UNDOUBTEDLY YUMOTO HOT SPRINGS

THE ICONIC DAY TRIP "SAHAKO-NO-YU"

THEY EVEN HAVE HORSE SPAS FOR REHABILITATING RACEHORSES.

HERE'S A SPRING NEAR ROAD STATION NARAHA, BUT IT'S SADLY NOT IN BUSINESS

1-F

2-F

TENJIN-MISAKI HOT SPRINGS, SHIOKAZE-SO (REOPENED IN 2015!)

J-VILLAGE

KANIARAI HOT SPRINGS

NAKANOYU, PUBLIC BATH NEAR IWAKI STATION (SEE PAGE 282)

IWAKI YUMOTO HOT SPRINGS

JIKIRI HOT SPRINGS

THIS IS THE NAME FOR WHEN A CRANE PAYLOAD LIFTS OFF THE GROUND. WE LOVE IT!

SPA RESORT HAWAIIANS

HULA GIRLS! ♡

NOTHING HITS THE SPOT AFTER A BATH LIKE THIS!

IWAKI HEALTH CENTER

SEKINOYU, NAKOSO HOT SPRINGS

6

TORYANSE, NAKAGO HOT SPRINGS

URARA-NO-YU (SEE PAGE 513)

IWAKI'S FAMOUS KIMURA MILK

HAND ON YOUR WAIST

HORIZON KAMINE (SEE PAGE 458)

AND THAT'S STILL NOT ALL! THERE ARE HIDDEN SPOTS ALL OVER THE PLACE!

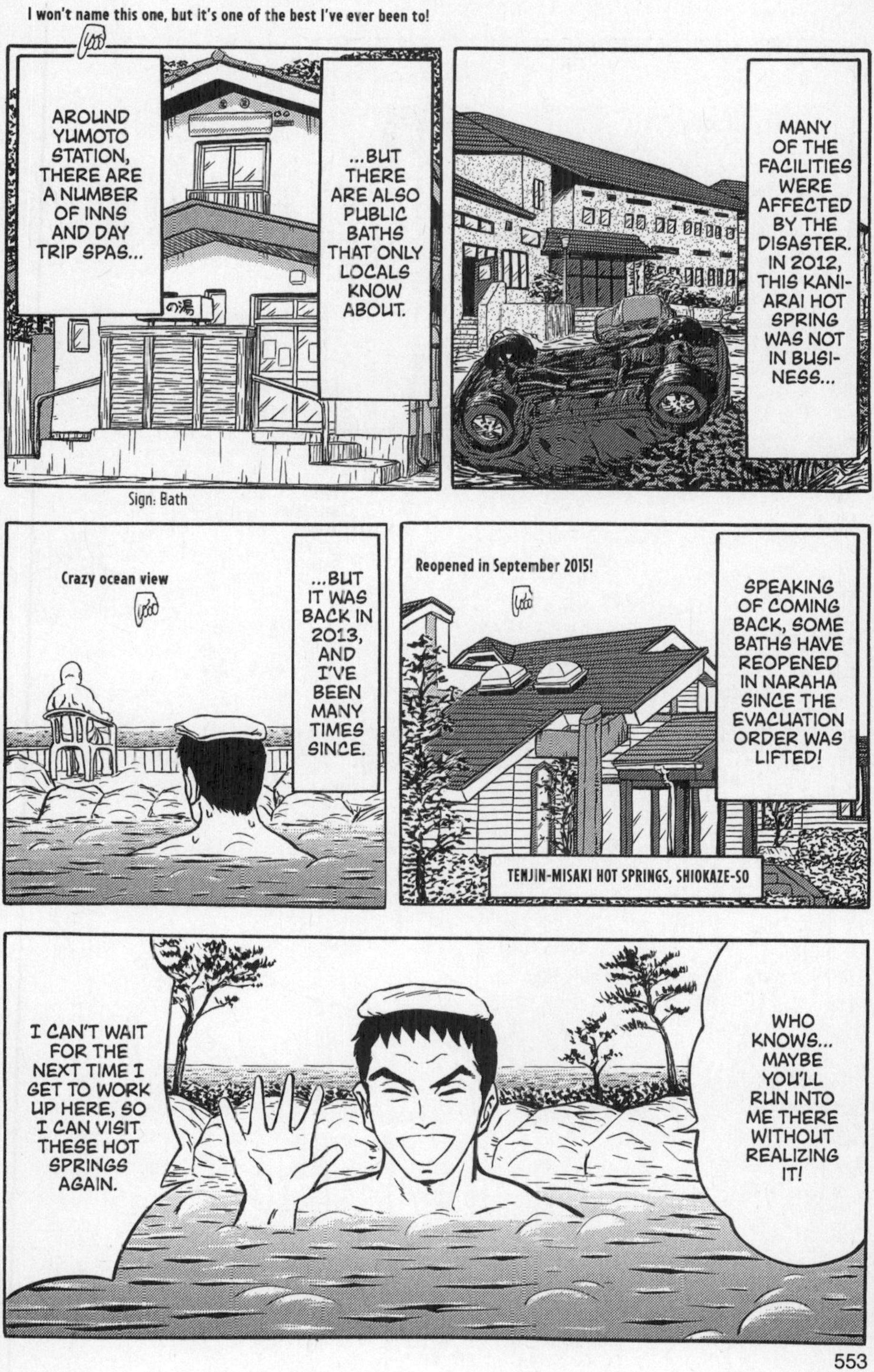
I won't name this one, but it's one of the best I've ever been to!
AROUND YUMOTO STATION, THERE ARE A NUMBER OF INNS AND DAY TRIP SPAS...
...BUT THERE ARE ALSO PUBLIC BATHS THAT ONLY LOCALS KNOW ABOUT.
の湯
Sign: Bath
MANY OF THE FACILITIES WERE AFFECTED BY THE DISASTER. IN 2012, THIS KANI-ARAI HOT SPRING WAS NOT IN BUSINESS...
Crazy ocean view
...BUT IT WAS BACK IN 2013, AND I'VE BEEN MANY TIMES SINCE.
Reopened in September 2015!
SPEAKING OF COMING BACK, SOME BATHS HAVE REOPENED IN NARAHA SINCE THE EVACUATION ORDER WAS LIFTED!
TENJIN-MISAKI HOT SPRINGS, SHIOKAZE-SO
I CAN'T WAIT FOR THE NEXT TIME I GET TO WORK UP HERE, SO I CAN VISIT THESE HOT SPRINGS AGAIN.
WHO KNOWS... MAYBE YOU'LL RUN INTO ME THERE WITHOUT REALIZING IT!

TRANSLATION NOTES, PART 3

I COULD GO THE TOTAL FICTION ROUTE ...
I CONSIDERED THROWING IN A BUNCH OF WHITE-KNUCKLE ACTION TO MAKE IT EXCITING.
STV
勢刈
"THE SILENT POWER PLANT"
WHEN TERRORISTS TAKE OVER FUKUSHIMA DAIICHI,
ONE FORMER SPECIAL OPS AGENT TURNED RADIATION SURVEY WORKER FIGHTS BACK!!

THE SILENT POWER PLANT, PAGE 386

A play on the famous *Silent Service* manga series by Kaiji Kawaguchi, master of Clancy-esque military/political thrillers. The series, started in the late 1980s just before the end of the Cold War, revolves around a nuclear submarine jointly developed by the US Navy and Japanese Naval SDF. When the Japanese captain declares the submarine its own independent state, it causes dramatic shifts in Cold War relations and results in tense underwater battles and political intrigue.

PINE CORRIDOR, PAGE 473

The Great Pine Corridor was a part of the old Edo Castle. It was a 50-meter-long open hallway along a courtyard, so named for the wall screens depicting pine trees along its length. Its fame comes from its part in the incident of the "Forty-Seven Ronin," which has been dramatized in books, TV, and movies. The lord Asano Naganori was forced to commit seppuku for the crime of attacking a court official who insulted him. The attack took place in the Pine Corridor. The forty-seven samurai who followed Asano planned and executed a revenge killing of the official to restore their late master's honor, after which the shogun allowed them to commit seppuku and maintain their honor, rather than being executed as criminals. While the tale may be somewhat altered from the actual events, its grisly nature and deep themes of loyalty and honor make it a popular one to this day.

SDF, PAGE 478

Article 9 of the Constitution of Japan outlaws war as a means of settling international disputes, effectively ruling out the possibility of a military. Instead, the armed forces of Japan are called "Self-Defense Forces" (SDF), or *jiei-tai* in Japanese, a small peacekeeping force that essentially functions under the United Nations. The SDF is technically classified as an extension of the national police and, in accordance with Article 9, is held to a level below that of "war potential." This article has been the subject of much national debate over the decades since its establishment in 1947, especially in recent years.

Former Naval SDF

MOCHI, PAGE 529

A kind of sticky rice cake. Traditionally, the rice is ceremonially pounded flat in a rounded wooden bowl with a heavy wooden hammer called a *kine*. One person pounds the mochi and another flips it over in a precise fashion; the rhythm is very important to avoid injury. Mochi can be eaten as-is or flavored in various ways. It's a traditional treat in the New Year's period, and, due to the extreme stickiness, it's a consistent choking hazard. Chew carefully!

TO MY AMERICAN READERS...
STAY SAFE!

KAZUTO TATSUTA

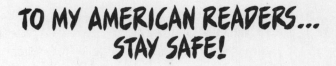

The author drew this original illustration for the American edition of *Ichi-F.*

Q&A WITH KAZUTO TATSUTA, AUTHOR OF *ICHI-F*

This exclusive interview appears only in the U.S. edition of *Ichi-F*, and was conducted on December 7, 2016, between staff at Kodansha Comics, Kazuto Tatsuta, and Mr. Tatsuta's editor.

KODANSHA COMICS: Let's start with something light. You've said that you do visit Fukushima from time to time. Is there anything you really miss about it? Food, places, etc.?

KAZUTO TATSUTA: That's a good question. Things I miss... I really miss the workplace. It's been over a year since I had a work assignment there. I'd love to see what it looks like at this moment.

KODANSHA COMICS: What about aside from work?

KAZUTO TATSUTA: Well, any place aside from the power plant, I can just visit anytime I want. But you can't actually go inside Ichi-F, which only makes the pull stronger. Also, since I was last there, they've built a much more comprehensive shelter area with a cafeteria, and a convenience store, and everything. I want to check it out and see how the food at the cafeteria is.

KODANSHA COMICS: I'm sure you've gotten many questions about the role of nuclear power and nuclear power plants before. There's worldwide concern about the impact of nuclear power. In previous interviews, you've claimed that your experiences are not meant to be commentary on the decommissioning effort. Is that still your stance on the matter?

KAZUTO TATSUTA: That's right. As the author of *Ichi-F*, I'm not trying to argue for or against nuclear power plants, or question their role in society. That's not the point of the comic.

KODANSHA COMICS: This will be your first published work in English. Is there anything you want the English-speaking readers of Ichi-F to know or understand about your experiences there?

KAZUTO TATSUTA: Mainly, just that Fukushima Daiichi isn't really some terrifying place full of negligent, unsafe conditions where people are practically forced into slave labor, as some might have you believe. The folks working there are all just ordinary old guys, most of whom are locals from Fukushima, and the rest coming from all over the country to help. That's what I want you to know.

KODANSHA COMICS: Are there foreign workers, too?

KAZUTO TATSUTA: Not that I've seen. Or should I say, I've never seen a worker who was clearly foreign in origin. I've seen news reports about Brazilian workers, but if they're there, it's a very small number.

KODANSHA COMICS: This report on your experiences will seem at times very distant, and yet also quite familiar to readers abroad. What can foreign readers do, if anything, to offer support or help with the decommissioning effort?

KAZUTO TATSUTA: Well, we're certainly busy enough handling the power plant on our own, so I don't think there's any point to attempting to come help the decommissioning process. What would make me happiest is for people not to view Fukushima through tinted glasses. Don't be afraid of food from Japan. Don't be afraid to come and visit Japan. I think that's enough for us.

KODANSHA COMICS: So, don't be shy about traveling to Japan to see the country?

KAZUTO TATSUTA: Fukushima is a wonderful place. It seems like many tourists in Japan will travel away from Tokyo to the southwest, to Kyushu, but far fewer of them go up north to the Tohoku region. Fukushima isn't the only tsunami-affected area that's struggling up there due to lower tourism—surrounding regions like Miyagi and Iwate are, too. It would make me really happy for you to visit them. Not to gawk at the damage or treat them with tender sympathy, but just to go and treat them like normal. That would be more than enough.

KODANSHA COMICS: This year (2017) marks six years since the initial incident. How do you think the public's perception of Ichi-F has changed?

KAZUTO TATSUTA: I feel like it largely hasn't changed. It seems like it's still misunderstood and feared by much of the public. But a lot of the initial panic about it being the "end of Japan as we know it" has disappeared as time has passed, so I hope that the fears continue to ease.

KODANSHA COMICS: What about you? How has your personal perception changed?

KAZUTO TATSUTA: It certainly has changed since the first time I went there. I was quite apprehensive about going in there, and while it's certainly not all just a walk in the park, when it comes to doing the actual work, I found that it was controlled in a way that removed nearly all of that concern

In many ways, it's just like any ordinary work site with ordinary people there. Since then, my view hasn't changed much. Mostly, I just feel frustration that this hasn't been expressed to the rest of society very well. Whenever something happens at Ichi-F, even now, it gets treated as this massive emergency that leads to crazy rumors and stories. That's always been frustrating to me. And there was that aftershock recently.

KODANSHA COMICS: We were going to ask you about that. There was another fairly large earthquake in Fukushima quite recently (November 2016), with tsunami waves of around a meter high. Could you talk a little about your feelings on that?

KAZUTO TATSUTA: Well, I was in the Tokyo area when it happened, and we got a fair amount of shaking, somewhere around magnitude 5. It took a while from the first jolt for the real shaking to start, so I realized it was pretty far off, and wondered if it was up north again. Once I was able to see the news reports, and they mentioned the height of the tsunami, I knew it would be all right. As a matter of fact, I actually visited Fukushima later that day—it was already in my plans. I left at midday and got there in the evening, and it was totally business as usual in Fukushima. Meanwhile, the cooling system at the spent fuel pool at Fukushima Daini stopped temporarily, and it turned into a big media panic. But as you'll know if you read *Ichi-F,* the cooling system gets turned off all the time during work, so an hour of inactivity is nothing. TEPCO announced that, and the media explained it as well before the day was done, but of course, some people are still going to call it the end of Japan. I get a little discouraged because every time something happens, there are always some people who don't get the message.

MR. TATSUTA'S EDITOR: You put out some very calm and rational commentary on Twitter, and it got a bunch of retweets.

KAZUTO TATSUTA: Over ten thousand retweets, in fact. I also gained about a thousand followers. Basically, I was just saying that they turn off the cooling system to the pool in order to do work on it fairly often, and that people shouldn't exaggerate the issue and cause undue panic.

EDITOR: So the fact that your tweets were getting spread around is a good sign that some people are getting the message.

KAZUTO TATSUTA: It was good to see it spread, but it also made me realize that a lot of people are still worried about that kind of stuff.

KODANSHA COMICS: How do you think this aftershock might affect the recovery and decommissioning process?

KAZUTO TATSUTA: Fundamentally, it won't have any effect. If anything, I think it's shown that a magnitude 7 or so won't have any effect on Ichi-F. They had a one-meter tsunami, and that didn't do any damage.

KODANSHA COMICS: There were quite a few aftershocks when you were working there in 2012. Was the operation able to continue without too much trouble back then?

KAZUTO TATSUTA: Well, they've done a lot of analysis on what level of earthquake is safe to keep working through, so the crews themselves aren't worried about it. Of course, there's the possibility of something unexpected happening, but that's true of anything, anywhere. I doubt a magnitude 7 would cause any problems. If there was another 8 or 9, and it caused another big tsunami—well, the plant isn't operational anymore. So it's almost impossible to have some kind of doomsday explosion or vast spread of contamination at this point.

KODANSHA COMICS: What is your next plan as a manga artist, or any other profession?

KAZUTO TATSUTA: Well, I plan to make a living as a musician now *(laughs)*. I'm joking, of course. I've told a number of subcontractors in Fukushima that I'm available for work, so I'm always ready to do another stint if it comes around, but it's an infrequent thing, and I haven't heard from them. As far as *Ichi-F* goes, I can't really continue onward unless I have another work experience to depict. There are a few little stories and angles that I'd still like to show off to the readers. I'm trying to come up with manga drafts for them, but I'm sad to say that the progress is very slow *(laughs)*.

EDITOR: Let's just say that we're hoping to have some new material this year.

KODANSHA COMICS: You mentioned music. Is there any other area you're interested in?

KAZUTO TATSUTA: For now, I think it's just the music.

KODANSHA COMICS: What about drawing something related to music?

KAZUTO TATSUTA: Good point. Shoot, I should have brought one of my CDs!

KODANSHA COMICS: You played live music over in Fukushima, correct?

KAZUTO TATSUTA: Yes, and I write some songs themed on what I saw there. In fact, I even have some that I wrote while I was there in 2012. I can't believe I didn't bring them!

KODANSHA COMICS: You did include some scenes of yourself playing music in *Ichi-F*, so I suppose the people who have read it are familiar with that side of you.

KAZUTO TATSUTA: After the most recent earthquake, I did go and play another show for a senior home. And I do them around Tokyo, too. In fact, I'm performing in Kawasaki this Saturday. I've got Kawasaki this week, Hachioji next week, then Sagamihara and Soshigaya-Okura the week after that. It's a little national tour. Or a Kanto region tour, I suppose...Maybe I should try an American tour, too *(laughs)*.

KODANSHA COMICS: Is there any last message you'd like to send to the readers in America?

KAZUTO TATSUTA: Wow, a serious question after we just got a little silly *(laughs)*. Well, I'm sure the Americans have a lot on their hands right now. We're watching what's unfolding there from Japan, too. As far as Fukushima Daiichi Nuclear Power Plant is concerned, based on the opinions of those working there, the plant itself is very stable now, and the chances of a sudden dangerous turn are practically nil. So continue to pay attention, if you can, but don't worry too much. And most of all, try to think of Fukushima like you would of any other city or area—don't treat it like a disaster area or subject of pity, and that would make everyone happiest.

KODANSHA COMICS: Thank you.

UNIFORM LIST

Here is a list of the names as they are written on the uniforms for those interested. Most are surnames, but deviations from this naming convention are listed as they appear.

竜田/タツタ - Tatsuta
大野 - Ono
木戸 - Kido
赤井 - Akai
田代 - Tashiro
大洋- Taiyo (COMPANY NAME)
中塚 - Nakatsuka
カトウ - Kato
キリヤマ - Kiriyama
クラタ - Kurata
タケナカ - Takenaka
佐竹 - Satake
三沢 - Misawa
近藤 - Kondo
ソガ - Soga
フルハシ - Furuhashi
泉 - Izumi
伊吹 - Ibuki
岸田 - Kishida
上野 - Ueno
アマギ - Amagi
ノムラ - Nomura
南 - Minami
秋山 - Akiyama
矢住 - Yasumi
サトウ - Sato
塩田 - Shioda
玉名 - Tamana
関本 - Sekimoto
江田 - Eda
北目 - Kitame
川前 - Kawamae
ナカジマ - Nakajima
小川 - Ogawa
ツルシバ - Tsurushiba
里中 - Satonaka (COMPANY NAME)

オノ - Ono
明石 - Akashi
宮田 - Miyata
クボ - Kubo
松木工業 - Matsuki Industries
ツルオカ - Tsuruoka
山洋 - Sanyo (COMPANY NAME)
沖田 - Okita
金谷 - Kanaya
タカハシ - Takahashi
マツダ - Matsuda
本多 - Honda
井口 - Iguchi
長町 - Nagamachi
大畑 - Obata
立栄 - Ritsuei (COMPANY NAME)
ウメモト - Umemoto
高木 - Takagi
長橋 - Nagahashi
尼子 - Amako
ミサキ - Misaki
ヤシキ - Yashiki
ツルミ - Tsurumi
大原 - Ohara
タケ - Take
植田 - Ueda
牛込 - Ushigome
中郷 - Nakago
タカハギ - Takahagi
坂元 - Sakamoto
磯原 - Isohara
前泊 - Maedomari
田町工業 - Tamachi Industrial (COMPANY NAME)
オオシマ - Oshima
シライワ - Shiraiwa

ACKNOWLEDGEMENTS

The publication of this important, wonderful book in the United States would not have been possible without the cooperation and support of many people. Thank you first and foremost to Kazuto Tatsuta, who allowed us to work with him to re-create the *Ichi-F* experience in a left-to-right reading format; to his editor and the staff of Kodansha (Yae Sahashi, Masae Watanabe, Naho Yamada, and Kana Koide, to name a few!) for their constant support and championship of the book; to Ben Applegate, Stephen Pakula, and the rest of my colleagues at Penguin Random House and Kodansha Comics, for acquiring the book, and supporting it all the way through from translation to release; to Stephen Paul, for not only his fantastic translation, but his research and his dedication to getting this book exactly right; to James Dashiell and Deron Bennett/AndWorld Design, for their tireless retouching and lettering, and their boundless patience; to Phil Balsman for his extraordinary cover design; and to all others who have supported the book and made this whole thing possible.

We hope this book entertains, educates, and enlightens, and that through this book, we can provide a glimpse into the world of Ichi-F.

Thank you for reading!

Lauren Scanlan,
Editor, Kodansha Comics

A Kodansha Comics Trade Paperback Original

Published in the United States by Kodansha Comics, an imprint of Kodansha USA Publishing, LLC, New York.

Publication rights for this English edition arranged through Kodansha Ltd, Tokyo.

First published in Japan between 2014-2015 by Kodansha Ltd., Tokyo as *Ichi-Efu*, volumes 1-3.

ISBN 978-1-63236-355-8

Kodansha Comics edition cover and logo design by Phil Balsman

Printed in the United States of America.

www.kodanshacomics.com

9 8 7 6 5 4 3 2 1
Translation: Stephen Paul
Retouching: James Dashiell
Lettering: AndWorld Design
Editing: Lauren Scanlan
Editorial assistance: Ben Applegate